The Allyn & Bacon Handbook— a text for any class

The Allyn & Bacon Handbook is a unique textbook: it's the only one you'll ever buy that will be relevant to *every* class you take. This is because unlike other texts – even other handbooks – *The Allyn & Bacon Handbook* is filled with information on the kinds of academic reading, writing and *thinking* that you will need to master in order to be successful throughout your college career. In addition to the conventions of grammar and usage, you will find information on how to find, evaluate, integrate, and cite sources for research papers no matter what discipline you are working in. Special features like the "Spotlight on Common Errors," "Critical Decisions" boxes and "Across the Curriculum" boxes make the text relevant, and the information easy to find and use, whether you're writing a lab report in chemistry or a gallery review for art history.

And, when your college career is coming to a close, *The Allyn & Bacon Handbook* will help you write a job application letter, compose a resume, even show you how to post one online. So go ahead and turn the page and see how this one text can help you make the most out of every class you take ...

i

TO SPOT-CHECK FOR COMMON ERRORS

■ **Check the back endpaper chart.** The nine sections in this chart cover over 90 percent of the most common sentence and punctuation errors you are likely to make. Look in these sections for sentence patterns and word forms close to what you have written. If any of the examples or explanations lead you to suspect an error in your work, follow the references to one of the text chapters.

IV. SENTENCE STRUCTURE: FRAGMENTS See SPOTLIGHT (page 273).

Mark where sentences end, usually with a period. Avoid a FRAGMENT—a word group that lacks a full subject and predicate and cannot stand alone.

Faulty	*Revised*
If our cousins arrive today. [Fragment]	Our cousins may arrive today.
	If our cousins arrive today, we'll have a picnic.

■ **Go to the orange-tinted "spotlight" summary page that matches your situation.** Colored "spotlight" pages in nine chapters give basic recognition patterns and sentences that fit common error situations.

Spotlight on Common Errors—SENTENCE CONSTRUCTION AND FRAGMENTS

■ **Narrow the search. Find a sentence or situation that** more closely resembles a sentence you have written. *Note* the revision suggested. Do you suspect a possible error? If so, *note* the reference to the chapter section where this revision is explained.

■ **Go to the** *Handbook* **section; find a usage guideline and example that** describes the possible error in your work. Challenge your sentence: Does it meet the *Handbook*'s usage guideline? Make a decision about revising your sentence.

SELECTED LIST OF USEFUL CHECKLISTS, SUMMARIES, AND BOXES

Critical Decisions Boxes

Across the Curriculum Boxes

Use the "Critical Decisions" boxes. These boxes will help you examine the choices you have to make throughout the writing process and give you practical advice you can use at every step.

CRITICAL DECISIONS

Thinking Critically

Develop habits of mind that prompt you to think critically about what you read. *Critical* in this sense does not mean "negative" but, rather, "active" and "alert." Critical habits include being alert to similarities and differences, posing questions, setting issues in broader contexts, and forming and supporting opinions. Developing the habits of a critical thinker will prepare you for working with the source materials on which you will base much of your writing.

Use the "Across the Curriculum" boxes. These boxes will help you to understand key differences – and similarities – when working in various disciplines.

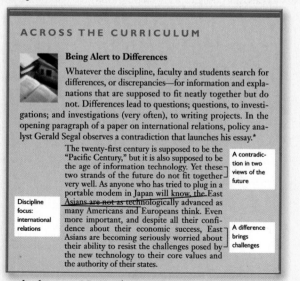

ACROSS THE CURRICULUM

Being Alert to Differences

Whatever the discipline, faculty and students search for differences, or discrepancies—for information and explanations that are supposed to fit neatly together but do not. Differences lead to questions; questions, to investigations; and investigations (very often), to writing projects. In the opening paragraph of a paper on international relations, policy analyst Gerald Segal observes a contradiction that launches his essay.*

> The twenty-first century is supposed to be the "Pacific Century," but it is also supposed to be the age of information technology. Yet these two strands of the future do not fit together very well. As anyone who has tried to plug in a portable modem in Japan will know, the East Asians are not as technologically advanced as many Americans and Europeans think. Even more important, and despite all their confidence about their economic success, East Asians are becoming seriously worried about their ability to resist the challenges posed by the new technology to their core values and the authority of their states.

A contradiction in two views of the future

Discipline focus: international relations

A difference brings challenges

Also: consult chapters 38-40 when writing or researching a paper for a specific discipline.

iii

Check the computer tips. The tips located throughout this text will help you get the most out of your computer.

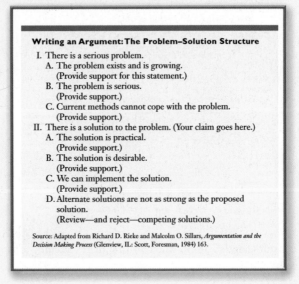

COMPUTER TIPS

Electronic Democracy at Its Best . . . and Worst

Usenet newsgroups represent perhaps the pinnacle of democracy and free speech. The exchanges in this new medium can be uninhibited, unrestrained, and uncensored. But that free flow of information increases the critical thinking challenge for researchers. Everybody from world-renowned experts in a field to ignorant, malicious crackpots has equal access to the medium, and it may be difficult to tell one group from the other. Be careful when using a Usenet posting as evidence in your writing. If

Check the summary boxes and checklists. Numerous checklists, summary boxes, and illustrations throughout give you quick advice on key procedures of composing and revising your paper.

Writing an Argument: The Problem–Solution Structure

I. There is a serious problem.
   A. The problem exists and is growing.
      (Provide support for this statement.)
   B. The problem is serious.
      (Provide support.)
   C. Current methods cannot cope with the problem.
      (Provide support.)
II. There is a solution to the problem. (Your claim goes here.)
   A. The solution is practical.
      (Provide support.)
   B. The solution is desirable.
      (Provide support.)
   C. We can implement the solution.
      (Provide support.)
   D. Alternate solutions are not as strong as the proposed solution.
      (Review—and reject—competing solutions.)

Source: Adapted from Richard D. Rieke and Malcolm O. Sillars, *Argumentation and the Decision Making Process* (Glenview, IL: Scott, Foresman, 1984) 163.

To Find Key Terms and Topics

Use these information locators:

Front endpapers: The compact contents chart provides an overview of the section and page numbers of the major topics.

Main contents: This detailed listing shows sections and pages for all topics and usage guidelines.

Index: This alphabetical listing shows the page numbers of every key term, word, or topic.

Revision symbols—inside back endpaper: This guide to common instructor markings will help locate discussions of revision topics.

Useful checklists, summaries, and boxes—inside front endpaper: Locates the special panels that provide rapid checklists of basic procedures.

"Spotlight on Common Errors": See page ii.

To narrow the search, look for these features on each page:

Tab shows the section-number combination for every topic. A *symbol* next to the tab shows typical instructor markings used to call attention to the topic.

Boxed checklists, summaries or "critical decisions" boxes are in shaded panels.

Explanations describe how or why processes or usage guidelines operate. *Bold type* identifies key terms being defined on location or in a cross-reference.

Revision examples are labeled to identify problems and the best revisions. In the nine chapters devoted to the most common errors, additional examples appear beneath the headings as an aid to spotting errors.

Section number gives chapter and section letter accompanying the *heading* that states or identifies a usage guideline.

Footer briefly identifies chapter section topics.

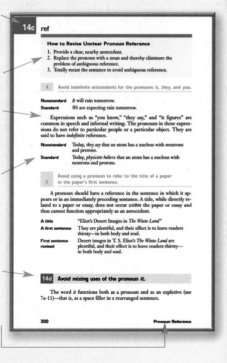

Check out the book's Companion Website. Numbered **Web icons** appearing in the margins of the page show where additional content and activities can be found on the companion website:

http://www.ablongman.com/rosen

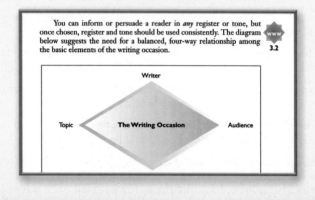

You can inform or persuade a reader in *any* register or tone, but once chosen, register and tone should be used consistently. The diagram below suggests the need for a balanced, four-way relationship among the basic elements of the writing occasion.

3.2

Writer

Topic — **The Writing Occasion** — Audience

Check out the Companion Website's interactive features. Self-scoring exercises and Writing Across the Curriculum Tutorials allow you to practice what you learn and get immediate feedback.

| Intro | Aut & Aud | Interpretation | Structure | Language | Thesis | Send |

Author and Audience

Any reader of a text will want to know as much as possible about the historical and cultural realities of the author and the audience. Literary texts themselves provide some evidence about the culture in which they are produced, and our reading of them can be deepened by considering what we can learn about the external social

What are the main differences between Homer's literary world and our own? Hint

Look at what Edwards says about orality and public performance.

What do the epics themselves suggest about the roles of poetry in Homeric society? Hint

response...

To what degree can our interpretation of the Homeric texts be shaped by our knowledge of its oral composition and subsequent commitment to written form? Hint

response...

When you have entered a response, click Next.   ◀ BACK   NEXT ▶

Interpreting Literary Texts   Instructions

From Mark Edwards, *Homer: Poet of the* Iliad. Baltimore: Johns Hopkins University Press, 1987.

...The poet Homer does not introduce himself. ...The epics are presented as history, as the facts of the past, which the singer (with the Muse's help) has only to relate with knowledge and truth. ...So nothing is known of Homer himself. ...Of the performance of the poems, we can safely conjecture only that it was a performance; not an individual reading to himself from a text, nor one person reading it to others, but a recitation, perhaps close to a dramatic performance.

...The poet's pride in his creation, his awareness of the immortality it will bring him and his characters, is sometimes openly expressed. [For example,]...Helen laments, "Upon [Paris and myself] Zeus has laid a hard lot, so that even afterwards we may become subjects of song for men still to be born" (*Iliad* 6.357-58)...In the *Iliad*, the superb description of the craftsmanship of Hephaestus, as he depicts by his artistic skill the circumstances of human life on the shield of Achilles, may well be thought a conscious parallel

The
ALLYN & BACON
Handbook
Fifth Edition

LEONARD J. ROSEN

LAURENCE BEHRENS
University of California, Santa Barbara

PEARSON
Longman

New York San Francisco Boston
London Toronto Sydney Tokyo Singapore Madrid
Mexico City Munich Paris Cape Town Hong Kong Montreal

In Memoriam

E.R.R.

Senior Vice President/Publisher: Joseph Opiela
Marketing Manager: Christopher Bennem
Supplements Editor: Donna Campion
Media Supplements Editor: Nancy Garcia
Production Manager: Charles Annis
*Project Coordination, Text Design, and
Electronic Page Makeup:* Pre-Press Company, Inc.
Cover Design Manager: Wendy Fredericks
Cover Designer: Silver Design
Cover Backgrounds: © Creatas
Manufacturing Manager: Roy Pickering
Printer and Binder: R.R. Donnelley & Sons, Crawfordsville
Cover Printer: Coral Graphics Services

For permission to use copyrighted material, grateful acknowledgment is
made to the copyright holders on pp. 881–882, which are hereby made part
of this copyright page.

Library of Congress Cataloging-in-Publication Data

Rosen, Leonard J.
    The Allyn & Bacon handbook / Leonard J. Rosen, Laurence
Behrens.—5th ed.
    p. cm.
Includes bibliographical references and index.
ISBN 0-321-20246-5
    1. English language—Rhetoric—Handbooks, manuals, etc.
    2. English language—Grammar—Handbooks, manuals, etc.
    3. Report writing—Handbooks, manuals, etc. I. Title: Allyn and
Bacon handbook. II. Behrens, Laurence. III. Title.

PE1408 .R677 2003
808'.042—dc21

2002066110

Please visit our Web site at http://www.ablongman.com/Rosen

ISBN 0-321-20246-5

1 2 3 4 5 6 7 8 9 10—DOC—05 04 03

Contents

Contents

Appendices   841

Preface to the Instructor

Welcome to the fifth edition.

Through four editions, *The Allyn & Bacon Handbook* has been unique in preparing students for academic writing by linking the skills of critical thinking, reading, and writing—both in the composition classroom and throughout the curriculum. The success of this approach has encouraged us to build further on what has proved most useful. We have continued to strengthen the book's signature features—critical thinking and writing across the curriculum—in three significant ways:

- To emphasize the importance of critical, writerly thinking beyond the composition classroom, we have added more than twenty-five new "Across the Curriculum" and "Critical Decisions" boxes throughout the text.
- In Part IX, "Writing the Research Paper" (Chapters 33–37), a new student essay on Web-based relationships illustrates a research paper in the making. We pay especially close attention to the gathering and evaluation of sources—both online and in the library, the formulation of a research question, the writing and revision of a thesis, and the drafting process. Of prime concern throughout is the close connection between skills of critical reading and thinking learned in Chapters 1 and 2 and the writing of an effective source-based paper.
- The book's thoroughly revised writing and thinking in the disciplines chapters now feature a new, more open and accessible format. Students will find new example readings throughout and two new example research papers on child labor (Chapter 39, Social Science) and black hole flares (Chapter 40, Science). Chapter 38, "Writing and Reading in the Humanities," continues to feature the full text of Kate Chopin's "A Shameful Affair" and an example of literary analysis based on the short story.

We have made other significant changes as well:

- The *Handbook* now conforms to style and editorial guidelines in the new (2001) *Publication Manual* of the APA.
- A new Chapter 45 on making oral presentations is both theory-based and at the same time practical, helping students to draft, rehearse, and deliver effective presentations.
- A totally revised Chapter 41, "Writing for the Web," offers students the latest strategies for devising and producing effective Web pages.

■ Heavily revised Chapters 1–4 follow a new student essay (on reducing teenage smoking) to illustrate the process of writing and revision. Developed through four chapters, the paper takes students through the process of reading, thinking, drafting, and revision necessary for producing competent, college-level work. The paper shows examples of Internet- and library-based sources in use. In all, the fifth edition has four new student papers.

Notwithstanding these important changes, the fifth edition retains *The Allyn and Bacon Handbook*'s comprehensive core features.

Core Features

Critical thinking   With its opening chapters—"Critical Thinking and Reading" and "Critical Thinking and Writing"—*The Allyn & Bacon Handbook* continues to mark a departure in the world of handbooks. We open with specific strategies for developing critical thinking skills that students can apply immediately to their reading assignments and to the writing that follows from these assignments. This approach, based on a survey of current research in the field, follows our conviction that writing at the college level is most often based on reading. If students want to write well, they must also read well. We develop these points on critical thinking and its relation to the writing process in two key places: in the rhetoric section (Chapters 1–4) and in the research section (Chapters 33–37). The evolving papers in both places show student writers changing their thinking as they work through a real writing process. Chapters 1 and 2 use a refined group of fresh examples (focused on the topic of reducing teenage smoking) to serve as continuous source readings for demonstrating student thinking and writing skills.

The new reading selections in Chapters 1 and 2 provide occasions for critical thinking, but also serve as background material for the essay developed in Chapters 3 and 4, where the student writer's emerging ideas are sparked by earlier reading.

Writing as a process   Chapters 3 through 6 on writing processes are designed to serve both as a quick-reference tool and as a mini-rhetoric, with assignments that call on students to write and revise paragraphs and whole papers. *Revision*, here, is key: the process of writing, discovery, and rediscovery through revision yields an example student paper that undergoes fundamental changes in its thinking—changes that would have been impossible had the writer not worked recursively from invention to multiple drafts through to a final effort. Similarly, the student paper in the research chapters (Part IX, Chapters 33–37) demonstrates how a writer's thinking evolves through reading, writing, and rewriting. Throughout these sections of the text, and in the sections devoted to sentence construction and word choice, we emphasize the role of revision in clarifying meaning and achieving a clean, spare style.

Because we have found that writing improves significantly when students give careful and sustained attention to a paper's governing sentence, we have made our discussion of thesis far more extensive than is commonly found in handbooks.

Writing across the curriculum and argumentation   Our comprehensive cross-curricular chapters (38, 39, and 40) orient students to the kinds of thinking, reading, and writing they will be called on to do in their various courses. After a general introduction devoted to characteristic assumptions and questions, each cross-curricular chapter reviews patterns for writing to inform and for making arguments in its discipline area; it reviews typical kinds of reading and audience situations; and it presents types of assignments found in the discipline, a complete student paper, and a listing of specialized reference materials.

Writing about literature.   A guiding assumption of this book is that college-level writing is based to a great extent on reading. Recognizing that for some composition classrooms reading involves literature as a context for writing, Chapter 38 includes material on writing about literature. The chapter retains its unique detail on making arguments throughout the humanities, but it also develops principles for writing about literature by providing specific guidelines and examples, including the story and student paper on Kate Chopin's "A Shameful Affair."

Argumentation in the disciplines.   As an outgrowth of this book's pervasive attention to critical thinking and its emphasis on writing and evaluating arguments, Chapters 38–40 provide the only handbook treatment of foundations for making claims in each discipline across the curriculum. Chapter 6, the first in a handbook to offer a Toulmin-based model for constructing arguments, uses basic terminology that composition students can put to use in any discipline. Combined, these chapters offer more depth than any handbook available in constructing claims and arguments across the disciplines.

Our "Across the Curriculum" panels highlight the ways in which writers beyond the composition classroom use strategies discussed in the handbook to advance their written work—for instance, the use of analogies by a physicist, or the use of subordination and coordination by an economist. To expand our already distinctive discussion of claims and evidence for writing in each of the disciplines, we wanted to demonstrate how the specific, writerly strategies we emphasize in the composition classroom are highly valued when students write in other courses. Finally, student researchers using the cross-curricular chapters will find numerous discipline-specific Web sites.

The research paper Integrating discussions found elsewhere on critical thinking, the writing process, and writing across the curriculum, this *Handbook*'s five chapters on research offer a wealth of practical, direct advice for launching college-level research projects. The research section draws heavily on critical thinking concepts from Chapters 1 and 2 in the use of sources; it incorporates phases of the writing process from Chapters 3–6; it also looks ahead to research assignments in the three major discipline areas (Chapters 38 through 40). The result is a strong treatment on the use and evaluation of sources and their integration into students' writing. In addition, the documentation coverage in Chapter 37 treats four different conventions: the MLA system, the APA system, the footnote style (based on the *Chicago Manual of Style*), and the CSE systems used in the sciences. Also addressed are the most current conventions from the Modern Language Association and from the American Psychological Association for citing electronic sources. These sections, with their research paper samples from a variety of discipline areas, provide comprehensive coverage on research.

Forming the backbone of the research chapters is the continuing example of a student paper, entitled "Computer-Mediated Communication: How Will It Affect Interpersonal Relationships?" These chapters on research clearly emphasize what we want our students to know: that the process of research is a process of challenging and clarifying one's thinking through a judicious use of source materials.

The Internet as resource The fifth edition presents an extremely thorough introduction to the Internet and to using Internet resources in research. Chapter 34, devoted to "Using Electronic Sources," provides the following important information:

- Strategies for formulating good queries
- Strategies for conducting *multiple* searches using different (specialized) search engines and directories
- Criteria for evaluating Internet-based sources (based on the work of Alexander and Tate at Widener University)
- A catalog of excellent general resources available on the Internet

Chapter 1, on "Critical Thinking and Reading," illustrates in an extended example how general principles of close, critical reading can be applied to claims made on a Web site. The cross-curricular chapters, 38–40, provide a wealth of excellent discipline-specific Web sites. Chapter 41 introduces students to the opportunities for "Writing for the Web." Chapter 43 includes a section on preparing online and scannable résumés. And dozens of margin icons throughout the *Handbook* alert students to pertinent Web resources on topics ranging from critical thinking to dictionary use to parallelism.

Guidelines and choices in sentence revision   Any experienced writer knows that there is often more than one solution to a common sentence error. Therefore, when appropriate, we discuss alternative solutions and encourage students in their role as writers to make decisions. When usage is a matter of strict convention, we offer firm, clear guidelines for eliminating common errors and understanding key concepts of grammar, usage, and style. We have used student and professional writing from the disciplines as the basis for more than 90 percent of the exercises *and* example sentences. Both exercises *and* examples almost always feature connected discourse from a variety of disciplines—on topics as varied as micro-breweries and Elizabethan stagecraft. To make the book easy to use as a reference tool and visually appealing, we have created numerous boxes that summarize important information, provide useful lists, or apply critical thinking to decisions and choices.

The "Spotlight" system: An alternative way to locate errors   To help students identify remedies for the most common trouble spots in grammar and usage, this handbook has developed the unique "Spotlight on Common Errors." This system offers an alternative for students who may be uncomfortable or unfamiliar with the formal terminology of grammar needed to locate errors in a traditional index. Students can find their way to remedies for common errors using the three parts of the "Spotlight" system:

1. The Spotlight chart on the back endpaper, with its broad view of error patterns, refers students to
2. The color-tinted "Spotlight" summary pages in selected chapters, which provide error recognition and brief remedies, in turn referring students to
3. Chapter sections with detailed explanations and revisions.

A few basic recognition examples are featured in all three elements of the "Spotlight" system. The use of the "Spotlight" system is described on the back endpaper and on the "Spotlight" summary pages.

Comprehensive ESL coverage   Students whose native language is not English have been entering mainstream composition courses in increasing numbers, with varying degrees of prior preparation from specialized English as a Second Language (ESL) courses. As a result, composition instructors have been called on to help international students cope with features of English that have not traditionally caused problems for native speakers. This handbook provides international students with unique help at these levels:

ESL notes in the text: These notes briefly identify troublesome English language features before referring readers to pertinent descriptive units in ESL Chapters 46–48.

Three ESL chapters: The chapters of the ESL section, developed with help from Will Van Dorp of Northern Essex Community College, summarize troublesome features of English language usage in three functional areas: nouns and related structures (Chapter 46); verbs and related structures (Chapter 47); and modifying structures (Chapter 48). Idioms and constructions with prepositions and particles—especially troublesome forms for international students—are treated in appropriate sections in all three chapters.

Acknowledgments

A number of people have helped us with special contributions to key elements of the text and supplements of this edition. Special thanks go to Mark Gallaher for his timely, expert help throughout the revision. Thanks also to Sarah Lefton for her help in designing and creating Chapter 41, "Writing for the Web." Thanks to Rick Branscomb (Salem State College, Massachusetts), Keith Gresham (University of Colorado at Boulder), and Michael Bergman (The WebTools Company), whose work we consulted in preparing Chapter 34, on using Internet Resources. Thanks to Eric Wirth of the Modern Language Association, who patiently answered our questions concerning recent changes in MLA recommended style for researchers. Thanks to Kathleen Shine Cain of Merrimack College for her fine work on the instructor's annotations, and to Professors Andrew and Gina Macdonald of Loyola University for their wisdom and experience in the "ESL Cue" notes based on work with both ESL and composition sections over many years. In the text we are most grateful to H. Eric Branscomb of Salem State College for contributions on electronic resources, and also to Will Van Dorp of Bradford College and Northern Essex Community College, for his apt examples and descriptions on ESL topics in Part XII.

For their reviews of the fourth edition, thanks to Rick Branscomb, Salem State College; Janet Eldred, University of Kentucky; Anne Fitzsimmons, Syracuse University; David Franke, SUNY-Cortland; Richard Keenan, University of Maryland-Eastern Shore; Deborah Kirkman, University of Kentucky; and Patricia McClure, West Virginia State College.

Many others helped us along the way; their particular contributions are too numerous to list, but we gratefully acknowledge their assistance. From Bentley College, we thank Tim Anderson, Christy Bell, Lindsey Carpenter, Robert Crooks, Nancy Esposito, Barbara Gottfried, Sherman Hayes, Tom Heeney, Richard Kyte, Donald McIntyre, Kathy Meade, and George Radford. We thank other colleagues as well: John Clarke of the University of Vermont, whose work on critical thinking aided the formulating of our pedagogy for the book, and Carol Gibbens of the University of California, Santa Barbara, for suggestions on the reference unit. Thanks also go to Burke Brown, University of Southern

Alabama; Eric Godfrey, Ripon College; Clarence Ivie, University of Southern Alabama; John Laucus, University Librarian, Boston University; William Leap, The American University; Larry Renbaum; Carol G. Schneider, Association of American Colleges; Alison Tschopp, Boston University; and Arthur White, Western Michigan University.

As writers we are indeed fortunate to work with an editorial, production, marketing, and sales staff as fine as the team at Longman Publishers. Joe Opiela, shared and helped to shape our vision for this book. Joe has proved himself a tireless advocate and a steady source of helpful ideas. Chris Bennem has worked tirelessly to promote the message of this book to faculty. Editorial Assistant Julie Hallett provided much of the administrative help that kept this project on track. And Elsa van Bergen shepherded the manuscript through production with an unfailing eye for style and detail. To all we offer hearty thanks for work well done.

> Leonard Rosen
> Laurence Behrens, University of California, Santa Barbara

The
ALLYN & BACON
Handbook

Critical Thinking and Reading

E specially in college, to be successful as a writer you must be an effective reader, making thoughtful, informed decisions about what you read. This opening chapter of a book that will serve your reference needs throughout college and beyond has a twofold purpose: first, to suggest general habits of mind that will prepare you for thinking critically about college-level reading materials, and second, to provide you with *particular* strategies for understanding and beginning to write about sources.[1]

CRITICAL DECISIONS

Thinking Critically

Develop habits of mind that prompt you to think critically about what you read. *Critical* in this sense does not mean "negative" but, rather, "active" and "alert." Critical habits include being alert to similarities and differences, posing questions, setting issues in broader contexts, and forming and supporting opinions. Developing the habits of a critical thinker will prepare you for working with the source materials on which you will base much of your writing.

ACTIVE, CRITICAL HABITS OF MIND

1a Active, critical thinkers search for and question similarities and differences.

Two or more sources on a particular topic will nearly always present similarities and differences concerning facts, interpretations of facts,

---

[1]We use the terms *source materials*, *sources*, and *texts* interchangeably to mean any reading selection.

value judgments, or policies that the writers think ought to be pursued. You can approach similarities and differences with questions that will get you thinking critically. Freshman writer Paul Guzman demonstrates how you can do so, using two sources on the effects of advertising in prompting adolescents to smoke. You will follow Paul and this topic through several chapters as Paul begins thinking about an essay and works through the process of writing to arrive at a finished essay (see 4e). Watch closely how Paul's observation of similarities and differences leads to questions that deepen his investigation into the topic.

Weblink

http://www.criticalthinking.org

The Center for Critical Thinking, a repository of information about the theory and practice of critical thinking.

FROM "TOBACCO ADS, PROMOTIONAL ITEMS LINKED WITH TEEN SMOKING" (1998)

Even if a teenager has no intention to start smoking, tobacco advertising and promotional items can lead one-third of them to try, according to an article in the February 18 issue of *The Journal of the American Medical Association* (*JAMA*).

John P. Pierce, Ph.D., from the University of California, San Diego, in La Jolla, and colleagues conducted the first longitudinal study on the effect of cigarette promotion on teenagers. In 1993, they interviewed 1,752 California adolescents (age 12 to 17 years old) who had never smoked and who had said they had no plans to start smoking, even if a friend offers them a cigarette. The adolescents were reinterviewed in 1996.

They write: "From these data, we estimate that 34 percent of all experimentation in California between 1993 and 1996 can be attributed to tobacco promotional activities."

The researchers found that those who had a favorite cigarette advertisement in 1993 were twice as likely as those who did not, to either have started smoking by 1996 or were willing to start smoking.

FROM "COWBOYS, CAMELS, AND KIDS" (1998)

Several studies have found that teenagers who smoke (or who say they might) are more apt to recall cigarette advertising and to view it favorably. Such findings do not necessarily mean that advertising makes adolescents more likely to smoke. It is just as plausible to suppose that teenagers pay more attention to cigarette ads after they start smoking, or that teenagers who are inclined to smoke for other reasons are also more likely to have a positive view of cigarette ads.

In reporting on research in this area, the mainstream press tends to ignore such alternative interpretations. Consider the coverage of a 1995 study published in the *Journal of the National Cancer Institute*. The study, co-authored by John Pierce, found that teenagers who scored high on a "receptivity" index— which included "recognition of advertising messages, having a favorite advertisement, naming a brand [they] might buy, owning a tobacco-related promotional item, and willingness to use a tobacco-related promotional item"—were more likely to say they could not rule out smoking in the near future.

Those who owned a cigarette promotional item or who were willing to use one in 1993 were nearly three times as likely to progress to smoking by 1996 than those unwilling to use a cigarette promotional item.

The researchers write: "This longitudinal study provides clear evidence that tobacco industry advertising and promotional activities can influence nonsusceptible never smokers to start the process of becoming addicted to cigarettes. . . . Our data establish that the influence of tobacco promotional activities was present before adolescents showed any susceptibility to become smokers."

They also write: "Exposure to other smokers in this analysis does not appear to significantly influence which adolescents begin the smoking uptake process, which is somewhat contradictory to previous studies."

—*SCIENCE NEWS UPDATE*, AMERICAN MEDICAL ASSOCIATION

Such "receptivity" was more strongly associated with an inclination to smoke than was smoking among parents and peers.

According to *The New York Times*, these results meant that "[t]obacco advertising is a stronger factor than peer pressure in encouraging children under 18 to smoke." . . . In reality, the study showed only that teenagers who like smoking-related messages and merchandise are more receptive to the idea of smoking—not exactly a startling finding.

—JACOB SULLUM

As a reader, prepare yourself to find similarities and differences in the articles you read. Here are Paul Guzman's observations on the selections concerning advertising and teenage smoking.

Similarities

- Both the *Science News Update* report and Sullum cite data reported by John Pierce and his colleagues showing that teenagers who are susceptible to smoking are more likely than others to have a favorite cigarette advertisement or be interested in promotional items distributed by tobacco companies.
- Both report Pierce's findings that exposure to other smokers is a lesser factor in terms of encouraging adolescents to smoke.

Differences

- The *Science News Update* report endorses the findings of Pierce and his colleagues, presenting them without critical comment. Pierce's research, as reported in *Science News*, points to a cause-and-effect relationship between advertising and youth smoking. Sullum acknowledges a *correlation* but not *causation*.

- The *Science News Update* report quotes extensively from the original article it summarizes, presenting specific statistics. Sullum quotes only briefly, apparently with the intention of questioning the definition of "receptivity," and includes no statistics.
- Sullum criticizes how the media reported on the study to which he refers. In neutrally summarizing Pierce's journal article for general readers, the *Science News Update* report is providing the media with a viewpoint that, at least to Sullum, is questionable.

Spotting similarities or differences in your reading is one way to begin having a conversation with your sources and, more generally, with a given topic. Based on your observations of differences, try posing questions. The more questions you pose and attempt to answer, the better you will know a reading selection.

Question similarities.

If two statements look alike, ask *why*.

1. Are the facts the same? Are the interpretations of facts the same?
2. Have facts been established in the same way? If two or more authors share the same opinion, what does this suggest? Is the reasoning or value system underlying these views necessarily the same?
3. What social conditions might explain the similarities?

Other questions are possible. The point is that your awareness of similarity marks a *beginning* point for your thinking.

Here's how Paul Guzman works with the similarities he's noticed:

Even though the two articles are reporting on two separate studies by John Pierce and his colleagues, the findings of each of these studies are so close that they are virtually identical. So both articles focus on similar information about advertising and teenage smoking. Although Sullum attempts to cast doubt on the interpretation of Pierce's findings, he doesn't really argue with Pierce's methods or the hard data.

Questions

1. Exactly how did Pierce and his colleagues collect their data? What questions did they ask of teenagers? Can the teenagers' reports about smoking be trusted? Were the subjects themselves asked why they smoked or were inclined to do so?
2. How did Pierce and his colleagues determine that exposure to other smokers had little influence on young people being receptive to smoking? Are there other studies on this?
3. How high are the rates of teenage smoking? At what age are most smokers likely to begin?

4. To what extent is tobacco advertising aimed at young people?
5. What other factors might influence adolescents to start smoking?

Questions such as these can prompt new inquiry—perhaps even a search for new sources. In Paul's case, these questions helped to focus his emerging paper.

Question differences.

Differences also point to questions. When authors disagree about facts, you should ask *why*.

1. Do methods of determining facts differ?
2. Which presentation of facts seems more authoritative?
3. What logic and what values underlie differing opinions? Do their analyses of problems differ? Are their assumptions about correct or ethical behaviors different?

Many questions are possible based on differences. Your awareness of differences marks a beginning point for thinking.

Here's how Paul Guzman explores the differences he's noticed:

Obviously, the *Science News Update* report and Sullum draw very different conclusions from the findings of Pierce and his colleagues. The *Update* essentially states that tobacco advertising has a strong influence in terms of making adolescents open to smoking. Sullum, on the other hand, suggests that as young people become more receptive to the idea of smoking, they respond more positively to cigarette advertising and promotion. I wonder if both views don't oversimplify the issue.

Questions

1. How have other experts responded to the findings of Pierce and his colleagues?
2. Has other research been conducted into the relationship between cigarette advertising and teenage smoking?
3. Should cigarette smoking be banned? Is such a ban feasible under freedom of speech protections? How can we be sure that such a ban would reduce teenage smoking?
4. How about antismoking advertising? Does it affect the views of teenagers and lead them not to smoke?
5. What might be the most effective ways of keeping young people from experimenting with cigarettes?

Again, questions prompt new investigation. Paul Guzman found himself particularly interested in Question 5. He pursued the question of how to keep teenagers from smoking, as you will see in his use of two other sources for his paper.

EXERCISE 1

Every day for a week, read three or more newspapers—your town's local paper(s) and one or more of the following: the *New York Times*, the *Wall Street Journal*, and *USA Today*. Pay special attention to each paper's coverage of a single news event. Read the accounts and observe differences. Pose questions based on these differences.

1b   **Active, critical thinkers challenge and are challenged by sources.**

Beyond searching for similarities and differences, try to maintain a generally questioning attitude when you read. Some questions you can direct to a source; others, to yourself. In both cases, your goal is to begin exploring the source and the issues it raises. Many readers consider the following guidelines to be useful:

Weblink
http://www.kcmetro.cc.mo.us/longview/ctac/reading.htm
How to apply critical thinking skills to reading.

1   **Challenge the author: Ask questions of the source.**

Every reading invites specific questions, but the following basic questions can get you started in your effort to read any text critically:

- What central problem, issue, or subject does the text explore? If the text explores a problem, what are the reasons for this problem? What are the effects of this problem?
- What is the most important or the most striking statement the author makes? Why is it important or striking?
- Who is the author, and what are the author's credentials for writing on this topic? What is the author's stake in writing this text? What does the author have to gain?
- How can I use this selection? What can I learn from it?

2   **Challenge yourself: Ask questions of yourself.**

A critical reading points in two directions: to the text(s) you are reading and to *you*. The questions you ask about what you read can prompt you to investigate your experience, values, and opinions. As part of any critical reading, allow the issues that are important to the text to *challenge* you. Question yourself and respond until you know your views about a topic. Pose the following questions to yourself:

- What can I learn from this text? Will this knowledge change me?
- How will my experience on this topic affect my reading?

COMPUTER TIPS

Electronic Democracy at Its Best ... and Worst

Usenet newsgroups represent perhaps the pinnacle of democracy and free speech. The exchanges in this new medium can be uninhibited, unrestrained, and uncensored. But that free flow of information increases the critical thinking challenge for researchers. Everybody from world-renowned experts in a field to ignorant, malicious crackpots has equal access to the medium, and it may be difficult to tell one group from the other. Be careful when using a Usenet posting as evidence in your writing. If possible, try to verify the information first in another, more reliable source.

ACROSS THE CURRICULUM

www

1.2

Being Alert to Differences

Whatever the discipline, faculty and students search for differences, or discrepancies—for information and explanations that are supposed to fit neatly together but do not. Differences lead to questions; questions, to investigations; and investigations (very often), to writing projects. In the opening paragraph of a paper on international relations, policy analyst Gerald Segal observes a contradiction that launches his essay.*

> The twenty-first century is supposed to be the "Pacific Century," but it is also supposed to be the age of information technology. Yet these two strands of the future do not fit together very well. As anyone who has tried to plug in a portable modem in Japan will know, the East Asians are not as technologically advanced as many Americans and Europeans think. Even more important, and despite all their confidence about their economic success, East Asians are becoming seriously worried about their ability to resist the challenges posed by the new technology to their core values and the authority of their states.

A contradiction in two views of the future

Discipline focus: international relations

A difference brings challenges

*Gerald Segal is a senior fellow at the International Institute for Strategic Studies. His article "Asians in Cyberia" appeared in the *Washington Quarterly* 18.3 (1995).

- What is the origin of my views on the topic?
- What new interest, or what new question or observation, does this text spark in me?
- If I turned the topic of this selection into a question on which people voted, how would I vote—and why?

Here are Paul Guzman's thoughts on his background with teenage smoking:

As an adult ex-smoker who started as a teenager, I'm not sure I accept that advertising played a very great role in leading me to start smoking. Movie images that glamorized smoking probably played a larger role, along with the fact that it was pretty easy to buy cigarettes. I'm not sure why I started. Even knowing the dangers of cigarettes, which were being advertised heavily, didn't stop me. Why do kids start, knowing the risks full well? And what can be done to discourage them?

EXERCISE 2

Reread the three newspaper articles you selected for Exercise 1. Based on suggestions in the preceding section, pose questions that challenge the underlying assumptions in each piece. Also, use one or two of the pieces as a basis for posing questions that challenge *you*.

1c **Active, critical thinkers set issues in a broader context.**

Whenever possible, identify the issues that are important to a single reading selection and then assume that every particular issue exists in a larger cluster of related issues. This larger context will not always be obvious. Here is a set of techniques for discovering it:

Weblink

http://writing.colostate.edu/
references/reading/toulmin/

A Web site devoted to philosopher Stephen Toulmin's model of critically analyzing texts.

- Begin by identifying one or more issues that you feel are important to a text.
- Assume that each issue is an instance, or example, of something larger. Your job is to speculate on this larger something.

- Write the name of the issue at the top of a page, followed by a question: "What is this a part of?" Write a one-paragraph response.
- Reread your response, and briefly state the broader context.
- Use this broader context to stimulate more thought on the reading selection and to generate questions about issues of interest.
- Option: Investigate other reading selections about the issues you've defined.

Paul Guzman found a Web page titled "Tobacco Use among Youth" that helped him set the issue of youth smoking in broader context. Located at a site sponsored by the Campaign for Tobacco-Free Kids (http://www.tobaccofreekids.org), it provided some important statistics. Here are some of Paul's responses to these statistics.

It's amazing, but smoking rates among teenagers are higher than those for adults. According to recent studies by the Department of Health and Human Services and the Centers for Disease Control, 31.4 percent of high school students smoke, while only 24.1% of adults do. Even more disturbing is that almost 90% of adults who smoke began smoking by the age of 18. Very few people begin smoking once they enter adulthood. This suggests that the best way to reduce smoking rates across the board is to find ways to decrease the number of people under 20 years of age who start smoking.

EXERCISE 3

Explore the larger context suggested by the differing news accounts of the three articles that you found for Exercise 1. Create a phrase that summarizes one issue, subject, or problem that you think is important to these accounts. Place that phrase at the top of a page and the question "What is this a part of?" below it. Write an answer in order to identify a broader context. What research activity could follow from your writing?

1d **Active, critical thinkers will form and support opinions.**

Know what you think about what you see and read. Have an opinion and be able to support it. Opinions generally follow from responses to questions such as these:

- Has the author explained things clearly?
- In what ways does this topic confuse me?
- Has the author convinced me of his or her main argument?
- What is my view on this topic?
- Would I recommend this source to others?

Whatever your opinion, be prepared to support it with comments that are based on details about what you have seen or read. Later in this chapter (see 1g), you will learn techniques for reading to evaluate a source. And in Chapter 2 (see 2b), you will learn techniques for writing an evaluation—a type of writing in which you formally present your opinions and give reasons for holding them. It is not practical or necessary for you to develop a formal response (oral or written) to every source you read. Just the same, as a critical and active thinker, you should be able to offer reasons for believing as you do.

Here's Paul Guzman's opinion, based on his own background and what he'd read about teenage smoking. This opinion becomes a fundamental part of his first-draft essay.

It goes without saying at this point that cigarettes are highly addictive and that smoking has serious health consequences. Most young people are made aware of these dangers from an early age, yet this information does not stop significant numbers of adolescents from experimenting with smoking and eventually becoming smokers. Tobacco advertising has been blamed for luring kids into smoking, but I'm not sure that banning cigarette ads would have much of an effect. More important, I think, is to make it harder for those under 18 to get cigarettes. Also we should find ways to make smoking less glamorous to young people, even giving adolescents themselves opportunities to help develop antismoking campaigns they would find effective.

You and your classmates will agree and disagree about the ideas expressed in a source. You should be able to have an informed discussion about these ideas. You do so by stating and supporting opinions. See Chapter 6 for advice when you want to convert your opinions to a formal argument.

EXERCISE 4

Use the suggestions in the preceding section to develop an opinion based on one or more of the articles you selected for Exercise 1. In writing, state your opinion in a sentence or two. Then, in a brief paragraph, support your opinion by pointing to particular paragraphs or sentences in the news accounts.

COMPONENTS OF A CLOSE, CRITICAL READING

Noticing differences, challenging and being challenged by sources, setting issues in a broader context, and forming and supporting opinions do not necessarily lead you to formal statements about the materials you encounter. When you read and use source materials as a basis for writing, however, you *will* need to formalize and systematize your critical thinking skills. A close, critical reading requires that you read to understand, respond, evaluate, and synthesize. These are the tasks that you will find discussed in this section. The forms of writing associated with close reading—summary, evaluation, analysis, and synthesis—are discussed in Chapter 2.

Reading and rereading

To read closely and critically, experienced readers often must read a text two or more times. We discuss the types of close, critical reading in four sections (1e–1h), but we do *not* mean to suggest that you must read sources four times in order to understand them thoroughly. Still, you should commit yourself to reading however much is necessary to understand, respond, evaluate, and synthesize.

1e Critical reading (1): Reading to understand

Every use to which you can put a source is based on your ability to understand it. Without understanding you can do nothing, so understanding must be your first goal as a critical reader.

1 Setting goals for reading to understand

The steps in reading to understand can be summarized as follows:
- *Identify the author's purpose.* This will likely be to inform or to argue.
- *Identify the author's intended audience.* The text will be written with particular readers in mind. Determine whether you are the intended audience.
- *Locate the author's main point.* Every competently written text has a main point that you should be able to express in your own words.
- *Understand the structure of the text.* If the author is arguing, locate the main point and supporting points; if the author is presenting information, locate the main point and identify sections of the presentation.
- *Identify as carefully as possible what you do not understand.*

Read the following selection, which is typical of the reading you might encounter in working with sources. (This is a source that Paul Guzman used in writing his essay on teenagers and smoking.) Throughout this chapter, we will add layers of notes to this passage in order to demonstrate strategies for reading to understand, respond, evaluate, and synthesize. The notes you see on the passage here illustrate how you might read to understand. Techniques for annotating in this way follow the passage itself.

Preventing Tobacco Problems
By Robert Schwebel
FROM SAYING NO IS NOT ENOUGH *(1998)*

What can tobacco do for you? What can you expect to get from smoking or chewing tobacco? Let's consider the perspective of an adolescent. Adolescents are experiencing a tumultuous period in life when they are supposed to establish their own independent identities. They are looking for answers to the questions: Who am I? What is the meaning of life? What is

Question to be answered

1

Teenagers vulnerable

important to me? As they seek to set their own course, there is a period of uncertainty, experimentation, and vulnerability. They no longer take for granted everything their parents have taught them. They are looking for new answers. Tobacco advertisers have played on the vulnerability by portraying a positive image of smokers. They present images that appeal to adolescents trying to form an identity. They portray smokers as extremely attractive young men and women having a great time in outdoor and glamorous settings. The smokers are slender. They are engaged in healthy activities and are independent, which is what adolescents are striving to become. They are adventurous, a characteristic admired by adolescents. Advertisers try to capture the imaginations of adolescents and show them a way to improve their self-images. Smoking is presented as self-enhancing: It relaxes people, leads to fun and adventure in life, and makes you attractive—important to adolescents, who are maturing physically and thinking about sexual relationships. It is an exciting pastime, essential to popularity, and a way to bond with peers.

Tobacco advertising is a hotly contested political issue. Whatever the outcome of the political battles, the impact of advertising and the need for parents to deal with it will remain for the foreseeable future. If all tobacco advertising were to be banned immediately, we still would have to deal with the legacy of these images. We would probably also have to deal with teens who have an increased desire to engage in an activity that is "so bad it is banned." Even if advertisers were prohibited from taking direct aim at young people with cartoon characters and teen "gear" giveaways, they would still find subtle ways to appeal to the emotions and vulnerability of teens and adolescents. Furthermore, the recent sales pitches to children and adolescents has probably contributed to the increased glamorization of tobacco in Hollywood, as reflected in films with lead actors and actresses lighting up on screen. This, too, is part of the legacy of tobacco advertising. At this time, tobacco smoking and chewing is seen as attractive by a large sub-set of the adolescent population.

Advertising also fosters the perception that smoking is more common than it is, and therefore acceptable. On the average, children and adolescents think that the prevalence of smoking is two or three times higher than the actual rate. Those with the highest

Section I: Effects of advertising

Tobacco advertising images aimed at teenagers' desires

2 Banning advertising not an immediate solution

Hollywood images contribute to glamorization

3 Another effect of advertising

Critical Thinking and Reading

overestimates are more likely to become smokers than are those with the most accurate perceptions. [. . .]

HARM THAT SPEAKS TO KIDS

Section II: Practical information can deter kids from smoking (not long-term risks)

As children get older and consider the possibility of smoking, there are certain negative consequences that seem most persuasive against tobacco use. It is not the long-term health risk that worries most young people. Rather, they are much more concerned with the economic cost of smoking and the fact that smoking causes bad breath, stains teeth, and makes their hair and clothing smell bad.

4

Young people also are interested in such information as the results of a survey, conducted by the American Cancer Society, that showed that 78 percent of boys twelve to seventeen say they don't want to date someone who smokes. Among girls, 69 percent say they prefer to date someone who doesn't smoke. Another concern of some young people is diminished athletic performance. Smoking reduces the amount of oxygen that the bloodstream can deliver to the body. Most coaches forbid their athletes from smoking.

5

SO WHY DO PEOPLE SMOKE?

Section III: Kids need to know addictive effects

With all the convincing evidence about the harmfulness of tobacco and the reality of bad smells and stained teeth, a smart child may ask: "So why do people still smoke or chew? Why don't they stop?" This line of questioning presents an opportunity to launch a full-scale discussion about the advertising and promotion of the tobacco industry. You can talk about how this industry attempts to make smoking seem desirable so that people will start using tobacco products. Later you can talk about how people get hooked on smoking and then can't stop.

6

People start smoking because they see it as meeting certain needs. Tobacco is portrayed in advertising as a way to be cool; a grown-up thing to do; an attractive, sexy, and glamorous activity; a way to have fun; a way to be comfortable with other people and a way to enhance self-image. The legacy of advertising is further reflected in popular cultural trends that make tobacco seem appealing to some people. People also start smoking because they are curious about the effects of tobacco, because they believe it will alter their mood,

Standard reasons teens start smoking

7

Other reasons

and sometimes because smoking is forbidden, and they want to rebel or defy their parents. When a large group of peers smoke for these or other reasons, others follow suit to fit in with the crowd.

*Most young people see smoking as something temporary. They start out by experimenting. They are curious or looking for a little fun or excitement, and think of it as a short term activity. They know tobacco is addictive but think, "I can't get hurt—I'm just dabbling." Practically no one thinks they will get hooked. Most expect to stop sometime in the future. As they smoke more, they begin to discover that tobacco has a positive effect on their mood. We should be honest with this information, as with other drugs. Many people derive pleasure from tobacco. If they like the effect, they begin to seek it. Eventually, many of them are surprised to discover that they have become addicted. So when children ask why people smoke, we can tell them the truth about the good feeling. But we also should emphasize our conviction that the great harm from tobacco far outweighs the benefits, and that there are other, healthier, more positive ways to feel good.

*Be honest with teens about pleasures of smoking: outweighed by harms

Important point: think they won't become addicted

8

| 2 | Applying techniques for reading to understand |

When you know that you must base later writing on a source you are reading, you should consciously adopt a system for reading to understand. There are many systems you can follow, but each commonly entails reading in three stages.

Preview   Skim the text, reading quickly both to identify the author's purpose and to recall what you know about the topic.

Read   Read with pen in hand, making notes (on separate sheets or on photocopied pages) about the content and the structure of the text. Stop periodically to monitor your progress.

Review   Skim the text a second time to consolidate your notes: jot down questions and highlight especially important passages.

Following are techniques for taking notes on information important to understanding a source.

Preview the text.

- *Read titles, openings, and closings in full.* This preview will give you a sense of topic, audience, purpose, and main point. Read the title, and guess the relationship between the title and text. If you are

reading an article or a chapter of a book, read the opening and closing paragraphs in full. If you are reading a book, read the preface
along with the first and last chapters.

- *Skim the rest of the text.* A brief look at the text will help you to understand its structure, or layout. When skimming an article, read all
headings, along with a few sentences from every second or third
paragraph. When skimming a book, review the table of contents,
and then read the opening and closing paragraphs of each chapter.
- *Recall what you know about the topic.* A review of your experience with
a topic will prepare you to be interested and ready with questions.
After skimming, think about the topic: reflect on your experience.
- *Predict what you will learn from reading.* Based on your quick review
of the text and your knowledge of the topic, predict what you will
learn. Predictions keep you focused on the content and alert to potential difficulties.

Read the text.

Read with a pen or pencil in hand, and make notes that will help
you understand.

- *Identify the author's purpose.* The author's purpose will likely be to inform or to argue. Locate passages that illustrate this purpose.
- *Underline important phrases and sentences.* Your underlining or highlighting of important information should work with your notes (see
below) so that you can return to the text and spot the author's main
topic at a glance.
- *Write notes that summarize your underlining.* You can summarize important points of an explanation or an argument by writing brief
phrases in the margins. This will help you to understand as you
read and to recall important information as you reread.
- *Identify sections.* A section of a text is a grouping of related paragraphs
(see 5a). Sometimes, an author will provide section headings. At
other times, you will need to write them. In either case, your awareness of sections will help you understand the structure of a text.
- *Identify difficult passages.* Use a question mark to identify passages
that confuse you, and circle unfamiliar words. Unless a particular
word is repeated often and seems central to the meaning of a text,
postpone using a dictionary until you complete your reading. Frequent interruptions to check the meaning of words will fragment
your reading and disrupt your understanding (see 22e).
- *Periodically ask: Am I understanding?* Stop at least once during your
reading to ask this question. If you are having trouble, change your
plan for reading. For especially difficult selections, divide the text
into small sections, and read one section at a sitting. Read until you
understand each section, or until you can identify what you do not
understand.

Review the text.

After reading and making notes, spend a few minutes consolidating what you have learned. Focus on the content of the passage and its structure. Understand the pattern by which the author has presented ideas and information. These additional minutes of review will crystallize what you have learned and be a real help later on, when you are asked to refer to and *use* the selection, perhaps for an exam or paper.

■ *Consolidate information.* Skim the passage, and reread your notes. Clarify them, if necessary, so that they accurately represent the selection. Reread and highlight (with boxes or stars) what you consider to be the author's significant sentences or paragraphs.

■ *Organize your questions.* Review the various terms and concepts you have had trouble understanding. Organize your questions concerning vocabulary and content. Use dictionaries. Seek out fellow students or an instructor to clarify especially difficult points. Your questions, gathered into one place, such as a journal, will be an excellent place to begin reviewing for an exam.

EXERCISE 5

Using the techniques discussed in the preceding section, read to understand (a) an editorial from a newspaper's OP-ED page or (b) any article in which a writer clearly expresses an opinion on a topic of interest to you. On a photocopy of the article, underline what you consider to be important sentences and phrases, and make notes that summarize important ideas and information. Also, identify the different sections of the passage.

1f Critical reading (2): Reading to respond

Your personal response to a text is the second component of a critical, comprehensive reading. If your responses are to be informed, you must understand what you have read. This done, focus on yourself. Aside from the merits of the text (for instance, whether it is well written and accurate), explore your responses. What reactions do particular lines or paragraphs spark in you? The focus here is on you. Soon enough, you will turn your attention to the text (when you evaluate). For the moment, react. Are you intrigued? Surprised? Angered?

1 Setting goals for reading to respond

The overall goal of reading to respond is to identify and explore *your* reactions to a text. More specifically, these goals are as follows:

■ Reflect on your experience and associations with the topic of a text. Know what you feel about a text—know your emotional response.

- Let the text challenge you.
- Use the text to spark new, imaginative thinking.

Following is a portion of the passage by Robert Schwebel that you read in 1e-1, along with Paul Guzman's comments. Reread the passage, this time observing the second layer of notes in blue, which represent Paul's response to the passage. Recommended techniques for highlighting in this way follow. You will have a chance to practice these techniques on the passage you chose for Exercise 5.

Preventing Tobacco Problems
By Robert Schwebel

FROM SAYING NO IS NOT ENOUGH *(1998)*

What can tobacco do for you? What can you expect to get from smoking or chewing tobacco? Let's consider the perspective of an adolescent. Adolescents are experiencing a tumultuous period in life when they are supposed to establish their own independent identities. They are looking for answers to the questions: Who am I? What is the meaning of life? What is important to me? As they seek to set their own course, there is a period of uncertainty, experimentation, and vulnerability. They no longer take for granted everything their parents have taught them. They are looking for new answers. Tobacco advertisers have played on the vulnerability by portraying a positive image of smokers. They present images that appeal to adolescents trying to form an identity. They portray smokers as extremely attractive young men and women having a great time in outdoor and glamorous settings. The smokers are slender. They are engaged in healthy activities and are independent, which is what adolescents are striving to become. They are adventurous, a characteristic admired by adolescents. Advertisers try to capture the imaginations of adolescents and show them a way to improve their self-images. Smoking is presented as self-enhancing: It relaxes people, leads to fun and adventure in life, and makes you attractive—important to adolescents, who are maturing physically and thinking about sexual relationships. It is an exciting pastime, essential to popularity, and a way to bond with peers.

Tobacco advertising is a hotly contested political issue. Whatever the outcome of the political battles, the impact of advertising and the need for parents to deal with it will remain for the foreseeable future. If all tobacco advertising were to be banned immediately, we still would have to deal with the legacy of

Side notes:

Question to be answered

Teenagers vulnerable

Section I: Effects of advertising

Tobacco advertising images aimed at teenagers' desires

1

How might these positive images be combatted?

2

these images. We would probably also have to deal with teens who have an increased desire to engage in an activity that is "so bad it is banned." Even if advertisers were prohibited from taking direct aim at young people with cartoon characters and teen "gear" giveaways, they would still find subtle ways to appeal to the emotions and vulnerability of teens and adolescents. Furthermore, the recent sales pitches to children and adolescents has probably contributed to the increased glamorization of tobacco in Hollywood, as reflected in films with lead actors and actresses lighting up on screen. This, too, is part of the legacy of tobacco advertising. At this time, tobacco smoking and chewing is seen as attractive by a large sub-set of the adolescent population.

Advertising also fosters the perception that smoking is more common than it is, and therefore acceptable. On the average, children and adolescents think that the prevalence of smoking is two or three times higher than the actual rate. Those with the highest overestimates are more likely to become smokers than are those with the most accurate perceptions. . . .

Margin notes (left):
- I wonder if a ban on advertising would work
- Yes. Smoking is glamorized by Hollywood
- Does advertising cause this?

Margin notes (right):
- Banning advertising not an immediate solution
- Hollywood images contribute to glamorization
- Another effect of advertising

3

HARM THAT SPEAKS TO KIDS

As children get older and consider the possibility of smoking, there are certain negative consequences that seem most persuasive against tobacco use. It is not the long-term health risk that worries most young people. Rather, they are much more concerned with the economic cost of smoking and the fact that smoking causes bad breath, stains teeth, and makes their hair and clothing smell bad.

Young people also are interested in such information as the results of a survey, conducted by the American Cancer Society, that showed that 78 percent of boys twelve to seventeen say they don't want to date someone who smokes. Among girls, 69 percent say they prefer to date someone who doesn't smoke. Another concern of some young people is diminished athletic performance. Smoking reduces the amount of oxygen that the bloodstream can deliver to the body. Most coaches forbid their athletes from smoking.

Margin notes (left):
- Section II: Practical information can deter kids from smoking (not long-term risks)

Margin notes (right):
- Kids not thinking about the future

4

5

SO WHY DO PEOPLE SMOKE?

With all the convincing evidence about the harmfulness of tobacco and the reality of bad smells and stained teeth, a smart child may ask: "So why do

6

Section III:
Kids need
to know
addictive
effects

people still smoke or chew? Why don't they stop?"
This line of questioning presents an opportunity to launch a full-scale discussion about the advertising and promotion of the tobacco industry. You can talk about how this industry attempts to make smoking seem desirable so that people will start using tobacco products. Later you can talk about how people get hooked on smoking and then can't stop.

Interesting:
make kids
more media
savvy

People start smoking because they see it as meeting certain needs. Tobacco is portrayed in advertising as a way to be cool; a grown-up thing to do; an attractive, sexy, and glamorous activity; a way to have fun; a way to be comfortable with other people and a way to enhance self-image. The legacy of advertising is further reflected in popular cultural trends that make tobacco seem appealing to some people. People also start smoking because they are curious about the effects of tobacco, because they believe it will alter their mood, and sometimes because smoking is forbidden, and they want to rebel or defy their parents. When a large group of peers smoke for these or other reasons, others follow suit to fit in with the crowd.

Standard
reasons
teens start
smoking

7

Other
reasons

*Be honest
with teens
about
pleasures of
smoking:
outweighed
by harms

*Most young people see smoking as something temporary. They start out by experimenting. They are curious or looking for a little fun or excitement, and think of it as a short term activity. They know tobacco is addictive but think, "I can't get hurt—I'm just dabbling." Practically no one thinks they will get hooked. Most expect to stop sometime in the future. As they smoke more, they begin to discover that tobacco has a positive effect on their mood. We should be honest with this information, as with other drugs. Many people derive pleasure from tobacco. If they like the effect, they begin to seek it. Eventually, many of them are surprised to discover that they have become addicted. So when children ask why people smoke, we can tell them the truth about the good feeling. But we also should emphasize our conviction that the great harm from tobacco far outweighs the benefits, and that there are other, healthier, more positive ways to feel good.

Important
point: think
they won't
become
addicted

8

Kids need
to know
that
pleasure
leads to
addiction

---

2   Applying techniques for reading to respond

You can achieve the goals of reading to respond when you approach a text with a set of questions that continually return your focus to *you* and *your* reactions. Here is a sampling of such questions.

Questions that promote a personal response

- *Which one or two sentences did I respond to most strongly in this text? What was my response?* Explore your reasons for being excited, angry, thoughtful, surprised, or threatened. Keep the focus on you.
- *What is the origin of my views on this topic? Who else shares my views?* Explore where and under what circumstances you learned about the topic. Criticize the views of people who believe as you do. Apply this criticism to yourself.
- *If I turned the topic of this text into a question on which people voted, how would I vote—and why?* Locate a debate in the text and take sides.
- *What new interest, question, or observation does this text spark in me?* Use a text to spark your own thinking. Let the text help you pose new questions or make new observations. Use the text as a basis for speculation.

See 38d for a discussion of the special case of responding to literature.

Many of the techniques just discussed are illustrated in the passage by Robert Schwebel in 1f-1. Observe the personal nature of Paul Guzman's notes. Several of his comments clearly represent a point of view: "I wonder if a ban on advertising is feasible," for example, and "Yes. Smoking is glamorized by Hollywood." These comments differ in kind from those that summarize, such as "Tobacco advertising images aimed at teenagers' desires." Responses, by definition, are personal. They will differ from one reader to the next.

EXERCISE 6

Reread the passage you selected for Exercise 5, this time to respond. Write notes and underline phrases and sentences, based on your response. For your notes this time use a color of pen or pencil different from the one you used while reading to understand, so that you can recreate your various layers of reading.

1g Critical reading (3): Reading to evaluate

Evaluating a text is the third component of a close, critical reading. When you read to respond, you focus on personal associations with the text. Were you pleased or sympathetic? Surprised? Angry? A response is focused on you. When you evaluate, you turn systematic attention to the text in order to determine how effectively the author has presented material. Certainly a response can lead to an evaluation, as you reread the text to understand why you reacted as you did. At the end of an evaluation, you should be able to explain the extent to which the author succeeded and the points on which you and the author agree or disagree.

VERY
IMPORTANT

You have four goals in reading to evaluate:

- Distinguish between an author's use of facts and use of opinions.
- Distinguish between an author's assumptions (fundamental beliefs about the world) and your own.
- Judge the effectiveness of an explanation.
- Judge the effectiveness of an argument.

Following is part of the passage by Robert Schwebel that you read in 1e-1, where you saw summary notes, and again in 1f-1, where you saw response notes. Reread the passage, this time observing a third layer of notes in red, Paul Guzman's evaluation of the passage. Recommended techniques for reading to evaluate follow.

Preventing Tobacco Problems
By Robert Schwebel
FROM SAYING NO IS NOT ENOUGH (1998)

What can tobacco do for you? What can you expect to get from smoking or chewing tobacco? Let's consider the perspective of an adolescent. Adolescents are experiencing a tumultuous period in life when they are supposed to establish their own independent identities. They are looking for answers to the questions: Who am I? What is the meaning of life? What is important to me? As they seek to set their own course, there is a period of uncertainty, experimentation, and vulnerability. They no longer take for granted everything their parents have taught them. They are looking for new answers. Tobacco advertisers have played on the vulnerability by portraying a positive image of smokers. They present images that appeal to adolescents trying to form an identity. They portray smokers as extremely attractive young men and women having a great time in outdoor and glamorous settings. The smokers are slender. They are engaged in healthy activities and are independent, which is what adolescents are striving to become. They are adventurous, a characteristic admired by adolescents. Advertisers try to capture the imaginations of adolescents and show them a way to improve their self-images. Smoking is presented as self-enhancing: It relaxes people, leads to fun and adventure in life, and makes you attractive—important to adolescents, who are maturing physically and thinking about sexual relationships. It is an exciting pastime, essential to popularity, and a way to bond with peers.

Question to be answered

Teenagers vulnerable

Section I: Effects of advertising

Tobacco advertising images aimed at teenagers' desires

Do these generalizations about advertising hold true?

How might these positive images be combatted?

Tobacco advertising is a hotly contested political issue. Whatever the outcome of the political battles, the impact of advertising and the need for parents to deal with it will remain for the foreseeable future. If all tobacco advertising were to be banned immediately, we still would have to deal with the legacy of these images. We would probably also have to deal with teens who have an increased desire to engage in an activity that is "so bad it is banned." Even if advertisers were prohibited from taking direct aim at young people with cartoon characters and teen "gear" giveaways, they would still find subtle ways to appeal to the emotions and vulnerability of teens and adolescents. Furthermore, the recent sales pitches to children and adolescents has probably contributed to the increased glamorization of tobacco in Hollywood, as reflected in films with lead actors and actresses lighting up on screen. This, too, is part of the legacy of tobacco advertising. At this time, tobacco smoking and chewing is seen as attractive by a large sub-set of the adolescent population.

[margin left: I wonder if a ban on advertising would work]

[margin left: Yes. Smoking is glamorized by Hollywood]

[margin right: Banning advertising not an immediate solution]

[margin right: "Subtle ways" is awfully vague]

[margin right: Hollywood images contribute to glamorization]

[margin right: 2]

Advertising also fosters the perception that smoking is more common than it is, and therefore acceptable. On the average, children and adolescents think that the prevalence of smoking is two or three times higher than the actual rate. Those with the highest overestimates are more likely to become smokers than are those with the most accurate perceptions. . . .

[margin left: Does advertising cause this?]

[margin right: Another effect of advertising]

[margin right: 3]

HARM THAT SPEAKS TO KIDS

As children get older and consider the possibility of smoking, there are certain negative consequences that seem most persuasive against tobacco use. It is not the long-term health risk that worries most young people. Rather, they are much more concerned with the economic cost of smoking and the fact that smoking causes bad breath, stains teeth, and makes their hair and clothing smell bad.

[margin left: Section II: Practical information can deter kids from smoking (not long-term risks)]

[margin right: Kids not thinking about the future]

[margin right: 4]

Young people also are interested in such information as the results of a survey, conducted by the American Cancer Society, that showed that 78 percent of boys twelve to seventeen say they don't want to date someone who smokes. Among girls, 69 percent say they prefer to date someone who doesn't smoke. Another concern of some young people is diminished athletic performance. Smoking reduces the amount of oxygen that the bloodstream

[margin left: Only applies to athletes— small percentage]

[margin right: 5]

can deliver to the body. Most coaches forbid their athletes from smoking.

SO WHY DO PEOPLE SMOKE?

Section III:
Kids need
to know
addictive
effects

With all the convincing evidence about the harmfulness of tobacco and the reality of bad smells and stained teeth, a smart child may ask: "So why do people still smoke or chew? Why don't they stop?" This line of questioning presents an opportunity to launch a full-scale discussion about the advertising and promotion of the tobacco industry. You can talk about how this industry attempts to make smoking seem desirable so that people will start using tobacco products. Later you can talk about how people get hooked on smoking and then can't stop.

Interesting:
make kids
more media
savvy

6

People start smoking because they see it as meeting certain needs. Tobacco is portrayed in advertising as a way to be cool; a grown-up thing to do; an attractive, sexy, and glamorous activity; a way to have fun; a way to be comfortable with other people and a way to enhance self-image. The legacy of advertising is further reflected in popular cultural trends that make tobacco seem appealing to some people. People also start smoking because they are curious about the effects of tobacco, because they believe it will alter their mood, and sometimes because smoking is forbidden, and they want to rebel or defy their parents. When a large group of peers smoke for these or other reasons, others follow suit to fit in with the crowd.

Any strong
evidence
linking ads
to teen
smoking?

Standard
reasons teens
start smoking

7

Other
reasons

*Most young people see smoking as something temporary. They start out by experimenting. They are curious or looking for a little fun or excitement, and think of it as a short term activity. They know tobacco is addictive but think, "I can't get hurt—I'm just dabbling." Practically no one thinks they will get hooked. Most expect to stop sometime in the future. As they smoke more, they begin to discover that tobacco has a positive effect on their mood. We should be honest with this information, as with other drugs. Many people derive pleasure from tobacco. If they like the effect, they begin to seek it. Eventually, many of them are surprised to discover that they have become addicted. So when children ask why people smoke, we can tell them the truth about the good feeling. But we also should emphasize our conviction that the great harm from tobacco far outweighs the benefits, and that there are other, healthier, more positive ways to feel good.

*Be honest
with teens
about
pleasures of
smoking:
outweighed
by harms

Important
point: think
they won't
become
addicted

8

Kids need to
know that
pleasure leads
to addiction

When you are reading to evaluate, you want to be alert to an author's use of *facts, opinions,* and *definitions,* and his or her *assumed views of the world.* You also want to know if an author's purpose is primarily to inform or to argue, so that you can pose specific questions accordingly.

Distinguish facts from opinions.

Before you can evaluate a statement, you should know whether it is being presented to you as a fact or an opinion. A **fact** is any statement that can be verified.

Nationwide, the cost of college tuition is rising.

New York lies at a more southerly latitude than Paris.

Andrew Johnson was the seventeenth president of the United States.

These statements, if challenged, can be established as true or false through appropriate research. As a reader evaluating a selection, you might question the accuracy of a fact or how the fact was shown to be true. You might doubt, for instance, that Paris is a more northerly city than New York. The argument is quickly settled by reference to agreed-upon sources—in the case of Paris, a map.

Weblink
http://www.kcmetro.cc.mo.us/
longview/ctac/opinion.htm
Useful tutorial on distinguishing fact from opinion.

An **opinion** is a statement of interpretation and judgment. Opinions are not true or false in the way that statements of fact are. Opinions are more or less well supported. If a friend says, "That movie was terrible," this is an opinion. If you ask why and your friend responds, "Because I didn't like it," you are faced with a statement that is unsupported and that makes no claim on you for a response. If an opinion is supported by an entire essay, then the author is, in effect, demanding a response from you.

Identify the strongly stated.opinions in what you read, and then write *comment notes:* in the margin, jot down a brief note summarizing your response to each opinion. Agree or disagree. Later, your notes will help you crystallize your reactions to the selection.

Distinguish your assumptions from those of an author.

An **assumption** is a fundamental belief that shapes people's views. If your friend says that a painting is "beautiful," she is basing that statement, which is an opinion, on another, more fundamental opinion—an assumed view of beauty. Whether or not your friend directly states what qualities make a painting beautiful, she is *assuming* these qualities and is basing her judgment on them. If the basis of her judgment is that the painting is "lifelike," this is an assumption. Perhaps she dislikes abstract paintings, and you like them. If you challenged each other on the point or asked *why*, you both might answer, "I don't know why I think this way. I just do." Sometimes assumptions are based on clearly defined reasons, and other times (as in the painting example) they are based on ill-defined feelings. Either way, the opinions that people have (if they are not direct expressions of assumptions themselves) can be better understood by identifying the underlying assumptions.

Consider two sets of assumptions.

When you read a source, two sets of assumed views about the world come into play: yours and the author's. The extent of your agreement with an author depends largely on the extent to which your assumptions coincide. Therefore, in evaluating a source, you want to understand the author's assumptions concerning the topic at hand, as well as your own. To do so, you must perform two related tasks: identify an author's opinions, and determine whether each opinion is based on some other opinion or assumed view.

Identify direct and indirect assumptions.

Assumptions may be stated directly or indirectly. In either case, your job as a critical reader is to identify and determine the extent to which you agree with them.

Assumption stated directly

#1 A nation is justified in going to war when hostile forces threaten its borders.

#2 A nation is justified in going to war when hostile forces threaten its interests.

At times, an author hints at, but does not directly state, an assumed view—as in this example:

Assumption not stated

#3 A conflict 7,000 miles from our border does not in any way threaten this nation, and we are therefore not justified in fighting a war that far from home.

Sentence 3 is based on the assumption expressed in Sentence 1. Suppose you were reading an editorial and came across Sentence 3. In a close, critical reading you would see in this statement an unexpressed assumption about the reasons nations *should* go to war. If you can show that an author's assumed views (whether directly or indirectly expressed) are flawed, then you can argue that all opinions based on them are flawed and should be rejected, or at least challenged.

Distinguish your definitions of terms from those of an author.

Consider this statement: *Machines can explore space as well as, and in some cases better than, humans.* What do the words *as well as* and *better than* mean? If you and an author define these words differently, you are sure to disagree. In evaluating a source, identify words that are important to the presentation. If the author does not define these words directly, then state what you believe the definitions to be. At times you will need to make educated guesses based on your close reading.

Question sources that explain and sources that argue.

Outside of the literature classroom, you will read sources that are written primarily to inform or to argue. As a critical reader engaged in evaluating a source, determine the author's primary purpose, and pose questions accordingly.

Sources that explain

When a selection asks you to accept an explanation, a description, or a procedure as accurate, pose—and respond to—these questions:

- For whom has the author intended the explanation, description, or procedure? The general public—nonexperts? Someone involved in the same business or process? An observer, such as an evaluator or a supervisor?
- What does the text define and explain? How successful is the presentation, given its intended audience?
- How trustworthy is the author's information? How current is it? If it is not current, are the points being made still applicable, assuming more recent information could be obtained?
- If the author presents a procedure, what is its purpose or outcome? Who would carry out this procedure? When? For what reasons? Does the author present the stages of the procedure?

Sources that argue

When a selection asks you to accept an argument, pose—and respond to—these questions:

- What conclusion am I being asked to accept?
- What reasons and evidence has the author offered for me to accept this conclusion? Are the reasons logical? Is the evidence fair? Has the author acknowledged and responded to other points of view?
- To what extent is the author appealing to logic? To my emotions? To my respect for authorities?[2]

Many of the techniques just discussed are illustrated in the notes made for the sample passage by Robert Schwebel in 1g-1. The third layer of comments that you see (in red) would prepare a reader for writing a formal evaluation of the passage.

---

[2]See 6g for a full discussion of evaluating arguments.

EXERCISE 7

Reread the passage you selected for Exercise 5, this time to evaluate the success of the author's presentation. Write notes and underline phrases and sentences, based on the discussion in the preceding section. Use a different color of pen or pencil for your notes than the ones you used while reading to understand and reading to respond, so that you can recreate your various layers of reading.

3   Applying evaluation techniques to Web-based sources[3]

You can find a great deal of current, useful information on the World Wide Web. But as a researcher, you should approach Web-based information and arguments with special caution and questions because people can "publish" on the Web without their materials being scrutinized for accuracy or fairness. Caution is required, as well, because of the distinctive nature of electronic online information.

- Web pages that appear to be informational may in fact be advertisements.
- Search engines tend to retrieve links unrelated to a query.
- Web pages, as well as the hyperlinks that connect one page to another, tend to be unstable and can disappear.

Weblink

http://www.library.ucla.edu/
libraries/college/help/critical/
index.htm
Advice for applying critical thinking to Internet material, including discipline-based sources.

A highly useful approach to evaluating information on the Web has been provided by Janet E. Alexander and Marsha A. Tate, reference librarians at the Wolfgram Memorial Library at Widener University. In 34c you will find a more extensive discussion of their strategy for evaluating Web-based sources. We summarize that discussion here. Alexander and Tate categorize Web pages into five major types:

1. Advocacy Web pages attempt to influence public opinion.
2. Business/marketing Web pages seek to generate money.
3. News Web pages try to provide extremely current information.
4. Informational Web pages seek to provide factual information.
5. Personal Web pages vary in purpose, depending on the intentions of the authors.

[3]This section is taken in large part from the Web site "Evaluating Web Resources" (http://www2.widener.edu/Wolfgram-Memorial-Library/webeval.htm, copyright 1996–1999), which complements the book *Web Wisdom: How to Evaluate and Create Information Quality on the Web* (1999) by Janet Alexander and Marsha Ann Tate.

In addition to posing the basic questions for evaluation developed in this chapter, you can ask the following questions in analyzing the five types of Web sites:

- Does the page or its related links help you establish that the information comes from credible sources?
- Does the page provide source information that will help you verify facts?
- Are the organization's or the individual's biases clearly stated?
- Is the page current, and does it provide basic bibliographic information?
- How thoroughly and persuasively does the page address its stated topic?

Be an informed, critical consumer of Web sites. Be aware of the kinds of sites you are viewing, and ask questions accordingly.

ILLUSTRATION: EVALUATING A WEB PAGE

Let's consider how some of these criteria apply to a particular Web page. Following is the home page for Women In Technology International (WITI), found at <http://www.witi.com>. WITI is an organization founded to promote the interests and competencies of women in technology and science. Following the home page is the text of a WITI research report found at <http://www.witi.com/center/researchstatist/researchpaper/researchpaper.pdf>, which is linked to the home page. The example evaluation is based on the opening paragraphs of the research report.

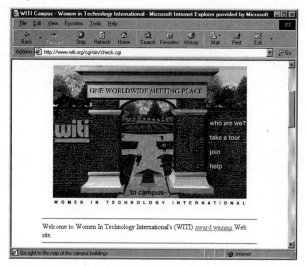

Business Impact

By Women in Science and Technology
A WITI Research Paper

- Women-owned firms will make approximately $50 million in computer-related purchases this year.
- 39% of business influencers, defined as those who are involved in the purchase of computers and related products for their organizations, are women. This is a universe of 9.2 million female business influencers.
- Women-owned businesses now employ 35% more people in the U.S. than the *Fortune* 500 companies employ worldwide.
- Women-owned businesses number 7.7 million, provide jobs for 15.5 million people and generate nearly $1.4 trillion in sales.
- Ten years ago, women made up only 10% of online users. Today it has grown to 43%.

"It's no longer a question, it's a fact—women have major impact as both influencers and purchasers of technology. Those companies committed to hiring women at every level of the organization today will have a significant competitive advantage in the 21st century!"

—CAROLYN LEIGHTON, executive director,
Women In Technology International (WITI)

Evaluation

The WITI Web site can be classified as an advocacy site, according to the categories set out by Alexander and Tate. On this page and linked pages, WITI states its biases clearly as being an organization "dedicated to breaking barriers" that women face in high-tech careers. The page provides phone numbers and e-mail addresses and seems willing to be contacted for follow-up questions. WITI clearly stands by its published work.

The page presents as facts four items of information about the influence of women in technology. The information appears to be legitimate. But given that (1) the sources for this information are not provided and (2) the purpose of WITI is to promote women's interests in technology, these facts—which show the significant influence of women in technology—should be verified in at least one other source. From all indications, fact checking would confirm the WITI information.

As for the conclusion drawn from WITI's facts, readers should be cautious. Will "companies committed to hiring women at every level of the organization today . . . have a significant competitive advantage in the 21st century"? If the preceding facts are true, the statement is at best an educated guess. Until the facts were verified, however, a researcher would not want to accept the statement attributed to the executive director of WITI.

EXERCISE 8

Evaluate one or more of the following Web sites.[4] Apply the criteria of *authority, accuracy, objectivity, currency,* and *coverage* to each site. (Note: To fully evaluate a site, once you have arrived at a home page you will need to follow some of the links to other pages.)

- *OncoLink* <http://oncolink.upenn.edu>
- *The Smoking Section* <http://www.smokingsection.com>
- *Americans for Nonsmokers' Rights* <http://www.no-smoke.org>
- *The True but Little Known Facts About Women and Aids, with documentation* <http://147.129.1.10/library/lib2/AIDSFACTS.html>
- *Feline Reactions to Bearded Men* <http://www.improb.com/airchives/classical/cat/cat.html>
- *Roget's Thesaurus* <http://humanities.uchicago.edu/forms_unrest/ROGET.html>
- *Webster's Revised Unabridged Dictionary,* 1913 Edition <http://humanities.uchicago.edu/forms_unrest/webster.form.html>

1h Critical reading (4): Reading to synthesize

Once you have understood, responded to, and evaluated a single source, you are in a position to link that source with others. By establishing links between one author and others (including yourself), you achieve a synthesis: an *integration* of sources. Synthesis is the fourth and in some ways the most complex component of a close, critical reading: it requires that you read and understand *all* your source materials and that you respond to and evaluate each one.

1 Setting goals for reading to synthesize

You are the organizing force of a synthesis. Without your active involvement with source materials, without your creative and integrating ideas, synthesis is impossible. You have four goals in reading to synthesize:

- Read to understand, respond to, and evaluate multiple sources on a subject, problem, or issue.
- Understand your own views on the subject, problem, or issue. Be able to state these views in a sentence or two.

---

[4]These sites are based on a list compiled by Janet E. Alexander and Marsha A. Tate (http://www2.widener.edu/Wolfgram-Memorial-Library/examples.htm, copyright 1996–1999).

■ Forge relationships among source materials, according to your purpose. In a synthesis, *your* views should predominate. Use the works of various authors to support what you think.

■ Generally, try to create a conversation among sources. Be sure that yours is the major voice in the conversation.

Applying techniques for reading to synthesize

When you are reading to synthesize, you want to be alert to the ways in which various sources "talk to" each other concerning a particular topic. Seek out relationships among sources. Be sure to consider yourself as a source—and a valuable one.

Students find the following plan helpful when writing syntheses:

■ *Read, respond to, and evaluate multiple sources on a topic.* It is very likely that the authors will have different observations to make. Because you are working with the different sources, you are in a unique position to find relationships among them.

■ *Subdivide the topic into parts, and give each part a brief title.* Call the topic that the several authors discuss *X*. What are all the parts, or the subdivisions, of *X* that the authors discuss? List the separate parts, giving each one a brief title.

■ *Write cross-references for each part.* For each subdivision of the topic, list *specific* page references to whichever sources discuss that part. This is called *cross-referencing*. Once you have cross-referenced each of the topic's parts, you will have created an index to your reading selections.

■ *Summarize each author's information or ideas about each part.* Now that you have generated cross-references that show you which authors discuss which parts of topic *X*, take up one part at a time, and reread all the passages you have cross-referenced. Summarize what each author has written on particular parts of the topic.

■ *Forge relationships among reading selections.* Study your notes, and try to link sources. Here are several relationships that you might establish:

Comparison: One author *agrees* with another.

Contrast: One author *disagrees* with another.

Example: Material in one source *illustrates* a statement in another.

Definition: Material from several sources, considered together, may help you *define* or redefine a term.

Cause and effect: Material from one source may allow you to *explain directly* why certain events occur in other sources.

Personal response: You find yourself agreeing or disagreeing with points made in one or more sources. Ask yourself *why*, and then develop an answer by referring to specific passages.

For ways to synthesize details you've observed in a work of literature, see 38d.

Cross-reference each part and summarize.

In actual course work, your reading selections will come from different journals, newspapers, and books—and cross-referencing should prove useful. Assume that you have identified parts of your topic and have listed page numbers from your sources that relate to each part. Following the page references, write a brief note summarizing the author's information or ideas. Exercise 9 asks you to do just this.

Forge relationships among your sources.

Based on your close reading of each selection and on your cross-references and notes, you should be able to establish relationships among the readings. Five general questions should get you started:

1. Which authors agree?
2. Which authors disagree?
3. Are there examples in one source of statements or ideas expressed in another source?
4. What definitions can you offer, based on the readings?
5. Do you detect a cause-and-effect relationship in any of the readings?

1.4

EXERCISE 9

Paul Guzman gathered several sources on the topic of teenage smoking. Read the excerpts that follow, and you'll find that you can make several connections across sources, linking the facts and ideas presented by one author with those presented by others:

> You have to give advertising some credit: It has helped to transform what might otherwise seem a strange and nasty habit—the deliberate inhalation of noxious fumes, followed by a bit of littering—into something with a certain glamorous allure. This little bit of glamour—heightened by the cigarette's bad-boy (and bad-girl) image in popular culture, may be enough of a lure to get a certain number of new smokers hooked every year. But ads aren't the only reason young people light up, and restrictions on ads often prove ineffective. In Canada, the percentage of smokers has actually *increased* slightly in the eight years since the country instituted a cigarette ad ban.
>
> —DAVID FUTRELLE, "Smoke and Mirrors" (1997)

> Eighty-six percent of youth (12–17) smokers prefer Marlboro, Camel and Newport—the three most heavily advertised brands. Marlboro, the most heavily advertised brand, constitutes almost 55 percent of the youth market but only about 35 percent of smokers over age 25.
>
> —CAMPAIGN FOR TOBACCO-FREE KIDS, "Tobacco Use among Youth" (2000)

[R]esearch indicates that the most important factors influencing whether a teenager will smoke are the behavior of his peers, his perceptions of the risks and benefits of smoking, and the presence of smokers in his home. Exposure to advertising does not independently predict the decision to smoke, and smokers themselves rarely cite advertising as an important influence on their behavior.

Critics of the industry have been quick to seize upon studies indicating that teenage smokers disproportionately prefer the most advertised cigarette brands. But such research suggests only that advertising has an impact on brand preferences, which the tobacco companies have conceded all along.

—JACOB SULLUM, "Cowboys, Camels, and Kids" (1998)

A long-term decline in trends of both per capita cigarette consumption and in the proportion of adolescents initiating smoking started in 1973, shortly after the advertising ban on the broadcast media. . . . Recently released confidential tobacco industry documents clearly indicate the concern of senior members of the tobacco industry shortly after this decline became manifest and reveal their solution to focus on the youth market.

The major innovative campaign, predicted by these confidential industry documents, was the Joe Camel campaign, which was launched in 1987. . . . This cartoon character was very attractive to young children as well as to young adolescents, and it was noted that increases in market share had occurred mainly in younger smokers. The unprecedented decline in adolescent smoking over a 12-year period was halted, and the incidence of initiation of smoking in the 14- to 17-year-old age group began to increase again.

—JOHN PIERCE, "Advertising and Promotion" (1998)

[T]he tobacco industry starts early in aiming its six-billion-dollar-a-year advertising and promotional programs at your children. Until recently they have used cartoon characters for the young ones and awarded prizes (gym bags, hats, t-shirts and other gear) that appeal to teen smokers. Your children are the target of their business minds as they attempt to replace smokers who die or quit with new and younger ones. *Advertisers know that nearly all first use of tobacco occurs before high-school graduation and that children are the chief source of new customers.*

—ROBERT SCHWEBEL, "Preventing Tobacco Problems," *Saying No Is Not Enough* (1998)

Based on your reading of the excerpts, make a connection across readings for each of the following categories:

1. Connections between advertising and smoking
2. Evidence that tobacco advertisers target teenagers
3. Evidence that advertising does/does not influence young people to smoke

Write a brief note on how each author offers a fact or idea about a specific category. Note that each author will not have something to say for each of these categories. Finally, be sure to consider yourself as a source: you should offer a comment about the category as well.

CHAPTER 2

Critical Thinking and Writing

You will often be asked to demonstrate your understanding of sources by writing summaries, evaluations, analyses, and syntheses—four forms of writing that are fundamental to college-level work. Each form emphasizes a particular way of thinking about texts, and each is built on particular skills in critical reading.[1]

Forms of writing that build on reading

- **Summary.** Briefly—and neutrally—restate the main points of a text. Summary draws on your skills of reading to understand (see 1e).
- **Evaluation.** Judge the effectiveness of an author's presentation and explain your agreement or disagreement. Evaluation draws on your skills of reading to understand (1e), reading to respond (1f), and reading to evaluate (1g).
- **Analysis.** Apply the clearly defined principles set out by one or more authors to investigate the work of other authors (or to investigate various situations in the world). Analysis draws on your skills of reading to understand (1e), reading to respond (1f), and reading to evaluate (1g).
- **Synthesis.** Gather the work of various authors according to *your* purpose. Synthesis draws on your skills of reading to understand (1e), reading to respond (1f), reading to evaluate (1g), and reading to synthesize (1h).

The cumulative layers of writing

The forms of writing discussed in this chapter are interrelated. Before you evaluate an author's presentation, you must demonstrate through summary that you understand the text. When you gather and synthesize multiple texts for a research paper, you will summarize *and* evaluate the texts as you forge relationships among them. When you conduct an analysis, you must have thoroughly understood and evaluated the principles you apply. This calls for written summary and evaluation as part of your analysis.

[1] We use the term *text* interchangeably with *source* to mean any reading selection.

CRITICAL D0CISIONS

Knowing When to Write Summaries, Evaluations, Analyses, and Syntheses

Whether a writing assignment calls for a summary, an evaluation, an analysis, or a synthesis depends largely on how it is worded. Of course, if an assignment explicitly asks you to "summarize," "evaluate," "analyze," or "synthesize," then your choice is clear. Often, however, the directions will not be so explicit, so you will need to read the assignment carefully to understand what is required. The introductions to sections 2a, 2b, 2c, and 2d that follow offer examples of assignments requiring each of these forms of writing, along with advice for determining which form is appropriate.

WWW

2.1

These forms of academic writing are cumulative: one builds on the next in much the same way that strategies for reading comprehensively do. For clarity of presentation, we discuss summary, evaluation, analysis, and synthesis in separate sections and as separate tasks. In practice—in the texts you read and in the papers you write—you will find that these forms of writing and thinking merge.

2a Writing a summary

The **summary**—a brief, neutral restatement of a text—is fundamental to working with sources in any academic setting. You will read texts in every course, and before you can comment on them or otherwise put them to use, you must show that you understand the authors on their own terms. Like any piece of writing, a summary calls for you to make decisions and to plan, draft, and revise. While sometimes called for on exams, a summary more typically appears as part of evaluations, analyses, and syntheses. The following three assignments require summaries.

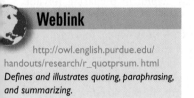

Weblink

http://owl.english.purdue.edu/
handouts/research/r_quotprsum.html
Defines and illustrates quoting, paraphrasing, and summarizing.

Assignments that explicitly call for a summary

Mathematics   Read the article "Structuring Mathematical Proofs," by Uri Leron [*The American Mathematical Monthly* 90 (March 1983): 174–185]. In two to four typed pages, summarize the concept of linear proof, giving one good example from the course.

| Film studies | Summarize Harvey Greenberg's discussion of *The Wizard of Oz*. |
| Social psychology | Write a summary of your textbook's discussion of the "realistic conflict theory." Make sure that you address the theory's explanation of prejudice as an intergroup conflict. |

An assignment may not explicitly call for a summary but may require it just the same, as in the following example. In completing this assignment, a student would need to summarize the Mary Shea argument.

Assignment that implies the need for a summary

| Business ethics | In "Good Riddance to Corporate America," Mary Shea argues that highly credentialed female MBAs are beginning to quit corporate America because of its "essential emptiness." How does she support this assertion? |

1 Setting goals for writing a summary

The focus of a summary is on a specific text, *not* on your reactions to it. Overall, your goal is to restate the text, as briefly as possible, in your own words. More specifically, you should aim to meet these goals:

- Clearly state the author's purpose in writing.
- Clearly state the author's thesis.
- Clearly state the author's main points in support of this thesis.

2 Understanding techniques for writing a summary

Summary begins with reading to understand. In 1e you were advised to make notes as you previewed, read, and reviewed a text.

Students find the following process helpful in preparing for and writing a summary:

- Determine the purpose of the source—for instance, to inform, explain, argue, justify, defend, compare, contrast, or illustrate.
- Summarize the thesis. Based on the notes you have made and the phrases or sentences you have highlighted while reading, restate the author's main point in your own words. In this statement, refer to the author by name; indicate the author's purpose (for example, to argue or inform); and refer to the title.
- Summarize the body of the text.

  STRATEGY 1: Write a one- or two-sentence summary of every paragraph. Summarize points important to supporting the author's thesis. Omit minor points and illustrations. Do not simply translate phrase for phrase from sentences in the text.

STRATEGY 2: Identify sections (groupings of related paragraphs), and write a two- or three-sentence summary of each section.

- Study your paragraph or section summaries. Determine how the paragraphs or sections work together to support the thesis.
- Write the summary. Join your paragraph or section summaries with your summary of the thesis, emphasizing the relationship between the parts of the text and the thesis.
- Revise for clarity and for style. Quote sparingly. Provide transitions where needed.

COMPUTER TIPS

Use a Scratchpad to Record Your Thoughts

When you're writing or when you're reading online material, it is useful to keep a second file window open for jotting down thoughts, ideas, and questions. If you have a big enough computer screen, you can even keep both windows visible at the same time and just switch between them. Some computers have small notepad utilities that simplify this process. Be sure to save this file each time you record questions you may have, tangential material you think of, or bibliographic citations and URLs you need to remember.

3 Applying techniques for writing summaries

The techniques for writing summaries can now be applied to an example passage found in Chapter 1: Robert Schwebel's "Preventing Tobacco Problems" (see 1e-1). You may want to reread the selection so that you can better understand the preparations for summary that follow.

2.2

Prepare: Make notes for a summary.

These preparatory notes are based on the above plan for writing summaries. The first note concerns Schwebel's purpose. The second is a clear statement of the thesis—in the writer's own words, not the author's. Finally, there is a one-sentence summary of each paragraph in the article.

Purpose To explain and advise

Thesis In order to counter the effects of tobacco advertising in terms of encouraging adolescents to smoke, we must provide young people with information regarding the harms of smoking that will speak to them directly and make sure they understand how addictive smoking really is.

Identify sections

Section 1 (¶s 1–3): Describes the role of tobacco advertising in encouraging adolescents to smoke

¶1: Adolescents are discovering their identities, and tobacco advertisers
appeal to this vulnerability by portraying smokers as popular, free-
spirited, and attracted to adventure, qualities that many young people
aspire to.

¶2: Banning cigarette advertising is not going to stop tobacco companies
from getting their message out to teenagers, who also find tobacco use
appealing because of favorite movie stars who smoke on screen.

¶3: Because of advertising, many young people overestimate the number of
people who smoke, and their overestimates lead many to try smoking.

Section 2 (¶s 4–5): Suggests negatives about smoking that teenagers
respond to

¶4: Adverse health consequences over the long term are of less concern
to potential adolescent smokers than more immediate issues: the price
of cigarettes and the hygienic negatives of smoking.

¶5: Also persuasive to adolescents are statistics reporting that most
teenagers don't want to go out with a person who smokes, as well as
smoking's effects on athletic ability.

Section 3 (¶s 6–8): Suggests that young people need to understand how
addictive smoking is

¶6: Young people need to know that advertising making smoking appear
attractive leads people to try cigarettes; then they get addicted and find
it impossible to quit.

¶7: In addition to the influence of advertising, young people are led to
experiment with cigarettes out of curiosity, rebelliousness, and a need
for peer acceptance.

¶8: Teenagers who experiment with smoking think they'll be able to give
it up when they want to, but the mood-enhancing effects of cigarettes
can quickly lead to addiction; in trying to prevent young people from
smoking, parents and educators need to be honest about why people
enjoy smoking and encourage potential smokers to find less health-
threatening outlets for lifting their mood.

Write the summary.

Join paragraph or section summaries to the thesis, and emphasize the
relationship of parts. Revise as needed to ensure a smooth flow of ideas.

In the chapter "Preventing Tobacco Problems" from his book *Saying
No Is Not Enough*, Dr. Robert Schwebel advises that in order to counter
the effect tobacco advertising has on encouraging adolescents to
smoke, we must provide young people with information regarding the
harms of smoking that will speak to them directly and make sure they
understand how addictive smoking really is. Adolescents are discovering their identities, and tobacco advertisers appeal to this vulnerability
by portraying smokers as popular, free-spirited, and attracted to adventure, qualities that many young people aspire to. There have been calls
to ban cigarette advertising altogether, but doing so is not going to

stop tobacco companies from getting their message out to teenagers, who also find tobacco use appealing because of favorite movie stars who smoke on screen. Ironically, because of advertising and other media images, many young people overestimate the number of people who smoke, and these overestimates lead them to try smoking.

To offset these influences, according to Schwebel, we must be realistic about what will persuade young people not to smoke. Adverse health consequences over the long term are of less concern to potential adolescent smokers than more immediate issues: the price of cigarettes and the hygienic negatives of smoking. Also persuasive to adolescents are statistics reporting that most teenagers don't want to go out with a person who smokes, as well as smoking's negative effects on athletic ability. Young people need to know that advertising making smoking appear attractive leads people to try cigarettes; then they get addicted and find it impossible to quit. In addition to the influence of advertising, young people are led to experiment with cigarettes out of curiosity, rebelliousness, and a need for peer acceptance. Teenagers who experiment with smoking think they'll be able to give it up when they want to, but the mood-enhancing effects of cigarettes can quickly lead to addiction. In trying to prevent young people from smoking, parents and educators need to be honest about why people enjoy smoking and encourage potential smokers to find less health-threatening outlets for lifting their mood.

EXERCISE I

Working with the article you selected for Exercises 5–7 in Chapter 1, and with the notes you made while reading that selection, write a summary. For specific help in doing so, follow the advice given in this section.

2b   Writing an evaluation

In an **evaluation** you judge the effectiveness and reliability of a text and discuss the extent to which you agree or disagree with its author. Consider the following assignments, which call for evaluation.

Sociology   Write a review of Christopher Lasch's *Culture of Narcissism.*

History   In "Everyman His Own Historian," Carl L. Becker argues for a definition of history as "the memory of things said and done." Based on your reading in this course, evaluate Becker's definition.

Physics   Write a review of *Surely You're Joking, Mr. Feynman!*

Writing an evaluation formalizes the process of reading to evaluate, which, in turn, depends on reading to understand and to respond (see 1e,f). Evaluation will always entail summary writing (see 2a), since before you can reasonably agree or disagree with an author's work or determine its effectiveness, you must show that you understand and can restate it.

I   Setting goals for writing an evaluation

You have two primary goals when writing to evaluate, and both depend on a critical, comprehensive reading: (1) to judge the effectiveness of the author's presentation, focusing for the moment only on the *quality* of the presentation; then (2) to agree and/or disagree with the author and explain your responses.

2   Understanding techniques for writing an evaluation

The basic pattern of evaluation is as follows:

1. Offer a judgment about the text.
2. Refer to a specific passage—summarize, quote, or paraphrase.
3. Explain your judgment in light of the passage referred to.

Using these components of evaluation, you will help to establish your authority as someone whose insights a reader can trust.

Prepare: Make notes on the effectiveness of the presentation.

Evaluate the effectiveness and reliability of a presentation according to the author's purpose for writing. If the author is attempting to persuade you, you use one set of criteria, or standards of judgment, to evaluate the text. If the author is informing—providing explanations or presenting procedures or descriptions—you use another set of criteria.

Criteria for texts that inform or persuade

Use the following criteria to judge the effectiveness of any text. Remember to support your evaluation by referring to and discussing a specific passage.

Accuracy   Are the author's facts accurate?

Definitions   Have terms important to the discussion been clearly defined—and if not, has lack of definition confused matters?

Development   Does each part of the presentation seem well developed, satisfying to you in the extent of its treatment? Is each main point adequately illustrated and supported with evidence?

Criteria for texts that inform

When an author writes to inform, you can evaluate the presentation based on any of the preceding criteria, as well as on the ones discussed in this section. Remember to support your evaluation by referring to and discussing a specific passage.

Audience   Is the author writing for a clearly defined audience who will know what to do with the information presented? Is the author consistent in presenting information to one audience?

Clarity	How clear has the author been in defining and explaining? Is information presented in a way that is useful? Will readers be able to understand an explanation or follow a procedure?
Procedure	Has the author presented the stages of a process? Is the reader clear about the purpose of the process—about who does it and why?

Criteria for texts that persuade

When an author writes to persuade, you can evaluate the presentation based on any of the preceding criteria, as well as on the ones that follow. Remember to support your evaluation by referring to and discussing specific passages.

Fairness	If the issue being discussed is controversial, has the author presented opposing points of view? Has the author seriously considered and responded to these points? (See 6e.)
Logic	Has the author adhered to standards of logic? Has the author avoided, for instance, fallacies such as personal attacks and faulty generalization? (See 6g.)
Evidence	Do facts and examples fairly represent the available data on the topic? Are the author's facts and examples current? Has the author included negative examples? (See 6g.)
Authority	Are the experts that the author refers to qualified to speak on the topic? Are the experts neutral? (See 6d-3 and 6g.)[2]

Prepare: Make notes on your agreement and disagreement with the author.

By applying the criteria above, you may decide that a selection is well written. Just the same, you may disagree with the author in part or in whole, or you may agree. In any case, you should examine the reasons for your reactions.

Whatever your reaction to a text, you should (1) identify an author's views, pointing out particular passages in which these views are apparent; (2) identify your own views; and (3) examine the basis on which you and the author agree or disagree. For the most part, you can explain agreements and disagreements by examining both your assumptions and the author's. Recall from Chapter 1 that an assumption is a fundamental belief that shapes people's opinions. Here is a format for distinguishing your views from the author's. (For an example of note making that follows this format, see 2b-3.)

Author's view on topic *X:*

Author's assumption:

My view:

My assumption:

[2]In 6g you will find an extended discussion of evaluating arguments.

Prepare: Organize your notes and gain a general impression.

Once you have prepared for writing an evaluation by making notes, review your material and develop an overall impression of the reading. In writing an evaluation, you will have enough space to review at least two, but probably not more than four or five, aspects of an author's work. Therefore, be selective in the points you choose to evaluate. Review your notes concerning the quality of the presentation and the extent of your agreement with the author. Select the points that will best support your overall impression of the reading. As with any piece of formal writing, plan your evaluation carefully. If you are going to discuss three points concerning a selection, do so in a particular order, for good reasons. Readers will expect a logical, well-developed discussion.

Students find these steps helpful in preparing evaluations:

- Introduce the topic and author: one paragraph. One sentence in the introduction should hint at your general impression of the piece.
- Summarize the author's work: one to three paragraphs. If brief, the summary can be joined to the introduction.
- Briefly review the key points in the author's work that you will evaluate: one paragraph.
- Identify key points in the author's presentation; discuss each in detail: three to six paragraphs. If you are evaluating the quality of the author's presentation, state your criteria for evaluation explicitly. If you are agreeing or disagreeing with opinions, try to identify the underlying assumptions (yours and the author's).
- Conclude with your overall assessment of the author's work.

The order of parts in the written evaluation may not match the actual order of writing. You may be unable to write the third section of the evaluation without first having evaluated the author's key points—the next section. The evaluation will take shape over multiple drafts.

3 Applying techniques for writing evaluations

Robert Schwebel's essay about teenagers and smoking (1e-1) provides an opportunity to demonstrate how you can evaluate a text. The first step of evaluation, neutrally presenting the author's views in a summary, was developed earlier in this chapter (2a-3). Beyond the summary, your evaluation will address one or both of these questions: How effective and reliable is the author's presentation? Do I agree with the author?

How effective and reliable is the author's presentation?

In 2b-2 you found ten criteria, or standards of judgment, one or more of which you can use to determine the effectiveness and reliability of a source: accuracy, definitions, development, audience, clarity, procedure, fairness, logic, evidence, and authority. Following is an example of how three of these standards—clarity, audience, and development—

become criteria for evaluating Schwebel's discussion. This evaluation assumes that the author is writing to inform.

Clarity	The author's presentation is clear and direct, and it is easy to follow the points he makes. He presents his ideas concretely, and offers advice that seems to be immediately useful for concerned readers.
Audience	The author is writing for an audience of parents and educators concerned about how to prevent smoking among teenagers. The information and advice he offers is tailored specifically for this audience. He writes in a friendly tone that is helpful and reassuring and that inspires a reader's confidence in his authority.
Development	Schwebel doesn't fully develop his two main points—the relationship between tobacco advertising and teenage smoking and what can realistically be done to prevent young people from experimenting with smoking. Although he does describe the imagery of tobacco advertising in detail and makes a persuasive case that such imagery would be likely to appeal to adolescents, he doesn't prove a direct connection between such advertising and teenage smoking. More objective information would be required for him to establish this connection. His specific suggestions for discouraging young people from smoking seem reasonable. However, a variety of other courses could be explored, including reducing the accessibility of cigarettes and involving teens themselves in the development of antismoking campaigns.

Do I agree with the author?

One of your jobs as an alert reader is to respond (see 1f). When you do so, make notes: point out specific passages that illustrate the author's view, summarize that view, respond, and then explain the assumptions underlying both your view and the author's. In a thoroughly active reading, you would point to many such passages and make notes. When you write a formal evaluation, choose the passages that seem the most interesting to you and that appear to involve the author's main point most directly. Here's an example response to a point made by Robert Schwebel:

Schwebel's view	To discourage young people from smoking, we need to provide information about the harms of smoking that appeals to adolescent concerns and make it clear just how addictive smoking is.
Schwebel's assumption	Most young people will listen to reason when it comes to smoking and respond to the cosmetic negatives of using tobacco and to the fear of becoming addicted to nicotine.
My view	We need to go further and make tobacco products less accessible to young people and create more effective

antismoking campaigns based on what adolescents themselves say would deter them from smoking.

My evaluation Notwithstanding reasonable arguments to the contrary, a
sizeable number of young people are going to be attracted
to smoking no matter what parents and educators say.
We must therefore do more than just talk to young
people about smoking and take more public efforts to
discourage tobacco use.

```
        Evaluation of "Preventing Tobacco Problems"
               from Saying No Is Not Enough
                    by Robert Schwebel
      Most people today would agree that cigarette
smoking poses serious long-term health risks to
those who smoke and a major financial burden in
terms of public and private health-care resources.
It would seem reasonable that young people, know-
ing the risks of smoking, could easily be per-
suaded not to start or even experiment with
cigarettes. Yet this is not the case. According
to various recent surveys, smoking rates among
teenagers are alarmingly high, significantly
higher than in the early 1990s. Many attribute
this at least in part to tobacco advertising in-
creasingly directed at children and adolescents.
What might be done to discourage young people from
smoking? In the chapter "Preventing Tobacco Prob-
lems" from his book Saying No Is Not Enough, Dr.
Robert Schwebel advises that in order to counter
the effect tobacco advertising has on encouraging
adolescents to smoke, we must provide young people
with information regarding the harms of smoking
that will speak to them directly and make sure
they understand how addictive smoking really is.
      According to Schwebel, a clinical psycholo-
gist and expert in drug prevention and treatment,
adolescents are discovering their identities, and
tobacco advertisers appeal to this vulnerability
by portraying smokers as popular, free-spirited,
```

Summary

and attracted to adventure, qualities that many young people aspire to. There have been calls to ban cigarette advertising altogether, but Schwebel feels that doing so is not going to stop tobacco companies from getting their message out to teenagers, who also find tobacco use appealing because of favorite movie stars who smoke on screen. Ironically, because of advertising and other media images, many young people overestimate the number of people who smoke, and these overestimates lead them to try smoking.

To offset these influences, according to Schwebel, we must be realistic about what will persuade young people not to smoke. Adverse health consequences over the long term are of less concern to potential adolescent smokers than more immediate issues: the price of cigarettes and the hygienic negatives of smoking. Also persuasive to adolescents are statistics reporting that most teenagers don't want to go out with a person who smokes, as well as smoking's negative effects on athletic ability. Young people need to know that advertising making smoking appear attractive leads people to try cigarettes; then they get addicted and find it impossible to quit. In addition to the influence of advertising, young people are led to experiment with cigarettes out of curiosity, rebelliousness, and a need for peer acceptance. Teenagers who experiment with smoking think they'll be able to give it up when they want to, but the mood-enhancing effects of cigarettes can quickly lead to addiction. In trying to prevent young people from smoking, parents and educators need to be honest about why people enjoy smoking and encourage potential smokers to find less health-threatening outlets for lifting their mood.

Writing an Evaluation

The advice Schwebel offers certainly seems reasonable, particularly as it suggests concrete action parents and educators can take in dealing with young people who might be attracted to smoking. Because he focuses so narrowly on the role of parents and educators, however, he doesn't address larger and perhaps more important public policy goals that might have an effect on reducing teen smoking.

Schwebel makes a number of useful and persuasive points. It seems true that many young people are unlikely to be scared into not smoking by constantly being warned of the long-term health risks involved. They see too many adult smokers around them who do not exhibit such problems. So focusing on issues such as bad breath, stained teeth, and the fact that most teens don't want to date a smoker probably is a better deterrent. More important, teens should be encouraged to think about what motivates people to start smoking and to analyze the images of smokers presented in tobacco advertising. Thinking critically about matters like these could very well permit large numbers of young people to say no to that first cigarette. Finally, the addictive power of nicotine deserves particular stress. Hearing from unhappy smokers in their twenties about how easily they became addicted could scare off teenagers more than warnings about long-term health risks.

However useful, though, Schwebel's advice may not go far enough. Perhaps a ban on tobacco advertising would make a difference. Is this a goal parents should lobby for? More important, despite reasonable appeals against smoking by parents and educators, young people are still going to be attracted to cigarettes. So a

Preview of key points of evaluation

Agreement with main points

Qualified agreement: main points must be expanded

variety of other courses could be explored. For example, we could reduce the accessibility of cigarettes, perhaps through taxes that make them financially out of reach for most teenagers or by penalizing merchants who sell tobacco products to people under the age of 18. Involving teens themselves in the development of antismoking campaigns might also have a strong effect. How might concerned parents and educators work to develop and fund such campaigns?

Ultimately, the battle against youth smoking must be fought on several fronts. In Saying No Is Not Enough, Robert Schwebel offers sound advice for parents and educators dealing with adolescents at risk for smoking. In the long run, however, broader and more comprehensive measures will be required if we are to seriously deter adolescents from trying cigarettes.

Conclusion: evaluator agrees but offers additional suggestions

Works Cited

Schwebel, Robert. Saying No Is Not Enough. 2nd ed. New York: Newmarket, 1998.

EXERCISE 2

Write an evaluation of the article you summarized in Exercise 1. In preparing for your evaluation, take notes both on the author's presentation—for instance, its fairness and use of evidence and logic—and on your response to the author's key points. In writing the evaluation, use the summary you have written, but be aware that you may need to alter it by dividing it into several parts—presenting first a one-paragraph overall summary and then more sharply focused summaries of individual points you wish to evaluate.

2c   Writing an analysis (an application paper)

An **analysis** is an investigation that you conduct by applying a principle or definition to an activity or object in order to see how that activity or object works, what it might mean, or why it might be significant. Analysis enables you to make interpretations. You might analyze, for instance, an event, condition, behavior, painting, novel, play, or television show. As an illustration of the range of ways analysis can be used, read the following assignments from different disciplines. Notice how each asks students to apply a principle or a definition.

Literature   Apply principles of Jungian psychology—that is, an archetypal approach to literature—to Hawthorne's "Young Goodman Brown." In your reading of the story, apply Jung's concepts of the *shadow*, *persona*, and *anima*.

Physics   Use Newton's Second Law ($F = ma$) to analyze the acceleration of a fixed pulley, from which two weights hang: m_1 (.45 kg) and m_2 (.90 kg). Having worked the numbers, explain in a paragraph the principle of Newton's law and your method of applying it to solve a problem. Assume that your reader is not comfortable with mathematical explanations: do not use equations in your paragraph.

Finance   Using Guilford C. Babcock's "Concept of Sustainable Growth" [*Financial Analysts Journal* 26 (May–June 1998): 108–114], analyze the stock price appreciation of the XYZ Corporation, figures for which are attached.

In these assignments, students are asked to analyze a short story, the acceleration of a pulley, and the stock performance of a corporation. In every discipline, certain principles and definitions play a key role in helping researchers to pose questions from a particular point of view in order to better understand the activities and objects under study. Teachers will assign analyses to determine the extent to which you have understood principles and definitions important to your coursework. A key test of understanding is *application:* can you apply what you have learned to new situations? By writing an analysis, you show that you can. Analysis builds on skills of reading to understand (1e) and writing summaries (2a).

> ### Setting goals for writing the analysis/application paper

An analysis should show readers how an activity or object works, what it might mean, or why it is significant. The specific goals of analysis follow:

- Understand a principle or definition and demonstrate your understanding by using it to study an activity or an object.
- Thoroughly apply this principle or definition to all significant parts of the activity or object under study.
- Create for the reader a sense that your analysis makes the activity or object being studied understandable—if not for the first time, then at least in a new way.

Different analyses lead to different interpretations.

What you discover through analysis depends entirely on which principles you apply to the activity or object under study. One event or text, analyzed according to different principles, will yield different interpretations. For example, over the years many writers have analyzed the L. Frank Baum classic, *The Wizard of Oz*, and the movie based on it. These writers have arrived at different interpretations, according to the different principles or definitions they applied to the story. Consider three specific insights into *The Wizard of Oz*, based on an application of three different principles.

Psychological analysis
At the dawn of adolescence, the very time she should start to distance herself from Aunt Em and Uncle Henry, the surrogate parents who raised her on their Kansas farm, Dorothy Gale experiences a hurtful reawakening of her fear that these loved ones will be rudely ripped from her, especially her Aunt (Em—M for Mother!). [Harvey Greenberg, *The Movies on Your Mind* (New York: Dutton, 1975).]

Political analysis
[*The Wizard of Oz*] was originally written as a political allegory about grass-roots protest. It may seem harder to believe than Emerald City, but the Tin Woodsman is the industrial worker, the Scarecrow [is] the struggling farmer, and the Wizard is the president, who is powerful only as long as he succeeds in deceiving the people. [Peter Dreier, "Oz Was Almost Reality," *Cleveland Plain Dealer* 3 Sept. 1989.]

Literary analysis
The Kansas described by Frank Baum is a depressing place. Everything in it is gray as far as the eye can see: the prairie is gray, and so is the house in which Dorothy lives. As for Auntie Em, "The sun and wind . . . had taken the sparkle from her eyes and left them a sober gray; they had taken the red from her cheeks and lips, and they were gray also. She was thin and gaunt, and never smiled now." And "Uncle Henry never laughed. . . . He was gray also, from his long beard to his rough boots." The sky? It was "even grayer than usual." [Salman Rushdie, "Out of Kansas," *New Yorker* 11 May 1992.]

Different analytical approaches yield different insights, and no analysis can be ultimately correct. There will be as many different interpretations of *The Wizard of Oz*, for instance, as there are principles of analysis; and each, potentially, has something to teach us. Not every analysis will be equally useful, however. An analysis is useful or authoritative to the extent that a writer (1) clearly defines a principle or definition to be applied; (2) applies this principle or definition thoroughly and systematically; and in so doing (3) reveals new and convincing insights into the activity or object being analyzed.

**Prepare: Turn the principle or definition you are using
to guide your analysis into a question—and then *probe*.**

When preparing to write an analysis, you must be satisfied that you thoroughly understand the definition or principle you will be using. Read and reread the material that will become your analytical tool, and think of this material as a lens through which you will see new elements of the object under analysis. Turn your material into a series of questions that you will direct at the object under analysis.

Before writing your analysis, direct as many questions as possible to the object under study, and make many notes. In your final written piece, you will not draw on every note, but only on those that prove most revealing—and you won't be able to tell which notes these are until you actually begin posing questions. Many students find the following guide for writing analyses helpful. (The third point assumes you've made a preliminary analysis and are choosing to incorporate the most revealing insights into your essay.)

- Introduce and summarize the activity or object to be analyzed. Whatever parts of this activity or object you intend to analyze should be mentioned here.
- Introduce and summarize the key definition or principle that will form the basis of your analysis.
- Analyze. Systematically apply elements of this definition or principle to parts of the activity or object under study. Part by part, discuss what you find.
- Conclude by reviewing all the parts you have analyzed. To what extent has your application of the definition or principle helped you to explain how the activity or object works, what it might mean, or why it is significant?

3 Applying techniques for writing analyses/application papers

The most common error in writing analyses is to present your readers with a summary only. Summary is naturally a *part* of analysis: you will need to summarize the object or activity you are examining and the principle or definition with which you are working, if this is not known to your readers. You must then take the next step and *apply* the principle or definition, using it as an investigative tool.

EXERCISE 3

Choose one of the three lines of analysis presented at the start of 2c-1—approaches to analyzing the classic *The Wizard of Oz* from a psychological, political, or literary view. Apply one of these analytic schemes to the movie, identifying key elements of the movie that can be explained in terms of the analytic principles offered.

www
2.3

ACROSS THE CURRICULUM

Writing an Analysis

Faculty and students across the curriculum write analyses. Consider two parts of an essay written by a freshman sociology student, Edward Peselman, "The Coming Apart of a Dorm Society." Peselman (1) introduces a principle (how powerful people get their way) that will guide his analysis and (2) applies that principle. You will follow similar organizational steps in writing analyses for courses across the curriculum.

First, Edward introduces a concept:

> According to sociologist Randall Collins, what a powerful person wishes to happen must be achieved by controlling others (61).

Next, Edward applies this concept. He turns it into a question (though the question never appears in the essay itself): How does Collins's observation about power help to explain what happened in my dorm? Edward's *answer* becomes part of the analysis:

> Collins's observation helps define who had how much power in our dormitory's social group. Marc and Eric clearly had the most power. Everyone feared them and agreed to do pretty much what they wanted. Through violent words or threats of violence, they got their way. I was next in line: I wouldn't dare to manipulate Marc or Eric, but the others I could manage through occasional sarcasm. To avoid my quips, Benjamin became very cooperative. Up and down the pecking order, we exercised power through macho taunts, challenges, and biting language.

<h2>2d Writing a synthesis</h2>

A **synthesis** is a written discussion in which you gather and present source materials according to a well-defined purpose. In the process of writing a synthesis you answer these questions: (1) Which authors have written on my topic? (2) In what ways can I link the work of these authors to one another and to my own thinking? (3) How can I best use the material I've gathered to create a discussion that supports *my* views? The following assignment calls for synthesis:

Sociology   This semester we have read a number of books, articles, and essays on the general topic of marriage: its legal, religious, economic, and social aspects. In a five-page paper, reflect on these materials, and discuss the extent to which they have helped to clarify or confuse your understanding of this "sacred institution."

The word *synthesis* does not appear in this assignment; nonetheless, the professor is asking students to gather and discuss sources. Note the importance of the writer here. Given multiple sources, a dozen students working on this sociology assignment would produce a dozen different papers; what would distinguish one paper from the next and make each uniquely valuable are the *particular* insights of each student. You are the most important source in any synthesis. However much material you gather into a discussion, your voice should predominate.

No synthesis is possible without a critical, comprehensive reading of sources. The quality of a synthesis is tied directly to the quality of prior reading. You have the best possible chance of producing a meaningful synthesis when you have read sources to understand (1e), respond (1f), evaluate (1g), and synthesize (1h). At one point or another, a synthesis will draw on all your skills of critical reading and writing; synthesis therefore represents some of the most sophisticated and challenging writing you will do in college.

Ensuring that your voice is heard

2.4

When writing a synthesis, avoid letting sources dominate a discussion unless you are being asked to write a literature review (see 40c-2—though even in this case your point of view dominates in that you select the articles to be discussed and determine the principles that organize discussion). In its most extreme form, the error of allowing sources to dominate leads to a series of summaries in which the writer, making no attempt at merging sources, disappears. The problem can be avoided if you remember that a synthesis should draw on your insights first, and only then on the insights of others. *A paper organized as a series of summaries of separate sources, introduced by a statement such as "Many authors have discussed topic* X,*" is* not *a synthesis, because it makes no attempt to merge ideas.*

Do Not Become Invisible in Your Papers

The DANGER signs:

1. Your paragraphs are devoted wholly to the work of the authors you are synthesizing.
2. Virtually every sentence introduces someone else's ideas.
3. The impulse to use the first-person *I* never arises.

Instead of writing a string of paragraphs organized around the work of others, write paragraphs organized around your own statements. In the context of a paper on advertising, for example, a discussion organized as summaries of separate sources would leave you invisible. Generally, a statement such as the one that follows indicates that the writer will never appear:

> Several authors have discussed the topic of advertising.

This statement, and the paper likely to be built on it, is *source* based and exhibits all the danger signals mentioned in the preceding box. By contrast, a paper in which the author is present will show an active, interested mind engaged with the reading material and headed in some clear direction, with a purpose:

> The topic of advertising is guaranteed to generate debate whenever it is discussed. It is rare to find a person who does not have strong, specific opinions about advertising and its effects on our culture.

This statement is *writer* based. The writer's purpose and direction are made known, and we sense the reading material will not overshadow the writer. If you find source materials monopolizing your work, re-examine your thesis, and make it into a writer-based statement.

1 Setting goals for writing a synthesis

Your goal in writing a synthesis is to create and participate in a discussion, joining your views on a topic with the views of others. Specifically, you want to do the following:

- Understand your purpose for writing.
- Define your topic and your thesis (see 3d).
- Locate the work of others who have written on this topic, and read to understand, respond, and evaluate.
- Forge relationships among sources; link the thinking of others to your own thinking.
- Create a discussion governed by your views; draw on sources as contributors to a discussion that you design and control.

2 Understanding techniques for writing a synthesis

In writing a synthesis, you will at some point write partial summaries, evaluations, and analyses. Synthesis draws on these forms and is larger and more ambitious than any one of them. Summary and evaluation treat single sources; analysis is limited to an application of one source (or set of ideas) to a second source; but synthesis merges sources and looks for larger patterns of relationship.

Cross-referencing ideas

A synthesis organized by *ideas* shows that you are intellectually present and involved with the material you have gathered. To organize a paper by ideas, you must first divide the topic into the component parts that the various authors take up in their discussions. These component parts then become the key ideas around which you organize your paper. You can follow this method when your writing is based on library research. Cross-referencing is a necessary step in the process (see 1h-2); once you have identified a component part of a topic and cross-referenced authors' discussions, you are nearly ready to write. In response to Exercise 9 in Chapter 1, you worked on completing a note sheet. If you have not completed this assignment, do so now.

Clarifying relationships among authors

Your cross-referenced notes enable you to lay out and examine what several authors have written about *particular* parts of a topic, in this case gender and technology. Working with what your sources say on a particular point, you can now forge relationships. Sources can be related in a variety of ways, but you will find that patterns emerge, which can be identified by asking several questions:

Which authors agree?

Which authors disagree?

Are there any examples in one source of statements made in another?

Can you offer any definitions?

Are any readings related by cause and effect?

Pose these questions (and others that occur to you) to get a conversation started among the particular parts of the topic you've identified. Ask: If these authors could talk to one another, what would they say—based on what they've written? What would *you* say to each of them? With whom do you agree? Why? Who seems right, or more authoritative? Take notes in response to these questions. When the time comes for writing, you may not use all your notes, but you will be prepared to launch a discussion in which you and your sources participate.

Many students find the following guidelines helpful when synthesizing source materials:

- Read sources on the topic; subdivide the topic into parts, and infer relationships among parts, cross-referencing sources when possible.
- Clarify relationships among authors by posing questions (for example, Which authors agree? Which authors disagree? and so on).
- Write a thesis (see 3d) that ensures your voice is heard and that allows you to develop sections of the paper in which you refer to sources.
- Sketch an outline of your paper (3d-4), organizing your discussion by *idea*, not by summary. Enter the names of authors into your out-

line, along with notes indicating how these authors will contribute to your discussion.

■ Write a draft of your paper and revise, following strategies discussed in Chapter 4.

3   Applying techniques for writing a synthesis

Since the writer's own views should predominate in a synthesis, no two syntheses, even if based on the same source materials, will be the same. Below is an example of how Paul Guzman generated a conversation among his sources. In an early stage of note taking, Paul listed his authors and cross-referenced the passages in which the authors commented on a particular point that interested him: the influence of advertising on leading young people to start smoking. Here, Paul summarizes each author's position on the point; he states what each would say to at least one other author; and then he responds personally to each author. (Paul is working with source materials from Chapter 1. See excerpts in Exercise 9, page 32.)

Tobacco advertising and teenage smoking

Futrelle	Futrelle suggests that advertising has some influence on getting young people to start smoking by associating smoking with glamour and rebelliousness, but he also says that there are other reasons teenagers begin to smoke. More importantly, he notes that after tobacco advertising was banned in Canada, the number of cigarette smokers increased, which suggests that advertising does not play a primary role.
Tobacco-Free Kids	The Campaign for Tobacco-Free Kids quotes statistics linking tobacco advertising to teenage smoking: the three brands of cigarettes that are most heavily advertised are the favorites among young smokers. Marlboro, which advertises the most, is smoked by 55% of teenage smokers but just 35% of adults. These statistics stand in contrast to those cited by Futrelle.
Sullum	Sullum argues that advertising has little influence on teenagers who start smoking and cites studies that point to peer pressure, individual views of the dangers of tobacco, and other smokers at home as better predictors. He claims that research such as that cited by the Campaign for Tobacco-Free Kids only proves that advertising affects choice of brand, a claim also made by tobacco producers.
Pierce	Pierce points to the decline in adolescent smoking that began in 1973 after television advertising of cigarettes was banned. He refers to papers now available that show the tobacco industry's plan to regain the teenage market with the introduction of advertising attractive

to young people, in particular the Joe Camel campaign beginning in 1987. From this point forward, youth smoking began to rise again, which suggests a connection between advertising and rates of teenage smoking.

Schwebel   Schwebel makes the point that most people who smoke start before they graduate from high school so the tobacco industry has an interest in recruiting youthful smokers with cartoon characters and promotional items designed with them in mind. Pierce also suggests that tobacco producers have good reason to appeal to the teenage market.

Guzman   Clearly, it is very difficult to prove a direct cause-and-effect link between rates of teenage smoking and tobacco advertising, even though such a connection seems reasonable. The evidence is contradictory and subject to different interpretations, and, as Sullum notes, people who smoke usually don't point to advertising as a major influence. The question of whether a ban on tobacco advertising would reduce teen smoking rates is crucial because of freedom of speech issues.

Once you have narrowed a topic, identified its parts, and assembled sources that discuss these parts, you are in a position (as Paul Guzman has demonstrated) to get a conversation started among your sources. The next step is to write your synthesis, which will require you to think critically not only about what other writers say on a topic but also about what *you* have to say. Your voice and your insights are crucial elements in a synthesis; they are the elements that distinguish your efforts from those of others writing on the same topic. In Chapter 3, you will follow Paul Guzman's progress as he draws relationships among sources and, just as important, draws on his own experience to create an effective essay.

EXERCISE 4

You have seen Paul Guzman's efforts to forge relationships among various selections on tobacco advertising and teenage smoking rates. Consider the example readings on this topic in Chapter 1: the *Science News Update* article, Sullum, the Campaign for Tobacco-Free Kids Web page, Schwebel, Futrelle, and Pierce. Given that no two readers respond to a passage in quite the same way, take your turn at forging relationships among these sources. Identify two or three parts of the larger topic of tobacco advertising and teen smoking rates that these articles discuss. Then follow Paul Guzman's lead, and generate a conversation among your sources.

Planning, Developing, and Writing a Draft

A writer's thoughts take shape through the very act of writing and rewriting. When you write you are also thinking, and when you revise you are thinking again about your topic. The many decision points you will face in the process of drafting and revising are discussed in this and the next chapter.

An Overview of the Writing Process

Preparing to write

3a **Discovering your topic, purpose, and audience.** Know your topic and, if necessary, research it. Let your purpose for writing generate and organize ideas. Keep specific readers in mind as you write.

3b **Generating ideas and information.** Use strategies such as freewriting to generate ideas and information for your draft.

3c **Reviewing and categorizing ideas and information.** Review the material you have generated, and group like ideas and information into categories.

3d **Writing a thesis and sketching your paper.** Study your material and write a working thesis, a statement that will give your draft a single, controlling idea. Based on your thesis, sketch your draft.

Writing

3e **Writing a draft.** Write a draft by adopting a strategy suited to your temperament. As you write, expect to depart from your sketch.

Revising

4a **Early revision: Rediscovering your main idea.** Refine your thesis. Use it to check that the broad sections of your document, as well as paragraphs, are coherent and logically arranged.

4b **Later revision: Bringing your main idea into focus.** Clarify individual sentences. Check grammar, usage, punctuation, and spelling.

Weblink

http://www.csuohio.edu/
writingcenter/writproc.html>

A hyperlinked map of the steps of the writing process, with a discussion of each.

The three stages of writing are, broadly speaking, distinct. Different activities take place in each stage, and the stages unfold more or less in this order: preparing to write, writing, and revising. But the stages also blend into each other. In the middle of a first draft, you may pause to revise an important sentence or paragraph, deciding to make one part of your document nearly finished while other parts remain rough or not yet written. In a first draft, you may discover new approaches to your topic and stop to write new lists and make new outlines, activities associated with preparing to write. Typically, writers loop backward and forward through the three stages of writing—several times for any one document. The process of writing is **recursive**: it bends and it circles, and it is illustrated well with a wheel.

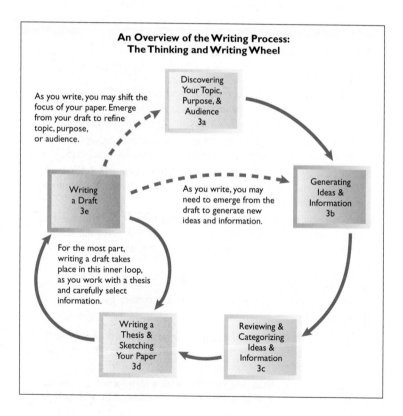

**An Overview of the Writing Process:
The Thinking and Writing Wheel**

Discovering
Your Topic,
Purpose, &
Audience
3a

As you write, you may shift the focus of your paper. Emerge from your draft to refine topic, purpose, or audience.

Writing
a Draft
3e

As you write, you may need to emerge from the draft to generate new ideas and information.

Generating
Ideas &
Information
3b

For the most part, writing a draft takes place in this inner loop, as you work with a thesis and carefully select information.

Writing a
Thesis &
Sketching
Your Paper
3d

Reviewing &
Categorizing
Ideas &
Information
3c

Discovering your topic, purpose, and audience

I Understanding your topic

In both college and business, you can expect to be assigned topics for writing and to define topics for yourself. In either case, in order to write most efficiently and with greatest impact, you should write about what you know (or what you can learn in sufficient time); find some way to own your topic; and sufficiently narrow your topic so that you can write on it fully within an allotted number of pages.

Know your topic.

Knowing your topic will usually require some investigation on your part. The following suggestions may help you to investigate and refine your topic:

Read: If you do not know a topic well, read and gather information: letters, photographs, articles, lecture notes, and so on.

Interview: Locate knowledgeable people and interview them. Avoid questions that can be answered with basic research. Develop questions that yield information and ideas unique to this source. (See 33g-2 for help on generating questions.)

Reflect: What is your personal commitment to the topic? What experiences have you had that influence your thinking? Issues on which you write may require that you take a stand. Know your position. (See 1b for strategies that can aid reflection.)

Own your topic.

Effective writing is produced by those who understand *and* are committed to a topic. If you are assigned a topic that does not, at first, stimulate you, try these strategies:

■ *Stretch the topic to fit your interests.* Redefine the assignment so that it touches on your experience and at the same time is acceptable to your professor.

■ *Identify a debate.* Try to understand why the topic is debatable (if it is) and whom the topic affects, as well as the merits and limitations of each side of the debate. Personalize the debate. Take a position.

■ *Talk with friends.* Informal conversations may help you to identify elements of a topic that interest you. Get a conversation going, listen, and participate.

Restrict and define your topic.

Know how long your assignment is expected to be, and limit your writing accordingly. Avoid the frustration of choosing a broad topic (for example, the issue of privacy on the Internet) for a brief paper or report—a mistake that will guarantee a superficial product. The following guidelines will help you to restrict a topic:

■ *Divide the topic into parts.* What are the component parts of this topic? What parts (or subtopics) do I know most about? Can I link subtopics in meaningful ways? In which subtopic am I most interested?

■ *Ask a journalist's questions.* To focus on a subtopic that interests you, pose questions: *who, what, where, when, why, how?* A response to one or more of these questions can become the focus of a paper.

ACROSS THE CURRICULUM

Broadening the Context

Across the curriculum, both faculty and students create occasions to think critically by asking: *How are the details of what I'm studying an instance or example of something larger?* Read the opening sentences of an article by media researcher Shelley Stamp Lindsey.* Observe how she takes a particular event, "the fight for female enfranchisement"—or the right to vote—and identifies it as a particular, interesting example of a larger issue.

> Much more than the vote was at stake in the campaign for women's suffrage. As the fight for female enfranchisement escalated in America during the early teens, the debate grew to encompass issues far beyond the ballot, or even the larger question of gender equality. Competing claims furnished a landscape where new ideals of feminine behavior could be tested— *and contested*—against women's increasing prominence in civic affairs. Indeed, female voting rights engaged a struggle over the very definition of modern womanhood.
>
> With the image of femininity at stake, much of the debate was waged in *visual* terms, in posters, cartoons, pageants, marches, and ultimately on movie screens where conservatives and activists fought over appropriate manifestations of "womanliness."

Initial topic is women's suffrage

Writer broadens topic to "modern womanhood"

Discipline focus: study will be in visual arts

*Lindsey's article "*Eighty Million Women Want*—? Women's Suffrage, Female Viewers, and the Body Politic" appeared in *Quarterly Review of Film and Video* 16.1 (1995).

EXERCISE I

List three topics with which you are intimately familiar and about which you can write for *public* view. Subdivide each topic into as many parts as you can. Eventually, you will select from these parts a focus for your paper.

EXERCISE 2

Of the topics you have narrowed in Exercise 1, which do you care most about? Write a brief paragraph in which you explain to yourself the *reasons* you are interested in one of these narrowed topics.

2 Identifying your purpose

There are four basic purposes or aims for writing: to *inform*, to *persuade*, to *express*, and to *entertain*. Since you will generally be asked to produce informative and persuasive pieces in college, this book primarily addresses these types of writing.

Informative writing

When writing to *inform*, you explain, define, or describe a topic so that the reader understands its component parts, its method of operation, its uses, and so on. The following assignments call for informative writing:

Literature   Cite three examples of metaphor in *Great Expectations*, and explain how each works.

Chemistry   Explain the chemical process by which water, when boiled, becomes steam.

Psychology   What is "cognitive dissonance," and in what ways does it contribute to the development of personality?

What the reader already knows about the topic will in large part determine the level of language you use and the difficulty of the information that you present. An engineer discussing the flight of planes would use one vocabulary with fellow engineers and another vocabulary with a nontechnical audience. (See 3a-3.)

Persuasive writing

When writing to *persuade*, you attempt to change a reader's views. As with informative writing, the persuasive writer carefully considers the reader's prior knowledge in order to provide the background information needed for understanding. If you knew nothing about international business, you might not be persuaded about the need to master a foreign language in college. The person urging you to learn Japanese would need to inform you, first, of certain facts and trends. As a persuasive writer, you will provide information both to establish understanding and to provide a base for building an argument. (See Chapter 6, which is devoted entirely to argumentation.) The following assignments call for persuasive writing:

Astronomy   Given limited government money available for the construction and updating of astronomical observatories, which of the projects discussed this semester deserve continued funding? Argue for your choices based on the types of discoveries you expect the various projects to make in the next five years.

Sociology   You have read two theories on emotions: the Cannon-Bard theory and the James-Lange theory. Which seems the more convincing to you? Why?

Marketing   Select three ads that describe similar products. Which ad is most effective? Why?

Expressive writing and writing to entertain

Through *expressive* writing you explore your own ideas and emotions. When private, expressive writing can lead you to be more experimental, less guarded, perhaps even more honest than in a paper meant for others. When public, expressive writing will not be a journal entry, but rather an essay in which you reflect your impressions. In many composition courses, the first part of a semester or an entire semester will be devoted to expressive writing.

The least frequent purpose of academic writing is to *entertain*. Possibly you will write a poem, story, or play in your college career, and certainly you will read forms of writing that are intended to entertain readers. What makes a piece of writing entertaining is subject to debate. It suffices to say here that writing to entertain need not only be writing that evokes smiles.

Purposes for writing may overlap: in a single essay, you may inform, persuade, and entertain a reader. But if an essay is to succeed, you should identify a *single*, primary purpose for writing.

COMPUTER TIPS

Compose Alternative Versions

Even if you're a worse-than-average typist, drafting is probably easier on a computer, because it allows you to make changes quickly and easily. Take advantage of this ease by composing multiple versions of sentences and paragraphs, particularly at crucial points in your papers, such as beginnings and endings. Type each version into your draft, and then simply delete the ones you don't like during revision.

EXERCISE 3

Return to the writing you produced for Exercises 1 and 2. This will become your topic for a five-page paper. Write a brief paragraph explaining your purpose for this paper. Although purposes may overlap to some extent, decide on one of two primary purposes: to inform *or* persuade your reader. If the topics in Exercises 1 and 2 left you uninspired, choose a new topic.

3 Defining your audience

Whether your intent is primarily to inform or to persuade, you must know your audience, since what you write will depend greatly on who will read your work. Questions that you ask about an audience *before you write a first draft* can help you make decisions concerning your paper's content and level of language.

Analyze the Needs of Your Audience

Pose these general questions, regardless of your purpose:

3.1

- Who is the reader? What is the reader's age, sex, religious background, educational background, ethnic heritage?
- What is my relationship with the reader?
- What impact on my presentation—on choice of words, level of complexity, and choice of examples—will the reader have?
- Why will the reader be interested? How can I spark interest?

If you are writing to inform, pose these questions as well:

- What does the reader know about the topic's history?
- How well does the reader understand the topic's technical details?
- What does the reader need to know? Want to know?
- What level of language and content will I use in discussing the topic, given the reader's understanding?

If you are writing to persuade, pose both sets of questions above, as well as the following:

- What are the reader's views on the topic? Given what I know about the reader (from the preceding questions), is the reader likely to agree with my view on the topic? To disagree? To be neutral?
- What factors are likely to affect the reader's beliefs about the topic? What special circumstances (work, religious conviction, political views, etc.) should I be aware of that will affect the reader's views?
- How can I shape my argument to encourage the reader's support, given his or her present level of interest, level of understanding, and beliefs?

EXERCISE 4

Return to the topic you selected in Exercise 3, where you wrote a paragraph explaining your purpose for a proposed five-page paper. Working with your topic and your purpose (to inform or persuade), answer the questions in the box "Analyze the Needs of Your Audience" three times, once for each of three different audiences: a friend at another school, your parents, and some other audience of your choosing. Select one of these as the audience for your paper.

4 Analyzing topic, purpose, audience—and the writing occasion

Each new writing project constitutes a distinct occasion for writing and requires that you consider the relationship of topic, purpose, and audience. Depending on the writing occasion, you will decide on the tone and the register for your project.

Tone is a writer's general attitude toward the reader and the subject. Every paper cannot help but have a characteristic tone. English offers numerous ways of saying the same thing. For example, the most simple request can be worded to reflect a variety of tones:

May I have the salt?   Give me that salt!

Choose words to create a tone that you think is appropriate to your topic, purpose, and audience. Mismatching tone and topic can create problems. Imagine discussing some grim event with a lighthearted, devil-may-care tone. Readers would turn away, and the purpose of communication would be defeated.

Register is the degree of formality in your writing.

- In a **formal register,** you follow all the rules and conventions of writing expected in the professional and academic worlds. Formal writing is precise and concise. It avoids colloquial expressions, and it is thorough in content and tightly structured.
- The **informal register** is common in personal correspondence and journals, and it tends to be conversational. Word choice is freely colloquial and structure need not be as tightly reasoned as in a formal paper. Occasional lapses in grammar, usage, spelling, or punctuation matter little in personal correspondence and not at all in personal journal writing.
- The **popular register** is typical of most general interest magazines. It adheres to all conventions of grammar, usage, spelling, and punctuation. It is also carefully organized. The language, however, is more conversational than that found in formal writing. Heavy emphasis is placed on engaging readers and maintaining their interest. For suggestions on matching tone and register to the writing occasion, see 21e, on the use of formal English.

CRITICAL DECISIONS

When Does Your Audience Need to Know More?
Consider these points when deciding whether your audience needs to know more about a key term or person.

■ Major personalities referred to in textbooks or in lectures will help constitute the general, shared knowledge of a discipline. In all cases, *refer to people in your papers either by their* last *names or by their first* and *last names.* Do not identify "giants of a field" with explanatory tags like *who was an important inventor in the early part of the twentieth century.*

■ Terms that have been defined at length in a textbook or lecture also constitute the general, shared knowledge of a discipline. Once you have understood these terms, use them in your papers—but do not define them. Demonstrate your understanding by using the terms accurately.

■ The same people and terms not requiring definition in an academic context may need to be defined in a nonacademic one. Decide what information to include based on a careful audience analysis.

You can inform or persuade a reader in *any* register or tone, but once chosen, register and tone should be used consistently. The diagram below suggests the need for a balanced, four-way relationship among the basic elements of the writing occasion.

3.2

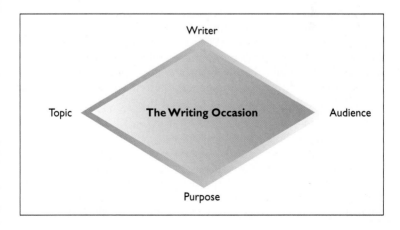

EXERCISE 5

Write a series of three brief letters to a mail-order business. Ask why you have not received the computer software you ordered and paid for. The letters should show a change in tone, moving from a neutral inquiry in the first letter to annoyed concern in the second to controlled anger in the third. In each case, maintain a formal tone. Avoid using colloquial expressions.

EXERCISE 6

Given the audience and the purpose you have chosen for the paper you are planning (see your answers to Exercises 3 and 4), decide on the tone and register you should adopt.

3b   Generating ideas and information

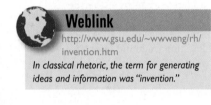

Weblink

http://www.gsu.edu/~wwweng/rh/
invention.htm

In classical rhetoric, the term for generating ideas and information was "invention."

At times you may stare at a topic you intend to write about and feel as though there is *nothing* to say. When you are feeling frantic, try proven strategies in this section for generating ideas and information. As you review these strategies, bear in mind this "User's Manual":

- No one method will work for all topics.
- Some methods may not suit your style of discovery.
- Some methods work well when combined.
- Move quickly to a new strategy if one does not work.
- Tell your internal critic to take a vacation.

The invention strategies discussed in this section can complement each other; you will generate one type of information using one strategy and other types using others. When you examine *all* the material you have generated, you should find ample opportunities to advance to the next stage of writing. The work of a single student, Paul Guzman (whose completed paper appears in 4e), illustrates how you might put the various strategies to use.

1   Reading

Most academic writing is based on reading. Early in the writing process, when you are still not precisely sure what your topic will be, reading can be an excellent stimulus. Source materials may present compelling facts or strongly worded opinions with which to agree or

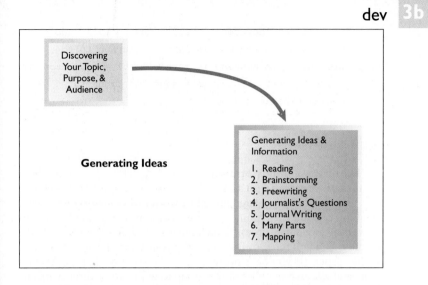

disagree. Be alert to your responses and jot them down; they may later become important to your paper. (See Chapter 1 and the discussion of strategies for reading effectively.) If you are writing a paper that will not draw heavily on sources, use your reading mainly as a stimulus. If you are writing a research report, read to generate the information you will then use to write the paper. In this case, realize that you will need to cite sources (see Chapter 37).

In browsing the Web site for the Campaign for Tobacco-Free Kids, Paul Guzman found an essay on young people and smoking that sparked his interest. His tentative topic was "how to prevent youth smoking." Paul made the following notes.

ILLUSTRATION: PAUL GUZMAN'S PAPER

READING

I hadn't realized how many young people have tried their first cigarette before they are even teenagers. One survey of fifth graders in the state of Washington reported by the Campaign for Tobacco-Free Kids indicates that 30% of them had already smoked at least one cigarette. Apparently it is by the age 11 or 12 that most smoking experimentation begins, but a good percentage of kids have tried cigarettes by the time they are 10 or even 9. It's hard to understand why children would be attracted to cigarettes so early. Advertising?

Peer pressure? They don't realize how lethally addictive tobacco can be. Obviously one solution to the
problem of youth smoking is more effective education
programs to cast smoking in a negative light for
potential experimenters.

2   Brainstorming

The object of **brainstorming** is to write quickly and, once finished, to return to your work with a critical eye. Place your topic at the top of a page, and then list any related phrase or word that comes to mind. Set a time limit of five or ten minutes, and list items as quickly as you can. To brainstorm in a small group, a technique that allows the ideas of one person to build on those of another, write your topic on a board or sheet of easel paper. (If you have no topic, see "Freewriting," 3b-3.) Sit in a circle, and ask each member of the group to offer two or three words or phrases for your list. Work around the circle a second time, asking each member to add another one or two ideas. Finally, open the floor to anyone who can add more ideas.

After you have generated your list, group related items, and set aside items that do not fit into a grouping. Groupings with the greatest number of items indicate areas that should prove fertile in developing your paper. Save the results of your brainstorming session for your next step in the planning process: selecting, organizing, and expanding information.

ILLUSTRATION: PAUL GUZMAN'S PAPER

BRAINSTORMING

<u>Reasons young people smoke</u>

peers smoking--want to fit in or go along with the crowd
advertising--how much of an influence is this on young
    people who start smoking?
merchants sell to underage buyers--this must be breaking
    the law
price within reason--a pack of cigarettes costs about as
    much as a magazine
curiosity--kids just want to know what smoking is like
parents/relatives smoke--bad role model, although some
    kids really hate their parents smoking
glamorous image in movies, etc.--popular movie stars
    like Gwyneth Paltrow are shown smoking

unaware of the health hazards--though most kids probably
know that cigarettes aren't good for them
think they're stronger than cigarettes--kids don't
realize how addictive tobacco is
rebellious--you're not supposed to smoke, so to rebel
you do
vending machines--it just occurs to me that kids can get
cigarettes from unsupervised vending machines
sponsorships--tobacco companies sponsor popular events
like car racing; get their image out

Paul grouped his list as follows. The question mark denotes the "leftover" category, which includes items Paul didn't have a primary category for.

<u>Personal</u>
curiosity
think they're stronger than cigarettes
rebellious

<u>Media-related</u>
advertising
glamorous image in movies, etc.
sponsorships

<u>Marketed-related</u>
merchants sell to underage buyers
price within reason
vending machines

?
peers smoking
parents/relatives smoke
unaware of health hazards

COMPUTER TIPS

Writing in the Dark

If you're a fairly speedy typist, one interesting use of your computer is to turn off the monitor and just type. You can either freewrite or compose a rough draft in this manner. It removes the fear of making mistakes, the urge to reread at inappropriate times, and the hypnotic effect of your works on the screen. Just type; then turn on the monitor to see what you have.

Freewriting is a technique to try when you are asked to write but have no topic. Think for a moment about the subject area in which you have been asked to write. Recall lectures or chapters read in textbooks. Choose a broad area of interest, and then start writing for some predetermined amount of time—say, five or ten minutes. Alternatively, you can write until you have filled a certain number of pages (typically one or two). As you write, do not stop to puzzle over word choice or punctuation. Once you have reached your time limit or page allotment, read over what you have done. Circle ideas that could become paper topics. To generate ideas about these specific topics, you may then try a more focused strategy for invention: brainstorming, focused freewriting, or any of the other strategies that will be discussed in later sections.

Focused freewriting gives you the benefits of freewriting, but on a *specific* topic. The end result of this strategy is the same as brainstorming, and so the choice of invention strategies is one of style: do you prefer making lists or writing sentences? Begin with a definite topic. Write for five or ten minutes. Then reread your work, and circle any words, phrases, or sentences that look potentially useful. Draw lines that link circled words, and make notes to explain the linkages. Then clarify these linkages on a separate sheet of paper. The result will be a grouping of items, some in sentence form, that looks like the result of brainstorming. Save your work for the next step in planning: selecting, organizing, and expanding information.

Following is a portion of Paul's focused freewriting on the topic "the allure of smoking."

........**ILLUSTRATION: PAUL GUZMAN'S PAPER**

FOCUSED FREEWRITING

Why is such a nasty habit as (smoking attractive) to young people? I guess it doesn't seem so nasty at first, particularly when you are (sneaking a few cigarettes with your friends.) But (I don't think I started smoking because of friends) or ("peer pressure.") As I recall, not many of my friends even smoked, although they didn't try to get me to stop. (Advertising?) I grew up after the tobacco companies stopped running ads on television, and (I don't really remember any cigarette ads) in magazines and so forth that drew me to smoking. But the (effect may have been more subliminal) than I realized. I was always a good kid--never got into real trouble, good student.

and all that. Maybe it was my need to be a little bit
rebellious. I wanted to appear cool too, and for some
reason I thought smoking did that for me. Why? I guess
because it was something "adults" did, that people in
movies did. Particularly old movies from the thirties and
forties that I enjoyed watching. Smoking was glamorous
then, and it seems like movies in the last 10 years or
so have glamorized smoking again ("Pulp Fiction," for
example).

Paul organized his freewriting on why teens start smoking into these
categories:

Peer pressure
Sneaking cigarettes with friends is exciting
Not sure peers led me to smoke
Advertising
Don't really remember ads
Effect may have been subliminal
Rebelliousness
To look cool
To seem more adult
Glamorous as in movie images

---

4   The journalist's questions

You have read or heard of the journalist's questions: *who, what,
when, where, why,* and *how.* In answering the questions, you can define,
compare, contrast, or investigate cause and effect. Again, the assumption is that by thinking about parts, you will have more to write about
than if you focus on a topic as a whole. The journalist's questions can
help you to restrict and define a topic (see 3a-1), giving you the option
to concentrate, say, on any three parts of the whole: perhaps the *who,
what,* and *why* of the topic. Under the topic of mapping (3b-7), you will
find the notes Paul Guzman made in response to four of the journalist's
questions.

5   Journal writing

You might keep a journal in conjunction with your writing course.
A *journal* is a set of private, reflective notes in which you describe your
reactions to lectures, readings, discussions, films, current events—any

topic touching on your course work. A journal borrows from both diary writing and course notebooks.

- As in a diary, your journal entries are private, reflective, and "safe" in the sense that you know no one is looking over your shoulder. Thus, you are free to experiment with ideas and to express your thoughts honestly.
- Unlike a diary, a journal focuses on matters relating to your course work and not on matters of your private life, unless such observations tie in with your course work.

Journal writing gives you an opportunity to converse with yourself in your own language about your studies. You pose questions, develop ideas, reflect on readings, speculate and explore, and try to pinpoint confusions. The more you write, the more you clarify what you know and, equally important, what you do not know.

Punctuation is not important as long as you can reread your journal entries. Periodically review your journal entries, looking for ideas in which you seemed particularly interested. As with freewriting, use these ideas as the basis for a more focused strategy of invention.[1]

6   The "many parts" strategy[2]

Another method for generating ideas about a topic is to list its parts. Number the items on your list. Then ask, "What are the uses of Number 1? Number 2? Number 3?" and so on. If *uses of* does not seem to work for the parts in question, try *consequences of*: "What are the consequences of Number 1?" The *many parts* strategy lets you be far more specific and imaginative in thinking about the topic as a whole than you might be ordinarily. Once you have responded to your questions about the uses or consequences of some part, you might pursue the one or two most promising responses in a focused freewrite.

ILLUSTRATION: PAUL GUZMAN'S PAPER

THE "MANY PARTS" STRATEGY

```
I. What are the parts of young people and smoking?
   1. Smoking rates among those under 21 are
      higher than smoking rates among adults.
   2. Most adult smokers started smoking before
      the age of 18.
```

[1]Discussion of journal writing here is based on Toby Fulwiler, ed., *The Journal Book* (Portsmouth, NH: Boynton/Cook-Heinemann, 1987) 1–7.

[2]This strategy is adapted from John C. Bean and John D. Ramage, *Form and Surprise in Composition: Writing and Thinking across the Curriculum* (New York: Macmillan, 1986) 170–71.

3. Young people are attracted to smoking even
   though they know its dangers.

One part, explored:

II. Why are young people attracted to smoking even
    though they know its dangers?
    --media images make smoking appear attractive
    --smoking is a way of rebelling against
      authority
    --if their friends smoke, some young people
      start smoking to fit in
    --girls may start to smoke because they think
      it will help them lose weight
    --young people mistakenly think they will be
      able to stop smoking when they decide that
      they want to

---

7 Mapping

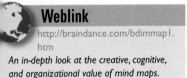

Weblink

http://braindance.com/bdimmap1.htm

An in-depth look at the creative, cognitive, and organizational value of mind maps.

If you enjoy thinking visually, try **mapping** your ideas. Begin by writing your topic as briefly as possible (a single word is best). Circle the topic, and draw three, four, or five short spokes from the circle. At the end of each spoke, place one of the journalist's questions, making a major branch off the spoke for every answer to a question. Now, working with each answer individually, pose one of the six journalist's questions once again. After you have completed the exercise, you will have a page that places ideas in relation to one another. Notice how the "map" distinguishes between major points and supporting information.

EXERCISE 7

Generate ideas about three of the following topics, using *two* of the previously mentioned methods of invention for each idea.

river rafting	current films	dorm life
a cousin	compulsory draft	space flight

EXERCISE 8

If you are preparing a paper as you read this chapter, use any *three* methods of invention to generate ideas about your topic. The end result of your work should be several categories of grouped ideas.

MAPPING THE JOURNALIST'S QUESTIONS

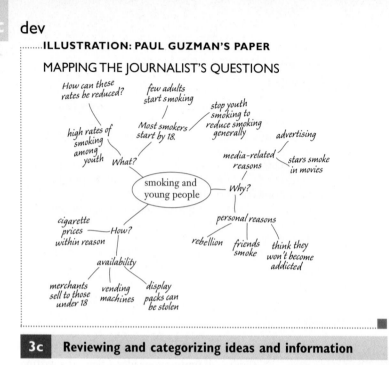

3c Reviewing and categorizing ideas and information

Not all of the information you have generated will be equally useful. Therefore, your next task in the writing process is to select those ideas that look most promising. *Promising* in this context is an inexact term because at this stage of the writing process there is no way to be exact. Until you have completed a first draft, you cannot know for certain the content of your paper. Despite the plans you make when preparing to write, your actual writing is where you will discover much of your content. For this reason, the choices you make about which ideas and information to include in a paper must be based on hunches: informed guesses about what will work.

1 Reviewing ideas and making meaningful categories

Make sense of the information you have generated by creating categories. A category is akin to a file drawer into which you place related materials. Your job is to consolidate: take all the ideas and information you have generated; spread your notes out before you; and then take a clean sheet of paper and group ideas. Give each new grouping a general category name. Beneath each category name, list subordinate, or supporting, information.

Paul Guzman generated three categories of information on which he could base a paper. Following is one of those categories, with information consolidated from the results of four different methods for generating information.

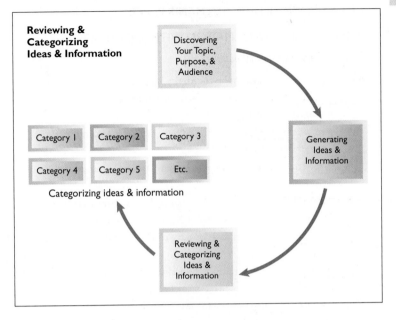

SELECTING INFORMATION INTO CATEGORIES

<u>Reasons that young people start smoking</u>

--young people are influenced by others to start smoking

--media images may influence young people to start smoking

--some natural tendencies of adolescence lead young people
    to start smoking

--young people often don't appreciate the dangers of
    smoking

--access to cigarettes is often too easy for young
    people

| 2 | Organizing information *within* categories |

Organize information within categories to clarify your ideas and their relation to one another. First, you will need to identify main, or *general*, points within each category and the subordinate, or *specific*, points supporting them, which is exactly what you will do when writing a paper. Use an informal outline or a tree diagram to organize major and supporting points within a category.

······ILLUSTRATION: PAUL GUZMAN'S PAPER

ORGANIZING INFORMATION WITHIN CATEGORIES

Organization by informal outline

Reasons that young people start smoking

Major point: Young people are influenced by others
    to start smoking.

> Supporting point: They often start smoking because
> their friends smoke.

Major point: Media images may influence young people to
    start smoking.

> Supporting points: (1) Cigarette advertising appears
> in general-interest magazines that young people
> read; (2) Film stars popular with young people are
> shown smoking.

Major point: Some natural tendencies of adolescence lead
    young people to start smoking.

> Supporting points: (1) Adolescence is a time of
> rebellion for many young people; (2) Teenagers think
> they're indestructible and won't become addicted.

Organization by tree diagram

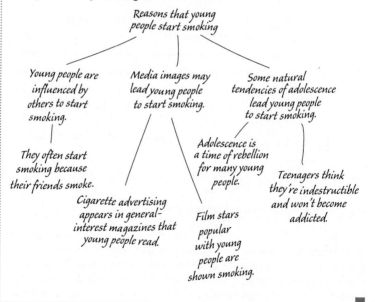

Planning, Developing, and Writing a Draft

Organizing material within a category is an excellent technique for revealing which of your main points will need further development once you begin writing a first draft. When Paul Guzman organized his category on the reasons young people smoke, he realized that he had neglected to generate enough supporting materials for his point about the influence of other people. Answers came quickly when Paul asked, "What other examples of young people being influenced by others can I point to?" An asterisk marks the two additions to the category.

Major point: Young people are influenced by others to
    start smoking.
    Supporting point: (1) They often start smoking
        because their friends smoke.
    * Young people are more likely to smoke if someone
        in the home smokes.
    * Girls sometimes start smoking because a boyfriend
        smokes.

Look to each of your main points to see how you might add supporting points. You may need to read additional sources to fill in gaps. Developing categories fully at this stage will maximize the information you will have to work with when devising a thesis.

EXERCISE 9

Select the most promising information from your efforts to generate ideas about your topic, as defined in Exercise 8. *Form categories:* consolidate information from all three invention strategies. Write a brief sentence or phrase of definition for each category. *Organize each category* into a main point and supporting points. Finally, *expand information:* fill in gaps, and if you are interested (or if your professor requires it), seek out source material that you can use in your paper. At the conclusion of this exercise, each category should have a main point supported by at least two specific, subordinate points.

3d   Writing a thesis and sketching your paper

A **thesis** is a general statement that you make about your topic, usually in the form of a single sentence, that summarizes the controlling idea of your paper. You cannot produce a fully accurate **final thesis** until you have written a complete draft. When sitting down to a first draft, you will at best have a **working thesis**—a statement that, based on everything you know about your topic, should prove to be a reasonably accurate summary of what you will write.

A thesis, like any other sentence, has a subject and a predicate. The subject announces the person, place, or thing that the sentence is about. The predicate makes a claim concerning the subject: it states that the subject takes a certain action, exists (or should exist), has a certain value, and so on.

Subject	Predicate
Alex	smiles.
Patricia	opens the door.

Weblink

http://www.indiana.edu/~wts/wts/thesis.html

An extended look at the process of composing and revising a thesis statement.

What distinguishes the thesis from other sentences is that it invites development and discussion. The sentence *Alex smiles* offers a subject and an action taken by that subject, but once stated, the sentence completes its own meaning. By contrast, a thesis is more complex: it invites—and requires—follow-up discussion, because its meaning is not yet complete. The job of the essay or research paper is to develop and complete the thesis. Consider this example:

Subject	Predicate
A largely invisible but rich biological world	can be found in the three inches of grass and topsoil immediately below our feet.

Notice that this example is more complicated than *Alex smiles*. The thesis asks the reader to accept as true or desirable a complex statement about how the world works or should work. Readers might be willing to accept the statement as true or desirable, but not on face value.

Informational versus argumentative theses

When a thesis is not likely to spark debate, its development will be purely informational—as, for instance, would be the development about the biological world just under our feet. Following such a thesis, you would expect a good deal of information to follow. There would not be much debate about the thesis, assuming the information presented was trustworthy.

When a thesis can reasonably be expected to spark disagreement, then development will take the form of an argument that provides reasons to encourage agreement. The thesis—*Human space flight can no longer be justified*—is argumentative. Some people might immediately accept the statement. Others might disagree. When the writer expects disagreement, an argument that supports and completes the thesis should follow. (See Chapter 6 for an extended discussion of how to write and support an argumentative thesis.)

Realize that your ideas for a paper and, consequently, for your thesis develop and change as your paper develops. Don't be bound by a single sentence at the beginning of your draft. Your working thesis *will* change. Nonetheless, you must depend on it to get you started.

1 Focusing on the subject of your thesis

As much as possible, you want the subject of your thesis statement to name something that is relatively specific and well defined. You want to name something you can discuss thoroughly within the allotted number of pages. How will you focus your subject?

Build on the fact that you have organized your information into categories. To settle on a subject for your thesis, review your categories, and select from among them your most promising and interesting material. Most likely, you will focus on only a fraction of this material in your actual paper.

Focusing the Subject of a Thesis with Questions

One useful way to limit and focus the subject of your thesis is to pose a journalist's questions: *who*, *what*, *when*, *where*, and *which aspects*.

Subject (too broad): wilderness

Limiting questions: which aspects?

Focused subject: wilderness camping

2 Basing your thesis on a relationship you want to clarify

Once you have focused your subject, you must make an assertion about it; that is, you must complete the predicate part of your thesis. If you have generated ideas on your own, you have several pages of notes. If you have conducted research, you have filled out perhaps fifty file cards. You cannot write until you have begun to forge relationships among the ideas and information that you have generated. It is only *in the process* of forging relationships—trying to make logical connections one way, seeing that a certain tactic does not work, trying other tactics, and constantly making adjustments—that sense emerges and you come to know what you think about your material.

In examining the notes you have generated and organized into categories, ask yourself, What new statement can I make that ties all—or part—of my material together? You will express this relationship in the predicate part of your thesis.

Whether you intend to inform or persuade, the relationship that you assert in your thesis can be more or less ambitious. When the assertion is ambitious, your thesis and the paper that you build from it will be, too. What determines the ambition of a thesis is the complexity of the relationship you establish between the predicate part of the sentence and the subject. In the example theses that follow, the predicates are underlined.

Least Ambitious Thesis

1. Wilderness camping <u>poses many challenges.</u>
   —Challenge #1
   —Challenge #2, etc.
2. Paul Guzman's thesis:
   Young people <u>start smoking for a variety of reasons.</u>
   —Some of these reasons are related to the media, such as the influence of tobacco advertising.
   —Some are related to the personal traits of teenagers, particularly their sense of indestructibility.

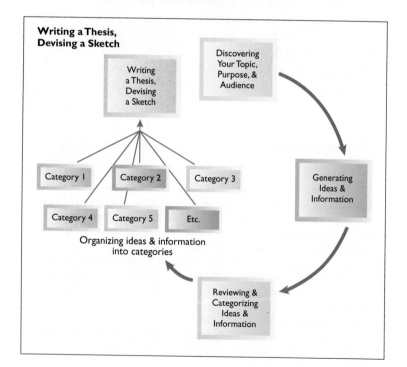

Each thesis requires little more than a summary of the topic's component elements. The writers make no attempt to forge relationships among these elements.

Moderately Ambitious Thesis

1. Like holding a mirror to your personality, wilderness camping shows you to yourself—for better and worse.
   —Wilderness camping described
   —The camper in the wilderness, described
   —Ways in which the wilderness elicits personal response, positive and negative
2. Paul Guzman's thesis:
   If we hope to deter young people from smoking, we must identify the factors that motivate them to start smoking in the first place.
   —Smoking rates among young people are alarmingly high and need to be lowered.
   —They are influenced to smoke by reasons related to the media and to their own vulnerabilities as teenagers.
   —Significantly reducing the rate of smoking among young people will require parents, educators, and others to work to lessen these influences.

(Note that this is the working thesis Paul Guzman used as the basis for his first-draft paper, which appears at the end of this chapter.)

Each thesis forges a relationship between two previously unrelated elements: between wilderness camping and self-reflection and between the causes of teen smoking and prevention. The writers will be reasoning with the facts, not merely presenting them in summary form. They will be making connections.

Most Ambitious Thesis

1. Wilderness camping teaches that we must preserve what is brutal in Nature, even at the expense of public safety.
   —Rigors of wilderness camping
   —Potential danger to public
   —Paradox: dangers notwithstanding, wilderness must be maintained
2. Paul Guzman's thesis:
   Although young people become smokers for a variety of reasons, to deter youth smoking, we must identify and develop strategies to combat those specific influences over which we can have most effective control.
   —While studies linking cigarette advertising with youth smoking may not be conclusive, there does seem to be a correlation. Yet is a ban on all cigarette advertising feasible?

—Young people's accessibility to cigarettes is clearly a problem that could be dealt with in part by enforcing bans on selling cigarettes to minors.

—Education efforts must speak more directly to the personal reasons that lead young people to become smokers.

—Paradox: Young people start smoking based on a cycle of influences. While we can identify any number of these influences, not all are equally important, and, more important, not all are equally subject to parents' and educators' control.

(Note that this is the revised thesis that Paul Guzman used as the basis for his final-draft paper, which appears at the end of Chapter 4.)

Each thesis broadens the scope of the paper and creates interest through paradoxical opposites. Each thesis promises a paper that will be argumentative. In addition to making connections where none existed previously, each thesis shows a writer willing to take intellectual risks. That is, the writer is willing to expand the scope of the paper, widening its context in order to take up a broader, more complex, and (if executed well) more important discussion. A fully ambitious thesis will create a paradox, a tension among its parts, by setting opposites against each other.[3] In a thesis with tension, you often find the conjunctions *although* and *even if*. The writer's job is to navigate between paradoxical opposites. The reader, sensing tension, wants to know what happens and why.

What sort of paper are you writing?

An ambitious thesis leads to an ambitious paper. Sometimes you will understand the ambition of your paper before you set out to write it; at other times you will not have a clear sense of how "large" a paper you are writing until you get midway through a draft and discover or challenge your ideas. In any event, you should know what sort of paper you are writing as you sit down to *revise* your first draft. Reread the draft; see what you have; and determine how ambitious your final draft should be. You will choose your final thesis, and shape your final paper, accordingly.

EXERCISE 10

Refer to your results from Exercise 9. Given the ideas you generated, write three theses for this topic—each with a different level of ambition.

---

[3]The term *tension*, as it relates to the thesis statement, is borrowed from John C. Beam and John D. Ramage, *Form and Surprise in Composition: Writing and Thinking across the Curriculum* (New York: Macmillan, 1986) 168–69.

Generating a Working Thesis

1. Focus and restrict your subject so that you will be able to write specifically on it in the number of pages allotted.
2. Assemble the notes—arranged in categories—that you have generated.
3. Forge a relationship that clarifies the material you have assembled.
4. Devise a sentence—a working thesis—that links the relationship you have forged with your focused subject.
5. Determine how ambitious you will be with your thesis—and your paper.
6. Let your thesis evolve as you develop and challenge your thoughts.

EXERCISE 11

Classify the following theses as least, moderately, or most ambitious. Explain your classifications:

1. In a national trend that has blurred the line between private and public, several cities and states have agreed to spend public funds to finance the construction of new stadiums.
2. Several cities and states have agreed to spend public funds to finance the construction of new stadiums.
3. In a national trend that has blurred the line between private and public, several cities and states have buckled to the demands of sports teams and agreed to spend public funds to finance the construction of new stadiums.

---

4   Devising a sketch of your paper or developing a formal outline

Look to your working thesis for clues about the ideas you will need to develop in your essay. For your academic paper to succeed, you must develop all directly stated or implied ideas in the thesis. You may want to regard your thesis as a contract between you and your reader. The thesis promises the reader a discussion of certain material, and the paper delivers on that promise.

Identifying significant parts of your thesis

Write the working thesis at the top of a page, and circle its significant words. Then ask questions of, or make comments about, each circled element. If you are thorough in quizzing your thesis, you will identify most of its significant parts. (You may not discover some parts until

CRITICAL DECISIONS

Quizzing Your Working Thesis to Determine Major Sections of Your Paper

In writing a thesis, you compress a great deal of information into a single sentence. In writing a paper based on this thesis, you will need to "unpack" and discuss this information. Use the following technique as an aid to unpacking: challenge, or quiz, your thesis with questions (see box on page 85), which will lead to a sketch of your paper.

Following is an example of how Paul Guzman analyzed his working thesis and sketched out the first draft of his paper.

— Define scope of problem

If we hope (to deter young people from smoking,) we must (identify the factors that motivate them to start smoking) in the first place.

What are these specifically?

Sketching the paper
—Define the problem: high rates of smoking among young people and relation to smoking among adults
—Discuss the influences that lead young people to experiment with smoking:
    tobacco advertising
    easy access to cigarettes
    personal reasons related to adolescence
—Discuss solutions

To see how Paul analyzed and unpacked the more ambitious thesis for his final paper, see the illustration on page 99 in Chapter 4.

you write a first draft.) Having identified these significant parts, briefly sketch the paper you intend to write.

Option: Preparing a formal outline of your paper

Many writers feel that a rough sketch (as illustrated in the Critical Decisions box above) is sufficient for beginning the first draft of a paper. Others feel more comfortable with a formal plan of action—an outline with clearly delineated major and minor points. In collaborative writing situations, with different writers responsible for various sections of the project, a formal outline is probably the only way to reach agreement on what each writer will contribute.

Question or Make Comments about Your Thesis in Order to Identify Major Sections of Your Paper

Questions

how does/will it happen?
how to describe?
what are some examples?
what are the reasons for?
what is my view?
compared with what?
what is the cause?
any stories to tell?
how?
when?

what has prevented/will prevent it
from happening?
who is involved?
what are the key features?
what are the reasons against?
how often?
possible to classify types or parts?
what is the effect of this?
which ones?

Comments

define
review the facts

review the reasoning
explain the contrast or paradox

A formal outline establishes the major sections and subsections of your paper. The outline shows how each section is supported by points you plan to discuss (see 18e). It also shows how these points are themselves supported. The goal of a formal outline is to make visible the material you plan to use in the paper. Standard outline form is as follows:

1. Uppercase roman numerals indicate the most general level of heading in the outline; headings in this level correspond with major sections of your paper.
2. Uppercase letters mark the major points you will use in developing each heading.
3. Arabic numbers mark the supporting points you will use in developing main points.
4. Lowercase letters mark further subordination—support of supporting points.

Note that the entries at each level of heading are grammatically parallel (see 18e); that each level of heading has at least two entries; and that only the first letter of an entry is capitalized. A formal outline need not show plans for your introduction or conclusion.

Useful as an outline can be, you will still need to discover the important elements of your paper during the process of writing, and your outline or sketch will change as the writing takes shape.

...........**ILLUSTRATION: FORMAL OUTLINE**

Following is an outline based on Paul Guzman's working thesis.

Thesis: If we hope to deter young people from smoking, we must identify the factors that motivate them to start smoking in the first place.

I. Problem (¶ 1)
   A. Large numbers of young smokers
      1. More than 3 million currently
      2. Numbers have been rising
   B. Most adult smokers started by age 18
II. Causal factors
   A. Tobacco advertising (¶ 2)
      1. Drop in smoking after TV ad ban in 1970s, rise in rates after Joe Camel campaign
      2. Teens interested in ads or brand-related items more likely to start smoking
   B. Access to cigarettes (¶ 3)
      1. Price within reach of young people
      2. Vendors who sell illegally to minors
      3. Make teenage possession illegal
   C. Personal reasons (¶ 4)
      1. Adolescent sense of rebelliousness, peer pressure, indestructibility
      2. Better education efforts needed
         a. Scare tactics don't work
         b. Young people more swayed by personal reasons
III. Solutions: parents, educators, and communities working together (¶ 5)

...........**ILLUSTRATION: FORMAL OUTLINE WITH SENTENCES**

Each item of a formal outline can also be written as a sentence, which you may prefer in your efforts to begin writing. The following is one section of the preceding outline, written in sentence form:

   C. Young people smoke for personal reasons related to adolescence.
      1. Such reasons include pressure from friends, the desire to appear more mature, rebelliousness, and a sense of indestructibility.
      2. To counteract such influences, more effective education efforts are needed.
         a. Young people are not much persuaded by the long-term risks of smoking.
         b. Personal reasons, such as attractiveness to potential dating partners, are more persuasive.

EXERCISE 12

Turn to the theses you wrote in Exercise 10. Circle significant words or phrases, pose development questions, and prepare an informal or formal outline of your paper. Then expand your outline into a first draft of your paper (3e).

ACROSS THE CURRICULUM

Organizing Scientific Writing

In *Scientific and Technical Writing: A Manual of Style,** writers are advised to create an "obvious," easily understood organization that is highlighted with clear "guideposts" (such as headings and cross-references). The editors offer the following overview of "typical organizational approaches" found in scientific and technical writing:

- Be sure that a document's organization explains and logically arranges all necessary ideas. Although there is no perfect organization for any technical or scientific document, some organizational methods will be more appropriate than others, depending on the document's audience and purpose.

- Typical organizational approaches include chronological, spatial, climactic, and task-oriented. Some documents may need an organization that combines more than one of these approaches.

- Use chronological organization when time is the organizing principle. It orders information according to when concepts develop, events occur, or actions happen, generally from the earliest to the latest.

- Use spatial organization when placement or geography is the organizing principle. Consider, for instance, describing equipment by parts or components, or presenting product sales figures or health statistics by geographic region.

- Use climactic organization to progress from least to greatest impact, concluding with the most interesting or forceful concepts, ideas, or facts. Brochures, when convincing readers to take action or make a decision, use this organization.

- Use task-oriented organization when readers will use information to do something. Thus, an instruction manual organizes its information into procedures or activities users perform.

*Philip Rubens, ed. (New York: Henry Holt, 1992) 15–16.

3e   Writing a draft

Your working thesis and your sketch or outline are essential for giving you the confidence to begin a first draft. Realize, however, that your final paper will *not* be identical to your original plans. Once begun, writing will lead you to discard and revise some of your original ideas and will lead to new ideas as well.

The object of a first draft is to get ideas down on paper, to explore them, and to establish the shape of your paper. The object is *not* to produce a final piece of work. Finished, readable documents come through revision. If you plan to revise, you will free yourself to write quickly—and imperfectly. Your draft will put you well on the way toward achieving a final product.

Strategies for Drafting

3.4   Working yourself through the draft

1a. Write *one* section of the paper at a time: write a general statement that supports some part of your thesis, then provide details about the supporting statement. Once you have finished a section, take a break. Then return to write another section, working incrementally in this fashion until you have completed the draft.

b. Alternatively, write one section of the paper and take a break. Then reread and revise that one section before moving to the next. Continue to work in this fashion, one section at a time, until you complete the draft.

2. Accept *two* drafts, minimum, as the standard for writing any formal paper. In this way, you give yourself permission to write a first draft that is not perfect.

3. If you have prepared adequately for writing, then trust that you will discover what to write *as* you write.

4. Save substantial revisions concerning grammar, punctuation, usage, and spelling for later. In your first draft(s), focus on discovery and content.

<hr>

1   Beating writer's block

Everybody avoids writing at some point or another. Odd as it may seem, this information can be of comfort. If you avoid writing, be assured that avoidance does *not* mean that you have done things poorly or that you do not "have what it takes" to be a competent writer. Avoidance and the anxiety that causes it are natural parts of the writing process, though

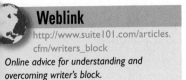
if you devote sufficient time to preparing yourself to write, you minimize the danger of writer's block. Still, preparing is not the same as writing a draft, and you inevitably face a moment in which you decide to take a step—or not. Think about the feelings you get when you do not want to write. When you are stuck as a writer, what might you be telling yourself? And how might you get unstuck?

Stuck	*I cannot get started.* I am afraid of the blank page or the empty computer screen. As I try to write, what I *have not* written seems so vast that I cannot start.
Unstuck	*Prepare yourself mentally to write one section of the paper, not the entire paper.* Three-page papers, just like 500-page books, get written one section at a time. When you sit down to write a draft, identify a *section:* a grouping of related paragraphs that you can write in a single sitting.
Stuck	*I want my writing to be perfect.* My early attempts to express anything are messy. I get a sinking feeling when I reread my work and see how much revision is needed. Whenever I cannot think of the right word, I freeze up.
Unstuck	*Plunge in, knowing this is a first attempt.* When you understand that you will rewrite the first draft of all formal papers or letters, you can give yourself permission to write a first draft quickly and at times imprecisely.
Stuck	*Why advertise my problems?* I worry about grammar, punctuation, and spelling, and I do not want to embarrass myself.
Unstuck	*Use a writer's reference tools.* Many people are nervous about these errors. The fear is real. However, as long as you know how to use standard desk references—a dictionary and a handbook—there is no need to memorize rules of grammar, punctuation, and spelling. Of course, knowing the rules *does* save you time.

2 Working with your sketch or outline

Following are three strategies for using your sketch or outline as a basis for writing. None is *correct* in the sense that one produces a better draft than the others. All will get you a first draft, and all have advantages and disadvantages. How you choose to use a sketch or outline is a matter of your temperament as a writer.

Adhering closely to your outline

One strategy for writing a draft is to follow closely the sketch or outline you made prior to actual drafting. To make full and frequent use of the outline you have assembled makes a great deal of sense, as long as you are aware that your paper *will* deviate from the outline.

Advantages

By regularly consulting your outline, you will feel that you are making progress toward the completion of your paper.

Disadvantages

A comprehensive outline can so focus your vision that you will not allow yourself to stray and discover the true territory of your paper. The paper planned will be the paper written, for better or worse.

COMPUTER TIPS

Break the Paper Habit

If you are in the habit of handwriting your first drafts, experiment with writing at the keyboard. There will be times when you need to print out a paper copy of your draft and edit it, but much of your revising, editing, and proofreading can (and should) be done quickly and efficiently on the screen. You may decide that preparing first drafts of one type of writing (for example, academic papers) works well at the keyboard, whereas drafting other types of writing (poetry) does not. Experiment and learn your preferences.

Adhering loosely to your outline

You may prefer to use a sketch or outline exclusively as a strategy for preparing. In the actual drafting of the paper, you can abandon your plan in favor of one that you generate *while* writing the draft. Examine your outline, studying its first section carefully, and then begin writing. Set aside the outline, and once writing is under way, create a new outline for each section of the paper you are about to write, based on the material you have just written. As you complete each section, update and adjust your outline.

Advantages

This strategy gives you the best chance of discovering material, since each new section of the paper is based on the writing you have just completed and not on an outline prepared in advance.

Disadvantages

The same freedom that gives you room to be creative can result in paragraphs that do not lead logically from one to the next and whole groupings of paragraphs that drift away from the working thesis.

Combining strategies

You may prefer more freedom than close adherence to a predraft outline allows, but still like more structure than the outline-as-you-go approach provides. If so, borrow from both methods. First, carefully review your predraft outline for each section of the paper before writing it. Then write the section *without* further reference to the outline. At the end of each section, compare your work against the outline, and plan to add or delete material as needed. Also look ahead to the next section and revise the outline, if necessary.

How to Write One Section of a Paper

1. **Prepare to write.** Identify your purpose and define your audience. Generate and organize your ideas and information. Devise a working thesis.
2. **Identify sections of the paper.** Ask of your thesis, What parts must I develop in order to deliver on the promise of this statement? Your answer of perhaps three or four points will identify the sections you need to write to complete that statement.
3. **Plan to write one section of your paper at a sitting.** If a section is long, divide it into manageable parts, and write one part at a sitting.
4. **Write individual paragraphs.** Each paragraph will be related to others in the section. As you begin a second paragraph, clearly relate it to the first. Relate the third paragraph to the second, and so on until you finish writing the section. Then take a break.
5. **Write other sections, one at a time.** Continue writing, building one section incrementally on the next, until you complete your first draft.

3 Working collaboratively

Your instructor may ask you to work collaboratively—that is, in a group. The great advantage of creating and writing a document collaboratively is that you can put the power of several minds to work on a task that might prove overwhelming for one person. Both in content and in presentation, however, your group's work should read as though *one* person had written it, even if several people have been involved in the actual writing.

- To minimize rewriting, meet as a group before any writing takes place. Agree on a structure for the overall document, and then assign parts to individuals. Agree on a consistent point of view for the paper.

CRITICAL DECISIONS

Overcome Obstacles to Writing: Identifying and resolving problems in mid-draft

At some point in the writing process you may find yourself unable to steam ahead, one section after the next. Perhaps your work in one section of the paper is not as good as it is elsewhere, or that after several attempts at writing a section you find the effort too difficult. When you are feeling especially frustrated, stop. Step back from your work, and decide how you will get past this obstacle. Ask, Why am I having trouble? Here are several possibilities:

1. You do not have enough information to write. You have not gathered enough information, or if you have, you may not thoroughly understand it.
2. You do not understand the point you planned to make or its relation to the rest of your paper.
3. The point you planned to make no longer seems relevant or correct, given what you have discovered about your subject while writing.
4. You recognize a gap in the structure of your paper, and you suddenly see the need to expand an existing section or to write an entirely new section.
5. The material in the section seems inappropriate for your audience.
6. You have said what you need to say in a page, but must write ten pages.

Each of these obstacles can frustrate your attempts at writing. You will come of age as a writer the moment you can realize you are having trouble and can then step away to name your problem and find a solution.

- At a second meeting after writing has just begun, ask each group member to outline his or her section and to discuss its structure. As a group, think of the ways in which one section will build from and lead to another. Also raise and address any problems encountered thus far in the writing.
- At the completion of a first draft, distribute the assembled document to the entire group, and have each member revise for content and consistency of perspective.
- Incorporate all agreed-upon revisions in a single version of the document. *One* member of the group should then take responsibility for rewriting the paper in order to ensure continuity of style and voice.

3f   Sample student paper: Rough draft

Here is Paul Guzman's rough draft, preparations for which you have followed throughout Chapters 1 through 3. His instructor's comments appear in the margins and at the end of the draft. You'll see this draft revised a second time in Chapter 4. Paul's thesis is underlined.

Teenagers and Smoking: Fighting the Battle on Every Front
(First Draft)

Surveys of adult smokers show that 90% were smoking by the time they were 18: Almost no one starts smoking in adulthood ("Tobacco Use"). The way to lower the number of smokers is to reduce the number of teenagers who start smoking. If we hope to deter young people from smoking, we must identify the factors that motivate them to start smoking in the first place.

Cigarette advertising plays a major role in encouraging young people to start smoking, and a definite correlation between advertising and teen smoking does seem to exist. For example, after the national television networks stopped running cigarette ads in the early 1970s, smoking declined significantly among teenagers (as well as among all other age groups) for more than a decade. Then, with the introduction in 1987 of the Joe Camel campaign--clearly appealing to young people whether intentionally or not--the number of adolescent smokers began to rise again.

Another factor motivating teenagers to begin smoking is that teenagers have such easy access to cigarettes. First of all, the price of a pack of cigarettes is within easy reach of most young people-- less than the cost of most "value meals" at fast-food restaurants. One way to make cigarettes less affordable to young people is to tax cigarette sales more heavily, effectively doubling the price of a pack to five dollars or more. Also, establishments that sell

Marginal comments:

Beginning with the facts. Any personal motivation for writing?

Revise the thesis to anticipate solutions. See note 1.

Is there any evidence to suggest ads not so important?

Good--you have an interest in solutions. But see note 4.

cigarettes should be more closely monitored using "sting" operations similar to those currently employed by local police to catch merchants who sell alcohol to minors.

What would be the penalty for someone who's caught?

Obviously, teenagers begin to smoke for a variety of personal reasons as well: the fact that their friends smoke, a sense of curiosity about smoking, the desire to appear more mature, rebelliousness, and a belief in their own indestructibility and ability to resist becoming addicted. Stronger education efforts are going to be key in counteracting these motivations. At this point, I think, programs to discourage adolescents from smoking have relied too heavily on scare tactics that just don't succeed in many cases. Teenagers can see adult smokers all around them who don't exhibit the dire symptoms they're warned cigarette smoking will lead to, so the claims can easily seem to them exaggerated. As youth addiction specialist Robert Schwebel notes, young people are less concerned about long-term health risks of smoking than about the results of an American Cancer Society study showing that large majorities of teenagers prefer not to date someone who smokes (143).

Could this turn into an antismoking ad?

It is likely that nothing will accomplish as much to help a young person resist the urge to smoke as loving parental involvement. At the same time, I believe that as a community and as a society we need to work together to find ways to reduce smoking levels more generally and to create a climate in which all children will be less likely to try cigarettes. If we can cut in half the number of adolescents who begin to smoke before they turn 20, then current patterns suggest that we can virtually cut in half the number of future smokers nationwide.

Again, a personal motive for writing would help.

Works Cited

Pierce, John P. "Advertising and Promotion."
    Addicted to Nicotine: A National Research
    Forum, "Section III: Nicotine-Environmental
    Risk Factors of Initiation." 27 July 1998.
    21 Sept. 2001 <http://www.nida.nih.gov/
    Meetsum/Nicotine/Pierce.html>.
Schwebel, Robert. Saying No Is Not Enough. New York:
    Newmarket Press, 1998.
"Tobacco Use among Youth." Campaign for
    Tobacco-Free Kids. 5 May 2001. 22
    Sept. 2001 <http://tobaccofreekids.org/
    research/factsheets/pdf/0002.pdf>.

Paul:

A good start. From what I can tell, you have half written a problem-solution essay. You're clear about the nature of the problem re: teenage smoking. But you could be much more definite about your proposed solutions. See my margin notes throughout and the numbered comments below.

(1) Thesis: The topic of teenage smoking certainly invites a problem-solution approach, and the general structure of your draft works. However, you barely hint at your interest in solutions in your thesis--which creates an inconsistency, since you're very direct about offering a solution ("sting" operations) in par. 3. Revise your thesis so that it better anticipates a fully developed problem and solution essay.

(2) Personal motivation: What is your personal connection to this topic? I don't feel your burning interest just yet. Do you care about teenage smoking? Why?

(3) Generally, you need to present more evidence in this paper: In par. 2, for instance, can you provide more evidence that cigarette advertising plays a major role in encouraging youths to begin smoking? And there are significant omissions: You have not mentioned the landmark 1998 settlement between the U.S.

Government and the tobacco industry. Nor have you discussed any solutions, such as banning tobacco advertising. Some more research is needed.

(4)   Develop proposed solutions: in par. 4 you've commented on antismoking programs that do <u>not</u> work. Can you be more specific about efforts that <u>might</u> work?

(5)   Remember that in offering solutions, you need to anticipate possible objections and also show that specific problems exist (for example, in terms of your discussion in paragraph 3 of cigarettes sold to minors).

You're definitely heading in the right direction with this draft. I think the issue for you in revision will be follow-through. Just about everything I've asked for above you have sown the seeds for in your draft. Now you need to nurture those seeds: let them develop.

The Process of Revision

L ike a first draft, revision is an act of creation. In a first draft you work to give a document potential. The writing may be incomplete, but you are working toward an important, controlling idea. In your subsequent drafts, you work to make an earlier draft's potential *real*, making decisions about content and structure. By adding, altering, or deleting sentences and paragraphs, you clarify your main point for yourself and, on the strength of that, for your reader.

CRITICAL DECISIONS

Focusing on the Stages of Revision
Think of revision as occurring in three stages—early, later, and final:

4a **Early revision:** Reread your first draft and rediscover or redefine your main idea. What you *intended* to write is not always what you *in fact* have written.

4b **Later revision:** Make all significant parts of your document work together in support of your main idea.

4c **Final revision (editing):** Correct errors at the sentence level that divert attention from your main point.

4a Early revision: Rediscovering your main idea

Weblink
http://www.powa.org/revifrms.htm
Detailed view of revision from the
Paradigm Online Writing Assistant.

Successful writing clearly communicates an idea, and it is the process of revision that helps to clarify this idea. The key to a successful revision is the commitment to rework drafts until they express your meaning *exactly*. Early revision involves adding, altering, or deleting entire paragraphs with the sole purpose of clarifying your main idea. Commit yourself to real and meaningful revision, and your writing will be good consistently. Back away from this commitment, and your efforts will likely falter.

Strategies for Early Revision

Pose three questions to get started on early revision. Your goal is to rediscover and clarify what you have written in a first draft.

■ What I *intended* to write in my first draft may not be what I have *in fact* written. What is the main idea of this first draft?

Underline one sentence in your draft in answer to this question. If you cannot find such a sentence, write one.

Choose a title for your second draft. The title will help you to clarify your main idea.

■ Does what I have written in this draft satisfy my original purpose for writing?

Review the assignment that began your writing project. Restate the purpose of that assignment. To the degree that you have not met the expectation of the assignment, revise.

■ Does my writing communicate clearly to my audience?

Think of your audience. If need be, revise your level of language, your choice of illustrations, and your general treatment of the topic in order to help your audience understand.

---

1   Choosing a revision strategy that suits you

There are as many different strategies for revising a paper as there are for writing one, and the strategy you choose will depend on your temperament:

■ Some first-draft writers work on individual paragraphs, revising until they achieve their idea for a particular paragraph before they move on.

■ Others work on one section of their paper at a time, revising a grouping of related paragraphs until that grouping functions as a single, seamless unit.

■ Still other writers complete an entire first draft and then revise.

The approach to revision advocated here is that a writer make several "passes" over a draft and on each pass revise with a different focus. *First*, revise the largest elements (the sections). *On the next pass*, revise paragraphs within sections. *On the final pass (or passes)*, revise individual sentences within paragraphs.

The overall objective of your first revision is to rediscover or re-define your main idea. Has the paper developed your working thesis? If so, fine. Still, what you intended to write may not be what you have written. Now is the time to check.

Reread your first draft with care, looking for some sentence other than your working thesis that more accurately describes what you have written. Often, such a "competing" thesis appears near the end of the draft, the place where you have forced yourself to summarize. If you can find no competing thesis, but are sure that your original working thesis does not fit the paper you have written, modify the existing working thesis, or write a new one. Be prepared to quiz the new thesis as you did before. See the box in 3d-4 to review techniques for doing this.

........**ILLUSTRATION: PAUL GUZMAN'S PAPER**

REVISING THE THESIS

As Paul reread his rough draft and his instructor's comments, he saw that he had developed his essay based on a thesis that could be considered only "moderately ambitious" (see 3d-3). This original thesis had not allowed him to pursue his topic as fully as he now felt he could. Challenged to add to his evidence and research, Paul recognized that he needed to explore in greater detail both possible solutions for reducing teen smoking *and* objections that might be raised regarding these proposed solutions. Based on his additional exploration, Paul revised his working thesis:

First-draft thesis

If we hope to deter young people from smoking, we must identify the factors that motivate them to start smoking in the first place.

Second-draft thesis

Although young people become smokers for a variety of reasons, to deter youth smoking we must identify and de-velop strategies to combat those specific influences over which we can have most effective control.

Paul's new thesis created the possibility for his essay to explore the im-portant paradox (indicated by the opening clause beginning with *although*) that, of the many causes leading to the problem of youth smoking, not all have equally viable solutions.

Paradox: Young people start smoking based on a cycle of influences. While we can identify any number of these influences, not all are equally important, and, more important, not all are equally subject to parents' and educators' control.

4a dev

Outline the sections of a revised paper.

A *section* of your paper is a group of related paragraphs (see 5a-1). Based on your revised thesis and on your questions and comments about that thesis, outline the sections of a revised paper.

ILLUSTRATION: PAUL GUZMAN'S PAPER

REVISING THE OUTLINE

Once Paul revised his thesis, he also had to revise the body of his essay to reflect his new emphasis on exploring solutions for reducing youth smoking as well as potential objections to those solutions. Compare the outline of Paul's first draft with the outline of the draft for his proposed revision.

Draft 1

Problem (¶ 1)
    Large numbers of young smokers
    Most adult smokers start by age 18
Causal factors
    Tobacco advertising (¶ 2)
    Access to cigarettes (¶ 3)
    Personal reasons (¶ 4)
Solutions: parents, educators, and communities working together (¶ 5)

Draft 2

Introduction and problem: high rates of youth smoking (¶s 1–2)
Possible cause/solution #1: banning <u>advertising</u>
    Some evidence linking ads to youth smoking (¶ 3)
    Correlation not same as causal link (¶ 4)
    Banning ads difficult because of First Amendment (¶ 5)
Possible cause/solution #2: limiting <u>access</u>
    Enforcement of laws barring sales to minors (¶ 6)
    Answer objections regarding strict enforcement (¶ 7)
Possible cause/solution #3: education dealing with <u>personal motives</u>
    Current scare tactics not working (¶ 8)
    Speak to teen concerns more directly (¶s 9–10)
Conclusion (¶ 11)

The Process of Revision

Incorporate sections of your first draft into your revised outline.

Study your new outline. Reexamine your first draft to determine how much of it will fit, with or without changes, into your plans for the final paper. Then retrieve your first draft, and cut and paste usable sections of this draft into your final outline. Be sure to reread each sentence of first-draft writing that you move into the second draft. Every sentence must contribute toward developing the meaning of your newly conceived thesis.

Write new sections of the final outline, as needed.

The preceding step will leave you with a partial paper: a detailed outline, some of the sections of which (imported from your first draft) are close to being complete, other sections of which are indicated by a phrase in your outline. You will need to write these sections from scratch. Before beginning a new section of your paper, write a section thesis to help focus your efforts (see 5a-2).

3 Reconsidering purpose and audience

Purpose

At some point in the process of revision you will want to reconsider your earliest reasons for writing. You may have been asked to explain, describe, argue, compare, analyze, summarize, define, discuss, illustrate, evaluate, or prove. (See explanations of these and other important word meanings in assignments in 44b.) With your purpose firmly in mind, evaluate your first draft to determine the extent to which you have met that purpose. Alter your revision plans, if necessary, to satisfy your reason for writing.

- Identify the key verb in the assignment, and define that verb with reference to your topic. (See 44b.)
- If you have trouble understanding the purpose, talk to your instructor. Bring your draft to a conference, and explain the direction you've taken.
- Once you identify the parts of a paper that will achieve a stated purpose, incorporate those parts into your plans for a revised draft.

Audience

Revisit your initial audience analysis (see 3a-3). Will your audience be classmates, fellow majors, or an instructor? Take whatever conclusions you reached in your analysis, and use them as a tool for evaluating your first draft. You may find it useful to pose these questions:

- How will this subject appeal to my readers?
- Is the level of difficulty with which I have treated this subject appropriate for my readers?

Early Revision: Rediscovering Your Main Idea   **101**

An Overview of the Revision Process

Use the Thinking and Writing Wheel adapted from Chapter 3 to guide you through the revision process:

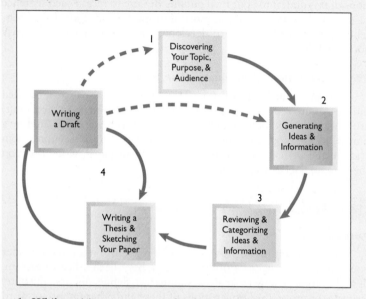

4.1

1. While revising, you may need to leave the draft to reconsider your topic, purpose, or audience. You may also need to pursue and develop new ideas.
2. You may need to leave the draft and return to your source materials, searching for additional supporting materials.
3. Fresh materials need to be integrated into a coherent and unified essay.
4. (a) **Early Revision:** If necessary, revise major elements of your draft to clarify your topic, purpose, and audience; to generate new materials; and to incorporate new elements into the revision.
   (b) **Later Revision:** You will probably not need to leave this inner loop for new materials. Concentrate on the ways in which paragraphs work together to support the essay's main idea.
   (c) **Final Revision:** Revise, refining your essay's tone, sentence structure, and word choice.

- Is my choice of language, in both its tone (see 3a-4) and its level of difficulty, appropriate for my readers?
- Are my examples appropriate in interest and complexity for my readers?

Make changes to your revision plans according to your analysis of the first draft.

4   Choosing and using a title

Before rewriting your paper, use your revised thesis to devise a title. A title creates a context for your readers. It alerts readers to your topic and your intentions for treating it. Forcing yourself to devise a title before beginning your major revision will help you to clarify your main idea. A *descriptive* title directly announces the content of a paper and is appropriate for reports and write-ups of experiments: occasions when you are expected to be direct. An *evocative* title is a playful, intriguing, or otherwise indirect attempt to pique a reader's interest. Both descriptive and evocative titles should be brief (no longer than ten words).

EXERCISE 1

Following advice offered in this section, revise the first draft of the paper you wrote in response to Exercise 12 in Chapter 3. Your early revision may be a major one, requiring you to rework your thesis and to redefine major sections of the paper.

4b   Later revision: Bringing your main idea into focus

Your first major revision of a draft (if you completed Exercise 1) requires the courage to look deep into your paper and make fundamental changes in order to present a single idea clearly. Later revisions will not be so dramatic or far-reaching and will require, for the most part, that you understand and are able to systematically apply certain principles of organization. Three principles of organization important to a later revision are unity, coherence, and balance.

1   Focusing the paper through unity

A paper is unified when the writer discusses only those elements of the subject implied by its thesis. A unified discussion also will not stray from the sentence that organizes and focuses any one of the principal parts of the paper. At each level of the essay, use a general statement to guide you in assembling specific, supporting parts.

Essay-level unity	The thesis (the most general statement in the essay) governs your choice of sections in a paper.
Section-level unity	Section theses (the second-most-general statements in the essay) govern your choice of paragraphs in a section.

coh

Paragraph-level unity	Topic sentences (the third-most-general statements in the essay) govern your choice of sentences in a paragraph.

A unified section of a paper is a discussion of those topics implied by your section thesis (see 5a-2). Every topic generated by quizzing the thesis will become a *section* of your final paper. You will devote at least one paragraph, and maybe more, to developing each section, or subtopic, of the thesis. In a unified paragraph, you discuss only one topic, the one implied by your topic sentence (see 5c).

COMPUTER TIPS

Don't Delete It—You May Want to Recycle It

Word processors have made the concept of discrete drafts obsolete. When handwriting or typewriting, you can be certain when a draft is finished and another one begins. Composing, revising, and editing on a word processor, however, is usually one long, seamless process. It is wise to save a version of your paper in a separate file (using the "Save As" function and a new file name) from time to time, especially if you're embarking on some major changes. Later in the process, you may decide to restore a sentence or paragraph that you discarded.

---

2 Focusing the paper through coherence

Coherence describes the clarity of the relationship between one unit of meaning and another: between sections of a paper, between paragraphs within sections, and between sentences within paragraphs.

- A *whole paper* is coherent when its sections (groupings of related paragraphs) follow one another in a sensible order.
- A *section* of the paper is coherent when the individual paragraphs that constitute it follow one another in a sensible order.
- A *paragraph* is coherent when the individual sentences in it follow one another in a sensible order.

At every level of a paper, you establish coherence by building logical bridges, or transitions, between thoughts. A **transition** may be a word, a sentence, or a paragraph devoted to building a smooth, logical relationship. In all cases, a transition has a double function: to remind readers of what they have just read and then to forecast for them what they are about to read. Transitional expressions include *additionally; likewise; first, second,* and so on; *afterward; for example; of course; accordingly; however; in conclusion;* and *on the whole.* (See 5d-3 for a detailed discussion of transitions and a more complete list.)

Transitions serve to highlight relationships that already exist. If you have trouble finding a word or sentence to serve as an effective transition, reexamine the sentences, paragraphs, or sections that you are trying to link. You may not have arranged them coherently and may need to rearrange them.

As you revise your paper, pause to analyze its sections *in relation* to each other. Rearrange sections, if need be, in order to improve the logical flow of ideas among the largest units of meaning, the paper's sections.

3   Focusing the paper through balance

Balance is a principle of development that guides you in expanding, condensing, and cutting material as you revise. First drafts are typically uneven in the amount of attention given to each section of a paper. In revision, one of your jobs is to review the extent of development you have given each of the topics you have discussed and to determine

---

ACROSS THE CURRICULUM

www

4.2

Sentence-Level Revision

Computer scientist Linda Cohen revises a brief paragraph on the automation of semiconductor (computer-chip) manufacturing:

First draft: Because technicians introduce particulate matter into the environment, automated equipment and robots are used in the manufacture of semiconductor chips. Oil from the skin, dust, hairs from eyelashes, and even residual smoke from the lungs can contaminate the chips, rendering them worthless.

Revisions: Because ^Human technicians introduce ^dirt ~~particulate matter~~ into the ^cleanroom environment, ~~automated equipment and robots are used in the manufacture~~ of semiconductor ^manufacturing chips. Oil from the skin, dust, hairs from eyelashes, and even residual smoke from the lungs can contaminate the chips, rendering them worthless. ^For this reason, the process is now automated.

Final draft: Human technicians introduce dirt into the cleanroom environment of semiconductor manufacturing. Oil from the skin, dust, hairs from eyelashes, and even residual smoke from the lungs can contaminate the chips, rendering them worthless. For this reason, the process is now automated.

---

whether it is appropriate to the importance of that particular point. At times, you will need to *expand:* to add material, in which case you will need to return to the notes you made in preparing to write. You may need to generate new information by reflecting on your subject, by conducting additional library research, or both. At times you will need to *condense:* to take a lengthy paragraph, for example, and reduce it to two sentences. At other times you will need to *cut:* to delete sentences because they are off the point or because they give too much attention to a subordinate point.

EXERCISE 2

Revise your first draft for unity, coherence, and balance following the guidelines discussed in this chapter.

4c   Final revision

I   Editing

Editing is revision at the sentence level: the level at which you attend to style, grammar, punctuation, and word choice. Depending on their preferences, writers will edit (just as they revise) throughout the writing process, from the first draft through to the last. It would be misleading to state flatly that the process of sentence-level rewriting should wait until all issues of unity and coherence are resolved. Still, to the extent that you *can* hold off, save editing until the later drafts, once you are relatively confident that your paper has a final thesis and that the major sections of the paper are in order.

A suggestion made in the Preface is worth repeating here: take an hour to read the introductions to each of the chapters in the handbook. If such a review is not realistic, then read the introductions to the chapters on sentence errors (see 12–16), effective sentences (see 17–20), and punctuation (see 24–29). Your review will give you a sense of the types of errors to watch for when editing. In addition, you can use the "Spotlight on Common Errors" in the endpapers and in key chapters of this book. Use the "Spotlight" pages as checklists for uncovering and revising the most common sentence and punctuation errors.

2   Proofreading

Before you call a paper finished, check for minor errors that may annoy readers and embarrass you. Reread your paper to identify and

Weblink

http://www.ucc.vt.edu/stdysk/
proofing.html

*Hints for effective proofreading from
Virginia Tech.*

correct misspelled words; words (often prepositions) omitted from sentences; words that have been doubled; punctuation that you tend to forget; and homonyms (writing *there* instead of *their*). If you have trouble spotting these minor errors in your writing, find a way to disrupt your usual pattern of reading so that the errors will become visible to you.

- One technique is to photocopy your work and have a friend read it aloud. You read along and make corrections.
- Another technique is to read each line of your paper in reverse order, from the last word on the line to the first. This approach forces you to focus on one word at a time.
- Besides checking for minor errors, review your writing assignment one last time to make sure you have prepared your manuscript in an appropriate form. (See Appendix A on Manuscript Form and Preparation.)

3   Determining when a final draft is *final*

At some point you must stop writing. In the age of word processing, deciding when to stop is not always easy, since you can make that one last correction and print a new page with relative ease. When changes seem not to improve the product, then you have reached an end to revision and editing. To consider a draft final, make sure your paper has met these standards:

- The paper has a clearly stated main point to communicate.
- It has met all requirements of unity and coherence at the levels of the paper, section, and paragraph.
- It is punctuated correctly and is free of errors in grammar and usage.

Stylistically, you could edit your papers ad infinitum. Stylistic editing can mean the difference between a good work and an excellent one. Eventually, however, you will reach a point at which changes do not improve the quality of your paper. When you reach this point, stop.

> **EXERCISE 3**
>
> Edit the draft of the paper you have revised for unity, coherence, and balance. Realize that you may need to make several passes at your draft to put it into final form. Now proofread your final draft.

www

4d Responding to editorial advice from peers or professors

4.3   One of your jobs as a writer is to give and receive editorial advice. All writers can benefit from an editor, a person whose fresh perspective can identify trouble spots that escaped the writer's view.

1 Receiving advice

As the writer of a paper that does not yet succeed, be aware that critical comments, provided they come from a responsible source, are being directed at your work and not at you.

Weblink

http://www.urich.edu/~writing/
wweb/peeredit.html

An outline of the steps in peer editing.

You have the prerogative to accept, to accept partially, or to reject editorial advice. If you truly disagree with your editor, even one who will at some point be grading you, then you should hold your ground and *thoughtfully* explain what you were trying to do in the paper, what you would like to do, and why you cannot accept a particular suggestion for revision. But remember that if the editor is responsible, he or she has the interests of your paper in mind and is making suggestions to improve your effort. These suggestions deserve an honest hearing.

2 Giving advice

As an editor, you must allow the writer his or her topic and interest in it. Do not criticize because a topic does not interest you. Also, realize

Guidelines for Peer Editing

1. Understand your role as an editor. Your goal is to work to improve the paper according to the author's needs, not your own.
2. Ask the writer to identify elements of the paper to which you should pay special attention.
3. Questions you might consider as you are reading:
   Is the writer helping me to become interested in this topic?
   Do all the parts of this paper seem to be present? Are general points backed up with specific examples?
   Is the writing at the sentence level sharp?
   How much help does the writer need with the nuts and bolts of grammar and punctuation?
4. Begin with the positive. Whether you are writing your editorial comments or are delivering them in conference, begin with the parts of the paper that you liked. If at all possible, find *something* that is worthy of a compliment.
5. Be specific with criticism. When you see room for improvement, identify specific words, sentences, or paragraphs, and state specifically what you think needs changing and why. If possible, build your constructive criticisms on earlier strengths:
   Avoid statements such as "This is vague."
   Strive for statements such as "Your sentences in this section don't have the same vivid detail as your earlier sentences."
6. End your editorial advice with a summary of what you have observed. Then suggest a point-by-point action plan for the writer. That is, advise the writer on specific steps to take that will lead to an improved paper.

Weblink

http://www-richmond.edu/
~writing/wweb/peeredit.html

An online booklet devoted to "Groupwork and Collaborative Writing" from UC Davis.

that this is not your paper that you are commenting on. Do not attempt in your comments to make the paper yours. Realize as well the power of your criticism. Many people feel fragile about their writing, and when you must criticize, be respectful. Most writing has something good in it. Start there, and be specific with your praise. State, "I like this sentence," and say why. Then compare passages that don't work with those that do, and explain the differences you see. Be honest with your criticism.

The better you edit other people's work, the more proficient you will become at editing your own. Whatever your editorial skills, you can benefit from the editorial advice of others precisely because they are not you and can therefore offer a fresh perspective. In developing your own guidelines for giving editorial advice, you may want to build on the notes in the box above.

The process of writing a draft and responding to criticism clarified for Paul Guzman several problems with his thinking about the problem of teen smoking. In the process of writing, he discovered a *new* thesis—the basis of which you can find in his earliest responses to the sources he read on his topic.

As you will see, Paul spent time refining his sentences so that they would read effortlessly. You will find in his essay the paradox evident in all good writing: when sentences are clear and easy to read, they mask the considerable effort that went into making them. Good writing looks to readers as if it took no work at all; the writer knows otherwise.

Teenagers and Smoking: How Can We Stop the Cycle?
(Final Draft)

I had my first cigarette when I was 14 and within a year I was an addicted, pack-a-day smoker. It wasn't until 12 years later, when my wife and I had our first child last summer, that I summoned up the will power to stop. The process was difficult, even agonizing at times, but I didn't want our baby to be parented by a father who smoked. More important, I didn't want her ever to become a smoker herself.

It's startling to realize how many young smokers there are. More than 3 million 12- to 17-year-old Americans smoke, according to a 2000 government study, and, despite various antismoking efforts, teenage smoking rates grew dramatically over much of the 1990s. Just as startling are surveys of adult smokers showing that 90% were smoking by the time they were 18: Almost no one starts smoking in adulthood ("Tobacco Use"). The way to lower the number of smokers, then, is to reduce the number of teenagers who start smoking. Although young people become smokers for a variety of reasons, to deter youth smoking we must identify and develop strategies to combat those specific influences over which we can have the most effective control.

Many critics of the tobacco industry argue that cigarette advertising plays a major role in encouraging young

people to start smoking, and some evidence seems to show such
a correlation. For example, after the national television
networks stopped running cigarette ads in the early 1970s,
smoking declined significantly among teenagers (as well as
among all other age groups) for more than a decade. Then,
with the introduction in 1987 of the Joe Camel campaign--
clearly appealing to young people whether intentionally or
not--the number of adolescent smokers began to rise again.
Furthermore, research studies have shown that nonsmoking
teenagers who remember specific cigarette ads or who express
an interest in owning a brand-related promotional item are
more likely than others to become smokers (Pierce).

Still, does this mean cigarette advertising should be
banned? Though it seems a fair assumption, there is really
no clear proof that advertising contributes significantly to
teen smoking. After R. J. Reynolds abandoned its Joe Camel
campaign in response to public criticism, teen smoking rates
continued to go up. And under a 1998 settlement with the
United States government, tobacco companies no longer place
cigarette ads in publications aimed specifically at teens.
Critics charge that the brands most popular with teenagers--
Marlboro, Camel, and Newport--are still heavily promoted in
general magazines with a high readership among young people,
mostly those focusing on fashion, sports, music, and popular
culture. However, the fact that teens are drawn to heavily
advertised brands or that teens already receptive to cigarette advertising are more likely than others to become
smokers can't by itself prove that a significant number of
young people are drawn to smoking primarily by advertising.
As Reason columnist Jacob Sullum puts it, "It is just as
plausible to suppose that teenagers pay more attention to
cigarette ads after they start smoking, or that teenagers
who are inclined to smoke for other reasons are also more
likely to have a positive view of cigarette ads" (38).

At any rate, a total ban on cigarette advertising is
unlikely because of freedom of speech protections under the
First Amendment. In June 2001, for example, the Supreme
Court struck down Massachusetts regulations banning any

public advertising of tobacco products 1,000 feet or closer to a school or playground, along with other restrictions on such advertising in retail stores. Writing for the majority, Justice Sandra Day O'Connor said, "The First Amendment . . . constrains state efforts to limit advertising of tobacco products, because so long as the sale and use of tobacco is lawful for adults, the tobacco industry has a protected interest in communicating information about its products and adult customers have an interest in receiving that information" (Lorillard). Similar reasoning would probably apply to any proposed ban on advertising in magazines aimed at both adult and teenage readers.

More feasible is legislation limiting teenagers' access to cigarettes. One possibility is to raise taxes on cigarettes to make them less affordable to teenagers. But because such taxes would also affect the pocketbooks of adult smokers, such a plan would clearly meet with resistance from a large bloc of voters. However, existing federal law already makes the sale of cigarettes to anyone under the age of 18 illegal. Unfortunately, most communities continue to fail in enforcing these rules. In a 1999 study Joseph DiFranza of the University of Massachusetts Medical School examined government documents regarding state enforcement of federal law relating to tobacco sales to minors. DiFranza discovered that retail merchants face virtually no risk for selling cigarettes to underage buyers: "I find evidence of possibly about a thousand episodes in which merchants were penalized for selling tobacco to kids. So just roughly about a billion packs of cigarettes [sold to minors] and a thousand penalties means if you sell tobacco to kids the likelihood of getting caught is one in a million" (qtd. in "Researcher").

Officials at both the state and local level will argue, of course, that enforcement is expensive and that it takes police away from more important duties. But there is a solution. Outlets that sell cigarettes could be licensed just as licenses are now required of merchants selling alcohol. The resulting revenues could be used to fund additional personnel to monitor merchant compliance with cigarette (and alcohol) age restrictions. Along with heavy fines and the threat of perhaps losing one's license, such policies should provide clear incentives for merchants to card more diligently. Such enforcement could easily be accompanied by regulations requiring that cigarettes not be displayed openly (to prevent theft) and either banning cigarette-vending machines or requiring that they be located in places where they can be closely supervised.

I don't mean to suggest that regulations like these would fully succeed in keeping cigarettes out of the hands of underage smokers, so other efforts would also be needed. Obviously, teenagers begin to smoke for a variety of personal reasons: the fact that their friends smoke, a sense of curiosity about smoking, the desire to appear more mature, rebelliousness, and a belief in their own indestructibility and ability to resist becoming addicted. Stronger education efforts are going to be key in counteracting these motivations. At this point, I think, programs to discourage adolescents from smoking have relied too heavily on scare tactics that just don't succeed in many cases. Teenagers can see adult smokers all around them who don't exhibit the dire symptoms they're warned cigarette smoking will lead to, so the claims can easily seem to them exaggerated.

While information about the health risks associated with smoking shouldn't be downplayed, it should be supplemented with other, more immediately persuasive information. For example, youth addiction specialist Robert Schwebel notes that young people are less concerned about long-term health risks of smoking than by the results of an American Cancer Society study showing that large majorities of teenagers prefer not to date someone who smokes (143). Teenagers also underestimate the addictive nature of cigarettes, thinking they can easily quit whenever they decide to. Testimonials from self-described nicotine addicts in their early twenties who deeply regret they ever started smoking could have a great impact on deterring young smokers. Involving teenagers in helping to create such messages, messages that they themselves would find effective, could go a long way toward helping young people to resist that first cigarette.

In fact, the state of Florida developed one such successful campaign using funds from its multibillion-dollar settlement with the tobacco companies. Devised largely by student members of the state group Students Working Against Tobacco (SWAT), the campaign satirized smoking and particularly the efforts of tobacco industry executives to manipulate teenagers into smoking. In a single year, the smoking rate among all Florida teenagers declined by 10% and that among 12- to 14-year-olds by 19% ("In Florida"). Unfortunately, Florida lawmakers significantly decreased the budget for the campaign in the state's 2000 budget, basically ending it for the foreseeable future. Its success, however, could be imitated elsewhere with funding from private foundations.

It is likely that nothing will accomplish as much to help a young person resist the urge to smoke as loving parental involvement, and I plan to do everything I can to discourage my little girl from ever feeling the need to light up as she grows older. At the same time, I believe that as a community and as a society we need to work together to find ways to reduce smoking levels more generally and to create a climate in which all children will be less likely to try cigarettes. If we can cut in half the number of adolescents who begin to smoke before they turn 20, then current patterns suggest that we can virtually cut in half the number of future smokers nationwide. Our goal must be to find solutions that are both effective and realizable.

Works Cited

"In Florida, Kicking Butts." The Economist
        24 Apr. 1999: 28.
Lorillard Tobacco Company v. Reilly. 28 June 2001.
        18 Sept. 2001 <http://supct.law.cornell.edu/
        supct/html/00-596.ZO.html>.

Pierce, John P. "Advertising and Promotion."
     Addicted to Nicotine: A National Research
     Forum, "Section III: Nicotine-Environmental
     Risk Factors of Initiation." 27 July 1998.
     21 Sept. 2001 <http://www.nida.nih.gov/
     Meetsum/Nicotine/Pierce.html>.

"Researcher: Penalty Risk Isn't Stopping Tobacco
     Sales to Kids." CNN.com: 13 Oct. 1999.
     19 Sept. 2001 <http://cgi.cnn.com/US/9910/13/
     tobacco.kids/>.

Schwebel, Robert. Saying No Is Not Enough. 2nd ed.
     New York: Newmarket, 1998.

Sullum, Jacob. "Cowboys, Camels, and Kids." Reason
     Apr. 1998: 34-39.

"Tobacco Use Among Youth." Campaign for Tobacco-
     Free Kids. 5 May 2001. 22 Sept. 2001
     <http://tobaccofreekids.org/research/
     factsheets/pdf/0002.pdf>.

CHAPTER 5

The Paragraph and the Paper

It is easy enough to define a paragraph: a group of related sentences organized by a single, controlling idea and marked by an indented first word (typically five spaces from the left margin). More complicated, however, is determining what makes a paragraph effective. As this chapter will clarify, an effective paragraph is unified, coherent, and well developed. During the process of drafting and revising you will need to make certain that each paragraph in your paper exhibits these qualities. Well-written paragraphs are so important to the development of a paper that discussion of paragraphs warrants its own chapter.[1]

5a The relationship of single paragraphs to a whole paper

Paragraphs rarely stand alone. They are extended units of thought that, carefully pieced together, build the content of a paper through strategic decisions you make in the writing and revision process.

The relationship of paragraphs to sections

Just as sentences make up individual paragraphs, paragraphs make up whole letters, essays, and reports. Aside from specialized occasions for writing, such as summaries and short-answer essay exams, you will seldom write a single, isolated paragraph. Usually, a paragraph will be part of a grouping—a **section**—within a larger document. Except at the beginning and the end of a paper (see 5f), any one paragraph will be involved directly with at least two others: the one immediately preceding and the one that follows.

The following paragraphs form a section—one part of an essay by David Rothenberg, a philosophy professor at the New Jersey Institute of Technology.

Weblink

http://www2.actden.com/writ_den/tips/paragrap/index.htm

WritingDEN's online guide to writing and developing paragraphs.

[1]Example paragraphs from various sources are consecutively numbered throughout the chapter for ease of reference.

CRITICAL DECISIONS

Determining Paragraph Length

A paragraph can be as brief as a sentence or as long as a page. Because there is no formula regarding paragraph length, writers must determine for themselves what is appropriate given their purpose, subject, and audience.

As you draft, concentrate on the content of your paragraphs. Save your concerns about paragraph length for the later stages of revision, when you are relatively satisfied with your work. Then think of your reader and the way your paragraphs appear on the page. Keep the following guidelines in mind:

■ Consistently short paragraphs (two or three sentences) may send the signal that your ideas are not well developed. Do you need to combine paragraphs? Or do many of your paragraphs actually require further development?

■ Consistently long paragraphs (nine or ten sentences) may give the impression that your writing is dense or that your ideas are not well differentiated. Think about dividing long paragraphs in a logical way. The new paragraph does not need its own topic sentence as long as it is clearly a continuation of the paragraph that precedes it.

■ One-sentence paragraphs are rarely appropriate for academic writing. In other writing situations, however, a one-sentence paragraph may be useful to emphasize a point, to provide a transition, or to offer a summary.

Titled "How the Web Destroys the Quality of Students' Research Papers," the essay originally appeared in the *Chronicle of Higher Education* in 1997.

It's easy to spot a research paper that is based primarily on information collected from the Web. First, the bibliography cites no books, just articles or pointers to places in that virtual land somewhere off any map: http://www.etc. Then a strange preponderance of material in the bibliography is curiously out of date. A lot of stuff on the Web that is advertised as timely is actually at least a few years old. (One student submitted a research paper last semester in which all of his sources were articles published between September and December 1995; that was probably the time span of the Web page on which he found them.)   1

Another clue is the beautiful pictures and graphs that are inserted neatly into the body of the student's text. They look impressive, as though they were the result of careful work and analysis, but actually they often bear little relation to the precise subject of   2 the paper. Cut and pasted from the vast realm of what's out there for the taking, they masquerade as original work.

Accompanying them are unattributed quotes (in which one can't tell who made the statement or in what context) and curiously detailed references to the kinds of things that are easy to find on the Web (pages and pages of federal documents, corporate propaganda, or snippets of commentary by people whose credibility is difficult to assess). Sadly, one finds few references to careful, in-depth commentaries on the subject of the paper, the kind of analysis that requires a book, rather than an article, for its full development. **3**

> —DAVID ROTHENBERG, "How the Web
> Destroys the Quality of Students'
> Research Papers," from *Chronicle of
> Higher Education*, August 15, 1997

2 The relationship of sections to the whole paper

A **thesis** states the topic you will address in a paper and either directly or indirectly suggests the points you will make about that topic (see 3d). You will probably devote one section of your paper to discussing each point you wish to develop. For each section of your paper you will write a **section thesis,** a statement that explicitly announces the point you will address in the section and either directly or indirectly suggests what you will discuss relating to this point. You will organize your discussion in paragraphs.

The section thesis organizing the paragraphs by David Rothenberg appears at the beginning of ¶1: *"It's easy to spot a research paper that is based primarily on information collected from the Web."* The rest of this paragraph and the two following paragraphs focus on developing this statement.

¶1 Evidence of primarily Web-based research based on the bibliography.

¶2 Evidence of primarily Web-based research based on pictures and graphs.

¶3 Evidence of primarily Web-based research based on information cited.

These paragraphs make up a distinct section of Rothenberg's essay. The section as a whole is *unified* and *well developed* in that the three paragraphs focus on and amply discuss a single controlling idea, the section thesis. Each paragraph is also unified and well developed, focusing on its own, more narrowly defined controlling idea. And because each paragraph builds on the one that precedes it and is positioned according to a clear plan, the whole section is *coherent*. In the same way, every paragraph in the section is itself coherent, since the sentences of each establish a clear pattern of relation.

EXERCISE I

Locate an article in a magazine or a chapter of a book (a textbook will do), and divide the article or chapter into its component sections. Analyze the paragraphs in one section as follows: (1) identify the controlling idea, or section thesis; and (2) explain how the section is unified, developed, and coherent.

5b The paragraph: Essential features

To develop an idea well, you will need to make sure that the sentences of your paragraphs are unified: sentences in any given paragraph should refer to one organizing idea. The paragraph should also be *well developed:* sentences should explain or defend well the main point of the paragraph. In addition, the paragraph should be *coherent:* sentences of the paragraph should be arranged in a clear order.

Here is an example of a well-written paragraph from a biology text.

Life on this planet began in water, and today, almost wherever water is found, life is also present. There are one-celled organisms that eke out their entire existence in no more water than that which can cling to a grain of sand. Some species of algae are found only on the melting undersurfaces of polar ice floes. Certain species of bacteria and certain blue-green algae can tolerate the near-boiling water of hot springs. In the desert, plants race through an entire life 4 cycle—seed to flower to seed—following a single rainfall. In the jungle, the water cupped in the leaves of a tropical plant forms a microcosm in which a myriad of small organisms are born, spawn, and die. We are interested in whether the soil of Mars and the dense atmosphere surrounding Venus contain water principally because we want to know whether life is there. On our planet, and probably on others where life exists, life and water have been companions since life first began.

—HELENA CURTIS, "Water"

Examine the qualities that make this grouping of sentences a paragraph, a unit of thought. First, the sentences of Curtis's paragraph are narrowly focused by a single, controlling idea: *water* and its relation to life. Given this focus, the grouping of sentences is unified. Observe as well that Curtis develops her central idea according to a clear plan. In the first six sentences, she associates water with life on earth. Notice how she moves from an extreme presented in one sentence to an opposite extreme presented in the next.

Curtis's next-to-last sentence, about water on Mars or Venus, extends observations made concerning water and life on earth to other planets, and once again she drives home her point, which she repeats by way of summary in the paragraph's last sentence. She has taken care to present eight *unified* sentences that *develop* a central idea and that are arranged in a meaningful, *coherent* order.

> ### EXERCISE 2
>
> Choose any numbered paragraph in this chapter, and explain why it can justifiably be called a paragraph. (1) identify the central, organizing idea that unifies the sentences; (2) identify the parts of the paragraph that explain or defend this central idea; and (3) explain how the sentences are organized according to a definite, coherent plan.

5c   Writing and revising to achieve paragraph unity

A unified paragraph will focus on, develop, and not stray from the paragraph's central, controlling idea generally expressed in a **topic sentence.** Recall that a *thesis* announces and controls the content of an entire essay. Just so, a *topic sentence* announces and controls the content of sentences in a single paragraph. Think of the topic sentence as a paragraph-level *thesis*, and you will see the principle of unity at work at *all* levels of the paper. At each level a general statement guides you in assembling specific, supporting parts.

A topic sentence can appear anywhere within a paragraph, provided that you recognize it and can lead up to and away from it with some method in mind.

1   Placing the topic sentence at the beginning of a paragraph

Writers often open paragraphs with a topic sentence when their purpose is to inform or persuade and they wish to be as direct as possible, as in the following example:

> The college town is an American institution. Throughout the 19th century, it was common practice to locate private colleges in small towns like Amherst in Massachusetts, Middlebury in Vermont and Pomona in California. The idea was that bucolic surroundings **5** would provide the appropriate atmosphere for the pursuit of learning and (not incidentally) remove students from the distractions and temptations of the big city. The influence of the small college on its town was minimal, however, beyond providing a few local residents with service jobs.
>
> —WITOLD RYBCYNSKI, "Big City Amenities"

Rybcynski begins the paragraph with a direct statement: *The college town is an American institution.* Every subsequent sentence focuses on and develops this topic sentence.

2   Placing the topic sentence in the middle of a paragraph

When a paragraph presents material on two sides of an issue, consider placing the topic sentence in the middle. Lead up to the topic sentence with supporting material concerning its first part, then follow the topic sentence with material concerning its second part:

> A host of simple-minded cliches about Moslems and Islam exists. When the hostage crisis in Iran occurred, most Westerners began to view all Moslems, the followers of Islam, as Arab or Iranian militants seeking to return the world to the 14th century. There is, however, great diversity in Islam, a religion that covers one-seventh of the earth's inhabitable area and includes a sixth of its population. To judge all Moslems as the same is as futile as judging all Christians and Jews in the same way. Most of the world's 800 million Moslems are not fatalistic radicals. Like most Christians and Jews, they, too, devoutly believe in and respect God and seek to live a good life in peace with others.   **6**
>
> —JACK SHAHEEN, "In Search of the Arab"

Shaheen's topic sentence is the pivot on which this paragraph turns: *There is, however, great diversity in Islam, a religion that covers one-seventh of the earth's inhabitable area and includes a sixth of its population.* Two sentences lead up to this topic sentence, preparing for it, and three sentences follow and develop it.

3   Placing the topic sentence at the end of a paragraph

In some cases you may want to postpone the topic sentence until the end, especially if you want to make sure that readers can consider all the sentences in the paragraph before coming to your main point. The strategy works especially well when you are arguing:

> It is a fact that many children today are watching a great deal of televised fare that is inappropriate for their age and sophistication level. This concern raises two possible courses of action. If we take the position of technology determinist Neil Postman that "it is pointless to spend time or energy deploring television or even making proposals to improve it," then the only response is to lock the television set up, or do whatever is necessary to keep it away from the innocent eyes of children. But if we believe that television can offer the potential to complement and enliven children's literacy experiences, it is imperative that greater efforts be made to improve both the quality of programming, and children's viewing habits.   **7**
>
> —SUSAN B. NEUMAN, "The Myth of the TV Effect"

If you move the last sentence of this paragraph to the beginning, you see that subsequent sentences support and develop the idea that *greater efforts be made to improve both the quality of programming, and children's viewing habits.* This statement is debatable, a fact that Neuman acknowledges by presenting two positions on the problem she notes (that children are watching television inappropriate for their age and level of sophistication). She rejects the first position, and then offers her own. By delaying her paragraph's main idea, Neuman ensures that her audience will have some background on the problem and some reason to agree with her position.

4   Omitting the topic sentence from the paragraph

In narrative and descriptive papers, and much less frequently in informative and persuasive papers, writers will occasionally omit the topic sentence from a paragraph. In a narrative paragraph that is part of a story, including the topic sentence may be so heavy-handed that it ruins an otherwise subtle effect. The subject of descriptive writing may be so obvious that including a topic sentence seems redundant. When you decide to omit a topic sentence, take care to write the paragraph with a clear topic sentence in mind. Focus each sentence on the implied topic and do not include any sentence that strays from that topic.

Here is an example of an informative paragraph with an implied topic sentence:

> Glossy brochures [from colleges to prospective high-school applicants] tend to portray a diverse group of beaming students frolicking happily and thinking deep thoughts on every page. "They're all the same," recalled one college freshman, happy to be finished with the process. Each brochure speaks of "rich diversity" and "academic rigor" and dozens of other high-minded ideals that are often in reality nothing more than hollow catch-phrases. Likewise, any campus can look beautiful through the lens of an admissions office photographer. Just remember, the building that looks so picturesque in the fading twilight could be part of the law school, miles from where the undergraduates study.
>
> —*YALE DAILY NEWS* STAFF, "The Insider's Guide to the Colleges" 8

The sentence that comes closest to being a topic sentence is the paragraph's final one. Yet this sentence only implies the following main idea: *When reviewing glossy college brochures, high-school students should not assume that they are being presented with a fully accurate portrayal of undergraduate life.* Placed at the head of the paragraph, the italicized sentence would function adequately as a topic sentence. Every sentence in the paragraph is governed by this implied sentence, just as if it had been stated directly.

EXERCISE 3

Reread several paragraphs that you have recently written for one of your classes. Choose one paragraph to revise for unity: add, delete, or modify sentences as needed.

EXERCISE 4

Locate the topic sentence of the paragraphs in the section you worked with in Exercise 1. Analyze each paragraph, and be prepared to discuss how every sentence contributes to the paragraph's unity.

5d Writing and revising to achieve paragraph coherence

When paragraphs are coherent, readers recognize a logical movement from one sentence to the next. While drafting a paper, you may not initially have a plan to ensure paragraph coherence. You may not even have a clear idea of every paragraph's main point. Revision is the time to sort these matters out—when you can make certain that each paragraph has a clear purpose and a clear, coherent plan for achieving that purpose.

I   Arranging sentences to achieve coherence

Writers use some standard patterns for arranging paragraphs, the most common of which are by space, by time, and by importance. If it occurs to you as you write a first draft that one of these patterns lends itself to the point you are discussing, then by all means write your paragraph with that pattern in mind. Very often, you will want to revise paragraphs with one of these patterns in mind as well.

Arrangement by space

In description, you can help readers visualize your subject by arranging a paragraph spatially. Start at a well-defined position with respect to the object you are describing, and then move from that position to others taking systematic steps, one at a time. Your description might proceed from front to back, right to left, top to bottom, outside to inside, and so on.

> By the 17th and 18th centuries, Edinburgh was already overbuilt. Gray stone buildings filled every nook and cranny along the city's maze of roads and alleys. Space was so scarce inside the city walls that doctors, merchants and other professionals conducted their business in the pubs that lined the streets. . . . When Edinburgh needed more room to pack in people, the resourceful **9** Scots had to expand upward. It was not uncommon . . . for some buildings to go up 12 to 14 stories. The higher floors were reserved for the upper crust of Scottish society. The richer you were, the farther away you lived from the dark, wet and always filthy Edinburgh streets.
>
> —GEORGE HOMSY, "From Kings to Caddies in Edinburgh"

The spatial organization in this paragraph rests on a principle of upward movement. The lower stories of buildings are associated with squalor. The upper stories are literally the realm of the upper class.

Arrangement by time

You can achieve coherence by arranging a paragraph according to a sequence of events. Start with a particular event, then move forward or backward in time in some definite order. Give your readers signals that emphasize the forward or backward movement. In the following paragraphs about the rise of homelessness in the 1980s, the writer moves readers forward in time with the highlighted phrases.

5.1

> If the large numbers of the homeless lived in hospitals before they reappeared in subway stations and in public shelters, we need to ask where they were and what they had been doing from 1972 to 1980. Were they living under bridges? Were they waiting out the decade in the basements of deserted buildings?
>
> No. The bulk of those who had been psychiatric patients and were released from hospitals **during the 1960s and early 1970s** had been living in the meantime in low-income housing, many in skid-row hotels or boarding houses. Such housing—commonly known as SRO (single-room occupancy) units—was drastically diminished by the gentrification of our cities **that began in 1970.** Almost 50 percent of SRO housing was replaced by luxury apartments or by office buildings **between 1970 and 1980,** and the remaining units have been disappearing at even faster rates. **As recently as 1986,** after New York City had issued a prohibition against conversion of such housing, a well-known developer hired a demolition team to destroy a building in Times Square that had previously been home to indigent people. The demolition took place in the middle of the night. In order to avoid imprisonment, the developer was allowed to make a philanthropic gift to homeless people as a token of atonement. This incident, bizarre as it appears, reminds us that the profit motive for displacement of the poor is very great in every major city. It also indicates a more realistic explanation for the growth of homelessness **during the 1980s.**
>
> —JONATHAN KOZOL, "Distancing the Homeless"

Arrangement by importance

Arrangement by importance is largely determined by where you position the topic sentence. How will your sentences lead up to or away from the topic sentence? You should be aware of two basic patterns: general to specific and specific to general.

General to specific: When the topic sentence begins the paragraph

By far the most common method for arranging sentences in a paragraph is to begin with a topic sentence and follow with specific, supporting details. When beginning a paragraph this way, decide how to order the information that will follow. You might ask, What does this paragraph's topic sentence obligate me to discuss? What are the *parts* of this paragraph, and in what order will I discuss them? In this paragraph, Jerry Dennis explains how birds increase the chances that their fledglings will survive.

> There is a simple reason so many birds remain with one mate: the kids. The demands of raising young often take the full attention of two adults. Biologists like to discuss the behavior in economic terms, speaking of parental "investment," and pointing out that it is more profitable for a male bird intent on propagating his own genes to stick with one mate and ensure the survival of a brood than to impregnate many females haphazardly. Once committed to monogamy, a male bird takes the job seriously. He may help build nests, take turns brooding the eggs, gather food, and stand watch. In studies where the male has been removed, the percentages of eggs that hatch and fledglings that survive decline dramatically.
>
> —JERRY DENNIS, "Mates for Life"

12

Specific to general: When the topic sentence ends the paragraph

When you are writing a description or narration or arguing a point, you may want to delay your topic sentence until the final sentence of a paragraph. Here you reverse the standard arrangement of a paragraph and move from specific details to a general, concluding statement. The goal is to build one sentence on the next so securely that the final sentence strikes the reader as inevitable.

> Einstein . . . wrote: "The most beautiful experience we can have is the mysterious. It is the fundamental emotion which stands at the cradle of all true art and true science." At first, this might seem a strange thought. We are frequently asked to believe that science is the antithesis of mystery. Nothing could be further from the truth. Mystery invites the attention of the curious mind. Unless we perceive the world as mysterious—queer and wonderful—we will never be curious about what makes it tick.
>
> —CHET RAYMO, "To Light the Fire of Science, Start with Some Fantasy and Wonder"

13

Raymo begins with a specific quotation from Albert Einstein. He develops the paragraph by exploring Einstein's use of the word *mysterious*. In so doing, he moves from the specific (the quotation) to the general, his larger point, which he locates in the paragraph's final sentence.

| 2 | Achieving coherence with cues |

When sentences are arranged with care, you need only highlight their arrangement so that readers can move easily through a paragraph. To highlight paragraph coherence, use **cues,** words and phrases that remind readers as they move from sentence to sentence that (1) they continue to read about the same topic and (2) ideas are unfolding logically.

Pronouns

The most direct way to remind readers that they continue to read about the same topic as they move from sentence to sentence is to repeat the most important noun, or the subject, of your topic sentence. To prevent repetition from becoming tiresome, use a pronoun to take the place of this important noun.

5.2

ILLUSTRATION: PRONOUN SUBSTITUTION

The choice of Peter Hall to supply vigorous entrepreneurial leadership was logical. Only twenty-nine, he was already an eminent director. He had earned his credentials with the theatre work he began at Cambridge and continued with the Elizabethan Theatre Company, formed by Oxford and Cambridge students to tour Shakespeare plays. More impressive and attention-getting was his direction of the 1955 premiere at the London Arts Theatre of Samuel Beckett's *Waiting for Godot*, an event that alone would have entered Hall's name into theatre history.

—ROGER CORNISH AND VIOLET KETELS,
Landmarks of Modern British Drama

Repetition

While unintentional repetition can make sentences awkward, planned repetition can contribute significantly to a paragraph's coherence. Either repeat an important word identically or use a clear substitution. As with pronoun use, repetition cues readers, reminding them of the paragraph's important information. In the following example, combinations of the following four words are repeated eight times: *performance/performer*, *minstrels*, *scops*, and *gleemen*.

5.3

ILLUSTRATION: WORD REPETITION

Although the performance practices of the Church held considerable power and influence, the medieval audience was familiar with other types of performance events. The jongleurs and the troubadours of southern France were professional performers who glorified heroic life and courtly love in verse, often singing of love in rather earthy terms. In Anglo-Saxon England, such performers were called (scops and gleemen;) later, they were known as (minstrels.) Usually accompanying themselves with a harp, (minstrels) probably composed such literary texts as *Widsith*, *Doer's Lament*, and *Beowulf.* Just as important, each of these texts offers a picture of the (minstrels' performance work.)

—RONALD J. PELIAS, *Performance Studies*

Parallelism

Chapter 18 is devoted entirely to a discussion of **parallelism:** the use of grammatically equivalent words, phrases, and sentences to achieve coherence and balance in your writing. A sentence whose structure parallels that of an earlier sentence has an echo-like effect, linking the content of the second sentence to the content of the first.

ILLUSTRATION: PARALLELISM

STUDENT EXAMPLE: JIM WALKER

5.4

```
All students need to be aware of what some students
know by instinct: that you can divert or reduce ag-
gression with a quick apology or with humor. This is
what social psychologists call reducing levels of
arousal by introducing an incompatible response.
Also, the school can implement Peer Mediation where
if students feel a physical or emotional threat they
can report it and discuss it with other students.
Students talk through the issues with each other--and
talking, it turns out, is the important thing: get-
ting two sides together to talk rather than using
weapons or fists to solve differences. Talking can
also show students that disagreements are not worth a
trip to the emergency room or worth the legal prob-
lems or medical bills--the consequences of violence
that movies and rap videos don't usually show. If
more students would have used these simple measures
at my high school, I'm convinced that at least sev-
eral fights could have been avoided.
```

16

Parallel structures found *within* sentences are:

you can divert or reduce

with a quick apology or with humor

what social psychologists call reducing levels of arousal by
    introducing

if students feel a physical or emotional threat

they can report it and discuss it

getting two sides together to talk rather than using

disagreements are not worth a trip to the emergency room or
    worth the legal problems

that movies and rap videos

---

3 **Highlighting coherence with transitions**

Transitions establish logical relationships between sentences, between paragraphs, and between whole sections of an essay. A transition can
be a single word, a phrase, a sentence, or an entire paragraph. In each case
a transition helps the reader anticipate what is to come. For example, when
you read the word *however*, you are immediately aware that the material
you are about to read will contrast with the material you have just read.

CRITICAL DECISIONS

Revising Paragraphs for Coherence

As a writer, you probably have too much to do in a first
draft to monitor the relationships among sentences and
paragraphs or to develop coherence. In a second or third
draft, however, you should evaluate your sentences in the broader context of paragraphs, and paragraphs in the broader context of sections.

- **Revise every paragraph within its section.** To revise an individual paragraph, examine it in relation to the ones that come before
  and after. Develop the habit of including transitional words at the
  beginning or end of paragraphs to help readers move from one
  paragraph to the next.

- **Revise every sentence within its paragraph.** Once you are sure of
  a paragraph's place in your paper, revise for coherence. Use cues—
  pronouns, parallelism, repetition, and transitions—to help move the
  reader from one sentence to the next through a paragraph.

5.5

Within a paragraph, transitions tend to be single words or short
phrases. A transition between paragraphs can be a word or two—*however*,
for example, *similarly*—a phrase, or a sentence. At times, you may want to
write a paragraph-length transition between sections of a paper.

To illustrate the use of transitions within and between paragraphs,
see paragraphs 1–3 in 5a, a section of David Rothenberg's essay on

"How the Web Destroys the Quality of Students' Research Papers." In the second sentence of paragraph 1, with the use of "First," Rothenberg promises a sequence of reasons to support his section thesis—that teachers can easily recognize Web-based research papers. In the third sentence, "Then" promises a continuation of this sequence, as does "Another" at the beginning of paragraph 2. Paragraph 3 begins with a transition that announces a third example: "Accompanying them"—that is, accompanying the previous examples. Brief as these transitions are, they let readers know what to expect on moving from sentence to sentence within a paragraph and from one paragraph to the next.

Transitions serve to highlight relationships writers have already created between the content of sentences or paragraphs. If you have difficulty writing a particular transition, rethink the logical connection between its elements. A rough transition, always a disruption to the smooth flow of ideas, is a sign of faulty logic.

The following box lists the most common transitions, arranged by type of relationship.

Transitional Expressions

To show addition	additionally, again, also, and, as well, besides, equally important, further, furthermore, in addition, moreover
To show similarity	also, in the same way, just as . . . so too, likewise, similarly
To show an exception	but, however, in spite of, on the one hand . . . on the other hand, nevertheless, nonetheless, notwithstanding, in contrast, on the contrary, still, yet
To indicate sequence	first, second, third, . . . next, then, finally
To show time	after, afterwards, at last, before, currently, during, earlier, immediately, later, meanwhile, now, recently, simultaneously, subsequently, then
To provide an example	for example, for instance, namely, specifically, to illustrate
To emphasize a point	even, indeed, in fact, of course, truly
To indicate place	above, adjacent, below, beyond, here, in front, in back, nearby, there
To show cause and effect	accordingly, consequently, hence, so, therefore, thus
To conclude or repeat	finally, in a word, in brief, in conclusion, in the end, on the whole, thus, to conclude, to summarize

---

Writing and Revising to Achieve Paragraph Coherence

Experienced writers often combine the four techniques just discussed to establish coherence within a paragraph. A skillful mix of pronouns, repeated words and phrases, parallel structures, and transitions will help to maintain the focus of a paragraph and will provide multiple cues, or signposts, that help readers find their way from one sentence to the next.

ILLUSTRATION: ACHIEVING COHERENCE

For many people the years after age sixty are filled with excitement. Financially, two-thirds of American workers are covered by pension plans provided by their employers. Socially, most maintain close friendships and stay in touch with family members. Some, however, experience financial problems, while others experience loneliness and isolation because many of their friends and relatives [17] have died or they have lost touch with their families. In the United States, there are now as many people over the age of sixty as there are under the age of seven, yet funding for programs involving the health and psychological well-being of older people is relatively limited.

—LESTER LEFTON, *Psychology*

In this paragraph, Lefton combines techniques for achieving coherence. He sets up parallel sentences with the words *Financially* and *Socially*. He also uses parallelism within sentences—for instance, *as many people over the age of sixty as there are under the age of seven.* As pronoun substitutes for the word *people*, Lefton uses *most, Some, others, their,* and *they.* He uses the transitional words *however* and *yet.* And he keeps the paragraph focused by repeating the word *people*, using several logical subsets of that general term: *workers, family members, friends, relatives,* and *older people.*

EXERCISE 5

Choose any four example paragraphs in this chapter. For each paragraph, identify the techniques that the author uses to establish coherence. Show the use of pronouns, repetition, parallel structures, and transitions. In addition, identify the use of transitions between paragraphs.

EXERCISE 6

Reread a paragraph you have recently written, and circle all words that help to establish coherence. Photocopy your paragraph and then revise it for coherence, using the techniques discussed previously: arrange sentences according to a pattern and then highlight that arrangement with pronouns, repeated words, parallel structures, and transitions. Write a clean copy of the paragraph, and make photocopies of both the original and the revision for class discussion.

5e Writing and revising to achieve well-developed paragraphs

One important element of effective writing is the level of detail you offer in support of a paragraph's topic sentence. To *develop* a paragraph means to discuss its core idea in a block of sentences that explains or illustrates or supports with reasons or facts. The most common technique is **topical development:** announcing your topic in the opening sentence, dividing that topic into two or three parts (in the case of chronological arrangement, into various *times*), and then developing each part within the paragraph. The various strategies presented here will help you to develop paragraphs that inform and persuade.

Developing Paragraphs: Essential Features

In determining whether a paragraph is well or even adequately developed, you should be able to answer three questions without hesitation:

- **What is the main point of the paragraph?**
- **Why should readers accept this main point?** (That is, what reasons or information have you provided that would convince a reader that your main point is accurate or reasonable?)
- **Why should readers care about the main point of this paragraph?**

When writing the first draft of a paper, you may not stop to think about how you are developing the central idea of every paragraph. There is no need to be this deliberate in first-draft writing. By the second draft, however, you will want to be conscious of fully developing your paragraphs.

Try combining methods of developing a paragraph's core idea, as needed. The same paragraph that shows an example may also show a comparison or contrast. No firm rules constrain you in developing a paragraph. Let your common sense and an interest in helping your reader understand your subject be your guides.

1   Narration and description

Telling stories (*narration*) and describing events or scenes (*description*) are two strategies for developing effective paragraphs. The two are usually used in combination. A narrative's main purpose is to make a point that is pertinent to the larger essay. Brief stories are often used as examples. Most often, narratives are sequenced chronologically and occur in an essay either as a single paragraph or as a grouping of paragraphs. The challenge in writing a narrative is to keep readers involved both in the events you are relating and in the people involved in those events. Vivid description helps to maintain this involvement.

It was a chilly, 60 degree night in southern Arizona last Monday. The moon was full, and Amtrak's 12-car Sunset Limited, bearing 248 passengers and 20 crew members, was doing between 50 and 55 m.p.h. as it approached a gentle curve not too far from the tiny town of Hyder. It was 1:20 A.M., and most of the passengers on the train, which is especially popular among retirees traveling from Los Angeles to Miami and back, were in bed. Suddenly, they were not so much awakened as catapulted from sleep. Those who kept their wits about them remember a terrible, prolonged shriek of metal against metal. For others, their waking sensation was pain, as they smashed into a wall or a chair or a sink. The Limited's two diesel locomotives had safely crossed a 30-ft.-high trestle over a desert gulch. But the next four cars—a dormitory car for crew members, two sleeping cars for passengers and a dining car—had jumped the rails. One hit the ground below; the other three hung down from the trestle like beads in a giant's necklace. **18**

—DAVID VAN BIEMA, "Murder on the Sunset Limited"

2   Example

An example is a particular case of a more general point. After topical development, development by example is probably the most common method of supporting the core idea of a paragraph. Examples *show* readers what you mean; if an example is vivid, readers will have a better chance of remembering your general point. The topic sentence of a paragraph may be developed with one extended example or several briefer ones.

Nervousness . . . is absolutely and entirely normal [in a college interview]. The best way to handle it is to admit it, out loud, to the interviewer. Miles Uhrig, director of admission at Tufts University, sometimes relates this true story to his apprehensive applicants: One extremely agitated young applicant sat opposite him for her interview with her legs crossed, wearing loafers on **19**

         The Paragraph and the Paper

her feet. She swung her top leg back and forth to some inaudible rhythm. The loafer on her top foot flew off her foot, hit him in the head, ricocheted to the desk lamp and broke it. She looked at him in terror, but when their glances met, they both dissolved in laughter. The moral of the story—the person on the other side of the desk is also a human being and wants to put you at ease. So admit to your anxiety and don't swing your foot if you're wearing loafers! (By the way, she was admitted.)

—ANTHONY F. CAPRARO III, "The Interview"

Several transitions are commonly used to introduce examples: *for example, for instance, a case in point, to illustrate.*

3   Sequential order/process

A paragraph that presents a process will show carefully sequenced events. The range of possibilities is endless: What is the process by which people fall in love? By which children learn? By which a computer chip is manufactured? These cases, different as they are, require a clear delineation of steps. In paragraphs organized as a process, you may want to use transitions that show sequence in time: *first, second, after, before, once, next, then,* and *finally.*

The first and simplest type of iron furnace was called a bloomery, in which wrought iron was produced directly from the ore. The ore was heated with charcoal in a small open furnace, usually made of stone and blown upon with bellows. Most of the impurities would burn out, leaving a spongy mass of iron mixed with siliceous slag (iron silicate). This spongy mass was then refined by hammering, reheating, and hammering some more, until **20** it reached the desired fibrous consistency. During the hammering, the glasslike slag would be evenly distributed throughout the iron mass. This hammered slab of wrought iron, or "bloom," was then ready to forge into some usable object.

—ELIOT WIGGINTON, "Furnaces"

4   Definition

Paragraphs of definition are always important. In informative writing, readers can learn the meaning of terms needed for understanding difficult concepts. In essays intended to persuade, writers define terms in order to establish a common language with the reader, an important first step toward gaining the reader's agreement. Once a term is defined, it can be clarified with examples, comparisons, or descriptions.

The hallmark signs of an obsessive-compulsive disorder are the presence of frequently intrusive and unwanted thoughts (obses- **21** sions) and repetitive behaviors (compulsions). In general, the anxiety created by the obsession is relieved through acting out the compulsive behavior. The individual becomes enmeshed in a cycle of feeling anxious over and over, and each time feeling as if he or she has to undertake a particular behavior to relieve the anxiety. These obsessions (and subsequent compulsions) are so disturbing that they interfere with everyday functioning including work, school, and relationships with others. The person who has an obsessive-compulsive disorder knows that the thoughts and the need for repetitive actions are excessive and time-consuming and reflect far more than simple concerns about everyday responsibilities and situations. This *intact insight,* knowing that these thoughts are not normal, is a characteristic of an obsessive-compulsive disorder.

—PETER E. NATHAN, JACK M. GORMAN, AND NEIL J. SALKIND,
Treating Mental Disorders: A Guide to What Works

5	Division and classification

Division (also called *analysis*) and classification are closely related operations. A writer who divides a topic into parts to see what it is made of performs an analysis.

COMPUTER TIPS

Use the TAB Key for Paragraph Indentation

One major difference between word processors and typewriters is that the former uses a proportional font: each letter takes up a different amount of space. Typewriters use monospaced fonts: each letter takes up exactly the same amount of space. Starting a paragraph with five taps on the typewriter space bar always gives you exactly the same indentation, but this is not true for a word processor. Depending on the font and size, typographical distinctions (boldface or italics), and the page justification setting, the amount of space taken up by five spaces varies quite a bit. Use the TAB key for paragraph indentations; it's one keystroke, it's absolutely consistent, and the command can be easily deleted.

A *classification* is a grouping of like items. Working with notes, the writer begins with what may appear at first to be bits of unrelated information. Gradually, patterns of similarity emerge that can be expressed as a paragraph that establishes categories for grouping. Most often, the writer devotes a sentence or two to developing each category.

Archaeological sites are most commonly classified according to the activities that occurred there. Thus, cemeteries and other sepulchers like

Tutankhamun's tomb are referred to as (burial sites.) A 20,000-year-old Stone Age site in the Dnieper Valley of the Ukraine, with mammoth-bone houses, hearths, and other signs of domestic activity, is a (habitation site.) So too are many other sites, such as caves and rock-shelters, early Mesoamerican farming villages, and Mesopotamian cities—in all, people lived and carried out greatly diverse activities. (Kill sites) consist of bones of slaughtered game animals and the weapons that killed them. They are found in East Africa and on the North American Great Plains. (Quarry sites) are another type of specialist site, where people mined stone or metals to make specific tools. Prized raw materials, such as obsidian, a volcanic glass used for fine knives, were widely traded in prehistoric times and profoundly interest the archaeologist. Then there are such spectacular (religious sites) as the stone circles of Stonehenge in southern England, the Temple of Amun at Karnak, Egypt, and the great ceremonial precincts of lowland Maya centers in Central America at *Tikal*, Copán, and Palenque. (Art sites) are common in southwestern France, southern Africa, and parts of North America, where prehistoric people painted or engraved magnificent displays of art.

—BRIAN FAGAN, *Archaeology*

6 Comparison/contrast

To *compare* is to discuss the similarities between people, places, objects, events, or ideas. To *contrast* is to discuss differences. The writer developing a paragraph that uses comparison and contrast conducts an analysis of two or more subjects, studying the parts of each and then discussing the subjects in relation to each other. Specific points of comparison and contrast make the discussion possible.

Paragraphs of comparison and contrast should be put to some definite use in a paper. It is not enough to point out similarities and differences; you should use this information to make a point. Paragraphs developed by comparison and contrast use transition words such as *similarly, also, as well, just so, by contrast, but, however, on the one hand/on the other hand*, and *yet*. When writing your paragraph, consider two common methods of arrangement: by subject or point by point.

In the following example, Stephen Jay Gould organizes his comparative discussion by subject. Note that when a comparative discussion b ecomes relatively long, you have the option of splitting it into two paragraphs.

Science works with testable proposals. If . . . new information continues to affirm a hypothesis, we may accept it provisionally and gain confidence as further evidence mounts. We can never be completely sure that a hypothesis is right, though we may be able to show with   23
confidence that it is wrong. The best scientific hypotheses are also generous and expansive: they suggest extensions and implications that enlighten related, and even far distant, subjects. Simply consider how the idea of evolution has influenced virtually every intellectual field.

Useless speculation, on the other hand, is restrictive. It generates no testable hypothesis, and offers no way to obtain potentially refuting evidence. Please note that I am not speaking of truth or falsity. The speculation may well be true; still, if it provides, in principle, no material for affirmation or rejection, we can make nothing   24
of it. It must simply stand forever as an intriguing idea. Useless speculation turns in on itself and leads nowhere; good science, containing both seeds for its potential refutation and implications for more and different testable knowledge, reaches out.

—STEPHEN JAY GOULD, "Sex, Drugs, Disasters"

Organizing a Paragraph of Comparison and Contrast

Comparison and contrast is a type of analysis in which parts of two (or more) subjects are discussed in terms of one another. Particular points of comparison and contrast allow a writer to observe similarities and differences. A comparative analysis is usually arranged in one of two ways.

Arrangement by subject

Topic sentence (may be shifted to other positions in the paragraph)

Introduce Subject A
   Discuss Subject A in terms of the first point
   Discuss Subject A in terms of the second point

Introduce Subject B
   Discuss Subject B in terms of the first point
   Discuss Subject B in terms of the second point

Conclude with a summary of similarities and differences.

Arrangement point by point

Topic sentence (may be shifted to other positions in the paragraph)

Introduce the first point to be compared and contrasted
   Discuss Subject A in terms of this point
   Discuss Subject B in terms of this point

Introduce the second point to be compared and contrasted
   Discuss Subject A in terms of this point
   Discuss Subject B in terms of this point

When comparisons are relatively brief, arrangement by subject works well. When comparisons are longer and more complex, a point-by-point discussion works best.

In the next paragraph, student Michele Pelletier uses a point-by-point arrangement to compare and contrast two types of armies of the fifteenth and sixteenth centuries. Pelletier uses her comparisons to make a point: both the mercenary and militia experiences "have found their way into American military history of the past thirty years."

Armies of volunteers and conscripts are today's versions of the militias and mercenary forces that existed in the 15th and 16th centuries. Militias were armies made up of citizens who were fighting for their home country. Mercenaries were professional soldiers who, better trained than militia men (they were always men), were hired by foreign countries to fight wars. Mercenaries had no cause other than a paycheck: if the country that hired them did not pay, they would quit **25** the battlefield. Mercenaries may have been fickle, but technically they were good fighters. Militia men may not have been as technically proficient as mercenaries, but they had the will to fight. Both of these traditions—fighting for a cause and fighting for money—have found their way into American military history of the past thirty years.

7	Analogy

An **analogy** is a comparison of two subjects that, on first appearance, seem unrelated. An analogy gains force by surprising a reader, by demonstrating that an unlikely comparison is not only likely but in fact is illuminating. Well-chosen analogies can clarify difficult concepts. In the following example, theoretical physicist Stephen Hawking describes the birth of a star, helping nonspecialists to understand difficult concepts through the use of two analogies:

A star is formed when a large amount of gas (mostly hydrogen) starts to collapse in on itself due to its gravitational attraction. As it contracts the atoms of the gas collide with each other more and more frequently and at greater and greater speeds—the gas heats up. Eventually, the gas will be so hot that when the hydrogen atoms collide they no longer bounce off each other, but instead coalesce to form helium. The heat released in this reaction, which is like a controlled hydrogen bomb explosion, is what makes the star shine. This additional heat also increases the pressure of the gas until it is sufficient to balance **26** the gravitational attraction, and then the gas stops contracting. It is a bit like a balloon—there is a balance between the pressure of the air inside, which is trying to make the balloon expand, and the tension on the rubber, which is trying to make the balloon smaller. Stars will remain stable like this for a long time, with heat from the nuclear reactions balancing the gravitational attraction.

—STEPHEN HAWKING, *A Brief History of Time*

The words *like* and *analogous to* often signal the beginning of an analogy. After describing the first of the two subjects of the comparison, the writer may follow with an expression such as *just so* or *similarly* and then continue with the second subject.

Development by cause and effect shows how an event or condition has come to occur—which requires careful analysis. As discussed elsewhere (see 6d-1), causes are usually complex, and a writer must avoid the temptation to oversimplify. Frequently, therefore, cause-and-effect reasoning is developed over several paragraphs. When you are developing a causal connection, avoid the mistake of suggesting that because one event precedes another in time, the first event causes the second. A causal relationship is not always so clear-cut, a point that James Watts and Alan Davis acknowledge in the following paragraph on the Great Depression of the 1930s. Paragraphs developed by cause and effect frequently use these transition words: *therefore, thus,* and *consequently.*

> The depression was precipitated by the stock market crash in October 1929, but the actual cause of the collapse was an unhealthy economy. While the ability of the manufacturing industry to produce consumer goods had increased rapidly, mass purchasing power had remained relatively static. Most laborers, farmers, and white-collar workers, therefore, could not afford to buy the automobiles and refrigerators turned out by factories in the 1920s, because their incomes were too low. At the same time, the federal government increased the problem through economic policies that tended to encourage the very rich to over-save. [27]
>
> —JAMES WATTS AND ALAN F. DAVIS,
> *Your Family in Modern American History*

EXERCISE 7

Return to Exercise 1 (page 119), in which you selected one section of a magazine article or book chapter to study in depth. If you have not done so, complete that exercise, and then for that same block of paragraphs analyze each paragraph and identify its pattern of development.

EXERCISE 8

Reread a paper you have recently written, and select a paragraph to revise so that its topic sentence is thoroughly developed. Use any of the patterns of development presented here so that you are able, without hesitation, to answer the three questions in the box on page 131. Make photocopies of your original paragraph and your revision; plan to address a small group of classmates and explain the choices you have made in revision.

| 5f | **Writing and revising paragraphs of introduction and conclusion** |

The introduction and conclusion to a paper can be understood as a type of transition. At the beginning of a paper, the introduction serves as a transition by moving the reader from the world outside of your paper to the world within. At the end of the paper, the conclusion works in the opposite direction by moving readers from the world of your paper back to their own world—with, you hope, something gained by their effort.

Introductions

Writing an introduction is often easier once you know what you are introducing. For this reason many writers choose not to work seriously on an introduction until they have finished a draft and can see the overall shape and content of the paper. Other writers, however, need to begin with a carefully written introduction. If this is your preference, remember not to demand perfection of a first draft, especially since the material you will be introducing has yet to be written. Once it is written, your introduction may need to change.

COMPUTER TIPS

Save Frequently

This is probably the most frequently given advice in all guides to writing with computers, and it's certainly the most ignored: **Save your writing frequently.** Everything that you've typed since the last save will be lost if there's a power failure or someone walks by and accidentally kicks the plug out of your computer. How long would it take you to reconstruct and retype all that material? It takes almost no time or effort to execute the keystroke combination necessary to save. Get in the habit of doing it automatically, mindlessly, whenever you stop to think, to reread, to rest, to get up from the computer for any reason.

Newer word-processing software allows you even more options for protecting your work. It saves your work automatically at regular timed intervals, allows you to work with a copy of your document rather than the original, and provides automatic backups. However, with multiple versions of your papers such as copies and backups, you need to be careful when you resume work at your next session: be sure you're using the most current version of your paper.

The introduction as a frame of reference

Introductions establish frames of reference. On completing an introduction, readers know the general topic of your paper, the disciplinary perspective from which you will discuss this topic, and the standards they will use in evaluating your work. Readers quickly learn from an introduction if you are a laboratory researcher, a field researcher, a theorist, an essayist, a reporter, a student with a general interest, and so

www
5.6

trans

on. Each of these possible identities implies for readers different standards of evidence and reasoning for evaluating your work. Consider the paragraph that follows. The introduction, explicitly in the thesis and implicitly in the writer's choice of vocabulary, establishes a frame of reference that alerts readers to the type of language, evidence, and logic that will be used in the subsequent paper. Thus situated, readers are better able to anticipate and evaluate what they will read.

ILLUSTRATION: WRITING IN THE HUMANITIES

STUDENT EXAMPLE: SARIKA CHONDRA

James Joyce's "Counterparts" tells the story
of a man, Farrington, who is abused by his boss
for not doing his job right. Farrington spends a
long time drinking after work; and when he finally
arrives home, he in turn abuses--he beats--his son
28 Tom. In eleven pages, Joyce tells much more than
a story of yet another alcoholic venting failures
and frustrations on family members. *In "Counterparts," Farrington turns to drink in order to gain
power--in much the same way his wife and children
turn to the Church.*

Language of literary analysis

Evidence: based on close reading of a story

Logic: generalization

Drinking and church going related to a need for power. Also comparison/contrast

By comparison, read the following introduction to a paper written from a sociological perspective. This paragraph introduces a paper you will find in Chapter 39, Writing and Reading in the Social Sciences.

ILLUSTRATION: WRITING IN THE SOCIAL SCIENCES

STUDENT EXAMPLE: KRISTY BELL

Currently, in the United States, there are at
least two million women alcoholics (Unterberger,
1989, p.1150). Americans are largely unaware of the
extent of this debilitating disease among women and
the problems it presents. Numerous women dependent
29 on alcohol remain invisible largely because friends,
family, co-workers, and the women themselves refuse
to acknowledge the problem. *This denial amounts to
a virtual conspiracy of silence and greatly complicates the process of* diagnosis *and* treatment.

Language of sociology

Evidence: based on review of sociological literature

Logic: cause and effect. Will show how denial complicates diagnosis and treatment

The Paragraph and the Paper

The introduction as an invitation to continue reading

Aside from establishing a frame of reference and set of expectations about language, evidence, and logic, an introduction should also motivate your reader to *continue* reading. A complete introduction provides background information needed to understand a paper. An especially effective introduction gains the reader's attention and gradually turns that attention toward the writer's thesis and the rest of the paper. Writers typically adopt specialized strategies for introducing their work. The examples that follow suggest several such strategies, though they by no means exhaust the possibilities available to you for opening your papers.

Student Example: Daniel Burke, "Defense of Fraternities"

A revolutionary event took place at Raleigh Tavern in 1776, an event that has added an important dimension to my life at college. In fact, nearly all American undergraduates are affected in some way by the actions of several students from the College of William **30** and Mary on December 5, 1776. The formation of the first Greek-letter fraternity, Phi Beta Kappa, started the American college fraternity-sorority tradition that today can be an important addition to your undergraduate education.

In this example, student writer Daniel Burke provides pertinent historical information that sets a context for the paper. By linking a "revolutionary event" in 1776 to his own life over two hundred years later, Burke captures the reader's interest.

The following example begins with a question, the response to which leads to the author's thesis.

Student Example: Bonnie Michaels, "What's the Good of Government?"

Is government the solution, or is it the problem? Many Americans believe that government plays an essential role in making our lives safer and our society more productive and more fair. But many others believe that government is too powerful and intrusive, and that it stifles personal initiative. Within the government itself, there are deep divisions: conservatives typically argue for "less government" and for "getting government off the backs of Americans"; liberals argue for a "humane govern- **31** ment" that defends the interests of the poor and elderly and, generally, of groups that cannot defend themselves. These diametrically opposed viewpoints about the proper role of government have created a productive tension that benefits our country.

See 5f-3 for two additional strategies for opening a paper: using a quotation and telling a story.

Strategies for Writing Introductions

1. Announce your topic, using vocabulary that hints at the perspective from which you will be writing. On completing your introduction, readers should be able to anticipate the type of language, evidence, and logic you will use in your paper.
2. If readers lack the background needed to understand your paper, then provide this background. In a paragraph or two, choose and develop a strategy that will both orient readers to your subject and interest them in it: define terms, present a brief history, or review a controversy.
3. If readers know something of your subject, then devote less (or no) time to developing background information and more time to stimulating interest. In a paragraph or two, choose and develop a strategy that will gain the reader's attention: raise a question, quote a source familiar to the reader, tell a story, or begin directly with a statement of the thesis.
4. Once you have provided background information and gained the reader's attention with an opening strategy, gradually turn that attention toward your thesis, which you will position as the last sentence of the introductory paragraph(s).

2   Conclusions

At minimum, a conclusion will summarize your work, but often you will want to do more than write a summary. Provided you have written carefully, you have earned the right to expand on your paper's thesis in a conclusion: to point the reader back to the larger world and to suggest the significance of your ideas.

ACROSS THE CURRICULUM

Introductory Paragraphs in Academic Writing

Academic writers, particularly in the sciences and social sciences, often state directly in the introduction to their papers the purpose for their research and writing. Note the following example from the work of an anthropologist. The writer's clearly stated goal is underlined:

As an anthropologist, I am intrigued by the possibility that culture shapes how biological scientists describe what they discover about the natural world. If this were so, we would be learning about more than the natural world in high school biology class; we would be learning about cultural beliefs and practices as if they were part of nature. In the course of my research I realized that the picture of the egg and sperm drawn in popular as well as scientific accounts of reproductive biology relies on stereotypes central to our cultural definitions of male and female. The stereotypes imply not only that female biological processes are less worthy than their male counterparts but also that women are less worthy than men. Part of my goal in writing this article is to shine a bright light on the gender stereotypes hidden within the scientific language of biology. Exposed in such a way, I hope they will lose much of their power to harm us.*

*Emily Martin, "The Egg and the Sperm: How Science Has Constructed a Romance Based on Stereotypical Male-Female Roles" (*Signs*, 1991).

Strategies for Writing Conclusions

1. **Summary.** The simplest conclusion is a summary, a brief restatement of your paper's main points. Avoid conclusions that repeat exactly material presented elsewhere in the paper.
2. **Summary and comment.** More emphatic conclusions build on a summary in one of several ways. These conclusions will:

set ideas in the paper in a larger context	purposefully confuse or trouble the reader
call for action (or research)	raise a question
speculate or warn	quote a familiar or authoritative source
tell a story	

Weblink

http://leo.stcloudstate.edu/acadwrite/conclude.html

Strategies for writing conclusions, with many examples.

A conclusion gives you an opportunity to answer a challenge that all readers raise—*So what? Why should this paper matter to me? What actions should I take?* A well-written conclusion will answer these questions and will leave readers with a trace of your thinking as they turn away from your paper and back to their own business.

The sample conclusions that follow do not exhaust the strategies for closing your papers; they should, however, give you a taste of the variety of techniques available. Here is a paragraph that presents the simplest possible conclusion: a summary—in this case, of an argument that colleges must cut costs and rethink their educational missions if they are to avoid going bankrupt. This concluding paragraph summarizes the author's key points:

> Already most colleges are looking carefully at ways to cut costs. But this cost-cutting is not examining basic questions about how a college is organized to provide for the advancement of knowledge and student learning. It is time to ask basic questions, to conceptualize fundamentally different ways—less costly ways—of providing education. Higher education will have to make hard choices. It will not be able to satisfy every need or respond to every constituent. The colleges that ask, and answer, basic questions about how to educate students in less expensive ways will be the colleges that survive.
>   —DANIEL S. CHEEVER, JR., "Higher and Higher Ed"

32

A more ambitious conclusion will move beyond a summary and call for involvement on the reader's part. For instance, you might ask the reader to address a puzzling or troubling question, to speculate on the future, or to reflect on the past. In the next example, by student Alison Tschopp the reader is given a challenge.

> The task of shaping children's values, like their diets, is better addressed through ongoing discussions between parents and children than through limiting the right of free speech. There is no need to silence advertisers in order to teach values or protect the innocent and unskeptical. The right to free speech is protected by the Constitution because as a nation we believe that no one person is capable of determining which ideas are true and rational. Like media critic Jean Kilbourne, we may disagree with some of the messages being conveyed through advertising—say, the message that women are attractive only when they are young and thin (44). Like Peggy Charren, we can agree that advertisements can create stresses in a family's life (15). Nevertheless, we must allow all ideas a place in the market place. As Charles O'Neil, an advertiser and a defender of the medium, suggests, "[a]dvertising is only a reflection of society; slaying the messenger will not alter the fact" that potentially damaging or offensive ideas exist (196). If we disagree with the message sent in an ad, it is our responsibility to send children a different message.

33

3   The opening and closing frame

You might consider creating an introductory and concluding frame for your papers. The strategy is to use the same story, quotation, question—any device that serves the purpose—as an occasion both to introduce your subject and, when the time is right, to conclude emphatically. Provided the body of a paper is unified, coherent, and well developed, an opening and closing frame will give the paper a pleasing symmetry. In the following example, Rachel L. Jones works with a quotation.

Introduction

William Labov, a noted linguist, once said about the use of black English, "It is the goal of most black Americans to acquire full control of the standard language without giving up their own culture." He also suggested that there are certain advantages to having two ways to express one's feelings. I wonder if the good doctor might also consider the goals of those black Americans who have full control of standard English but who are every now **34** and then troubled by that colorful, grammar-to-the-winds patois that is black English. Case in point—me.

Conclusion

I would have to disagree with Labov in one respect. My goal is not so much to acquire full control of both standard and black English, but to one day see more black people less dependent on a dialect that excludes them from full participation in the world we **35** live in. I don't think I talk white; I think I talk right.

—Rachel L. Jones, "What's Wrong with Black English"

EXERCISE 9

Locate a collection of essays and/or articles: any textbook that is an edited collection of readings will work. Read three articles, and examine the strategies the authors use to introduce and conclude their work. Choose one article to analyze more closely. Examine the strategies for beginning and ending the selection, and relate these strategies to the selection itself. Why has the writer chosen these *particular* strategies? Be prepared to discuss your findings in a small group.

EXERCISE 10

In connection with a paper you are writing, draft *two* opening and *two* closing paragraphs, using different strategies. Set your work aside for a day or two, and then choose which paragraphs appeal to you the most. Be prepared to discuss your choices in a small group.

CHAPTER

Writing and Evaluating Arguments

Argument is fundamental to academic thinking and writing. While the information you learn from textbooks and lectures might seem to be factual and beyond dispute, much of what we know about the world begins in argumentation. Academic researchers experiment, read critically, observe, and take surveys of people's behavior. Then, finding certain patterns, they make statements about their findings—the validity of which they try to demonstrate to others through arguments. In this chapter you will learn the elements of argument in any context. Chapters 38–40 discuss how to adapt these elements according to the discipline in which you are writing.[1]

6a   An overview of argument

Weblink

http://www.kcmetro.cc.mo.us/
longview/ctac/flowpt1.htm

Hypertext flow chart for evaluating arguments.

An **argument** is a process of influencing others, of changing minds through reasoned discussion. Arguments consist of three parts: claim, support, and reasoning. To construct an argument, you engage in a writing process (with phases of discovery, drafting, and revising—see Chapters 3 and 4). You develop a claim, or point you want to argue. Then you develop support for accepting this claim. Support consists of two elements:

- Evidence—facts, statistics, examples, and expert opinions that you gather.
- The reasoning by which you connect that evidence to your claim.

The process of constructing an argument is illustrated here, with examples from the student argument that begins on page 150.

[1]The approach to argument taken here is based on the work of Stephen Toulmin, as developed in *The Uses of Argument* (Cambridge: The University Press, 1958).

Writing and Evaluating Arguments

CRITICAL DECISIONS

Arguing Effectively

Writing arguments requires making a number of important choices. Here are a few.

■ Based on your observations and research, you must decide what claim you can make about your subject and how best to articulate that claim.

■ You must decide what evidence that you have discovered will best serve to convince your intended audience of your claim. This requires making a number of decisions about your readers' knowledge and opinions about your subject.

■ You must decide how to deal with any objections readers may have regarding your claim and evidence, as well as how to deal with any evidence that might potentially appear to contradict your claim.

■ You must decide how best to structure your argument to gain readers' support for your claim.

To write an argument, follow these steps:

1. **Make a *claim*.** Choose a subject; then make an assertion about the subject (see 6b). Here is the claim from the sample argument:

   Although women are certainly underrepresented at present in the computer industry, changing cultural and market forces will inevitably bring about a more equitable proportion of women to men.

2. **Gather *evidence*.** Carefully choose facts, statistics, opinions, and examples that support the claim. Group related evidence into clusters (see 6c). Here are the five clusters of evidence that support the claim in the sample argument:

   Cluster 1: Interviews show that sexism is not as big a problem as it has been.
   Cluster 2: Female computer professionals are forming mentoring groups.
   Cluster 3: Computing jobs no longer require background in math and science.
   Cluster 4: The Web has emerged as a marketplace emphasizing communication.
   Cluster 5: Women are buying more high-tech equipment.

3. ***Link evidence to the claim* with a clear line of reasoning.** Evidence by itself does not advance an argument's claim. To advance an argument, provide clear reasoning that shows how and why each item of evidence makes the claim more believable.

Choose from three types of reasoning to link evidence and claim:

■ *Reasoning with logic:* appeal to the reader's respect for clear, orderly thinking. Types of logic used: generalization, cause, sign, analogy, and parallel case.

■ *Reasoning with authority:* appeal to the reader's respect for an expert who says, "I believe this claim to be true (or desirable)."

■ *Reasoning with emotion:* move readers to agreement by an appeal to their emotions.

In academic settings, you will most often link evidence to claim by reasoning with logic (see 6d).

Evidence	A clear line of reasoning	
[Facts, examples, statistics, opinions] +	[Appeals to logic, authority, emotions]	→ **Claim**
		Supports

A typical argument will present three or more supports for the claim. The claim in the sample argument offers five supports—that is, five items of evidence, each linked to the claim with a specific line of reasoning. The student writer uses appeals to logic—but no appeals to authority or emotion:

Evidence	+	**Line of reasoning**	
Less sexism is evident.		This is a **sign** that women are facing improved conditions in the computer industry.	*support*
Evidence	+	**Line of reasoning**	
Female mentoring groups are emerging.		This is a **sign** that women are facing improved conditions in the computer industry.	*support*
Evidence	+	**Line of reasoning**	
There is a shift in the computer industry away from a reliance on math.		This shift will **cause** a more equitable split of jobs between women and men.	*support*
Evidence	+	**Line of reasoning**	
The Web has emerged as a marketplace of communication.		This development will **cause** a more equitable split of jobs between women and men.	*support*
Evidence	+	**Line of reasoning**	
Women have emerged as consumers of high-tech equipment.		This development will **cause** a more equitable split of jobs between women and men.	*support*

Claim: Although women are certainly underrepresented at present in the computer industry, changing cultural and market forces will inevitably bring about a more equitable proportion of women to men.

4. *Rebut* (argue against) *counterarguments* (see 6e).

Counterargument:	Women are not biologically equal to men in technical fields.
Rebuttal:	1. Socialization explains all the differences. 2. There are many examples of superb female engineers.

5. **Decide on a *structure* for your argument.** Will you place your claim at the beginning, middle, or end of the argument? Ask: Why this placement as opposed to another? Determine where you will raise and challenge counterarguments (see 6f).

Outline of the Sample Argument

In the sample argument that follows, the claim appears at the beginning.

Introduction:	Women are not getting senior management jobs in the computer industry.
Claim:	Although women are certainly underrepresented at present in the computer industry, changing cultural and market forces will inevitably bring about a more equitable proportion of women to men.
Counterargument and rebuttal:	Women are not naturally geared toward math/science.
Supporting claim:	Evidence + clear lines of reasoning: #1 Less sexism evident—sign that times are changing. #2 Emergence of female mentoring groups—sign that times are changing. #3 Shift of industry away from reliance on math—will cause changes. #4 Emergence of Web as a marketplace—will cause changes. #5 Emergence of women as consumers of high-tech equipment—will cause changes.
Conclusion:	Cultural and market forces are changing high-tech business. Signs are already present that changes are taking place. In the future, women *will* have greater access to senior management jobs.

The argument, "Women and Computing: Beyond the Glass Ceiling," uses (with some modification) the classic five-part structure for writing arguments presented on page 176. Marie Hobahn begins her argument by introducing her topic (the difficulty women have with securing senior management positions in the computer industry) and stating her claim. Before moving to directly support her claim, she first raises and rebuts arguments that challenge her own. She then turns to supporting her argument, linking distinct clusters of evidence to her claim with five lines of reasoning: two signs that conditions are improving for women, and three causes that will improve the employment of women in the computer industry.

Women and Computing: Beyond the Glass Ceiling
By Marie Hobahn

How well are women doing in the professional world of computing? There's no use denying it: the numbers don't look good. It is estimated that no more than 10% of technology companies are headed by a female CEO (Mayfield 2). Women fill less than 30% of programming, engineering, and management jobs at high-tech companies. Companies created or run by women received just 1.6% of the venture capital invested in high-tech firms from 1991 to 1996 (Crain; Hamm). The glass ceiling that keeps women from advancing seems real. According to D. J. Young, a software quality assurance manager at the software firm Intuit, "More women are . . . reaching that first level of management, but . . . the higher [they] go, the harder it is to get to the next level" (qtd. in DeBare 1). Considering this discouraging news, it might seem a hopeless act of faith to believe that things will get better anytime soon. But that faith would, in fact, be justified. <u>Although women are certainly underrepresented at present in the computer industry, changing cultural and market forces will inevitably bring about a more equitable proportion of women to men.</u>

Introduction

Claim
(argumentative
thesis)

Let's first establish that there is no biological reason why women should not be the equal of men
in the world of computing. Arguments like those used
by opponents of women in the military--they have
smaller, weaker bodies, and so are unsuited for com-
bat--cannot be used here. True, some traditionalists
will argue that male superiority in technology is genetic. George Gilder, a fellow at the Discovery Institute, insists that the dominance of males in mathematics, logic, and physics (not to mention business
and politics) is "not an effect of socialization
since they arise in all societies known to anthropology" ("Women and Computers" 16). Some also argue that
the left hemisphere of the brain, which controls
logic and analytic ability, dominates in men, while
the right hemisphere, which controls emotions, dominates in women (Bulkeley).

Rebuttal

But few accept such arguments today. As Susan
Merritt, dean of the School of Computer Science at
Pace University, points out, "The belief that women
will have less affinity for computing is more myth
than reality." Whatever differences exist between
men and women in computer aptitude can be attributed
to learned behavior. Jo Sanders, who runs the Gender
Equity Program at the City University of New York,
maintains that "looking for the functional equivalent of a computer gene [to explain why there are
more men in the computer industry than women] is at
best misguided and at worst a cynical attempt to
keep women out of computing" ("Women and Computers"
16). Up to around the fifth grade, girls and boys
demonstrate equal interest in, and ability with,
computers. After that point, because of subtle
(sometimes not-so-subtle) messages, patterns of
reinforcement, and the presence or absence of role
models, boys' interest in technology rises and
girls' drops off (Kantrowitz 51). Then we begin
to see a familiar gender distinction of men being
fascinated by power and speed and women being more

interested in utility and communication (Brunner and Bennett 46). One male writer states:

> When I talk about computers with other men, we chat about them the way we do--or used to--about cars. We boast about the speed of the processors and the size of our hard drives. . . . On the other hand, I think most women are . . . more interested in whether the computer works well enough to do what they want it to do. (Nicholson 21)

Despite the effects of socialization, women's achievements in computing have been numerous and substantial enough to disprove any doubts about female aptitude for programming. Charles Babbage, the nineteenth-century mathematician generally credited with inventing the computer, received substantial assistance from Ada Byron (daughter of the poet). Her plan to calculate Bernoulli numbers is now generally regarded as the first computer program. In 1979 the Defense Department named a software language "Ada" in her honor (Toole). During World War II, the army assigned the name computers to the women who were calculating trajectories for artillery gunners. Some of these women were assigned to enable the first modern computer, ENIAC, to perform these calculations; they called the process "programming" (Petzinger). Another woman, Grace Hopper, who was trained as a mathematician and who rose to the rank of rear admiral in the U.S. Navy, helped program the UNIVAC, the first large commercial computer (Lee 273). Many other notable women have participated in historic events in the computer industry, and some are celebrated and discussed in a growing number of academic Web sites. (See, for instance, the "ADA Project" at <http://www.cs.yale.edu/HTML/YALE/CS/HyPlans/tap/> and "Past Notable Women of Computing" at <http://www.cs.yale.edu/homes/tap/past-women-cs.html>.)

Clearly, women in the computer industry have the ability to excel. Still, the skeptic may wonder on

Rebuttal

what basis anyone can predict that the position of
women in the world of computing will significantly
improve in the near future. Based on the marginal
opportunities for women in the computer industry to
date, this skepticism seems fair--but only until one
examines changing market forces and signs of an
already improved status for women.

One sign that the computer industry is becoming
a more hospitable place for women is that increasing
numbers of women are advancing without encountering
sexist attitudes. While no one is suggesting that the
traditional male-dominated computer industry is a
thing of the past, a 1996 survey of twenty female
high-tech entrepreneurs conducted by Nina Munk and
Suzanne Oliver revealed that none of the respondents
felt limited by on-the-job sexism (105). In early
1998, Computerworld's senior editor for security and
network operating systems, Laura DiDio, interviewed
four female information services (IS) executives.
One, Pauline Nist, told DiDio, "The 'woman thing' is
not so important as long as you're technically competent" (76). The other women agreed so heartily that
DiDio was able to conclude: "These women all had one
thing in common: They . . . saw the glass ceiling as
just another obstacle. They paid no attention to it
and kept on going" ("Crashing" 77).

Another sign that women are emerging as a force
is the growing presence of mentoring programs in which
women computer professionals serve as role models for
younger women contemplating careers in the industry.
Such programs include PipeLINK, organized by two
Rensselaer Polytechnic Institute professors; the "Young
Women in Technology" program sponsored by the Idaho
Department of Vocational Education; and Jo Sanders's
Computer Equity Training Project at the Women's Action
Alliance in New York (Holzberg 43-45). Other groups
include Girls, Inc., EQUALS, Screenplay, and the
Women's Education Equity Act (Koch 23). The presence
of these mentors suggests that women have established

Argument
from sign
(another
sign that
conditions are
improving)

An Overview of Argument

secure enough footholds in the high-tech workforce to
believe that they can actually help others. The idea of
mentoring young women is beginning to influence univer-
sity-level computer science programs as well. Carnegie
Mellon, for example, instituted such a mentoring system
in the mid-1990s, along with other measures designed to
make computer science more attractive to female students. The result: while only 8% of first-year computer
science majors in 1995 were women, by 2001 that number
had risen to nearly 40% (Michaud).

Opportunities are expanding for women, and gains
are being made. In the next few years these gains
will broaden as three important changes sweep through
the computer industry. The first involves a shift in
the world of computing away from a strict reliance on
math and science and toward areas of strength traditionally associated with women--communications and visual design. Researchers Pamela E. Kramer and Sheila
Lehman characterize the old associations of computers
with skills in math as "increasingly inaccurate":

> Metaphors for computer technology are moving
> away from the number-crunching computer
> . . . and toward an understanding of computing
> as an interactive process in which the com-
> puter becomes an intelligent participant in
> and facilitator of individual and group com-
> munication. This shift reflects the fact
> that creative computing now relies at least
> as much upon language, visual design, prob-
> lem definition, and organizational skills
> as upon quantitative analysis. (170-71)

In other words, computing is moving away from those
areas in which men have been socialized to excel and
toward other areas in which women have been socialized to excel. The fact that computers may be (as one
headline writer suggested) "A Tool for Women, a Toy
for Men" (Bulkeley) should work to boost women's opportunities now that the personal computer as "toy" is
giving way to the personal computer as "tool."

Argument from cause (a shift in the industry will help women)

Writing and Evaluating Arguments

A second market force that is changing the availability of senior management jobs for women in high-tech industries is the emergence of the World Wide Web as a place for information exchange, commerce, and communication. With raw computing power doubling every nine months, personal computers have not come close to reaching the limits of their potential power and speed. But however fast the machines become, almost all computer professionals predict that the future of computing is going to be improved not by raw power but by the Internet and Web applications. People want to be able to communicate more easily and more systematically, both globally and on small local networks. Ease of communication and the design of interfaces to enhance communication will be key areas of growth. In these areas, socialization works to favor women (Holzberg).

Argument from cause (a second shift that will help women)

The third force that is creating greater opportunities for women in high-tech industries is the emerging importance of women both as users and as potential consumers of technology. According to a recent note in Byte, "women may be geekier than you think": In a 1996 survey, 66% of women had purchased a computer in the last two years ("Geekette"). More than 30% had installed the PC themselves. A 1997 study by Women in Technology International revealed that women-owned business would make $50 million in purchases that year ("Women's Buying Power"). In a change of strategy, advertising agencies are beginning to depict women in computer ads, and they are doing so in ways that don't imply that women use computers only for storing recipes (Pope B1). A columnist in Advertising Age remarks: "I think it would be beneficial to show girls that their moms have no trouble handling computers. Calgon could create a commercial of a mother printing out her daughters' hectic schedules from her laptop, then having enough time left over for a relaxing bath" (Crain).

Argument from cause (a final shift that will help women)

The signs are present that conditions for women in the computing industry are already improving. Cultural and market forces will gather momentum and change the face of the computing industry, creating a need for senior managers who understand the changing market and can exploit it. The obvious choice for such managers will be women. And as more women managers take their places in the boardrooms, the messages that get communicated to girls in the schoolroom will be clear: computing is a career for women. Inevitably, more girls will choose high-tech careers. Not immediately, perhaps, but sooner rather than later, the era of male dominance in the world of computing is coming to an end. Here and there "dinosaur" attitudes will persist, but in general there is no future for sexist attitudes and practices in the high-tech workplace. Conclusion

Works Cited

"ADA Project: Tapping Internet Resources for Women in Computer Science." 20 July 1998. 7 May 2000 <http://www.cs.yale.edu/HTML/YALE/CS/HyPlans/tap/>.

Brunner, Cornelia, and Dorothy Bennett. "Technology Perceptions by Gender." Education Digest Feb. 1998: 43-51.

Bulkeley, William M. "A Tool for Women, a Toy for Men." Wall Street Journal 16 Mar. 1996: B1.

Crain, Rance. "Helping Women Embrace Computers." Advertising Age 8 July 1996: 15.

DeBare, Ilana. "Voices: Women in the Computer Industry." Sacramento Bee 1996. 18 July 1998. <http://www.sacbee.com/news/projects/women/wcvoices.html>.

DiDio, Laura. "Crashing the Glass Ceiling." Computerworld 26 Jan. 1998: 73+.

"Geekette Power." Byte Jan. 1997: 26.

Hamm, Steve. "Why Women Are So Invisible in Silicon Valley." Business Week 25 Aug. 1998: 136.

Holzberg, Carol S. "Computer Technology: It's a
Girl Thing." Technology and Learning May–June
1997: 42–48.

Kantrowitz, Barbara. "Men, Women and Computers."
Newsweek 16 May 1994: 48–55.

Koch, Melissa. "Opening Up Technology to Both Gen-
ders." Education Digest Nov. 1994: 18–23.

Kramer, Pamela E., and Sheila Lehman. "'Mismeasur-
ing Women': A Critique of Research on Computer
Ability and Avoidance." Signs: Journal of
Women in Culture and Society 16.1 (1990):
158–72.

"Leading Women Visionaries to Converge in the Silicon Valley for Women in Technology International (WITI) 1998 Technology Summit." 20 July
1998. 20 Mar. 2000 <http://www.witi.com/
Center/Offices/Witinews/Summit/060198.html>.

Lee, J. A. N. "Grace Hopper." Annals of the History
of Computing 9.3 (1987): 273.

Mayfield, Kendra. "The Push to Push Women Higher."
Wired News. 19 June 2001. 15 Nov. 2001
<http://www.wired.com/news/print/
0,1294,44519,00.html>.

Merritt, Susan. "For Women, a Central Role in Computers." Letter. New York Times 27 July 1986:
A26.

Michaud, Anne. "The Computer Gender Gap." Boston
Globe. 31 July 2001: C1.

Munk, Nina, and Suzanne Oliver. "Women of the
Valley." Forbes 30 Dec. 1996: 102–08.

Nicholson, David. "Stereotype Does Not Compute."
Washington Post 4 Mar. 1996: Business 15+.

"Past Notable Women of Computing." 20 July 1998.
24 Mar. 2000 <http://www.cs.yale.edu/homes/
tap/past-women-cs.html>.

Petzinger, Thomas. "History of Software Begins with
the Work of Some Brainy Women." Wall Street
Journal 15 Nov. 1996: B1.

Pope, Kyle. "High-Tech Marketers Try to Attract
    Women without Causing Offense." Wall Street
    Journal 17 Mar. 1996: B1+.

Toole, Betty. "Ada Byron, Lady Lovelace
    (1815–1852)." 30 July 1998. 16 Apr. 2000
    <http://www.cs.yale.edu/homes/tap/Files/
    ada-bio.html>.

"Women and Computers: Nature or Nurture?" Panel
    discussion. Los Angeles Times 11 Apr. 1997:
    Supp. 16+.

"Women's Buying Power." Computerworld 16 June 1997: 41.

ACROSS THE CURRICULUM

6.1

Writing Arguments in the Sciences

A teacher of biology and freshman composition at Colgate University, Victoria McMillan explains that the papers and reports you write for science courses are—or should be—arguments, even though the word *argument* may not appear in your assignments:

Although a scientific paper may be descriptive, it is also a well-structured *argument* founded on supporting evidence. Scientific papers provide a forum for presenting one's own findings and conclusions and for arguing for or against competing hypotheses. . . .

Academic assignments such as laboratory reports and independent research projects also incorporate the principles of scientific argument. . . . They force you not only to think like a scientist, but also to write like one. And most important, they show you that data cannot speak for themselves: you still have to incorporate them into a coherent, meaningful story, a scientific argument, that supports your conclusions.*

*Writing Papers in the Biological Sciences. New York: St. Martins, 1988. 1–2.

6b   Making a claim (an argumentative thesis)

Every paper that you write in college will have a thesis (an extended discussion of which you will find in 3d). An argumentative paper has an argumentative thesis, or claim, which differs from theses for papers that intend to inform. Consider two sample theses. Assume that each introduces a paper and, like any thesis, summarizes in a single statement an entire discussion. Which thesis promises an argument?

> Beginning in the eighteenth century and continuing through to our day, researchers and philosophers have speculated on the possibility that, aside from human beings, there exists other intelligent life in the universe.

> Given the urgent nutritional and health needs of people around the world, governments today are spending obscene amounts of money searching the cosmos for signs of intelligent life.

Although both theses address the same general subject, the search for intelligent life in the universe, clearly the second is the one that promises an argument. An argumentative thesis, or claim, makes a point about which reasonable people can be expected to disagree. An informational thesis, in contrast, is not likely to spark debate. Provided the writer of the first thesis writes a paper that adequately explains how, over the past three centuries, different people have speculated about intelligent life in the cosmos, readers will likely accept the information as legitimate and informative. In contrast, the argumentative thesis—the claim—addresses the same topic but casts it as a debate in which the writer takes a position.

1 Answering one of three questions with your claim

Generally, there are three kinds of debates in the context of which you will write arguments based on claims: debates about what is a fact, what is the best policy, and what is valuable. You can confirm that you've written an argumentative claim by making sure it answers a question about fact, policy, or value.

Claims that answer questions of fact

A question of *fact* can take the following forms:

Does X exist?

Does X lead to Y?

How can we define X?

The answer to any of these questions will be an argumentative claim—as, for instance, the claim of the sample argument:

> Although women are certainly underrepresented at present in the computer industry, changing cultural and market forces will inevitably bring about a more equitable proportion of women to men.

This claim is a prediction: it answers a question about a (future) fact. The present fact is that "women are . . . underrepresented in the computer industry." By claiming that this fact will change in the future, the writer obligates herself to an argument. She will need to support her claim.

Once established, a fact can be used in other arguments—for instance, in problem–solution arguments (see the box on page 175). In a problem–solution argument, the writer may need to argue that a problem exists. Then, having established the problem, the writer can proceed with a solution—an argument about policy, about what should be done.

Claims that answer questions of policy

A question of *policy* takes the following form:

What action should we take?

Politics and social action are major arenas in which arguments about policy occur. These arguments help to determine which legislative actions are taken and how money is spent. The sample claim about searching for intelligent life promises an argument about policy:

> Given the urgent nutritional and health needs of people around the world, governments today are spending obscene amounts of money searching the cosmos for signs of intelligent life.

The writer is taking a clear stand that certain policies should *not* be followed. Notice that with the mention of nutritional and health needs, the claim suggests the type of support the writer will use in arguing for the claim.

Claims that answer questions of value

A question of *value* takes the following form:

What is *X* worth?

X can be a movie, a book, a college course, a theory, a vacation—any topic about which people might have differing opinions. Essentially, the writer who enters into an argument about value commits to rating and defending that rating. In the argument itself, the writer must define the standards by which *X* is being evaluated. Notice how each of these claims about value has embedded in it a term of judgment:

> The tickets to professional sports games are overpriced.
>
> *Great Expectations* is the best novel that Dickens wrote.
>
> Despite some problems, the Internet-based course I took this summer was a success.

Overpriced, best, some problems, and *success* are all terms signaling that an evaluation is about to take place. (See the discussion at 2b, "Writing an evaluation.")

An argument creates a discussion between the writer and readers. For any discussion to succeed, all participants must use key terms in the same way. In a written argument, it is the writer's responsibility to define all key words in the claim so that readers are debating the same topic. Consider this claim:

The United States should not support totalitarian regimes.

Unless the term *totalitarian regimes* is clearly defined (and distinguished from, say, *authoritarian regimes*), the argument cannot succeed. Examine your claims. If one or another word requires it, incorporate a definition into your argument. Take special care to define terms when you are sure that readers will disagree with your definitions. At times, entire arguments are needed to define complex terms, such as *honor*. If a key term in your claim is not complicated, a paragraph or even a sentence of definition will do.

Here are the sample claims presented in this section. Boldfaced terms need definition. In each case, the writer could not reasonably support the claim without first defining key terms:

Market forces will inevitably bring about **a more equitable proportion** of women to men.

Governments today are spending **obscene amounts** of money searching the cosmos for signs of intelligent life.

The tickets to professional sports games are **overpriced.**

Great Expectations is the **best** novel that Dickens wrote.

Despite some **problems,** the Internet-based course I took this summer was a **success.**

EXERCISE I

In a paragraph, recall an argument that you had recently in which some issue of importance to you was debated. With whom did you argue? What positions did you and the other person (people) argue? What was the outcome? To what extent did your powers of persuasion affect the argument's outcome?

EXERCISE 2

Choose two subjects, and pose questions of fact, policy, and value about them. Of each topic, ask, Does *X* exist? (or Does *X* lead to *Y*? or How can we define *X*?). What should we do with regard to *X*? and What is the value of *X*? Answer these questions with statements that could serve as claims for later arguments. Possible topics: artificial intelligence, post-traumatic stress disorder, ozone holes, and stem cell research.

ACROSS THE CURRICULUM

Making Claims in Different Subject Areas

Compare how the claims a writer will make change from one discipline area to the next.

In Chapter 38 (Writing and Reading in the Humanities), you learn the following:

To make a claim about literature, first find a pattern of meaning in a text. Confirm and refine that pattern and then make a claim. (See 38a-2.)

In Chapter 39 (Writing and Reading in the Social Sciences), you learn this:

Claims in the social sciences will often commit you to observing the actions of individuals or groups and to stating how these actions are significant, both for certain individuals and for the people responding to them. (See 39a-2.)

And in Chapter 40 (Writing and Reading in the Sciences), you learn this:

Scientific arguments often involve two sorts of claims. The first takes the form *X is a problem* or *X is somehow puzzling.* This claim establishes some issue as worthy of investigation, and it is on the basis of this claim that experiments are designed. [. . .] The process continues when you make a second claim that attempts to explain the anomaly. Such a claim takes this form: *X can be explained as follows.* (See 40a-2.)

6c Gathering evidence

6.2

By definition, an argument requires support. Support for an argument consists of both evidence and a clear line of reasoning. In this section we consider evidence.

Evidence can be of three types:

■ Facts and statistics.
■ Opinions of experts (and of others affected by the outcome of the argument).
■ Examples that illustrate the point you are making.

Evidence in and of itself does not advance a claim. To do that, you need to link the evidence to the claim, as you will learn to do in the next section. For the moment, concentrate on the types of evidence that can provide the basis for good, strong support for a claim. Every argument requires that you carefully examine its claim and ask:

What combination of facts, opinions, and examples will readers need in order to accept my claim as true, probable, or desirable?

To the degree you will need to do research in order to gather evidence for your argument, see Chapters 33 and 34 for assistance. Through research, you will gather relevant facts, opinions, and examples.

CRITICAL DECISIONS

What Will Convince Your Readers?

Once you have decided on a claim, turn your attention to gathering evidence that will convince readers to accept your view as true, probable, or desirable. Assemble support from the following categories:

- **Facts and statistics:** Find sources on your topic. Take notes on any facts or statistics that you think are pertinent. Remember that the facts you gather should accurately represent the available data. The U.S. Government Printing Office publishes volumes of statistics on life in the United States. These are often the source for statistics used in other studies.

- **Expert opinions:** Locate experts by reviewing source materials and checking for people whose work is referred to repeatedly. Also compare bibliographies, and look for names in common. Within a week or so of moderately intensive research, you will identify acknowledged experts on a topic. Quote experts when their language is particularly powerful or succinct; otherwise, summarize or paraphrase.

- **Examples:** Examples allow you to demonstrate in real and practical terms the points you wish to make in an argument. Such concrete, understandable examples may be more memorable than your abstract claim. Readers will recall your example and then your point—and you will have communicated effectively.

Organizing your evidence

Having gathered facts, examples, and opinions that will help to advance your claim, organize your evidence into topical clusters. For the sample argument (6a) on women in the high-tech workplace, writer Marie Hobahn conducted research and located some fifty pieces of evidence she considered using for her argument. From various sources, she found closely related evidence that she grouped into five categories:

Gathering Evidence   **163**

Less sexism evident.

Emergence of female mentoring groups.

Shift of industry away from reliance on math.

Emergence of Web as a marketplace.

Emergence of women as consumers of high-tech equipment.

Within each category, Marie looked to combine the facts, examples, and expert opinions she had gathered. For instance, in the first category ("Less sexism evident"), Marie grouped the three related pieces of evidence—facts, survey results of twenty female high-tech entrepreneurs, and expert opinions—from two analysts.

EXERCISE 3

Provide paragraph-length examples for two of the following general statements. If you feel that the statement is inaccurate, revise it to your liking. Then provide an example based on your own experience.

1. During the first weeks of their first semester, freshmen are unsure of themselves socially.
2. Assignments at the college level are much more demanding than those in high school.
3. My friend _____ (you provide the name) usually offers sound advice.

EXERCISE 4

With pen in hand, reread the paragraphs you wrote in answer to Exercise 3. Circle your statements of opinion. Underline your statements of fact. Do any patterns emerge? (Instead of working with your own paragraphs, you might switch papers with a classmate.)

6d Linking evidence to your claim

As already noted, support for a claim consists of two elements: the evidence you have gathered (facts, opinions, and examples) and a clear line of reasoning that links the evidence to your claim. You can use any of five types of logic to connect evidence to a claim:

Generalization	You argue that your evidence shows that your claim is true in all (or most) cases.
Causation	You argue that your evidence has caused (or will cause) the claim to be true.
Sign	You argue that your evidence is a clear sign that the claim is true.

Analogy	You argue that another case—a set of circumstances seemingly unrelated to the facts of your case—actually clarifies your case and the claim you are making about it.
Parallel case	You produce as evidence a case (B) that is very similar to the facts of your case (A). You argue that the claim you are making about your case A is proven by the circumstances of the parallel case B.

Using any of these appeals to *logic*, you attempt to convince readers that your claim is reasonable. You can link evidence to your claim with two other sorts of appeals, which you'll also learn about in this section: to the reader's regard for *authority* and the reader's *emotions*.

1	**Appealing to logic**

An appeal to logic is by far the most common basis for arguing in the academic world. This section demonstrates five of the most common logical appeals: generalization, causation, sign, analogy, and parallel case.

Argument from generalization

Given several representative examples of a group (of people, animals, paintings, trees, washing machines, whatever), you can infer a general principle or *generalization* that applies to other examples of that group. In order for a generalization to be fair, you must select an adequate number of examples that are typical of the entire group. You must also acknowledge any examples that apparently disprove the generalization. Arguments from generalization allow you to support claims that answer questions of fact and value.

Sample argument

As litter, plastic is unsightly and deadly. Birds and small animals die after getting stuck in plastic, six-pack beverage rings. Pelicans accidentally hang themselves with discarded plastic fishing line. Turtles choke on plastic bags or starve when their stomachs become clogged with hard-to-excrete, crumbled plastic. Sea lions poke their heads into plastic rings and have their jaws locked permanently shut. Authorities estimate that plastic refuse annually kills up to 2 million birds and at least 100,000 mammals.

—GARY TURBAK, "60 Billion Pounds of Trouble"

Claim	Plastic litter kills animals. [Answers a question of fact]
Evidence	Birds, turtles, sea lions, and various mammals have died from plastic litter.
Reasoning	Generalization. Danger to the animals cited can be generalized to other animals that come into contact with plastic litter.

Argument from causation

In an argument from causation, you begin with a fact or set of facts about your topic. (If readers are likely to contest these facts, you must first make an argument to establish your facts before pushing on with an argument from causation.) An argument from *causation* enables you to claim that a particular action or condition leads to a specific result or effect: Sunspots cause the aurora borealis. Dieting causes weight loss. Smoking causes lung cancer. Working in the opposite direction, you can begin with what you presume to be an effect of some prior cause: the swing of a pendulum, inattention among schoolchildren, tornadoes. Of this presumed effect, you ask: "What causes this?" Establishing a direct causal link is seldom easy, for usually multiple causes may contribute to a single condition (think of the inattentive child at school). In arguing causation, therefore, you need to be sensitive to complexity. Arguments of causation allow you to support a claim that answers a question of fact or of policy. Cause-and-effect reasoning also allows you to use a problem-solution structure in your arguments. (See the box on page 175.)

Sample argument

Under primitive agricultural conditions the farmer had few insect problems. Those arose with the intensification of agriculture—the devotion of immense acreages to a single crop. Such a system set the stage for explosive increases in specific insect populations. Single-crop farming does not take advantage of the principles by which nature works; it is agriculture as an engineer might conceive it to be. Nature has introduced great variety into the landscape, but man has displayed a passion for simplifying it. Thus he undoes the built-in checks and balances by which nature holds the species within bounds. One important natural check is a limit on the amount of suitable habitat for each species. Obviously then, an insect that lives on wheat can build up its population to much higher levels on a farm devoted to wheat than on one in which wheat is intermingled with other crops to which the insect is not adapted.

—Rachel Carson, *Silent Spring*

Claim	Insect problems arose with the practice of intensive, single-crop farming. [Answers a question of fact]
Evidence	The variety of vegetation in natural habitats discourages infestation; natural habitats have "checks and balances."
Reasoning	Cause and effect. By creating one-crop farms and eliminating the checks and balances of natural habitats, farmers caused their own insect problems.

Argument from sign

A sore throat and fever are signs of flu. Black smoke billowing from a window is a sign of fire. Risk taking is a sign of creativity. In an argument from *sign*, two things are correlated; that is, one tends to occur in the presence of the other. A sign is *not* a cause, however. If your big toe aches at the approach of thunderstorms, your aching toe may be a sign of approaching storms, but it surely does not cause them. Economists routinely look to certain indexes (housing starts, for instance) as indicators, or signs, of the economy's health. Housing starts are *correlated with* economic health, often by means of a statistical comparison. If a sign has proven to be a particularly reliable indicator, then you can use it to support a claim that answers a question of fact.

Sample argument

Advertisments are constructed to make women anxious about the moisture content of their skin. In the language of advertising, dry skin is "a sign of a woman who is all dried up and is not sexually responsive—and who may also be sterile. This is because water is connected, in our psyches, with birth. It is also tied to purity, as in baptismal rites when sin is cleansed from a person. All of this suggests that words and images that picture a body of a woman as being dehydrated and losing water have great resonance."

—ARTHUR ASA BERGER, "Sex as Symbol in Fashion Advertising"

Claim	In advertisements, images of dehydration resonate for readers and viewers. [Answers a question of fact]
Evidence	Readers have profound psychological associations with dryness.
Reasoning	Sign. Dry skin is a sign of sterility and infertility, deeply resonant themes for men and women.

Argument from analogy

An argument from *analogy* sets up a comparison between the topic of your argument and another topic that initially appears unrelated. While suggestive and at times persuasive, an analogy actually proves nothing. There is always a point at which an analogy will break down, and it is usually a mistake to build an argument on analogy alone. Use analogies as you would seasonings in cooking. As one of several attempts to persuade your reader, an analogy spices your argument and makes it memorable. You can use analogies in support of claims that answer questions of fact, policy, and value.

Sample argument

In closing, we might describe learning with an analogy to a well-orchestrated symphony, aimed to blend both familiar and new sounds. A symphony is the complex interplay of composer, conductor, the repertoire of instruments, and the various dimensions of music. Each instrument is used strategically to interact with other instruments toward a rich construction of themes progressing in phases, with some themes recurring and others driving the movement forward toward a conclusion or resolution. Finally, each symphony stands alone in its meaning, yet has a relationship to the symphonies that came before and those that will come later. Similarly, learning is a complex interaction of the learner, the instructional materials, the repertoire of available learning strategies, and the context, including the teacher. The skilled learner approaches each task strategically toward the goal of constructing meaning. Some strategies focus on understanding the incoming information, others strive to relate the meaning to earlier predictions, and still others work to integrate the new information with prior knowledge.

—BEAU FLY JONES ET AL., "Learning and Thinking"

Claim	Learning involves a complex blend of learner, materials, and context. [Answers a question of fact]
Evidence	In a symphony orchestra, meaning (sound) is created through interaction of musicians, conductor, composer, and history.
Reasoning	Analogy. The complex interactions needed to create symphonic music are analogous to the interaction needed to create meaning for a learner.

Argument from parallel case

While an analogy argues a relationship between two apparently unrelated topics, an argument from *parallel case* argues a relationship between people, objects, events, or conditions that are directly related. The implicit logic is this: the way a situation turned out in a closely related case is the way it will (or should) turn out in this one. Lawyers argue from parallel case whenever they cite a prior court case in which the legal question involved was similar to the question involved in a current case. Because the earlier case ended a certain way (with the conviction or acquittal of a defendant, or with a particular monetary award), so too should the present case have this outcome. An argument from parallel case requires that situations presented as parallel be alike in essential ways. If this requirement is not met, the argument loses force. The argument would also be weakened if someone could present a more closely parallel case than yours. You can use a parallel case in support of claims that answer questions of fact, policy, or value.

Sample argument

By the year 2000, women and minorities will account for 68 per cent of the new workers. Coupled with the fact that, if current trends continue, the United States will face a shortage of scientists and physicians by the end of the century, it is safe to say that sustaining America's scientific and biomedical preeminence depends upon attracting—and retaining—talented women and minorities.

If we are to ensure our country's future competitiveness, we must change the prevailing [male-dominated] culture [of science and technology]—the rules of the game—in our classrooms, boardrooms, laboratories, and faculty lounges. To do so, we must recognize that brains, not brawn, will dominate the next century, and that means more than ever we must tap into the brain power of women. . . .

Eighty years ago, when British women were trying to win the right to vote, they played by men's rules: They broke windows in Parliament Square. Many of the women were treated brutally and arrested. Their leader, Emmeline Pankhurst, pointed out that every advance of men's rights has been marked by violence and the destruction of property. She defended the women's actions, saying, "Why should women go to Parliament Square and be battered about and insulted, and most important of all, produce less effect than when they throw stones? We tried it long enough. We submitted for years patiently in insult and assault. Women had their health injured. Women lost their lives. . . . After all, is not a woman's life, is not her health, are not her limbs more valuable than panes of glass? There is no doubt of that, but most important of all, does not the breaking of glass produce more effect upon the Government?"

While I am not advocating that American women in science resort to such behaviors—or even to the breaking of test tubes—it is clear that all of us in the scientific community have a lot of breaking to do—especially old rules, self-defeating habits, and glass ceilings.

—BERNADINE HEALY, former director
of the National Institutes of Health,
The Chronicle of Higher Education

Claim	To take their rightful place in the scientific community, women must first challenge the male-dominated culture of science. [Answers a question of policy]
Evidence	In the early twentieth century, British women who fought to gain entry into the political community (by winning the right to vote) first had to challenge the male-dominated culture of British politics. Women protested at Parliament Square and broke windows.
Reasoning	Parallel case. Just as during the early twentieth century women needed to fight to enter British politics, women today need to fight to enter and advance in scientific fields.

2   Appealing to authority

Two types of authority are important in arguments: the authority you yourself bring as a writer and the authority of those who have expert knowledge on the topic that concerns you.

Establishing yourself as an authority

Before readers will agree with a claim you are making, they need to trust you, the writer. As a maker of arguments, you must therefore work to establish your trustworthiness—your authority to speak and make a claim. *Authority* in this sense is not the same as having expert knowledge. It has to do, rather, with establishing a presence that readers can yield to in a self-respecting way.

There are several things you can do to help establish this trust:

- *Be honest*, first of all. The point is so obvious it hardly seems worth making, but readers generally have a good nose for dishonesty.
- *Strike a reasonable tone* (see 21e).
- *Choose a level of language appropriate for the occasion* (see 3a-4).
- *Read thoroughly on your topic.* Learn enough to have an opinion worth considering.

Referring readers to experts

As a writer, you greatly help your cause when you can quote experts who support your point of view. Which experts should you choose? See the box below.

Once you have determined to the best of your ability that a writer you wish to quote is indeed expert, you must then identify those places in your argument where appeals to authority will serve you well. Appeals to authority can be used to support claims that answer questions of fact, policy, and value.

CRITICAL DECISIONS

Using Authoritative Sources

Read critically to determine which sources you can confidently draw on in a paper. Use the following criteria to help you make your decisions:

1. Prefer acknowledged authorities to self-proclaimed ones.
2. Prefer an authority working within his or her field of expertise to one who is reporting conclusions about another subject.
3. Prefer first-hand accounts over those from sources who were separated by time or space from the events reported.
4. Prefer unbiased and disinterested sources over those who can reasonably be suspected of having a motive for influencing the way others see the subject under investigation.
5. Prefer public records to private documents in questionable cases.
6. Prefer accounts that are specific and complete to those that are vague and evasive.
7. Prefer evidence that is credible on its own terms to that which is internally inconsistent or demonstrably false to any known facts.
8. In general, prefer a recently published report to an older one.
9. In general, prefer works by standard publishers to those of unknown or "vanity" presses [and Web sites of established organizations to those of individuals].

10. In general, prefer authors who themselves follow [standard] report-writing conventions. . . .
11. When possible, prefer an authority known to your audience to one they have never heard of

Source: Thomas E. Gaston and Bret H. Smith, *The Research Paper: A Common-Sense Approach* (Englewood Cliffs, NJ: Prentice Hall, 1988) 31–33.

Sample argument

Leo Marx claims that Melville's "Bartleby the Scrivener" is autobiographical.

Claim   Herman Melville's "Bartleby the Scrivener" is a story about Melville.

Evidence   Leo Marx says so.

Reasoning Authority. Leo Marx is a respected literary critic; his insights are valuable and are worth examining.

Use appeals to authority to support claims that answer questions about facts, policy, and value.

3	Appealing to emotion

Appeals to reason are based on the force of logic, and appeals to authority are based on the reader's respect for the opinions of experts. By contrast, appeals to *emotion* are designed to tap the audience's needs and values. Arguments based on appeals to reason and authority may well turn out to be valid, but validity does not guarantee that readers will *endorse* your position. For instance, you might establish with impeccable logic that the physical condition of your community's public schools has deteriorated badly, to the point of affecting the performance of students. While true, your claim may not carry force enough to persuade the town council to vote on a bond issue or to raise money to renovate several buildings. To succeed in your effort (or in any appeal to emotion), you must make your readers feel the same urgency to act that you do. Appeals to emotion can be used to support claims that answer questions about policy and value. The following paragraphs were written as part of a holiday charity drive by a writer and editor for the *New York Times*. Anna Quindlen's argumentative claim (not stated in the example paragraphs) was *People should give what they can afford to the needy.*

Sample argument

There are the ones who are born with acquired immune deficiency syndrome, born to die because their parents used dirty needles. There are the ones who are left in hospitals to lie in the metal cribs, their only stimulation the occasional visit from a nurse. There are those who are freezing, and starving, and those who are beaten and bruised.

A doctor in the neonatal intensive care unit at one city hospital looked around at the incubators one afternoon and wondered aloud about the tubes, the medicines needed to make the premature thrive and the sickly ones bloom. It was not at all uncommon, she said, to find that an infant who had been coaxed from near death to life in the confines of that overly warm room, in one of those little plastic wombs, had turned up two or three years later in the emergency room with cigarette burns, broken bones, or malnutrition.

—ANNA QUINDLEN, "A City's Needy"

Claim	People should give what they can to the needy.
Evidence	There are children in New York suffering terribly, through no fault of their own.
Reasoning	Emotion. The plight of these blameless, helpless children touches the reader, who almost certainly lives in better circumstances. Quindlen moves the reader to pity, and pity may prompt a contribution.

Making an Emotional Appeal

1. List the needs of your audience with respect to your subject. These needs might be physical, psychological, humanitarian, environmental, or financial.
2. Select the category of needs best suited to your audience, and identify emotional appeals that you think will be persuasive.
3. Place the issue you are arguing in your reader's lap. Get the reader to respond to the issue emotionally.
4. Call on the reader to agree with you on a course of action.

Plan your emotional appeal by beginning with a claim that has already been supported by evidence and appeals to reason and authority. In your efforts to raise taxes for school renovation, you could show photographs, produce a list of items in need of repair, and quote expert witnesses who believe that children's learning suffers in deteriorating environments. Having argued by such appeals, you can then plan an emotional appeal.

In the real world, even the best argument may fail to achieve its objective. Some subjects—for example, abortion or capital punishment—are so controversial or so tied to preexisting religious or moral beliefs that many people have long since made up their minds one way or the other and will never change. Such subjects are so fraught with emotion that logical arguments are ineffective in persuading people to rethink their positions. Sometimes, also, your audience has a vested interest in *not* being persuaded by your arguments. (Perhaps your audience has a financial stake in holding to an opposing position.) When your audience feels significantly threatened by the prospect of your victory, it is futile to insist on the validity of your argument.

EXERCISE 5

Write the outline of an argument, your claim for which should be based on the following scenario:

> Imagine yourself a student at a college or university where the board of trustees has voted to institute a curfew on dormitory visitors. After 11 P.M. on weekdays and 1 A.M. on weekends, no student may have a guest in his or her dormitory room. The rule simply put: no overnight guests.

> Decide on a claim, and determine whether it answers a question of fact, policy, or value. Plan a discussion in which you argue three ways in support of your claim.

6e   Making rebuttals

By definition, arguments are subject to challenge, or to counterarguments. Because reasonable people will disagree, you must be prepared to acknowledge differences of opinion and to address them—for two reasons. First, by raising a challenge to your own position, you force yourself to see an issue from someone else's perspective. This can be a valuable lesson, prompting you to reevaluate and refine your views. In addition, challenges pique a reader's interest. Research shows that when tension (that is, disagreement) exists in an argument, readers maintain interest. They want to know what happens or how the argument is resolved.

Once you acknowledge opposing views, respond with a *rebuttal*, an argument that addresses and rejects these views. If you can, point out the faulty logic on which they are based. If you do not raise objections, your readers inevitably will. Better that you raise them on your terms so that you can control the debate.

You should also be open to accepting the views of others. Readers will appreciate your ability to concede at least some of your opposition's points, and they will take it as a sign of your reasonableness.

CRITICAL DECISIONS

Responding to Opposing Points of View

Expect opposition. When you have located opposing points of view, use the occasion to extend your thinking. Let disagreement enhance the quality of your argument.

- **The facts are in dispute.** When the facts in an argument are disputed, investigate the validity of your facts and the opposition's.

  Check the credibility of sources. Be sure that your sources are reliable. If you discover some dispute about reliability, raise it in your argument, and establish the trustworthiness of your information. If you cannot, abandon questionable sources, and thank your opposition.

  If sources (yours and the opposition's) are equally reliable, ask, Through what process were the facts established? Different methods lead to different perceptions of fact. Acknowledge these methods, and state clearly which methods you (or your sources) have relied on.

- **Expert opinions are in dispute.** Experts *will* disagree. Respond to differences of expert opinion by checking qualifications. These strategies should help:

  Strategy 1: Ask: Is the author referred to in several sources?

  Strategy 2: Locate two reviews of a book written by the person in question, and you will learn something of the author's reputation.

  If the experts holding opposing views are reliable, acknowledge the disagreement in your argument, and attempt to explain it.

6f   Preparing to write an argument

Devising strategies for argument

There are two time-honored strategies for arranging arguments: the problem–solution structure and the classic five-part structure are summarized in boxes in this section. In these structures, each part of the argument may be a paragraph or a section consisting of several paragraphs.

Inductive and deductive arrangements

An inductively arranged argument moves from support—particular facts, examples, and opinions—to a claim. A great deal of scientific and technological argument proceeds this way. The writer makes certain observations, finds patterns in those observations, and then makes a claim about them.

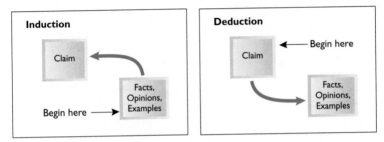

A deductively arranged argument moves from a claim to support—to particular facts, opinions, and examples. A good deal of writing in the humanities, in politics, and in law proceeds this way. The writer begins with a general principle or claim, the truth, likelihood, or desirability of which is then proven.

Writing an Argument: The Problem–Solution Structure

I. There is a serious problem.
   A. The problem exists and is growing.
      (Provide support for this statement.)
   B. The problem is serious.
      (Provide support.)
   C. Current methods cannot cope with the problem.
      (Provide support.)
II. There is a solution to the problem. (Your claim goes here.)
   A. The solution is practical.
      (Provide support.)
   B. The solution is desirable.
      (Provide support.)
   C. We can implement the solution.
      (Provide support.)
   D. Alternate solutions are not as strong as the proposed solution.
      (Review—and reject—competing solutions.)

Source: Adapted from Richard D. Rieke and Malcolm O. Sillars, *Argumentation and the Decision Making Process* (Glenview, IL: Scott, Foresman, 1984) 163.

Regardless of whether you use an inductive or a deductive arrangement for your argument, realize that in either case, you know before you begin drafting what your claim, support, and lines of reasoning will be. The decision to move inductively or deductively is a decision about strategy.

You can position the claim in your argument at the beginning, middle, or end of the presentation. In the problem–solution structure, you see that the claim is made only after the writer introduces a problem. Working with the five-part structure, you have more flexibility in positioning your claim. One factor that can help determine placement is considering your audience's likelihood of agreeing with you:

- When an audience is likely to be neutral or supportive, you can make your claim early on with the assurance that you will not alienate readers.
- When an audience is likely to disagree, plan to make your claim toward the end of the presentation. In that way you give yourself space to build consensus with your readers, step by step, until you reach a conclusion.

Writing an Argument: The Classic Five-Part Structure

1. **Introduction:** Introduce topic to be argued and establish its importance. Provide background information.
2. **Claim:** State your claim (your argumentative thesis).
3. **Supporting the claim:** Construct reasons for accepting the claim.

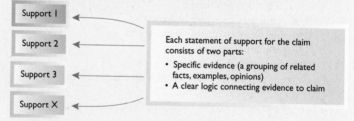

Each statement of support for the claim consists of two parts:

- Specific evidence (a grouping of related facts, examples, opinions)
- A clear logic connecting evidence to claim

4. **Counterargument/rebuttal:** Raise arguments against the claim; challenge them.
5. **Conclusion:** Summarize the argument; remind readers of what you want them to believe or do.

Depending on the writing occasion, you will want to rearrange elements of this typical argumentative structure. For instance, you may want to raise and rebut counterarguments first (as the writer does in the sample argument in 6a), or you may want to raise counterarguments immediately after (or before) every support you offer for the claim. You may want to locate the claim at the end of the argument. Be flexible. Adapt your approach according to your needs.

Readers tend to remember most clearly what they read last. Thus, you may want to present your reasons in support of your claim in the order of least to most emphatic. Conversely, you may want to offer your most emphatic reasons at the very beginning of the argument. In one strong move you might gain the reader's agreement and then cement that agreement with reasons of secondary importance. Decisions you make about placing your claim and arranging your points of support will depend on your assessment of your audience's probable reactions to your views.

EXERCISE 6

Return to the argument you outlined in Exercise 5, and introduce in this outline an argument counter to your own. In a paragraph, discuss how you would rebut the counterargument or accept it in part.

Establishing your claim

Drafting an argument is more a recreation of thinking than an act of exploration. Exploration—through writing or through talking with friends—comes prior to writing a first draft. Consider writing a *pre*draft: a brief paper, intended for your eyes only, in which you explore the position you want to take in your argument. Whatever your method for doing so, arrive at your views on a topic—your claim—*before* you sit down to write the draft. As you begin, you should understand the support you

---

Gathering Materials for Your Argument

1. Gather material on your subject. Generate information on your own—see 3b. If necessary, conduct research—see Chapters 33–35.
2. Review your material. Decide what you think about the topic, and in a single sentence answer a question of fact, policy, or value. Your one-sentence answer will be the claim of your argument.
3. Understand your audience: What do they know about the topic? What do they need to know? To what sorts of appeals will they respond?
4. Plan out the lines of reasoning you will present to link your evidence with your claim.
5. Identify strong counterarguments, and plan to rebut and neutralize them. Possibly concede some of your opposition's points.
6. Sketch your argument, deciding on placement of your claim and arrangement of your lines of reasoning.
7. Draft your argument, realizing that you will need to backtrack on occasion to get new information or to rethink your strategy. See Chapter 3 on the necessary uncertainties in preparing for and writing a first draft.
8. Revise two or three times. See Chapter 4 for advice.

will present and the lines of reasoning you will use to link that support to your claim. You will flesh out the discussion as you write, but the backbone of your argument should be carefully established ahead of time.

EXERCISE 7

Based on your outline in Exercise 6, write the draft of an argument.

6g Evaluating arguments and avoiding common errors

Whether you are evaluating your own arguments (in an effort to revise them) or someone else's, there are several common errors to watch for. Correct these errors in your own writing, and raise a challenge when you find them in the writing of others.

1 Defining terms

Your evaluation of an argument should begin with its claim. Locate the claim, and be sure that all terms are well defined. If they are not, determine whether the lack of definition creates ambiguities in the argument itself. For example, if you define the word *generosity* one way and others define it differently, there is bound to be disagreement. If a word such as *generosity* slips into the claim, informed argument cannot likely begin until the word is carefully defined. With especially ambiguous words, sometimes whole paragraphs of definition are needed.

2 Examining appeals to logic

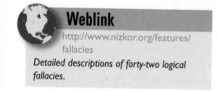

Weblink

http://www.nizkor.org/features/
fallacies

Detailed descriptions of forty-two logical fallacies.

As you have seen in 6d, the lines of reasoning that a writer develops—generalization, causation, and so on—establish logical support for a claim. If you as a reader feel that an argument's logic is not valid, then you are entitled to raise a challenge. If the logic is flawed, the validity of the claim may be in doubt. Any of the following seven types of fallacies, or flaws, will undermine an argument's logic. The first four flaws specifically address the lines of reasoning you will use to make arguments: generalization, causation, sign, and analogy.

1. *Faulty generalization.* Generalizations may be flawed if they are offered on the basis of insufficient evidence. It would not be valid, for instance, to make the generalization that left-handed people are clumsy because all three lefties you know are clumsy. A more academic example: It would be a faulty generalization to claim on the

basis of one survey of a single dorm that students on your campus are evenly split on joining fraternities and sororities. In order for your generalization to be accurate, the survey would need to have been administered campus-wide—if not to every student, then at least to a representative cross-section.

2. *Faulty cause and effect.* Two fallacies can lead a writer to infer incorrectly that one event causes another. The first concerns the ordering of events in time. The fact that one event occurs before another does *not* prove that the first event caused the second. (In Latin, this fallacy is known as *post hoc*, a brief form of *post hoc, ergo propter hoc*—"after this, therefore because of this.") If the planets Venus and Jupiter were in rare alignment on the morning of the Mt. St. Helens eruption, it would not be logical to argue that the alignment caused the eruption.

   The second flaw: the belief that events must have *single* causes. Many factors usually contribute to the occurrence of an event. What caused the layoff of production-line workers at the General Motors plant in Framingham, Massachusetts? Likely, several issues: increased competition from foreign auto manufacturers, a downturn in the economy, the cost of modernizing the Framingham assembly line, a need to show stockholders that there were fewer employees on the payroll, and a decision to build more cars out of the country. To claim that *one* of these is the sole cause of the plant shutdown would be to ignore the complexity of the event.

3. *Confusing correlation with causation.* There is a well-known saying among researchers that *correlation does not imply causation*. In one study on creativity, researchers correlated *risk taking* and *a preference for the unconventional* with groups of people classified as creative. It would not be logical to infer from this correlation that creativity *causes* risk taking or that this trait *causes* creativity. The most that can be said is that the traits are associated or correlated with—they tend to appear in the presence of—creative people. Arguments made with statistical evidence are usually subject to this limitation.

4. *Faulty analogy.* The key components of an analogy must very nearly parallel the issues central to the argument you are making. The wrong analogy not only will *not* clarify, but also will positively confuse. For instance, an attempt to liken the process of writing to climbing a flight of stairs would create some confusion. The analogy suggests that the writing process occurs in clearly delineated steps, when progress in actual writing is seldom so direct. Analogies should enhance, not obscure, understanding.

5. *Either/or reasoning.* Assume that someone is trying to persuade you that the United States ought to intervene militarily in a certain conflict many thousands of miles from U.S. territory. At one point in the argument you hear this: "Either we demonstrate through force that the United States continues to be a world power or we take a

backseat, passive role in world affairs. The choice is clear." Actually, the choice is not at all clear. The person arguing has presented two options and has argued for one. But many possibilities for conducting U.S. foreign policy exist besides going to war or becoming passive. Be wary of an argument whose author preselects two possibilities from among many and then attempts to force a choice.

6. *Personal attacks.* Personal attacks, known in Latin as *ad hominem* arguments, challenge the person presenting a view rather than the view itself. You are entitled to object when you read or hear this type of attack: "The child psychologist on that talk show has no kids, so how can he recommend anything useful to me concerning my children?" Notice that the challenge sidesteps the issue in an argument to dismiss an apparently useful observation by dismissing the person who offers it. At the very least, statements should be evaluated on their merits.

7. *The begged question.* Writers who assume the validity of a point that they should be proving by argument are guilty of begging the question. For instance, the statement "All patriotic Americans should support the president" begs a question of definition: What *is* a patriotic American? The person making this statement assumes a definition that he or she should in fact be arguing.

3   **Examining evidence**

Arguments also can falter when they are not adequately or legitimately supported by facts, examples, statistics, or opinions. Refer to the following guidelines when using evidence.

Facts and examples

6.3

1. *Facts and examples should fairly represent the available data.* An example cannot be forced. If you find yourself sifting through a great deal of evidence in order to find one confirming fact or example, take your difficulty as a sign, and rethink your point.

2. *Facts and examples should be current.* Facts and examples need to be current, especially when you are arguing about recent events or are drawing information from a field in which information is changing rapidly. If, for example, you are arguing a claim about the likelihood of incumbent politicians being reelected, you should find sources that report on the most recent elections. If you are trying to show a trend, your facts and examples should also be drawn from sources going back several years, if not decades.

3. *Facts and examples should be sufficient to establish validity.* A generalization must be based on an adequate number of examples and on representative examples. To establish the existence of a problem concerning college sports, for instance, it would not do to claim

that because transcripts were forged for a handful of student-athletes at two schools, a problem exists nationwide.

4. *Negative instances of facts and examples should be acknowledged.* If an argument is to be honest, you should identify facts and examples that constitute evidence *against* your position. Tactically, you are better off being the one to raise the inconvenient example than having someone else do this for you in the context of a challenge.

Statistics

5. *Statistics from reliable and current sources should be used.* Statistics are a numerical compression of information. Assuming that you do not have the expertise to evaluate the procedures by which statistics are generated, you should take certain commonsense precautions when selecting statistical evidence. First, cite statistics from reliable sources. If you have no other way of checking reliability, you can assume that the same source cited in several places is reliable. The U.S. government publishes volumes of statistical information and is considered a reliable source. Just as with facts and examples, statistics should be current when you are arguing about a topic of current interest.

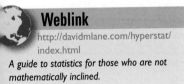

Weblink

http://davidmlane.com/hyperstat/index.html

A guide to statistics for those who are not mathematically inclined.

6. *Comparative statistics should compare items of the same logical class.* If you found statistical information on housing starts in New England in one source and in a second source found information on housing starts in the Southwest, you would naturally want to compare the numbers. The comparison would be valid only if the term *housing starts* was defined clearly in both sources. Lacking a definition, you might plunge ahead and cite the statistics in a paper, not realizing that one figure included apartment buildings in its definition of *housing*, while the other included only single-family homes. Such a comparison would be faulty.

Expert opinions

7. *"Experts" who give opinions should be qualified to do so.* Anyone can speak on a topic, but experts speak with authority by virtue of their experience. You will want to be sure that your experts are, in fact, expert, and evaluating the quality of what they say can be troublesome when you do not know a great deal about a topic. You can trust a so-called expert if you see that person cited as an authority in several sources. For experts who are not likely to be cited in academic articles or books, use your common sense. (See the box in 6d-2 for more on evaluating expert opinions and choosing authoritative sources.)

8. *Experts should be neutral.* You can disqualify an expert's testimony for possible use in your argument if you find that the expert will profit somehow from the opinions or interpretations offered.

Evaluating Arguments and Avoiding Common Errors　　　**181**

CHAPTER 7

Constructing Sentences

If you are a lifelong speaker of English, then you are an expert in the language. You may not realize this, however, because in all likelihood your knowledge of the language is *implicit*. For example, even though you correctly use participles every day, you may not know the textbook definition of *participle*. Yet understanding the basic terminology of English grammar can help you make sentence-level decisions that will improve your writing.

CRITICAL DECISIONS

Conveying Meaning Clearly
The sentence is our basic unit of communication. Sentences, of course, are composed of words, each of which can be classified as a part of speech—a noun, a verb, an adjective, and so forth. Remember, though, that these are parts of a whole: meaning in language is based on the *relationship* among words. As a writer, you must make careful decisions not only about individual words, but also about their arrangement, in order to convey your intended meaning.

7a   Understanding sentence parts

7.1   I   The basics: Recognizing subjects and predicates

The fundamental relationship in a sentence is the one between a subject and its predicate. Every sentence has a **subject:** a noun or noun substitute, along with any modifiers, that performs the main action of the sentence or is described by the sentence. Likewise, every sentence has a **predicate:** a verb and other words associated with it that state the action performed by a subject or describe the subject's condition.

Constructing Sentences

A **simple subject** is the single noun or pronoun that identifies what the sentence is about. The **simple predicate** is the main sentence verb. You can gain a great deal of confidence from your ability to divide a sentence into its subject and predicate parts.

Simple Subject	Simple Predicate
Alcohol	acts as a stimulant.

2   Nouns

A **noun** is the part of speech that names a person, place, thing, or idea.[1] Only nouns can be introduced by an **article.** The **indefinite article** *a* appears before a noun or an adjective describing a noun when these begin with a consonant: *a* book, *a* large book. Also, words that begin with the letter *u* when it's pronounced *yoo* are preceded by *a*: *a* unit, *a* useful device. The word *an* is placed before a noun beginning with a vowel or unpronounced *h*—as in *hour*: *an* hour, *an* ant. The **definite article,** *the*, denotes a specific noun: *the* book. Nouns can also be accompanied by certain classes of words that limit what they refer to. The most common limiting words (and their categories) are *this, that, these, those* (demonstrative); *any, each, some* (indefinite); *one, two, first, second*, etc. (numerical); and *which, that, whose,* etc. (relative).

Weblink

http://owl.english.purdue.edu/handouts/print/#parts

Handouts on the parts of speech from the Purdue Online Writing Lab.

ESL NOTE   The use of articles and of various limiting words indicates whether an English noun names a person or thing that is specific or definite. Nouns that name something generic, nonspecific, or abstract are generally used without these words (see 46a-2 and 46b).

Nouns change their form to show **number;** they can be made singular or plural: *boy/boys, child/children, herd/herds.* They also change in form to show **possession,** but unlike pronouns (see 7a-7), they do this only with the addition of an apostrophe and usually an *s: girl's, children's, herd's.* Finally, nouns can be classified according to categories of meaning that affect the way they are used, as shown in the box on page 184.
Specific uses of nouns are addressed in several places in this text:

Nouns: agreement with verbs: 10a	Nouns: phrases: 7d-2, 3
Nouns: as clauses: 7e-3	Nouns: as subjects: 7b
Nouns: as complements: 7b	Nouns: showing possession: 8c, 27a
Nouns: as modifiers: 11g	Nouns with articles: 46b
Nouns: as objects: 7b	

[1]We owe our discussions of the parts of speech to Hulon Willis, *Modern Descriptive English Grammar* (San Francisco: Chandler, 1972).

Classification of Nouns

Proper nouns are capitalized and name particular persons, places, or things:

Sandra Day O'Connor, Chevrolet, "To His Coy Mistress"

Common nouns refer to general persons, places, or things and are not capitalized:

judge, automobile, poem

Count nouns can be counted:

cubes, cups, forks, rocks

Mass nouns cannot be counted:

sugar, water, air, dirt

Concrete nouns name tangible objects:

lips, clock, dollar

Abstract nouns name intangible ideas, emotions, or qualities:

love, eternity, ambition

Collective nouns are singular in form but plural in sense:

crowd, family, group, herd

---

3   **Verbs**

A **verb,** the main word in the predicate of a sentence, expresses an action, describes an occurrence, or establishes a state of being.

Action	Eleanor *kicked* the ball.
Occurrence	A hush *descended* on the crowd.
State of being	Thomas *was* pious.

Verbs change form on the basis of their **principal parts.** Building from the **infinitive** or **base form** (often accompanied by **to**), these parts are the **past tense,** the **present participle,** and the **past participle.**

Base form	Past tense	Present participle	Past participle
to escape	escaped	am escaping	escaped
to ring	rang	am ringing	rung

The principal parts of a verb have a major role in showing **tense.** Tense expresses the verb's action in time relative to a present statement.

There are four varieties of verbs in English. Each establishes a different relationship among sentence parts, as shown in the box.

Classification of Verbs

Transitive verbs transfer action from an actor—the subject of the sentence—to a person, place, or thing receiving that action (see 9d-1).

> *buy, build, kick, kiss, write*
> Wanda *built* a snowman.

Intransitive verbs show action, yet no person, place, or thing is acted on (see 9d-1).

> *fall, laugh, sing, smile*
> Stock prices *fell*.

Linking verbs allow the word or words following the verb to complete the meaning of a subject (see 11d).

> *be (am, is, are, was, were, has/have been), look, remain, sound, seem, taste*
> Harold *seems* happy.

Helping or **auxiliary verbs** help to show the tense and mood of a verb (see 9c and 47d).

> *be (am, is, are, was, were), has, have, had, do, did, will*
> I *am* going. I *will* go. I *have* gone. I *did* go.

Modal auxiliaries such as *might, would, could,* and *must* help a verb to express urgency, obligation, and likelihood (see 9c-1 and 47d).

> I *should* go. I *might* go. I *could* go.

ESL NOTE   To determine whether a word in a sentence is a verb, apply the test sequence described in 12a (on sentence fragments).

See Chapter 9 for a detailed discussion of verbs. The following list provides a brief index to more information on verb use.

A **verbal** is a verb form that functions as an adjective, an adverb, or a noun. There are three types of verbals: gerunds, participles, and infinitives.

A **gerund,** the *-ing* form of a verb, functions as a noun.

Editing is both a skill and an art. [The gerund is the subject of the sentence.]

I am tired of *editing*. [The gerund is an object of a preposition.]

A **participle** modifies nouns and pronouns. Its present and past forms make up two of the verb's principal parts, as shown previously.

The *edited* manuscript was 700 pages. [The past participle modifies the noun *manuscript*.]

The man *editing* your manuscript is Max Perkins. [The present participle modifies the noun *man*.]

An **infinitive,** often preceded by *to*, is the base form of the verb. An infinitive can function as a noun, adjective, or adverb.

To edit well requires patience. [The infinitive functions as the noun subject of the sentence.]

The person *to edit* your work is Max Perkins. [The infinitive functions as an adjective.]

He waited *to edit* the manuscript. [The infinitive functions as an adverb.]

The following list is a brief index to other information on verbals.

CRITICAL DECISIONS

Checking for Key Sentence Elements
When rereading sentences you have written, check three key relationships:

1. Does the sentence have a subject and a verb? A word grouping that lacks a subject, a verb, or both is considered a fragment. See Chapter 12.

Incomplete	At the beginning of the meeting. [no subject or verb.]
Revised	At the beginning of the meeting, the treasurer gave her report.

2. Does the sentence have a subject and verb that *agree in number?* A subject and verb must both be singular or plural.

Inconsistent	The treasurer are a dynamic speaker. [The plural verb does not match the singular subject.]
Revised	The treasurer is a dynamic speaker.

3. Does the sentence have a subject close enough to the verb to ensure clarity? Meaning can be confused if the subject/verb pairing is interrupted with a lengthy modifier. See Chapter 15 for a discussion of misplaced modifiers.

Interrupted	We because of our dire financial situation have called this meeting.
Revised	We have called this meeting because of our dire financial situation.

5   Adjectives

An **adjective** modifies or describes a noun or pronoun and can provide crucial defining and limiting information in a sentence. It can also provide less crucial but compelling information to help readers see, hear, feel, taste, or smell something named. Adjectives include the present and past participle forms of verbs, such as *fighting* Irish, *baked* potato, and *written* remarks. The single-word adjectives in the following sentences are italicized.

> Climate plays an *important* part in determining the *average* numbers of a species, and *periodical* seasons of *extreme* cold or drought I believe to be the most *effective* of *all* checks.
>
> —CHARLES DARWIN, *On the Origin of Species*

6   Adverbs

An **adverb** can modify a verb, an adjective, an adverb, or an entire sentence. Adverbs describe, define, or otherwise limit, generally answering these questions: *when, how, where, how often, to what extent,* and *to what degree.* Although many adverbs in English are formed by adding the suffix *-ly* to an adjective, some are not: *after, ahead, already, always, back, behind, here, there, up, down, inside, outside.*

Descriptive adverbs describe individual words within a sentence.

The poor *unwittingly* subsidize the rich. [The adverb modifies the verb *subsidize*.]

Poverty *almost* always can be eliminated at a higher cost to the rich. [The adverb modifies the adverb *always*.]

Widespread poverty imposes an *increasingly* severe strain on our social fabric. [The adverb modifies the adjective *severe*.]

Conjunctive adverbs establish adverb-like relationships between whole sentences. These words—*moreover, however, consequently, thus, therefore*, and so on—play a special role in linking ideas and sentences. (See 7a-9 and 19a-3.) Chapter 11 provides a detailed discussion of adjectives and adverbs. The following is a brief index to more information on adjectives and adverbs.

7 Pronouns

Pronouns substitute for nouns. The word that a pronoun refers to and renames is called its **antecedent.** Like a noun, a pronoun shows **number**—it can be singular or plural. Depending on its function in a sentence, a pronoun will change form—that is, its **case.** It will change from **subjective** to **objective** to **possessive.** The following examples show this change in case for the pronoun *he*, which in each instance is a substitute for the noun *Jake*.

antecedent — pronoun (subjective)

Jake reads a magazine. *He* reads a magazine.

antecedent — pronoun (objective)

The magazine was given to Jake. The magazine was given to *him*.

antecedent — pronoun (possessive)

Jake's subscription is running out. *His* subscription is running out.

There are eight classes of pronouns.

Personal pronouns (*I, me, you, us, his, hers*, etc.) refer to people and things.

When sugar dissolves in water, the sugar molecules break *their* close connection within the sugar crystal.

Relative pronouns (*who, whose, which, that*, etc.) begin dependent clauses (see 7e) and refer to people and things.

The presence of the sugar, *which* is now in solution, changes many of the properties of the water.

Demonstrative pronouns (*this*, *these*, *that*, *those*) point to the nouns they replace.

These changes involve the water's density, boiling point, and more.

Interrogative pronouns (*who*, *which*, *what*, *whose*, etc.) form questions.

What does boiling sugar water have to do with coating caramel apples?

Intensive pronouns (*herself*, *themselves*, and other compounds formed with *-self* or *-selves*) repeat and emphasize a noun or pronoun.

The sugar *itself* can be recovered from the water by the simple act of boiling.

Reflexive pronouns (*herself*, *themselves*, and other compounds formed with *-self* or *-selves*) rename—reflect back to—a preceding noun or pronoun.

The ease of recovery demonstrates that sugar molecules do not bind *themselves* strongly to water molecules.

Indefinite pronouns (*one*, *anyone*, *somebody*, *nobody*, *everybody*, etc.) refer to general, or nonspecific, persons or things.

Anyone who has stained a shirt with salad dressing knows that water will not dissolve oil.

Reciprocal pronouns (*one another*, *each other*) refer to the separate parts of a plural noun.

The many solvents available to chemists complement *one another.*

The following is a brief index to more information on pronouns.

Pronouns: agreement in person and number: 10a, b

Pronouns: case—subjective, objective, possessive: 8a–d

Pronouns: reference to antecedent: 14a–e

Pronouns: relative pronouns: 8f, 14e

---

8   Prepositions

A **preposition** links a noun (or word group substituting for a noun) to other words in a sentence. *In*, *at*, *of*, *for*, *on*, and *by* are all prepositions. Many common prepositions are shown in the following box. With the words that follow them, prepositions form **prepositional phrases,** which function as adjectives or adverbs. In the following sentence, arrows lead from the (three) prepositional phrases to the (three) words modified. Note that the middle prepositional phrase modifies the word *evolution* in the first prepositional phrase.

The theory *of evolution by natural selection* was proposed *in the 1850s.*

ESL NOTE Prepositions occur in a very wide variety of English constructions that are often highly idiomatic. They are often followed by a noun or pronoun in the objective form or case (see 8b-1 and 46c), thus forming a modifying prepositional phrase (see 7d-1).

The following is a brief index to more information on prepositions.

Common Prepositions
Single-word prepositions

about	beyond	off
above	by	on
across	concerning	onto
after	despite	out
against	down	outside
along	during	over
among	except	through
around	for	to
as	from	toward
before	in	under
behind	into	until
below	like	up
beneath	near	with
between	of	

Multiword prepositions

according to	contrary to	on account of
along with	except for	on top of
apart from	in addition to	outside of
as for	in back of	owing to
because of	in case of	with regard to
by means of	in spite of	with respect to

9   Conjunctions

Conjunctions join sentence elements or entire sentences in one of two ways: either by establishing a coordinate or *equal* relationship among joined parts or by establishing a subordinate or *unequal* relationship. Briefly, conjunctions are classified in four ways: as coordinating conjunctions, conjunctive adverbs, correlative conjunctions, and subordinating conjunctions.

Coordinating conjunctions join parallel elements within a sentence or join two or more sentences into a single sentence: *and, but, or, nor, for, so, yet.* (For uses of coordinating conjunctions see 10a-2, 3, 19a-1, and 25b.)

Infants only cry at birth, *but* within a few short years they speak in complete sentences.

Conjunctive adverbs create special logical relationships between the clauses or sentences joined: *however, therefore, thus, consequently,* etc. (For uses of conjunctive adverbs see 13b-4, 19a-3, and 26b.)

Infants can only cry at birth; *however,* within a few short years they can speak in complete sentences.

Correlative conjunctions are pairs of coordinating conjunctions that place extra emphasis on the relationship between the parts of the coordinated construction: *both/and, neither/nor, not only/but also,* etc. (For uses of correlative conjunctions see 10a-3.)

Three-year-olds *not only* speak in complete sentences *but also* possess vocabularies of hundreds or even thousands of words.

Subordinating conjunctions connect subordinate clauses to main clauses: *when, while, although, because, if, since, whereas,* etc. (For uses of subordinating conjunctions see 7e-1 and 19b-1.)

When children reach the age of three, they can usually carry on complete conversations with their peers and with adults.

10   Interjections

An **interjection** is an emphatic word or phrase. When it stands alone, it is frequently followed by an exclamation point. As part of a sentence, the interjection is usually set off by commas.

Oh, they're here.   Never!

11   Expletives

An **expletive** is a word that fills a slot left in a sentence that has been rearranged. *It* and *there* function as expletives—as filler words without meanings of their own—in the following examples.

Basic sentence   A sad fact is that too few Americans vote.
With expletive   It is a sad fact that too few Americans vote.
Basic sentence   Millions of people are not voting.
With expletive   There are millions of people not voting.

Expletives are used with the verb *be* in sentences with a delayed subject. Sentences with expletives can usually be rearranged back to their basic form. Try to delete expletives from your writing to achieve a spare, concise style (see Chapter 17).

EXERCISE 1

Place a slash (/) between the subject and predicate parts of the following sentences. Identify the simple subject and simple predicate of each sentence with the abbreviations "ss" and "sp." Circle prepositions.

>   ss   sp
> *Example:* The physics (of) particle behavior / is important (for) designing safe and efficient processing plants.

1. Vega, the hapless hit man of *Pulp Fiction*, brought new life to John Travolta's career.
2. The actor earned his second Oscar nomination for playing Vega.
3. The first, of course, came in 1977 for his breakthrough in *Saturday Night Fever.*
4. Between the poles of these two pictures, Travolta had gone from household name to all-but-employable.
5. But now Travolta is once again at the top of his game.

7b   Understanding basic sentence patterns

English has five basic patterns from which virtually all sentences are built. Each of the five patterns consists of a subject and a predicate. Depending on the sentence's structure, the predicate may contain a **direct object,** an **indirect object,** or a subject or object **complement.** The basic pattern diagrams that follow include definitions of these key terms and concepts.

	⌐ Predicate ⌐
Pattern 1:	Subject verb
	We *look.*

Subject   a noun or noun substitute, and any modifiers, that performs the main action of the sentence or is described by the sentence.

Predicate   a verb, and other words associated with it, that states the action undertaken by the subject or describes the subject's condition.

	⌐——— Predicate ———⌐
Pattern 2:	Subject verb (tr.) direct object
	Stories *excite* *the imagination.*

Direct object   a noun, or group of words substituting for a noun, that receives the action of a transitive verb (tr.). A direct object answers the question *What or who is acted upon?*

Pattern 3:

Predicate

Subject	verb (tr.)	indirect object	direct object
Stories	*offer*	*us*	*relief.*

Indirect object   a noun, or group of words substituting for a noun, that is indirectly affected by the action of a verb. Indirect objects typically follow transitive verbs such as *buy, bring, do, give, offer, teach, tell, play,* or *write.* The indirect object answers the question *To whom or for whom has the main action of this sentence occurred?*

Pattern 4:

Predicate

Subject	verb (tr.)	direct object	object complement
They	*make*	*us*	*tense.*

Object   an adjective or noun that completes the meaning of a direct
complement   object by renaming or describing it. Typically, object complements follow verbs such as *appoint, call, choose, consider, declare, elect, find, make, select,* or *show.*

Pattern 5:

Predicate

Subject	verb (linking)	subject complement
We	*are*	*readers.*

Subject   a noun or adjective that completes the meaning of a subject
complement   by renaming or describing it. Subject complements follow linking verbs such as *appear, feel, seem,* and *remain,* as well as all forms of *be.*

EXERCISE 2

Working with a topic of your choice, write a paragraph in which you use each of the five basic sentence patterns.

> *Example:* The curtain finally rose. [Sentence Pattern 1] The set was lavish. [Sentence Pattern 5] The actors wore period costumes. [Sentence Pattern 2] The set design gave the audience a feast for the eyes. [Sentence Pattern 3] The critics declared it an absolute smash. [Sentence Pattern 4]

7.2

7c   Expanding sentences with single-word modifiers

Principles of sentence expansion can be found at work in virtually any paragraph you read. The first technique for expanding sentences is to add modifiers. The nouns and verbs in the five basic sentence patterns can be modified by adjectives and adverbs.

1   Modifying nouns and verbs with adjectives and adverbs

Noun modified by adjective   A novel will engage an *active* imagination.
Verb modified by adverb   I read *thoroughly.*

Depending on its location, an adverb will change the meaning of a sentence or the rhythm. When placing an adverb, take care that it modifies the word you intend it to modify.

Shifted meaning	I am *only* moving my bed (that is, doing nothing more important than moving).
	I am moving *only* my bed (that is, no other furniture).
Shifted rhythm	*Sometimes,* stories can provide emotional relief.
	Stories *sometimes* can provide emotional relief.
	Stories can provide emotional relief *sometimes.*

A single-word adjective is often positioned directly before the noun it modifies, although writers make many variations on this pattern. When an adjective could describe more than one noun in a sentence, take particular care to place the adjective closest to the noun it modifies. See Chapter 15, on editing to correct misplaced modifiers, and 48b for the sequence of adjective modifiers in a typical English sentence.

A *good* story will excite a reader.   [*Story* is the word modified.]

A story will excite a *good* reader.   [*Reader* is the word modified.]

EXERCISE 3

Use single-word adjectives or adverbs to modify the nouns and verbs in the following sentences.

> *Example:* A man walked down a street.
>
> An *old* man walked *slowly* down a *tree-lined* street.

1. College tuition rises. [Sentence Pattern 1]
2. Students hold jobs. [Sentence Pattern 2]
3. The jobs give them wages. [Sentence Pattern 3]
4. Joblessness makes the students tense. [Sentence Pattern 4]
5. The wages are vital. [Sentence Pattern 5]

EXERCISE 4

Take the paragraph you wrote for Exercise 2, and modify its nouns and verbs as you have done in Exercise 3.

7d   Modifying and expanding sentences with phrases

A **phrase** does not express a complete thought, nor can it stand alone as a sentence. Phrases consist of nouns and the words associated with them, or verb forms not functioning as verbs (*verbals*) and the words associated with them. Phrases function in a sentence as modifiers and as objects, subjects, or complements. As such, they can be integrated into any of the five sentence patterns (see 7b) to add detail.

1   Adding prepositional phrases

A preposition together with its noun, called an *object*, forms a **prepositional phrase,** which functions in a sentence as a modifier.

Adjective   Stories can excite the imaginations *of young people.*
Adverb   Paul reads *in the evening.*

2   Adding verbals: Infinitive phrases

A verbal is a verb form functioning as a noun, adjective, or adverb. An infinitive—the base form of a verb—often is preceded by the word *to.* Infinitives function as adjectives, adverbs, or nouns, but they behave as verbs in that they can be modified with adverbs and followed by direct and indirect objects. Infinitives and the various words associated with them form **infinitive phrases.**

Noun subject   *To read in the evening* is a great pleasure.
Noun object   Some children start *to read at an early age.*
Adjective   Stories offer us a chance *to escape dull routines.*
Adverb   We read *to gain knowledge.*

3   Adding verbals: Gerund and participial phrases

When it appears without its helping verbs, the *-ing* form of the verb functions as a noun and is called a **gerund.** Without its helping verb, the present or past participle can function as an adjective. A noun or pronoun appearing before a gerund must be written in its possessive form.

Gerund   We did not approve of *Paul's* reading all night. [The gerund phrase functions as the object of the preposition *of.* A noun in the possessive case is used before the gerund.]
Faulty   We did not approve of *him* reading all night. [The pronoun before the gerund does not use the possessive case.]
Revised   We did not approve of *his* reading all night.

Modifying and Expanding Sentences with Phrases   **195**

4   Adding noun phrases

A **noun phrase** consists of a noun accompanied by all of its modifying words. A noun phrase can be quite lengthy, but it always functions as a single noun—as the subject of a sentence, as the object of a verb or preposition, or as a complement.

Subject   *Even horror stories with their gruesome endings* can delight readers.

Direct object A tale of horror will affect *anyone who is at all suggestible.*

Complement   Paul is *someone who likes to read horror stories.* [Subject complement]

5   Adding absolute phrases

Unlike other phrases, **absolute phrases** consist of a subject and an incomplete predicate. Absolute phrases modify entire sentences, not individual words. When you use an absolute phrase, set it off from your sentence with a comma or pair of commas (see Chapter 25). An absolute phrase is formed by deleting the linking verb *be* from a sentence.

Sentence   His hands were weak with exhaustion.

Absolute phrase   his hands weak with exhaustion

New sentence   His hands weak with exhaustion, Paul lifted the book off its shelf. [The phrase modifies the basic sentence, *Paul lifted. . . .*]

An absolute phrase may also be formed by changing the main verb of a sentence to its *-ing* form, without using an auxiliary.

Sentence   His hands trembled with exhaustion.

Absolute phrase   his hands trembling with exhaustion

New sentence   His hands trembling with exhaustion, Paul lifted the book off its shelf.

6   Adding appositive phrases

Appositive phrases rename nouns. The word *appositive* describes the positioning of the phrase *in apposition to*, or beside, the noun. Appositives are actually "clipped" sentences—the predicate part (minus the verb) of Sentence Pattern 5.

		Predicate	
Pattern 5:	Subject	verb (linking)	subject complement
	Paul	*is*	*an old college friend.*

| Appositive phrase | an old college friend |
| New sentence | Paul, an old college friend, is an avid reader. |

EXERCISE 5

In the sentences that follow, circle all single-word modifiers and underline all modifying phrases.

> *Example:* (Recently,) Stephen W. Hawking published a (popularized) version of his ideas about space and time.

- ■ *Recently* is an adverb and modifies the verb *published*.
- ■ *Popularized* is an adjective and modifies the noun *version*.
- ■ Two prepositional phrases—*of his ideas about space and time*—function as an adjective by modifying the noun *version*.
- ■ The second prepositional phrase, *about space and time*, functions as an adjective by modifying the object of the preceding phrase, *ideas*.

1. On a clear, moonless night, he says, the brightest objects in the sky are the planets nearest Earth.
2. Looking more closely, we can see that the stars near Earth appear to be fixed, but they are not.
3. To measure the distance of a star from Earth, scientists calculate the number of years it takes the star's light to reach us.
4. His calculations having proved it, Sir William Herschel confirmed that our galaxy (the Milky Way) forms a spiral.
5. We now know that our galaxy is only one of some hundred thousand million galaxies.
6. Each of those hundred thousand million galaxies contains a hundred thousand million stars.

WWW

7.3

7e Modifying and expanding sentences with dependent clauses

Weblink

http://www.writing.ucsb.edu/
faculty/behrens/ex_scomb.htm#A
*A sentence-combining self-quiz from the UC
Santa Barbara writing program.*

A **clause** is any grouping of words that has both a subject and a predicate. There are two types of clauses. An **independent** or **main clause** can stand alone as a sentence. Any sentence fitting one of the five structural patterns reviewed in 7b is an independent clause. A **dependent** or **subordinate clause** cannot stand alone as a sentence, because it is usually introduced either with a subordinating conjunction (e.g., *while*) or with a relative pronoun (e.g., *who*). There are three types of dependent clauses: adverb, adjective, and noun clauses.

1 Adding dependent adverb clauses

Dependent **adverb clauses** modify verbs, adjectives, and other adverbs. They begin with subordinating conjunctions and answer the question *when, how, where, how often, to what extent,* or *to what degree.* Placed at the head of a sentence, a subordinating conjunction makes that (independent) clause grammatically dependent on another. For example, when the subordinating conjunction *if* is placed at the head of a sentence, that sentence becomes grammatically dependent, unable to stand alone.

Main clause plus   *if* + Food is repeatedly frozen and thawed.
subordinating conjunction

Dependent clause   if food is repeatedly frozen and thawed

Although it consists of a subject and predicate, this last grouping of words is no longer a sentence. To make sense, this clause must be set in a dependent relationship with an independent clause.

If food is repeatedly frozen and thawed, it will spoil.

For guidance on punctuating sentences with dependent clauses, see 25a-1.

Subordinating Conjunctions and the Logical Relationships They Establish

To show condition: *if, even if, unless,* and *provided that*
To show contrast: *though, although, even though,* and *as if*
To show cause: *because* and *since*
To show time: *when, whenever, while, as, before, after, since, once,* and *until*
To show place: *where* and *wherever*
To show purpose: *so that, in order that,* and *that*

See 7a-9 for a discussion of conjunctions.

---

2 Adding dependent adjective clauses

Like adjectives, **adjective clauses** modify nouns. The clauses usually begin with the relative pronoun *which, that, who, whom,* or *whose.* The following shows an adjective clause modifying a subject.

People *who lived through the Depression of the 1930s* remember it well.

A country *that had prospered in the first two decades of the century* now saw massive unemployment and hardship.

For a discussion of when to use which relative pronoun, see 8f.

Noun clauses function exactly as single-word nouns do: as subjects, objects, complements, and appositives. Noun clauses are introduced with the pronoun *which, whichever, that, who, whoever, whom, whomever,* or *whose* or with the word *how, when, why, where, whether,* or *whatever.*

Subject	*That ozone holes have already caused blindness and skin cancer in grazing animals* suggests the need for immediate legislative action.
Object	Apparently, few inhabitants of populous northern cities are aware of *how the depletion of ozone in the upper atmosphere can harm living organisms—humans included.*
Complement	The looming danger that ozone depletion poses is *why researchers have sounded an alarm.*

EXERCISE 6

Combine each of the sentence pairs that follow by using a subordinating conjunction.

> *Example:* Competition in the job market is intense. Job seekers need to approach their task strategically.
>
> *Because* competition in the job market is intense, job seekers need to approach their task strategically.

1. Job seekers tend to deemphasize interpersonal skills. This is a poor strategy in a business climate that seeks those who can communicate effectively and work as team members.
2. Even in a high-tech world, people still have to eat. Many people are studying the culinary arts.
3. Parents are entering the workforce in increasing numbers. The need for child-care workers and preschool workers expands.
4. You should find a job that fulfills you personally. That love will eventually help your career in terms of dollars and cents.
5. A shortage of labor in entry-level construction jobs seems likely in the near future. The construction industry is offering training and making outreach efforts.

7.4

7f Classifying sentences

Sentences are classified by function and by structure.

I Functional definitions

There are four functional sentence types: statements, questions, exclamations, and commands.

- Statements, called **declarative** sentences, are by far the most common and make direct assertions about a subject.
- A question, or **interrogative** sentence, is formed either by inverting a sentence's usual word order (*She did sing./Did she sing?*) or by preceding the sentence with a word such as *who, whom, which, when, where, why,* or *how.*
- An exclamation, or **exclamatory** sentence, used rarely in academic writing, serves as a direct expression of a speaker's or writer's strong emotion.
- Commands, or **imperative** sentences, express an order or instruction addressed to a second person, with the pronoun *you* implied.

Declarative	The driver turned on the ignition.
Interrogative	Was the engine flooded?
Exclamatory	What an awful fire! How terrible!
Imperative	Put away your textbooks.

2   Structural definitions

There are four structural classes of sentences in English: simple, compound, complex, and compound-complex.

Each of the five basic sentence patterns discussed in 7b qualifies as a **simple sentence:** each has a single subject and a single predicate. The designation "simple" refers to a sentence's structure, not its content. A simple sentence, with all its modifying words and phrases, can be long.

> Vampires play a prominent role in two major works of literary criticism from the first half of this century—Mario Praz's *The Romantic Agony* and D. H. Lawrence's *Studies in Classical American Literature.* [This sentence consists of one subject, *vampires,* and one simple predicate, *play.*]

Compound sentences have two subjects and two predicates. They are created when two independent clauses are joined with a coordinating or correlative conjunction or with a conjunctive adverb. For details on how coordination can be used to create sentence emphasis, see 19a.

> The vampire casts no shadow and has no reflection, but he (or she) manifests prominent canine teeth. [The conjunction *but* joins two independent clauses.]

Complex sentences consist of an independent clause and one or more dependent clauses.

> Stoker's Dracula is dignified and still *until* he explodes into ravenous action. [The subordinating conjunction *until* signals a dependent adverb clause.]

Compound-complex sentences consist of at least two independent clauses and one subordinate, dependent clause.

Anne Rice's vampires seem to regard vampirism amorally, *and* their scruples about their predatory nature gradually subside *as* they become increasingly inhuman. [The coordinating conjunction *and* signals a compound sentence, and the subordinating conjunction *as* signals a dependent clause in a complex sentence.]

One way to maintain a reader's interest is to vary sentence types as well as sentence lengths. See Chapter 20 for suggestions for controlling sentence length and rhythm.

EXERCISE 7

Use the clauses and phrases provided to build up the core sentence. Add conjunctions when they are necessary to the logic of your expanded sentence.

> *Example:* Athol Fugard is a South African playwright. (a) plays confront difficulties (b) interracial relations (c) his troubled country
>
> Athol Fugard is a South African playwright whose plays confront the difficulties of interracial relations in his troubled country.

1. A common thread connects Fugard's work. (a) respect for humanity (b) search for human dignity (c) struggle to cultivate trust and hope in a demeaning world

2. Fugard's looks reflect his struggles. (a) tenacious (b) weathered

3. Fugard handwrites his plays. (a) in this computer age (b) with a tortoise-shell Parker pen (c) which include *A Lesson from Aloes, The Road to Mecca,* "*Master Harold*" . . . *and the Boys,* and *My Children, My Africa,* all successfully produced in America

4. South Africa is changing. (a) for Fugard there are signs (b) the freeing of Nelson Mandela (c) the lifting of the ban on the African National Congress (d) the government's willingness to negotiate

5. Fugard continued writing. (a) during the mid-1960s (b) he staged classic plays with the Serpent players (c) the country's first nonwhite theater troupe

CHAPTER 8

Case in Nouns and Pronouns

Weblink

http://www.uottawa.ca/academic/
arts/writcent/hypergrammar/
prntrcky.html

Explanations of some tricky points of pronoun usage.

The primary decision you will need to make in using nouns and pronouns is which *case* to use with these words. The term **case** refers to a noun's or a pronoun's change in form, depending on its function in a sentence. Such decisions are more troublesome with pronouns than with nouns because nouns change form only to show possession, whereas pronouns change form both to show possession and to show a change in function from subject to object.

CRITICAL DECISIONS

Determining the Function of Personal Pronouns

The personal pronouns are *I, we, you, he, she, it,* and *they,* along with their other forms. As personal pronouns (except *you* and *it*) change their function in a sentence, they also change their form. (For example: *I* am happy. Pass *me* the salad.) The relative pronouns *who* and *whoever* also change form to *whom* and *whomever* when their function changes from subject to object. You need to be alert to the function of these pronouns in order to decide whether to use the subjective or the objective case. Most of this chapter is devoted to personal and relative pronouns.

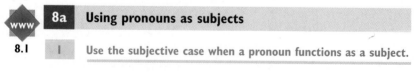

8a | **Using pronouns as subjects**

www

8.1 | Use the subjective case when a pronoun functions as a subject.

She speaks forcefully.

The executive officers—and only *they*—can meet here.

Subject of an independent clause	In September 1908, Orville Wright began demonstration flights of the Wright brothers' "Signal Corps Flyer"; *he* invited Thomas Selfridge to be a passenger.
Subject of a dependent clause	When *they* attempted a fourth circuit of the parade grounds, the Flyer's right propeller hit a bracing wire and cracked.
Appositive that renames a subject	Thomas Selfridge—*he* alone—bears the grim distinction of being the first person to be killed in the crash of a powered airplane.

Pronouns Used as Subjects		
	Singular	*Plural*
1st person	I	we
2nd person	you	you
3rd person	he, she, it	they

2   Use the subjective case for pronouns following the linking verb *be*.

This is *she*.   These are *they*.   It is *I*.

The linking verb *be* in a sentence serves as a grammatical "equals" sign (see 11d). It links the subject of the sentence to a completing or "complement" word that is identical to the subject. When pronouns are involved in this equation, they take the subjective form.

Bush *was* President.   It was *he*, the president, who spoke.

In nonstandard or informal usage it is fairly common to hear a linking-verb construction using an objective form, as in "It's me" or "This is her." But in academic English these constructions should be revised using a subjective pronoun that maintains sentence logic and consistency: "It's I" and "This is she." If such a construct sounds stilted, the best remedy is to rewrite, as in "This is Ellen," or "Here she is."

8b   Using pronouns as objects

I   Use the objective form for pronouns functioning as objects.

The governor handed *her* the report.   The job appealed to *me*.
We enjoyed taking *them* to dinner.

www
8.2

Pronouns functioning as the object of a preposition, as the object or indirect object of a verb, or as the object of a verbal take the objective form.

Spotlight on Common Errors—CASE FORMS

These are the errors most commonly associated with a pronoun's case. For full explanations and suggested revisions, follow the cross-references to chapter sections.

CASE FORM ERRORS occur when writers misunderstand a pronoun's function in a sentence as a subject, object, or indicator of possession.

When a noun or an indefinite pronoun (such as *one*, *anyone*, *somebody*) shows possession, use an apostrophe (see 27a-b).

Faulty	**Revised**
This is Alberts signature.	This is Albert's signature.
The families decision was final.	The family's decision was final.
Somebodies book is here.	Somebody's book is here.
This is anyones guess.	This is anyone's guess.

A personal pronoun that shows possession (such as *his*, *her*, *mine*, *ours*) uses NO apostrophe (see 8c-1 and 27a-2).

Faulty	**Revised**
This coat is her's.	This coat is hers. (This is her coat.)
Give the cat it's food.	Give the cat its food.
These coats are their's.	These coats are theirs. (These are their coats.)
Your's are the first hands to touch this.	Yours are the first hands to touch this. (Your hands are the first hands to touch this.)

After a form of the verb *be* (*is*, *are*, *was*, *were*), use a pronoun's subjective form (*I*, *you*, *he*, *she*, *we*, *they*) or its possessive form (*mine*, *yours*, *his*, *hers*, *theirs*, *ours*) with no apostrophe (see 8a-2 and 8c-1).

Faulty	**Revised**
This is her. This is him.	This is *she*. This is *he*.
Is that her? It is me.	Is that *she*? It is *I*.
This is our's. That is her's.	This is *ours*. That is *hers*.

> **When a personal pronoun (such as *I, me, you, he, she, it*) follows the word *and*, choose the pronoun's form as if the pronoun were alone in the sentence (see 8d and 8b-1).**

Faulty

Sally and me went to the movies.

She and me went.
Her and me went.

Tom went with Sally and I.

It's a secret between you and I.

That's between he and Sally.

Revised

Sally and *I* went to the movies.
[Test: I went to the movies alone.]

She and *I* went.
[Test: She went. I went.]

Tom went with Sally and *me*.
[Test: Tom went with me.]

It's a secret between you and *me*.
[Test: It's a secret between me and a friend.]

That's between *him* and Sally.
[Test: That's between him and a friend.]

> **Use *its* to show possession; use *it's* ONLY for a contraction of *it is* (see 27a-2).**

Faulty

A dog hates it's fleas.
Its raining.

Revised

A dog hates *its* fleas.
It's raining. (It is raining.)

> **For a contraction with the verb *be* (*is, are*), use an apostrophe (see 27a-2).**

Faulty

Its a difficult position.

Their coming home.

There coming home.

Shes home.
Your home.
Whos there?

Revised

It's a difficult position.
(It is a difficult position.)

They're coming home.
(They are coming home.)

They're coming home.
(They are coming home.)

She's home. (She is home.)
You're home. (You are home.)
Who's there? (Who is there?)

Pronouns Used as Objects		
	Singular	Plural
1st person	me	us
2nd person	you	you
3rd person	him, her, it	them

Object or indirect object of verb (see 7b)

Aerospace engineer Lonnie Johnson has been tinkering as an inventor almost all his life. A robot he created as a high school senior in 1968 won *him* first prize in a college science fair. [*Him* is the indirect object of *won*.]

Object of preposition (see 7d-1)

While Johnson was working on a powerful hydraulic cooling device in 1982, it occurred to *him* that his machine could be turned into a new kind of toy water gun. [*Him* is the object of the preposition *to*.]

Appositive that renames the object (see 7d-6)

The inventor created a prototype for his daughter and discovered it was a hit with many children, *both her and neighborhood friends alike*. [The appositive phrase *both her and neighborhood friends alike* renames and clarifies *many children*, the object of the preposition *with*. The pronoun in the appositive must be in the objective case: *her*.]

Object of verbal (see 7a-4)

Thus Johnson created the powerful Super Soaker water gun, earning *him* toy industry immortality. [*Him* is the indirect object of the present participle—or verbal—*earning*.]

> **2** Use the objective form for pronouns functioning as the subject of an infinitive.

Study enabled *us* to reach the goal.

When a pronoun appears between a verb and an infinitive, it takes the objective form. In this position, the pronoun is called the subject of the infinitive.

With infinitive   Babe Ruth's 60 home runs in 1927 helped *him* to reach a level of stardom unmatched by other athletes of his era. [The objective-form pronoun appears between the verb *helped* and the infinitive *to reach*.]

Babe Ruth's home runs helped *him* reach stardom. [The subject of the infinitive *reach* uses the objective form, *him*.]

8c Using nouns and pronouns in the possessive case

Use a possessive noun or pronoun before a noun to indicate ownership of that noun (or noun substitute).

Eleanor Roosevelt gave the Civil Works Administration *her* enthusiastic support for hiring 100,000 women by the end of 1933.

ESL NOTE English nouns are made possessive either with the possessive case (*a woman's voice*) or with the noun as object of the preposition *of* (*voice of a woman*). With some inanimate nouns the prepositional form is standard, and the possessive case form is seldom used (NOT *a house's color* BUT *color of a house*). See 46c-1.

Possessive Forms of Pronouns		
	Singular	Plural
1st person	my, mine	our, ours
2nd person	your, yours	your, yours
3rd person	his, her, hers, its	their, theirs

1 Certain possessive pronouns are used as subjects or subject complements to indicate possession.

Yours are the first hands to touch this. These are *theirs*.

The possessive pronouns *mine, ours, yours, his, hers*, and *theirs* are used in place of a noun as subjects or subject complements.

Ours is a country of opportunity for both men and women, Eleanor Roosevelt argued. This opportunity is *ours*. (*mine, yours, his, hers, theirs*)

2 Use a possessive noun or pronoun before a gerund to indicate possession.

The group argued for *Lynette's* getting the new job.

Be careful not to mistake a gerund for a participle, which has the same *-ing* form but functions as an adjective. A participle is often preceded by an objective pronoun.

Participle with objective pronoun	Sir Laurence Olivier's popularity kept *him acting* in film until shortly before his death. [*Him*, an objective pronoun, is modified by the participle *acting*.]
Gerund with possessive pronoun	Critics admired *his acting* from Olivier's earliest stage appearances.

Confusion between an *-ing* word's function—as a gerund or as a participle—can lead to errors.

Faulty Hard work resulted in *them* getting government jobs. [*Getting* is mistakenly treated as a participle and is incorrectly preceded by an objective pronoun.]

Revised Hard work resulted in *their* getting government jobs. [*Their* indicates possession of the gerund *getting government jobs*.]

EXERCISE 1

Based on your analysis of each of the following sentences, fill in the blanks with an appropriate subjective, objective, or possessive pronoun: *I/we, you, he/she/it/they; me/us, you, him/her/it/them; my/mine/our/ours, your/yours, his/her/hers/its/their/theirs.*

> **Example:** _____ changing costumes, mid-performance, amused the audience.
>
> *Changing costumes* is a gerund phrase and takes a possessive pronoun. *His* (or *her*) changing costumes, mid-performance, amused the audience.

1. Delegates to the convention watched _____ changing positions on important issues and deserted the candidacy.
2. Delegates wanted _____ to remain steadier under challenges from contenders.
3. After _____ left the convention, the delegates searched for a restaurant.
4. The newly elected president arrived and said the delegates had worked so effectively that she wanted to give _____ a banquet.
5. "_____ is an organization that recognizes honest effort," the president said.

EXERCISE 2

Complete the sentences that follow by filling in the blanks with pronouns or nouns of the appropriate form.

1. Presenting the newly discovered evidence—the intruder's gloves—to the district attorney, the chief inspector said: "These are _____ ."
2. It is _____ who has won.
3. It is _____ who have won.
4. This is _____ contest.
5. Mark answered the phone and, listening to a person asking for him, said: "Yes, this is _____ ."

8d In a compound construction, use pronouns in the objective or subjective form according to their function in the sentence.

Sally and *I* went to the movies. Tom went with Sally and *me*.

The coordinating conjunction *and* can create a compound construction—a doubled subject or object. These can sometimes mask how a pronoun functions in a sentence. When you have difficulty choosing between a subjective or objective pronoun in a compound construction, try this test: *Create a simplified sentence by dropping out the compound.* Then *try choosing the pronoun.* With the compound gone in the simpler construction, you should be able to tell whether the pronoun operates as a subject or an object.

Compound subject

Pierre and Marie Curie worked collaboratively; together Marie and *he* discovered polonium and radium. [The subjective pronoun forms the second part of a compound subject.]

Confusing   Marie and *him* received the Nobel Prize in physics in 1903. [The pronoun subject is mistakenly put in the objective form.]

Simplified   *He* received the Nobel Prize in 1903. [In the simplified construction, the need for the subjective pronoun is clear.]

Revised   Marie and *he* received the Nobel Prize in 1903.

Compound object

The 1903 Nobel Prize in physics was awarded to Pierre and *her* for their work on radioactivity. [The objective pronoun is the object of a preposition in a compound construction.]

Confusing   The Nobel Prize was presented to Pierre and *she* in 1903. [In this construction, the pronoun functions as part of the preposition's compound object. Mistakenly, the pronoun is made subjective.]

Simplified   The Nobel Prize was presented to *her* in 1903.

Revised   The Nobel Prize was presented to Pierre and *her* in 1903.

8e Pronouns paired with a noun take the same case as the noun.

For first-person plural pronouns (*we, us*) paired with a noun, use the same case as the noun.

We first-year students face important challenges.

Transitions can be challenging for *us* first-year students.

The first-person plural pronoun *we* or *us* is sometimes placed before a plural noun to help establish the identity of the noun. Use the subjective-case *we* when the pronoun is paired with a subject or complement. Use the objective-case *us* when the pronoun is paired with an object of a verb, verbal, or preposition. To test for the correct pronoun, simplify the sentence and *drop out* the paired noun. In the simpler sentence, you should be able to determine which pronoun case is required.

Nonstandard	*Us* strikers demand compensation. [*Strikers* is the subject of the sentence, and the pronoun paired with it should be the subjective-case *we*.]
Simplified	*We* . . . demand compensation. [The need for the subjective-case *we* is now clear.]
Revised	*We* strikers demand compensation.
Nonstandard	Give *we* strikers a fair share. [*Strikers* is the indirect object of the verb *give*, and the pronoun paired with it should be the objective-case *us*.]
Simplified	Give *us* . . . a fair share. [The need for the objective-case *us* is now clear.]
Revised	Give *us* strikers a fair share.

In an appositive, a pronoun's case should match the case of the noun it renames.

The executive officers—and only *they*—can attend. [Renamed subject]

Give this report to Linda—*her* and no one else. [Renamed object]

Pronouns may occur in an **appositive**—a word or phrase that identifies or renames a noun. If so, the pronoun must take the same case as the noun being renamed. Once again, you can test for pronoun choice by simplifying the sentence: *Drop the noun being renamed out of the sentence.* The simpler sentence that remains will usually reveal what pronoun case is required.

Renamed object	The inventor created a prototype for his daughter and discovered it was a hit with many children, both *her* and neighborhood friends alike.
Confusing	The prototype was a hit with many children, both *she* and neighborhood friends.
Simplified	The prototype was a hit with *her* and neighborhood friends.

Choose the appropriate form of the pronouns *whose*, *who*, *whom*, *whoever*, and *whomever* depending on the pronoun's function.

The basic forms of the relative pronouns *whose, who, whom, whoever,* and *whomever* are shown in the following table. A relative pronoun's form depends on its function within its own clause.

Forms of the Relative Pronoun Who(m)/Who(m)ever		
Subjective	*Objective*	*Possessive*
who	whom	whose
whoever	whomever	—

1 In a question, choose a subjective, objective, or possessive form of *who(m)* or *who(m)ever* according to the pronoun's function.

Who is going?   To *whom* are you writing?   *Whose* birthday is it?

To test the correct choice for these pronouns at the beginning of a question, mentally *answer* the question, substituting the personal pronouns *I/me, we/us, he/him,* or *she/her* for *the relative pronoun.* Your choice of the subjective or objective form in the answer sentence will likely be quite clear, and it will be the same choice to make for the form of *who(m)* or *who(m)ever.*

Question (Who/whom) are you addressing?
Answer You are addressing (he/*him*). [The choice of the objective form is clear.]
Revised *Whom* are you addressing? [The objective form is correct.]

Question For (who/whom) are you writing?
Answer You are writing for (she/*her*). [The choice of the objective form is clear.]
Revised For *whom* are you writing? [The objective form is correct.]

The possessive form *whose* can begin a question if the pronoun shows possession of the noun that immediately follows. To determine whether a possessive pronoun is correct for a sentence, replace the initial pronoun in the question with *what,* and then mentally answer that question. If the answer requires that you use *his, her, their,* or *its* in place of the relative pronoun, then choose the possessive form, *whose.*

Question What name goes on the envelope?
Answer *Her* name goes on the envelope.
Possessive *Whose* name goes on the envelope?

2   In a dependent clause, choose the subjective, objective, or possessive form of *who(m)* or *who(m)ever* according to the pronoun's function within the clause.

Henry Taylor, *who* writes poems, lives in Virginia. Taylor, *whom* critics have praised, has a new book. The poet, *whose* book won a prize, rides horses.

To choose the correct case for a relative pronoun in a dependent clause, eliminate the main clause temporarily. Consider the pronoun's function *only* in the dependent clause. When deciding between the subjective or objective forms, apply the following tests.

Determine whether the relative pronoun functions as the subject of a dependent clause.

If the relative pronoun is followed immediately by a verb, you should probably use the subjective-case *who* or *whoever*. To be sure that the choice of pronouns is correct, detach the dependent clause. Then substitute the word *I, we, you, he,* or *she* for *who* or *whoever*. Does this yield a legitimate sentence? If so, the choice of the subjective case is correct.

Subjective	Your request will be of concern to (whoever/whomever) gets it.
Simplified	(Whoever/whomever) gets it. [*He* gets it. (Legitimate sentence)]
Revised	Your request will be of concern to *whoever* gets it.

Determine whether the relative pronoun functions as an object in the dependent clause.

If the relative pronoun is followed immediately by a noun or by the pronoun *I, we, you, he, she, few, some, many, most, it,* or *they,* you should probably use the objective-case *whom* or *whomever*. To be sure of the choice, detach the dependent clause. Then rearrange the clause into normal word order, and substitute the word *him, her,* or *them* for the relative pronoun. If one of these substituted pronouns fits into the sentence as an object of a verb, verbal, or preposition, then the choice of the objective-case *whom* or *whomever* is correct.

Objective	Please send this to (whoever/whomever) it might interest.
Simplified	It might interest (whoever/whomever). [It might interest *them*. (*Them* is the object of the verb.)]
Revised	Please send this to *whomever* it might interest.

Determine whether the relative pronoun needs to show possession.

If the relative pronoun beginning a dependent clause needs to show possession, use the possessive-case *whose*. Confirm the choice by substituting the word *his, her, their,* or *its* for the relative pronoun. A sentence should result when the dependent clause is considered by itself.

Possessive   Daly, *whose* theories on urban wildlife have generated heated discussion, believes that we can profit by finding nature in our cities. [The possessive-case *his* yields a sentence: "*His* theories on urban wildlife . . ."]

8g   **Choose the case of a pronoun in the second part of a comparison depending on the meaning intended.**

I studied Keats more than *him* (more than I studied Arnold—him).

I studied Keats more than *she* (more than Margo—she—studied Keats).

The words *than* and *as* create a comparison.

Calcutta is more densely populated *than* New York.

The new magneto engines are as efficient *as* traditional combustion engines.

For brevity's sake, writers and speakers often omit the second part of a comparison. Written in their complete form, the preceding examples would read as follows.

Calcutta is more densely populated than New York is densely populated.

The new magneto engines are as efficient as traditional combustion engines are efficient.

A comparison links two complete clauses. The brief form of a comparison is its "clipped" form; the fully expressed comparison, its "complete" form. When you compare people and use pronouns in the second part of your comparison, be sure to express your exact meaning.

At times, the pronoun in the second part of a comparison will take the place of a noun functioning as a subject. In this case, use the subjective form: *he, she, we.*

Complete   Some think that Prospero is a more perplexing figure than Hamlet is perplexing. [*Hamlet* functions as a subject in the second part of the comparison. A pronoun replacement for *Hamlet* would take the subjective form.]

Complete   Some think that Prospero is a more perplexing figure than *he* is perplexing.

Clipped   Some think that Prospero is a more perplexing figure than *he.*

At times, the pronoun in the second part of a comparison will take the place of a noun functioning as an object. In this case, use the objective form: *him, her, us.*

Complete   Many critics are more intrigued by Prospero than they are intrigued by Hamlet. [*Hamlet* functions as the object of the preposition *by* in the second part of the comparison. A pronoun replacement for *Hamlet* would take the objective form.]

Complete   Many critics are more intrigued by Prospero than they are intrigued by *him.*

Clipped   Many critics are more intrigued by Prospero than by *him.*

Avoid "clipping" the second part of a comparison unless all its parts are obvious. If you do clip the comparison, mentally recreate the full comparison to determine the function of the noun your pronoun is replacing. When that noun functions as a subject, use pronouns in the subjective form. When that noun functions as an object, use pronouns in the objective form.

CRITICAL DECISIONS

Applying a Test for *who* and *whom*

In a clause the relative pronouns *who* and *whom* take the place of nouns (or pronouns) that function as subjects or objects. Choosing the correct relative pronoun requires that you see that pronoun in relation to the words immediately following. You must examine the broader context of the clause in which the pronoun is located. Two questions should help you to choose between *who* and *whom* correctly.

■ **Is the relative pronoun followed by a verb?**

—"Yes": choose the subjective-case *who* or *whoever.*
A relative pronoun followed by a verb indicates the pronoun occupies the subject position of the clause. To confirm this choice, substitute *I, we, you, he,* or *she* for the pronoun.

Cycler Lance Armstrong, *who* survived a serious bout with cancer, won his third Tour de France in 2001. [*Who* is followed by a verb, and when it is converted to *he* it yields a sentence: "*He* survived a bout with cancer."]

—"No": choose the objective-case *whom* or *whomever.* See the next test.

■ **Is the relative pronoun followed by a noun or by any of these pronouns: *I, we, you, he, she, few, some, many, most, it, they*?**

—"Yes": choose the objective-case *whom* or *whomever*.

A relative pronoun followed by a noun or one of the listed pronouns indicates that the normal order of the clause (subject-verb-object) has been rearranged, suggesting the need for a pronoun in its objective form. To confirm your choice of *whom* or *whomever*, rearrange the pronoun and the words immediately following. Then substitute *him, her,* or *them* for the relative pronoun.

Armstrong, *whom* most analysts consider one of the greatest bike racers ever, clocked the third fastest tour in the history of the race. [*Whom* is followed by *most*, and when it is converted to *him* it yields a sentence: "Most analysts consider *him*. . . ."]

EXERCISE 3

In the following sentences, correct the usage of the italicized pronouns. If a pronoun choice is correct, circle the pronoun.

8.4

> *Example:* Anne told me it was Simon's fault; but between you and *I*, she's as much to blame as *him*.
>
> Anne told me it was Simon's fault; but between you and *me*, she's as much to blame as *he*. [Pronouns that follow a preposition must be objective case: thus, between you and me. The second part of the comparison requires a subjective-case pronoun: She is to blame as much as *he is to blame*.]

1. It was *her* who wanted to leave early.
2. *She* is a better manager than *he*.
3. "*Who* do you want to reach?" asked the operator.
4. *He* is an employee in *whom* the firm has placed great trust.
5. Eric prepared a meal for both *you* and *he*.
6. *You* and *he* have been out of town for two months.
7. Maintaining discipline in the classroom is a problem *us* teachers face.
8. Maintaining discipline in the classroom is a problem facing *us* teachers.
9. *Whoever* drew the shortest straw would take our complaints to the principal.
10. Beth, *who* drew the shortest straw, cheerfully accepted her unpleasant task.
11. *She* being so willing and pleasant was an inspiration to *us* all.

CHAPTER **9**

Verbs

Weblink

http://cctc2.commnet.edu/grammar/
verbs.html

*A resource on verbs, including quizzes and
graphics.*

The decisions you make about verb forms will convey three important messages that are the focus of this chapter: *tense*—an indication of when the action or state of being described in your sentence occurred; *voice*—your judgment about the relative importance of the actor versus the object acted on in your sentence; and *mood*—your judgment as to whether a statement is a fact, a command, or an unreal or hypothetical condition contrary to fact.

CRITICAL DECISIONS

Making Other Decisions about Verbs

Although this chapter focuses on decisions about tense, voice, and mood, using verbs effectively requires care in other areas as well. For example, you must make sure that verbs agree with their subjects (see pages 242–251) and that verbs are near enough to their subjects and objects so that readers don't get confused (see Section 15e). You also need to choose verbs that are precise and that lend vigor to your writing. (See 17b.)

VERB FORMS

9a Using the principal parts of regular verbs consistently

Weblink

http://www.uottawa.ca/academic/arts/
writcent/hypergrammar/grammar.html

*A "HyperGrammar" from the University of
Ottawa, with an extensive section on verbs.*

All English verbs, other than *be*, have two basic forms and three principal parts: base form, present tense (*-s* form), past tense, past participle, and present participle.

		The Principal Parts of Regular Verbs		
Base form	Present tense (-s form)	Past tense	Past participle	Present participle
share	shares	shared	shared	sharing
start	starts	started	started	starting
climb	climbs	climbed	climbed	climbing

Most verbs are **regular** in that they follow the simple, predictable pattern shown in the box, in which the past tense and past participle are identical. (For regular verbs, only base forms appear in most dictionaries.)

1   Recognizing the forms of regular verbs

Alison *walks* to the theater.   Yesterday, she *walked* there.

She *has walked* often.   She *is walking* there now.

Base form and present tense (-s form)

The **base** (or infinitive) **form** of a verb—often called its **dictionary form**—is the base from which all changes are made. For plural nouns or for the personal pronouns *I, we, you,* or *they,* use the base form of a verb with *no* ending when the action of a verb is present.

Alaska's Pacific mountains *create* a region of high peaks and broad valleys.

Use the **-s form** of a verb (creates, tries, loves) with third-person, singular subjects when an action is in the present. A verb's -s form (add -s or -es to a verb) is used in three instances: with the personal pronouns *he, she,* or *it;* with any noun that can be replaced by these pronouns; and with a number of indefinite pronouns (such as *something* or *no one*) that are often considered singular.

Alaska's north slope *consists* of plateaus and coastal regions.

Difficulties with subject–verb agreement occur when a writer is unsure whether to use a verb's base form or -s form in a sentence. For a discussion of subject–verb agreement, see Chapter 10.

Past-tense form

The **past tense** of a verb indicates that an action has been completed in the past. The regular verbs follow a predictable pattern in forming the past tense by taking the suffix -ed or -d.

Secretary of State William H. Seward *arranged* for the purchase of Alaska.

Using the Principal Parts of Regular Verbs Consistently   **217**

Two participle forms

For regular verbs, the form of the **past participle** is identical to that of the past tense. A verb's past participle is used in three ways.

- Paired with *has* or *have*, the past participle functions as a main verb.
- Paired with *be*, the past participle forms a passive construction.
- Paired with a noun or pronoun, the past participle functions as an adjective.

> The Crimean War *had depleted* [main verb] the tsar's treasury. With the treasury *depleted* [adjective], the tsar needed to raise money. Selling land to fill the treasury *was considered* [passive construction] a devil's bargain by some.

ESL NOTE   Both past and present participles have uses as adjective modifiers, usually placed before the nouns or pronouns modified—as in *a confused speaker* or *a confusing speaker*. Note that while the past and present participles from this verb are related in meaning, they work in opposite directions on the word modified (see 48a-1).

The **present participle,** the *-ing* form of the verb, has three uses.

- It functions as a main verb of a sentence and shows continuing action when paired with a form of *be (am, are, is, was, were).*
- It functions as an adjective when paired with a noun or pronoun.
- It functions as a noun, in which case it is called a *gerund* (see 7a).

> The *decimating* [gerund] of seal herds *was proceeding* [main verb] at an *alarming* [adjective] rate.

ESL NOTE   The role of a gerund in a sentence is determined by the verb being used. Certain verbs pair idiomatically with gerunds, as in *go swimming* or *enjoy swimming* (see 47e-2). Gerunds can be objects of certain prepositions that are idiomatically determined by the preceding verb: *I have reasons for coming* versus *I decided on walking.* Certain other verbs are paired idiomatically with the other verbal noun form, the infinitive (see 47e-2).

2   Revising nonstandard verb forms by using standard *-s* and *-ed* forms

| Nonstandard | He walk home. |
| Revised | He walked home. |

In rapid conversation, many people skip over *-s* and *-ed* endings. In some dialects the base (or infinitive) form of the verb is used in place of verbs with *-s* and *-ed* endings. Writers of standard academic English, however, need to observe the regular forms.

Nonstandard	She was *ask* to read this assignment. She *like* to stay up late, and she still *be* wide awake.
Revised	She was *asked* to read it. She *likes* to stay up late, and she *is* still wide awake. [Base forms have been replaced by standard verb forms with *-s* and *-ed* endings.]

Rapid speech often skips or "swallows" an *-ed* ending when it forms an "st" sound, as in two common expressions, *used to* (meaning *accustomed to*) and *supposed to* (meaning *expected to*). Writers must be especially careful to supply the standard forms.

Nonstandard	We were *suppose to* be home early, but we are *use to* walking slowly.
Revised	We were *supposed to* be home early, but we are *used to* walking slowly.

The same speech patterns may also swallow final *-ed* endings in common modifiers (adjectives in past participle form) such as *prejudiced* or *iced*. These often need attention in proofreading.

Nonstandard	They were *prejudice* against drinking *ice* tea.
Revised	They were *prejudiced* against drinking *iced* tea.

9b Learning the forms of irregular verbs

An irregular verb forms its past tense and past participle by altering the spelling of the base verb, as in *build/built*. A dictionary entry will show you when a verb is irregular.

Be

The most frequently used verb in our language, *be*, is also the only verb with more than five forms. It functions both as the main verb in a sentence and as a frequently used auxiliary verb (see 9c and 7a-3). The eight forms of *be* are shown in the box.

The Principal Parts of *be*		
Base form	Present tense	Past tense
(to) be	he, she, it *is*	he, she, it *was*
	I *am*	I *was*
	we, you, they *are*	we, you, they *were*
	Past participle	Present participle
	been	*being*

Spotlight on Common Errors—VERBS

These are errors most commonly associated with verb use. For full explanations and suggested revisions, follow the cross-references to chapter sections.

TENSE ERRORS: Keep clear the time relationships among two or more verbs in closely linked clauses or sentences.

> **If you refer to *past events occurring at roughly the same time*, use past-tense verbs (see 9f).**

Faulty

Tom *had traveled* where jobs *presented* themselves. [past perfect/past]

Tom *traveled* where jobs *had presented* themselves. [past/past perfect]

[Different tenses wrongly suggest the events happened at different times.]

Revised

   past event   past event

Tom *traveled* where jobs *presented* themselves. [past/past]

[The sentence refers to events that occurred at the same time.]

> **If you refer to *past events occurring one before the other*, use the past tense for the more recent event and the past perfect for the earlier event.**

Faulty

I *remembered* Mrs. Smith, who *showed* me kindness. [past/past]

[The tenses wrongly suggest that actions occurred at the same time.]

Revised

   later event   earlier event

I *remembered* Mrs. Smith, who *had shown* me kindness. [past/past perfect]

[Mrs. Smith's "showing" occurred before the remembering.]

BUT if a key word (such as *before* or *after*) establishes a clear time relation, then the past perfect form of the verb is not used.

earlier event   later event

I *was* unable to follow current events, *before* Mrs. Smith *showed* me how to read. [past/past]

> **Avoid tense shifts between closely linked sentences (see 16b).**

Faulty tense shift

The problem started when Fred *forgot* his appointment. Today he *comes* in late again. [past/present]

Revised

The problem started when Fred *forgot* his appointment. Today he *came* in late again. [All action is in the past tense.]

ERRORS OF VERB FORM occur when writers confuse regular verbs with irregular verbs, the moods of verbs, and transitive verbs such as *lay* with intransitive verbs such as *lie*.

> **Regular/irregular: Know whether a verb is regular or irregular (see 9b).**

Faulty	**Revised**
I begun the story.	I *began* the story.
I had drank three full glasses.	I *had drunk* three full glasses.

> **Mood: When writing about an event that is unreal or hypothetical, use a verb's subjunctive forms. Expressions such as *recommend*, *suggest*, and *it is important* signal an unreal or hypothetical event (see 9h).**

Faulty	**Revised**
I recommend that Sarah builds a playhouse.	I recommend that Sarah *build* a playhouse.

In sentences expressing unreal conditions and beginning with *if*, use *were* in the first part of the sentence and *would* as a helping verb in the second part (see 9h).

Faulty	**Revised**
If it was any colder, the pipes will freeze.	*If it were* any colder, the pipes *would freeze.*

> **Transitive/intransitive: Use a transitive verb (*set, lay, raise*) to show an action transferred from an actor to an object. Use an intransitive verb (*sit, lie, rise*) to limit action to the subject (see 9d).**

Faulty	**Revised**
Sit the books on the table.	*Set* the books on the table. [Transitive]
It hurts only when I set.	It hurts only when I *sit*. [Intransitive]
I think I'll lay down.	I think I'll *lie* down. [Intransitive]
Lie the blanket in the corner.	*Lay* the blanket in the corner.[Transitive]

The forms of *lie* and *lay* are particularly tricky. (See pages 225–226.)

Faulty	**Revised**
Yesterday, I laid down to rest.	Yesterday, I *lay* down to rest.
I had lain the book on the table.	I had *laid* the book on the table.

The following box contains the principal parts for a partial list of irregular verbs. (See the *Handbook* Web site for an expanded list.) Remember that the past participle is the form of the verb used with the auxiliaries *has* and *have*. Without the auxiliary, it functions as an adjective.

Some Irregular Verb Forms

Base form	Past tense	Past participle
become	became	become
begin	began	begun
break	broke	broken
bring	brought	brought
catch	caught	caught
cut	cut	cut
dig	dug	dug
dive	dove, dived	dived
do (does)	did	done
fight	fought	fought
find	found	found
forbid	forbade, forbad	forbidden *or* forbid
give	gave	given
have (has)	had	had
know	knew	known
leave	left	left
lose	lost	lost
prove	proved	proved *or* proven
read	read	read
ride	rode	ridden
ring	rang	rung
sing	sang	sung
sink	sank	sunk
teach	taught	taught
tear	tore	torn
wake	woke, waked	waked, woken
write	wrote	written

9c Using auxiliary verbs

An **auxiliary** (or helping) **verb** is combined with the base form of a verb or the present or past participle form to establish tense, mood, and voice in a sentence. This combination of verbs creates a **verb phrase.** The most frequently used auxiliaries are *be, have,* and *do.*

■ *Be* functions as an auxiliary when it combines with the *-ing* form of a verb to create the progressive tenses (as in I *am going*).

■ *Have* functions as an auxiliary when it combines with the past participle form of a verb to create the perfect tenses (as in I *have gone*).

■ *Do* functions as an auxiliary when it combines with the base form of a verb to form questions, to show emphasis, and to show negation. (*Do* you care? I *do* care. I *don't* care.)

ESL NOTE For illustrations of the varied uses for auxiliary verbs in English, see 47c–d.

<blockquote>**I** Use modal auxiliaries to refine meaning.</blockquote>

The producers *should* agree to this.   They *must* agree.

When paired with the base form of a verb, a **modal auxiliary** expresses urgency, obligation, likelihood, possibility, and so on: *can/could, may, might, must, ought to, should, would*. Unlike the auxiliaries *be, have,* and *do*, most of these modal auxiliaries do not change form.

Observe how meaning in a sentence changes depending on the choice of modal auxiliary:

I must resign.   I ought to resign.   I would resign.

I could resign.   I can resign.   I might resign.

Modal auxiliaries can combine with other auxiliaries to create complex verbal phrases that require careful use.

I ought to have resigned.   I could have been resigning.

The auxiliaries *will* and *shall* establish the future tense.

When shall I resign?   She will resign then.

Avoid careless *of* usage when *have* is part of past tenses used with modals.

Rapid speaking sometimes forms contractions with *have* following modals such as *could, would, should, must, may, might*. Thus, *would have* can become *would've* or *might have* can become *might've*. Such colloquial usages can translate into sounds like "would of" or even "woulda," "might of," or "mighta," leading some into a careless habit of writing *of* when *have* is the form intended.

| **Careless** | She should *of* told me about it; then I might *of* had time to avoid it. |
| **Revised** | She should *have* told me about it; then I might *have* had time to avoid it. |

ESL NOTE For illustrations of how modal auxiliaries affect word order and verb constructions, see 47d.

Using Auxiliary Verbs   **223**

2   Revise nonstandard auxiliaries by using standard forms of *be*.

Faulty   She going to class.
Revised   She is going to class.

Some dialects form present-tense auxiliary constructions with variations on the base form of *be*. For written academic English, these forms must be revised.

Nonstandard   She *be* singing beautifully. [The base form of *be* is a non-standard usage here. The *-s* form of the verb is needed.]
Nonstandard   She singing a beautiful melody. [The *be* form has been dropped.]
Revised   She *is* singing a beautiful melody. [The auxiliary is now the standard *-s* form.]

EXERCISE I

Identify the main verb and any auxiliary verb associated with it in the sentences that follow.

> *Example:* Peru presents many contrasts to a traveler. (The verb is *presents*.)

1. Peru has both modern cities, such as Lima, and ancient ones, such as Cuzco.
2. Anthropologists believe Cuzco to be the oldest continuously inhabited city in the Western Hemisphere.
3. In fact, the city's population is actually growing.
4. Travelers have long admired the city's massive walls.
5. Craftsmen began work on the cathedral in 1659 and finished nearly one hundred years later.
6. The Pizzeria Giorgio Gourmet exemplifies the old and the new.
7. The restaurant serves a thoroughly modern food—pizza; yet the restaurant incorporates into its architecture an Inca-built wall.

EXERCISE 2

In the sentences that follow, use the appropriate form of the irregular verb.

> *Example:* Over the past five years, nearly every woman in our therapy groups [confess] to a negative body image. [confessed]

Most of the women we interviewed had negative body images, not because they [have] _____ *1* _____ homely bodies but because they [see] _____ *2* _____ themselves incorrectly. Their images of their bodies [be] _____ *3* _____ distorted. In the cases of some women, this distortion was so extreme that their bodies [become] _____ *4* _____ caricatures. Many of the women also [feel] _____5_____ to some extent alienated from their own bodies. This estrangement is probably inevitable, given the fact that women have been [teach] _____6_____ to perceive the mind as divorced from the body.

9d Using transitive and intransitive verbs

Action verbs are classified as *transitive* and *intransitive*. A **transitive verb** (marked with the abbreviation **tr.** in the dictionary) transfers an action from a subject to an object. The action of an **intransitive verb** is limited to the subject of a sentence.

 Distinguish between verbs that take direct objects and those that do not.

Sharon studied.   Sharon studied her lecture notes.

A large number of verbs regularly take a direct object and are always transitive. Others never take an object and are always intransitive.

Transitive   The politician kissed the baby. [The transitive verb *kissed* transfers action from *politician* to *baby*.]

Intransitive   The politician smiled. [An action is performed, but no object is acted on.]

Many verbs can have both a transitive and an intransitive sense. Such "two-way" verbs will take a direct object or not, depending on their use.

Intransitive   She runs every day. [The verb takes no object.]

Transitive   She runs a big business. [The verb has changed meaning and now takes an object.]

ESL NOTE   Note that a transitive verb is the *only* type that can be made passive (see 9g). Neither intransitive nor most linking verbs can take a passive form in modern English. For specifics on transitive verbs and passive constructions, see 47a-1.

2   Avoid confusion between the verbs *sit/set*, *lie/lay*, *rise/raise*.

Set the books on the table.

It hurts only when I *sit*.

I think I'll *lie* down for a rest.

Lay the blanket in the corner.

Difficulties in distinguishing between transitive and intransitive verbs lead to misuse of *sit/set*, *lie/lay*, and *rise/raise*. The forms of these verbs are shown in the box below. Because the meaning of the verbs in each pairing is somewhat similar, the verbs are sometimes used interchangeably in speech. In formal writing, however, careful distinctions should be maintained. The first verb in each pair is intransitive—it takes no object—while the second verb is transitive.

Sit is normally an intransitive verb. Its action is limited to the subject.

> adverb
> You sit *on the bench*.

Set is a transitive verb. It transfers action to an object, which must be present in the sentence.

> object   adverb
> You set *the papers* on the bench.

Lie is an intransitive verb. Its action is limited to the subject.

> adverb
> I lie *on the couch*.

Lay is a transitive verb. It transfers action to an object, which must be present in the sentence.

> object   adverb
> I lay *the pillow* on the couch.

Rise is an intransitive verb. Its action is limited to the subject.

> adverb
> I rise *in the morning*.

Raise is a transitive verb. It transfers action to an object, which must be present in the sentence.

> object   adverb
> I raise *the flag each morning*.

The Principal Parts of *sit/set*, *lie/lay*, and *rise/raise*				
Base form	Present tense	Past tense	Past participle	Present participle
sit	sits	sat	sat	sitting
set	sets	set	set	setting
lie	lies	lay	lain	lying
lay	lays	laid	laid	laying
rise	rises	rose	risen	rising
raise	raises	raised	raised	raising

EXERCISE 3

Choose the appropriate form of *sit/set*, *lie/lay*, or *rise/raise* in these sentences.

> **Example:** A squirrel was [sit/set] _____ on a picnic table.
> A squirrel was *sitting* on a picnic table.

1. A man walked by and [sit/set] _____ a newspaper on a nearby table.
2. He then [sit/set] _____ down and unfolded the paper.
3. From one pocket he produced a tomato, which he [lie/lay] _____ on the paper.
4. From another pocket came a salt shaker, which he [rise/raise] _____ ceremoniously.
5. The squirrel [rise/raise] _____ at the scent of food.

EXERCISE 4

In the following sentences, fill in the blanks with the appropriate form of the verb indicated in parentheses.

> **Example:** The First World War [begin] _____ as an Old World War.
> The First World War *began* as an Old World War.

1. Everything about the war expressed the world that Americans [hope] _____ they had [leave] _____ behind.
2. That Old World [be] _____ a battlefield of national ambitions, religious persecutions, and language barriers.
3. European armies had [fight] _____ over whether a nation's boundary should [be] _____ on one side or the other of a narrow river.
4. Old World monarchs had [transfer] _____ land from one flag to another, [barter] _____ people as if they [be] _____ mere real estate.
5. In the 1800s, the English, French, and German empires [expand] _____ across the globe.

TENSE

9e Understanding the uses of verb tenses

A verb's **tense** indicates when an action has occurred or when a subject exists in a given state. There are three basic tenses in English: *past*, *present*, and *future*. Each has a **perfect** form, which indicates a completed action. Each has a **progressive** form, which indicates ongoing action. And each has a **perfect progressive** form, which indicates ongoing action that will be completed at some definite time. The time relationships among these tenses are charted in the box on page 233.

The varied uses of the present tense

Present: I start the engine.
> **Present perfect:** I have started the engine.
> **Present progressive:** I am starting the engine.
> **Present perfect progressive:** I have been starting the engine.

The simple present tense

A verb's base form is the present-tense form for first- and second-person subjects, singular or plural (*I, we, you* play), as well as plural third-person subjects (*they* play). A present-tense verb for a third-person, singular noun or pronoun ends with the suffix *-s* (*he* plays). The **simple present tense** indicates an action taking place in the writer's present time: *You see these words.* But the present tense in combination with other time-specific expressions (such as *after, before, when,* or *next week*) indicates other time references, such as ongoing action or future action (see 9f-1).

> After I *arrive*, they can announce where I *am* staying.

> Before I *depart*, my bags should be packed.

> Tomorrow we *walk* to school.

> Next week, Nelson *dances* in New York.

The historical present tense

The so-called **historical present tense** is used when referring to actions in an already existing work: a book, a report, an essay, a movie, a television show, an article, and so on.

> In *The Songlines*, Bruce Chatwin *explores* the origins and meanings of Aboriginal "walkabouts" in Australia.

> In *Blade Runner*, Harrison Ford *plays* a world-weary detective whose job it *is* to disable renegade, humanlike robots.

Additionally, the present tense is used to express information that, according to current scientific knowledge or accepted wisdom, is true or likely to be true.

> Evidence *indicates* that Alzheimer's patients *show* a decrease in an important brain transmitter substance.

> Absence *makes* the heart grow fonder.

> She *is* an excellent dentist.

The present tense is also used to indicate a generalized time or a customary, repeated action.

Time *flies.*

Each Tuesday I *walk* to the bakery.

The present perfect tense

The **present perfect tense** is formed with the auxiliary *have* or *has* and the verb's past participle. This tense indicates an action completed at an indefinite past time.

I *have returned* and she *has left.*

The present perfect tense also indicates an action that, although begun at some past time, continues to have an impact in the present.

He *has* recently *given* support to museums.

ESL NOTE   Expressions for duration of time, such as *since* and *for,* require the use of the perfect tense.

Faulty   I *was* here *since* four o'clock and *waited* here *for* many hours. [The simple past is not used with these expressions showing duration of time.]

Revised   I *have been* here *since* four o'clock and *have waited* here for many hours. [The present perfect is used.]

In constructions that indicate a specific past time using phrases or clauses (with *when, after, before, while*), the simple past is required.

Faulty   I *have met* him at eight o'clock and I *have left* after he arrived. [These expressions for a specific past time or event do not use the perfect.]

Revised   I *met* him at eight o'clock, and I *left* after he arrived.

For more information on the use of tenses with time expressions, see 47b-2.

The present progressive tense

The **present progressive tense** is formed with the auxiliary *is, am,* or *are* and the verb's present participle. This tense indicates a present, ongoing action that may continue into the future.

She *is considering* a move to Alaska.

ESL NOTE   Certain verbs, such as *have,* are generally not used in a progressive tense, except with some idioms: *having a good time; having a baby* (see 47b-1).

The present perfect progressive tense

The **present perfect progressive tense** is formed with the auxiliary *has been* or *have been* and the verb's present participle. This tense indicates an action that began in the past, is continuing in the present, and may continue into the future.

She *has been studying* English for a year.

| 2 | The past and future tenses |

PAST TENSES

Past: I started the engine.
    Past perfect: I had started the engine.
    Past progressive: I was starting the engine.
    Past perfect progressive: I had been starting the engine.

The simple past tense

Regular verbs form the **simple past tense** by adding *-d* or *-ed* to the infinitive of the verb. Irregular verbs form the past tense in less predictable ways and are best memorized or verified in a dictionary. The simple past tense indicates an action completed at a definite time in the past.

Mothers *found* themselves unable to give their daughters accurate and positive perceptions about their bodies, since they themselves *were* preoccupied with faulty body images of their own.

The past perfect tense

The **past perfect tense** is formed with the auxiliary *had* and the verb's past participle. This tense indicates a past action that has occurred prior to another action.

By the time a girl reached puberty, she *had* already *developed* a negative body image.

The past progressive tense

The **past progressive tense** is formed with the auxiliary *was* or *were* and the verb's present participle. This tense indicates an ongoing action conducted—and completed—in the past.

In the 70s women *were striving* for a thin, boyish figure.

The past perfect progressive tense

The **past perfect progressive tense** is formed with the auxiliary *had been* and the verb's present participle. This tense indicates a past, on-going action completed prior to some other past action.

> During the three decades preceding the 70s, however, women *had been trying* to project a more full-figured look.

FUTURE TENSES

Future: I will start the engine.
> **Future perfect:** I will have started the engine.
> **Future progressive:** I will be starting the engine.
> **Future perfect progressive:** I will have been starting the engine.

The future tense

The **future tense** consists of the base form of the verb, along with the auxiliary *will* for all nouns and pronouns. This tense indicates an action or state of being that will begin in the future. In very formal writing, the first person *I* and *we* have traditionally taken the auxiliary *shall*. Increasingly, this word is reserved for opening (first-person) questions implying obligation: "Shall I?"

> Even if a woman does match the current ideal body image, she still must realize that she *will* not *fit* the mold forever.

ESL NOTE English has no simple future tense but expresses future events with a variety of constructions, including some uses of the present tense (described above), as well as auxiliaries and such expressions as *going to* or *about to* (see 47b-3).

The future perfect tense

The **future perfect tense** is formed with the verb's past participle and the auxiliary *will have*. This tense indicates an action occurring in the future, prior to some other action.

> By the time many girls reach the age of 16, they *will have spent* hundreds of dollars on such products as reducing aids, diet foods, and fitness equipment.

The future progressive tense

The **future progressive tense** is formed with the auxiliary *will be* (or *shall be*) and the verb's present participle. This tense indicates an on-going action in the future.

Many young women believe that if they do not maintain a standard of physical loveliness, they *will be enduring* loneliness for the rest of their lives.

The future perfect progressive tense

The **future perfect progressive tense** is formed with the auxiliary *will have been* and the verb's present participle. This tense indicates an ongoing action in the future that will occur before some specified future time.

By the year 2005, many women born in the early 1960s *will have been dieting* for as long as 30 years.

9f Sequencing verb tenses

Although a sentence will always have a main verb located in its independent clause, it may have other verbs as well. A complex sentence will have a second verb in its dependent clause, and a sentence with an infinitive or participle (verb forms that function as adjectives, adverbs, and nouns) will also have at least two verbs or verb forms. Since every verb shows tense, any sentence with more than one verb may indicate actions that occur at different times. Unless the sequence of these actions is precisely set, confusion will result.

Unclear	Before I *leave*, I *reported* on my plans. [This sentence suggests that two events (one in each clause) are related, but the time sequencing of the events—one future, the other past—makes the relationship impossible.]
Clear	Before I *leave*, I *will report* on my plans. [The two actions take place in the future, one action earlier than the other.]
Clear	Before I *left*, I *reported* on my plans. [The two actions take place in the past, one action earlier than the other.]

1   Sequence the events in complex sentences with care.

Jones *attacked* Representative Kaye, who *had proposed* the amendment.

Jones *has spent* months preparing for the trial that *will begin* next week.

9.2 A complex sentence joins an independent and a dependent clause, forming a close relationship between events described by two verbs. Look at the logical relationship of time sequence in the two clauses, and choose verb tenses that clarify that relationship. Make a decision about tenses as shown in the Critical Decisions box on page 233.

ESL NOTE   Indirect quotation or reported speech is a common case of tense sequence involving two verbs. A main verb, such as *says*, makes the report while another makes the indirect quotation in a *that . . .* clause— often occurring at a different time from the report: *She says that she will go.* When one event occurs before another, the verb sequence requires careful attention (see 47b-4).

CRITICAL DECISIONS

Maintaining Clear Time Relationships among Closely Linked Verbs

If you refer to *past events occurring at roughly the same time*, use past-tense verbs.

Faulty

Tom *had traveled* where jobs *presented* themselves. [past perfect/past]
[The different tenses wrongly suggest that the events happened at different times.]

Revised

past event   past event
Tom *traveled* where jobs *presented* themselves. [past/past]

If you refer to *past events occurring one before the other*, use the past tense for the more recent event and the past perfect for the earlier event.

Faulty

I *remembered* Mrs. Smith, who *showed* me kindness. [past/past]
[The tenses wrongly suggest that actions occurred at the same time.]

Revised

later event   earlier event
I *remembered* Mrs. Smith, who *had shown* me kindness. [past/past perfect]

BUT if a key word (such as *before* or *after*) establishes a clear time relationship, then the past perfect form of the verb is not used.

earlier event   later event
I *was* unable to follow current events *before* Mrs. Smith *showed* me how to read. [past/past]

2 Choose verb tense in an infinitive phrase based on your choice of verb in the main clause.

> Ellen hoped to get rich.   To have voted was critical.

An **infinitive phrase** begins with the word *to* placed before a verb. A present infinitive shows an action that occurs at the same time as or later than the action of the main verb. In the following sentences, the main verb is underlined.

> With her supporting performance in *Gone with the Wind*, Hattie McDaniel <u>became</u> the first black actor *to win* an Academy Award. [*To win* shows an action at the same time as *became*.]

> Many critics <u>expected</u> Morgan Freeman *to win* the award for best actor in 1989. [*To win* shows a possible action in the future, later than *expected*.]

A perfect infinitive is formed by placing the auxiliary *have* between the word *to* and the past participle of the verb. A perfect infinitive phrase shows an action that occurs before the action of the main verb.

> Sidney Poitier and Denzel Washington <u>remain</u> the only black actors *to have won* an Academy Award for an appearance in a leading role. [*To have won* refers to an action prior to the present indicated by *remain*.]

3 Choose the verb tense of a participle based on your choice of verb in the main clause.

> *Arriving* early, the speaker <u>had</u> time to relax.

> *Having* thoroughly *studied* the matter, the judge <u>made</u> her decision.

> *Impressed* with the novel, Marie <u>recommended</u> it to friends.

Participles, past and present, function as adjectives in a sentence. A participle in its present *(-ing)* form indicates an action that occurs at the same time as the action of the sentence's main verb. The main verb in each of the following examples is underlined, and the participial phrase is italicized.

> *Playing as part of the Los Angeles Rams "Bull Elephant" backfield*, fullback Dan Towler <u>was named</u> most valuable player in the 1952 Pro Bowl game. [Towler's playing occurred at the same time that he was named most valuable player.]

A participle's present perfect form (the past participle preceded by the auxiliary *having*) shows an action that occurs before that of the main verb.

> *Having graduated from Washington & Jefferson College*, Towler <u>joined</u> the Rams in 1950. [Towler graduated before he joined the Los Angeles team.]

A participle in its past form (the base form + *-ed* for regular verbs) shows an action that occurs at the same time as or earlier than the action of the main verb.

> *Interested primarily in studying for the ministry*, Towler pursued a master's degree in theology while playing for the Rams. [Towler's interest in studying for the ministry existed both before and while he pursued his master's degree.]

EXERCISE 5

In each sentence that follows, identify the tense of the italicized verb. Then choose the appropriate tense for subsequent verbs in each sentence.

> *Example:*   Personality *is* the unique but stable set of characteristics and behavior that [set] _____ each individual apart from all others.
>
> *is*   present tense   *sets*   present tense

1. Most people *have accepted* the view that human beings [possess] _____ specific traits that [be] _____ fairly constant over time.

2. You *may be* surprised [learn] _____ that until recently a heated debate [exist] _____ in the behavioral sciences over the definition's accuracy.

3. On one side of this debate *were* scientists who [contend] _____ that people [do] _____ not [possess] _____ lasting traits.

4. According to these researchers (whom we *will term* the "anti-personality" camp), behavior [be] _____ shaped largely by external factors.

5. On the other side of the controversy *were* scientists who [hold] _____ , equally strongly, that stable traits [do] _____ exist.

WWW

VOICE

9.3

9g Using the active and passive voices

Voice refers to the emphasis a writer gives to the actor in a sentence or to the object acted upon. Because only transitive verbs (see 9d) transfer action from an actor to an object, these verbs can form the active and passive voices. The **active voice** emphasizes the actor of a sentence.

> Brenda scored the winning goal.
>
> Thomas played the violin.

In each case, an actor, or agent, is *doing* something. In a **passive-voice** sentence, the object acted on is emphasized.

> The winning goal was scored by Brenda.

> The violin was played by Thomas.

The emphasis on the object of a passive-voice sentence requires a rearrangement of words—the movement of the object, which normally follows a verb, to the first position in a sentence. A passive-voice construction also requires a form of the verb *be (is, are, was, were, has been, have been)* and often the preposition *by.*

| Brenda | **was** | scored | the winning goal | **by** |

> The winning goal was scored by Brenda.

You can make the original actor/subject disappear altogether by deleting the prepositional phrase.

> The winning goal was scored.

I   Use a strong active voice for clear, direct assertions.

Stronger   A guidance counselor recommended the book.

Weaker   A book was recommended.

In active-voice sentences, people or other agents *do* things. Active-voice sentences help create a direct, lively attitude between the subject and the reader. By contrast, passive-voice sentences are inherently wordy and reliant on the weak verb *be.* Unintended overuse of the passive voice makes prose dull. Unless you have a specific reason for choosing the passive voice (see the following discussion), use the active voice.

You can make a passive-voice sentence active by restoring a subject/verb sequence. Rewording will eliminate both the preposition *by* and the form of *be.* Note that if an actor of a passive-voice sentence is not named, you will need to provide a name.

Passive (weak)   In 1858, Stephen Douglas was challenged to a series of historic debates. [The "challenger" is not named.]

Active (stronger)   In 1858, Abraham Lincoln challenged Stephen Douglas to a series of historic debates.

Passive (weak)   The Senate race was won by Douglas, but a national reputation was established by Lincoln.

Active (stronger)   Douglas won the Senate race, but Lincoln established a national reputation.

ACROSS THE CURRICULUM

Using Active Verbs in Legal Writing

Richard H. Weisberg, professor of law at Benjamin N. Cardozo School of Law (Yeshiva University), advises lawyers to use active-voice verbs in their writing:

To reinvigorate the active verbal juices flowing through even the most seasoned legal writer, [s/]he must periodically recite five simple sentences.

1. "I love the law."
2. "The law needs good writers."
3. "Good writers seek brevity."
4. "Brevity thrives where strong verbs abound."
5. "I love strong verbs."

[. . .]

The language redounds with vividly descriptive words of action. When the legal writer finds such a verb and uses it to link [a] subject directly to an object, the sentence is almost inevitably strong.*

*Richard H. Weisberg, *When Lawyers Write* (Boston: Little, Brown, 1987), 61–63.

---

2   Use the passive voice to emphasize an object or to deemphasize an unknown subject.

Object emphasized   The funding goal was reached earlier than expected.

Actor(s) emphasized   We reached the funding goal earlier than expected.

While you should generally prefer the active voice for making direct statements, you will find the passive voice indispensable on two occasions: to emphasize an object and to deemphasize an unknown subject/actor.

Emphasize an object with a passive construction.

When the subject/actor of a sentence is relatively unimportant compared with what is acted on, use the passive voice both to deemphasize the subject/actor and to emphasize the object. The passive voice will shift the subject/actor to a prepositional phrase at a later position in the clause. You may then delete the phrase.

Active	We require twelve molecules of water to provide twelve atoms of oxygen.
Passive (actor retained)	Twelve molecules of water are required by us to provide twelve atoms of oxygen.
Passive (actor deleted)	Twelve molecules of water are required to provide twelve atoms of oxygen.

Deemphasize an unknown subject with the passive voice.

You may deemphasize or delete an *unknown* subject/actor by using the passive voice. Instead of writing an indefinite subject/actor (such as *someone* or *people*) into a sentence, use the passive voice to shift the subject/actor to a prepositional phrase. You may then delete the phrase.

Active	People mastered the use of fire some 400,000 years ago.
Passive (actor retained)	The use of fire was mastered by people some 400,000 years ago.
Passive (actor deleted)	The use of fire was mastered some 400,000 years ago.

EXERCISE 6

Change the passive-voice sentences that follow to the active voice, and change active-voice sentences to passive. Invent a subject if need be for the active-voice sentences.

> *Example:* A trillion dollars will be claimed by retirement plans in the next few years. [The passive voice involves the verb *will be claimed*.]
>
> Retirement plans will claim a trillion dollars in the next few years. [The verb *will claim* is expressed in the active voice.]

1. Nearly 18.5 million Americans maintain 401(k) retirement plans.
2. The 401(k) plan is recommended by economists, politicians, and investment advisers as a key to a comfortable retirement.
3. In practice, however, the 401(k) is often mismanaged by the plan-holder's employer.
4. Some workers have voiced their concerns about the structuring and funds allocation of their 401(k)s.
5. As it turns out, the company executives who choose 401(k) plans for their employees do not investigate alternative, possibly better plans.

MOOD

9h | **Understanding the uses of mood**

The **mood** of a verb indicates whether a statement is a fact, a command, or an unreal or hypothetical condition contrary to fact. In the

indicative mood, a writer states a fact, opinion, or question. Most of our writing and speech is in the indicative mood.

> The mayor has held office for eight years. [fact]

> The mayor is not especially responsive. [opinion]

> Did you vote for the mayor? [question]

In the **imperative mood,** a writer gives a command, the subject of which is "you," the person being addressed. In this book, for example, the imperative addresses readers with specific guidelines for writing or making revisions. An imperative uses the verb in its base form. Often, the subject of a command is omitted, but occasionally it is expressed directly.

> Follow me!

> Do not touch that switch.

> Don't you touch that switch!

By using the **subjunctive mood,** a writer shows that he or she believes an action or situation is unreal or hypothetical. With a subjunctive verb, a writer can also make a recommendation or express a wish or requirement, usually preceded by such a verb construction as *recommend,* *suggest, insist, it is necessary,* or *it is important.* The **present subjunctive** uses the base form (infinitive) of the verb for all subjects.

> I recommend that he *develop* his math skills before applying.

> I insist that they *be* disciplined.

The **past subjunctive** uses the past-tense form of the verb—or, in the case of *be*—the form *were.*

> If management *assumed* traveling costs, the team would be happier.

> He wished he *were* four inches taller.

ESL NOTE *If* constructions require a subjunctive verb form only when they express a condition that is considered unreal or hypothetical. Section 47b-5 demonstrates differences between real and unreal conditions with *if* constructions.

| 1 | Use the subjunctive mood with certain *if* constructions. |

> If I owned a dog, I would walk it every day.

When an *if* clause expresses an unreal or hypothetical condition, use the subjunctive mood. In a subjunctive *if* construction, the modal auxiliary *would, could, might,* or *should* is used in the main clause. (See 9c-1 for a discussion of modals.)

Faulty	If Tom was more considerate, he would have called. [Clearly, Tom was not considerate (he did not call), and so the indicative or "factual" mood is at odds with the meaning of the sentence.]
Subjunctive	If Tom *were* more considerate, he would have called.
Subjunctive	If I *were* elected, I might raise taxes.

Note: When an *if* construction is used to establish a cause-and-effect relationship, the writer assumes that the facts presented in a sentence either are true or could very possibly be true. Therefore, the writer uses an indicative ("factual") mood with normal subject–verb agreement.

| Faulty | If I were late, I apologize. |
| Revised | If I was late, I apologize. [The lateness is assumed to be a likely or possible fact.] |

> **2** Use the subjunctive mood with *as if* and *as though* constructions.

He dances as though he were weightless.

When an *as if* or *as though* construction sets up a purely hypothetical comparison, use the subjunctive mood.

Faulty	She swims as if she *was* part fish. [But since the speaker knows she is not, the indicative ("factual") mood is inconsistent.]
Revised	She swims as if she *were* part fish.
Subjunctive	He writes quickly, as though he *were* running out of time. [The sentence assumes that he is not running out of time.]

> **3** Revise to eliminate auxiliary *would* or *could* in subjunctive clauses with *if, as if,* or *as though.*

| Clear | If I had listened, I would have avoided the problem. |
| Confusing | If I would have listened, I would have avoided the problem. |

In subjunctive constructions, the modal auxiliary verbs *would, could,* or *should* may appear in the main clause to help indicate that its action is unreal or conditional. The auxiliaries *would* and *could* cannot appear in the *if* clause, however, since this creates a kind of "double conditional." These auxiliaries must be replaced with the appropriate subjunctive form.

| Faulty | If the pilot *would have* been alerted, the oil spill would have been avoided. |
| Revised | If the pilot *had* been alerted, the oil spill would have been avoided. |

Faulty	He could have acted as though he *could have* seen the reef.
Revised	He could have acted as though he *had* seen it.

4   Use the subjunctive mood with a *that* construction.

I think it is important that he arrive early.

Use the subjunctive mood with subordinate *that* constructions expressing a requirement, request, urging, belief, wish, recommendation, or doubt. In each of these constructions, the word *that* may be omitted.

The rules require that we *be* present.

I wish that I *were* a painter.

We recommend that he *accept* the transfer.

ESL NOTE   *That* clauses can occur in a variety of sentences not requiring a subjunctive form. See 47b-6 for rules in constructions involving *wish that*.

EXERCISE 7

Use the subjunctive mood, as appropriate, in revising the sentences that follow.

> *Example:*   Some experts claim that unmarried couples living together would be happier if they would make finances and spending an explicit topic of discussion and negotiation.
>
> Some experts claim that unmarried couples living together would be happier if they made finances and spending an explicit topic of discussion and negotiation.

1. The couples often wish that there are more precedents to help them decide who pays for what.

2. If each partner communicated his or her expectations to the other, there are fewer squabbles over "your crackers" and "my paper towels."

3. Some experts recommend that each partner keeps a separate bank account but also open a joint checking account to cover household expenses.

4. Experts suggest that each party should be fully informed about the discretionary spending of the other.

5. One specialist, in her book *Financial Planning for Couples*, recommends that the partner with the higher income pays a proportionately higher share of joint household expenses.

10

Agreement

T he term **agreement** describes two significant relationships in a sentence: that between a subject and a verb and between a pronoun and an antecedent. A singular subject must take a singular verb, and a plural subject must take a plural verb. Likewise, a singular pronoun functions with a singular antecedent, and a plural pronoun with a plural antecedent. You will need to make decisions about agreement in every sentence you write.

CRITICAL DECISIONS

Recognizing Singular and Plural

Making correct decisions about agreement requires recognizing whether certain sentence parts are regarded as singular or plural. This is easy enough with nouns because most form the plural with the addition of *–s* or *–es*, although there are exceptions (see 23e-5). Problems can arise, however, with indefinite pronouns (such as *everyone*, *none*, *neither*), collective nouns *(staff, band)*, and some other sentence elements, because their form and function are not so clearly singular or plural. This chapter provides information to help you make this crucial distinction.

SUBJECT–VERB AGREEMENT

Weblink

http://www.asu.edu/duas/wcenter/
subject.html

Subject–verb online handout from Arizona State University.

Subjects and verbs must agree in both number and person. The term **number** indicates whether a noun is singular (denoting one person, place, or thing) or plural (denoting more than one). The term **person** identifies the subject of a sentence as the same

person who is speaking (the first person), someone who is spoken to (the second person), or someone or something being spoken about (the third person). Pronouns differ according to person.

	First-person subject	Second-person subject	Third-person subject
Singular	I	you	he, she, it
Plural	we	you	they

Agreement between a verb and first- or second-person pronoun subject does not vary. The pronouns *I*, *we*, and *you* take verbs *without* the letter *s*.

> I walk.   We walk.   You walk.

> I scream, you scream, we scream—for ice cream.

The forms of agreement for third-person subjects and verbs, however, can be confusing.

www

10.1

10a | **Make a third-person subject agree in number with its verb.**

The suffix *-s* or *-es*, affixed to a present-tense verb, signals a singular third-person subject (A frog do*es* this.). The suffix *-s* or *-es*, affixed to most nouns, indicates a plural (Frog*s* do this.).

The "tradeoff" technique

To remember the basic forms of third-person agreement for most verbs in the present tense, you may find it helpful to visualize something like a balanced tradeoff of *-s* endings between most noun subjects and their verbs: if one ends with an *-s*, then the other does not.

Singular   A boy__ hikes.   A girl__ swims.   A kid__ does it.

Plural   The boys hike__.   The girls swim__.   Kids do__ it.

If a noun or pronoun has a plural sense, even if it does not end with an *-s* (for example, *children*, *oxen*, *geese*, *they*, *these*), then the tradeoff technique still applies. Since the noun or pronoun is plural, the verb is also plural—that is, the verb now lacks its *-s* ending.

Singular   A child plays.   He plays.   He does it.

Plural   Children play __.   They play __.   They do__ it.

Note: The "tradeoff" technique does not apply when a verb is paired with an auxiliary (or helping) verb (see 9c). Verbs paired like this do *not* use *-s*.

A child will play.	He may play.	He might do it.
Children should play.	They could play.	They must do it.

Spotlight on Common Errors—AGREEMENT

 These are the errors most commonly associated with agreement between subject and verb or pronoun and antecedent. For full explanations and suggested revisions, follow the cross-references to chapter sections.

AGREEMENT ERRORS occur when the writer loses sight of the close link between paired subjects and verbs, or between pronouns and the words they refer to (antecedents). Paired items should both be singular or both be plural.

> **A subject and its verb should both be singular or plural whether or not they are interrupted by a word or word group (see 10a-1). Match subject and verb. Disregard interrupting words.**

Faulty

Some people, when not paying attention, easily *forgets* names.

Revised

Some **people,** when not paying attention, easily *forget* names.

> **A sentence with a singular subject needs a singular form of the verb *be (am, is, was);* a sentence with a plural subject needs a plural form of the verb *be (are, were)* (see 10a-7). To ensure agreement, ignore words following the verb *be*.**

Faulty

The reason for her success *are* her friends.

Revised

The **reason** for her success *is* her friends.

When the subject comes after the verb in sentences beginning with *it* or *there*, verb and subject must still agree. Ignore the word *it* or *there*.

Faulty

There *is* seven hills in Rome.

Revised

There *are* **seven hills** in Rome. [The subject, *hills*, needs a plural verb.]

> **When *and* joins words to create a two-part pronoun referent or a two-part subject, the sense is usually plural, and so the matching pronoun or verb must be plural (see 10a-2 and 10b-1). When *or/nor* creates a two-part pronoun referent or a two-part subject, the nearer word determines whether the matching pronoun or verb is singular or plural (see 10a-3 and 10b-2).**

Faulty

A cat and a dog often *shares* **its** food.

Revised

A cat and a dog often *share* **their** food. [The plural pronoun and verb match a two-part referent and subject, *cat and dog*.]

Faulty

Neither the rats nor the dog *chase* **their** tail.

Revised

Neither the rats nor the dog *chases* **its** tail. [The singular pronoun and verb match the nearer singular subject, *dog*.]

Revising nonstandard verb and noun forms to observe *-s*
and *-es* endings

In rapid conversation people sometimes skip over the *-s* or *-es* endings of verbs that are paired with singular nouns. In some English dialects, the base (or infinitive) form of the verb is used for singular nouns.
Standard academic English, however, requires that writers observe   **10.2**
subject–verb agreement.

Nonstandard	He read the book.	**Nonstandard**	She do it.
Standard	He reads the book.	**Standard**	She does it.

ACROSS THE CURRICULUM

Plurals in Academic Writing

Academic writing often uses nouns derived from Latin
and Greek that form the plural by changing the final
syllable from *–um* to *–a*, *-us* to *–i*, or *–on* to *–a*:

medi*um*/medi*a*   curricul*um*/curricul*a*   dat*um*/dat*a*
stimul*us*/stimul*i*   syllab*us*/syllab*i*   alumn*us*/alumn*i*
criteri*on*/criteri*a*   phenomen*on*/phenomen*a*

Make sure to use a plural verb with such irregular plural nouns.

Bacteria surround (not *surrounds*) us.

The media bombard (not *bombards*) the public with cultural stereotypes.

| A subject agrees with its verb regardless of whether any
| phrase or clause separates them.

The *purpose* of practicing daily for several hours <u>is</u> to excel.

Often a subject may be followed by a lengthy phrase or clause that
comes between it and the verb, confusing the basic pattern of agreement.
To clarify the matching of the subject with the verb, mentally strike out
or ignore phrases or clauses separating them. Verbs in the following examples are underlined; subjects are italicized.

Downward mobility—a swift plunge down America's social and economic ladders—<u>poses</u> an immediate and pressing problem. [The verb
poses agrees with its singular subject, *downward mobility*, not with the
plural *ladders* in the interrupting phrase.]

One of my friends in a nearby town <u>has</u> heard this. [The prepositional
phrases must be ignored to make the singular *one* agree with *has*.]

The words *each* and *every* have a singular sense. When either of these words precedes a compound subject joined by *and,* use a singular verb.

> *Every* city and county in Massachusetts <u>has</u> struggled with the problem of downward mobility.

Exception: When *each* follows a compound subject, the sense is plural, and the plural verb is used.

> Boston and New York *each* <u>are</u> launching programs to reeducate workers.

Note: Phrases beginning with *in addition to, along with, as well as, together with,* or *accompanied by* may come between a subject and its verb. Although they add material, these phrases do *not* create a plural subject. They must be mentally stricken out to determine the correct number of the verb.

Faulty *The anthropologist,* as well as social researchers, <u>are</u> always looking for indicators of change in status. [The interrupting phrase before the verb gives a false impression of a plural subject.]

Revised *The anthropologist,* as well as social researchers, <u>is</u> always looking for indicators of change in status. [The singular subject *anthropologist* agrees with the singular verb.]

> **2** A compound subject linked by the conjunction *and* is in most cases plural.

UPS and Federal Express <u>compete</u> with the U.S. postal system.

When a compound subject linked by *and* refers to two or more people, places, or things, it is usually considered plural.

Plural *Statistical information* and *the analysis based upon it* <u>allow</u> an anthropologist to piece together significant cultural patterns. [The compound subject has a plural sense. Thus the verb, *allow,* is plural.]

Exception: When a compound subject refers to a single person, place, or thing, it is considered singular.

Singular Whatever culture she studies, *this anthropologist* and *researcher* <u>concerns</u> herself with kinship relations. [The compound has a singular sense—it refers to one person and can be replaced by the singular pronoun *she.* Thus the verb, *concerns,* is singular.]

> **3** When parts of a compound subject are linked by the conjunction *or* or *nor,* the verb should agree in number with the nearer part of the subject.

Neither the crew members nor the *captain* <u>speaks</u> Arabic.

When all parts of the compound subject are the same number, agreement with the verb is fairly straightforward.

Either John or *Maria* sings today.

Either the Smiths or the *Taylors* sing today.

When one part of the compound subject is singular and another plural, the subject nearer the verb determines the number of the verb. If the nearer subject is singular, the verb is singular.

Singular To most Americans, either poor habits or *ineptitude* is responsible for an individual's failure. [The singular subject, *ineptitude*, is nearer to the verb; therefore the verb, *is*, is singular.]

When the subject nearer the verb is plural, the verb is plural.

Plural Neither the downwardly mobile individual nor the *people* surrounding him realize that losing a job is often due to impersonal economic factors. [The plural subject, *people*, is nearer to the verb; therefore the verb, *realize*, is plural.]

A compound subject is sometimes preceded by a verb in sentences with inverted word order. Here, too, the verb agrees in number with the part of the subject that is nearer to the verb. (See 10a-8.)

There is neither a *dentist* nor any doctors in that remote village.

Note: Subject–verb agreement in this situation may appear to be mismatched. Avoid such awkwardness by revising to place the plural part closest to the verb.

---

4 Most indefinite pronouns have a singular sense and take a singular verb.

Virtually *everybody* in developed countries travels by bus.

Many who live elsewhere have no choice but to walk.

Indefinite pronouns (such as *any* and *each*) do not have specific antecedents—they rename no particular person, place, or thing and thus raise questions about subject–verb agreement.

The following indefinite pronouns have a singular sense:

another	each one	more	one
any	either	much	other
anybody	every	neither	somebody
anyone	everybody	nobody	someone
anything	everyone	none, no one	something
each	everything	nothing	

Singular *Much* of the law concerning the admissibility or exclusion of evidence involves standards of truth and fairness.

Singular Although some evidence indicated the defendant's guilt, *nothing* was sufficient to prove beyond a reasonable doubt that he was guilty.

The indefinite pronouns *both*, *ones*, and *others* have a plural sense and take a plural verb.

Plural   F. Lee Bailey and Johnny Cochrane are highly successful defense attorneys, and *both* <u>generate</u> extensive controversy.

The indefinite pronouns *all*, *any*, *more*, *many*, *enough*, *none*, *some*, *few*, and *most* have a singular or plural sense, depending on the meaning of a sentence.

Try substituting *he*, *she*, *it*, *we*, or *they* for the indefinite pronoun. The context of a sentence will give you clues about the number of its subject.

Plural   Millions of Americans are called for jury duty each year, but *most* never actually <u>serve</u> on a jury. [*Most* (Americans) has a plural sense. It can be replaced with the pronoun *they*, and thus takes a plural verb, *serve*.]

Singular Some trial testimony can be highly dramatic, but *most* <u>remains</u> fairly tedious. [*Most* (trial testimony) can be replaced by the pronoun *it*. The singular sense here creates the need for a singular verb, *remains*.]

> **5** Collective nouns have a plural or a singular sense, depending on the meaning of a sentence.

At this school, the *faculty* <u>meets</u> as a group with the president.

When a collective noun, such as *audience*, *band*, *bunch*, *crew*, *crowd*, *faculty*, *family*, *group*, *staff*, *team*, and *tribe*, refers to a single unit, the sense of the noun is singular and the noun takes a singular verb. The context of a sentence will give you clues about the number of its subject.

Singular The *jury* <u>hears</u> all the evidence presented by both the prosecution and the defense. [The *jury* is referred to as a single unit. It has a singular sense and takes a singular verb, *hears*.]

When the collective noun refers to individuals and their separate actions within a group, the sense of the noun is plural and the noun takes a plural verb.

Plural   The *jury* often <u>have</u> diverse reactions to the evidence they hear. [*Jury* in this case emphasizes the actions of individual members. Thus, it has a plural sense and takes a plural verb, *have*.]

If this plural use sounds awkward to you, add a plural noun to the sentence to clarify matters.

Plural   The *jury members* often <u>have</u> diverse reactions to the evidence.

6   **Nouns plural in form but singular in sense take singular verbs.**

Economics depends heavily on mathematics.

The nouns *athletics, economics, mathematics, news, physics,* and *politics* all end with the letter *-s,* but they nonetheless denote a single activity.

Note: *Politics* can be considered plural, depending on the sense of a sentence.

News of a layoff causes some people to feel alone and blame themselves.

Politics often comes into play. [*Politics* has a singular sense and takes a singular verb.]

Note: The nouns *pants* and *scissors* are considered singular, but they take a plural verb.

The scissors *are* handy.   The pants *need* to be cut and hemmed.

7   **A linking verb agrees in number with its subject, not with the subject complement.**

One *reason* for his success is his friends.

His *friends* are one reason for his success.

In a sentence with a linking verb, identify the singular or plural subject when deciding the number of the verb. Disregard the subject complement *following* the linking verb.

Singular   The *reason* for the acquittal was the many mistakes made by the police in gathering evidence. [The singular verb *was* agrees with the singular subject *reason,* not with the plural subject complement *mistakes.*]

Plural   The many *mistakes* made by the police in gathering evidence were the reason for the acquittal. [The plural verb *were* agrees with the plural subject *mistakes* not with the singular subject complement *reason.*]

8   **In sentences with inverted word order, a verb should agree in number with its subject.**

Here *is* Michael.   Here *are* Janice and Michael.   There *is* a strategy.

The subject of an English sentence is normally placed before a verb. When this order is rearranged, the subject and verb continue to agree in number. Most errors with rearranged sentences occur with the verb *be.*

Here and *there* as adverbs

When inverted sentences begin with *here* and *there* as adverbs, the verb will agree in number with the subject (which follows the verb), not with the adverb.

Make a Third-Person Subject Agree in Number with Its Verb   **249**

Normal	The adviser said, "The Pattersons are here." [The plural subject, *Pattersons*, needs a plural verb.]
Rearranged	The adviser said, "Here *are* the Pattersons."
Singular	The adviser said, "Here *is* David Patterson."

Expletives

The words *it* and *there* often function as **expletives,** words that fill gaps in a sentence when normal word order is reversed (see 7a-11). *There* can never serve as the subject of a sentence. Disregard it when determining whether the sentence has a singular or plural subject.

Plural	There were several *factors* that influenced the outcome of the trial. [*There* is disregarded. The plural subject, *factors*, needs to agree with a plural verb, *were*.]
Singular	There was a single *factor*, however, that was most significant—the lack of high-quality evidence. [*There* is disregarded. The singular subject, *factor*, needs to agree with a singular verb, *was*.]

Notice that the expletive *it* is always followed by a singular verb.

Singular	It is a very good *idea* to help them.

When an expletive and a verb precede a compound subject with *or/nor*, the verb still agrees in number with the part of the subject that is nearer to the verb.

There is neither a *dentist* nor any doctors on the Sioux reservation.

ESL NOTE See 7a-11 and 47a-2 for ways to use expletives. See 14e and 17a for ways to avoid wasting words with expletives.

Questions

Inverting a sentence's word order is one method of forming a question. The relocated verb must still agree in number with the subject.

Statement	He really *wants* to hold on to that idea.
Question	Does he really want to hold on to that idea? [The verb *does want* agrees with the subject *he*.]

Many questions are formed with *wh* words (*what, where, when, why*), with a verb following the *wh* word and a noun following that. The verb and noun should agree in number.

Singular	What is *the cost* to him of abandoning it?
Plural	What are *the costs* aside from that?

When the verb in a question precedes a compound subject with *or/nor*, make the verb agree in number with the part of the subject that is nearer to the verb.

Have either *nurses* or a doctor been seen entering the hospital area?

> **9** The verb of a dependent clause introduced by the pronoun *which, that, who,* or *whom* should agree in number with the pronoun's antecedent.

In such a dependent clause, both the pronoun (*which, that,* etc.) and verb are dependent for their number on an antecedent in the main clause.

The *books, which* <u>are</u> old, <u>are</u> falling apart.

> **10** Phrases and clauses that function as subjects are treated as singular and take singular verbs.

Often a noun clause or a phrase with a gerund or infinitive will act as the subject of a sentence. Such a construction is always regarded as singular.

To swim well <u>is</u> the first prerequisite for scuba diving.

That the child is able to cough <u>is</u> a good sign.

> **11** Titled works, key words used as terms, and companies are treated as singular in number and take singular verbs.

Titles of works, names of companies or corporations, underlined or italicized words referred to as words, numbers, and units of money are regarded as singular entities in a sentence and take singular verbs.

Classics <u>is</u> an overused word.   "The Killers" <u>is</u> a Hemingway story.

EXERCISE 1

In the following sentences, determine whether a subject is singular or plural. Choose the correct form in parentheses, and be able to explain your choice.

> *Example:* How (do/does) we get other people to agree with us?
>
> How *do* we get other people to agree with us? [The subject of the sentence is the plural pronoun, *we.* The full verb (including the auxiliary *do*) and the subject must agree in number.]

1. One reason for making a purchase (is/are) a buyer's emotional needs.
2. There (is/are) no single method that (assure/assures) success in persuading others; still, several methods (seem/seems) helpful.
3. One effective way of impressing others (is/are) to get them to like us.
4. Flattery (has/have) a long history.
5. Both flattering people and getting them to talk about themselves (work/works) in surprisingly consistent ways.

PRONOUN–ANTECEDENT AGREEMENT

CRITICAL DECISIONS

Recognizing Antecedents

An **antecedent** is a word—usually a noun, sometimes a pronoun—that is renamed by a pronoun. To correct problems of pronoun agreement or reference, you need to identify each pronoun's antecedent and then make decisions about pronoun form and placement. If you're not sure of a pronoun's antecedent—that is, if you can't easily substitute a noun for the pronoun—then your sentence is likely faulty.

A pronoun and antecedent must agree in *number*, *person*, and *gender*. **Gender** refers to whether a noun or pronoun is feminine, masculine, or neuter.

Mary flies planes.	<u>She</u> flies planes. (feminine)
Bob rides trolleys.	<u>He</u> rides trolleys. (masculine)
A trolley runs on tracks.	<u>It</u> runs on tracks. (neuter)

In cases such as these, a pronoun is easily matched to its antecedent in terms of person (first, second, or third), number (singular or plural), and gender (masculine or feminine). At times, however, choosing the right pronoun requires careful attention.

10b **Pronouns and their antecedents should agree in number.**

Weblink

http://leo.stcloudstate.edu/style/
genderbias.html

Advice on avoiding gender bias in pronouns from St. Cloud State.

The *number* of a noun (either as subject or antecedent) is not always clear. The following conventions will help you to determine whether an antecedent is singular or plural.

1 A compound antecedent linked by the conjunction *and* is usually plural.

Watson and Crick were awarded a Nobel Prize for <u>their</u> achievement.

Plural In early classifications, living things were separated into *the plant kingdom* and *the animal kingdom*. <u>These</u> were then subdivided in various ways. [The compound antecedent has a plural sense; therefore, the pronoun renaming it is plural in form.]

Plural   In the 4th century B.C., *Aristotle* studied the animal kingdom, and *Theophrastus* studied the plant kingdom. Their classification systems led to many insights. [The compound antecedent has a plural sense; therefore, the pronoun renaming it is plural in form.]

Exception: When a compound antecedent with parts joined by the conjunction *and* has a singular sense, use a singular pronoun.

Singular   *One English naturalist* and *writer*, Thomas Blythe, used his classification scheme to identify more than 18,000 different types of plants. [The compound antecedent refers to one person— Thomas Blythe; therefore, the pronoun renaming it is singular.]

The words *each* and *every* have a singular sense. When either of these words precedes an antecedent joined by *and*, use a singular pronoun.

Singular   Every *visible organism* and *microscopic organism* has its own distinctive, two-word Latin name according to the system designed by Carolus Linnaeus.

Exception: When *each* follows an antecedent joined by *and*, the sense is plural, and the plural pronoun is used.

Plural   Daly and Blythe *each* made their contribution to biological classification.

> **2**   When parts of a compound antecedent are linked by the conjunction *or* or *nor*, a pronoun should agree in number with the nearer part of the antecedent.

Neither the captain nor the *crew members* understood *their* predicament.

This pattern of agreement with *or* or *nor* follows the same convention as does subject–verb agreement (10a-3).

Singular   Neither the traditional two-kingdom systems nor the recent five-kingdom *system* is complete in its classification of organisms. [The pronoun is nearer to the singular *system* and so agrees in the singular.]

Note: Avoid awkward pronoun use by revising to place the plural part of the compound antecedent nearer to the pronoun.

Revised   Neither the five-kingdom system nor the traditional two-kingdom *systems* are complete in their classifications.

> **3**   Make pronouns agree in number with indefinite pronoun antecedents.

Each one has her own job.   *Both* have begun their research.

Indefinite pronouns (such as *each*, *anyone*, and *everyone*) do not refer to particular persons, places, or things. Most often these indefinite pronouns have a singular sense as an antecedent and will be renamed with a singular pronoun. (See the complete list of singular and plural indefinite pronouns in 10a-4.) Writers sometimes forget that the pronouns *anyone* and *everyone* are singular and must agree with a singular pronoun.

Faulty   *Everyone* seems to have their own idea about *each* of the millions of organisms and their purpose.

Revised   *Everyone* seems to have his or her own idea about *each* of the millions of organisms and its purpose. [See 10c for choosing gender-appropriate pronouns.]

When an indefinite pronoun (such as *both* or *others*) functions as an antecedent and has a plural sense, rename it with a plural pronoun.

Plural   Some organisms are readily classified as animal or plant; *others*, most often the simplest organisms, find themselves classified in different ways.

A few indefinite pronouns (such as *some*, *more*, or *most*) can have a singular or a plural sense, depending on the context of a sentence. Determine the number of an indefinite pronoun antecedent before selecting a pronoun replacement.

Plural   *Some* of the simplest living organisms defy classification, by virtue of their diversity. [*Some* has a plural sense.]

Singular   *Some* of the recent research made possible by microscopes is startling in its findings.

---

4   Make pronouns agree in number with collective noun antecedents.

A well-informed group, the *faculty* is outspoken in its opinions.

The *faculty* at the gathering shared their thoughts on the issue.

Collective nouns are singular or plural depending on the meaning of a sentence. When a collective noun such as *audience*, *band*, *group*, or *team* refers to a *single unit*, its sense as an antecedent is singular, and it takes a singular pronoun.

Singular   A *group* of similar organisms that interbreed in nature is called a species and is given its own distinct Latin name. [*Group* has a singular sense.]

When a collective noun refers to individuals and their *separate actions* within a group, the sense of the noun as an antecedent is plural, and the noun takes a plural pronoun.

Plural   Human beings are the only *group* of primates who walk on two legs, without the aid of <u>their</u> hands. [*Group* has a plural sense.]

10c **Rename indefinite antecedents with gender-appropriate pronouns.**

A lawyer serves *his or her* clients. Lawyers serve *their* clients.

Gender-specific pronoun use can be inaccurate and offensive. To avoid unintentional sexism, use four techniques, either alone or in combination. (For more discussion on gender reference, see 21g.)

Use the constructions *he or she*, *his or her*, or *him or her* in referring to an indefinite pronoun or noun.

Choose this option when the antecedent of a pronoun must have a singular sense. Realize, however, that some readers object to the *he or she* device as cumbersome.

Singular   To some extent, *a biologist* must decide which system of classification <u>he or she</u> will use.

Make a pronoun's antecedent plural, if the accuracy of a sentence will permit a plural antecedent.

Plural   To some extent, *biologists* must decide for <u>themselves</u> which system of classification *they* will use.

Reconstruct the statement to avoid pronouns altogether.

Neutral   To some extent, *a biologist* must decide which system of classification to use. [The infinitive *to use* avoids the *he or she* difficulty.]

Arbitrarily assign gender identity.

Assign a masculine identity to one indefinite antecedent and a feminine identity to another. Maintain these assignments throughout a document.

Alternate   A *biologist* must decide which system of classification <u>she</u> will
gender   use. An *anthropologist* must also choose when selecting the
assignments technological attributes <u>he</u> will use in distinguishing ancient
                 objects.

10.3

EXERCISE 2

Revise the following sentences to ensure agreement between pronouns and antecedents. Eliminate the generic *he*. Place a check before the sentences in which a pronoun agrees in number with its antecedent.

Example: The characters, plots, and settings of Stephen King's stories have haunted readers with its believable eeriness.

The characters, plots, and settings of Stephen King's stories have haunted readers with *their* believable eeriness.

1. In one of these novels, a 1958 Plymouth Fury is a jealous monster who seeks out and destroys the enemies of her male owner.
2. Anyone who considers himself a horror connoisseur has read at least some of the novels of Stephen King.
3. Whenever King's novels become motion pictures, it grosses millions.
4. In their adaptation of King's short novel *The Body* into the full-length feature film *Stand by Me*, artist and director Rob Reiner created a tender-hearted crowd pleaser, quite unlike other movies made from King's novels.

EXERCISE 3

Revise the following gender-biased sentences so that they do not stereotype males or females or restrict references to males. When you make singular nouns plural, other words in the sentence will change.

Example: The behaviorist theory assumes that man's response to his environment is similar to the response of other animals.

The behaviorist theory assumes that humans respond to their environment in the same ways that other animals do.

1. Each operator answers her phone.
2. As part of her job, a nurse prepares injections for her patients.
3. A miner would take a canary below ground to make sure the air was safe for him to breathe.
4. A pilot, today, takes much of his training in flight simulators.
5. Recent research has suggested a relationship between the amount of time a child watches television and his later performance in school.

EXERCISE 4

Revise the following paragraph to ensure agreement between subject and verb and between pronoun and antecedent. Also, revise any sentence in which the generic *he* is used.

The haunted house loom large in American literature and film. Some of the most famous has been Poe's castle in "The Masque of the Red Death," his "house" of Usher, Shirley Jackson's Hill House, the Bates mansion in Hitchcock's *Psycho*, and the suburban home in *The Amityville Horror*. A relatively recent haunted house story, a genre piece in the tradition of horror classics, were King's *The Shining*. Any reader of the book or viewer of the movie was sure to satisfy his need for chills and thrills. As is the case in so many stories of the haunted house, none of the characters are ever entirely sure where he fits into the house's scheme of things.

ACROSS THE CURRICULUM

Using Words Precisely to Avoid Bias in Social Scientific Writing

The Publication Manual of the American Psychological Association, fifth edition, advises writers to choose words precisely when characterizing groups—both to maintain accuracy and to avoid giving offense:

Precision is a necessity in scientific writing; when you refer to a person or persons, choose words that are accurate, clear, and free from bias. . . . For example, using *man* to refer to all human beings is simply not as accurate as the phrase *men and women.* To describe age groups, it is better to give a specific age range ("ages 65–83") instead of a broad category ("over 65"; see Schaie, 1993). When describing racial and ethnic groups, be appropriately specific and sensitive to issues of labeling. For example, instead of describing participants as Asian American or Hispanic American, it may be helpful to describe them by their nation or region of origin (e.g., Chinese Americans, Mexican Americans). . . .

Part of writing without bias is recognizing that differences should be mentioned only when relevant. Marital status, sexual orientation, racial and ethnic identity, or the fact that a person has a disability should not be mentioned gratuitously.*

*The Publication Manual of the American Psychological Association, 5th ed. (Washington: APA, 2001) 62–63.

CHAPTER

11

Adjectives and Adverbs

Adjectives and adverbs are **modifiers**—descriptive words, phrases, or clauses that enliven sentences with vivid detail. In Chapter 7 you learned how phrases and clauses function as modifiers. To make effective decisions about single-word modifiers, you need to understand the differences between the two main types: adjectives and adverbs.

11a Distinguishing between adjectives and adverbs

The following Critical Decisions box can help you decide whether to use an adjective or an adverb in your sentence.

CRITICAL DECISIONS

Choosing Between Adjectives and Adverbs

Ask questions: Adjectives and adverbs answer different questions.

An **adjective** modifies a noun or pronoun and answers these questions:

Which: The *latest* news arrived.

What kind: An *insignificant* difference remained.

How many: The *two* sides would resolve their differences.

An **adverb** modifies a verb and answers these questions:

When: *Tomorrow* the temperature will drop.

How: The temperature will drop *sharply*.

How often: Weather patterns change *frequently*.

Where: The weather patterns *here* change frequently.

An **adverb** also modifies adjectives, adverbs, and entire clauses:

Modifying an adjective: An *especially* large group enrolled.

Modifying an adverb: Courses at this school *almost* never get closed.

Modifying a clause: *Consequently*, the registrar closed the course.

When choosing between an adjective and adverb form, identify the word being modified, and determine its part of speech. Then follow the conventions presented in this chapter.

1 Identifying and using adjectives

Weblink
http://www.uottawa.ca/academic/
arts/writcent/hypergrammar/
rvadvadj.html
An interactive quiz on using adjectives and adverbs from the University of Ottawa.

An **adjective** modifies a noun or pronoun by answering these questions: **Which?** the *tall* child; **What kind?** the *artistic* child; **How many?** *five* children. Pure adjectives are not derived from other words: *large, small, simple, difficult, thick, thin, cold, hot.* Many adjectives, however, are derived from nouns.

Base noun	Suffix	Adjective
science	-ic	scientific
region	-al	regional
book	-ish	bookish

Adjectives are also derived from verbs.

Base verb	Suffix	Adjective
respect	-ful	respectful
demonstrate	-ive	demonstrative
hesitate	-ant	hesitant
confuse	-ed	confused (past participle)
confuse	-ing	confusing (present participle)

ESL NOTE The past and present participles formed from the same basic verb are related in meaning. Consider, though, how two forms derived from a transitive verb (such as *confuse*) may work in opposite directions on the word modified: *a confused speaker* experiences confusion, while *a confusing speaker* gives others this experience (see 48a-1).

Placement

A single-word adjective is usually placed before the word it modifies. Occasionally an adjective will appear after a noun or pronoun—usually when the adjective is formed by a phrase or clause.

The speaker was received with *enthusiastic* applause.

The speaker, *bookish* and *hesitant*, approached the podium.

ESL NOTE In most English sentences, two or more adjectives that accumulate as modifiers before a noun or pronoun are typically given a standard order or sequence. For example, adjectives describing nationality and color are typically placed nearer than others to the noun or pronoun.

| Confusing | *a blue Japanese cheerful flower* |
| Typical | *a cheerful blue Japanese flower* |

Section 48f-1–2 describes typical patterns for placement of English adjective modifiers.

COMPUTER TIPS

Beware of Grammar Checkers

Avoid using a grammar checker, no matter how tempted you are by the concept of a software program that will "correct" your grammar mistakes. The technology required to support such a function effectively is still years away. Unfortunately, today's grammar checkers literally make more mistakes than they correct: they might tell you that a certain sentence is a run-on, for example, when it's not. If your mastery of grammar is already nearly perfect, then grammar software may have some value. You can test your writing decisions against the recommendations of the program and then decide whether your approach is valid. However, remember to proceed cautiously.

---

2 Identifying and using adverbs

An **adverb** modifies a verb by answering several questions: **When?** *Yesterday*, the child sang. **How?** The child sang *beautifully*. **How often?** The child sings *regularly*. **Where?** The child sang *here*.

In addition, adverbs modify adjectives: The child sang an *extremely* intricate melody. Adverbs can modify other adverbs: The child sings *almost* continuously. And certain adverbs can modify entire sentences: *Consequently*, the child's voice has improved.

Pure adverbs are not derived from other words: *again, almost, always, never, here, there, now, often, seldom, well.* Many adverbs, however, are formed from adjectives. These adverbs may be formed simply by adding the suffix *-ly* to adjectives.

Adjective	Add -ly	Adverb
beautiful		beautifully
strange		strangely
clever		cleverly
respectful		respectfully

However, an *-ly* ending alone is not sufficient to establish a word as an adverb. Certain adjectives also show this ending: a friend*ly* conversation, a love*ly* afternoon. In any standard dictionary look for the abbreviations **adj.** and **adv.**, which will distinguish between the forms of a word.

Placement

The location of an adverb may be shifted in a sentence, depending on the rhythm and emphasis a writer wants to achieve.

Formerly, Zimbabwe was known as Rhodesia.

Zimbabwe was *formerly* known as Rhodesia.

Zimbabwe was known as Rhodesia, *formerly.*

A note of caution: Lengthy adverb phrases and clauses should not split sentence elements that occur in pairs, such as a subject and verb or a verb and its object (see 15d,e). Also, limiting modifiers such as *only, almost,* or *nearly* must be carefully placed close to the word they modify (see 15b).

ESL NOTE While the placement of most English adverbs is flexible, limiting adverbs and others require specific positions in the sentence, as described in 48c-1–2.

Thousands of words in our language have both adjective and adverb forms. Consider modifiers formed from the noun *grace. Graceful* and *gracious* are adjectives, and *graciously, gracefully,* and *gracelessly* are adverbs.

EXERCISE 1

Identify the single-word adjectives and adverbs in the following sentences; also identify the words being modified.

adj   adj
Example: Every personality has its introverted and extroverted parts.

adv
American culture greatly exaggerates the virtues of extroversion.

1. Our culture prefers the assertive, flexible, and extroverted individual over the introverted, cautious, and inhibited individual.

2. The popular perception is that the introverted personality is uptight, socially isolated, unable to achieve goals, and prone to melancholy.

3. One could argue, however, that since introverted behavior is not rewarded by our culture, introverts should naturally feel underappreciated.

4. Some theorists correctly observe that such individuals have been responsible for much of the artistic, scientific, and scholarly achievement of the human race.

5. Social scientists theorize that in earlier historical epochs, introverts contributed subtly to social stability.

EXERCISE 2

Convert the following nouns and verbs to adjectives and adverbs; convert the adjectives to adverbs. (Use a dictionary for help, if necessary.) Then use each newly converted word in a sentence.

> *Example:* courtesy   courteous   courteously
>
>   (noun)   (adjective)   (adverb)
>
>   A courteous driver will signal before turning.

substance   hope   argue

reason   understand

ACROSS THE CURRICULUM

The Importance of Modifiers

Modifiers are central to even the most formal and technical of academic writing. Consider the following passage from a work by a psychology professor on the development of the human mind. He is writing here about the concept of spiritual possession.

> Always the patients are uneducated, usually illiterate, and all heartily believe in spirits or demons or similar beings and live in a society which does. The attacks usually last from several minutes to an hour or two, the patient being relatively normal between attacks and recalling little of them. Contrary to horror fiction stories, negatory possession is chiefly a linguistic phenomenon, not one of actual conduct. In all the cases I have studied, it is rare to find one of criminal behavior against other persons. The stricken individual does not run off and behave like a demon; he just talks like one.*

Notice how little would be communicated if the underlined adjectives and adverbs were deleted.

*Julian Jaynes, *The Origin of Consciousness in the Breakdown of the Bicameral Mind* (Houghton Mifflin, 1976).

11b Use an adverb (not an adjective) to modify verbs as well as verbals.

Adverbs are used to modify verbs even when a direct object stands between the verb and its modifier.

Faulty	If you measure an object in Denver *precise*, it will weigh some-what less than the same object measured in Washington. [The adjective *precise*—following a direct object—is used incorrectly to modify the verb *measured*.]
Revised	If you measure an object in Denver *precisely*, it will weigh some-what less than the same object measured in Washington.
Faulty	A *precise* measured object in Denver will weigh somewhat less than the same object measured in Washington. [The adjective *precise* incorrectly modifies the participle *measured*.]
Revised	A *precisely* measured object in Denver will weigh somewhat less than the same object measured in Washington.
Faulty	An object's weight can be determined by measuring it *careful* against a known weight. [The adjective *careful* incorrectly modi-fies the gerund *measuring*.]
Revised	An object's weight can be determined by measuring it *carefully* against a known weight.

11c Use an adverb (not an adjective) to modify another adverb or an adjective.

Although informal or nonstandard usage occasionally finds adjectives like *real* or *sure* functioning as adverbs ("a real bad time," "it sure was good"), standard academic usage requires that adverbs modify adjectives and other adverbs.

Nonstandard	A *reasonable* accurate scale can measure hundredths of a gram. [The adjective *reasonable* incorrectly modifies the adjective *accurate*.]
Revised	A *reasonably* accurate scale can measure hundredths of a gram.
Faulty	An object on the Moon weighs *significant* less than it does on Earth. [The adjective *significant* incorrectly modifies the adverb *less*.]
Revised	An object on the Moon weighs *significantly* less than it does on Earth.

11d Use an adjective (not an adverb) after a linking verb to describe a subject.

The following verbs are linking verbs: forms of *be* (*is, are, was, were, has been, have been*), *look, smell, taste, sound, feel, appear, become, grow, remain, seem, turn*, and *stay*. A sentence with a linking verb establishes, in effect, an equation between the first part of the sentence and the second:

A LINKING VERB B, or $A = B$.

In this construction, the predicate part, *B*, is called the *subject comple-ment*. The function of a **subject complement** is to rename or modify the noun subject of a sentence. The subject complement may be a noun, pronoun, or adjective—but *not* an adverb. Below, the linking verbs are followed by adjectives that describe a subject.

Linking	The dessert looks *delicious.*
	The crowd turned *violent.*
	The pilots were *thirsty.*

Important exceptions: Several linking verbs, especially those associated with the five senses, can also express action. When they do, they are considered *action* (not linking) *verbs* and are modified by adverbs.

Action	Palmer looked *menacingly* at the batter. [*Looked* is an action verb with an adverb modifier.]
Linking	Palmer looked angry and *menacing.* [*Looked* is now a linking verb meaning "appeared." The adjective *menacing* describes the subject's attitude.]
Action	The storm turned *violently* toward land. [*Turned* is an action verb with an adverb modifier.]
Linking	The storm turned *violent.* [*Turned* is now a linking verb meaning "became." The adjective *violent* is linked as a modifier to *storm.*]

1 Good, well, bad, badly

The words *good* and *well*, along with *bad* and *badly*, are not inter-changeable in formal writing (though they tend to be interchangeable in conversation). The common linking verbs associated with appearance or feeling—*looks, seems, appears, feels*—can cause special problems. The rules of usage follow.

Good and *well*

Good is an adjective, used either before a noun or after a linking verb to describe the condition of a subject.

Acceptable	Kyle looks good. [After a linking verb, *good* describes the subject's appearance.]
	Kyle is a good dancer. [*Good* modifies the noun *dancer.*]
Nonstandard	Susan drives good. [*Drives* is an action verb requiring an adverb.]
Revised	Susan drives well.

The word *well* can be used as either an adjective or an adverb. It has limited use as an adjective only after certain linking verbs (*looks, seems, be/am/is/are*) that describe the subject's good health.

Acceptable	Robert looks well. [*Looks* is a linking verb. The sense of this sentence is that Robert seems to be healthy.]

Well functions as an adverb whenever it follows an action verb.

Nonstandard	Janet sings good. [*Sings* is an action verb and requires an adverb as modifier.]
Revised	Janet sings well.

Bad and badly

Bad is an adjective, used before a noun and after a linking verb to describe a subject. Again, the linking verbs that involve appearance or feeling—*looks, seems, appears, feels*—can cause special problems.

Faulty	Marie feels badly. [*Feels* is a linking verb and must tie the subject, *Marie*, to an adjective.]
Revised	Marie feels bad. [As an adjective, *bad* is linked to the subject to describe *Marie* and her mental state.]

Exception: The verb *feels* could possibly be an action verb indicating a sense of touch: "The blind reader feels braille letters carefully and well." Only in this limited meaning would the phrases *feels badly* or *feels well* be used properly to show how that sense is operating.

Badly is an adverb, used after an action verb or used to modify an adjective or adverb.

Nonstandard	John cooks bad. [*Cooks* is an action verb and must be modified by an adverb.]
Revised	John cooks badly.

EXERCISE 3

Browse through a dictionary, and locate five words that have both adjective and adverb forms. Write a sentence for the two uses of each word—ten sentences in all. Draw an arrow from each adjective or adverb to the word modified.

> *Example: patient*   The people in the waiting room were patient.
>
> *patiently*   The people waited patiently.

EXERCISE 4

Fill in the blank in each sentence with *good, well, bad,* or *badly,* and draw an arrow from the word chosen to the word modified.

> *Example:* The team's prospects are _____.
>
> The team's prospects are *good.*

1. Tom has been looking _____.
2. If he were under a doctor's supervision, he might look _____.
3. He certainly sleeps _____.
4. A _____ sleeper can put in eight hours a night.
5. Sleeping _____ can make one feel old in a hurry.

www

11.1

Use comparative and superlative forms of adjectives and adverbs.

Both adjectives and adverbs change form to express comparative relationships. The base form of an adjective or adverb is called its **positive** form. The **comparative** form is used to express a relationship between two elements, and the **superlative** form is used to express a relationship among three or more elements. Most single-syllable adverbs and adjectives, and many two-syllable adjectives, show comparisons with the suffix *-er* and superlatives with *-est*.

	Positive	Comparative	Superlative
Adjective	crazy	crazier	craziest
	crafty	craftier	craftiest
Adverb	near	nearer	nearest
	far	farther	farthest

Adverbs of two or more syllables and adjectives of three or more syllables change to the comparative and superlative forms with the words *more* and *most*. Adjectives and adverbs show downward (or negative) comparisons with the words *less* and *least* placed before the positive form. If you are uncertain of an adjective's or adverb's form, refer to a dictionary.

	Positive	Comparative	Superlative
Adjective	elegant	more/less elegant	most/least elegant
	logical	more/less logical	most/least logical
Adverb	beautifully	more/less beautifully	most/least beautifully
	strangely	more/less strangely	most/least strangely

Use irregular adjectives and adverbs with care.

Some adjectives and adverbs are irregular in forming comparatives and superlatives and must be memorized. Consult the following box for these basic forms.

Irregular Forms of Comparison			
	Positive	*Comparative*	*Superlative*
Adjective	good	better	best
	bad	worse	worst
	little	less	least
	many	more	most
	much	more	most
	some	more	most
Adverb	well (also adj.)	better	best
	badly	worse	worst

> **2** Express comparative and superlative relationships accurately, completely, and logically.

Accuracy

Use the comparative form of adverbs and adjectives to show a relationship between two items. Use the superlative form when relating three or more items.

Two items	In the winter months, New York is colder than Miami.
Two items	First-year students are often more conscientious about their studies than second-year students.
Multiples	Eudora Welty is considered one of the finest American writers of the twentieth century.

Completeness

Be sure to provide enough context so that comparisons make sense.

Incomplete	Jason is more efficient. [More efficient than whom? at what?]
Revised	Jason is the more efficient runner. [Two runners are being compared.]
	OR
	Jason is a more efficient runner than Dylan.

Logic

Certain adjectives have an absolute meaning—they cannot be logically compared. For instance, one cannot discuss greater or lesser degrees of *perfect*. *Perfect* represents a logical endpoint of comparison, as do the words *unique, first, final, last, absolute, infinite,* and *dead.* While a concert performance might be *nearly* perfect or a patient on an operating table *almost* dead, once *perfection* or *death* is reached, comparisons literally make no sense.

Illogical	The story was submitted in its most final form.
Revised	The story was submitted in its final form.
	OR
	The story was submitted in nearly final form.

11f Avoid double comparisons, double superlatives, and double negatives.

Double comparisons/superlatives

11.2

Adjectives and adverbs show comparative and superlative relationships either with a suffix (*-er/-est*) or with the words *more, most, less,* or *least*. It is redundant and awkward to use the *-er/-est* suffix with *more/most* or *less/least*.

CRITICAL DECISIONS

Applying a Test for Choosing Comparative Forms—
few/fewer/fewest, little/less/least, many, much

When making comparisons, note the differences between nouns that can be counted and those that cannot (see 7a-2 and 45a-1). Then choose the appropriate form for your comparison.

■ **For nouns that can be counted, downward comparisons must be made with *few, fewer,* or *fewest*.**

| Faulty | Frozen yogurt has *less* calories than ice cream. [Since *calories* can be counted, *less* is the wrong comparative term.] |
| Revised | Frozen yogurt has *fewer* calories than ice cream. |

■ **For mass nouns, which cannot be counted (see 7a-2), downward comparisons must be made with *little, less,* or *least*.**

| Faulty | "Drinker's Delight" coffee has *fewer* caffeine than regular coffee. [Since *caffeine* is a mass noun and cannot be counted, *fewer* is the wrong comparative term.] |
| Revised | "Drinker's Delight" coffee has *less* caffeine than regular coffee. |

■ **For nouns that can be counted, use the adjective *many*, not *much*.**

| Faulty | Ice cream has *much* calories. [Since *calories* can be counted, *much* is the incorrect adjective form.] |
| Revised | Ice cream has *many* calories. |

Faulty The Empire State Building is more taller than the Chrysler Building.

Revised The Empire State Building is taller than the Chrysler Building.

Faulty That is the least likeliest conclusion to the story.

Revised That is the least likely conclusion to the story.

Double negatives

Double negatives—the presence of two modifiers that say "no" in the same sentence—are redundant and sometimes confusing, though fairly common in nonstandard usage. A clear negation should be expressed only once. Combine the negatives *not*, *never*, *neither/nor*, *hardly*, or *scarcely* with *any*, *anything*, or *anyone*. Do not combine these negatives with the negatives *no*, *none*, *nothing*, or *no one*.

Nonstandard I didn't have none.
I didn't have no cash. [These double negatives risk the implication that the speaker in fact has cash.]

Revised I had none.
I didn't have any cash.

Nonstandard I hardly had none.

Revised I hardly had any.

Nonstandard I never had nothing.

Revised I never had anything.
I had nothing.

11g Avoid overusing nouns as modifiers.

A noun can modify another noun and thus function as an adjective: *gate* keeper, *toll* booth, *cell* block. Noun modifiers provide handy shortcuts, but when two or more nouns are stacked before a third noun to function as adjectives, the result is logically and stylistically disastrous.

Unclear The textbook Civil War chapter review questions are due tomorrow.

The sentence falters because five different nouns could serve as the subject: *textbook*, *Civil War*, *chapter*, *review*, and *questions*. Unstack noun modifiers by moving the subject to the beginning of the sentence and arranging modifying nouns into phrases.

                        subject   prep. phrase with possessive   prep. phrase
Revised The review questions from the textbook's chapter on the Civil War are due tomorrow.

ESL NOTE With noun modifiers, sequence and placement are more critical than with adjectives or adverbs (see 44a-2 on noun modifiers). Some of the conventions for ordering cumulative adjective modifiers may also apply to nouns (see 48f).

EXERCISE 5

Correct the problems with comparative and superlative forms in the following sentences.

> *Example:* Of the three Brontë sisters, Emily was the taller.
>
> Of the three Brontë sisters, Emily was the tallest. [The superlative is needed to differentiate among three or more people.]

1. Anne Brontë, the younger sister, wrote *Agnes Grey* and *The Tenant of Wildfell Hall.*
2. Charlotte is better known for *Jane Eyre.*
3. Charlotte was the longest-lived of the three sisters.
4. Emily was the stubbornest: though seriously ill, she refused to see a doctor.
5. Emily was the more private of the three, even with her family.

12

Sentence Fragments

A central goal of writing is to keep readers focused on clearly stated ideas. Few errors are more disruptive of this goal than the sentence fragment. In drafting and editing your work, it is important that you determine how best to spot and correct this error.

CRITICAL DECISIONS

Keeping the Needs of Readers in Mind

One way to spot sentence fragments is to think carefully about your readers. With a critical eye, read every group of words you have set off as a complete sentence. Individually, is the intended meaning of each complete and clear? Is the relationship among ideas easy to follow? If not, use the tests for determining sentence fragments discussed in this chapter.

Weblink

http://leo.stcloudstate.edu/punct/
fragmentcauses.html

A succinct bottom-up view of the causes of sentence fragments, from LEO: Literacy Education Online.

The **sentence fragment** is a partial sentence punctuated as if it were a complete sentence. Because it is only a partial sentence, a fragment leaves readers confused, trying to guess at what claims or statements are being made. To be a sentence, a group of words must first have a subject and a predicate. A sentence fragment may lack either a subject or a predicate—and sometimes both. A fragment may also be a dependent clause that has not been joined to an independent (or main) clause.

12a   Check for completeness of sentences.

Avoid writing fragments by checking your sentences for grammatical completeness. There are three tests you can conduct:

1. Locate a verb.
2. Locate the verb's subject.
3. Check for subordinating conjunctions or relative pronouns.

First test: Locate a verb.

To be sure you've written a sentence, find the verb. Note that verbs ending in -*ing* must be preceded by a form of *be* (for example, *is*, *are*, *were*, *was*, etc.) in order to function as sentence verbs.

Fragment	The wind blowing in great gusts. [*Blowing* is not preceded by a form of *be*.]
Revised	The wind *was blowing* in great gusts.

Be sure that the word you settle on as the sentence verb is not a participle, a verb form that functions as a modifier (see 7a-4).

Fragment	A pair of boots caked with mud by the door. [*Caked* serves as a modifier describing *pair of boots*.]
Revised	A pair of boots caked with mud *sat* by the door.

Verb forms introduced with the infinitive marker *to* never function as sentence verbs. Another verb must be added to make a sentence.

Fragment	A way to solve the problem. [*To solve* is an infinitive, not a sentence verb.]
Revised	A way to solve the problem *exists*.

Second test: Locate the verb's subject.

Once you have located a verb, ask *who* or *what* makes its assertion or action, and you will find the subject.

Fragment	Separated visible light into a spectrum of colors. [Who separated?]
Revised	*Isaac Newton* separated visible light into a spectrum of colors. [The new subject, *Isaac Newton*, answers the question.]
Fragment	First attempted an analysis of the short story. [Who attempted?]
Revised	*Edgar Allan Poe* first attempted an analysis of the short story. [The new subject, *Edgar Allan Poe*, answers the question.]

Imperative sentences—commands—often lack a subject. Still, they are considered sentences, since the implied subject is understood to be *you*.

Imperative sentence	**Understood as**
Come here, please.	You come here, please.

ESL NOTE The subject of a sentence in English, unlike that in many other languages, is expressed directly as a separate word in one location

Spotlight on Common Errors—SENTENCE CONSTRUCTION AND FRAGMENTS

These are the errors most commonly associated with sentence construction and fragments. For full explanations and suggested revisions, follow the cross-references to chapter sections.

FRAGMENT ERRORS arise when writers incorrectly mark a group of words as a sentence. Apply a three-part test to confirm that a grouping of words can stand alone as a sentence (see 12a).

Test 1: Locate a verb: A sentence must have a verb.

Churchill *was* a leader.	**A leader of great distinction.**	**When he *became* prime minister.**
[Verb—*was*]	[No verb—this grouping of words cannot be a sentence; it is a FRAGMENT.]	[Verb—*became*—BUT this word grouping fails Test 3 below, so it is still a FRAGMENT.]

Revised   Churchill was *a leader of great distinction*.

Note: Be sure the word selected as a verb is not a verbal, which looks like a verb but actually serves as a subject, object, or modifier (see 7a-4).

After *serving* his country in the First World War.

[Verbal: *serving* looks like a verb but is actually an object in the prepositional phrase beginning with *after*. This grouping of words is therefore a FRAGMENT.]

Revised   **After serving his country in the First World War,** he became prime minister.

Test 2: Locate the verb's subject: A sentence must have a subject.

Churchill was a leader.	**When he became prime minister.**
[Subject—*Churchill*]	[Subject—*he*—BUT this word grouping fails Test 3, so it is still a FRAGMENT.]

Test 3: Be sure that words such as *when, while, because* or *who, which, that* do not prevent the word group from being a sentence (see subordinating conjunctions and relative pronouns, 19b-1–2).

Sentence   Churchill *was* a leader.

[No words prevent the grouping from being a sentence.]

Fragments   *When* he became prime minister.   *Who* became prime minister.

[*When* (a subordinating conjunction) and *who* (a relative pronoun) prevent these word groups from standing alone as sentences.]

Revised   **He became prime minister.**

See 12b–12d for ways to correct fragments once you have identified them.

only. Because the subject is not implied in the form of a verb (other than the imperative) or other sentence part, identifying the subject with a specific word is critical to the structure of an English sentence (see 7a-1 and 7b).

Third test: Check for subordinating conjunctions or relative pronouns.

Subordinating conjunctions

after	because	provided that	until
although	before	since	whenever
as if	how	though	where
assuming that	if	unless	while

A word grouping that consists of a subject and predicate is still a fragment if it contains an opening subordinating conjunction. Eliminate the conjunction, and the clause will stand as a sentence. Combine the dependent clause with another sentence, and the new dependent clause will function as an adverb.

Fragment   Though people may have a personality disorder. [The conjunction *though* makes the clause dependent on another statement.]

Revised   ~~Though~~ People may have a personality disorder. [Dropping the conjunction makes a simple sentence.]

Revised   Though people may have a personality disorder, *they may see their behavior as normal.* [The dependent clause now functions as an adverb.]

Note: A subordinating conjunction cannot be used as a transitional expression at the beginning of a sentence. Words like *therefore* or *however*, called *conjunctive adverbs*, *do* function as transitions (see 13b-4). Observe the differences:

Fragment   Whereas, Allen went to the second session.

Revised   Allen went to the second session.

Revised   However, Allen went to the second session.

The words *though*, *although*, and *whereas* are *not* interchangeable with *however* or *therefore*.

Relative pronouns

that	whichever	whoever	whomever
which	who	whom	

A relative pronoun signals that the clause is dependent and cannot stand alone as a sentence. If the pronoun is eliminated and a noun is present to function as the subject, the clause will stand as a sentence. If combined with another sentence, the dependent clause will function as an adjective.

Fragment   People who have a personality disorder. [*Who* takes the place of the subject *people*, creating a dependent clause.]

Revised   People ~~who~~ have a personality disorder. [Eliminating *who* leaves a simple sentence.]

Revised   People who have a personality disorder *see their behavior as acceptable.* [*People* is the subject of a verb, *see*, with a *who* clause as adjective modifier.]

Exception: When a relative pronoun introduces a question, it becomes an interrogative (questioning) pronoun. The resulting construction is not considered to be a fragment: *Who has a personality disorder?*

Note that fragments beginning with subordinating conjunctions and relative pronouns may be grammatically part of the preceding sentence. The fragments in the example below are italicized.

Fragments   The patient was diagnosed with a personality disorder. *Although she didn't accept the diagnosis.* She refused treatment. *Which troubled her doctor.*

Revised   The patient was diagnosed with a personality disorder although she didn't accept the diagnosis. She refused treatment, which troubled her doctor.

EXERCISE 1

Use the three-part test to identify fragments and to explain the cause of each fragment. Place a check before complete sentences, and circle the numbers of items that are fragments.

> *Example:* When the author of one study claims that groups moving in unison tend to think alike.
>
> Fragment—fails Test 3 (The word *when* prevents the clause from standing alone as a sentence.)

1. Rhythmic movements help to establish a group bond.
2. Giving the group a certain advantage over the other groups.
3. One reason why armies put so much emphasis on drilling new recruits.
4. Possibly movement in unison represents or fosters identical, in-group thinking.
5. The Nazi parade is a striking example of the connection between lockstep movement and lockstep thinking.

12b   **Eliminate fragments: Revise dependent clauses set off as sentences.**

A dependent clause functions as a modifier—either as an adverb (see 19b-1) or as an adjective (see 19b-2). A dependent clause that has been set off incorrectly as a sentence can be corrected in one of two ways:

> **1** Convert the dependent clause to an independent clause.

Fragment Even though the president attended the meeting.
Clear The president attended the meeting.

If the dependent clause begins with a subordinating conjunction, delete the conjunction, and you will have an independent clause—a sentence.

Fragment While Americans keep recycling the same old clichés.
Revised ~~While~~ Americans keep recycling the same old clichés.

If a dependent clause uses a relative pronoun, eliminate the relative pronoun, replacing it with a noun or personal pronoun, if necessary, and you will have an independent clause.

Fragment Many students, who might read more often.
Revised Many students~~, who~~ might read more often. [The eliminated relative pronoun leaves the noun, *students*, as the subject.]

> **2** Join the dependent clause to a new sentence.

Fragment Though the president attended.
Clear Though the president attended, she did not speak.

The dependent clause introduced by a subordinating conjunction can be made to function as an adverb by joining it to an independent clause. When the dependent clause introduces a sentence, set it off with a comma (see 25a-1). When the clause ends a sentence, do not use a comma (but see 25a-3).

Fragment If our culture did not portray reading as an almost antisocial activity.
Revised *Many students might read more often* if our culture did not portray reading as an almost antisocial activity.

A dependent clause fragment that uses a relative pronoun can be made to function as an adjective (a relative clause) by attaching it to an independent clause.

Fragment Levar Burton, an actor best known for his roles in *Roots* and *Star Trek: The Next Generation*, who has done much to promote literacy. [The noun and modifying clause have no verb.]

Revised Levar Burton, who has done much to promote literacy, is an actor best known for his roles in *Roots* and *Star Trek: The Next
Generation*. [The *who* clause serves as an adjective in a sentence
with a new verb, *is*.]

EXERCISE 2

Identify fragments in the following paragraph. Combine fragments to
make complete sentences.

12.2

Example: Even though Anheuser-Busch, Miller, G. Heileman,
Coors, and Pabst brew 95 percent of the 200 million
barrels of beer produced annually in the United States.
These companies are not the only producers of American beer.

Even though Anheuser-Busch, Miller, G. Heileman,
Coors, and Pabst brew 95 percent of the 200 million
barrels of beer produced annually in the United States,
these companies are not the only producers of American beer.

While only eight microbreweries existed in the United States
a decade ago. Today seventy microbreweries are brewing more
than 65,000 barrels of specialty beers a year. Microbreweries are
winning awards for the tastiness of their products. Which has
caused the large producers to alter their production and advertising techniques. Because microbrewery beer is often free of addi-
tives. It must be sold locally. Local production, distribution, and
advertising has become a key to microbrewery success. Which
depends on creating the perception among buyers of a freshness
and healthfulness not available in mass-market beers. Even though
image is important. Quality of the product is what has convinced
an increasing number of American beer drinkers to buy from local,
smaller breweries.

12c Eliminate fragments: Revise phrases set off as sentences.

Phrases consist of nouns and the words associated with them or
verb forms not functioning as verbs (called *verbals*) and the words associated with them. Phrases function as sentence parts—as modifiers,
subjects, objects, and complements—but never as sentences. The
various kinds of phrases are defined in 7d. As with dependent clauses
that form fragments, you may either convert phrases to complete
sentences by adding words, or you may join phrases to independent
clauses.

Eliminating Fragments from Your Writing

1. **Revise dependent clauses set off as sentences.**
   Convert the dependent clause to an independent clause.

   Fragment   Although computers may be revolutionizing the world.

   Revised   ~~Although~~ Computers may be revolutionizing the world.

   Join the dependent clause to a new sentence.

   Fragment   Although, computers may be revolutionizing the world.

   Revised   Although computers may be revolutionizing the world, *relatively few people understand how they function.*

2. **Revise phrases set off as sentences.**
   There are various kinds of phrases: verbal, prepositional, absolute, and appositive (see 7d). None can stand alone as a sentence.

   Fragment   After years of drought.

   Revised   ~~After~~ Years of drought *can devastate a national economy.*

   Revised   After years of drought, *a nation's economy can be devastated.*

3. **Revise repeating structures or compound predicates set off as sentences.**
   Repeating elements and compound predicates cannot stand alone. Incorporate such structures into an existing sentence, or add words to construct a new sentence.

   Fragment   College sports has long been conducted as a business. A profitable business. [The repeating element is a fragment.]

   Revised   College sports has long been conducted as a business—a profitable business. [The repeating element has been incorporated into an existing sentence.]

| | Revising verbal phrases |

Participial and gerund phrases (functioning as modifiers or nouns)

Fragment   Making his television debut in *Roots*.

Revised   Levar Burton ~~making~~ made his television debut in *Roots*. [The phrase is rewritten as a sentence.]

Revised   Making his television debut in *Roots*, Levar Burton received excellent reviews. [The participial phrase, functioning as an adjective, is joined to an independent clause.]

Infinitive phrases (functioning as nouns)

Fragment   To promote literacy among children.

Revised   One of Burton's goals is to promote literacy among children. [The phrase is rewritten as a sentence.]

2   Revising prepositional phrases (functioning as modifiers)

Fragment   With its emphasis on quick, informal communication.

Revised   With its emphasis on quick, informal communication, e-mail invites users to be careless about the rules of grammar and usage. [The phrase is joined to an independent clause.]

3   Revising absolute phrases (modifying an entire sentence)

Fragment   The need for unhindered movement being a defining quality of the American character.

Revised   The need for unhindered movement is a defining quality of the American character. [The phrase is rewritten as a sentence.]

Revised   The culture of the automobile first arose in the United States, the need for unhindered movement being a defining quality of the American character. [The phrase is joined as a modifier to an independent clause.]

4   Revising appositive phrases (renaming or describing other nouns)

Fragment   A tendency to drive first and think about environmental consequences later.

Revised   Americans have a tendency to drive first and think about environmental consequences later. [The phrase is rewritten as a sentence.]

Revised   Americans suffer from "Auto-mania," a tendency to drive first and think about environmental consequences later. [The phrase renames the final noun in the independent clause.]

EXERCISE 3

Identify the numbered units that are fragments, and correct them. Place a check before any sentence needing no revision.

> *Example:* Whereas, as children mature, they should learn to sort through conflicting messages. [*Whereas* is a subordinating conjunction. The clause that follows is dependent.]
>
> As children mature, they should learn to sort through conflicting messages.

(1) Children receive conflicting messages from a variety of sources. (2) Which cannot be silenced: teachers, books, friends, and television programs. We have, from time to time, experimented in this country with limiting access to potentially damaging or offensive materials (3) such as books and movies. (4) But these experiments have not withstood legal challenges. (5) The courts have decided that Americans have the right to choose what they see or hear and that writers and others have the right to create what they wish. (6) Although, certain extreme instances, like child pornography, are so offensive and damaging to the children being filmed that as a society we *have* said that such products are repugnant. (7) Which is the argument that Charren is making about advertisements directed at children. (8) But as a society having agreed to limit speech only in the most extreme cases. (9) There is nothing in the making of advertisements that is as purposefully vulgar or hurtful as there is in child pornography. (10) If anything, advertising more closely resembling the language of our everyday speech.

12d | **Eliminate fragments: Revise repeating structures or compound predicates set off as sentences.**

Fragment As large as the capitol's rotunda

Clear The foyer was large, as large as the capitol's rotunda.

Repetition can be an effective stylistic tool (see 19c-2). Repeated elements, however, are not sentences but sentence parts and should not be punctuated as sentences. Use a comma or dashes to set off repeated elements.

Fragment Children begin for the first time to differentiate themselves from others as they enter adolescence. *As they begin to develop a personal identity.* [The subordinate *as* clause cannot stand alone.]

Revised Children begin for the first time to differentiate themselves from others as they enter adolescence, as they begin to develop a personal identity. [The clause is subordinated.]

Fragment Adolescents want to know they belong in the social order. An order shaped by forces they barely understand. [The phrase and clause need a connection.]

Revised Adolescents want to know they belong in the social order—an order shaped by forces they barely understand. [The structure repeats and expands the term *social order*.]

Compound predicates consist of two sentence verbs (and their associated words) joined with a coordinating conjunction, such as *and* or *but*. The two predicates share the same subject and are part of the same sentence. When one half of the compound predicate is punctuated as a sentence, it becomes a fragment. To correct the fragment, join it to a sentence that contains an appropriate subject, or provide the fragment with its own subject.

Fragment   The process of maturation is lifelong. *But is most critical during the adolescent years.* [The last unit has no subject.]

Revised   The process of maturation is lifelong. But *the process* is most critical during the adolescent years. [The unit is given its own subject.]

Revised   The process of maturation is lifelong but is most critical during the adolescent years. [The phrase is joined to the preceding sentence as a compound predicate.]

EXERCISE 4

Identify which of the following units are fragments. Correct each by writing a new sentence or by joining the fragment to an independent clause.

> *Example:* Messiness in the workplace. How does it affect your productivity? [The first unit lacks a verb.]
>
> How does messiness in the workplace affect your productivity? [The fragment replaces the pronoun *it* and becomes the subject of the question.]

Specialists suggest that setting up a workable system to organize yourself is only a first step. A small one. The most significant organizing principle in life is a wastebasket in every room. And a willingness to use them. A common myth is that highly creative people are "naturally" messier and more chaotic than those who are relatively uncreative. That being organized and artistic are incompatible. A *Wall Street Journal* article reported that people spend an average of six weeks a year looking for things in their offices. Unbelievable!

12.3

COMPUTER TIPS

Help Online

Online Writing Labs (OWLs) are beginning to proliferate on the Internet. These resource centers offer writing services ranging from standard handbook information to reviewers who will actually read a draft and offer suggestions. Most provide help with specific questions on composition, research, grammar, and style. The most popular OWL is located at Purdue University: <http://owl.English.purdue.edu>.

| 12e | **Use fragments intentionally on rare occasions.** |

Whose business was it? No one's.

The speaker made his point. Barely.

Fragments are generally not suitable for academic writing. In personal essays and in fiction, experienced writers will occasionally use sentence fragments by design. These intentional uses are always carefully fitted to the context of a neighboring sentence, sometimes answering an implied question or completing a parallel structure that has been separated for emphasis. In academic prose, a fragment will probably be regarded as a lapse, not as a stylistic flourish.

ACROSS THE CURRICULUM

An Acceptable Use of Fragments

One potentially acceptable use of sentence fragments in academic writing is a fragment that answers a question posed by the writer in the sentence that immediately precedes it. Here is a historian writing about the depiction of Frontierland at the Disney theme parks:

Where is the frontier? *Evidently where New Mexico borders on the Mississippi River, where western gold and silver miners load their ore directly onto steamboats heading to New Orleans.**

Even so, such usage introduces a level of informality that some readers may find inappropriate.

*Patricia Nelson Limerick, "Travels in Frontierland" in *The Adventures of the Frontier in the Twentieth Century* (University of California Press, 1994).

13

Comma Splices and Fused Sentences

Sentence grammar is built on the fundamental rule that independent clauses—complete sentences—must be kept distinct from one another. When sentence boundaries are blurred, statements become confused. Readers must struggle to decipher which combinations of words might form meaningful units.

Sentence boundaries can become blurred in two ways. In the **fused** (or **run-on**) **sentence,** the writer fails to recognize the end of one independent clause and the beginning of the next. The writer of a **comma splice** recognizes the end of one independent clause and the beginning of the next, but marks the boundary between the two incorrectly—with a comma.

13a Identify fused sentences and comma splices.

Fused sentence	In the last election, voter turnout was low turnout should be higher.
Comma splice	In the last election, voter turnout was low, turnout should be higher.
Clear	In the last election, voter turnout was low. Turnout should be higher.

Before submitting a draft of your work to others, read your sentences aloud. Look for long sentences that seem to consist of two or more separate statements, or those that are so long they force you to stop midway to take a breath. Be on the alert for the following three circumstances in which fused sentences and comma splices are found.

1. **A sentence of explanation, expansion, or example** is frequently fused to or spliced together with another sentence that is being explained, expanded on, or illustrated. Even if the topics of the two sentences are closely related, the sentences themselves must remain distinct.

Spotlight on Common Errors— SENTENCE CONSTRUCTION AND SENTENCE BOUNDARIES

These are the errors most commonly associated with sentence construction and sentence boundaries. For full explanations and suggested revisions, follow the cross-references to chapter sections.

RECOGNIZING SENTENCE BOUNDARIES: The end of a sentence is usually marked with a period. Not clearly marking the end will result in a FUSED SENTENCE (see 13b-1) or a COMMA SPLICE (see 13b-1).

Correct	Winston Churchill became a leader. He served his country in the First World War. Churchill was a leader of distinction.
Fused sentences	Winston Churchill became a leader he served his country in the First World War Churchill was a leader of distinction.
Comma splices	Winston Churchill became a leader, he served his country in the First World War, Churchill was a leader of distinction.

REVISING ERRORS OF SENTENCE CONSTRUCTION

Separate independent clauses with a period (see 13b-1).

Winston Churchill served his country in the First World War. He became a leader of distinction.

Link by using a comma plus one of these conjunctions—*and, but, or, nor* (see coordinating conjunctions, 13b-2, 19a-1).

Winston Churchill served his country in the First World War, *and* he became a leader of distinction.

Link by using a semicolon (see 13b-3, 26a–c).

Winston Churchill served his country in the First World War; he became a leader of distinction.

Link by using a semicolon (or period) and a word such as *however, consequently,* or *therefore* (see conjunctive adverbs, 13b-4, 19a-3).

Winston Churchill served his country in the First World War; *subsequently,* he became a leader of distinction.

Link by using a word such as *when, while,* or *because* (see subordinating conjunctions, 13b-5, 19b).

After he served his country in the First World War, Winston Churchill became a leader of distinction.

Fused sentence	The Pre-Raphaelite Brotherhood was a group of painters, poets, and painter-poets their artistic aims varied widely.
Comma splice	The Pre-Raphaelite Brotherhood was a group of painters, poets, and painter-poets, their artistic aims varied widely.
Revised	The Pre-Raphaelite Brotherhood was a group of painters, poets, and painter-poets. Their artistic aims varied widely.

13.1

2. **The pronouns** *he, she, they, it, this,* and ***that,*** when renaming the subject of a sentence, can signal a comma splice or a fused sentence. Even when the subject named or renamed in adjacent sentences is identical, the sentences themselves must be kept distinct.

Fused sentence	Dante Gabriel Rossetti was a poet he was also a painter.
Comma splice	Dante Gabriel Rossetti was a poet, he was also a painter.
Revised	Dante Gabriel Rossetti was a poet, and he was a painter.

3. **Conjunctive adverbs** (words such as *however, furthermore, thus, therefore,* and *consequently*) and **transitional expressions** (phrases such as *for example* and *on the other hand*) are commonly found in fused or spliced clauses. Conjunctive adverbs and transitions always link complete sentences. Writers must reflect this linkage with appropriate punctuation: a period or semicolon. (For a complete list of conjunctive adverbs, see the Critical Decisions box at 19a-1.)

Fused sentence	The works of the Pre-Raphaelites were initially criticized as vulgar however the influential art critic John Ruskin soon took up their cause.
Comma splice	The works of the Pre-Raphaelites were initially criticized as vulgar, however, the influential art critic John Ruskin soon took up their cause.
Revised	The works of the Pre-Raphaelites were initially criticized as vulgar; however, the influential art critic John Ruskin soon took up their cause. [*However* starts a new main clause.]

EXERCISE I

Use a slash mark (/) to identify the points at which the following sentences are fused or spliced together.

> *Example:* Designers of advertisements for professional medical journals use multiple strategies for convincing their readers sometimes they use shocking visual images.
>
> Designers of advertisements for professional medical journals use multiple strategies for convincing readers / sometimes they use shocking visual images.

1. Advertisements for aspirin and other pain relievers are incredibly dull, they are so like one another, so unmemorable that we remember them only because of their sheer frequency.

2. Unlike most other advertising, pain reliever commercials are very modest in their claims, in other words, they promise only partial relief from minor aches and only relatively quickly.

3. One would expect that such commercials would press harder to represent both the intensity of the pain as well as the joy of relief however these advertisements never suggest that the sufferer was ever in acute pain or that the sufferer's relief is now total.

4. Oddly enough, ads for pain relievers claim very little, they are undramatic, uninteresting.

5. The advertisements that physicians and surgeons see in their professional journals do attempt to represent acute pain, the difference may be attributable to the fact that the audience in this case (doctors) is not experiencing pain itself, but rather is treating pain.

www

13.2

CRITICAL DECISIONS

Recognizing Independent Clauses

In order to avoid creating comma splices and fused sentences, it is essential that you be able to recognize independent clauses. An independent clause is a complete unit of thought that contains one subject (or a compound subject) and one verb (or a compound verb) and is not introduced by a subordinating conjunction or relative pronoun. Check your sentences for the presence of a second subject following the verb; if it is not the subject of a subordinate clause, then it is likely the start of a new independent clause. See Chapter 7 for more definitions.

13b Correct fused sentences and comma splices in one of five ways.

Separate independent clauses with a period
(and sometimes a colon).

Comma splice	Cotton was once the lead farm product in Alabama, today poultry has replaced it.
Clear	Cotton was once the lead farm product in Alabama. Today, poultry has replaced it.

Using a period is the most obvious way to repair a fused or spliced construction. Occasionally, writers use a colon between independent clauses when the first sentence is a formal and emphatic introduction to the second sentence.

Fused sentence	Logging is often the first step in deforestation it may be followed by complete clearing of trees and a shift to unsound land uses.
Comma splice	Logging is often the first step in deforestation, it may be followed by complete clearing of trees and a shift to unsound land uses.
Revised	Logging is often the first step in deforestation. It may be followed by complete clearing of trees and a shift to unsound land uses.
Revised	Logging is often the first step in deforestation: it may be followed by complete clearing of trees and a shift to unsound land uses. [The colon gives the opening clause an emphatic introductory function.]

2   Link clauses with a comma and a coordinating conjunction.

Weblink

http://parallel.park.uga.edu/
~sigalas/Commas/2ic.html
Here's an upbeat page with a handy mnemonic device for curing comma splices.

Fused sentence	January may be the coldest month it is a month of great productivity.
Clear	January may be the coldest month, **but** it is a month of great productivity.

Use a comma placed *before* a coordinating conjunction—*and, but, or, nor, for, so,* and *yet*—to link sentences that are closely related in content and that are equally important. (See 19a for a detailed discussion of co-ordinating conjunctions.)

Fused sentence	Deforestation has a severe environmental impact on soil in heavy tropical rains soil erodes quickly.
Comma splice	Deforestation has a severe environmental impact on soil, in heavy tropical rains soil erodes quickly.
Revised	Deforestation has a severe environmental impact on soil, **for** in heavy tropical rains soil erodes quickly.

3   Link clauses with a semicolon.

Fused sentence	Wind is one cause of erosion water is another cause.
Comma splice	Wind is one cause of erosion, water is another cause.
Clear	Wind is one cause of erosion; water is another cause.

Use a semicolon in place of a comma and a coordinating conjunction to link sentences that are closely related and equally important.

The semicolon links independent clauses without making the relationship between them explicit. You might choose a semicolon when the relationship between clauses is crystal clear and a conjunction would be redundant or when you want your readers to discover the exact relationship between clauses.

Fused sentence	Experience reinforces the argument that deforestation has not been a path to economic development it has instead been a costly drain on resources.
Comma splice	Experience reinforces the argument that deforestation has not been a path to economic development, it has instead been a costly drain on resources.
Revised	Experience reinforces the argument that deforestation has not been a path to economic development; it has instead been a costly drain on resources.

> **4** Link clauses with a semicolon (or period) and a conjunctive adverb.

Comma splice	Joyce Carol Oates is a novelist, essayist, playwright, and poet, she is a distinguished scholar.
Clear	Joyce Carol Oates is a novelist, essayist, playwright, and poet; **moreover,** she is a distinguished scholar.

Use conjunctive adverbs—words such as *however, furthermore, thus, therefore,* and *consequently*—to link closely related, equally important clauses. (See the Critical Decisions box at 19a-1 for a complete list of conjunctive adverbs.)

As with most adverbs, a conjunctive adverb can shift its location in a sentence. If placed at the beginning, the conjunctive adverb is usually followed by a comma. If placed in the middle, it is usually set off by a pair of commas. And if placed at the end, it is preceded by a comma. Wherever you place the adverb, be sure to use a period or a semicolon between the two clauses you have linked. Place a period between clauses when you want a full separation of ideas. Place a semicolon between clauses when you want to emphasize the link between ideas.

Fused sentence	Deforestation is not irreversible once a forest is cleared regeneration takes a lifetime.
Comma splice	Deforestation is not irreversible, once a forest is cleared regeneration takes a lifetime.
Revised	Deforestation is not irreversible; however, once a forest is cleared, regeneration takes a lifetime. [The semicolon emphasizes the link between ideas.]
Revised	Deforestation is not irreversible. Once a forest is cleared, however, regeneration takes a lifetime. [The period makes a full separation.]

CRITICAL DECISIONS

 Choosing a Method to Link Independent Clauses
A period helps readers focus on and understand one sentence at a time. To show the relationship *between* sentences, consider linking clauses. You have various options for doing so. Which option you choose depends on the relationship you want to establish between independent clauses.

■ **Use a colon to make one independent clause announce another.** (See 13b-1.)

Separated	The race was postponed for one reason. The sponsors withdrew their support.
Linked	The race was postponed for one reason: the sponsors withdrew their support.

■ **Use one of three options to maintain equal emphasis between two independent clauses.** (See 13b-2–4 and 19a.)

Coordinating conjunction with a comma

Separated	Runners had already arrived. They were angry with the postponement.
Linked	Runners had already arrived, **and** they were angry with the postponement.

Semicolon

Separated	One faction of runners wanted to boycott all future races in that city. Another faction wanted to stage a protest march.
Linked	One faction of runners wanted to boycott all future races in that city; another faction wanted to stage a protest march.

Conjunctive adverb with a semicolon or a period

Separated	The sponsors cited financial worries. They had political concerns as well.
Linked	The sponsors cited financial worries; **however,** they had political concerns as well.

■ **Use a subordinating conjunction to emphasize one independent clause more than the other.** (See 13b-5 and 19b.)

Separated	The press was embarrassing. The sponsors canceled the race permanently.
Linked	**Because** the press was embarrassing, the sponsors canceled the race permanently.

Comma splice	Hannibal crossed the Alps, he defeated the Romans in the Po Valley.
Clear	**After** Hannibal crossed the Alps, he defeated the Romans in the Po Valley.

Use a subordinating conjunction to join clauses by giving more emphasis to the idea in one clause than in the other. By placing a subordinating conjunction at the beginning of a clause, or by using a relative pronoun such as *who, whom, which,* or *that,* you make that clause dependent. The new dependent clause will function as a modifier. When the clause begins a sentence, a comma follows it. The dependent clause at the end of a sentence often does not use a comma. (See 19b and 25a-1 for discussions of subordination.)

Fused sentence	International agencies have begun to lend help a number of governments are now strengthening their forest-management programs.
Comma splice	International agencies have begun to lend help, a number of governments are now strengthening their forest-management programs.
Revised	**Because** international agencies have begun to lend help, a number of governments are now strengthening their forest-management programs. [A dependent clause begins the sentence.]
Revised	A number of governments are now strengthening their forest-management programs **because** international agencies have begun to lend help. [A dependent clause ends the sentence.]
Revised	A number of governments are now strengthening forest-management programs **that** have begun to get help from international agencies. [A dependent relative clause ends the sentence, creating a different meaning.]

ACROSS THE CURRICULUM

Comma Splices in Fiction

Novelists and short story writers occasionally use comma splices for literary effect, particularly to suggest that the events described in the independent clauses are happening almost simultaneously. Here is an example:

It was while the two were in midair, their hands about to meet, that lightning struck the main [circus tent] pole and sizzled down the guy wires, filling the air with blue heat and light that Harry must certainly have seen, even through the silk of his blindfold. *The tent buckled, the edifice toppled him forward.*

—Louise Erdrich, "Eleanor's Tale: The Leap"

As a student of literature, you should learn to recognize this dramatic narrative use of comma splices.

Conjunctions and Punctuation

Coordinating conjunctions

            and   but   so   or   for   nor   yet
Use coordinating conjunctions with punctuation in this pattern:
   Independent clause   ,   CONJUNCTION   independent clause.

Newton developed calculus, and he discovered laws of gravity.

Conjunctive adverbs

        however   furthermore   thus   therefore   consequently
Use conjunctive adverbs with punctuation in these patterns:
   Independent clause   ;   CONJUNCTION   ,   independent clause.
   Independent clause   .   CONJUNCTION   ,   independent clause.

Newton developed calculus; moreover, he discovered laws of gravity.

Newton developed calculus. Moreover, he discovered laws of gravity.

Subordinating conjunctions

        after   although   because   once   since   though   while
Use subordinating conjunctions with punctuation in these patterns:
     CONJUNCTION   clause   ,   independent clause
     Independent clause   CONJUNCTION   clause.

After Newton developed calculus, he discovered laws of gravity.

Newton discovered laws of gravity after he developed calculus.

EXERCISE 2

Using any of the strategies discussed in this chapter, correctly punctuate the following word groupings in which you find fused sentences or comma splices. In each case, name the error (or errors) you are correcting.

Example: Genetic engineering has been called the great scientific breakthrough of the century there are still many doubts concerning its potential effects on our environment.

Fused sentence. Genetic engineering has been called the great scientific breakthrough of the century. **However,** there are still many doubts concerning its potential effects on our environment.

1. Genetic engineering is the technique by which scientists alter or combine hereditary materials, genes are part of all living material they carry chemical information that determines every organism's characteristics.

2. The movement of creating genetically engineered organisms began in the early 1900s based on the earlier experiments of the Austrian monk Gregor Mendel he laid the foundation for future experiments with his work on cross-breeding in plants.

3. Scientists have discovered the benefits and uses of genetically engineered organisms in agriculture one of the first examples is the ice-minus bacterium created by Steve Lindow and Nicholas Panopoulos.

4. Lindow and Panopoulos realized that a bacterium commonly found in plants produces a protein that helps ice to form causing damaging frost, they removed this unfavorable gene, they prevented ice from forming on greenhouse plants.

5. Researchers hope in 20 to 30 years to create corn and wheat plants that can fix their own nitrogen in this way the plants would not need to be fertilized, this would save anywhere from $3 to $14 billion annually.

6. Geneticists have found beneficial uses of engineered organisms in agriculture, they have also found ways to use these organisms to clean up environmental hazards for instance, Dr. Anandra M. Chakrabarty has engineered an organism that breaks up oil spills.

13.3

EXERCISE 3

Correct the fused sentences and comma splices in the following paragraph, making use of all five strategies discussed in this chapter. One consideration governing your choice of corrections should be sentence variety. Vary methods for correcting fused and spliced clauses to avoid repeating sentence structures in consecutive sentences.

Whatever they may believe about what happens to the soul after death most cultures bury their dead. Given the grim fact of history that corpses can sometimes pile up at an alarming rate, it has not always been easy for managers of cemeteries, in a way cemetery planning is much like urban planning. Streets have to be mapped out and plots need to be sold, often, above-ground structures—mausoleums—have to be designed and executed. A chapel of some sort is usually called for—decorated Gothic or vertical Gothic, above all the cemetery must be landscaped in such a way as to afford comfort to the mourners.

Pronoun Reference

A **pronoun** substitutes for a noun, allowing you to talk about someone or something without having to repeat its name (see 7a-7). To
serve this function, a pronoun must make a clear and unmistakable
reference to the noun for which it substitutes—called its **antecedent.** **14.1**
When the reference is not clearly made to a specific noun, meaning can
become vague or confused.

Unclear   Michelangelo had a complex personality, as did Raphael, though
his was the more complex. *His* art was not nearly so typical of
the High Renaissance, and *he* was frequently irascible.

To whom do the pronouns *he* and *his* refer in these sentences? No one
can tell. The sentences need to be revised, and the pronouns and antecedents placed with care to keep readers moving forward.

Revised   Michelangelo had a complex personality, as did Raphael, though
Michelangelo's was the more complex. *His* art was not nearly so
typical of the High Renaissance, and *he* was frequently irascible.
[The proper noun replaces an unclear pronoun, providing a reference point for the pronouns that follow.]

14a   Make pronouns refer clearly to their antecedents.

Confusing   When Mark and Jay return home, *he* will call.
Clear   When Mark and Jay return home, *Mark* will call.

Revise a sentence whenever a pronoun can refer to more than one
antecedent. Use a noun in place of a pronoun, if needed for clarity; or
reposition a pronoun so that its antecedent is unmistakable.

Confusing   In 1949, astronomer Gerard Kuiper proposed the existence
of a comet-strewn belt girting our solar system, although the
same theory had been advanced by K. E. Edgewater two years
earlier. Astronomer Hal Levin comments that there is uncertainty as to whether Kuiper knew about *him*. [Does the pronoun *him* refer to Levin or Edgewater?]

ACROSS THE CURRICULUM

Precision in Academic Writing

The precision required of much academic writing makes the careful use of pronouns especially important. Note, for example, how few pronouns physicist Stephen Hawking uses in the following passage from his book *A Brief History of Time*:

For example, very accurate observations of the planet Mercury revealed a small difference between *its* motion and the predictions of Newton's theory of gravity. Einstein's general theory of relativity predicted a slightly different motion from Newton's theory. The fact that Einstein's predictions matched what was seen, while Newton's did not, was one of the crucial confirmations of the new theory. However, *we* still use Newton's theory for all practical purposes because the difference between *its* predictions and those of general relativity is very small in the situations that *we* normally deal with. (Newton's theory also has the great advantage that *it* is much simpler to work with than Einstein's.)*

Particularly in writing that makes comparisons, as this passage does, overuse of pronouns can lead to confusion.

*Stephen W. Hawking, *Our Picture of the Universe* (Bantam Books, 1988, p. 80).

Revised In 1949, astronomer Gerard Kuiper proposed the existence of a comet-strewn belt girting our solar system, although the same theory had been advanced by K. E. Edgewater two years earlier. Astronomer Hal Levin comments that there is uncertainty as to whether Kuiper knew about Edgewater.

Describing a person's speech indirectly can lead to unclear pronoun reference. Occasionally, if you can document what was said, you can convert indirect quotations to direct ones in order to clarify a pronoun's reference. Otherwise, you can restate the sentence carefully to avoid confusion among the nouns.

Confusing One astronomer told a reporter that *he* might be able to view the belt through a telescope but *he* couldn't be certain that *he* was looking at the home base of the comets. [Do any of the *he*s refer to the reporter?]

Direct statement As one astronomer told a reporter, "I might be able to view the belt through a telescope, but I can't be certain that I am looking at the home base of the comets."

Restatement One astronomer told a reporter that while it was possible to view the belt through a telescope, it was impossible to say with certainty that this was the home base of the comets.

ESL NOTE   In a standard English sentence, the subject is not repeated elsewhere in the sentence with an unnecessary pronoun. Pronouns are involved when the subject is renamed in a dependent clause (see 7e-2). Repeated subjects must be avoided in sentences with long dependent clauses separating subjects from verbs.

14b   Keep pronouns close to their antecedents.

Confusing   The *statement* that Dr. Parker made and that she issued as a formal warning infuriated the mayor, who knew *it* would alarm the public.

Clear   Issued as a formal warning, Dr. Parker's *statement* alarmed the public, and *it* infuriated the mayor.

Even when pronoun choice is correct, too many words between a pronoun and its antecedent can confuse readers. If, in a long sentence or in adjacent sentences, several nouns appear between a pronoun and its proper antecedent, these nouns will incorrectly claim the reader's attention as the word renamed by the pronoun.

Confusing   *Prehistoric peoples* used many organic substances, which survive at relatively few archaeological sites. Bone and antler were commonly used, especially in Europe some fifteen thousand years ago. *They* relied heavily on plant fibers and baskets for their material culture. [The pronoun *they* must refer to *prehistoric peoples*, since only people can *rely*, but the intervening nouns distract from this reference.]

Closer antecedent   *Prehistoric peoples* used many organic substances, which survive at relatively few archaeological sites. *They commonly used* bone and antler, especially in Europe some fifteen thousand years ago. *They* also relied heavily on plant fibers and baskets for their material culture.

Pronoun replaced   *Prehistoric peoples* used many organic substances, which survive at relatively few archaeological sites. Bone and antler were commonly used, especially in Europe some fifteen thousand years ago. *The desert peoples of western North America* relied heavily on plant fibers and baskets for their material culture.

The relative pronouns *who*, *which*, and *that*, when introducing a modifying adjective clause, should be placed close to the nouns they modify (see 19b-2).

Confusing   Archaeologists must base their findings on the few objects at sites occupied by prehistoric people that have survived. [Does *that* refer to *objects*, *sites*, or *people*?]

Closer antecedent   Archaeologists must base their findings on the few objects that have survived at sites occupied by prehistoric people.

14.2

Spotlight on Common Errors— PRONOUN REFERENCE

These are the errors most commonly associated with pronoun reference. For full explanations and suggested revisions, follow the cross-references to chapter sections.

PRONOUN REFERENCE ERRORS arise when a sentence leaves readers unable to link a pronoun with an *antecedent*—a specific noun that the pronoun refers to and renames (see 7a-7). If the identity of this antecedent is unclear, readers may miss the reference and become confused. Four error patterns lead to problems with pronoun reference.

> **A pronoun should refer clearly to a single noun. When the pronoun can refer to either of two (or more) nouns within a sentence or between sentences, revise sentences for clarity (see 14a).**

Within a sentence

Faulty

When Mark and Jay return home, *he* will call. [To whom does *he* refer?]

Revised

When Mark and Jay return home, *Mark* will call.

Between sentences

Faulty

The conversation between Clara and Nancy lasted two hours. At the end, *she* was exhausted. [Which one is *she*?]

Revised

The conversation between Clara and Nancy lasted two hours. At the end, *Clara* was exhausted.

> **A pronoun should be located close to the noun it renames. When a pronoun is too far from its antecedent, revise the sentence to narrow the distance and clarify meaning (see 14b).**

Within a sentence

Faulty

The statement that Dr. Parker made about a city water fountain and that she issued as a formal warning infuriated the mayor, who knew *it* would alarm the public. [Does *it* clearly refer to the faraway *statement* and not to something else?]

Revised

Issued as a formal warning, Dr. Parker's *statement* about a city water fountain alarmed the public, and *it* infuriated the mayor. [Less distance between the pronoun and antecedent makes the reference clear.]

Between sentences

Faulty	**Revised**
Major oil spills have fouled coastlines in Alaska, France, and England and have caused severe ecological damage. *Some* could almost certainly be avoided. [Does *some* refer to faraway *spills* or to *coastlines*?]	Major oil spills have fouled coastlines in Alaska, France, and England and have caused severe ecological damage. *Some spills* could almost certainly be avoided. [*Spills* is added to clear up the reference.]

> The pronouns *this* and *that* should refer to specific words. When either is used as a one-word summary of a preceding sentence, revise to clarify the reference between sentences by adding an additional word or phrase of summary (see 14c-3).

Faulty	**Revised**
The purpose of the conference was to explore the links between lung cancer and secondhand smoke. *This* was firmly established. [What was established?]	The purpose of the conference was to explore the links between lung cancer and secondhand smoke. *This connection* was firmly established. [A summary word added makes the reference clear.]

> Once you establish a pattern of first-person (*I/we*), second-person (*you*), or third-person pronouns (*he/she/it/they*) in a sentence or paragraph (see 8a, 8b), keep references to your subject *consistent*. Prevent confusion by avoiding shifts and revising sentences for consistency (see 16a-1).

Within a sentence

Faulty	**Revised**
Students generally fare better when *you* are given instruction on taking lecture notes. [Confusion arises between third-person *students* and second-person *you*. Who is the subject?]	*Students* generally fare better when *they* are given instruction on taking lecture notes. [Consistent third person] OR As a student, *you* will generally fare better when you are given instruction on taking lecture notes.

Between sentences

Faulty	**Revised**
Students fare better when given instruction on basic skills. *You* can improve *your* notetaking after getting help with the techniques. [Have *students* suddenly become *you*?]	*Students* fare better when given instruction on basic skills. *They* can improve *their* notetaking after getting help with the techniques.

Keep Pronouns Close to Their Antecedents

EXERCISE 1

Rewrite the sentences that follow so that pronouns are replaced or are close to and refer clearly to the nouns they rename. Place a check beside the sentences that need no revision.

> *Example:* When Bob talks with Joe by phone, he can hardly get a word in edgewise because he expects a more delayed response from him.
>
> When Bob talks with Joe by phone, Bob can hardly get a word in edgewise because he expects a more delayed response from Joe. [The pronouns are replaced with nouns.]

1. The ritual of greeting varies from one culture to another; for example, Americans ask, "How are you?" whereas Filipinos ask, "Where are you going?"—a question that seems prying to them.

2. Professor Deborah Tannen claims that while conducting research in a corporate environment, she found many women who rightly perceived themselves as highly successful; these women felt that their coworkers shared this perception but that higher-level management did not recognize it.

3. The men whom Tannen interviewed often told her that if she hadn't been promoted, it was because she didn't deserve it.

14c   **State a pronoun's antecedent clearly.**

To be clear, a pronoun's antecedent should be stated directly, either in the sentence in which the pronoun appears or in an immediately preceding sentence. If the antecedent is merely implied, the pronoun's meaning will be weak or imprecise, and the reader will probably be confused.

> **1**   Make a pronoun refer to a specific noun antecedent, not to a modifier that may imply the antecedent.

Confusing   From *animated* films such as *Fantasia* in 1940 to *Atlantis* in 2001, Disney studios have raised *it* to an art form.

Clear   From films such as *Fantasia* in 1940 to *Atlantis* in 2001, Disney studios have raised *animation* to an art form.

Although an adjective may imply the antecedent of a pronoun, an adjective cannot serve as an antecedent. Revise sentences so that a *noun* provides the reference for a pronoun.

Confusing	Two glass rods will repel each other when they are electrified. *It* is created from a buildup of positive and negative charges in the rods. [What does *it* refer to?]
Noun antecedent	Two glass rods will repel each other when they carry *electricity*. *It* is created from a buildup of positive and negative charges in the rods.
	OR
	Two glass rods will repel each other when they are electrified. *Electricity* is created from a buildup of positive and negative charges in the rods.

2 **Make a pronoun refer to a noun, not to the possessive form of a noun.**

Confusing	*Sally's* case is in trouble. Does *she* know that?
Clear	*Sally* is in trouble with this case. Does *she* know that?

Although the possessive form of a noun may imply the noun as the intended antecedent of a pronoun, this form cannot serve as an antecedent. Revise sentences so that a *noun* provides the reference for a pronoun. Alternatively, change the pronoun so that it, too, is in the possessive form.

Confusing	The *Greeks'* knowledge of magnetic forces was evident before 600 B.C. *They* observed that certain minerals attracted pieces of iron.
Noun antecedent	The *Greeks* had knowledge of magnetic forces before 600 B.C. *They* observed that certain minerals attracted pieces of iron. [The possessive form—*Greeks'*—is eliminated to provide an antecedent for the pronoun *they*.]
Pronoun replaced	The *Greeks'* knowledge of magnetic forces was evident before 600 B.C. *Their scientists* observed that certain minerals attracted pieces of iron.

3 Give the pronouns *that, this, which,* and *it* precise reference.

Confusing	The paper proposed to link cancer and secondary smoke. *This* was established.
Clear	The paper proposed to link cancer and secondary smoke. *This connection* was established.

The pronouns *that, this, which,* and *it* should refer to specific nouns. Avoid having them make vague reference to the overall sense of a preceding sentence.

Confusing	Like magnetic poles attract, while unlike poles repel each other. The reason for *this* was not well understood until the twentieth century. [What exactly does *this* refer to?]
Antecedent provided	Like magnetic poles attract, while unlike poles repel each other. The reason for *this phenomenon* was not well understood until the twentieth century.
Confusing	In the late nineteenth century, knowledge of atomic structure was advanced by J. J. Thomson, *which* established that one component of the atom is negatively charged. [*Which* does not refer to a particular noun.]
Antecedent provided	In the late nineteenth century, knowledge of atomic structure was advanced by J. J. Thomson, *who* established that one component of the atom is negatively charged. [*Who* now refers to Thomson.]

How to Revise Unclear Pronoun Reference

1. Provide a clear, nearby antecedent.
2. Replace the pronoun with a noun and thereby eliminate the problem of ambiguous reference.
3. Totally recast the sentence to avoid ambiguous reference.

---

4   Avoid indefinite antecedents for the pronouns *it*, *they*, and *you*.

Nonstandard	*It* will rain tomorrow.
Standard	*We* are expecting rain tomorrow.

Expressions such as "you know," "they say," and "it figures" are common in speech and informal writing. The pronouns in these expressions do not refer to particular people or a particular object. They are said to have *indefinite* reference. In academic writing, pronouns should refer to specific antecedents. *You* should be used either to address the reader directly or for a direct quotation. *It* and *they* should refer to particular things, ideas, or people.

Nonstandard	Today, *they say* that an atom has a nucleus with neutrons and protons.
Standard	Today, *physicists believe* that an atom has a nucleus with neutrons and protons.
Nonstandard	Because physicists work with abstract models and mathematical languages, *you* must almost take their reports as an item of faith.
Standard	Because physicists work with abstract models and mathematical languages, *nonscientists* must almost take their reports as an item of faith.

5	Avoid using a pronoun to refer to the title of a paper in the paper's first sentence.

A pronoun should have a reference in the sentence in which it appears or in an immediately preceding sentence. A title, while directly related to a paper or essay, does not occur *within* the paper or essay and thus cannot function appropriately as an antecedent.

A title	"Eliot's Desert Images in *The Waste Land*"
A first sentence	They are plentiful, and their effect is to leave readers thirsty—in both body and soul.
First sentence revised	Desert images in T. S. Eliot's *The Waste Land* are plentiful, and their effect is to leave readers thirsty—in both body and soul.

14d Avoid mixing uses of the pronoun *it*.

The word *it* functions both as a pronoun and as an expletive (see 7a-11)—that is, as a space filler in a rearranged sentence.

As an expletive	*It* is clear that the committee is resisting the initiative. [The clause *that the committee is resisting the initiative* functions as the subject.]
As a pronoun	Although the committee voted, *it* [that is, the committee] showed no leadership.

Avoid using the word *it* as both an expletive and a pronoun in the same sentence.

Confusing	*It* is clear that *it* is shirking *its* responsibilities.
Weak	*It* is clear that the committee is shirking *its* responsibilities.
Clear	Clearly, the committee is shirking *its* responsibilities.

14e Use the relative pronouns *who, which,* and *that* appropriately.

1 Selecting relative pronouns

Relative pronouns (see 7e-2) introduce dependent clauses that usually function as adjectives. The pronouns *who, which,* and *that* rename and refer to the nouns they follow. The pronoun *who* can refer to people, divinities, or personified animals.

> The most highly respected baseball player in the year 1911 was Ty Cobb, *who* had joined the Detroit Tigers in 1905.

That refers to animals, things, or people (when not referring to a *specific* person, in which case the pronoun *who* is used).

> For decades, Cobb held a record *that* remained unbreakable—until Pete Rose stroked his 4,192nd career hit in 1985.

Which refers to animals and things.

> His career, *which* lasted 24 years, was marked by extraordinary statistics—for example, a batting average of .367, 2,244 runs, and 892 stolen bases.

ESL NOTE   Avoid repeating the subject of a sentence with an unnecessary pronoun, especially when a long dependent clause separates a subject from its verb.

Avoid   The taller *man*, who ran away quickly, *he* recognized me. [An unnecessary pronoun repeats the subject.]

Revised   The taller man, who ran away quickly, recognized me.

---

2   **Using relative pronouns in essential and nonessential clauses**

Essential   People who are constantly angry become stressed.

Nonessential   Jim, who is constantly angry, has become stressed.

Use either *that* or *which*, depending on whether a clause begun by one of these words is essential or nonessential to the meaning of the noun being modified. Use *that* or *which* (with *no* commas around the dependent clause) to denote an **essential** (or restrictive) **modifier**—a word, phrase, or clause that provides information crucial for identifying a noun.

> As a young man, Gabriel García Márquez advocated many left-wing proposals for reform *that* [or *which*] were not in the end accepted.

As the noun being modified becomes more specific (for instance, when it identifies a *particular* person, place, or thing), then a modifying clause is no longer essential, since the core information of the noun is already established. Use *which* (with commas around the dependent clause) to denote a **nonessential** (or nonrestrictive) **modifier.**

> Norman, Oklahoma, *which* has been dubbed the "Storm-chasing capital of the U.S.," is the home of the National Severe Storm Laboratory. [Because the location is specifically identified, any modifying information is nonessential.]

CRITICAL DECISIONS

Applying a Test for Choosing *who*, *which*, or *that*— With or Without Commas

Writers can be unsure of themselves when choosing relative pronouns *(who, which, and that)* and when using commas with relative clauses. Relative pronouns begin relative clauses, and these function in a sentence as if they were adjectives: they modify nouns. You can apply three tests for deciding which pronoun to use and whether or not to use commas.

Identify the noun being modified.

■ **Is the noun the name of a *specific* person (George), place (Baltimore), or thing (the *Mona Lisa*)?** If yes, then use the pronoun *who*, *whom*, or *whose* (for a person) or *which* (for a place or thing) *with* commas. The noun does not need the modifying clause to specify its meaning. This clause is *nonessential*.

My friend George, *who* is constantly angry, has developed a stress disorder.

Baltimore, which is Maryland's largest city, is not the capital.

■ **Is the noun being modified an unspecified person (people), place (city), or thing (painting)?** If yes, then it is quite likely that the modifying information of the clause is essential for specifying the noun's identity. Use *who*, *whom*, or *whose* (for a person) and *which* or *that* (for a place or thing) *without* commas. The modifying clause is *essential*.

People *who* are constantly angry often develop stress disorders.

The painting *that* I liked best was quite expensive.

■ **Is the identity of the common noun being modified made clear and specific to the reader in the context of the paragraph?** If yes, then treat the common noun in the same way that you would a proper noun: use a relative clause, with commas.

The *Mona Lisa* is one of the world's best known works of art. The painting, which hangs in Paris's Louvre Museum, has been imitated and parodied countless times.

[The word *painting* in the second sentence renames the *Mona Lisa*. In context, the reader knows the specific painting being referred to, so the relative clause *(which hangs in Paris's Louvre Museum)* is nonessential and takes commas.]

Use *who* to denote either an essential or a nonessential modifier.

Essential   As recently as the 1970s, meteorologists *who* conducted storm chases were viewed as irresponsible by many of their colleagues. [Because there are many meteorologists and none is named, the information in the modifying clause is essential.]

Nonessential   Eric Rasmussen, who is a meteorologist on staff at the laboratory, makes the decision whether or not to send his "storm-chasing troopers." [Because a *particular* meteorologist is named, the modifying clause is nonessential.]

See 25d for a full discussion of essential and nonessential modifiers with commas.

3   Avoid a confusing overuse of *which* or *that.*

Writers who pile up too many modifying clauses using *which* or *that* may need to rethink sentences to clarify the main statement as distinct from the modifying clauses.

Confusing fragment   Norman, Oklahoma, *which* has been dubbed the "Storm-chasing capital of the U.S.," *which* is the home of the National Severe Storm Laboratory.

Revised   Norman, Oklahoma, *which* is the home of the National Severe Storm Laboratory, has been dubbed the "Storm-chasing capital of the U.S."

Revised   Norman, Oklahoma, *which* has been dubbed the "Storm-chasing capital of the U.S.," is the home of the National Severe Storm Laboratory.

WWW
14.3

EXERCISE 2

Revise the following sentences so that pronouns refer clearly to their antecedents. Place a check beside the sentences that need no revision.

Example: "Tornado Alley" gets its name from what is essentially a fight within the atmosphere that occurs seasonally over the Midwest. This is due to the collision of a cold current of air from the Rockies with warm, moist air drifting north from the Gulf of Mexico.

"Tornado Alley" gets its name from what is essentially a fight within the atmosphere that occurs seasonally over the Midwest. *This struggle* is due to the collision of a cold current of air from the Rockies with warm, moist air drifting north from the Gulf of Mexico.

1. Though storm experts generally understand the preconditions of severe storms, they are unsure of specific details—which is a problem for the millions who reside in Tornado Alley.

2. These have killed about 18,000 people over the course of the past 200 years.

3. It can contain winds of 200 miles per hour, or even higher.

4. The updraft of a tornado generally narrows, causing it to spin even faster. This can cause severe damage during the peak of the storm.

5. This tendency to spin (called *vorticity*) is a quality of the air itself which can interact with the updraft of a thunderstorm; it can spawn a tornado.

EXERCISE 3

The pronouns *this*, *that*, *these*, *which*, and *it* are often used ambiguously, especially when they refer to ideas, situations, or circumstances not previously identified or clearly explained. In the following sequence of sentences, avoid vagueness by rewriting sentences to provide clear references. Use information from adjoining sentences to provide references.

> *Example:* Archaeology offers a unique approach to studying long-term change in human societies. This has characterized the study of humankind in North America.
>
> Archaeology offers a unique approach to studying long-term change in human societies. *This approach* has characterized the study of humankind in North America.

1. Unfortunately, archaeologists have only recently undertaken it in the context of the European Contact Period.

2. In the past they somewhat rigidly saw it as the ending point of prehistory, when Native Americans came into the orbit of Western civilization.

3. This was apparent especially because archaeologists tended to be preoccupied with the classification of discrete periods in the past, rather than with the processes of cultural change.

4. These were given names such as Paleo-Indian, Archaic, Woodland, and so on.

5. In short, these narrowly constrained the interests of archaeologists.

6. Now they are taking a closer look at the phenomenon of European Contact as a part of long-term developments in that society.

15

Misplaced and Dangling Modifiers

A modifier can be a single word: a *sporty* car; a phrase: Joanne drove a car *with racing stripes;* or a dependent clause: *After she gained confidence driving a sporty car,* Joanne took up racing. As you write, you will need to make decisions about where to place modifiers within your sentences. In order to function most effectively, a modifier should be placed directly next to the word it modifies. If this placement disrupts meaning, then the modifier should be placed *as close as possible* to the word it modifies. The Critical Decisions box on page 312 poses three questions you can ask to determine if you have placed your modifiers well.

Weblink

http://www.uottawa.ca/academic/
arts/writcent/hypergrammar/
msplmod.html

How to correct misplaced and dangling modifiers in your writing.

MISPLACED MODIFIERS

15a | **Position modifiers so that they refer clearly to the words they should modify.**

Confusing   A truck rumbled down the street, gray with dirt.

Clear   A dirty, gray truck rumbled down the street. A truck rumbled down the gray, dirty street.

Readers expect a modifier to be linked clearly with the word the writer intended it to modify. When this link is broken, readers become confused or frustrated.

Confusing   This chair was designed for weekend athletes with extra padding.

Revised   This chair with extra padding was designed for weekend athletes.

Here is a more complicated example of a sentence made confusing by a misplaced modifier.

Confusing   The behavior of a chemical compound created in a laboratory is similar to the behavior of a compound created by nature that is identical.

Here, the modifying clause *that is identical* would seem to modify *nature*, but this meaning makes little sense. The writer has misplaced the modifying clause. When the clause is reduced to a single adjective and repositioned, the meaning becomes clear.

Revised   The behavior of a chemical compound created in a laboratory is similar to the behavior of an *identical* compound created by nature.

If a phrase or clause beginning a sentence functions as an adjective modifier, then the first words after the modifier—that is, the first words of the independent clause—should include the noun being modified.

Confusing   A small Green Mountain town, Calvin Coolidge was born in Plymouth, Vermont. [Who or what is a *Green Mountain town?*]

Revised   Calvin Coolidge was born in Plymouth, Vermont, a small Green Mountain town. [*Green Mountain town* now modifies *Plymouth, Vermont.*]

ESL NOTE   In most English sentences, two or more adjectives that accumulate as modifiers before a noun or pronoun are typically given a standard order or sequence. Section 48f-1–2 describes typical patterns for placement of English adjective modifiers.

ACROSS THE CURRICULUM

Using Modifiers

Modifiers are fundamental sentence elements, and writers use them in every discipline area. In the following example, historian Simon Schama uses modifiers of varying length and positionings to create rich detail in his discussion of Henry David Thoreau.

Returning to the cabin in the woods by Walden Pond, a catch of fish tied to his pole, Henry David Thoreau was seized with an overwhelming urge to eat raw woodchuck. It was not that he was particularly hungry. And he already knew the taste of woodchuck, at least cooked woodchuck, for he had killed and eaten an animal

(continued)

Using Modifiers *(continued)*

that had been complacently dining off his bean field. It was simply the force of wildness he suddenly felt possessing his body like an ancient rage.*

Modifying clause

the force of wildness *he suddenly felt possessing his body*

Modifying phrases

Returning to the cabin in the woods by Walden Pond, a catch of fish tied to his pole, Henry David Thoreau

he already knew the taste of woodchuck, *at least cooked woodchuck,*

possessing his body *like an ancient rage*

Modifying words

overwhelming urge   *raw* woodchuck   *particularly* hungry   *already* knew

complacently dining   his *bean* field   *suddenly* felt   an *ancient* rage

*The passage is excerpted from Simon Schama, *Landscape and Memory* (New York: Knopf, 1995) 571.

EXERCISE I

Reorganize or rewrite the following sentences so that the misplaced modifier is correctly placed. (You may need to add a word or two in some sentences and provide something specific for the modifier to describe.) Place a check mark beside any sentence in which modifiers are used clearly.

> *Example:* Turning to black subculture as an alternative to homogenized mainstream culture, black slang and music became increasingly common among American teenagers after 1950.
>
> Turning to black subculture as an alternative to homogenized mainstream culture, American teenagers after 1950 began using black slang and listening to black music. [The sentence is given a new subject, *American teenagers*, that can be modified by the introductory phrase.]

1. Black rhythm and blues, with its typical twelve-bar structure, among white teenagers became rock 'n' roll's most common format.

2. Organized by a disc jockey in Cleveland, Ohio, two-thirds of the audience for a stage show featuring black rhythm and blues acts in 1953 were white.

3. Strung down the center of the theater, black and white members of the audience were separated by a rope that was often gone by the end of the performance.

4. Combining elements of black rhythm and blues and white country western music, American teenagers found rock 'n' roll attractive.

15.1

Spotlight on Common Errors—MODIFIERS

Four errors are most commonly associated with modifiers. For full explanations and suggested revisions, follow the cross-references to chapter sections.

MODIFIER ERRORS arise under two conditions: when the word being modified is too far from the modifier (a misplaced modifier) and when the word being modified is implied but does not appear in the sentence (a dangling modifier). Both errors will confuse readers.

Position a modifier near the word it modifies (see 15a).

Faulty

A truck rumbled down the street, gray with dirt. [What is gray and dirty?]

Revised

A **dirty, gray** truck rumbled down the street.

A truck rumbled down the **gray, dirty** street.

Make a modifier refer clearly to one word (see 15c).

Faulty

The supervisor who was conducting the interview thoughtfully posed a final question. [Was this a thoughtful interview or thoughtful question?]

Revised

The supervisor who was conducting the interview posed a final, **thoughtful question.**

The supervisor, who was conducting a **thoughtful interview,** posed a final question.

Reposition a modifier that splits sentence elements (see 15d–15g).

Faulty

Vigorous exercise—complemented by a varied diet that includes nuts, grains, vegetables, and fruits—is one key to fitness. [The "key to fitness" is unclear.]

The agent signed, with her client seated beside her, the contract. [What is "signed" is unclear.]

Revised

Vigorous exercise, **one key to fitness,** should be complemented by a varied diet that includes nuts, grains, vegetables, and fruits.

With her client seated beside her, the agent **signed the contract.**

Make introductory phrases refer clearly to a *specific* word in the independent clause (see 15h-1–2).

Faulty

After considering his difficulty in the interview, the application was withdrawn. [Who withdrew the application?]

Revised

After considering his difficulty in the interview, **the candidate withdrew** his application.

15b Position limiting modifiers with care.

The children trusted only him.

Only the children trusted him.

In conversation, **limiting modifiers**—words such as *only*, *almost*, *just*, *nearly*, *even*, and *simply*—are often shifted within a sentence with little concern for their effect on meaning. When written, however, a limiting modifier is taken literally to restrict the meaning of the word placed directly after it.

Nearly 90 percent of the 200 people who served in presidential cabinets from 1897 to 1973 belonged to the social or business elite.

Ninety percent of the *nearly* 200 people who served in presidential cabinets from 1897 to 1973 belonged to the social or business elite.

Placement of the limiting modifier *nearly* fundamentally alters the meaning of these sentences.

EXERCISE 2

Use the limiting modifier in parentheses to rewrite each sentence two ways, giving each version a different meaning.

> *Example:* Acquiring a copy of one's own medical records is very difficult because medical records are the property of physicians and health-care facilities. (usually)
>
> Acquiring a copy of one's own medical records is *usually* very difficult because medical records are the property of physicians and health-care facilities.
>
> Acquiring a copy of one's own medical records is very difficult because medical records are *usually* the property of physicians and health-care facilities.

1. One study indicated that one-quarter to one-third of patient health records contain errors. (only)

2. For many years the Medical Information Bureau was known for being uncooperative with patients who desperately needed access to their records. (even)

3. Massachusetts patients have a right to see any medical document retained by a hospital supported or licensed by the state. (even)

4. Through the "patient advocate" of his or her hospital, any patient can obtain any personal health information. (almost)

Reposition modifiers that describe two elements simultaneously.

Confusing	The supervisor conducting the interview thoughtfully posed a final question.
Clear	The supervisor conducting the interview posed a final, thoughtful question.

A **squinting modifier** appears to modify two words in the sentence—the word preceding it and the word following it. To convey a clear meaning, the modifier must be repositioned so it can describe only a *single* word.

Confusing	The official being questioned aggressively shut the door. [Does *aggressively* describe how the official was being questioned or how the official shut the door?]
Revised	The official, who was being questioned aggressively, shut the door. [A clause is set off to become a nonessential modifier of *official*.]
Revised	The official who was being questioned shut the door aggressively. [*Aggressively* is moved to an unambiguous position and modifies *shut*.]

EXERCISE 3

The following sentences are made awkward by squinting modifiers. Revise each sentence twice so that the modifier describes a different word in each revision.

> *Example:* Sitting in the hot summer sun often accelerates the skin's aging process.
>
> Sitting *often* in the hot summer sun accelerates the skin's aging process. [*Often* modifies *sitting*—the sense being that one must sit in the sun many times to accelerate the skin's aging.]
>
> *Often*, sitting in the hot summer sun accelerates the skin's aging process. [The sense here is that sitting in the sun even once or a few times can accelerate the aging of the skin.]

1. Going to the movies sometimes makes me wish I were an actress.
2. The equation that Steven thought he had analyzed thoroughly confused him on the exam.
3. The father reprimanding his son angrily pushed the shopping cart down the supermarket aisle.

4. The suspect being questioned thoroughly believed his constitutional rights were being violated.
5. Taking long walks frequently helps me to relax.

CRITICAL DECISIONS

Questioning Your Placement of Modifiers

Modifiers provide much of the interest in a sentence, but when misused, they confuse readers. Pose three questions to know precisely *which* word in a sentence you are modifying.

■ **What modifiers am I using in this sentence?** You should be able to recognize modifiers when you write them. Single words, phrases, and clauses can function as modifiers.

Modifying word (see 7c)

Adverb   The artist succeeded *brilliantly.*

Modifying phrase (see 7d)

Adjective   The painting, *displayed on a dark wall*, glowed.

Modifying clause (see 7e)

Adverb   *After the gallery closed that evening*, the staff celebrated.

■ **What word is being modified? (See 15a–c.)**

The artist made a *deliberate* effort.

[The noun *effort* is being modified.]

The artist succeeded *brilliantly.*

[The verb *succeeded* is being modified.]

Confusing   Several patrons who returned repeatedly called the young artist "a wonder." [The single-word modifier *repeatedly* seems to modify two words, *returned* and *called.*]

■ **Does the modifying word, phrase, or clause clearly refer to this word? (See 15a–c, 15h.)**

Clear   On returning, several patrons repeatedly *called* the young artist "a wonder." [The modifier *repeatedly* now clearly modifies the verb *called.*]

15d

Reposition a lengthy modifier that splits a subject and its verb.

Confusing   One key to fitness—which should be complemented by a varied diet that includes nuts, grains, vegetables, and fruit—is exercise.

Clear One key to fitness is vigorous exercise; another is a varied diet that includes nuts, grains, vegetables, and fruit.

Lengthy modifiers disrupt the link between subject and verb and should be repositioned to keep that link clear.

Confusing Nutmeg, *which for most people today is associated primarily with holiday baking but was once highly prized for its supposed medicinal qualities as well as for its use in flavoring food*, has a fascinating history.

Revised *Associated today primarily with holiday baking but once highly prized for its supposed medicinal qualities as well as for its use in flavoring food*, nutmeg has a fascinating history. [Modifying elements have been shifted to the beginning of the sentence, so the core sentence is no longer interrupted.]

Revised Nutmeg, *which most people today associate primarily with holiday baking*, has a fascinating history. *It was once highly prized for its supposed medicinal qualities as well as for its use in flavoring food.* [The final modifying element has been revised and is now a separate sentence.]

EXERCISE 4

Reposition modifiers in rearranged, rephrased, or divided sentences to establish clear links between subjects and verbs. Try rewriting sentences in more than one way.

Example: "Hypermusic," a product of both musical instrument and computer, which blends the sounds produced by traditional instruments with simple-to-operate computer interfaces, thus allowing the player, whether musically trained or not, to sound like a virtuoso, is the brainchild of Tod Machover of MIT.

"Hypermusic," a product of both musical instrument and computer, blends the sounds produced by traditional instruments with simple-to-operate computer interfaces. The brainchild of Tod Machover of MIT, this new technology allows the player, whether musically trained or not, to sound like a virtuoso.

1. Hyperinstruments, which perform the chores of playing a musical instrument with the virtuosity of the most accomplished musician, allow the player to control the tempo and volume of the performance.

2. Machover, the child of a musician and a computer graphics specialist, who had thus been exposed to music and computers from childhood, eventually abandoned traditional instruments for electronic ones.

3. Machover, insisting that the average music lover is neglected while an elite corps of musicians receives all the serious attention, a system that deprives the average player of the joy of performance, favors democratizing music.

15e	**Reposition a modifier that splits a verb and its object or a verb and its complement.**

Confusing   The agent signed, with her client seated beside her, the contract.
Clear   With her client seated beside her, the agent signed the contract.

A lengthy adverb phrase or clause can create an awkward sentence if it splits a verb and its object or a verb and its complement. Reposition these adverbs by placing them at the beginning or the end of a sentence.

Awkward   A number of presidents have emphasized *in foreign disputes* nonintervention. [The verb and object are split.]

Revised   A number of presidents have emphasized nonintervention *in foreign disputes.*

Awkward   Millard Fillmore became, *after serving eight years as a U.S. representative from New York*, the elected vice president in 1848. [The verb and complement are split.]

Revised   *After serving eight years as a U.S. representative from New York,* Millard Fillmore was elected vice president in 1848.

Note that brief one- or two-word adverbial modifiers may appear before a direct object or complement.

Clear   Fillmore was *by 1850* the thirteenth president.

EXERCISE 5

Reposition modifiers in order to restore clear links between verbs and objects or complements in these sentences.

> *Example:* One of Machover's strangest inventions, the "hypercello," seamlessly blends, by programming the computer to "sense" the cellist's tiniest arm movements, musician and instrument.
>
> One of Machover's strangest inventions, the "hypercello," seamlessly blends musician and instrument by programming the computer to "sense" the cellist's tiniest arm movements.

1. The experience of listening to a hypercello performance is, since one can't tell where the player leaves off and the computer takes over, a strange one.

2. Machover is planning, given his emphasis on making musical performance available to the nonprofessional, an interactive event called *Brain Opera*.

3. Attendees at *Brain Opera* will learn to play, even though they may never have picked up a musical instrument in their lives, hyperinstruments.

4. The audience of *Brain Opera* will perform, after they have learned to play the easier types of hyperinstruments, followed by taking part in sessions involving increasingly complex music games, their very own opera.

5. One wonders what standards critics will use to judge *Brain Opera*, which is eccentric, visionary, and radical, a success.

15f	Reposition a modifier that splits the parts of an infinitive.

Confusing	Her wish to boldly and decisively break the record won many supporters.
Clear	Her wish to break the record, boldly and decisively, won many supporters.

An **infinitive** is the **base** form of a verb: *go, walk, see*. In a sentence, the infinitive form is often immediately preceded by the word *to: to go, to walk, to see*. In conversation, emphasis on a short adverbial modifier sometimes interrupts the two parts of an infinitive: *"Please try to quickly move up."* Such an interruption in long or complex written sentences can be disruptive to the intended meaning.

Move an adverb to a position before or after an infinitive, or rewrite the sentence and eliminate the infinitive.

Split	Many managers are unable *to* with difficult employees *establish* a moderate and reasonable tone.
Revised	Many managers are unable *to establish* a moderate and reasonable tone with difficult employees.

Split	One of a manager's responsibilities is *to* successfully *manage* conflict.
Revised	One of a manager's responsibilities is *to manage* conflict successfully.

Occasionally, a sentence with a split infinitive will sound more natural than a sentence rewritten to avoid the split. This will be the case when the object of the infinitive is a long phrase or clause and the adverbial modifier is short.

Split   Some managers like to *regularly* interview a variety of workers from different departments so that potential problems can be identified and averted.

Avoiding the split may become somewhat awkward.

No split   Some managers like to interview *regularly* a variety of workers from different departments so that potential problems can be identified and averted.

No split   Some managers like *regularly* to interview a variety of workers from different departments so that potential problems can be identified and averted.

Some readers do not accept split infinitives, no matter what the circumstances of a sentence. The safe course for a writer is to avoid the split by eliminating the infinitive or changing the modifier.

Modifier changed   *On a regular basis*, some managers like to interview a variety of workers from different departments so that potential problems can be identified and averted.

15g   Reposition a lengthy modifier that splits a verb phrase.

Confusing   The search for fairy tale origins has for over two centuries fascinated scholars.

Clear   The search for fairy tale origins has fascinated scholars for over two centuries.

A *verb phrase* consists of a main verb and its auxiliary or helping verb. Like an infinitive, a verb phrase is a grammatical unit. Unlike infinitives, verb phrases are commonly split with brief modifiers.

In developed countries, the commitment to children as a natural resource *has* long *been linked* to huge investments in education and health care.

The sense of a verb phrase is disrupted when the phrase is split by a lengthy modifying phrase or clause. Repair the split by relocating the modifier.

Confusing   Many third-world countries *have* in efforts to improve the health, well-being, and education of children *invested* large sums.

Revised   Many third-world countries *have invested* large sums in efforts to improve the health, well-being, and education of children.

EXERCISE 6

In the following sentences, reposition modifiers in order to repair split infinitives and restore clear links between auxiliary and main verbs.

Example: In one of Machover's music games, "Sonic Simon Says," players must try to, whatever their initial reservations, imitate simple melody patterns invented by the computer.

In one of Machover's music games, "Sonic Simon Says," players must try to imitate simple melody patterns invented by the computer, whatever their initial reservations.

1. To effectively play a musical instrument in most cases requires years of patient practice, but Machover's hyperinstruments may change all of that.
2. In another one of Machover's music games, "wild orchestration," players can, as music is being performed by the hyperorchestra, change the instrumentation of a given musical piece.
3. Enormous speakers will, as audience members come and go, blast the continuously evolving *Brain Opera* throughout the auditorium.
4. Machover's hyperinstruments make it possible for anyone to, musically creative or not, conduct an orchestra or play like a musical prodigy.
5. There are already some instruments on the market that allow players to, whether they are interested in composing or simply jamming with a favorite artist, live out the fantasy of playing like a pro.

15.3

DANGLING MODIFIERS

15h **Identify and revise dangling modifiers.**

Confusing After considering these issues, the decision was postponed.
Clear After considering these issues, the candidate postponed his decision.

A modifier is said to "dangle" when the word it modifies is not clearly a part of the same sentence. Correct the error by rewriting the sentence, making sure to include the word modified.

Give introductory clauses or phrases a specific word to modify.

First-draft sentences beginning with long introductory phrases or clauses often contain dangling modifiers. Revision involves asking what the opening clause or phrase modifies and rewriting the sentence to provide an answer.

Dangling	Dominated though they are by a few artists who repeatedly get the best roles, millions of people flock to the cinemas. [Who or what are dominated? If the *millions* are not, the main clause lacks a word to be modified.]
Revised	Dominated though they are by a few artists who repeatedly get the best roles, <u>movies</u> continue to attract millions of people. [The opening clause is now followed immediately by a noun it can modify.]
Dangling	After appearing in *The Maltese Falcon*, it was clear that Warner Brothers had a box-office star. [Who appeared in the film?]
Revised	After appearing in *The Maltese Falcon*, <u>Humphrey Bogart</u> became Warner Brothers' box-office star.

2   Rewrite passive constructions to provide active subjects.

Often a modifying phrase that begins a sentence will dangle because the independent clause is written in the passive voice (see 9g). Missing from this passive-voice sentence is the original subject, which would have been modified by the introductory phrase or clause. Correct the dangling modifier by rewriting the independent clause in the active voice.

Dangling	Drawn by his world-weary attitude, Bogart was defined as the persona of the private detective. [*Who* was drawn by his world-weary attitude?]
Revised	Drawn by his world-weary attitude, <u>the movie-going public</u> defined Bogart as the persona of the private detective.

CRITICAL DECISIONS

Revising to Maintain Passive Constructions

Occasionally, the original subject of a passive construction—either stated directly or implied—is not what a dangling modifier is meant to modify. In such cases, revise the modifier itself.

Dangling	After complaining to the authorities, the debris was cleared.
Revised	After I complained to the authorities, the debris was cleared.

EXERCISE 7

Repair the dangling modifiers that follow by restoring the word modified to each sentence. (You will find this word in parentheses.) Place a check in front of any sentence in which modifiers are used correctly.

Example: Having conquered an area stretching from the southern border of Colombia to central Chile, civilian and military rule was maintained for two hundred years before the Spanish discovery of America. (the Incas)

Having conquered an area stretching from the southern border of Colombia to central Chile, the Incas maintained civilian and military rule for two hundred years before the Spanish discovery of America.

1. Centering on the city of Cuzco in the Peruvian Andes, the coastal and mountain regions of Ecuador, Peru, and Bolivia were included. (the empire)

2. As the only true empire existing in the New World at the time of Columbus, wealth both in precious metals and in astronomical information had been assembled. (the Inca empire)

3. Knitting together the two disparate areas of Peru, mountain and desert, an economic and social synthesis was achieved. (the Incas)

4. Growing and weaving cotton and planting such domesticated crops as corn, squash, and beans, Peru had been settled dating from before 3000 B.C. (the Incas)

16

Shifts and
Mixed Constructions

onsistency is an essential quality of language, and we expect that within sentences writers will adhere to certain patterns. This means that the decisions you make in writing one part of a sentence must be in line with the decisions you make subsequently. If not, clear communication suffers.

CRITICAL DECISIONS

Recognizing Grammatical Inconsistency
Decisions regarding grammatical consistency can be challenging and complex. Careful rereading will generally help you spot shifts, which are discussed in the first section of this chapter, but recognizing mixed constructions and incomplete sentences (discussed in the second section) is often more complicated. To do so, you will need to understand how sentence elements can—and cannot—function. For example, a prepositional phrase cannot function as a subject, but a gerund phrase can (Playing an instrument well requires practice.) You will also need to examine every sentence as if you were another reader trying to make sense of it for the first time. If there is any possibility of confusion, then you will need to make the changes necessary to clarify your ideas.

SHIFTS

Aside from the content it communicates, a sentence expresses other important information: person, number, tense, mood, voice, and tone. Once writers make a decision about these matters, they should follow that decision conscientiously within any one sentence.

16a   Revise shifts in person and number.

The term **person** identifies whether the subject of a sentence is the person speaking (the first person), the person spoken to (the second person), or the person spoken about (the third person). **Number** denotes whether a person or thing is singular or plural (see 7a-2 and 7a-7).

> **1**   Revise shifts in person by keeping all references to a subject consistent.

A shift from one person form to another obscures a subject's identity, changing the reference by which the subject is known. Shifts in person often occur when a writer switches from the third person *(he, she, it)* to the second person *(you)*, and vice versa. You can avoid this difficulty by recognizing the second- or third-person orientation of your sentences and by maintaining consistency.

Inconsistent	A person who is a nonsmoker can develop lung troubles when you live with smokers.
Third person	A person who is a nonsmoker can develop lung troubles when he or she lives with smokers.
Second person	If you are a nonsmoker, you can develop lung troubles if you live with smokers.

> **2**   Revise shifts in number by maintaining consistent singular or plural forms.

Inconsistent	They had the best time of their life.
Revised	They had the best time of their lives.

You can avoid shifting number and confusing readers by maintaining a clear plural or singular sense in all significant words throughout a sentence. Any significant words related to a subject or object should match its number.

Inconsistent	The seven candidates for the judgeship have a liberal record.
Revised	The seven candidates for the judgeship have liberal records.

When, in an effort to avoid sexist language, you change the number of a pronoun from singular to plural, be sure to change the number of the subject (see 10c).

Sexist reference	Any candidate should file his papers by noon on December 1.
Revised but no agreement	Any candidate should file their papers by noon on December 1.
Revised	Any candidates should file their papers by noon on December 1.

EXERCISE 1

Correct shifts in person and number in the following sentences.

> *Example:* During the ninth and tenth centuries, leaders in the Catholic Church suggested that by using elements of stage drama, we could enhance the appeal of public worship.
>
> During the ninth and tenth centuries, leaders in the Catholic Church suggested that by using elements of stage drama, *the Church* could enhance the appeal of public worship.

1. A typical monastic community would usually confine their dramatic activities to Christmas, Easter, and perhaps one or two saints' days.
2. Although we can locate a number of saints' plays in the early drama of Western Europe, you can't find them all collected in one place.
3. Until the nineteenth century, comedy was inappropriate to serious religious dramas; they saw it as almost blasphemous.
4. The villainous characters in medieval drama are usually comic but not lovable; he is insensitive, even cruel.

16b **Revise shifts in tense, mood, and voice.**

Tense, mood, and *voice* denote important characteristics of main sentence verbs: when the action of the verb occurs, what a writer's attitude toward that action is, and whether the *doer* or *receiver* of the action is emphasized. When these characteristics are treated inconsistently, readers can be confused.

> **1** Revise shifts in tense by observing the appropriate sequence of verb tenses.

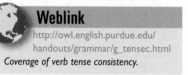

Weblink

http://owl.english.purdue.edu/
handouts/grammar/g_tensec.html
Coverage of verb tense consistency.

A verb's **tense** shows when an action occurs or when a subject exists in a certain state of being (see 9e and 9f). Tenses are often changed within sentences in regular and consistent patterns. Shifts in tense that disrupt these patterns strike readers as illogical, especially when the shifts alter the logic or time sequencing within or between sentences.

Inconsistent The road climbed from the Montezuma Castle National Monument, and the vegetation changes from desert scrub to scrub pines.

Consistent The road climbed from the Montezuma Castle National Monument, and the vegetation *changed* from desert scrub to scrub pines. [The past tense is used consistently.]

The "historical present tense" is often used in academic writing to refer to material in books or articles or to action in a film (see 9e-1).

Inconsistent   In her article, Karen Wright referred to Marshall McLuhan's global village and asks rhetorically, "Who today would quarrel with McLuhan's prophecy?" [The reference to Wright's work should either be past or "historically" present, but not both.]

Consistent   In her article, Karen Wright refers to Marshall McLuhan's global village and asks rhetorically, "Who today would quarrel with McLuhan's prophecy?"

Acceptable shifts of tense are needed to establish a proper sequence of events.

Acceptable   After he *had read* of experiments in electricity, Nathaniel Hawthorne *observed* that the world *was becoming* "a great nerve." [The tenses change from past perfect to past to past progressive. See Chapter 9 for a full discussion of tenses.]

2   Revise for shifts in mood.

A verb's **mood** indicates whether a writer judges a statement to be a fact, a command, or an occurrence contrary to fact (see 9h). Sentences in the **indicative mood,** by far the most common, are presented as fact. In the **imperative mood,** writers express commands—addressing them usually to an implicitly understood "you." In the **subjunctive mood,** writers express doubt or a condition contrary to fact (see 9h-1–4). When mood shifts in a sentence, readers cannot be sure of a writer's intentions. You can avoid confusion by choosing a mood and using it consistently.

Inconsistent   If he were more experienced, he will be able to help us. [The sentence shifts from the "doubtful" subjunctive to the "factual" indicative.

Consistent subjunctive   If he were more experienced, he would be able to help us.

3   Revise for shifts in voice.

A **transitive verb**—one that transfers action from a subject to an object—can be expressed in the active or passive voice (see 9g-1–2). If writers shift from one voice to the other in a single sentence, both emphasizing and deemphasizing a subject (or *doer* of an action), then readers will be confused. Avoid the difficulty by choosing an active *or* a passive voice in any one sentence.

Inconsistent	Columbus arrived in the New World, and it was believed he had found the coast of Asia. [The shift from active voice to passive leaves doubt about who believed this.]
Consistent	Columbus arrived in the New World and believed he had found the coast of Asia.

ACROSS THE CURRICULUM

Active and Passive Voice in Scientific Writing

Particularly in science and social science writing, which rely on the passive voice for objectivity, shifts to the active voice may sometimes be necessary to avoid awkwardness. Note the following example from a study of courtship patterns among women:

Finally, the *whisper* was used by most of the subjects in the sample. The woman moved her mouth near another person's ear and soft vocalizations presumedly were produced. Sometimes body contact was made.*

The shift to the active verb *move* in the second sentence avoids the awkwardness of "The woman's mouth was moved."

*Monica H. Moore, "Nonverbal Courtship Patterns in Women," *Ethology and Sociobiology*, Vol. 6, 1995.

16.1

EXERCISE 2

Correct the shifts in tense, voice, and mood in the following sentences.

> *Example:* Sports metaphors are popular in modern speech; they appeared most often in the language of advertising, business, and politics.
>
> Sports metaphors are popular in modern speech; they *appear* most often in the language of advertising, business, and politics.

1. Business has always been attracted by the language of football, for example, and it often will have invoked terms such as *team player*, *game plan*, and *optioned out*.
2. The connection is far from accidental in that both areas celebrated aggression.
3. If there were any doubt left about the connection between sports and business, recent surveys show that companies pay extravagant sums in order to rent private viewing suites at sports complexes.

4. Politicians will routinely use sports talk, and they use these figures of speech to curry favor with sports-minded voters.

5. Politicians and businesspeople use sports analogies, and complex ethical issues are often transformed into simple matters of strategy.

16c   Revise for shifts in tone.

Tone refers to the writer's attitude toward the subject and audience. Tone is a difficult element to revise, since so much determines it, including word choice, sentence structure, and sentence mood and voice. See 3a-4 and the box in 21e for more on matching the tone of a paper to your occasion for writing.

In papers that you prepare for your courses, your tone should be precise, logical, and formal, though not stuffy. Abrupt shifts from any established tone in a paper will be disconcerting to readers.

Disconcerting	In his famous painting *Persistence of Memory*, Salvador Dalí creates his most haunting allegory of empty space in which time is deader than a doornail. [The final slang expression creates an informal tone inconsistent with a formal analysis.]
Consistent	In his famous painting *Persistence of Memory*, Salvador Dalí creates his most haunting allegory of empty space in which time is at an end.

EXERCISE 3

Correct any shifts in tone in the following sentences so that the sentences are consistent.

> *Example:* Can you name a person who is always in a hurry, is extremely competitive, and blows his stack frequently?
>
> Can you name a person who is always in a hurry, is extremely competitive, and is often angry?

1. In contrast, can you think of someone who is so low-key that he's a couch potato, not very competitive, and easygoing in relations with others?

2. You now have in mind two *Homo sapiens* who could be described as showing Type A and Type B behavior patterns.

3. Type A individuals get frazzled by stress more easily and tend to suffer more coronary problems than Type Bs.

4. Type Bs have the patience of the blessed saints and perform well under high levels of stress and on tasks involving complex judgments and accuracy.

5. Who would make the better executive, the better spouse, the better party animal?

16d **Maintain consistent use of direct or indirect discourse.**

Direct discourse reproduces spoken or written language exactly, with quotation marks. **Indirect discourse** reproduces the language of others approximately, capturing its sense, though not its precise expression (see 28a-1).

Direct Lawrence asked, "Is that the telephone ringing?"

Indirect Lawrence asked whether the telephone was ringing.

Mixing discourse in one sentence can disorient a reader by raising doubts about what a speaker has actually said. You can avoid the problem by making a conscious choice to refer to another's speech either directly or indirectly.

16.2

CRITICAL DECISIONS

Distinguishing Between Direct and Indirect Discourse

Reported speech, or indirect discourse, is very different from directly quoted speech, which gives the exact verb tense of the original. The following table shows the patterns for changing verb tenses, verb forms, and modal auxiliaries in reported speech or indirect discourse.

Direct Speech	*Reported Speech*
Tenses:	
present	→ **past**
Ellie said, "I like horses."	Ellie said [that] she liked horses.
past	→ **past perfect**
Ellie said, "I rode the horse."	Ellie said [that] she had ridden the horse.
present progressive	→ **past progressive**
Ellie said, "I'm going riding."	Ellie said [that] she was going riding.
present perfect	→ **past perfect**
Ellie said, "I have ridden there."	Ellie said [that] she had ridden there.
past progressive	→ **past perfect progressive**
She said, "I was out riding."	She said [that] she had been out riding.
*****past perfect**	→ **past perfect**
She said, "I had ridden there."	She said [that] she had ridden there.

Direct Speech	Reported Speech
Auxiliary verbs:	
can →	**could**
She said, "I can show him."	She said [that] she could show him.
will →	**would**
She said, "I will ride again."	She said [that] she would ride again.
***could** →	**could**
She said, "I could ride."	She said [that] she could ride.
***would** →	**would**
She said, "I would go."	She said [that] she would go.

*These verbs do not change form as they undergo tense shifts.

EXERCISE 4

Correct the shifts in discourse in the following sentences by making direct quotations indirect.

> *Example:* As a boy in his teens, Albert Einstein asked how our view of the world would change if "I rode on a beam of light."
>
> As a boy in his teens, Albert Einstein asked how our view of the world would change if we rode on beams of light.

1. The great physicist Niels Bohr nailed a horseshoe on a wall in his cottage because "I understand it brings you luck whether you believe or not."

2. The mystery writer Agatha Christie believed that being married to an archaeologist, a man whose business it was to excavate antiquities, was a stroke of great good luck, because as she got older "he shows more interest in me."

3. In a feverish letter from a battlefield in Italy, Napoleon wrote Josephine that he had received her letters and that "do you have any idea, darling, what you are doing, writing to me in those terms?"

MIXED CONSTRUCTIONS

A **mixed construction** occurs when a sentence begins with a certain grammatical pattern and then concludes as if the sentence had begun differently. The resulting mix of incompatible sentence parts will confuse readers.

Mixed constructions are common in speech, but readers are likely to be sensitive to, and confused by, mixed constructions. Proofread carefully to identify and correct mixed constructions, which tend to occur in predictable patterns.

"The fact that"

The expression "the fact that" and words following it result in a mixed construction when writers forget that the expression begins a noun clause that functions as a subject or object. Writers see the subject and verb of the clause and mistakenly conclude that they have written a sentence.

Mixed The fact that design elements are as important to a play's success as actors. [Even though *are* is a verb and *design elements* functions as a subject, this is not a sentence. It is a noun clause that could take the place of a noun in another sentence, as below.]

Revised The fact that design elements are as important to a play's success as actors is often overlooked by beginning students of theater. [The noun clause now functions as the subject of the sentence.]

Revised Design elements are as important to a play's success as actors. [Deleting the words *the fact that* converts the dependent noun clause to an independent clause.]

An adverb clause

Adverb clauses begin with subordinating conjunctions—words such as *when*, *because*, and *although* (see the box in 19a). A mixed construction occurs when the final word of an introductory adverb clause also serves as the subject (or a word modifying the subject) of an independent clause.

Mixed When a set is successful design pleases actors and theatergoers alike. [The last word of the adverb clause, *successful*, is also used to modify the subject, *design*.]

Revised When a set is successful, the design pleases actors and theatergoers alike. [The adverb clause ends with *successful*; the independent clause begins with *the*.]

Revised A successfully designed set pleases actors and theatergoers alike.

A prepositional phrase

A prepositional phrase consists of a preposition (*by, of, in*, etc.) and a noun—the object of the preposition (see 7d-1). A noun functioning as the object of a prepositional phrase cannot simultaneously function as the subject of an independent clause.

Mixed	By creating a functional set design can help the audience believe the "place" on the stage is real. [The prepositional phrase *by creating a functional set design* operates incorrectly as the subject of the sentence.]
Revised	Creating a functional set design can help the audience view the stage as a believable other world. [*Creating a functional set design* operates as the subject of the independent clause. The preposition *by* is deleted.]
Revised	By creating a functional set design, a designer can help the audience view the stage as a believable other world. [The prepositional phrase remains, and a new subject, *a designer*, is added.]

16f Establish consistent relations between subjects and predicates.

A second type of mixed construction occurs when the predicate of a sentence does not logically complete its subject. The error is known as **faulty predication** and most often involves a form of the verb *be*, a linking verb that connects the subject complement with the subject.

Inconsistent	The electron microscope is keenly aware of life invisible to the human eye. [Can a microscope be keenly aware?]
Revised	The electron microscope helps us to be keenly aware of life invisible to the human eye. [Now it is people *(us)* who have been made aware.]
Revised	Aided by the electron microscope, we have grown keenly aware of life invisible to the human eye.

Faulty predication occurs in three other constructions involving the verb *be* and the sentence pattern *A is B* or *A = B*. If in writing a definition you begin the subject complement *(B)* with the words *when*, *if*, or *where*, or if in giving a reason you begin the subject complement with *because*, you may create a mixed construction.

Faulty	Electron illumination is if beams of electrons instead of light are used in a microscope. [In this sentence pattern, the subject *(electron illumination)* must be renamed by a noun or described by an adjective.]
Faulty	Electron illumination is when beams of electrons instead of light are used in a microscope. [In this sentence pattern, the subject *(electron illumination)* must be renamed by a noun or described by an adjective.]
Faulty	The reason electron microscopes have become essential to research is because their resolving power is so great. [In this sentence pattern, the subject *(reason)* must be renamed by a noun or described by an adjective.]

The sentence pattern of *subject/linking verb/subject complement* requires an adjective or a noun to serve as subject complement. The words *when, where, if,* and *because* begin adverb clauses and, thus, do not fit grammatically into the pattern. Revise a faulty predicate by changing the adverb clause to a noun clause or by changing the verb.

Revised   Electron illumination occurs when beams of electrons instead of light are used in a microscope.

Revised   The reason electron microscopes have become essential is that their resolving power is so great.

Verbs other than *be* can assert actions or states that are not logically consistent with a subject. Wherever you find faulty predication, correct it.

Faulty   The rate of Native American college enrollment has seen an improvement in the last ten years. [A *rate* cannot see.]

Revised   The rate of Native American college enrollment has increased in the last ten years.

Revised   Over the last ten years, educators have seen an increase in the rate of Native American college enrollment.

www
16.3

EXERCISE 5

Revise the sentences that follow in two ways, making each consistent in grammar or meaning. Place a check beside any sentence that needs no revision.

> *Example:* By implanting cats with microchip bar codes could resolve Novato, California's problem with strays.
>
> Implanting cats with microchip bar codes could resolve Novato, California's problem with strays.
>
> By implanting cats with microchip bar codes, the town of Novato, California, tried to resolve its problem with strays.

1. The fact that strays were overrunning the town and creating a health problem and a nuisance.

2. When minute, pellet-sized bar codes became available and created a radical alternative to neutering or destroying strays.

3. With the bar code implants, runaway cats could be identified and quickly returned to pet owners instead of being destroyed.

4. One sign of trouble was when animal rights groups protested the "indignity" of the solution and when comedians asked, "Are people next?"

5. Advanced, miniaturized technology used for instant identification breathes fear into those who vigilantly protect against invasions of privacy.

INCOMPLETE OR ILLOGICAL SENTENCES

An **incomplete sentence,** as its name implies, is one that lacks certain important elements. A fragment (see Chapter 12), the most extreme case of an incomplete sentence, may have no subject or predicate. In less extreme cases, a sentence may lack a word or two, which you can identify and correct with careful proofreading.

16g Edit elliptical constructions to avoid confusion.

Both in speech and in writing, we omit certain words in order to streamline communication. These "clipped" or shortened sentences are called **elliptical constructions.** But elliptical constructions may confuse readers if a writer omits words that are vital to sentence structure.

1 Use *that* when necessary to signal sentence relationships.

You can omit *that* and create an elliptical construction if the omission does not confuse readers.

Town planners in Novato, California, hoped (that) implanting cats with microchip ID tags could resolve the town's problem with strays.

If the omission confuses readers, then restore *that* to the sentence.

Unclear Thoughtful people honestly fear an implant of miniature ID tags in cats is a precursor to implants in humans. [The wording incorrectly points to *an implant* as the object of *fear.*]

Clear Thoughtful people honestly fear *that* an implant of miniature ID tags in cats is a precursor to implants in humans. [The word *that* now indicates that an entire noun clause will serve as the object of *fear.*]

ESL NOTE *That* clauses can occur in a variety of sentences. Notice that the noun clauses retain their structure even when the specific word *that* is omitted. For special rules in constructions involving *wish that,* see 47b-6.

Indirect quotation or reported speech is a very common special case of tense sequence involving two verbs in a *that* clause (see 47b-4).

2 Provide all the words needed for parallel constructions.

Elliptical constructions are found in sentences where words, phrases, or clauses are joined by the conjunction *and* or are otherwise made parallel. Grammatically, an omission is legitimate when a word or words are repeated *exactly* in all compound parts of the sentence, as in the following examples. Words that could be omitted are placed in parentheses. (See the discussion of parallelism at 18a–b.)

Parallel   According to one widely accepted theory, humans possess sensory (memory), short-term (memory), and long-term memory. [A word is omitted.]

Parallel   Information moves from short- (term memory) to long-term memory when we think about its meaning or (when we think) about its relationship to other information already in long-term memory. [A clause is omitted.]

An incomplete sentence results when words omitted in one part of an elliptical construction do not match identically the words appearing in another part.

Not parallel   Sensory and short-term memory *last* seconds or minutes, while long-term memory years or decades.

Parallel   Sensory and short-term memory *last* seconds or minutes, while long-term memory *lasts* years or decades.

The omitted word, *lasts*, is not identical to the word in the first part of the parallel structure, *last*. *Lasts* completes a singular subject and *last*, a plural subject.

3   **Use the necessary prepositions with verbs in parallel constructions.**

Elliptical constructions also result from the omission of a preposition that functions idiomatically as part of a complete verb phrase: believe *in*, hope *for*, looked *up*, tried *on*. When these expressions are doubled by the conjunction *and*, and you wish to omit the second preposition, be sure this preposition is identical to the one remaining in the sentence. In the following example, the doubled preposition is *on*: "relied *on*" and "ultimately thrived *on*."

In 1914, Henry Ford opened an auto manufacturing plant that relied and ultimately thrived on principles of assembly-line production.

If the prepositions are not identical, then *both* must appear in the sentence so that the full sense of each idiomatic expression is retained.

Faulty   Henry Ford believed and relied *on* the assembly line as a means to revolutionize American industry.

Revised   Henry Ford believed *in* and relied *on* the assembly line as a means to revolutionize American industry.

16h   Make comparisons consistent, complete, and clear.

To make comparisons effective, you should compare logically consistent elements and state comparisons completely and clearly. (In Chapter 11 you will find more on comparative forms of adjectives and adverbs.)

1   Keep the elements of a comparison logically related.

The elements you compare in a sentence must be of the same logical class.

Illogical   Modern atomic theory provides for fewer types of atoms than Democritus, the ancient Greek philosopher who conceived the idea of atoms. [Atoms are being compared incorrectly with Democritus, a person.]

Logical   Modern atomic theory provides for fewer types of atoms than did Democritus, the ancient Greek philosopher who conceived the idea of atoms.

2   Complete all elements of a comparison.

Comparisons must be made fully, so that readers understand which elements in a sentence are being compared.

Incomplete   Democritus believed there existed an infinite variety of atoms, each of which possessed unique characteristics—so that, for instance, atoms of water were smoother. [Smoother than what?]

Complete   Democritus believed there existed an infinite variety of atoms, each of which possessed unique characteristics—so that, for instance, atoms of water were smoother than atoms of fire.

Incomplete   The ideas of Democritus were based more on speculation. [More on speculation than on what?]

Complete   The ideas of Democritus were based more on speculation than on the hard evidence of experimentation.

3   Make sure comparisons are clear and unambiguous.

Clarify comparisons that invite alternative interpretations.

Unclear	Scientists today express more respect for Democritus than his contemporaries. [Two interpretations: (1) Democritus's contemporaries had little respect for him; (2) scientists respect the work of Democritus more than they respect the work of his contemporaries.]
Clear	Scientists today express more respect for Democritus than they do for his contemporaries.
Clear	Scientists today express more respect for Democritus than his contemporaries did.

EXERCISE 6

Revise the sentences that follow to eliminate problems with mixed constructions. Place a check beside any sentence that needs no revision.

> *Example:* We have a special reverence and fascination *with* fire.
>
> We have a special reverence *for* and fascination *with* fire.

1. Since ancient times, fire has been regarded more as a transforming element than sheer destructive power.
2. Medieval alchemists believed in fire resided magical properties.
3. In legend, Prometheus's gift of fire made humans better, and for this Prometheus was punished.
4. Although humans have used fire for about 400,000 years, not all people have known how to *make* fire.

CHAPTER 17

Being Clear, Concise, and Direct

Weblink

http://www.wisc.edu/writing/
Handbook/ClearConciseSentences.
html

A resource for writing clear, concise sentences.

Writing with clarity and directness involves making choices about wording that will help your audience understand your ideas. In most cases, you will achieve clear, concise, and direct expression through revision.

CRITICAL DECISIONS

Understanding the Need to Be Clear, Concise, and Direct

I have made this letter longer than usual, only because I have not had time to make it shorter.

—BLAISE PASCAL

Over three hundred years ago, the French mathematician and philosopher Blaise Pascal knew what writers know today: writing concisely is a challenge that takes time. The time spent in revising for clarity, conciseness, and directness is well spent—both for you and your readers.

Be clear, concise, and direct for yourself.

Writing becomes clearer as you revise to eliminate wordiness and to increase your use of active verbs. Revise for clarity, conciseness, and directness in order to be confident and satisfied that you have produced your best work.

Be clear, concise, and direct for your readers.

Revising for clarity, conciseness, and directness also has practical benefits. Readers can more clearly understand the points you want to make. Rather than wasting time trying to understand your meaning, they can respond directly to your points.

Wordiness can include unnecessary repetition, redundancy, and the use of buzzwords and long-winded, empty phrases. As you revise, look for places where you have said the same thing two different ways or used two words when one will do. It is a mistake to think that padded wording will make your writing sound more authoritative. And if you use filler simply to meet the length requirement of an assignment, your strategy will backfire by obscuring your message.

1 **Combine sentences that repeat material.**

A first draft may contain sentences that repeat material. When revising, combine sentences to eliminate wordiness and to sharpen focus.

Wordy The high *cost* of multimedia presentations is due to the combined *cost* of studio shoots and *expensive* video compression. The *costs* of graphic design and programmers are also high. [The word *cost* and its equivalents appear four times.]

Combined Studio shoots, video compression, graphic design, and programmers' work all contribute to the high cost of multimedia presentations.

2 **Eliminate wordiness from clauses and phrases.**

Eliminate wordiness by eliminating relative pronouns and by reducing adjective clauses to phrases or single words.

Complex Josephine Baker, *who was* the first black woman to become an international star, was born poor in St. Louis in 1906.

Concise Josephine Baker, the first black woman to become an international star, was born poor in St. Louis in 1906.

Complex Many were drawn by her vitality, *which was* infectious.

Concise Many were drawn by her infectious vitality.

Wordiness can also be eliminated by shortening phrases. When possible, reduce a phrase to a one-word modifier (see 7c).

Wordy *Recent revivals of* Baker's French films have included *rereleases of subtitled versions of Zou-Zou* and *Princess Tam-Tam.*

Concise *Recently* Baker's French films *Zou-Zou* and *Princess Tam-Tam* have been *rereleased with subtitles.* [The phrases are reduced to simpler modifiers.]

3 Revise sentences that begin with *it is, there is, there are,* and *there were.*

Expletive constructions *(it is, there is, there are, there were)* fill blanks in a sentence when a writer inverts normal word order (see 7a-11, 14d). Expletives are almost always unnecessary and should be replaced with direct, active verbs whenever possible.

Wordy   *There were many reasons why* Baker was more successful in Europe than in America.

Direct   Baker was more successful in Europe than in America for many reasons.

Wordy   *It is* because Europeans in the 1920s were interested in anything African *that* they so readily responded to Baker's outrageous style.

Direct   Because Europeans in the 1920s were interested in anything African, they readily responded to Baker's outrageous style.

4   Eliminate buzzwords.

Buzzwords are vague, often abstract expressions that add little but noise to a sentence. Buzzwords can be nouns: *area, aspect, case, character, element, factor, field, kind, sort, type, thing, nature, scope, situation, quality.* They can be adjectives, especially those with broad meanings: *nice, good, interesting, bad, important, fine, weird, significant, central, major.* And they can be adverbs: *basically, really, quite, very, definitely, actually, completely, literally, hopefully, absolutely.* Eliminate buzzwords. When appropriate, replace them with more precise expressions.

Wordy   *Those types of major* disciplinary problems are *really quite* difficult to solve.

Concise   Disciplinary problems are difficult to solve.

Wordy   *Basically,* she was *definitely* a *nice* person.

Concise   She was friendly. [*Kind, thoughtful, outgoing,* or any other more precise adjective could replace the vague *nice.*]

5   Eliminate redundant writing.

Intentional repetition can be a powerful technique for achieving emphasis (see 19c-2). Unintentional repetition, however, most often results in a tedious sentence. When you spot unintended repetition in your writing, eliminate it.

Redundant	James English believes that a lottery, *jackpot* mentality has undermined the will of Americans to succeed through hard work.
Revised	James English believes that a lottery mentality has undermined the will of Americans to succeed through hard work.
Redundant	Historically, immigrants *who came to this country* arrived in America expecting to work long hours. Even if they did not benefit directly *from their 70-hour weeks*, they believed their children would.
Revised	Historically, immigrants arrived in America expecting to work long hours. Even if they did not benefit directly from their efforts, they believed their children would.

Redundant phrases

A **redundant phrase** repeats a message unnecessarily. Redundant phrases include *small in size*, *few in number*, *continue to remain*, *green in color*, *free gift*, *extra gratuity*, *repeat again*, *combine together*, *add to each other*, and *final end*. Make your sentences concise by omitting one part of a redundant phrase.

Redundant	Today, the earlier belief in the value of hard work seems like naive *innocence*.
Concise	Today, the earlier belief in the value of hard work seems naive.
Redundant	The quickest route to expendable *extra* income is to hit the lottery.
Concise	The quickest route to expendable income is to hit the lottery.

6   Eliminate long-winded phrases.

Long-winded phrases such as *at this point in time* do not enhance the meaning or elegance of a sentence. Such expressions are tempting because they come to mind ready-made and seem to add formality, sophistication, and authority to your writing. But do not be fooled. Using such phrases muddies your sentences, making you sound either pretentious or inexperienced. Eliminate these phrases and strive for simple, clear, direct expression.

Wordy	*In the final analysis*, hard work is hard and *in a very real sense* explains why some people would rather bet on the lottery than work a 60-hour week.
Revised	The demands of working hard may explain why some people would rather bet on the lottery than work a 60-hour week.

Avoiding Wordy Expressions

Wordy	Direct
at this moment (point) in time	now, today
at the present time	now, today
due to the fact that	because
in order to utilize	to use
in view of the fact that	because
for the purpose of	for
in the event that	if
until such time as	until
is an example of	is
would see to be	is
the point I am trying to make*	———
in a very real sense*	———
in fact, as a matter of fact*	———

*These expressions are fillers and should be eliminated.

WWW

17.1

EXERCISE 1

Revise these sentences to eliminate wordiness by combining repeated material, reducing phrases and adjective clauses, and avoiding expletives.

Example: What type of consumer do you want to advertise to? Specifying the target or consumer that you want to reach with your product is the main step in advertising.

Effective advertising targets specific consumers.

1. When defining the purpose of advertising some experts admit that it is a manipulation of the public while others insist that advertising promotes the general well-being of its audience.
2. Advertising is one of the most eye-catching methods of selling a product. This is because advertising is a medium of information.
3. There are many consumers who are drawn to a product because the advertising campaign has been effectively utilized.
4. There are many qualities which an advertisement must have to lure the public to buy its product. The advertisement must be believable, convincing, informative, and persuasive. With these qualities in the ads, they will be the first ones to sell.
5. Like I mentioned before, it is not only women who are being portrayed sexually. Men are used in many advertisements also.
6. There exists a built-in sexual overtone in almost every commercial and advertisement around.

7. Advertising is one of several communications forces which performs its role when it moves the consumer through successive levels. These levels include unawareness, awareness, comprehension, conviction, and action.

EXERCISE 2

Revise the following sentences to eliminate wordiness.

Example: Early forms of advertisements were messages to inform the consumers of the benefits and the availability of a product.

Originally, advertisements informed consumers of a product's benefits and availability.

1. The producer must communicate with the product's possible customers in a way that is quite personal and quite appealing to the customer.
2. By identifying the product you start to narrow down the range of people you want to buy the product.
3. Advertising is a complex, but not mysterious, business.
4. To summarize a successful advertiser in today's world in one word, it would have to be opportunistic.
5. From campaign to campaign there are many different objectives and goals ads are trying to accomplish.
6. It used to be that women were mainly portrayed in the kitchen or in other places in the home.
7. We find advertising on television, on the radio, in newspapers and magazines, and in the phone book, just to name a few places.

17b Use strong verbs.

Strong verbs move sentences forward and make a subject's action clear for readers. One way to improve a draft is to circle all your verbs, revising as needed to ensure that each provides a crisp, direct statement.

1 Give preference to verbs in the active voice.

Sentences with verbs in the active voice emphasize the actor of a sentence rather than the object that is acted on (see 9g).

Active A cancer patient using the Internet can access volumes of medical information about his or her disease.

Passive Volumes of medical information about his or her disease can be accessed by a cancer patient using the Internet.

Passive Volumes of medical information about cancer can be accessed on the Internet. [The actor is not named.]

Unless a writer intends to focus on the object of the action, leaving the actor secondary or unnamed, the active voice is the strongest way to make a direct statement. When the actor needs to be named, a passive-voice sentence is wordier and thus weaker than an active-voice sentence.

Passive This widespread availability of medical information is not viewed favorably in all quarters. [The passive voice obscures the identity of those who hold negative views.]

Active Some doctors view the widespread availability of medical information unfavorably.

ACROSS THE CURRICULUM

Using Strong Verbs

Strong verbs heighten a reader's interest by establishing clear and vigorous relationships between the actors of a sentence and what is acted on. Unless you have good reason to deemphasize this relationship (see 9g-2), choose strong verbs when writing, regardless of discipline area. Observe the use of verbs in this introduction to a scientific article on the analysis of DNA fragments from mummified humans. (We have boldfaced the verbs.)

> Using sensitive techniques of molecular biology, we **have investigated** the possibility of recovering and analyzing genetic materials (deoxyribonucleic acid, DNA) from mummified human tissue and bone from selected archaeological sites in Greenland. Simple extraction procedures of both skin and bone samples **yielded** DNA material in purified form. Using human specific probes, we **demonstrated** that a minor, but distinct, portion of the purified DNA material was of human origin. Further analysis **showed** the remaining portion of the isolated DNA to consist mainly of DNA of fungal origin. The finding of DNA of human origin in mummified skin and bone samples, in particular, **opens up** the possibility for detailed anthropological genetic studies.*

In each of the five sentences excerpted here, the authors use a strong verb in the main clause. Cumulatively, these verb choices send a message to the reader: that the authors feel excitement for their work and think it significant.

*The passage is excerpted from Ingolf Thuesen and Jan Engberg, "Recovery and Analysis of Human Genetic Material from Mummified Tissue and Bone," *Journal of Archaeological Science* 17 (1990): 679.

Passive It is feared that the sheer volume, combined with the uncensored nature of Internet material, will mislead or confuse patients. [The passive voice conceals the identity of those who are in doubt.]

Active Some physicians fear that the sheer volume combined with the uncensored nature of Internet material will mislead or confuse patients.

2 Use forms of *be* and *have* as main verbs only when no alternatives exist.

The verb *be* is essential in forming certain tenses, such as a progressive tense.

The ability to retrieve medical information so readily *is fostering* in many patients an urge to question their care.

In a sentence of definition, *be* functions as an equal sign.

The National Cancer Institute and the National Institutes of Health *are* two institutions with Web sites that patients can consult.

Beyond these uses, *be* is a weak verb. Even weaker are the forms *seems to be* (or *seems that*) and *appears to be* (or *appears that*), which lack the courage to make a direct statement. When possible, replace these with strong, active-voice verbs.

Weak Many health-care professionals *are of the opinion* that the Internet is not the appropriate vehicle to teach people about health issues.

Stronger Many health-care professionals *claim* that the Internet is not the appropriate vehicle to teach people about health issues.

The verb *have* functions as an auxiliary in forming the perfect tenses. It tends to make a weak and indirect statement when used alone as the main verb of a sentence. Replace forms of *have* with strong, active-voice verbs.

Weak The easy accessibility of medical information *has* the effect of getting patients more involved in planning their treatment programs.

Stronger The easy accessibility of medical information *enables* patients to become more involved in planning their treatment programs.

3 Revise nouns derived from verbs.

A noun can be formed from a verb by adding a suffix: dismiss/dismiss*al*, repent/repent*ance*, devote/devo*tion*, develop/develop*ment*.

Often these constructions (sometimes called *nominalizations*) result in a weak, wordy sentence. The noun form replaces what was originally an active verb and requires the presence of a second verb. When possible, restore the original verb form of a noun derived from a verb.

Wordy   Many patients *made the discovery* that communication with other patients via the Internet *was helpful* in providing emotional support to everyone.

Direct   Many patients *discovered* that communicating with other patients via the Internet *helped* everyone emotionally.

Wordy   The Internet can act as a tool for the dissemination of health information.

Direct   The Internet can disseminate health information.

17.2

EXERCISE 3

Revise these sentences for clarity and directness by changing passive verbs to active verbs, replacing weak verbs with strong verbs, and converting nouns made from verbs back into verbs.

> *Example:* Both positive and negative reactions to a product should be expected.
>
> Consumers should expect both positive and negative reactions to products.

1. Advertising has always been generally understood as a form of communication between the buyer and the seller.
2. The aim of advertising is to give exposure of a certain product to a targeted audience.
3. Without catalogue viewership the product may be forgotten because the consumer will not have the ability to view it again.
4. There is a discussion of effective marketing in Thomas R. Forrest's article which is entitled "Such a Handsome Face: Advertising Male Cosmetics."
5. It has been noticed that in today's society a man's appearance is thought to be an important factor in his success.
6. There are several aspects of advertising that are seen to be essential to the successful marketing of a product.
7. Five questions should be asked before the implementation of a successful advertising campaign.
8. The association of a product with something that is desirable increases its visibility.

EXERCISE 4

Revise the following first draft of a student paper. Use all the techniques described in this and related chapters to achieve conciseness, clarity, and directness.

Advertising can be displayed in many different ways. One major way that advertisers try to sell their products is through the use of sexism. Sexism is portrayed in the majority of ads lately and it appears to be only getting worse.

It is now over twenty years after the feminist movement and sexism is as big of a problem as ever. Usually in the advertising industry it is the female that is used in the ad that portrays sexism: however, male sexism is found also. The latest problem occurred when Miller Beer tried to hook spring-break college bound kids with an ad insert for campus newspapers about annual trips to Florida that are often taken by college students. The ad included sketches of women in bikinis with hints of ways for these college kids to "pick up women." This ad insert drew a lot of attention from college students, mainly females that were outraged over it. There were even threats to boycott the product. However there were no results because the National Advertising Review Board has not issued guidelines on the use of women in ads since 1978. Also, there are very few agencies that have particular rules or regulations on sexism in ads. This could be due to the fact that the top managements are mostly male.

Everyone knows that sexism is used in advertisements all over the place but the question is, are they avoidable? Many advertising executives say no because they feel that advertisers have to address themselves to such a huge chunk of people that they are never going to be able to make everyone happy. This is why sexism and stereotyping in advertising is such a big problem today.

18

Maintaining Sentence Parallelism

I n writing, **parallelism** involves matching a sentence's structure to its content. When two or more ideas are parallel (that is, closely related or comparable), a writer can emphasize similarities as well as differences by creating parallel grammatical forms.

CRITICAL DECISIONS

Using Parallelism Effectively
Parallel structures help sentences to cohere by establishing clear relationships among sentence parts. To use parallelism effectively, you must make logical decisions about how to present parallel ideas for your readers. The parallel structures you choose should be those that most clearly suit your purpose and style. Consider the following:

They enjoy <u>dining</u> out, <u>going</u> to clubs, and <u>attending</u> concerts.

They like going out <u>to restaurants</u>, <u>to clubs</u>, and <u>to concerts</u>.

They frequent <u>restaurants</u>, <u>clubs</u>, and <u>concerts</u>.

Each of these constructions is parallel. What works best in a particular sentence would be up to the writer.

18a | **Use parallel words, phrases, and clauses with coordinating conjunctions.**

Whenever you use a coordinating conjunction (*and, but, for, or, nor, so, yet*), the joined words, phrases, or clauses become *compound* elements: compound subjects, objects, verbs, modifiers, and clauses. For sentence

Weblink

http://webster.commnet.edu/
grammar/parallelism.htm

Full coverage of parallelism, with examples and quizzes.

parts to be parallel in structure, the compound elements must share an equivalent, but not necessarily identical, grammatical form. If a verb in one part of a parallel structure is modified by a prepositional phrase, then a corresponding verb in the second part of the sentence should also be modified by a prepositional phrase—*but* that phrase need not begin with the same preposition.

1 Using parallel words

Not parallel The candidate was a visionary but insisting on realism.

Parallel The candidate was <u>visionary</u> *but* <u>realistic</u>.

Words that appear in a compound pair or series are related in content and should be parallel in form.

Not parallel Psychologist Howard Gardner identifies specific and a variety of types of intelligence, rather than one monolithic "IQ" score.

Determine the parallel elements.

Gardner identifies ___Slot 1___ and ___Slot 2___ types of intelligence, rather than one monolithic "IQ" score.

Gardner identifies *specific* and ___Slot 2___ types of intelligence, rather than one monolithic "IQ" score.

In this sentence the adjective *specific* completes Slot 1, and the noun *variety* completes Slot 2. In order for the sentence to be parallel, both slots must be filled by the same part of speech. In this case, both words should be adjectives, modifying the noun *types*.

Revise so that parallel elements have equivalent grammatical form.

Parallel Psychologist Howard Gardner identifies *specific* and *varied* types of intelligence, rather than one monolithic "IQ" score.

If the elements that should be logically parallel shift their function in a sentence, they may well shift their part of speech. In the following sentence, the parallel words are nouns—acting as a subject.

Parallel *Mathematics* and *art* are two of Gardner's seven types of intelligence. [The parallel terms are nouns.]

If these parallel words needed to modify the word *intelligence* in a second sentence, then the nouns would be changed to their adjective form:

Parallel   *Mathematical* and *artistic* intelligence are two of Gardner's seven types. [The parallel terms are adjectives.]

In parallel constructions, idiomatic terms must be expressed completely (see also 16g-3).

Not parallel   Other experts have been both intrigued and supportive of Gardner's claims.

Determine the parallel elements.

Other experts have been both ___Slot 1___ and ___Slot 2___ Gardner's claims.

The preposition *by* is needed to complete the first slot, since the idiom is *intrigued by*, not *intrigued of*.

Revise so that parallel elements have equivalent grammatical form.

Parallel   Other experts have been both intrigued *by* and supportive *of* Gardner's claims. [Each parallel item now has its own proper idiomatic preposition.]

2   Using parallel phrases

Not parallel   The judge had an ability to listen to conflicting testimony and deciding on probable guilt.

Parallel   The judge had an ability <u>to listen to conflicting testimony</u> *and* <u>to decide on probable guilt.</u>

To echo the idea expressed in a phrase in one part of a sentence, use a phrase with the same grammatical structure in another part.

Not parallel   Unstable technologies and searching for development funds have prompted some schools to cancel their online courses.

Determine the parallel elements.

___Slot 1___ and ___Slot 2___ have prompted

Unstable technologies and *searching for development funds* have prompted

Slot 1 is completed with a noun and modifier. Slot 2 is not parallel since it is completed with a gerund *(ing)* phrase.

Revise so the elements have equivalent grammatical form.

Parallel   *Unstable technologies* and *money shortages* have prompted some schools to cancel their online courses.

Both slots are now completed with a noun *(technologies, shortages)* and a modifier *(unstable, money)*. Note that the sentence can also be made parallel by completing both slots with gerund phrases:

18.1

coord //
Spotlight on Common Errors—PARALLELISM

These are the errors most commonly associated with parallelism. For full explanations and suggested revisions, follow the cross-references to chapter sections.

FAULTY PARALLELISM occurs when writers compare or contrast sentence parts without using similarly constructed wordings. In the examples that follow, parallel structures are highlighted.

Conjunctions suggest comparisons and require parallel structures.

Conjunctions such as *and* and *but* require parallel structures (see coordinating conjunctions, 18a).

Faulty

The candidate was a visionary but insisting on realism. [The verb forms *was a visionary* and *insisting* are not parallel.]

Revised

The candidate was **visionary** but **realistic.** [Similarly worded adjectives are linked by the conjunction *but*.]

Faulty

The candidate attended meetings, spoke at rallies, and she shook thousands of hands. [The candidate's three activities are not parallel.]

Revised

The candidate **attended meetings, spoke at rallies,** and **shook thousands of hands.** [The candidate's three activities are similarly worded.]

Paired conjunctions such as *either/or* and *both/and* require parallel structures (see correlative conjunctions, 18b).

Faulty

Depending on your tolerance for adventure, traveling without a map can either be exciting or you can be frustrated. [The words that describe *traveling—exciting* and *you can be frustrated*—are not parallel.]

Revised

Depending on your tolerance for adventure, traveling without a map can either be **exciting** or **frustrating.** [Similarly worded adjectives are joined by the paired conjunctions *either/or*.]

Faulty

Explorers can be both afraid of the unknown and, when they encounter something new, they want to understand it. [The verb forms *can be afraid* and *want to understand* are not parallel.]

Revised

Explorers can be both **afraid of the unknown** and **curious about it.** [Similarly worded adjectives and phrases are joined by the paired conjunctions *both/and*.]

Direct comparisons and contrasts require parallel structures (see 18c).

Faulty

The staff approved the first request for funding, not the second presenter requesting funds. [The objects *request* and *presenter* are not parallel.]

Revised

The staff approved **the first request for funding,** not **the second.** [The requests being contrasted share similar wording.]

Faulty

The old American frontier was frequently lawless, and so too anyone who surfs the Internet must grow accustomed to life without a central, regulating authority. [The compared items are not parallel.]

Revised

The Internet, no less than **the old American frontier,** is a lawless place that lacks a central, regulating authority. [Compared items, the *Internet* and the *frontier,* are similarly worded; both are now completed with the second part of the sentence: *is a lawless place.*]

Lists require parallel structures (see 18e).

Faulty

Make sure you pack the following in your kit:

—an alcohol solution that will cleanse wounds

—bandages

—Remove splinters with a tweezers

—matches

[Items in the list are not parallel.]

Revised

Make sure you pack the following in your kit:

—**alcohol**

—**bandages**

—**tweezers**

—**matches**

[Items in the list are similarly worded.]

Parallel   The dual problems of *coping with unstable technologies* and *searching for development funds* have prompted some schools to cancel their online courses.

In this revision two gerund phrases are used as objects of the preposition *of*. The two slots in the sentence are parallel. Both consist of a gerund followed by a prepositional phrase.

3   Using parallel clauses

Not parallel   Before the storm's end but after the worst was over, the captain radioed the Coast Guard.

Parallel   Before the storm had ended *but* after the worst was over, the captain radioed the Coast Guard.

A *clause* is a group of words that has a complete subject and predicate. Both independent clauses (that is, sentences) and dependent clauses can be made parallel, provided they are parallel in content.

In order to maintain parallel structure in sentences that have a pair or series of dependent relative clauses, you will need to repeat the relative pronouns *who, whom, which,* and *what.*

Not parallel   Roseate terns are small diving birds that are highly adept
(dependent   fliers, that habitate together in large colonies, and they are
clauses)   listed as an endangered species.

Determine the parallel elements.

Roseate terns are small diving birds   Slot 1 ,   Slot 2 , and   Slot 3 .

Roseate terns are small diving birds *that are highly adept fliers*,   Slot 2 , and   Slot 3 .

Slot 1 is completed with a relative clause beginning with the relative pronoun *that*. Slots 2 and 3 must have the same structure. Each slot must be completed with a clause that begins with the word *that*.

Revise so that parallel elements have equivalent grammatical form.

Parallel   Roseate terns are small diving birds *that* are highly adept fliers, *that* habitate together in large colonies, and *that* are listed as an endangered species.

Brief words that begin a series (for example, a relative pronoun such as *who*, a preposition such as *by* or *in*, and the infinitive *to*) may be written once at the beginning of the first item in the series and then omitted from all remaining items.

Parallel   Carl Sagan was an astronomer, physicist, and popular writer *who* advised NASA on the American space program, campaigned against nuclear proliferation, and brought science within the reach of nonexperts.

A caution: If one of these introductory words appears in more than one part of the series but not in *all* parts, the parallelism will be faulty.

Not parallel   I want *to* go home, wash up, and *to* eat.

Parallel   I want *to* go home, *to* wash up, and *to* eat.
I want *to* go home, wash up, and eat.

| 18b | Use parallelism with correlative conjunctions: *either/or*, *neither/nor*, *both/and*, *not only/but also*. |

Not parallel   Explorers can be both afraid of the unknown and, when they encounter something new, they want to understand it.

Parallel   Explorers can be *both* afraid of the unknown *and* curious about it.

Whenever you join parts of a sentence with pairs of words called *correlative conjunctions* (*either/or*, *neither/nor*, *both/and*, *not only/but also*), you must use the same grammatical form in both parts. Once again, think of the conjunction as creating parallel slots in the sentence. Whatever grammatical structure is used to complete the first slot must be used to complete the second.

Not parallel   After defeating Custer at Little Bighorn, Crazy Horse managed both to stay ahead of the army and *escape*.

Determine the parallel elements.

managed both __Slot 1__ and __Slot 2__ .

managed both *to stay ahead of the army* and __Slot 2__ .

Slot 2 must take the same form as Slot 1. Each must be a verb in its infinitive form: *to* _____.

Revise so that parallel elements have equivalent grammatical form.

Parallel   After defeating Custer at Little Bighorn, Crazy Horse managed both *to stay* ahead of the army and *to escape*.

Variation: By slightly modifying the sentence—by moving the word *to* outside of the parallel structure created by the correlative conjunction—you can eliminate the word *to* in both of the sentence's parallel slots.

managed *to* both   Slot 1   and   Slot 2 .

managed *to* both *stay ahead of the army* and   Slot 2 .

Parallel   After defeating Custer at Little Bighorn, Crazy Horse managed *to* both *stay ahead of the army* and *escape.*

ACROSS THE CURRICULUM

Parallelism

Making sentence elements parallel is a good strategy for giving sentences a professional polish. You will find writers in all disciplines using parallel structures to make their presentations concise, rhythmically balanced, and logical—as author Harold Livesay demonstrates in this excerpt from his biography of Andrew Carnegie. In three sentences, Livesay employs three sets of parallel structures.

Carnegie's twelve years' experience on the Pennsylvania Railroad shaped his subsequent career. On the railroad he assimilated the managerial skills, grasped the economic principles, and cemented the personal relationships that enabled him to become successively manager, capitalist, and entrepreneur. His most spectacular achievement—building Carnegie Steel into the world's largest steel producer—rested primarily on his successful transfer of the railroads' managerial methods to the manufacturing sector of the economy.*

Parallel structure   On the railroad he _A_, _B_, and _C_.

On the railroad he *assimilated* the managerial skills, *grasped* the economic principles, and *cemented* the personal relationships

Parallel structure   that enabled him to become successively _A_, _B_, and _C_.

that enabled him to become successively manager, capitalist, and entrepreneur.

Parallel structure   rested primarily on his successful transfer of _A_ to _B_.

rested primarily on his successful transfer of the railroads' managerial methods to the manufacturing sector of the economy.

*This passage is excerpted from Harold Livesay, *Andrew Carnegie and the Rise of Big Business* (Boston: Little, Brown, 1975) 29.

18c	**Use parallelism in sentences with compared and contrasted elements.**

Not parallel   The staff approved the first request for funding, not the second presenter who requested funds.

Parallel   The staff approved <u>the first request for funding</u>, *not* <u>the second request</u>.

When words, phrases, or clauses are compared or contrasted in a sentence, their logical and grammatical structures must be parallel (see 16h). Expressions that set up comparisons and contrasts include *rather than*, *as opposed to*, *on the other hand*, *not*, *like*, *unlike*, and *just as/so too*.

Not parallel   The word *mensch*, derived from Yiddish, describes a man who is assertive and affectionate, while a *schnook* is being spineless and sneaky.

Determine the parallel elements.

The word *mensch*, derived from Yiddish, Slot 1 , while a *schnook* Slot 2 .

The word *mensch*, derived from Yiddish, *describes a man who is assertive and affectionate*, while a *schnook* Slot 2 .

Slot 1 consists of a present-tense verb and a noun that is modified by a relative clause. Slot 2 begins with a verb in the present progressive tense *(is being)*, which is followed by two adjectives. Slot 2 should take the same basic form as Slot 1.

Revise so that parallel elements have equivalent grammatical form.

Parallel   The word *mensch*, derived from Yiddish, *describes a man who is assertive and affectionate*, while *schnook describes someone who is spineless and sneaky.*

EXERCISE 1

Revise the following sentences to correct the faulty parallel structure.

Example: Native Americans have one of the highest unemployment rates in the nation, the lowest educational attainment of any U.S. minority group, and they fare worst in the area of health.

Native Americans have one of the highest unemployment rates in the nation, the lowest educational attainment of any U.S. minority group, and *the worst record of health care.* [Each slot in the series now begins with an adjective in its superlative form: *highest, lowest, worst.* Each adjective is followed by a noun and each noun by a prepositional phrase.]

1. Designating Asian Americans as the "model minority" is problematic not only because the term obscures the diversity of the group but they are represented in only a small percentage of top-ranking positions in the United States.

2. Some sociologists say that racism is rooted in a preference for one's "own kind" rather than social causes.

3. Conflict theorists feel that racism results from competition for scarce resources and an unequal distribution of power and racial tension increases during periods of economic decline.

4. Corporate managers do not tend to wield the political power of professionals such as lawyers and doctors, nor workers whom they supervise.

5. Either the percentage of the elderly living below the poverty line has decreased or to underestimate the number of elderly living in poverty is prevalent.

18d Use parallelism among sentences to enhance paragraph coherence.

Like many other towns on the Great Plains, Nicodemus, Kansas, *was founded* in the 1870s. *Unlike any other* that still survives, *it was founded* by black homesteaders.

18.2

Parallelism can help to relate the parts of an *entire paragraph* by highlighting the logic a writer uses to move from one sentence to the next. Parallel structures bind a paragraph's sentences into a coherent unit.

Parallel sentences within a paragraph

A house divided against itself cannot stand. I believe this government cannot endure, permanently half slave and half free. I do not expect the Union to be dissolved. I do not expect the house to fall. But I do expect it will cease to be divided. It will become all one thing, or all the other.

—ABRAHAM LINCOLN, 1858

In this famous passage, Lincoln uses parallel structures to show relationships not only among single words or phrases but also among whole sentences. Elements of the first sentence *(house, divided)* are repeated near the end of the paragraph. Lincoln repeats the phrase *I do not expect* twice and then produces a parallel contrast with *But I do expect* in a third repetition. The final two sentences repeat *it will* with different verbs. The last sentence sets up a parallel opposition governed by *all*. Parallel structures give the paragraph an emphatic, memorable rhythm.

18e   Use parallel entries when writing lists or outlines.

A list or outline divides a single large subject into equal or coordinate elements. Elements in a list or outline may be written as words, phrases, or clauses. When preparing a paper or taking notes from a book, keep the elements of lists and outlines in equivalent grammatical form. Like parallel elements in a sentence, parallel elements in a list or outline highlight the logical similarities that underlie parallel content.

1   Making lists

A *list* is a series of items that are logically similar or comparable. A list that is not expressed in grammatically parallel form can be very confusing.

Not parallel

Those attending should be prepared to address these issues:

- morale of workers
- Why do we need so much overtime?
- getting more efficient
- We need better sales tools.

The preceding shows a list with four forms: a noun phrase, a question, a verb in its *-ing* form, and a sentence. Choosing any one of these forms as a standard would make the list parallel.

Parallel

Those attending should be prepared to address these issues:

- morale of workers
- necessity of overtime
- need for efficiency
- need for better sales tools

Parallel

Those attending should be prepared to address these issues:

- improving worker morale
- reducing the need for overtime
- improving efficiency
- reevaluating sales tools

2   Making outlines

An **outline** is a logically parallel list with further subdivisions and subsections under individual items. To make an outline that will help you write a paper or take summarizing notes from a book, follow the guidelines shown in 3d-4. Keep elements at the same level of generality in the outline parallel in form.

Not parallel

Chapter Title: Jefferson Takes Power [clause]

    A. The man and his policies [compound nouns]
    B. Buying Louisiana [*-ing* form of a verb]
    C. Jefferson, Marshall, and the courts [compound nouns]
    D. There's trouble on the seas [clause]

Subdivisions within the outlined chapter are written three ways: as an independent clause, as a noun or noun phrase, and as a verb in its *-ing* form. You need to choose *one* of these grammatical structures to make a logically parallel outline.

Parallel, with a subdivision

Chapter Title: Jefferson in Power

    A. The man and his policies
    B. The Louisiana Purchase
    C. Jefferson, Marshall, and the courts
    D. Trouble on the seas
        1. The benefits of neutrality
        2. The dangers of neutrality

As you expand the outline in greater detail and add subdivisions, once again present each entry of a subdivision in parallel form.

EXERCISE 2

Outline the major sections of any chapter in one of your textbooks, using the author's subheadings or your own. Then choose one section to outline in detail. Make parallel entries in your outline for every paragraph in that section, maintaining a consistent grammatical form.

EXERCISE 3

Repeat Exercise 2, using a paper you have recently written. Use the outline of your paper to evaluate the coherence of your work.

CHAPTER **19**

Building Emphasis with Coordination and Subordination

To emphasize a thought, you can assign special importance to particular words in a sentence and to particular sentences in a paragraph. Make decisions about emphasis once you have written a draft and have your main points clearly in mind. Then you can manipulate words, phrases, and clauses to create the effects that will make your writing memorable.

COORDINATION

The guidelines in the Critical Decisions box on page 358 will help you make decisions about when to use coordination.

19a Use coordinate structures to emphasize equal ideas.

One common technique for creating emphasis and eliminating wordiness is **coordination,** combining sentence elements with coordinating and correlative conjunctions and conjunctive adverbs. Elements in a coordinate relationship share equal grammatical status and equal emphasis.

19.1

 Give equal emphasis to elements with coordinating conjunctions.

The **coordinating conjunctions** *and, but, or, nor, so, for, yet* offer an efficient way of joining parallel elements from two or more sentences into a single sentence.

A market allows sellers *of goods* to interact with buyers.

A market allows sellers *of services* to interact with buyers.

Using the coordinating conjunction *or*, you can join these two ideas and eliminate repetition by coordinating the objects of the two prepositional phrases. In the following sentence, *goods* and *services* receive equal emphasis.

Combined   A market allows sellers of goods *or* services to interact with buyers.

CRITICAL DECISIONS

Knowing When to Coordinate Sentence Elements
Coordination links sentences and sentence parts. The following sentences can be joined in various ways to establish coordinate relationships.

(1) A complete suit of armor consisted of some 200 metal plates. (2) The armor of the fifteenth century offered protection from cross bows. (3) Armor offered protection from swords. (4) Armor offered protection from early muskets. (5) A suit of armor weighed 60 pounds. (6) A suit of armor would quickly exhaust the soldier it was meant to protect.

Why choose coordinate relationships?

Coordinating Conjunctions and the Relationships They Establish

To show addition: *and*	**To show contrast:** *but, yet*
To show choice: *or, nor*	**To show cause:** *for*
To show consequences: *so*	

Link sentences and emphasize specific words.

> The armor of the fifteenth century offered protection from cross bows, swords, *and* early muskets.

Link sentences and emphasize specific phrases.

> A complete suit of armor consisted of some 200 metal plates *and* weighed 60 pounds.

Link and give equal emphasis to whole sentences.

> The armor of the fifteenth century offered protection from cross bows, swords, and early muskets; *but* the armor would quickly exhaust the soldier it was meant to protect.

Conjunctive Adverbs and the Relationships They Establish

> **To show contrast:** *however, nevertheless, nonetheless,* and *still*
>
> **To show cause and effect:** *accordingly, consequently, thus,* and *therefore*

To show addition: *also, besides, furthermore,* and *moreover*
To show time: *afterward, subsequently,* and *then*
To show emphasis: *indeed*
To show condition: *otherwise*

Use conjunctive adverbs to link and give equal emphasis to two sentences. Conjunctive adverbs can be shifted from the beginning to either the middle or the end of the second sentence (which is not possible with coordinating conjunctions—see 19a-3).

The armor of the fifteenth century offered protection from cross bows, swords, *and* early muskets; *however,* the armor would quickly exhaust the soldier it was meant to protect.

Coordinating conjunctions express specific logical relationships between the elements they join. *And* joins elements by addition. *Or* and *nor* suggest choice or opposition. *But* and *yet* join elements by contrast. *For* suggests a cause of an occurrence. *So* suggests a result of some action. (Note that *for* and *so,* when used as coordinating conjunctions, join entire independent clauses. The other coordinating conjunctions may join sentence elements and entire sentences.)

Coordinating conjunctions must be used with appropriate punctuation to show that two ideas share the same emphasis.

To establish equality between words

Darwin was a naturalist *and* biologist with an exceptionally fertile mind.

To establish equality between phrases

Darwin theorized that evolutionary changes proceed not in jumps *but* in leaps.

To establish equality between clauses

Darwin's theory of natural selection was his most daring, *for* it dealt with the mechanism of evolutionary change.

2 Give equal emphasis to elements by using correlative conjunctions.

Correlative conjunctions are pairs of coordinating conjunctions that emphasize the relationship between the parts of the coordinated construction. The following are the common correlative conjunctions:

either/or	*both/and*	*not only/but*
neither/nor	*whether/or*	*not only/but also*

The first word of the correlative is placed before the first element to be joined, and the second word of the correlative is placed before the second element.

Both supply *and* demand are theoretical constructs, not fixed laws.

---

3 Use conjunctive adverbs to give balanced emphasis to sentence elements.

Conjunctive adverbs, also called *adverbial conjunctions,* create compound sentences in which the independent clauses that are joined share a logically balanced emphasis. Such conjunctions include *however, otherwise, indeed, nevertheless, afterward, still,* and others listed in the Critical Decisions box on page 358. (See 7a-9 and especially 13b-4 for uses of conjunctive adverbs.)

Linked sentences

As the price of a good or service increases, the quantity of the good or service demanded is expected to decrease. *Moreover,* as the price of a good or service decreases, the quantity of the good or service demanded is expected to increase.

Conjunctive adverbs, like most adverbs, can be moved around in a sentence.

We almost take for granted that rain will replenish whatever amount of water we may use up. Water, *however,* is not an infinitely renewable resource.

In the second sentence, the conjunctive adverb may be moved.

However, water is not an infinitely renewable resource.

Note: Because conjunctive adverbs have the force of transitional elements, they are usually set off in a sentence with commas. (See 13b-4 for avoiding comma splices when using conjunctive adverbs.)

---

4 Revise sentences that use illogical or excessive coordination.

Problems with coordination arise when writers use conjunctions aimlessly, stringing unrelated elements together without regard for an equal or balanced relationship of ideas.

Faulty coordination

Two elements linked by a conjunction show faulty coordination when they are not logically related. Revise or reorganize sentences to establish groupings that make sense, using coordination for elements of closely related importance.

ACROSS THE CURRICULUM

Emphasis Through Coordination

Coordination is a fundamental tool of sentence construction that gives writers in all discipline areas a means of controlling emphasis. Observe how economist Milton Friedman uses coordination to give elements equal weight.

In a free-enterprise, private property system, a corporate executive is an employee of the owners of the business. He has direct responsibility to his employers. That responsibility is to conduct the business in accordance with their desires, which generally will be to make as much money as possible while conforming to the basic rules of the society, both those embodied in law and those embodied in ethical custom. Of course, in some cases his employers may have a different objective. A group of persons might establish . . . for example, a hospital or a school. The manager of such a corporation will not have money profit as his objective but the rendering of certain services.*

Coordinate words

A, B system

free-enterprise, private property system (comma replaces *and*)

for example, A **or** B

for example, a hospital **or** a school

Coordinate phrases

both those in A **and** those in B

both those embodied in law **and** those embodied in ethical custom

will not have A **but** B

will not have money profit as his objective **but** the rendering of certain services

*The passage is excerpted from Milton Friedman, "The Social Responsibility of Business Is to Increase Its Profits," *New York Times Magazine* 13 Sept. 1970.

Faulty Spiders can be found in all sorts of habitats, from the tundra environment of mountain peaks to the deepest crevices of caves, and spiders are not particularly adaptable to new habitats. [The writer coordinates these sentences improperly. Clearly, the writer intends a contrast.]

Revised Spiders can be found in all sorts of habitats, from the tundra environment of mountain peaks to the deepest crevices of caves, but a given spider will not be particularly adaptable to a new habitat.

Excessive coordination

Readers look to a writer for signals about logical relationships among ideas. If a writer aimlessly uses coordinating conjunctions to join every statement to the next, readers will see no real connections among the ideas, and no idea will stand out. In reviewing first-draft writing, study your use of coordinating and correlative conjunctions and of conjunctive adverbs. Coordinate structures should be retained only when you have deliberately equated main ideas.

Faulty When the young princess Marie Antoinette of Austria was handed over by the Austrian government to the care of the French monarchy, she had to cross the national boundary line all alone, and she had to remove all her articles of Viennese clothing and replace them with French-made ones, and she could retain not even a keepsake.

Revised When the young princess Marie Antoinette of Austria was handed over by the Austrian government to the care of the French monarchy, she had to cross the national boundary line all alone. Next, she had to remove all her articles of Viennese clothing and replace them with French-made ones. She could retain not even a keepsake.

EXERCISE I

Combine the following sets of sentences so that whole sentences or parts of sentences show equal emphasis. Use coordinating conjunctions, correlative conjunctions, or conjunctive adverbs.

> *Example:*   Ostriches grow from egg to 150-pound bird in nine months. A young python of five pounds requires ten to twenty years to reach 120 pounds.
>
> Ostriches grow from egg to 150-pound bird in nine months, but a young python of five pounds requires ten to twenty years to reach 120 pounds.

1. Why living things evolve is only partly understood. How living things evolve is only partly understood.

2. Monkeys, apes, and humans are all good manipulators of hand-eye coordination. No mammal can rival the chameleon for eye-tongue coordination.

3. Snake anatomy contains the most clever feeding apparatus. Snake anatomy also contains the most intricately efficient feeding apparatus.

4. The snake opens its jaws. It begins to engulf the monkey. It is not hurried. It is deliberate. It is precise.

5. The Nunamiu Eskimo believe that wolves know where they are going when they set out to hunt caribou. They believe that wolves learn from ravens where caribou might be. They believe certain wolves in a pack never kill. Others, they believe, specialize in killing small game.

6. When the wolves come together, they make squeaking noises. They encircle each other. They rub and push one another. They poke their noses into each other's neck fur. They back away to stretch. They chase each other. They stand quietly together. Then they are gone down a vague trail.

7. Mexico still has a small population of wolves. Large populations remain in Alaska and Canada.

EXERCISE 2

Rewrite the sentences in the following paragraph by using coordinating conjunctions, correlative conjunctions, or conjunctive adverbs along with appropriate punctuation. Remember that you want to show equality between ideas or parts of ideas. Be sure that the revised paragraph is cohesive and coherent.

The smallest living creatures known are viroids. Each is composed of fewer than 10,000 atoms. They can cause several different diseases in plants. They have probably most recently developed from more complex organisms rather than less complicated ones. They are so simple in structure. One wonders how they could be alive at all. They survive because they are parasites. They take over much larger cells and force that cell to begin making more viroids like themselves.

EXERCISE 3

Rewrite the following sets of sentences to correct problems of faulty coordination.

1. Plants adapted to cold climates can conduct photosynthesis at temperatures far below those of their warmer-weather compatriots, and some evergreens still maintain the process at 0°C, and some algae that inhabit hot water springs can do likewise at 75°C, and yet most plants photosynthesize best between 10° and 35°C.

2. Many arthropods are definitely "dressed to kill." The scorpion sports sharp jaws, strong pincers, and it packs a nasty sting, but it is outclassed by the black widow spider, and her bite can be lethal if untreated, and yet centipedes will attack and paralyze prey twice their size with a bite.

Use Coordinate Structures to Emphasize Equal Ideas

19b   **Use subordinate structures to emphasize a main idea.**

Writers use **subordination** within sentences to emphasize one idea over another. The basic idea always appears in an **independent clause,** a statement that can stand alone as a sentence in itself. To state another idea closely linked to that core statement, writers add a **dependent clause,** which cannot stand by itself. A dependent clause begins with a subordinating conjunction, such as *if, although,* or *because* (see the Critical Decisions box on page 365 for a complete list), or with a relative pronoun: *who, which,* or *that.* A sentence with both dependent and independent clauses is known as a **complex sentence.** (See also 7e.)

	Use subordinating conjunctions to form dependent adverb clauses.

A subordinating conjunction placed at the beginning of an independent clause (a complete sentence) renders that clause *dependent.* Once dependent, this clause can be joined to an independent clause. To create a dependent adverb clause, begin with two sentences that you think could be combined.

> Married women could not leave the home for the twelve-hour work days required in the mills.

> They lost their ability to earn income.

When you place a subordinating conjunction at the head of the dependent clause, the clause will function like an adverb in the new complex sentence.

> Because married women could not leave the home for the twelve-hour work days required in the mills, they lost their ability to earn income.

Emphasis and logical sequence determine the placement of a dependent adverb clause.

At the beginning

> When the Triangle Shirtwaist Factory fire broke out in a rag bin on a quiet Saturday afternoon in 1911, it spread extraordinarily quickly.

In the middle

> The fire, though it claimed 146 lives, did result in the addition of 30 new ordinances to the New York City fire code.

At the end

> The terrorized, virtually all-female workforce was hampered in its efforts to leave because management had purposefully designed narrow escape passages in an effort to spot and catch pilferers.

CRITICAL DECISIONS

Knowing When to Subordinate Sentence Elements

Subordination links whole sentences. The following sentences can be joined to establish subordinate relationships.

A suit of armor weighed 60 pounds.

A suit of armor would quickly exhaust the soldier it was meant to protect.

Why choose subordinate relationships?

Subordinating Conjunctions and the Relationships They Establish

To show condition: *if, even if, unless, provided that, whether,* and *as though*

To show contrast: *though, although, even though, as if, rather than, than,* and *even if*

To show cause: *because, since, how, so,* and *why*

To show time: *when, whenever, while, as, before, after, since, once,* and *until*

To show place: *where* and *wherever*

To show purpose: *so that, in order that,* and *that*

Subordinating conjunctions link whole clauses but, in the process, give one clause greater emphasis. Use a subordinating conjunction when you want one of the two sentences you are linking to modify (that is, to describe or to comment on) the other.

Because it weighed 60 pounds, a suit of armor would quickly exhaust the soldier it was meant to protect.

Designate one sentence as subordinate by placing a conjunction at its head; thereafter, the sentence is referred to as a *dependent clause* (in this example, *Because it weighed 60 pounds*). Emphasis in a sentence linked with subordination is given to the *independent clause* (in this example, to the clause beginning with *a suit of armor* and ending with *protect*). See the discussion on relative pronouns (14e, 19b-2, 25d-1–2), which also begin dependent clauses.

---

2   Use *that, which,* and *who* to form dependent adjective clauses.

A dependent **adjective clause** modifies a noun in an independent clause. Adjective clauses are introduced by relative pronouns that rename and refer to the nouns they follow. The pronoun *who* can refer to people or to personified divinities or animals. *That* refers to people, animals, or things. *Which* refers to animals and things. To create a dependent adjective clause, begin with two sentences that you think could be combined.

> Belief in vampires has generated any number of folk tales, superstitions, and horror stories.

> It has existed for thousands of years.

Substitute a relative pronoun for the subject of the dependent clause, the clause that will function like an adjective in the new complex sentence.

> which has existed for thousands of years,

Join the now dependent clause to the independent clause.

> Belief in vampires, which has existed for thousands of years, has generated any number of folk tales, superstitions, and horror stories.

www

19.2

---

3   Use subordination accurately to avoid confusion.

Three errors are commonly associated with subordination: inappropriate and ambiguous use of subordinating conjunctions, illogical subordination, and excessive subordination.

Inappropriate and ambiguous use of subordinating conjunctions

The subordinating conjunction *as* is used to denote both time and comparison.

> As human beings became more advanced technologically, they learned to domesticate animals and plants rather than to forage and hunt.

As is occasionally used to indicate cause: *Mary didn't arrive this morning, as <u>she missed her plane</u>.* This usage is apt to confuse readers who expect *as* to indicate time or comparison. When you wish to establish cause and effect, use the subordinating conjunction *because*.

Confusing	*As* the plough is used as a wedge to divide the soil, it is the most powerful invention in all agriculture.
Revised	*Because* the plough is used as a wedge to divide the soil, it is the most powerful invention in all agriculture.

The preposition *like* is used as a subordinating conjunction in informal speech. In formal writing, use the subordinating conjunction *as* in place of *like* when a conjunction is needed.

Nonstandard	American agriculture did not have the plough and the wheel *like* Middle Eastern agriculture did.
Revised	American agriculture did not have the plough and the wheel *as* Middle Eastern agriculture did.

Illogical subordination

The problem of illogical subordination arises when a dependent clause does not establish a clear, logical relationship with an independent clause. To correct the problem, reexamine the clauses in question, and select a more accurate subordinating conjunction or, if the sentences warrant, a coordinating conjunction.

Faulty   *Although* she was agitated at being shut up in a matchbox for so long, the female scorpion seized the first opportunity to escape.

The subordinating conjunction *although* fails to establish a clear, logical relationship between the dependent and independent clauses. The content of the dependent clause gives no reason for the scorpion's wanting to escape.

Revised   *Because* she was agitated at being shut up in a matchbox for so long, the female scorpion seized the first opportunity to escape.

Excessive subordination

As with coordination, a writer may overuse subordination. When all or most parts of a long sentence are subordinate in structure, readers may have trouble identifying points of particular importance. Study your use of subordinating conjunctions and relative pronouns. Retain subordinate structures when you have deliberately made the ideas of one clause dependent on another. Choose other structures when clauses do not exist in a dependent/independent relationship.

Faulty

The manatee, which is a very tame beast, has a hippopotamus-like head and virtually no neck, so that one wonders how the creature could ever have been mistaken for the mermaid, although there are those who claim that if the animal is seen from sufficiently far away as it sits on the rocks, the lines of its head could convey the impression of flowing hair.

Revised

The manatee, which is a very tame beast, has a hippopotamus-like head and virtually no neck. One wonders how the creature could ever have been mistaken for the mermaid. There are those who claim, though, that if the animal is seen from sufficiently far away, the lines of its head could convey the impression of flowing hair.

EXERCISE 4

Revise the sentence pairs that follow by creating a complex sentence with one dependent clause and one independent clause. Place the dependent clause in whatever position best demonstrates the relationship of that clause to the main idea.

Use Subordinate Structures to Emphasize a Main Idea   367

Example: The Viennese naturalist Konrad Lorenz took a degree in medicine. Later, Konrad Lorenz became director of the Max Planck Institute for behavioral physiology.

After he took a degree in medicine, the Viennese naturalist Konrad Lorenz became director of the Max Planck Institute for behavioral physiology.

1. Social animals such as crows will attack or "mob" a nocturnal predator. The nocturnal predator sometimes appears during the day.

2. A fox is followed through the woods by a loudly screaming jay. The fox's hunting is spoiled.

3. Poisonous or foul-tasting animals have chosen the "warning" colors of red, white, and black. Predators associate these with unpleasant experiences.

4. Scent marks of cats act like railway signals. The scent marks prevent collision between two cats.

5. The surroundings become stranger and more intimidating to the animal. The readiness to fight decreases proportionately.

OTHER DEVICES FOR ACHIEVING EMPHASIS

19c   Use special techniques to achieve emphasis.

Coordination and subordination are fundamental to the structure of so many sentences that often they go unnoticed as devices for directing a reader's attention. Not so subtle are special stylistic techniques such as repetition and contrast, which writers use to achieve highly visible and at times dramatic prose. Precisely because they are so visible, you should mix these techniques both with subordination and coordination and with less emphatic simple sentences in a paragraph.

1   Punctuate, capitalize, and highlight to emphasize words.

Punctuation, capitalization, and highlighting work *with* sentence content to create emphasis. *Capitalizing* a word, especially if it is not a proper name and hence is usually not begun with an uppercase letter, is one sure way to create emphasis. Capitalizing all the letters of a word, as in FIRE, will attract even more attention. So, of course, will **boldfacing** or *italicizing* a word. In academic writing, strictly limit your use of these techniques and depend, instead, on the wording of your sentences to create emphasis. Occasionally, however, you might use uppercase letters for effect.

There does not seem to be any point in my knowing for the rest of my life that, during 1964, 720 tons of soot fell on every square mile of New York City, yet there it is in my notebook, labeled "FACT."

Punctuation can add emphasis to sentences in a number of ways:

■ An *exclamation point*, when used sparingly, will help a reader to share a writer's amazement, enthusiasm—or, in some cases, contempt (see 24c).

■ A *colon* at the end of a clause sets up a reader's expectation that important, closely related information will follow. The words following a colon are emphasized (see 29a).

■ A *dash*, which may also be typed as a double hyphen (--), creates a pause in a sentence and the expectation that something significant will follow. Used sparingly, a dash is an excellent tool for emphasis. Overused, it creates a choppy effect that can annoy readers (see 29b).

■ *Parentheses* are used to set off information from the body of a sentence. This information will be viewed by readers as an aside—interesting, useful, but ultimately nonessential. Thus, parentheses give material emphasis of a special sort, saying in effect pay attention but not *too much*. Material set off in parentheses is simultaneously emphasized and deemphasized (see 29c).

| 2 | Repeat words and phrases to emphasize ideas. |

Intentional repetition is another technique for creating emphasis. Note the repetition in the following sentence from an essay by writer Scott Russell Sanders:

> Before college, *the only people* I had ever known who were interested in art or music or literature, *the only ones* who read books, *the only ones* who ever seemed to enjoy a sense of ease and grace were the mothers and daughters.

Sanders could have written this sentence without repeating the subject modified by the three relative clauses: "Before college, the only people I had ever known who were interested in art or music, who read books, who ever seemed to enjoy a sense of ease and grace were the mothers and daughters." By repeating the phrase *the only ones*, however, he gives stronger emphasis to the point he is trying to make.

Similarly, in the following sentence from an essay criticizing the movie *Natural Born Killers*, novelist John Grisham repeats the subject in subsequent clauses rather than rename the subject with the pronoun *it*:

> Oliver Stone is saying that *murder* is cool and fun, *murder* is a high, a rush, *murder* is a drug to be used at will.

Again, the effect is to give the subject greater emphasis.

In both these examples, repetition serves to triple sentence elements, a common strategy for giving a sentence an arresting, memorable rhythm. Think of Lincoln's famous line from the Gettysburg Address: "government of the people, by the people, for the people." Be careful, though, with repetition that goes beyond three uses of a word or phrase. Too much repetition can dilute emphasis.

Repetition can also help to create striking effects across several sentences, especially if the repetition serves to reinforce parallel structures, as in one of the closing paragraphs from Martin Luther King Jr.'s "Letter from Birmingham Jail":

> If I have said anything in this letter that overstates the truth and indicates an unreasonable impatience, I beg you to forgive me. If I have said anything that understates the truth and indicates my having a patience that allows me to settle for anything less than brotherhood, I beg God to forgive me.

Here repetition provides a careful balance that strongly emphasizes King's meaning.

Be sure to use repetition thoughtfully and in moderation. Too much repetition in a paragraph can create a stilted, overly balanced effect.

3   Use contrasts to emphasize ideas.

Contrast, otherwise known as *antithesis* or *opposition*, creates emphasis by setting one idea against another, in the process emphasizing both. When using this technique, be sure that the elements you set in contrast have parallel structures.

> Requiring more skill to use and initially more unwieldy to master than the dictionary, *Roget's College Thesaurus* is, nonetheless, a valuable and time-saving aid for the struggling writer.

> If you apply to a college that won't promise to lock in its tuition rates, make sure to check the terms of your financial aid package. If you don't, you may find that after the freshman year your grants have been transformed into loans.

4   Use specialized sentences to create emphasis.

Sentence length depends both on a writer's preferences and on an audience's needs. Still, readers do not expect a steady diet of four- or five-word sentences. Nor do they expect one-sentence paragraphs. Purposefully violating these (and other) expectations regarding the sentence can create emphasis (see 20a and 20b).

The brief sentence

An especially brief sentence located anywhere in a paragraph will call attention to itself. The following paragraph concludes emphatically with a four-word sentence.

> If you apply to a college that won't promise to lock in its tuition rates, make sure to check the terms of your financial aid package. If you don't, you may find that after the freshman year your grants have been transformed into loans. That can be disastrous.

The one-sentence paragraph

Because it is so rare, a one-sentence paragraph calls attention to itself. Often these emphatic paragraphs begin or conclude an essay. In the following example, the one-sentence paragraph appears mid-essay and is both preceded and followed by long paragraphs.

> Not only are fruit seeds dispersed in the coyote's scat, the seeds' pericarp dissolves in his digestive tract, increasing the chance of germination by 85 percent.
>
> A coyote's breath is rumored to be so rank that he can stun his prey with it.
>
> Most people may never see a coyote—especially if they go looking for one—but everyone can hear them at night. They're most vocal from December to February, during the mating season. . . .

The periodic sentence

Most sentences can be classified as *cumulative*. They begin with a subject and gather both force and detail from beginning to end. The advantage of a cumulative sentence is that it directly and emphatically announces its business by beginning with its subject.

Cumulative sentence   Most people may never see a coyote—especially if they go looking for one—but everyone can hear them at night.

A *periodic* sentence delays the subject and verb in an effort to pique the reader's interest. Information placed at the head of the sentence draws readers in, creating a desire to find out what happens. Emphasis is given to the final part of the sentence, where the readers' need to know is satisfied.

Periodic sentence   Washing machines, garbage disposals, lawn mowers, furnaces, TV sets, tape recorders, slide projectors—all are in league with the automobile to take their turn at breaking down whenever life threatens to flow smoothly for their enemies.

19.3

EXERCISE 5

Read the sentences that follow, and underline the emphatic elements. Label the specific techniques the writer uses: coordination, subordination, punctuation, capitalization, repetition, contrast, or sentence length. Write your analysis in paragraph form.

> In books I've read since I was young I've searched for heroines who could serve as ideals, as models, as possibilities—some reflecting the secret self that dwelled inside me, others pointing to whole new ways that a woman (if only she dared!) might try to be. The person that I am today was shaped by Nancy Drew; by Jo March, Jane Eyre and Heathcliff's soul mate Cathy; and by other fictional females whose attractiveness or character or audacity for a time were the standards by which I measured myself.
>
> I return to some of these books to see if I still understand the powerful hold that these heroines once had on me. I still understand.
>
> —JUDITH VIORST

EXERCISE 6

Use the various techniques you have learned in this chapter to combine the short, choppy sentences that follow, rewording them to make an engaging paragraph.

> There are self-regulated devices in the body. One of these can provide long-term immunity from diseases such as mumps or measles. This same device somehow also causes the AIDS virus, if present, to infect the immune cells. This discovery was made by researchers. They work at Virginia Commonwealth University in Richmond. They found that the HIV virus can get coated with antibodies. Even so, the virus will attack the surrounding T-cells (immune cells).

CHAPTER **20**

Controlling Length and Rhythm

G ood writing depends, in part, on pacing—including how long a sentence takes to read and how the positioning of words and phrases creates a particular sentence rhythm. Focusing on length and rhythm will not, by itself, make a sentence memorable. But once the content of a passage has been established, sentence style can enhance that

20.1

CRITICAL DECISIONS

Considering the Relationship among Sentences

A writer cannot make effective decisions about the length and rhythm of an individual sentence without taking into account the sentences that surround it. For this reason, such decisions are best made not as you draft but during the process of revising and editing.

One helpful technique for examining a draft in terms of sentence length and rhythm is to read the draft aloud as if you were presenting your paper for an audience. Consider the following questions:

- Do any passages seem choppy or disjointed? If so, you may have grouped too many short sentences together. Look for ways of combining sentences to show a clearer relationship between ideas.
- Do any passages seem droning or monotonous? If so, the sentences may be too similar in length and type. Edit to add more variety.
- Do any passages seem wordy or hard to follow? If so, there may be too many long sentences in the passage. Look for ways of shortening sentences and simplifying sentence structure.

The advice in this chapter will help you make choices about the length and rhythm of your sentences.

---

content's effectiveness. As a writer, you will often need to make thoughtful decisions about the length and rhythm of your sentences.

20a   Monitoring sentence length

1   Track the length of your sentences.

Track the length of your sentences, especially in the late stages of revision, once you are certain of a paper's content. If you want to vary sentence length, you must be aware of the average length of your sentences. The information in the box on the next page will help you make that determination.

As you begin tracking sentence length, following a technique such as the one suggested here will not be necessary for long. Soon you will develop a writer's intuition about sentence length and will begin to make changes subconsciously.

2   Vary sentence length and alternate the length of consecutive sentences.

Regardless of average sentence length, good writers will (1) write sentences in a paragraph that vary from their average and (2) avoid placing two or more very short or very long sentences consecutively (see 19c-4).

The paragraph below was written by a student, Jenafer Trahar. At twenty words, Trahar's average sentence length is slightly less than that of other stylistically strong writers. She is careful both to vary length and to alternate lengths in consecutive sentences.

(1) One major problem with the commercialization of college sports is the exploitation of student-athletes, many of whom come to school on athletic scholarships. (2) Frequently, student-athletes don't deserve to be admitted to a school. (3) Many colleges routinely lower admissions requirements for their ball players, and some schools will even waive requirements for that exceptional athlete, who without his sports abilities might not have had a place on a college campus. (4) Most kids not interested in academics would normally shun a college education. (5) But for gifted athletes, college appears to be a road that leads to the pros. (6) Or so they think. (7) According to Richard Lapchick of the Center for the Study of Sport in Society, twelve thousand high school athletes participate in sports in any one year, but only one will subsequently play for a professional team.

—JENAFER TRAHAR

Analysis of sentence length

(20 word avg.)
1. 24 words (average)
2. 11 words (short)
3. 36 words (long)
4. 12 words (short)
5. 15 words (average)
6. 4 words (short)
7. 36 words (long)
    $138 \div 7 \approx 20$

Trahar's sentence lengths are varied: three short, two long, two average.

■ No short sentences are placed consecutively.
■ No long sentences are placed consecutively.
■ No sentences of average length are placed consecutively.

Notice that Trahar regularly alternates short sentences with long or average-length ones.

Tracking Sentence Length

Any given sentence in a paragraph is long or short in relation to the *average* number of words per sentence in that paragraph. A simple process of counting and dividing will reveal your average sentence length.

1. Number the sentences in a paragraph and write those numbers in a column on a piece of paper.
2. Count and record the number of words in each sentence.
3. Add the word counts to obtain the total number of words in the paragraph.
4. Divide the number of words by the number of sentences in the paragraph. This number is your average sentence length for the paragraph.

Consider a sentence to be *average* in length if it has *five words more or less* than your average. Consider a sentence *long* if it has six or more words more than your average and *short* if it has six or fewer words less than your average.

5. Return to the listing you made in step 2, and designate each sentence as *average* length, *short*, or *long*. (These designations apply to your writing only.)

EXERCISE 1

Choose three paragraphs you have written recently and analyze them for sentence length. Follow the steps laid out in the preceding box. On finishing your analysis, you should have figured your average sentence length for each paragraph and designated each sentence in the paragraph as *short*, *average*, or *long*. Write a brief paragraph in which you summarize your findings.

CRITICAL DECISIONS

Varying Sentence Length and Alternating the Length of Consecutive Sentences

No precise formula exists for determining how many long or short sentences should be used in a paragraph. But you may find these general principles helpful as you make decisions about how to revise:

- Determine the average length of sentences in a paragraph.
- Plan to vary from that average by using short and long sentences.
- Use short sentences to break up strings of longer ones.
- Avoid placing short sentences consecutively unless you are doing so for specific stylistic effect.
- Avoid placing more than two or three long sentences consecutively.
- Avoid placing more than three or four sentences of average length consecutively.

20b   Strategies for varying sentence length

20.2

The techniques discussed here for manipulating sentence length will be helpful *only* if you are working with sentences that are already concise and direct. Sentence length can always be reduced by eliminating wordiness, and revising for conciseness should be your first strategy. See Chapter 17 for advice.

I   Control the use of coordination.

Coordination is the use of coordinating and correlative conjunctions and of conjunctive adverbs to compound sentence elements. Coordination is a means of joining two or more sentences into a single sentence (see 19a). In its favor, coordination reduces the overall length of a paragraph by allowing a writer to combine sentence parts (or entire sentences) and eliminate redundancy.

> Between 12,000 and 10,000 B.C., the massive icecap began to recede. Huge land masses such as Britain and Scandinavia, once ice-covered, began to reappear. At the same time, the enormous quantities of melting ice caused the sea level to rise.

The cost of combining sentences with coordination is that the length of the revised sentence will increase:

Between 12,000 and 10,000 B.C., the massive icecap began to recede, huge land masses such as Britain and Scandinavia began to reappear, and the sea level rose as the enormous quantities of ice melted.

If combining three sentences using coordination as in this example seems too long, you might decide to break the combined sentence in two.

Between 12,000 and 10,000 B.C., the massive icecap began to recede. Huge land masses such as Britain and Scandinavia began to reappear, and the sea level rose as the enormous quantities of ice melted.

COMPUTER TIPS

Limited Use for a Grammar/Style Checker

Avoid relying on grammar checkers to evaluate and correct your usage. However, a grammar/style checker can help you identify with a high degree of accuracy style problems such as sexist language, repeated words, overly long or overly short sentences, clichés, and the use of passive voice. Of course, once you have found the problem, you still have to be the judge of what action to take.

---

2   Control the use of modifying phrases and clauses.

One way of controlling sentence length is through your use of modifying phrases and clauses (see 7d, e). If you determine that a sentence is too long in relation to its neighbors, you can reduce sentence length by converting a modifying clause into a phrase.

When a city is threatened with water shortages, drastic actions become necessary.

In times of drought, drastic actions become necessary. [The dependent clause is shortened to two prepositional phrases.]

Move modifying phrases from one sentence to another.

You may also shorten a sentence by moving a modifier from the sentence to an adjacent sentence (where it may have a new function).

In Los Angeles, *a city that has recently suffered through several severe droughts,* municipal leaders are now ready to look at long-term solutions to the persistent problem of water shortages. Engineers there have already considered desalination plants as one solution.

In Los Angeles municipal leaders are now ready to look at long-term solutions to the persistent problem of water shortages. Engineers *in that city, which has recently suffered through several severe droughts,* have already considered desalination plants as one solution.

Substitute a single-word modifier for a phrase- or clause-length modifier.

To shorten a sentence, you may be able to convert phrases or clauses to single-word adjectives or adverbs. In the following example, an important detail (about towing icebergs) is lost in the conversion and would need to be added to some other sentence. Still, the desired result, a briefer sentence, is achieved.

The melting of ice, *which would be towed south from the Arctic Ocean,* is one solution that would supply millions of gallons of fresh water.

The melting of *arctic* ice is one solution that would supply millions of gallons of fresh water.

> **3** Control the use of phrases and clauses used as nouns.

Sentences can be combined by converting the key words of one sentence into a phrase or clause that then functions as a noun (as a subject, object, or complement) in a second sentence. The disadvantage of the revision is that the newly combined sentence tends to be long.

The English during the Tudor period drank ale with their breakfast in place of water.

It was a widespread custom.

Combined   *To drink ale with one's breakfast,* rather than water, was a widespread custom in Tudor England. [The infinitive phrase functions as the subject.]

To shorten such a sentence, try moving the noun phrase or clause into its own sentence.

Sentence with   *The fact that much of the water was polluted* was one main
a noun clause   reason the Tudor English substituted ale for water.

Revision   Much of the water in Tudor England was polluted. This condition prompted many to substitute ale for water.

ESL NOTE   Noun clauses in English have several uses. Notice the special rules in constructions involving *wish that* (see 47b-6). Indirect quotation or reported speech is a very common special use involving *that* clauses. Section 47b-4 describes the tense sequences encountered in reported speech.

EXERCISE 2

Use any of the strategies discussed thus far in the chapter to combine the following sentences. Vary sentence length and alternate the length of consecutive sentences.

> I have been teaching English literature in a university. I have also been studying literature. I have been doing these things for twenty-five years. Certain questions stick in one's mind in this job; actually, they do in any job. They persist not only because people keep asking them. Such questions stick in one's mind because they are inspired by the very fact of being in a university. First one might ask what is the benefit of studying literature. Then one might ask whether literature helps us think more clearly, or whether it helps us feel more sensitively, or whether literature helps us live a better life than we could if we did not have it.

EXERCISE 3

Follow the instructions in Exercise 2 and revise the three paragraphs that you analyzed for sentence length in Exercise 1. Revise to vary sentence length and to alternate the length of consecutive sentences.

20c Strategies for controlling sentence rhythm

1 Use modifying phrases and clauses to alter sentence rhythm.

Sentences consist of subjects, verbs, and often objects or complements, any of which can be modified. It is primarily through placement of modifiers that sentences change rhythm.

Modifiers concentrated at the *beginning* of a sentence

> *Providing a sense of solidarity for the community,* the National Puerto Rican Forum voiced the concerns of its members and lobbied for new laws.

Modifiers concentrated in the *middle* of a sentence

> The Forum, *the first such organization on the mainland USA,* was established by members of the Puerto Rican community in New York City.

Modifiers concentrated at the *end* of a sentence

> The Forum and similar organizations have lobbied for laws *that outlaw discriminatory practices against Puerto Ricans in such matters as housing and employment.*

Sentence rhythm is also related to length. A brief sentence with relatively few modifiers offers a strong rhythmical contrast to longer, heavily modified sentences.

> The Commonwealth of Puerto Rico was created in 1952.

ACROSS THE CURRICULUM

Controlling Sentence Length and Rhythm

You will find writers in all discipline areas who vary sentence length and rhythm to achieve an effective style. In the following passage, psychologist David Shapiro attempts to define, in part, "rigid thinking." Observe how Shapiro varies sentence length, controls sentence rhythm with phrases and clauses, and uses different sentence types.

> What exactly is meant by rigidity of thinking? Consider as a commonplace example the sort of thinking one encounters in a discussion with a compulsive, rigid person, the kind of person we also call "dogmatic" or "opinionated." Even casual conversation with such a person is often very frustrating, and it is so for a particular reason. It is not simply that one meets with unexpected opposition. On the contrary, such discussion is typically frustrating just because one experiences neither real disagreement nor agreement. Instead, there is no meeting of minds at all, and the impression is simply of not being heard, of not receiving any but perfunctory attention.*

Sentence types: question, command, direct statement
Sentence structures: simple, compound, complex
Sentence length (based on an average length of 18 words): short, long, average, short, average, long
Purposeful repetition:
"a compulsive, rigid person, the kind of person we also call"
"the impression is simply of not being heard, of not receiving"

*The passage is excerpted from David Shapiro, *Neurotic Styles* (New York: Basic, 1965) 24.

Vary the position of phrases.

Phrases that function as adverbs may, like adverbs, be moved around in a sentence. Because such movement can change meaning as well as sentence rhythm, beware of altering the meaning of your sentences when revising for style.

I reached our new home *on Monday*, wondering whether the movers would arrive.

Shifted rhythm	*On Monday*, I reached our new home, wondering whether the movers would arrive.
Shifted meaning	I reached our new home, wondering whether the movers would arrive *on Monday*. [The timing of the movers' arrival has now become the issue.]

A phrase that functions as an adjective should be placed as close as possible to the noun it modifies to avoid confusion and faulty reference.

Faulty Zebulon Pike ventured west to the Rockies, *an explorer of the Mississippi.*

Revised Zebulon Pike, *an explorer of the Mississippi*, ventured west to the Rockies.

Shifted rhythm *An explorer of the Mississippi*, Zebulon Pike ventured west to the Rockies.

Vary the position of clauses.

Like single-word adverbs and phrases functioning as adverbs, adverb clauses can be moved around in a sentence. An adverb clause that begins a sentence can be shifted to the interior or to the end of the sentence. The placement of the clause determines its punctuation.

> *After so many white settlers had come from England*, it was not surprising that the English language and English customs dominated America.

> It was not surprising, *after so many white settlers had come from England*, that the English language and English customs dominated America.

> It was not surprising that the English language and English customs dominated America *after so many white settlers had come from England.*

Place a dependent clause that functions as an adjective next to the word it modifies. Neglecting to do so may confuse readers. (See Chapter 15 on revising to correct misplaced modifiers.)

Faulty The Great Pyramid at Giza has a base area of 13 acres which was built in the fourth dynasty for the pharaoh Khufu.

Revised The Great Pyramid at Giza, which was built in the fourth dynasty for the pharaoh Khufu, has a base area of 13 acres.

Shifted rhythm Built in the fourth dynasty for the pharaoh Khufu, the Great Pyramid at Giza has a base area of 13 acres. [The relative clause has been shortened to a phrase beginning with "built."]

Vary the position of transitions.

Transitions (see 5d-3) can also be moved around in a sentence. When their position changes, sentence rhythm changes. Brief transitions include *for instance, for example, in addition,* and *additionally.* Conjunctive adverbs also serve as transitions: *however, moreover, consequently,* and *therefore.*

> Advertising is an ancient art. *For example*, some early advertisements appear about three thousand B.C. as stenciled inscriptions on bricks.

> Advertising is an ancient art. Some early advertisements, *for example*, appear about three thousand B.C. as stenciled inscriptions on bricks.

2 Revise individual sentences with a disruptive rhythm.

A sentence that starts and stops a reader repeatedly has a disruptive rhythm and should be revised.

Disruptive Francisco Goya's *Los Caprichos*, a series of eighty etchings,
rhythm published in 1799, described by the author as a criticism of "human errors and vices," and now considered as one of his finest works, was a commercial failure.

Because its erratic, bumpy rhythm interferes with understanding, this sentence needs revision. Revision in this case might lead to two sentences:

Revised Francisco Goya's *Los Caprichos*, a series of eighty etchings, was published in 1799. Described by the author as a criticism of "human errors and vices," it is now considered as one of his finest works even though it was a commercial failure.

3 Vary sentence types.

Sentences are classified by structure and function. There are four functional types of sentences (7f-1): the direct statement, the question, the exclamation, and the command. For the most part, academic writing is restricted to statements and questions. The occasional question posed, aside from its contribution to content, will introduce a unique rhythm into a paragraph.

Varying Sentence Rhythm

Vary sentence structures and rhythms to make your writing stylistically strong. You may find the following general principles helpful.

■ Use phrases, clauses, and transitions to vary sentence beginnings.
■ Consciously shift the location of phrase- and clause-length modifiers in a paragraph. Locate modifiers at the beginning of some sentences, in the middle of others, and at the end of others.
■ Use short sentences to break up strings of long sentences.
■ Limit your concentration of phrase- and clause-length modifiers to one and possibly two locations in a sentence. Heavily modifying a sentence at the beginning, middle, *and* end will create a burden stylistically.
■ Vary sentence types.

Vary the structure of sentences.

There are four structural types of sentences: simple, compound, complex, and compound-complex. (See 7f-2.) Writing that is strong stylistically tends to mix all four types. As an illustration of a student's effective use of sentence variety, consider again the paragraph by Jenafer Trahar in 20a-2. Here are the types of sentences she used:

Structural type of sentence	Sentence opens with
complex	noun phrase functioning as the subject
simple	single-word modifier
compound-complex	subject
simple	subject
simple	coordinating conjunction and modifying phrase
simple	coordinating conjunction
compound	modifying phrase

While her sentences are declarative (typical of academic writing), Trahar makes use of all four structural sentence types. What is more, she nicely varies the openings of her sentences. The result is a stylistically sophisticated paragraph.

When revising for style, you may want to consult other chapters in this section on matters of conciseness (17), parallelism (18), and emphasis (19).

20.3

EXERCISE 4

Revise the following paragraph to eliminate the choppiness created by too many short sentences. In your revision, use all the techniques you have learned in this chapter for varying sentence length and rhythm.

> The term "derelicts" in naval usage refers to abandoned ships. Derelicts are rarely seen anymore. They were more frequently sighted in the days of the tall-masted sailing ships. At one time they were considered dangerous. In the days before radar, a passing ship could encounter a derelict with absolutely no warning. For example, in 1906, the *St. Louis* had a near-collision with the derelict *Dunmore*. Some derelicts managed to remain afloat for several months. The *Fanny Wolston* stayed afloat for at least 1408 days. Derelicts are to the sea what ghost towns are to the Old West. They become ghostly entities. They were floating haunted houses. The wreck inspires pity. The derelict evokes awe.

EXERCISE 5

Read the paragraph that follows, and analyze the component sentences for length and rhythm. Structure your analysis like the analysis of Jenafer Trahar's paragraph in 20a-2. Be sure to include a paragraph that summarizes your observations.

> For the past twenty-five years I have been teaching and studying English literature in a university. As in any other job, certain questions stick in one's mind, not because people keep asking them but because they're the questions inspired by the very fact of being in such a place. What good is the study of literature? Does it help us think more clearly, or feel more sensitively, or live a better life than we could without it?
>
> —NORTHROP FRYE

EXERCISE 6

Reexamine the three paragraphs that you revised for sentence length in Exercise 3. Revise these paragraphs a final time for sentence rhythm, using the techniques you have learned in this chapter.

Choosing the Right Word

D ecisions about your purpose as a writer and your intended audience profoundly affect your **diction**—your choice of words. Like the overall tone of a document, diction can be high or low, formal or informal, or any register between (see 3a-4). The English language usually gives you choices in selecting words. A document that shows little concern for word choice will quickly lose its readers.

CRITICAL DECISIONS

Choosing the Right Tone and Register for Your Papers

Choosing an appropriate tone requires that you carefully analyze the writing occasion—the topic, your purpose, and your audience—and that you then make decisions about your document's content, diction, and style.

Formal
- *Likely audience*—specialists or knowledgeable non-specialists.
- *Content*—choose content that goes beyond introductory material.
- *Diction*—use technical language whenever needed for precision.
- *Style*—adhere to all the rules and conventions expected of writing in the subject area. Use complicated sentences if needed for precision.

Popular or informal
- *Likely audience*—nonspecialists interested in the subject area.
- *Content*—similar to that of a formal presentation, but avoid examples or explanations that require specialized understanding. Emphasize content that will keep readers engaged.
- *Diction*—avoid specialized terms whenever possible.
- *Style*—adhere to all conventions of grammar, usage, and spelling. Use some slang or colloquial language, but keep it to a minimum.

21a Understanding denotation and connotation

21.1

Your first concern in selecting a word is to be sure that its **denotation,** or dictionary meaning, is appropriate. A careless writer might, for instance, state that in performing their jobs diplomats should know when to *precede.* Is this the intended meaning (when to go first), or did the writer mean that diplomats should know when to *proceed* (when to go forward)? Although these words look similar and sound nearly the same, their denotations are very different.

Once you are satisfied that you are using a word correctly according to its denotation, consider its **connotations**—its implications, associations, and nuances of meaning. Consider these sentences:

His speech was *brief.*
His speech was *concise.*
His speech was *curt.*
His speech was *abbreviated.*

Brief, concise, curt, and *abbreviated:* these adjectives suggest brevity—but only the word *brief* has this single meaning, with no other associations. The word *brief* suggests nothing about the content of what is said, aside from its duration. *Curt* suggests a brief remark made with a degree of rudeness. *Abbreviated* suggests that the speaker has more to say, but is being purposely brief. And *concise* suggests efforts to make one's statements as brief and accurate as possible. Your choice among words with their different connotations will make a difference in how readers react to your writing.

EXERCISE 1

Given the following set of words, state which word in each set you would prefer someone to use in describing you. Why? Choose one set of words and, in a paragraph, discuss what you understand to be the differences in connotation among the words. Use a dictionary, if necessary.

1. thrifty, economical, provident, frugal
2. reserved, inhibited, restrained, aloof
3. strange, bizarre, eccentric, peculiar, weird
4. lively, alert, enthusiastic, pert, spirited, sprightly
5. sentimental, emotional, maudlin, mushy

21b Revising awkward diction

At times you may find that an instructor has placed the abbreviation *AWK* in the margins of your papers, with a line leading to a phrase or to a particular word. *Awkward diction*, or word choice, calls attention to a word that is not quite right for a sentence. You can minimize awkward writing by guarding against four common errors: inappropriate connotation, inappropriate idiom, straining to sound learned, and unintentional euphony (rhyming, etc.).

1 Choosing words with an appropriate connotation

Frequently, *awkward diction* means that a word's connotation is inappropriate. The sentence in which the word appears is grammatical, and the word in question is the right part of speech. But the word's meaning seems only partially correct.

Awkward　The player *duplicated* his coach's actions. [*Duplicate* connotes an exact rendering of something else, such as a letter. Actions cannot be duplicated so exactly.]

Checking a dictionary entry for *duplicate*, you will find that there are synonyms for this word with nearly the same denotation but with a less awkward and limited connotation.

Revised　The player *copied* his coach's actions.
Revised　The player *imitated* his coach's actions.

2 Following standard English idioms

An **idiom** is a grouping of words, one of which is usually a preposition, whose meaning may not be apparent based solely on simple dictionary definitions. The grammar of idioms—particularly the choice of prepositions used with them—is a matter of customary usage and is often difficult to explain.

Not idiomatic　I ran *into* an old letter.
Idiomatic　I ran *across* an old letter.

Native speakers of English know intuitively that "running *across* an old letter" is a legitimate phrase, while "running *into* an old letter" is not. You can refer to the detailed listings in a dictionary to find some idioms. For others, you must listen carefully to the patterns of common usage. The box on page 388 shows some common idiomatic expressions in English.

3 Writing directly rather than straining to sound learned

In an effort to sound learned, some students will use words that do not exist in English.

Awkward	The character's grief and *upsetion* were extreme. [The word does not exist.]
Awkward	*Disconcern* is common among the employees at that factory. [*Disinterest, indifference,* or *unconcern* could be used.]

At times, students straining at sophistication will choose lengthy, complicated phrasings and pretentious language because they mistakenly believe this is the way learned people express themselves. The following sentence is *not* erudite.

Awkward	The eccentricities of the characters could not fail to endear them to this reader.
Revised	I found the eccentric characters appealing.

Some Common Idioms in American English

We *arrived at* a conclusion.

We *arrived in* time.

We *arrived on* time.

We *brought in* the cake.

We *brought up* the rear of the parade.

Except for my close friends, no one knows of my plan.

Don't call, *except in* emergencies.

I often *get into* jams.

Get up the courage to raise your hand.

I *got in* just under the deadline.

Good friends will *make up* after they argue.

How did you *make out* in your interview?

We'll *take out* the trash later.

Next week, the Red Sox *take on* the Orioles.

The senate will *take up* the issue tomorrow.

A large crowd *turned out*.

At midnight, we will *turn in*.

The request was *turned down*.

---

4   Listening for unintentional euphony

A sentence can be awkward when a writer unintentionally creates rhymes or alliterations (words that begin with the same consonant sound) that distract the reader from a sentence's meaning.

Awkward	Particularly in poetry, euphony is put to literary ends. [The rhymes and alliterations distract from the meaning.]
Simplified	In a poem, euphony is used for literary ends.

The surest way to avoid unintentional rhymes or alliterations is to listen for them as you read your work aloud.

21c Using general and specific language

Successful writers combine the general and the specific. The writer who concentrates on details and will not generalize gives the impression of being unable to see "the big picture." Conversely, the writer who makes nothing but general claims will leave readers restless for specific details that would support these claims. Read the following sets of sentences.

Retailers recognize that the placement of merchandise in a store should reflect customers' habits of mind. Customers aren't likely to notice displays at the very front of a store. Basic items should be placed at the back of the store.

Retailers recognize that the placement of merchandise in a store should reflect customers' habits of mind. According to one researcher, the very front of a store—the first five to fifteen feet—is a kind of decompression zone where shoppers adjust to the lighting and slow their pace. They aren't likely to notice displays of merchandise until they've reached the end of this zone. A retailer's goal is to get customers deep into the store so they will pass as much merchandise as possible. For this reason, retailers know to place basic items—those that people shop for most—at the very rear of the store. This is why, for example, supermarkets often locate their dairy sections along the back wall.

In the first paragraph, the writer makes a claim and supports it with two general examples, neither of which is developed. In the second paragraph, the writer makes the same claim. But this time, details are provided that give readers specific explanations about the placement of merchandise in retail stores. These details establish the writer's authority and provide reasons for accepting the writer's claim. Effective writers combine general claims and specific, supporting details.

EXERCISE 2

Create three lists, the first item of each being a very general word, the next item somewhat less general, the next still less general, and so on. The completed list, top to bottom, will proceed from general to specific.

Example: nation, state, county, city, neighborhood, street, house

EXERCISE 3

Choose a topic that you know well (sports, music, art, etc.) and write a general sentence about it. Then, in support of that sentence, write two additional sentences rich in specific detail.

> *Example:*   Topic—Cooking an omelette
> General sentence:
>> Making omelettes is a delicate operation.
>
> Specific sentences:
>> Use a well-seasoned omelette pan—cast iron, well greased, clean but never thoroughly scrubbed.
>>
>> Scramble the eggs with a splash of water (not milk), blending lightly so as not to toughen the cooked eggs.

21d   Using abstract and concrete language

Abstract words are broad. They name categories or ideas, such as *patriotism, evil,* and *friendship.* **Concrete** expressions (a *throbbing* headache, a *lemon-scented* perfume) provide details that give readers a chance to see, hear, and touch. Just as with general and specific language, seek a balance between the abstract and concrete—as in this example:

> Among all the symbols in biology, perhaps the most widely used and most ancient are the hand mirror of Venus (♀) and the shield and spear of Mars (♂), the biologists' shorthand for male and female. Ideas about the nature of biological inheritance—the role of male and female—are even older than these famous symbols. Very early, men must have noticed that certain characteristics—hair color, for example, a large nose, or a small chin—were passed from parent to offspring. And throughout history, the concept of biological inheritance has been an important factor in the social organizations of men, determining the distribution of wealth, power, land, and royal privileges.
>
> —HELENA CURTIS

Notice that the abstract term *symbol* is given two more concrete examples: the hand mirror of Venus and the shield and spear of Mars. The abstract term *characteristics* is given concrete examples: *hair color, a large nose, a small chin.* And the abstract phrasing *social organizations of men* is given more concrete examples: *power, wealth, land, social privileges.* Of these last examples, though, one can imagine more concrete cases (*what kinds of privileges?*). Even though Curtis does not provide these, she *does* weave the abstract with the concrete.

EXERCISE 4

Take an abstract word such as *honesty, truth, friendship,* or *chaos,* and, in two or three sentences, link that word with a specific person, place, or event. Then provide concrete, descriptive details that help give meaning to the abstraction.

21e Using formal English as an academic standard

Academic writing is expected to conform to standards of **formal English**—that is, the English described in this handbook. There are many standards, or dialects, of English in this country, all of which are rich with expressive possibilities. Academic writing avoids language that by virtue of its private references limits a reader's understanding or limits the audience. Slang, jargon, and regional or ethnic dialect are examples of language specific to particular groups. When you address an audience *beyond* the group, such language restricts what that audience can understand.

1 Revise most slang expressions into standard English.

Slang is the comfortable, in-group language of neighborhood friends, coworkers, teammates, and so forth. If you do not windsurf, and you happen to overhear a conversation between windsurfers in which someone says that she was *dialed in* or *completely powered*, you probably won't know what these words mean. Slang can be descriptive and precise for those who understand. It can just as readily be confusing and annoying to those who do not. In some cases, slang may mislead: the same expression can have different meanings for different groups. For example, *turbo charged* has distinctly different meanings for computer aficionados and for race-car enthusiasts. In the interest of writing accessibly to as many people as possible, avoid slang expressions in academic papers.

2 Replace regionalisms and dialect expressions with standard academic English.

Regionalisms are expressions specific to certain areas of the country. Depending on where you were born, you will use the word *tonic, soda, cola,* or *pop* to describe what you drink with your *sub, hoagie, grinder, po-boy,* or *hero*. Words that have a clear and vivid reference in some areas of the country may lack meaning in others or have an unrelated meaning. For instance, *muss* means "to make messy" in some places and "to fight" in others.

Dialect expressions are specific to certain social or ethnic groups, as well as regional groups. Like regionalisms, dialects can use a specialized vocabulary and sometimes a distinctive grammatical system. Especially with respect to verbs (see Chapter 9), regional and ethnic dialect usage may regularly differ from standard English in omitting auxiliary verb forms. ("I done everything I can" or "It taken him all day" omit the standard auxiliary *have, had,* or *has.* "They be doing all right" replaces the standard *are* with the infinitive or base form *be*.) These are grammatically consistent and correct usages within the dialects they represent, but they address their language to a specific and restricted group rather than to a general audience. Like slang, regionalisms and dialect usages should be avoided in academic writing.

> **3** Reduce colloquial language to maintain clarity and a consistent level of academic discourse.

Colloquial language is informal, conversational language. Colloquialisms do not pose barriers to understanding in the same way that slang, jargon, and regionalisms do. Virtually all long-time speakers of English will understand expressions like *tough break*, *nitty-gritty*, and *it's a cinch*. In formal English, however, colloquialisms are rewritten or "translated" to maintain precision and to keep the overall tone of a document consistent. A few translations follow.

Colloquial	Formal
it's a cinch	it is certain
tough break	unfortunate
got licked	was beaten

> **4** Revise to restrict the use of jargon.

Jargon is the in-group language of professionals, who may use acronyms (abbreviations of lengthy terms) and other linguistic devices to take shortcuts when speaking with colleagues. When writers in an engineering environment refer to RISC architecture, they mean machines designed to allow for **R**educed **I**nstruction **S**et **C**omputing. RISC is an easy-to-use acronym, and it is efficient—as long as one engineer is writing or speaking to another. The moment communication is directed outside the professional group, a writer must take care to adjust the level of language and to define terms. See the Across the Curriculum box in this section for an example.

EXERCISE 5

Think of a group—social, geographic, or professional—to which you belong and which you know well. Write a paragraph on some subject using in-group language: slang, jargon, or regionalisms. When finished, translate your paragraph into formal English, rewriting in-group expressions so that the paragraph can be read and understood by a general audience.

ACROSS THE CURRICULUM

Word Choice and Audience

In discussing a specialized topic, writers in any discipline should understand their audience's comfort with specialized language. An audience of experts will understand technical terms; an audience of nonexperts will not. And so you will find writers across the curriculum carefully controlling their word choice depending on an audience's needs. Observe, below, how paleontologist and evolutionary biologist Stephen Jay Gould shifts his vocabulary from technical to nontechnical.* To readers of the specialized journal *Evolution*, Gould (and co-author David Woodruff) use technical language to report on the shell of the snail *Cerion*:

> *Cerion* possesses an ideal shell for biometrical work. . . . It reaches a definitive adult size with a change in direction of coiling and secretion of a thickened apertural lip; hence, ontogenic and static variation are not confounded. (1026)

To readers of his *Hen's Teeth and Horse's Toes: Further Reflections in Natural History*, written for the general public, Gould avoids technical terms:

> In personal research on the West Indian land snail *Cerion*, my colleague David Woodruff and I find the same two morphologies again and again in all the northern islands of the Bahamas. Ribby, white, or solid-colored, thick and roughly rectangular shells inhabit rocky coasts at the edges of banks where islands drop abruptly into deep seas. Smooth, mottled, thinner, and barrel-shaped shells inhabit calmer and lower coasts at the interior edges of banks, where islands cede to miles of shallow water. (143)

In both cases, Gould's word choice is precise and concise. He chooses the *level* of his language, however, based on the needs of his audience, just as you should. The observation holds for all discipline areas: know your audience; choose your language accordingly.

*The first passage is from Stephen Jay Gould and David Woodruff, "Fifty Years of Interspecific Hybridization: Genetics and Morphometrics of a Controlled Experiment on the Land Snail *Cerion* in the Florida Keys," *Evolution* 41 (1987): 1026. The second passage is from Stephen Jay Gould, *Hen's Teeth and Horse's Toes* (New York: Norton, 1983), 143.

21f   Using figures of speech with care

Similes, analogies, and *metaphors* are **figures of speech,** carefully controlled comparisons that clarify or intensify meaning. Perhaps your spirit *soars* when you read a particular line of poetry. The figurative use of *soar* creates an image of birds in flight, of elevation and clear vision. Literally speaking, birds and planes soar; spirits do not. English allows for the pairing of unlikely, even totally opposite images to help readers feel and see as writers do. In academic writing, figurative language is used across disciplines, though in some disciplines more freely than in others.

1   Use similes, analogies, and metaphors.

A **simile** is a figure of speech in which two different things—one usually familiar, the other not—are explicitly compared. The properties of the thing known help to define what is unknown. Similes make comparison very explicit, often using the word *like* or *as* to set up the comparison.

> The wind whistled in the street and the music ghosted from the piano *as* leaves over a headstone and you could imagine you were in the presence of genius.
>
> —BRUCE CHATWIN, Traveler, writer

> A particle of spin 2 is *like* a double-headed arrow: it looks the same if one turns it round half a revolution (180 degrees).
>
> —STEPHEN HAWKING, Physicist

As with a simile, the purpose of an **analogy** is to make an explicit comparison that explains an unknown in terms of something known. Analogies most often use direct comparison to clarify a process or a difficult concept.

> Just as a trained mechanic can listen to a ping in a car's engine and then diagnose and correct a problem, so too an experienced writer can reread an awkward sentence and know exactly where it goes wrong and what must be done to correct it.

Extended analogies can be developed over a paragraph or several paragraphs. They usually begin and end with certain *cues*, or words that signal a reader that an analogy is about to be offered or concluded. Words that mark a transition to an analogy are *consider*, *by analogy*, and *just as*. The transition from analogy back to a main discussion is achieved with expressions such as *similarly*, *just so*, *so too*, and *in the same way*. (See 6d-1 for use of analogies in building an argument.)

A **metaphor** also illustrates or intensifies something relatively unknown by comparison with something familiar. In the case of metaphor, however, the comparison is implicit. In the expression *hand of time*, for instance, the abstract term *time* is given a physical attribute. *Like* and *as* or other signals of explicit comparison are not used in metaphors.

> In the mirror of his own death, each man would discover his individuality.
>
> —PHILIPPE ARIÈS, Historian

The metaphor suggests that contemplating death allows people to see themselves in revealing ways.

Metaphors are not restricted to poetry or academic writing; they are used everywhere in our daily speech when an abstract or unknown idea, thing, or activity is spoken of in terms associated with something else. For instance, when we say "round up everybody," we implicitly compare the activity to a cattle roundup. Such metaphorical comparisons, if not well matched to the situation, can create more confusion for the reader than clarity.

2   **Revise mixed metaphors.**

Keep your language focused on a single metaphorical image throughout a sentence. Otherwise, you risk a **mixed metaphor,** which will stop your readers for a hearty laugh—at your expense. You would not, for instance, want to be the author of this.

Mixed metaphor	This story weaves a web that herds characters and readers into the same camp. [The comparison mixes spiderwebs with cattle roundups.]
Consistent	This story weaves a web that tangles characters and readers alike.

3   **Replace worn-out metaphors (clichés) with fresh figures.**

In a famous essay, "Politics and the English Language," writer George Orwell warns against the *worn-out metaphor.*

A newly invented metaphor assists thought by evoking a visual image, while on the other hand a metaphor which is technically "dead" (e.g., *iron resolution*) has in effect reverted to being an ordinary word and can generally be used without loss of vividness. But in between these two classes there is a huge dump of worn-out metaphors which have lost all evocative power and are merely used because they save people the trouble of inventing phrases for themselves.

Weblink

http://www.mtholyoke.edu/acad/
intrel/orwell46.htm

*The complete text of Orwell's famous essay—
a must-read for everyone who aspires to clear
and concise writing.*

Orwell proceeds to offer his list of worn-out metaphors, also called **clichés.** These include *play into the hands of, no axe to grind, swan song,* and *hotbed.* These trite expressions, current when Orwell's essay was written in 1945, are with us still. Modern-day expressions that can be added to this list of clichés include *the game of life, counting chickens before they hatch, water over the dam* or *under the bridge,* and *burning bridges.* Work to create your own metaphors. Keep them vivid, and keep them consistent.

Using Figures of Speech with Care   **395**

EXERCISE 6

In a few sentences, use figurative language to describe the approach of a thunderstorm, the effect of a sunny morning on your mood, or the feeling of just having finished the last exam of a long and difficult semester.

21g Eliminating biased, dehumanizing language

Language is a tool. Just as tools can be used for building, they can also be used to dismantle. You have heard and seen the words that insensitive people use to denigrate whole groups. Equally repugnant is language used to stereotype. Any language that explicitly or subtly characterizes an individual in terms of a group is potentially offensive. Writers must also take care to show consideration for audiences by referring to any group using the terms that group uses to describe itself. Equally important is considering the sensibilities of readers who may differ from the writer in terms of gender, age, disability or illness, sexual orientation, and religion.

Sexism in diction

When referring to people, English has no gender-neutral pronoun in the third-person singular. Until recently, the designated "neutral" pronoun was usually masculine (A doctor should respect *his* patients), but changing times have made this usage both inaccurate and offensive. Gender-offensive language can also be found in such expressions as chair*man*, *man*kind, *man*power, *mother*ing, etc. Reread late drafts of your writing to identify potentially gender-offensive language. Unless the context of a paragraph clearly calls for a gender-specific reference, follow the suggestions given in the box on the facing page to avoid offending your readers. Also see 10c for avoiding gender-offensive pronoun use.

1	**Rewrite gender-stereotyping nouns as neutral nouns.**

Sexist A cover letter and résumé should be sent to the department *chairman*.

Neutral A cover letter and résumé should be sent to the department *chair*.

Sexist *Man's* need to compete may be instinctive.

Neutral *The human* need to compete may be instinctive.

Some Potentially Offensive Gender-Specific Nouns

Avoid: stewardess (and generally nouns ending with -*ess*)
Use: flight attendant

Avoid: chairman
Use: chair or chairperson

Avoid: woman driver; male nurse
Use: woman who was driving; driver; nurse; man on the nursing station

Avoid: mankind
Use: people; humanity; humankind

Avoid: workmen; manpower
Use: workers; work force; personnel

Avoid: the girl in the office
Use: the woman; the manager; the typist

Avoid: mothering
Use: parenting, nurturing

---

2   Balance references to the sexes.

Sexist   The *men* and *girls* in the office contributed generously to the Christmas Fund.

Neutral   The *men* and *women* in the office contributed generously to the Christmas Fund.

www

21.2

3   Make balanced use of plural and gender-specific pronouns.

See 10c for strategies that will help you to correct gender problems with pronoun use.

Sexist   A doctor should respect *his* patients.

Neutral   *Doctors* should respect *their* patients. [The plural strategy is used; see 10c.]

EXERCISE 7

Identify gender-offensive language in the following paragraph. Rewrite sentences in whatever way you feel is needed to make the gender references neutral.

> The elementary school teacher, especially at the early grades, has her hands full with helping children adjust to a formal learning environment. Not all of the girls and young men in her class will understand that school is not, primarily, a place for play. Learning, of course, should be fun; but the elementary school teacher must be sure that her students appreciate the distinctions between playground play and intellectual play. By the later grades, a teacher will want his students to understand that serious intellectual play is the business of school. Women and boys in high school must appreciate that ideas should be celebrated with, not hidden from, classmates.

21h Avoiding euphemistic and pretentious language

Sometimes writers betray an anxious, condescending, or self-inflated attitude through their word choices. These attitudes may arise from a variety of motives, but the result is almost always a loss of clear expression.

1 Restrict the use of euphemisms.

The **euphemism** is a polite rewording of a term that the writer feels will offend readers. Instead of *dead* or *died*, you will find *passed on*, *passed away*, *mortally wounded*. You may also find these clichés: *kicked the bucket*, *bit the dust*, and so on. If you are concerned about using expressions that might offend readers, create a context within a sentence or paragraph that may soften a potentially harsh word choice.

Euphemism   No one wanted to tell the child that his dog had gone to the Great Beyond.

Revised   Breaking the news to the child that his dog had died was very painful.

In nonacademic writing, use discretion in selecting a euphemism. Debate with yourself your use of language and then make your choice.

2 Eliminate pretentious language.

Pretentious language is unnecessarily ornate and puffed-up with its own importance. It suggests a writer's concern more with image than with clear communication. See 17a-2, 4, and 6 on eliminating wordiness. Pretentious writers will often choose the windy version of everyday expressions that seem too common.

Pretentious	Direct
It appears to me that	I believe
In the final analysis	In conclusion
The individual who	The person who
utilize	use
demonstrate	show
functionality	function

In specialized areas of study, you will find that writers need technical terms to communicate precisely. Writing that requires specialized terms is very different from pretentious writing that is calculated to bolster a writer's ego. In your own work, you can distinguish between a legitimate technical term and a pretentious one by being both concise and precise.

Adhering to these two principles—the one helping you to cut wordiness and the other helping you to maintain precision—should make you aware of pretentious language, which can *always* be cut from a sentence.

Pretentious language	Cross-cultural treatises give every indication that all cultures establish relatively distinct gender differentiation.
Direct language	Studies from around the world show that all cultures establish clear roles for men and women.
Specialized language (no revision needed)	Index futures differ from other futures contracts in that they are not based on any underlying commodity or financial instrument that can be delivered; therefore, there is no cash market associated with them.

This passage on "index futures" comes from a book on investing. Students of finance would understand, or would be expected to understand, the terms *index futures*, *futures contracts*, *commodity*, *financial instrument*, and *cash market*. None of the words in this legitimately technical passage is calculated to bolster the writer's ego, as was the case in the preceding example.

Distinguishing Pretentious Language from Legitimate Technical Language

Bear in mind two principles when attempting to eliminate pretentious language:

- **Be concise:** Use as few words as possible to communicate clearly. Delete whole sentences or reduce them to phrases that you incorporate into other sentences. Reduce phrases to single words. Choose briefer words over longer ones. (See 17a for a full discussion of conciseness.)
- **Be precise:** Make sure your sentences communicate your *exact* meaning. If you need to add clarifying words, add as few words as possible. Use technical language for precision only when no other language will do.

EXERCISE 8

In the sentences that follow, identify and revise what you feel are examples of pretentious writing. Find other samples of writing, perhaps from a current newspaper, and conduct a similar analysis.

In the final analysis, the one unending truth that we must as a nation uphold is mutual respect. Mutual respect, a tolerance for difference, is premised on the notion that we ought to expect from others the same considerations that we believe we ourselves are due. Setting aside, for the moment, high-minded rationales for respecting one another—the Judeo-Christian tradition, for instance, that we ought to love one another—we can observe that for very practical reasons mutual respect serves our own ends.

Dictionaries and Vocabulary

A living language is continually evolving, shifting, and changing. It is flexible and yet precise. English is just such a language. In part because contemporary English has drawn from so many other languages, it often offers a number of options in selecting words. Using dictionaries to help expand your vocabulary can allow you to make better decisions about choosing the words that will most precisely and effectively convey your meaning.

Weblink

http://www.yourdictionary.com
A useful vocabulary site with links to a number of general and specialized dictionaries.

USING DICTIONARIES

22a Understanding dictionary entries

Dictionaries give us far more than a list of words and their meanings. They not only define a given word, but also provide a brief description of its etymology, spelling, division, and pronunciation, as well as related words and forms. Here is a typical set of entries:

Word division — Grammatical functions — Pronunciation

Spelling — **proj·ect** (*for n.* prä′jekt′, präj′ikt; *Cdn* prō′jekt′, prä′jekt′; *for v.* prōjekt′, pr -) *n.* [ME *projecte* < L *projectum*, neut. of *projectus*, pp. of *projicere* < *pro-*, before, forward + *jacere*, to throw: see PRO-² & JET¹] **1** a proposal of something to be done; plan; scheme ☆**2** an organized undertaking; specif., *a)* a special unit of work, research, etc., as in a school, a laboratory, etc. *b)* an extensive public undertaking, as in conservation, construction, etc. ☆**3** a complex of inexpensive apartments or houses, esp. one that is publicly owned or financed in full: — Etymology, Meanings

Idiom — **housing project** — *vt.* **pro·ject′** **1** to propose (an act or plan of action) **2** to throw or hurl forward **3** *a)* to cause (one's voice) to be heard clearly and at a distance *b)* to get (ideas, feelings, etc.) across to others effectively **4** to send forth in one's thoughts or imagination [*to project* oneself into the future] **5** to cause to jut out **6** to cause (a shadow, image, etc.) to fall or appear upon a surface **7** EXTRAPOLATE **8** *Geom.* to transform the points of (a geometric figure) into the points of another figure, usually by means of lines of correspondence **9** *Psychol.* to externalize (a thought or feeling) so that it appears to have objective reality — *vi.* **1** to jut out; protrude **2** to be effective in the projection of one's voice, ideas, etc. —*SYN.* PLAN — Grammatical functions, Example, Field label

Synonym

CRITICAL DECISIONS

Expanding Your Vocabulary

As you read or while you are in class, jot down unfamiliar words. Collect them as follows.

■ Make a set of flash cards with a new word and the sentence in which it appears on one side of each card. Place the definition on the other side.

■ Review the cards regularly. Categorize them by discipline or by part of speech. Practice changing the vocabulary word's part of speech with suffixes.

■ Expand entries in your file when you find a previously filed word used in a new context.

■ Consciously work one or two new words into each paper that you write, especially when the new words allow you to be precise in ways you could not otherwise be.

1 Understanding standard entry information in dictionaries

Most dictionary entries include more information on words than many people expect. In a typical entry you can find:

22.1

■ *Spelling* (including variations)
■ *Word division* indicating syllabication and where a word should be divided
■ *Pronunciation* (including variations)
■ *Grammatical functions* (parts of speech)
■ *Grammatical forms* (plurals, principal parts of irregular verbs)
■ *Etymology* (a given word's history/derivation)
■ *Meanings* (arranged according to either frequency of use or earliest to most recent use)
■ *Examples* of the word in context
■ *Related words*, *synonyms* and *antonyms*
■ *Usage labels* (see 22a-2)
■ *Field labels* (for words that have discipline-specific meanings)
■ *Idioms* that include the word

2 Usage labels

Usage refers to how, where, and when a word has been used in speech and writing. When preparing papers in an academic or business setting, use formal English as a standard (see 21e), rather than words labeled as nonstandard. When you see the label *slang* assigned to the entry *prof*, for instance, you would probably decide not to use it in formal writing. There are other categories of restricted usage, and these are generally listed and explained in the front matter of most dictionaries: *colloquial*, *slang*, *obsolete*, *archaic*, and *dialect*.

COMPUTER TIPS

Thesauri

Electronic thesauri—both the kind that comes with your word processor and the ones available on the World Wide Web—are subject to the same limitations as printed thesauri. Use them as references only. Never replace a word you've written with a word suggested by a thesaurus unless you're absolutely sure of both its denotations and its connotations.

EXERCISE I

Consult your dictionary to answer the following questions about grammatical function.

1. Which of the following nouns can be used as verbs: *process, counsel, dialogue, hamper, instance?*
2. How do you make these nouns plural: *annals, humanity, armor, accountancy, deer, analysis, medium, sister-in-law, knife?*
3. What are the principal parts of these verbs: *hang, begin, break, forbid, rise, set?*
4. What are the comparative and superlative forms of these adverbs and adjectives: *unique, bad, mere, initial, playful?*

EXERCISE 2

Using two different dictionaries, list and comment on the usage restrictions that are recorded for the following words:

1. get-up
2. whither
3. hipster
4. maverick
5. hit
6. max

22b Choosing a dictionary

I Comparing abridged dictionaries

The most convenient and commonly used dictionaries in households, businesses, and schools are called "abridged"—or shortened.

("Unabridged" dictionaries are described in 22b-2.) An abridged dictionary tries to give as much information as possible in one portable volume. The following list includes only some of the more widely used abridged dictionaries.[1]

The American Heritage Dictionary, 4th ed. (Houghton Mifflin, 2000) includes about 200,000 entries. It presents the most contemporary meaning of a word first, rather than proceeding historically. Guidance to good usage is provided by extensive usage-context indicators and "Usage Notes" which reflect the opinions of a panel of usage experts. The dictionary contains many photographs, illustrations, and maps.

The Concise Oxford Dictionary of Current English, 9th ed. (Oxford University Press, 1995) is the briefest of the abridged dictionaries listed here. It is based on the work for the unabridged *Oxford English Dictionary* (see 22b-2) and includes current usage and illustrative quotations, scientific and technical terms, many colloquial and slang expressions, and both British and American spellings.

Merriam Webster's Collegiate Dictionary, 10th ed. (G. & C. Merriam, 1998) is based on *Webster's Third New International Dictionary of the English Language* (see 22b-2) and includes some 215,000 entries emphasizing "standard language." Labels indicating usage occur less frequently than in other desk dictionaries. Entries give full etymologies followed by definitions in chronological order, with the most recent meaning listed last. It includes extensive notes on synonyms and illustrative quotations.

EXERCISE 3

Look up the following words in one of the abridged dictionaries listed above. How many different meanings does each word have? From observing older meanings versus the more current meanings, how would you describe the overall shifts in meaning that some words have undergone over time?

1. double   3. conductor   5. cross
2. foul   4. weird   6. funky

---

[1]The descriptions of abridged, unabridged, and discipline-specific dictionaries that follow are adapted from entries in Eugene Sheehy, *Guide to Reference Books*, 10th ed. (Chicago: American Library Association, 1986); Diane Wheeler Strauss, *Handbook of Business Information: A Guide for Librarians, Students, and Researchers* (Englewood, CO: Libraries Unlimited, Inc., 1988); and Bohdan Wynar, *ARBA Guide to Subject Encyclopedias and Dictionaries* (Littleton, CO: Libraries Unlimited, 1986)

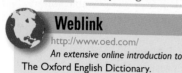

Weblink

http://www.oed.com/

An extensive online introduction to The Oxford English Dictionary.

The compilers of unabridged dictionaries attempt to be exhaustive both in recounting the history of a word and in describing its various usages. For quick reference—to check spelling or commonplace usage—an abridged dictionary will serve you well. But when you are curious about a word and its history (for instance, if you want to know the precise usage of a word in Shakespeare's day), you will want to consult an unabridged dictionary.

The second edition of *The Oxford English Dictionary* (Clarendon Press, 1989) includes the text of the first edition, the *Supplement* (1972–1986), and almost 5,000 new entries for a total of more than 500,000 words. It is the great dictionary of the English language, with meanings arranged chronologically to show the history of every word from the date of its entry into the language to its most recent usage, supported by almost two million quotations from the works of more than 5,000 authors since 1150. The *O.E.D.* is an invaluable source for scholars.

The Random House Webster's Unabridged Dictionary (Random House, 1997) is considerably briefer than the other unabridged dictionaries listed here, though it is particularly current and includes extensive usage notes.

Webster's Third New International Dictionary of the English Language (G. & C. Merriam, 1993) includes about 450,000 entries, with special attention to new scientific and technical terms. The third edition of 1986 emphasizes the language as currently used (though entries are arranged with the earliest uses first), with a descriptive approach to usage, construction, and punctuation.

EXERCISE 4

Choose two of the words you looked up in Exercise 3 and compare what you found with the entry for the same word in an unabridged dictionary, preferably *The Oxford English Dictionary*. Briefly characterize the history of each word, explaining how its meaning has shifted over time.

22c   Using specialized dictionaries of English

Specialized dictionaries focus on a specific kind of word or language information, such as slang, etymologies, synonyms, antonyms, and accepted usage. The following are some particularly useful specialized dictionaries.

1 Dictionaries of usage

When your questions regarding the usage of a word are not adequately addressed in a standard dictionary, consult one of the following:

A Dictionary of Contemporary American Usage, ed. Bergen Evans and Cornelia Evans

Dictionary of Modern English Usage, ed. H. W. Fowler

Dictionary of American-English Usage, ed. Margaret Nicholson

Modern American Usage, ed. Jacques Barzun

2 Dictionaries of synonyms

Dictionaries that present synonyms of words can be a great help for writers wanting to expand vocabulary. A caution, though: while synonyms have approximately the same denotation, their connotations differ. Before using a synonym, be sure that you thoroughly understand its connotation (see also 22e-3).

Webster's Dictionary of Synonyms

The New Roget's Thesaurus of the English Language in Dictionary Form

3 Other specialized dictionaries

Dictionaries of origins/etymologies

The information on word origins in basic dictionaries can be pursued in more detail in the following specialized references.

Dictionary of Word and Phrase Origins, ed. William Morris and Mary Morris

The Oxford Dictionary of English Etymology, ed. C. T. Onions

Origins: A Short Etymological Dictionary of Modern English, ed. Eric Partridge

Dictionaries of slang and idioms

Many terms omitted or given only brief notice in basic dictionaries are described in great detail in slang dictionaries.

The New Dictionary of American Slang, ed. Robert Chapman

Dictionary of Slang and Unconventional English, ed. Eric Partridge

Dictionary of American Slang, ed. Harold Wentworth and Stuart Berg Flexner

Using Specialized Dictionaries of English

EXERCISE 5

Look up the following words in a dictionary of usage and a dictionary of origins. Based on information you find out about the meanings, origins, and uses of each word from these specialized sources, characterize the kind of writing or the kind of audience for which each term seems most appropriate.

1. awesome 3. celebrate 5. ere
2. mews 4. groovy 6. flunk

BUILDING VOCABULARY

22d Learning root words, prefixes, and suffixes

Once a word enters the language, its core or *root* is often used as the basis of other words that are formed with *prefixes* and *suffixes*—letters coming before, or after, the root. When you can recognize root words, prefixes, and suffixes, often you will be able to understand the meaning of a new word without checking a dictionary.

I Becoming familiar with root words

A root anchors a plant in the ground and provides a base from which it can grow. The **root** of a word anchors it in language, providing a base from which meaning is built. When you encounter an unfamiliar word, try identifying its root. With help from the context of the surrounding sentence, you can often infer an appropriate definition. Consider the following sentence:

Beautiful and *beauteous* are paronymous words.

You have come upon an unfamiliar word, *paronymous*. You might say: "This reminds me of another word—*anonymous*." Immediately, you sense that the similar sounding words share a root: *nymous*. You know that *anonymous* means "having an unknown name." It is not so tremendous a leap to conclude that the root *nymous* means *name*. Now you examine the sentence once more and make an educated guess, or inference. What do the words *beautiful* and *beauteous* have to do with *names*? The words themselves tell you—that they are built on a single name: *beauty*. If you guessed that *paronymous* means "derived from the same word (or root)," you would be correct.

Whether you know a root word or make an educated guess about its meaning, your analysis will aid reading comprehension and, in the process, will improve your vocabulary. Many of the root words in English come from Latin and Greek.

22.2

Common Root Words

Root	Definition	Example
basis [Greek]	step, base	base, basis, basement, basic
bio- [Greek]	life	biography, biology, bionic
cognoscere [Latin]	to know	recognize, cognizant, cognition
ego [Latin]	I	ego, egocentric, egotistical
grandis [Latin]	large	grandiose, aggrandize
graphein [Greek]	to write	graph, graphic
hydro [Greek]	water	hydraulic, dehydrate
hypnos [Greek]	sleep	hypnosis, hypnotic
jur, jus [Latin]	law	jury, justice
lumen [Latin]	light	illuminate, luminary
manu- [Latin]	hand	manage, management, manual
mare [Latin]	sea	marine, marinate, marina
matr- [Latin]	mother	maternal, matrilineal
pathos [Greek]	suffering	empathy, sympathy
patr- [Latin]	father	paternal, patriarch
polis [Greek]	city	metropolis, police
primus [Latin]	first	primitive, prime, primary
psych [Greek]	soul	psychological, psyche
scrib, script [Latin]	to write	describe, manuscript
sentire [Latin]	to feel	sentiment, sentimental, sentient
sol [Latin]	sun	solstice, solar, solarium
solvere [Latin]	to release	solve, resolve, solution, dissolve
tele [Greek]	distant	telegraph, telemetry
therm [Greek]	heat	thermal, thermos
veritas [Latin]	truth	verity, verify, veritable
vocare [Latin]	to call	vocal, vocation, avocation

2 Recognizing prefixes

A **prefix**—letters joined to the beginning of a root word to qualify or add to its meaning—illustrates its own definition: the root *fix* comes from the Latin *fixus*, meaning "to fasten"; *pre* is a prefix, also from Latin, meaning "before." The prefix joined to a root creates a new word, the meaning of which is "to place before." The prefix and the root, considered together, will allow you to infer a meaning. Prefixes can indicate number, size, status, negation, and relations in time and space.

Prefixes indicating number

Prefix	Meaning	Example
uni-	one	unison, unicellular
bi-	two	bimonthly, bicentennial, bifocal
tri-	three	triangle, triumvirate
multi-	many, multiple	multiply, multifaceted
omni-	all, universally	omnivorous, omniscient
poly-	many, several	polytechnic, polygon

Prefixes indicating size

Prefix	Meaning	Example
micro-	very small	microscopic, microcosm
macro-	very large	macroeconomics
mega-	great	megalomania, megalith

Prefixes indicating status or condition

Prefix	Meaning	Example
hyper-	beyond, super	hyperactive, hypercritical
neo-	new	neonate, neophyte
para-	akin to	parachute, paramilitary
pseudo-	false	pseudoscience, pseudonym

Prefixes indicating negation

Prefix	Meaning	Example
anti-	against	antibiotic, antidote, anticlimax
counter-	contrary	counterintuitive, counterfeit
dis-	to do the opposite	disable, dislodge, disagree
mal-	bad, abnormal	maladjusted, malformed, malcontent
mis-	bad, wrong	misinform, mislead, misnomer
non-	not, reverse of	noncompliance, nonalcoholic

Prefixes indicating spatial relations

Prefix	Meaning	Example
circum-	around	circumspect, circumscribe
inter-	between	intercede, intercept
intra-	within	intravenous, intramural
intro-	inside	introvert, intrude

Prefixes indicating relations of time

Prefix	Meaning	Example
ante-	before	antecedent, anterior
paleo-	ancient	Paleolithic, paleography
post-	after	postdate, postwar, posterior
proto-	first	protohuman, prototype

3 Analyzing suffixes

A **suffix**—letters joined to the end of a word or a root—will change a word's grammatical function. Observe how with suffixes a writer can give a verb the forms of a noun, adjective, and adverb.

Verb	impress
Noun	impression
Adjective	impressive
Adverb	impressively

The following are some frequently used suffixes.

Noun-forming suffixes

Verb	+	Suffix	(Meaning)	=	Noun
betray		-al	(process of)		betrayal
participate		-ant	(one who)		participant
play		-er	(one who)		player
construct		-ion	(process of)		construction
conduct		-or	(one who)		conductor

Noun	+	Suffix	(Meaning)	=	Noun
king		-dom	(office, realm)		kingdom
sister		-hood	(state, condition of)		sisterhood
strategy		-ist	(one who)		strategist
Ohio		-an	(belonging to)		Ohioan
master		-y	(quality)		mastery

Adjective	+	Suffix	(Meaning)	=	Noun
pure		-ity	(state, quality of)		purity
gentle		-ness	(quality of, degree)		gentleness
active		-ism	(act, practice of)		activism

ww/d

Verb-forming suffixes

Noun	+	Suffix	(Meaning)	=	Verb
substance		-ate	(cause to become)		substantiate
code		-ify	(cause to become)		codify
serial		-ize	(cause to become)		serialize
Adjective	+	Suffix	(Meaning)	=	Verb
sharp		-en	(cause to become)		sharpen

Adjective-forming suffixes

Noun	+	Suffix	(Meaning)	=	Adjective
region		-al	(of, relating to)		regional
substance		-ial	(of, relating to)		substantial
response		-ible	(capable of, fit for)		responsible
history		-ic	(form of, being)		historic
Kurd		-ish	(of, relating to)		Kurdish
response		-ive	(tends toward)		responsive
Verb	+	Suffix	(Meaning)	=	Adjective
credit		-able	(capable of)		creditable
abort		-ive	(tends toward)		abortive

EXERCISE 6

Identify and initially define, without using a dictionary, the roots, pre-fixes, and suffixes of the following sets of words. Then check your definitions against dictionary entries.

1. photometry
   photogenic
   photograph
   photoelectric

2. excise
   concise
   precise
   incisive

3. conduce
   reduce
   deduce
   produce

4. optometrist
   optician
   ophthalmologist
   optical

5. discourse
   recourse

6. diverge
   converge

7. convert
   pervert
   revert

8. tenable
   tenacious
   retain

9. memoir
   remember

10. remorse
    morsel

I   Use contextual clues and dictionaries.

In college, you will spend a great deal of your time reading, and reading provides the best opportunities for expanding your vocabulary. When a new word resists your analysis of root and prefix or suffix, first let the context of a sentence provide clues to meaning. Contextual clues will often let you read a passage and infer fairly accurate definitions of new words—accurate enough to give you the sense of a passage. Indeed, using a dictionary to look up *every* new word in the name of thoroughness can so fragment a reading that you will frustrate—not aid—your attempts to understand. Focus first on the ideas of an entire passage. Circle or otherwise highlight new words, especially repeated words. Then, if the context has not revealed the meaning, reach for your dictionary.

In the passage that follows, possibly unfamiliar vocabulary is set in italics. Do not stop at these words. Note them, but then complete your reading of these paragraphs from an astronomy text by George O. Abell:

> Let us once again compare the *propagation* of light to the propagation of ocean waves. While an ocean wave travels forward, the water itself is *displaced* only in a *vertical* direction. A stick of wood floating in the water merely bobs up and down as the waves move along the surface of the water. Waves that propagate with this kind of motion are called *transverse* waves.

> Light also *propagates* with a transverse wave motion, and travels with its highest possible speed through a *perfect vacuum*. In this respect light differs markedly from sound, which is a physical vibration of matter. Sound does not travel at all through a vacuum. The *displacements* of the matter that carry a sound *impulse* are in a *longitudinal* direction, that is, in the direction of the propagation, rather than at right angles to it.

EXERCISE 7

Based on context alone, make an educated guess about the italicized words in the paragraphs on light and sound waves. Write down the definition you would give each word. Then look up each word in an unabridged dictionary. How do your definitions compare?

2   Collect words—and use them.

If a word is mentioned more than twice, you should know its formal definition since its repeated use indicates that the word is important. Look the word up if you are not sure of its meaning. When attempting to *increase* your vocabulary, proceed slowly when putting newly discovered words to use in your own writing and speech. As an aid to vocabulary building, you may want to create a file of new words, as described in the box on page 401.

3 Use the thesaurus with care.

A thesaurus (literally from the Greek word meaning "treasure") is a reference tool that lists the synonyms of words and, frequently, their antonyms. Because the thesaurus is found in many computerized word processing programs, its use has become dangerously easy. If you find yourself turning to a thesaurus merely to dress up your writing with significant-sounding language, spare yourself the trouble. Unfortunately, sentences like the one that follows are too often written in a transparent effort to impress—and the effect can be unintentionally comical.

Pretentious The *penultimate* chapter of this novel left me *rhapsodic.*

This sentence shares many of the problems associated with pretentious diction (see 21h-2). It also suggests how the *diction* (the level) of the two italicized words chosen from the thesaurus is likely to contrast sharply with the diction that characterizes the rest of a paper. Often, the sense of the word (its denotation or connotation) may be slightly off the mark—not precisely what the meaning of the sentence requires (see 21a). In either case, a sentence with such "treasures" usually stands out as awkward (see 21b). A more restrained choice of words would produce a better sentence.

Revised I was overwhelmed by the next to last chapter of this novel.

By no means should you ignore the thesaurus; it is, in fact, a treasury of language. But when you find a word, make sure you are comfortable with it—that it is *your* word—before appropriating it for use in a paper.

4 Build discipline-appropriate vocabularies.

Each discipline has a vocabulary that insiders, or professionals, use when addressing one another. One of your jobs as you move from class to class will be to recognize important words and add them to discipline-specific vocabularies that you will develop. The longer you study in a discipline, and especially if you should major in it, the larger and more versatile your specific vocabulary will be. Discipline-specific vocabularies consist of two types of words: those that are unique to the discipline and those that are found elsewhere, though with different meanings. For example, the word *gravity* occurs in contexts outside of the physics classroom. In a newspaper article or essay you might find *gravity* used to suggest great seriousness: *The gravity of the accusations caused Mr. Jones to hire a famous attorney.* Present-day physicists use the word *gravity* in an altogether different sense.

EXERCISE 8

Take an informal survey to see if you can identify five words or phrases unique to a particular group of people. Listen to fraternity or sorority members on campus addressing members of their own houses; listen closely in a locker room to members of a team with which you have practiced; or sit in on a campus club meeting or a session of the student government. List the five words or phrases; then define each expression and illustrate its community-specific use in a sentence.

EXERCISE 9

Review your notes and text for one course and identify five words or phrases particular to that subject. The words or phrases might well occur in contexts beyond the course but should have a course-specific meaning. List the words or phrases; then define each expression and illustrate its discipline-specific use in a sentence.

Spelling

You can improve your spelling by learning a few rules and the exceptions to those rules. Spelling "demons" can be overcome by recognizing the words you most commonly misspell and remembering devices for memorizing their correct spelling.

CRITICAL DECISIONS

Using a Dictionary to Check Correct Spellings

Marilyn vos Savant, the *Parade* magazine columnist who is said to have the world's highest IQ, once responded to a reader's question about spelling and intelligence. People who make the fewest spelling errors, she said, are generally those who know that when they are not sure of the correct spelling of a word, they should consult a dictionary. She went on to address the question "But if I don't know how to spell a word, how can I look it up?" Her answer was that if you know a word well enough to use it in a sentence, you know enough about how it is spelled to find it in a dictionary. It's a good idea to recognize when you're not sure of how to spell a word.

23a Overcoming spelling/pronunciation misconnections

Long-time speakers and readers of English have learned basic connections between sounds and letter combinations that help them spell a large number of words. However, for historical reasons certain combinations of letters are not always pronounced in the same way (for example: th*ough*t, b*ough*, thr*ough*, r*ough*, etc.). In addition, regional and dialect variations in pronunciation may drop or vary the pronunciation of certain

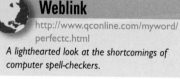

Weblink

http://www.qconline.com/myword/perfectc.html

A lighthearted look at the shortcomings of computer spell-checkers.

endings of auxiliary verbs. It is safer to try to keep a visual image of a word in your mind, rather than to rely on what you hear to help you to spell a word correctly.

| 1 | Recognizing homonyms and commonly confused words |

Weblink
http://www.earlham.edu/~peters/
writing/homofone.htm
*An English homophone (or homonym)
dictionary.*

One of the most common causes of spelling confusion is **homonyms**—words that sound alike, or almost alike, but that have different spellings and meanings—for example, *affect* and *effect*, *discrete* and *discreet*, and *lessen* and **23.1**
lesson. For a list of the most commonly confused homonyms and near homonyms, see the *Handbook*'s Web site.

EXERCISE 1

From each pair or trio of words in parentheses, circle the correct homonym. Then make up sentences using each of the other words correctly.

1. Funeral etiquette in some cultures dictates that you should pay (your/you're) respects to the deceased by making (sure/shore) to spend a few quiet moments at the (beer/bier).
2. (There/they're/their) child (threw/through) a rock at (hour/our) child.
3. With the release of the (imminent/eminent) physicist's groundbreaking discovery, the presentation of the Nobel prize seemed (immanent/imminent).
4. If (your/you're) harboring any (illusion/allusion) about becoming a concert pianist someday, (your/you're) bound to be disappointed.
5. The technical staff is devising a method by which the (devise/device) can be installed by even nontechnical personnel.

| 2 | Recognizing words with more than one form |

A subgroup of homonyms that many people find particularly troublesome consists of words that sometimes appear as one word and other times appear as two words.

We *always* work hard, in *all ways*.

By the time everyone was *all ready* to go, it was *already* too late.

It *may be* a question of etiquette, but *maybe* it's not.

Everyday attitudes are not always appropriate *every day*.

Overcoming Spelling/Pronunciation Misconnections **415**

Once we were *all together,* we were *altogether* happy to have met.

Unlike *always/all ways* and *already/all ready, all right* and *a lot* do not vary. They can be written only as two words.

Faulty   It's *alright* with me if Sally comes along.
Revised It's *all right* with me if Sally comes along.

Faulty   James has *alot* of homework to do tonight.
Revised James has *a lot* of homework to do tonight.

3   Memorizing words with silent letters or syllables

Weblink

http://webster.commnet.edu/
grammar/notorious.htm

*"Notorious Confusables": over 400 often
confused words, defined and illustrated
correctly in sentences that can be read
aloud on your computer.*

Many words contain silent letters, such as the *k* and the *w* in *k*no*w* or the *b* in dum*b*, or letters that are not pronounced in everyday speech, such as the first *r* in Feb*r*uary. The simplest way to remember the spelling of these words is to commit them to memory, mentally pronouncing the silent letters as you do so. Following is a list of frequently used words whose mispronunciation in everyday speech often leads to misspelling.

ai*s*le	condem*n*	gover*n*ment	*p*neumonia
can*d*idate	Feb*r*uary	int*e*rest	priv*i*lege
clim*b*	for*ei*gn	paradigm	prob*ab*ly

4   Distinguishing between noun and verb forms of the same word

Many spelling problems occur when noun and verb forms of a word have different spellings.

Verb	*Noun*
advise	advice
describe	description
enter	entrance
marry	marriage

5   Distinguishing American from British and Canadian spellings

The endings of various words differ depending on whether the American version or the British version of the word is being used. Though each is correct, when in America, do as the Americans do.

COMPUTER TIPS

Spelling Checkers

Spelling checkers are wonderful inventions. They are quick, accurate, and sharper than your own eye at catching mistakes. But use them wisely. First, wait until the end of your writing process. Spell-checking a rough draft or even an intermediate draft filled with words that you may delete later is a waste of time. Also, remember the limitations of spelling checkers: they will catch only words not in their built-in dictionaries. Because *there, their,* and *they're* are all spelled correctly, the spelling checker will not tell you if you've chosen the wrong one. When a correction is suggested, make sure you choose the correct one (consult a dictionary if you need to). If you've written *alot* and your spelling checker offers to substitute *allot,* be careful not to change your intended meaning. Finally, if your word processor has an ongoing spelling checking feature, consider turning it off. Few things are more damaging to the flow of your thoughts than being interrupted by a beep, a warning that you've misspelled a word, or the silent substitution of an incorrect word.

American	British
-or (humor, color)	-our (humour, colour)
-ment (judgment)	-ement (judgement)
-tion (connection)	-xion (connexion)
-ize (criticize, realize)	-ise (criticise, realise)
-er (center, theater)	-re (centre, theatre)
-led (traveled)	-lled (travelled)

Other American/British variations include gray/grey and check/cheque.

23b   Learn basic spelling rules for *ie/ei*.

The *i* before *e* rule you learned in grammar school still holds true: "*i* before *e* except after *c*, or when pronounced *ay*, as in n*ei*ghbor."

i before *e*

achieve	piece
belief/believe	field
brief	fiend/friend

Except after c

ceiling	receipt/receive
conceit	deceit/deceive
conceive	perceive

ei **pronounced** *ay*

beige	neighbor
eight(h)	heinous
freight	vein

Exceptions

ancient	foreign
height	seize
either	weird

Finally, if the *ie* is not pronounced as a unit, the rule does not apply: science, conscientious, atheist.

> **EXERCISE 2**
> Insert *ie* or *ei* in the following words. If necessary, use a dictionary to confirm your choice.
>
> | | | |
> |---|---|---|
> | forf___t | s___zure | p___rce |
> | financ___r | f___nt | pat___nce |
> | consc___nce | h___ress | counterf___t |
> | defic___nt | sl___ght | r___fy |

23c   Learn rules for using prefixes.

Prefixes are placed at the beginnings of words to qualify or add to their meaning. The addition of a prefix never affects the spelling of the root word. Do not drop a letter from or add a letter to the original word.

un	+	usual	=	unusual
mis	+	statement	=	misstatement
under	+	rate	=	underrate
de	+	emphasize	=	deemphasize

See 22d-2 for a list of prefixes.

23d Learn rules for using suffixes.

A **suffix** is an ending added to a word in order to change the word's function. For example, suffixes can change a present-tense verb to a past-tense verb (help, help*ed*); make an adjective an adverb (silent, silent*ly*); make a verb a noun (excite, excite*ment*); or change a noun to an adjective (force, forc*ible*). Spelling difficulties often arise when the root word must be changed before the suffix is added.

I Learn rules for keeping or dropping a final e.

Many words end with a silent *e* (hav*e*, mat*e*, rais*e*, confin*e*, procur*e*). When adding a suffix to these words, you can use the following rules.

Rule: If the suffix begins with a vowel, drop the final silent e.

| accuse | + | ation | = | accusation | sedate | + | ive | = | sedative |
| inquire | + | ing | = | inquiring | cube | + | ism | = | cubism |

Exceptions

The silent *e* is sometimes retained before a suffix that begins with a vowel in order to distinguish homonyms (dyeing/dying); to prevent mispronunciation (*mileage*, not milage); and especially, to keep the sound of *c* or *g* soft.

| courage | + | ous | = | courageous | embrace | + | able | = | embraceable |
| outrage | + | ous | = | outrageous | notice | + | able | = | noticeable |

Rule: If the suffix begins with a consonant, keep the final silent e.

| manage | + | ment | = | management | acute | + | ness | = | acuteness |
| sedate | + | ly | = | sedately | force | + | ful | = | forceful |

Exceptions

When the final silent *e* is preceded by another vowel, the *e* is dropped (*argument*, not arguement; *truly*, not truely).

Other exceptions include:

| judge | + | ment | = | judgment | awe | + | ful | = | awful |
| acknowledge | + | ment | = | acknowledgment | whole | + | ly | = | wholly |

EXERCISE 3

Combine the following words and suffixes, retaining or dropping the final *e* as needed. Check your choices in the dictionary to make sure they are correct.

1. investigate	+	ive	6. service	+	able
2. malice	+	ious	7. complete	+	ly
3. due	+	ly	8. mistake	+	en
4. trace	+	able	9. grieve	+	ance
5. singe	+	ing	10. binge	+	ing

2 Learn rules for keeping or dropping a final y.

When suffixes are added to words that end in a final *y*, use the following rules.

Rule: When the letter immediately before the y is a consonant, change the y to i and then add the suffix.

beauty	+	ful	=	beautiful	comply	+	ant	=	compliant
breezy	+	er	=	breezier	busy	+	ness	=	business

Exceptions
Keep the final *y* when the suffix to be added is *-ing*.

study + ing = studying   comply + ing = complying

Keep the final *y* for some one-syllable root words.

shy + er = shyer   wry + ly = wryly

Rule: Keep the final y when it is preceded by a vowel.

journey	+	ing	=	journeying	buoy	+	ant	=	buoyant
deploy	+	ment	=	deployment	play	+	ful	=	playful

EXERCISE 4

Combine the following root words and suffixes, changing the *y* to *i* when necessary.

1. supply	+	er	6. convey	+	ance
2. stultify	+	ing	7. cry	+	er
3. testy	+	er	8. Kennedy	+	s
4. rarefy	+	ed	9. plenty	+	ful
5. joy	+	ousness	10. day	+	ly

3   **Learn rule for adding -*ally*.**

Rule: Add -*ally* to make an adverb out of an adjective that ends with *ic*.

terrific   +   ally =   terrifically
caustic   +   ally =   caustically
fantastic   +   ally =   fantastically

Exception
public + ly = publicly

4   **Learn the rule for adding -*ly*.**

Rule: Add -*ly* to make an adverb out of an adjective that does not end with *ic*.

hesitant + ly = hesitantly   fastidious + ly = fastidiously
helpful + ly = helpfully   fortunate + ly = fortunately

5   **Learn the rule for adding -*cede*, -*ceed*, and -*sede*.**

Words that sound like *seed* are almost always spelled -*cede*.

| intercede | concede | precede |
| accede | recede | secede |

Exceptions
Only supersede uses -*sede*.
Only exceed, proceed, and succeed use -*ceed*.

6   **Learn rules for adding -*able* or -*ible*.**

These endings sound the same, but there is an easy way to remember which to use.

Rule: If the root word is an independent word, use the suffix -*able*. If the root is not an independent word, use the suffix -*ible*.

comfort + able = comfortable   audible
advise   + able = advisable   plausible
agree   + able = agreeable   compatible

Exceptions
culpable, probable, resistible

Learn Rules for Using Suffixes

A word that ends in a consonant sometimes doubles the final consonant when a suffix is added.

Rule: Double the final consonant when a one-syllable word ends in a consonant preceded by a single vowel.

flip	+	ant	=	fli**pp**ant	slip + er =	sli**pp**er
flat	+	en	=	fla**tt**en	split + ing =	spli**tt**ing

Rule: Double the final consonant when adding a suffix to a two-syllable word if a single vowel precedes the final consonant and if the final syllable is accented once the suffix is added.

control + er   = contro**ll**er
concur + ence = concu**rr**ence
commit + ing   = commi**tt**ing

Rule: Do not double the final consonant when it is preceded by two or more vowels, or by another consonant.

sustain + ing = sustaining
comport + ed   = comported

Rule: Do not double the final consonant if the suffix begins with a consonant.

commit + ment = commitment
fat   + ness = fatness

Rule: Do not double the final consonant if the word is *not* accented on the last syllable, or if the accent shifts from the last to the first syllable when the suffix is added.

beckon + ing   = beckoning
prefer + ence = preference

EXERCISE 5

Add the correct suffix to the following roots, changing the roots as necessary. Consult a dictionary as needed.

1. benefit   + ed
2. realistic + (-ly or -ally?)
3. contempt   + (-able or -ible?)
4. parallel   + ing
5. proceed   + ure
6. reverse   + (-able or -ible?)
7. allot   + ment
8. occur   + ence
9. room   + mate
10. control   + (-able or -ible?)

23e Learn rules for forming plurals.

There are several standard rules for making words plural.

I **Learn the basic rule for adding -s/-es.**

Adding -s

For most words, simply add -*s*.

gum/gums   automobile/automobiles

Adding -es

For words ending in -*s*, -*sh*, -*ss*, -*ch*, -*x*, or -*z*, add -*es*.

bus/buses   watch/watches
bush/bushes   tax/taxes
mistress/mistresses buzz/buzzes

For words ending in -*o*, add -*es* if the *o* is preceded by a consonant.

tomato/tomatoes   hero/heroes
potato/potatoes   veto/vetoes

Exceptions
pro/pros, piano/pianos, solo/solos
soprano/sopranos

Add -*s* if the final *o* is preceded by a vowel.

patio/patios   zoo/zoos

2 **Learn the rule for plurals of words ending in -f or -fe.**

To form the plural of some nouns ending in -*f* or -*fe*, change the ending to -*ve* before adding the -*s*.

half/halves   leaf/leaves
elf/elves   yourself/yourselves

Exceptions
scarf/scarfs/scarves   proof/proofs
belief/beliefs   motif/motifs
hoof/hoofs/hooves

Learn Rules for Forming Plurals   **423**

For words that end in a consonant followed by -*y*, change the *y* to *i* before adding -*es* to form the plural.

amenity/amenities   enemy/enemies

Exceptions
proper names such as McGinty/McGintys; Mary/Marys

For words ending in a vowel followed by -*y*, add -*s*.

monkey/monkeys   delay/delays

CRITICAL DECISIONS

Improving Your Spelling
In addition to learning the spelling rules detailed in this chapter, there are several ways to improve your spelling skills.

- Memorize commonly misspelled words.
- Keep track of the words that give you trouble. See if you can discern a pattern, and memorize the relevant rule.
- Use the dictionary. Check words whose spelling you are not sure of, and add them to your personal list of difficult-to-spell words. If you are not sure of the first few letters of a word, look up a synonym of that word to see if the word you need is listed as part of the definition.
- Pay attention when you read: your mind will retain a visual impression of a word that will help you remember how it is spelled.
- You may also develop mnemonic devices—techniques to improve memory—for particularly troublesome words. For instance, you might use the -*er* at the end of pap*er* and lett*er* as a reminder that stationery means writing pap*er*, while station*ary* means st*a*nding still.
- Edit and proofread carefully, paying particular attention to how the words look on the page. You will find as you train yourself that you will begin to recognize spelling errors, and that you actually know the correct spelling but have made an old mistake in haste or carelessness.
- On word processors, use a spell-checker, but realize that this computer aid will only identify misspelled words. If you have used an incorrect homonym, but have spelled it correctly, the spell-checker will not highlight the word.

---

4   Learn the rule for plurals of compound words.

When compound nouns are written as one word, add an *-s* or *-es* ending as you would to make any other plural.

snowball/snowballs   mailbox/mailboxes

When compound nouns are hyphenated or written as two words, the most important part of the compound word (usually a noun that is modified) is made plural.

sister-in-law/sisters-in-law   head of state/heads of state
nurse-midwife/nurse-midwives   city planner/city planners

5   Learn the irregular plurals.

Some words change internally to form plurals.

woman/women   goose/geese
mouse/mice   tooth/teeth

Some Latin and Greek words form plurals by changing their final *-um*, *-on*, or *-us* to *-a* or *-i*.

curricul*um*/curricul*a*   criteri*on*/criteri*a*
syllab*us*/syllab*i*   medi*um*/medi*a*
dat*um*/dat*a*   stimul*us*/stimul*i*
alumn*us*/alumn*i*

For some words, the singular and the plural forms are the same.

deer/deer   sheep/sheep   fish/fish
species/species moose/moose   **23.2**
elk/elk   rice/rice

EXERCISE 6
Make the following words plural. Check your answers in the dictionary.

1. calf   6. knife
2. memorandum   7. editor-in-chief
3. torch   8. heresy
4. chief   9. gas
5. kilowatt-hour   10. ego

End Punctuation

The ending of one sentence and the beginning of the next is a crucial boundary for readers. When sentence boundaries are blurred, readers have trouble grouping a writer's words into meaningful segments. To mark the end-of-sentence boundary in English you have three choices: a period, a question mark, or an exclamation point.

CRITICAL DECISIONS

Choosing End Punctuation

The choice between using a period and a question mark at the end of a sentence is a matter of function. Your main determination will be whether the sentence is a statement or a direct question. The choice of using an exclamation point, however, is more a matter of style and tone. Your main determination here will be whether using an exclamation point will serve your purpose for writing.

THE PERIOD

24a Using the period

| Placing a period to mark the end of a statement or a mild command

It is conventional to end statements or mild commands with a period.

For quite some time after the *Titanic*'s collision with the iceberg, the people on board did not believe themselves to be in danger.

"Women and children must get into the lifeboats."

A restatement of a question asked by someone else is called an **indirect question.** Since it is really a statement, it does not take a question mark.

Direct question	Many of the women who were being urged to board the life rafts asked, "Is this truly necessary?"
Statement	Many of the women who were being urged to board the life rafts asked whether this measure was truly necessary.

2 Placing periods in relation to end quotation marks and parentheses

A period is always placed inside a quotation mark that ends a sentence.

The rule was, at least on the port side of the ship, "Women and children only."

When a parenthesis ends a sentence, place a period outside the end parenthesis if the parenthetical remark is not a complete sentence (see 29c). If the parenthetical remark is a separate complete sentence, enclose it entirely in parentheses and punctuate it as a sentence—with its own period.

Faulty	No allowance had been made for life rafts for steerage passengers (that is, economy class—the cheapest fare.).
Revised	No allowance had been made for life rafts for steerage passengers (that is, economy class—the cheapest fare).
Revised	No allowance had been made for life rafts for steerage passengers. (Steerage was defined as economy class, the cheapest fare.)

3 Using a period with abbreviations

The following abbreviations conventionally end with a period:

Mr.   Mrs.   Ms. (even though this is not an abbreviation)
apt.   Ave.   St.   Dr.   Eccles.   mgr.

When an abbreviation ends a sentence, use a single period.

The lawyers addressed their questions to Susan Turner, Esq.

When an abbreviation falls in the middle of a sentence, punctuate as if the word abbreviated were spelled out.

The award envelope was presented to Susan Turner, Esq., who opened it calmly.

See 31a–e for a full discussion of abbreviations.

Use no periods with acronyms or certain long abbreviations.

Weblink

http://www.acronymfinder.com
Acronym Finder: A searchable data-base containing 84,000 common acronyms.

A number of abbreviations do not take periods—most often *acronyms* (NATO for *N*orth *A*tlantic *T*reaty *O*rganization), the names of large organizations (IBM for *I*nternational *B*usiness *M*achines), or government agencies (FTC for *F*ederal *T*rade *C*ommission). To be sure about the proper abbreviation of a word or organizational name, see the box at 31c and consult an appropriate reference.

ABC   NBA   NAFTA   MADD   ABM   FAA

EXERCISE I

Add, delete, or reposition periods in these sentences as needed.

> *Example:*   Organ transplants have increased since the development of immunosuppressive drugs such as cyclosporin
>
> Organ transplants have increased since the development of immunosuppressive drugs such as cyclosporin.

1. According to one expert, "roughly 5,000 patients are waiting at any given moment for replacement livers. Ten thousand wait for kidneys." (Thomas)

2. Modern transplant techniques have created a rush for human organs and have given rise to what is ghoulishly called the "meat market"

3. "The ethical dilemmas raised by organ transplants are enormous," says Dr. Philip Wier (an ethicist at the Longwood Institute.)

4. Some poor people, faced with the prospect of starving, sell off their kidneys (This practice is the subject of intense debate in some state legislatures)

THE QUESTION MARK

24b   Using the question mark

I   Using a question mark after a direct question

Why do children develop so little when they are isolated from others?

Why is the crime rate higher in the city than the country? Why do more males than females commit crimes?

Note: An indirect question restates a question put by someone else. The indirect question does not take a question mark.

> Researchers have asked why children develop so little when they are isolated from others.

Requests, worded as questions, are often followed by periods.

> Would you pour another glass of wine.

Questions in a series inside a sentence will take question marks if each denotes a separate question.

> When an automobile manufacturer knowingly sells a car that meets government safety standards but is defective, what are the manufacturer's legal responsibilities? moral responsibilities? financial responsibilities? [Note that these "clipped" questions do not require capitalization.]

When the sense of the questions in a series is not completed until the final question, use one question mark—at the end of the sentence.

> Will the agent be submitting the manuscript to one publishing house, two houses, or more?

2 Using a question mark after a quoted question within a statement

Placing the question mark *inside* the end quotation mark

When the question mark applies directly to the quoted material, place it inside the quotation mark.

> In a dream, Abraham Lincoln remembered a stranger asking, "Why are you so common looking?"

Place the question mark inside the end quotation mark when the mark applies to *both* the quoted material *and* the sentence as a whole.

> Don't you find it insulting that a person would comment directly to a president, "Why are you so common looking?"

Placing the question mark *outside* the end quotation mark

When the sentence as a whole forms a question but the quoted material does not, place the question mark outside the quotation.

> Was it Lincoln who observed, "The Lord prefers common-looking people; that's the reason he makes so many of them"?

Note: Do *not* combine a question mark with a period, a comma, or an exclamation point.

Faulty   "Are you going with him?!" asked Joan.
Revised   "Are you going with him?" asked Joan.

<table>
<tr><td>3</td><td>Using a question mark within parentheses to indicate that the accuracy of information is in doubt even after extensive research</td></tr>
</table>

The question mark can be used to indicate dates or numerical references known to be inexact. The following are equivalent in meaning:

Geoffrey Chaucer was born in 1340 **(?).**

Chaucer was born about 1340.

Chaucer was born c. 1340. (The c. is an abbreviation for *circa*, meaning "around.")

Note: Do *not* use the question mark in parentheses to make wry comments in your sentences.

Faulty We found the play a stimulating **(?)** experience.

Revised We found the play as dull as we expected.

EXERCISE 2

Add or delete question marks as needed. If necessary, reword sentences.

> *Example:* The candidates' forum provided an illuminating (?) hour of political debate.
>
> The candidates' forum failed to provide an illuminating debate.

1. Many people are quick to condemn politicians, so why don't more people run for elected office.

2. With polls shaping the agendas of politicians, is it any wonder that Americans turn cynical, refuse to vote, bemoan the absence of leadership.

3. Political scientists ask why Americans have one of the lowest voter turnouts among democratic nations?

4. Was it Marie Thompson who asked, "Why do we have so much difficulty rising to the challenge of our democratic traditions"?

5. Thompson reaches no firm answers when she concludes, "If the framers of the Constitution assumed an educated, caring citizenry, then we must wonder aloud—have we failed to meet the challenges laid down 200 years ago"?

24.1

THE EXCLAMATION POINT

<table>
<tr><td>24c</td><td>Using the exclamation point</td></tr>
</table>

In spoken conversation, exclamations are used freely, especially in moments of high passion. For some informal occasions, writers may be tempted to create with exclamation points what their tone of voice cannot show on paper. In academic writing, however, it is far more convincing to create emphasis by the force of your words, as opposed to the force of your punctuation.

Using the exclamation point—sparingly—to mark an emphatic statement or command

Save the exclamation point to call special attention to a unique, memorable sentence, the content of which creates its own emphasis.

Enterprising archaeologists visit their dentists regularly, if only to obtain supplies of worn-out dental instruments, which make first-rate fine digging tools**!**

Please**!** Let me do it myself**!** [The use of exclamation points with this emphatic exclamation and command is appropriate for duplicating spoken dialogue.]

2   Marking mild exclamations with periods or commas

Please, let me do it myself.

Note: Do not combine an exclamation point with a period, comma, or question mark.

Faulty   "Leave this room**!,**" demanded the judge.
Revised   "Leave this room**!**" demanded the judge.

EXERCISE 3

Read the following paragraphs on the subject of getting fired from a job and provide periods, question marks, and exclamation points as needed.

Many people who have lost their jobs report that the loss profoundly undermines their self-esteem They blame themselves They ask themselves "How can I be lovable, worthy, and competent if I have lost my job" Having to file an unemployment claim only serves to deepen their sense of shame

Even well-intentioned former coworkers are no source of comfort The newly unemployed often find that even the most sympathetic colleagues tend to abandon them These coworkers are terrified that the same thing might happen to them (in a climate of downsizing this fear is certainly justified) Others tell the victim that this loss is "the best thing that could ever happen to you" From the fired person's point of view, such people are merely trying to alleviate their own discomfort "They say that so that they won't have to worry about me" one woman commented The loss of one's job can cause a person to become cynical and suspicious

24.2

Commas

O ne important purpose of punctuation is to help readers identify clusters of related words. *Within* sentences, the most common mark for doing so is the **comma,** which is used primarily to signal that some element, a word or cluster of related words, is being set off

Weblink

http://webster.commnet.edu/
grammar/commas.htm

A hypertext guide to using commas.

from a main sentence for a reason. The choices you make about comma use should be tied to the logic of a sentence's structure.

CRITICAL DECISIONS

Understanding When to Use Commas

As a writer, you will make two main decisions about comma use. You will decide (1) when they are required by convention and (2) when they are not required. The lack of a comma when it is needed can be bothersome, even confusing, to readers, while the presence of an unneeded comma can cause just as much difficulty. In this chapter, sections 25a to 25e focus on when commas are required in sentences. Section 25f provides examples of occasions when novice writers may insert commas into sentences unnecessarily. It is just as important to recognize when commas *are not* needed as to recognize when they *are.*

25a Using commas with introductory and concluding expressions

| 1 | Place a comma after a modifying phrase or clause that begins a sentence. |

Yesterday, the faucet stopped working.

Once the weather turned cold, the faucet stopped working.

A sentence may begin with an opening phrase or clause that is neither the subject nor a simple modifier of the subject. If such an introductory element is longer than a few words, set it off from the main part of the sentence with a comma.

> According to landscape architect Robert Gibbs, urban shopping centers could learn a lot from suburban malls.

> Because Gibbs possesses a commercial shrewdness, he is able to spot the flaws in the most elegant street designs.

Option: The comma after an introductory word or brief phrase is optional.

> In fact a great many considerations are involved in mall design.

When an introductory element consists of two or more phrases, a comma is required.

> As a commercial space with a retailing bias, the mall should have a design that does not let the shopper become distracted from buying.

Note: An opening verbal phrase or clause is set off with a comma if it is used as a modifier. An opening verbal used as a subject is *not* set off.

Modifier   In creating a shopping environment that is too beautiful, commercial designers are failing to serve the needs of the merchants.

Subject   Creating a shopping environment that is too beautiful fails to serve the needs of the merchants.

| 2 | Place a comma after a transitional word, phrase, or clause that begins a sentence. |

Actually, we've had this problem for years.

A transition is a logical bridge between sentences or paragraphs. As an introductory element, it is set off with a comma.

> Once division of labor by sex arose, it must have produced several immediate benefits for the early hominids. *First of all,* nutrition would have improved owing to a balanced diet. *Second,* each male or female would have had to become expert in only part of the skills needed for subsistence.

When a transitional element is moved to the interior of a sentence, set it off with a *pair* of commas. At the end of a sentence, the transitional element is set off with a single comma.

> Lipid molecules, *of course,* can pass through cell membranes with ease.

> Lipid molecules can pass through cell membranes with ease, *to cite one example.*

3 Use a comma (or commas) to set off a modifying element that ends or interrupts a sentence *if* the modifier establishes a qualification, contrast, or exception.

The ships return to port at all hours, often at night.

The storm warning was broadcast on the A channel, not the B channel.

A qualification

The literary form *short story* is usually defined as a brief fictional prose narrative, *often involving one connected episode.*

A contrast

The U.S. government located a lucrative project for an atomic accelerator in Texas, *not Massachusetts.*

An exception

The children of the rich are the group most likely to go to private preparatory schools and elite colleges, *regardless of their grades.*

When phrases or clauses of contrast, qualification, and exception occur in the middle of a sentence, set them off with a *pair* of commas.

All seas, *except in the areas of circumpolar ice,* are navigable.

If a phrase or clause does *not* establish a qualification, contrast, or exception, do *not* use a comma to separate it from the sentence.

The faucet stopped working once the weather turned cold.

EXERCISE I

The following sentences contain transitional expressions and modifying words or phrases. Rewrite each sentence so that the transition or modifier will come at the *beginning* of the sentence **or** at the *end*. Use commas as needed.

> *Example:* Some of the Balkan nations of southeastern and south central Europe in 1912 declared war on the waning Ottoman Empire.
>
> In 1912, some of the Balkan nations of southeastern and south central Europe declared war on the waning Ottoman Empire.

1. Bulgaria attacked Serbia and Greece in 1913 in a second war over boundaries.

2. Bulgaria was carved up as a result of the 1913 war by its former Balkan allies and Turkey.

3. The assassination of Archduke Ferdinand of Austria the following year brought on the First World War.

4. A sprawling new nation, Yugoslavia, was formed after the Austro-Hungarian Empire collapsed.

5. The aspirations of Croats and other minorities in Yugoslavia were suppressed under the tenuous domination of the Serbs.
6. The collapse of the Ottoman Empire at the same time left many ethnic Turks subject to their longtime foes the Bulgarians.
7. A million Armenians were slaughtered at the same time as a result of attempts at forging a new Turkish state in Anatolia.
8. Undermined by corrupt and meddling monarchs and by ethnic passions, parliamentary governments of southeastern Europe rose and fell.
9. The fall of Communist regimes in eastern Europe today has led to a resurgence of ethnic fighting.
10. "Ethnic cleansing" reminiscent of Nazi atrocities has annihilated whole villages.

25b Using a comma before a coordinating conjunction to join two independent clauses

The faucet stopped working, and the sink leaks.

We can fix the problems ourselves, or we can call a plumber.

One of the principal ways to join two independent clauses is to link them with a comma and a coordinating conjunction: *and, but, or, nor, so* (see 19a-1).

The changes in *Homo erectus* are substantial over a million years, *but* they seem gradual by comparison with those that went before.

Homo erectus used stone tools, *and Homo erectus* was the first of early humanoids to use fire.

Note: When one or both clauses have internal punctuation, to prevent misreading use a semicolon instead of a comma before the conjunction.

Several thousand years ago, probably some lines of Neanderthal man and woman died out; but it seems likely that a line in the Middle East went directly to us, *Homo sapiens.*

25c Using commas between items in a series

I   Place a comma between items in a series.

www
25.1

We'll need a washer, a valve, and a wrench.

Items joined in a series should be parallel (see Chapter 18). Items can be single words, phrases, or clauses.

Spotlight on Common Errors—COMMA USE

These are clues to the errors most commonly associated with comma use. For full explanations and suggested revisions, follow the cross-references to chapter sections.

COMMA ERRORS arise when the use—or absence—of commas leaves readers unable to differentiate between a main sentence and the parts being set off. Five error patterns account for most of the difficulty with comma use.

Use a comma to set off introductory words or word groupings from the main part of the sentence (see 25a).

Faulty	**Revised**
Yesterday the faucet stopped working.	Yesterday, the faucet stopped working.

Faulty	**Revised**
Once the weather turned cold the faucet stopped working.	Once the weather turned cold, the faucet stopped working.

Do *not* use a comma to set off concluding words or word groupings from a main sentence (but see 25a-3 for exceptions).

Faulty	**Revised**
The faucet stopped working, yesterday.	The faucet stopped working yesterday.

Faulty	**Revised**
The faucet stopped working, once the weather turned cold.	The faucet stopped working once the weather turned cold.

Place a comma before the word *and, but, or, for,* or *so* when it joins two sentences (see 25b).

Faulty	**Revised**
The faucet stopped working *and* the sink leaks.	The faucet stopped working, *and* the sink leaks.

Faulty	**Revised**
I'll fix them myself *or* I can call a plumber.	I'll fix them myself, *or* I can call a plumber.

BUT use no comma if one key word, usually the subject, keeps the second grouping of words from being considered a sentence.

Faulty

I'll fix them myself, or call a plumber.

Revised

I'll fix them myself or call a plumber.

Use a comma to separate three or more items in a series (see 25c-1).

Faulty

I'll need a washer a valve and a wrench.

Revised

I'll need a washer, a valve, and a wrench.

or

I'll need a washer, a valve and a wrench.

Use a *pair* of commas to set off from a sentence any word or word group that adds nonessential information (see 25d).

Faulty

Ahorn Hardware which is just around the corner has the best prices.

Revised

Ahorn Hardware, which is just around the corner, has the best prices.

[Since a specific hardware store is named and its identity is clear, the added information is nonessential and is set off with a pair of commas.]

BUT use *no* commas if a word or word group adds essential information needed for identifying some other word in the sentence.

Faulty

The hardware store, which has the best prices, is just around the corner.

Revised

The hardware store which has the best prices is just around the corner.

[Since the added information is essential for identifying *which* hardware store (the one with the best prices), no commas are used. Note that in the case of essential information, many writers insist on using *that* to introduce the information.]

The hardware store **that** has the best prices is just around the corner.

Words   A Central Processing Unit contains a large number of special-purpose registers for storing *instructions*, *addresses*, and *data*.

Phrases   Booms and busts have plagued economic activity since the onset of industrialization, *sporadically ejecting many workers from their jobs*, *pushing many businesses into bankruptcy*, and *leaving many politicians out in the cold*.

Note: When at least one item in a series contains a comma, use a semicolon to separate items and prevent misreading (see Chapter 26). For the same reason, use semicolons to separate long independent clauses in a series.

> I believe that the sun is about ninety-three million miles from the earth; that it is a hot globe many times bigger than the earth; and that, owing to the earth's rotation, it rises every morning and will continue to do so indefinitely.

ACROSS THE CURRICULUM

Final Commas Separating Items in a Series

In separating items in a series, most academic writers include a comma before the conjunction that links the final item in the series to those that precede it:

> Geneticists frequently refer to the genome as the Bible, the Holy Grail, or the Book of Man. . . . Today, models of molecular biology are appropriated to support prevailing ideologies, traditional biases, and social stereotypes.
>
> —DOROTHY NELKIN, "The Grandiose Claims of Geneticists,"
> *The Chronicle of Higher Education*, Mar. 3, 1993

However, the style taught in departments of journalism specifically drops the comma before the conjunction. This is the style you will find in most newspapers and popular magazines:

> It is known that some species of flowers, insects, lizards and snakes can reproduce asexually. . . . But for decades scientists have known how to trick the eggs of mice, rabbits and other mammals into developing as if they had been fertilized by subjecting the eggs to various chemicals or to temperature changes, needle pricks or electrical shocks.
>
> —ANDREW POLLACK, "New Work May Provide Stem Cells
> While Taking Baby from Equation," *New York Times*,
> Nov. 6, 2001

If your preference is to drop the final comma before the conjunction in a series, be sure to do so consistently. You might also want to make sure that your instructor finds this usage acceptable.

2 Place a comma between two or more coordinate adjectives in a series if no coordinating conjunction joins them.

Getting under the sink can be a tricky, messy job.

A series of adjectives will often appear as a parallel sequence: the *playful, amusing* poet; an *intelligent, engaging* speaker. When the order of the adjectives can be reversed without affecting the meaning of the noun being modified, the adjectives are called **coordinate adjectives.** Coordinate adjectives can be linked by a comma or by a coordinating conjunction.

Series with commas

The stomach is a thick-walled, muscular sac that can expand to hold more than 2 liters of food or liquid.

Series with *and*

The stomach is a thick-walled *and* muscular sac that can expand to hold more than 2 liters of food or liquid.

Series with commas

The left hemisphere of the brain thinks sequential, analytical thoughts.

Series with *and*

The left hemisphere of the brain thinks sequential *and* analytical thoughts.

Note: The presence of two adjectives beside one another does not necessarily mean that they are coordinate. In the phrase "the wise old lady," the adjectives could not be reversed in sequence or joined by *and*. The adjective *wise* describes *old lady*, not *lady* alone. The same analysis holds for the phrase "the ugly green car." *Green car* is the element being modified by *ugly*. Only coordinate adjectives modifying the same noun are separated by commas.

EXERCISE 2

Combine the following sentences with the conjunction indicated in brackets, and decide whether you need to use a comma. Recall that unless a conjunction joins independent clauses, no comma is needed.

Example: Anthropologists are currently investigating whether early hominids (proto-humans) ate meat. [and] Did they obtain meat by hunting or scavenging?

Anthropologists are currently investigating whether early hominids (proto-humans) ate meat and whether they obtained it by hunting or scavenging.

1. Proto-humans did not walk as well on two feet as we do. [but] They were better than we are at climbing trees and suspending themselves from branches.

2. Ancestors of present-day leopards were contemporary with early hominids. [and] Ancestors of present-day leopards shared the same habitats as early hominids.

3. Leopards cannot defend their kills from scavenging by lions. [so] They store their kills in trees.

4. Archaeologist John Cavallo thinks that early tree-climbing hominids may have fed off leopard kills stashed in trees. [since] Leopards don't guard the carcasses of their kills.

EXERCISE 3

In each sentence, place a comma as needed between items in a series.

Example: Native American societies were based on close ties of kin and on notions of community mutual obligation and reciprocity.

Native American societies were based on close ties of kin and on notions of community, mutual obligation, and reciprocity.

1. They possessed complex religious beliefs symbolic world views radically different from those of Europeans and cultural values Europeans did not understand.

2. Like other native populations "discovered" after them, Native Americans were exploited decimated by exotic diseases robbed of their lands and ultimately stripped of their traditional cultures.

3. Survivors became serfs slaves or subordinate and often tangential elements in the new social order.

4. Therefore, for centuries Native Americans continued to resist Catholic missionaries explorers and settlers from all over Europe.

25d   Using commas to set off nonessential elements

  I Identify essential (restrictive) elements that need no commas.

The hardware store which has the best prices is just around the corner.

When a modifier provides information that is necessary for identifying a word, then the modifier is said to be **essential** (or **restrictive**), and it appears in its sentence *without* commas. Note that in the case of essential information, many writers insist on using *that* to introduce the information.

The world-renowned architect *commissioned to design a synagogue for the Beth Shalom congregation in Elkins Park* produced a masterpiece.

Weblink

http://www.wisc.edu/writetest/
Handbook/Commas.html#definitions
*Punctuating restrictive and nonrestrictive
modifiers: Definitions of nonrestrictive and restrictive modifiers with sample pairs of sentences and self-test sentences and answers.*

There have been many famous archi-
tects. This sentence refers to the *one*
architect hired by this congregation.
Without the modifying phrase *commissioned to design a synagogue for
the Beth Shalom congregation in Elkins
Park*, the subject of this sentence, *the
world-renowned architect*, could not be
conclusively identified. Therefore, the
modifying expression is essential, and no commas are used to set apart
the phrase from the sentence in which it appears.

An essential modifier can also be a single word (or single name).

The world-renowned architect *Frank Lloyd Wright* was born in 1869.

Without the name *Frank Lloyd Wright*, we would not know which world-
renowned architect was born in 1869.

An essential modifier can also be a clause.

The cyclotron is an instrument *that accelerates charged particles to very
high speeds.*

The noun modified—*instrument*—could be *any* instrument. The clause
that follows provides information essential to defining *which* or *what
kind of* instrument.

2	Use a pair of commas to set off nonessential (nonrestrictive) elements.

Ahorn Hardware, which is just around the corner, has the best prices.

If a word being modified is clearly defined (as, for instance, a
person with a specific name is clearly defined), then the modifying
element—though it might add interesting and useful information—is
nonessential. In this case, use commas to set the modifier apart from
the sentence.

Nonessential   Frank Lloyd Wright, *possibly the finest American architect of
the twentieth century,* died in 1959.

The subject of the sentence has already been defined adequately by his
name, *Frank Lloyd Wright.* The writer uses the modifying phrase not as a
matter of definition but as an occasion to add nonessential information.

The meaning of a sentence will change according to whether modifying elements are punctuated as essential or nonessential. The two
pairs of sentences that follow are worded identically. Punctuation gives
them different meanings.

Essential	The students *who have band practice after school* cannot attend the game.
Nonessential	The students, *who have band practice after school,* cannot attend the game.

The essential modifier precisely defines *which* students will not be able to attend the game—only those who have band practice. The meaning of this first sentence, then, is that some students *will* be able to attend—those who do *not* have band practice. The nonessential modifier communicates that *all* of the students have band practice and that none can attend.

Punctuating Modifying Clauses with *Who*, *Which*, and *That*

The relative pronouns *who*, *which*, and *that* begin modifying clauses that can interrupt or end sentences.

Who

Who can begin a clause that is essential to defining the word modified.

> Organizations designate managers *who help administrative units meet their specific goals.*

Who can also begin a nonessential clause. Note the presence of commas in this sentence.

> Frank Smith, *who is an administrative manager,* helps his administrative unit meet its goals.

Which

Similarly, *which* can begin an essential or a nonessential modifying clause.

> Two sites *which flourished in the dim yet documented past* are Saxon London and medieval Winchester. [essential]

> Some historical archaeologists excavate sites like Saxon London or medieval Winchester, *which flourished in the dim yet documented past.* [nonessential]

That

That always denotes an essential clause. Do not use commas to set off a modifying clause beginning with *that*.

> Two sites *that flourished in the dim yet documented past* are Saxon London and medieval Winchester. [essential]

---

3 **Use commas to set off parenthetical or repeating elements.**

The reasons she gave, all three of them, were convincing.

By definition, a parenthetical remark does not provide crucial information. Set off parenthetical expressions as you would any nonessential element.

Lizzie Borden, *despite the weight of evidence against her,* was acquitted of the murder of her father and her stepmother.

Options: You have the choice of setting off parenthetical elements by using commas, parentheses, or dashes. Base your decision on the level of emphasis you wish to give the parenthetical element. Dashes call the most attention to the element and parentheses the least attention.

CRITICAL DECISIONS

 Distinguishing Essential from Nonessential Information Within a Sentence

Comma placement often depends on a decision you make about whether certain qualifying (or additional) information is or is not essential to the meaning of a particular word in a sentence.

A test to determine whether qualifying information is essential or nonessential

1. Identify the single word in the sentence being qualified by a word group.
2. Identify the qualifying word group.
3. Drop the qualifying word group from the sentence.
4. Ask of the single word from #1, above: Do I understand which one or who?
   a. If you can give a single answer to this question, the qualifying information is nonessential. Set the information off from the sentence with a pair of commas.

   The train arrived early in Baltimore, the birthplace of Babe Ruth.

   b. If you cannot give a specific answer to the question, the qualifying information is essential. Include the information in the main sentence with no commas.

   The cities that have antiquated water systems need to modernize quickly or risk endangering public health.

Repeating elements

Repetition can both add useful information to a sentence and create pleasing sentence rhythms. By definition, a repeating element is nonessential, so the logic of setting off nonessential elements with commas applies. Set off a repeating element with a *pair* of commas if the element appears in the middle of a sentence. (You may also use a pair of dashes.) Use a comma or a dash and a period if the element concludes the sentence.

The police investigation, *a bungled affair from start to finish,* overlooked crucial evidence and even managed to lose notes taken at the scene of the crime.

Archaeologists working underwater have exactly the same intellectual goals as their dry-land colleagues—*to recover, reconstruct, and interpret the past.*

These bare facts have become so familiar, *so essential in the conduct of an interlocking world society,* that they are usually taken for granted.

Appositives

One class of repeating element is called an **appositive phrase,** the function of which is to rename a noun. The phrase is called *appositive* because it is placed in *apposition* to—that is, *side by side* with—the noun it repeats. In the first example, the appositive *a bungled affair from start to finish* renames the subject of the sentence, *investigation.* The sentence could be rewritten and repunctuated as follows:

A bungled affair from start to finish, the police investigation overlooked crucial evidence.

Exception: When a nonessential appositive phrase consists of a series of items separated by commas, set it off from a sentence with a pair of dashes—not commas—to prevent misreading.

Confusing   Motion sickness, nausea, dizziness, and sleepiness, is a dangerous and common malady among astronauts.

Revised   Motion sickness—nausea, dizziness, and sleepiness—is a
dangerous and common malady among astronauts.

EXERCISE 4

Combine the following pairs of sentences. Use commas to set off non-essential modifiers and omit commas when modifiers are essential.

> *Example:*   A number of Hollywood films have depicted historical
> events. Such films were painstakingly researched.
>
> A number of Hollywood films that have depicted historical
> events were painstakingly researched.

1. Film by its very nature is better able than prose to present the event
in all its intensity.

   Even the most sober historians are willing to admit that fact.

2. In some instances the film has turned out to be more historically
accurate than the original historical account.

   Vivien Leigh's portrayal of a spirited Scarlett O'Hara is now considered to be a fairly accurate interpretation of the not-so-helpless
Southern belle.

3. Of course there have been plenty of instances of mistakes in historical representation.

   A film might carefully reproduce the material culture of an era but skew the facts of the event.

4. Viewers are more comfortable if the film ratifies their personal biases.

   Hollywood history films tend to reflect the biases of their viewers, especially in political matters.

5. *Bonnie and Clyde* transformed a vapid Bonnie Parker into an aggressive moll.

   Anne of the Thousand Days transformed an ambitious and strong-willed Anne Boleyn into a lovesick, awestruck girl.

6. *A Man for All Seasons* presented a gentle, principled man.

   The historical Thomas More wrote that the execution of heretics was "lawful, necessary and well done."

7. *Bonnie and Clyde* and *Anne of the Thousand Days* were made only two years apart.

   These two films illustrate the rise of the generation gap of the 1960s.

<table>
<tr><td>**25e**</td><td>**Using commas to acknowledge conventions of quoting, naming, and various forms of separation**</td></tr>
</table>

1   Use a comma to introduce or to complete a quotation.

25.2

Tom said, "I'll be back in two hours."

Commas set a quotation apart from the words that introduce or conclude the quotation. Commas (and periods) are placed *inside* end quotation marks.

The prizefighter Rocky Graziano once said, "I had to leave fourth grade because of pneumonia—not because I had it but because I couldn't spell it."

Early in his career, Winston Churchill sported a mustache. At a fancy dinner, he argued with a woman. "Young man—I care for neither your politics nor your mustache," she snapped.

"Madam," responded Churchill, "you are unlikely to come into contact with either."

(For more on using commas with quotations, see Chapter 28.)

2

Use a comma to set off expressions of direct address.
If the expression interrupts a sentence, set the word off
with a *pair* of commas.

"Ed, did you bring your computer?"

"Please come out of the stockroom, Ed."

"Our business, Ed, is to sell shoes."

You will most often encounter expressions of direct address when writing dialogue or when quoting speakers addressing their audiences.

3

Use a comma to mark the omission of words
in a balanced sentence.

The first train will arrive at two o'clock; the second, at three o'clock.

Sentences are balanced when identical clause constructions are doubled or tripled in a series. So that repeating words in the clauses do not become tedious to a reader, omit these words and note the omission with a comma.

> Some southern novelists attribute the character of their fiction to the South's losing the Civil War; others, to the region's special blending of climate and race; and still others, to the salubrious powers of mint juleps.

In this example, the commas substitute for *attribute the character of their fiction.*

4

Place a comma between paired "more/less" constructions.

The less you smoke, the longer you'll live.

Some constructions involve a paired comparison of "more" of one element contrasted against "more" or "less" of another. Separate these elements with a comma.

> The more wires a database contains, the greater the number of bits it can move.

> The more some people get, the less they are willing to give.

5

Use a comma to set off tag questions that conclude a sentence.

This is the right house, isn't it?

A **tag question,** a brief question "tagged on" to a statement addressed to someone, should be set off from that statement.

You slipped into the office and read that letter, didn't you?

I have reached the only possible conclusion, haven't I?

6   Use a comma to set off yes/no remarks and mild exclamations.

"Yes, I'll call him right away."

"Oh well, I can put it off for another day."

7   Use commas according to convention in names, titles, dates, numbers, and addresses.

Commas with names and titles

Place a comma directly after a name if it is followed by a title.

Mr. Joe Smith, Executive Editor

Lucy Turner, Ph.D.

Robert Jones, Sr.

Set off a title in commas when writing a sentence.

Mr. Joe Smith, Executive Editor, signed for the package.

Lucy Turner, Ph.D., delivered the commencement address.

Robert Jones, Sr., attended the ceremony.

Commas with dates

Place a comma between the day of the month and year. If your reference is to a particular month in a year and no date is mentioned, do not use a comma.

January 7, 2002   but   January 2002

When a date is written out, as in an invitation, use the following convention:

the seventh of January, 2002

No commas are used in the military convention for writing dates.

7 January 2002

If you include a day of the week when writing a date, use the following convention:

The package will be delivered on Wednesday, January 7, 2002.

Commas with numbers

Place a comma to denote thousands, millions, and so forth.

543   5,430   54,300   543,000   5,430,000   5,430,000,000

Some writers place no comma in four-digit numbers that are multiples of fifty.

2550   1600   but   1,625

Do *not* use commas when writing phone numbers, addresses, page numbers, or years.

Commas with addresses

When writing an address, place a comma between a city (or county) and state.

Baltimore, Maryland Baltimore County, Maryland

Place no comma between a state and zip code.

Baltimore, Maryland 21215

When writing an address into a sentence, use commas to set off elements that would otherwise be placed on separate lines of the address. Set off the name of a state with a comma if no zip code follows it.

Mr. Abe Stein, Senior Engineer
Stein Engineering
1243 Slade Avenue
Bedford, Massachusetts 01730

The control boards were shipped to Mr. Abe Stein, Senior Engineer, Stein Engineering, 1243 Slade Avenue, Bedford, Massachusetts 01730.

The office in Bedford, Massachusetts, was not easy to find.

8   Use commas to prevent misreading.

Confusing   To help Mary carried the box.
Revised   To help, Mary carried the box.

Although no rule calls for it, a comma may be needed to prevent misreading. Misreading can occur when numbers are placed together.

Confusing   Down by twenty six members of the squad suddenly woke up.
Revised   Down by twenty, six members of the squad suddenly woke up.

Misreading can occur when words that are often used as auxiliary verbs (e.g., *will, should,* forms of *be, do*) function as main verbs and occur before other verbs.

Confusing   Those who do know exactly what must be done.
Revised   Those who do, know exactly what must be done.

Misreading can occur when a word that functions both as a preposition and as a modifier (e.g., *after, before, along, around, beneath, through*) is used as a modifier and is followed by a noun.

Confusing	Moments after the room began to tilt.
Revised	Moments after, the room began to tilt.

Misreading can occur when identical words are placed together.

Confusing	To speak speak into the microphone and press the button.
Revised	To speak, speak into the microphone and press the button.

EXERCISE 5

Decide whether commas are needed to clarify meaning in these sentences. Then make up three sentences of your own in which adding a comma will prevent misreading.

1. If you can come join us.
2. The doctor dressed and performed an emergency appendectomy.
3. The doctor dressed and sutured the wound.
4. From beneath the supports began to weaken.
5. By twos twenty children walked down the aisle.

25f Editing to avoid misuse or overuse of commas

I Eliminate the comma splice.

Confusing	She climbed the ladder, she slid down the slide.
Revised	She climbed the ladder. She slid down the slide.
	She climbed the ladder, **and** she slid down the slide.

The most frequent comma blunder, the **comma splice,** occurs when a writer joins independent clauses with a comma.

Faulty	Columbus is considered a master navigator today, he died in neglect.

To revise a comma splice, see the box on page 450 and Chapter 13.

2 Eliminate commas misused to set off essential (restrictive) elements.

Confusing	Athletes, who use steroids, invite disaster. [The sense is that *all* athletes use steroids, which is not true.]
Revised	Athletes who use steroids invite disaster. [Only those athletes who use steroids invite disaster.]

Four Ways to Avoid Comma Splices

1. Separate the two clauses with a period.

   Columbus is considered a master navigator today. He died in neglect.

2. Join the two clauses with a coordinating conjunction and a comma.

   Columbus is considered a master navigator today, but he died in neglect.

3. Join the two clauses with a conjunctive adverb and the appropriate punctuation.

   Columbus is considered a master navigator today; nevertheless, he died in neglect.

4. Join the two clauses by making one subordinate to the other.

   Although Columbus is considered a master navigator today, he died in neglect.

Commas are not used with essential elements. (See 25d.) The presence of commas can alter the meaning of otherwise identical sentences. Therefore, be sure of your meaning as you decide to punctuate (or not) a modifying element.

3 Eliminate commas that are misused in a series.

Confusing   For tomorrow, memorize the poem, and the song.

Revised   For tomorrow, memorize the poem and the song.

A comma is not placed before a coordinating conjunction if it connects only two elements in a series.

Faulty   You cannot learn much about prices, and the amount of goods traded from demand curves alone.

Revised   You cannot learn much about prices and the amount of goods traded from demand curves alone.

A comma is *not* used after a second coordinate adjective.

Faulty   Self-help books encourage individuals to imagine alternative, improved, selves.

Revised   Self-help books encourage individuals to imagine alternative, improved selves.

A comma is not placed before the first item in a series or after the last item, unless the comma is required because of a specific rule.

Faulty   A Central Processing Unit (CPU) has a fixed repertoire of instructions for carrying out tests involving**,** data manipulation, logical decision making, and control of the computer. [The comma should be eliminated before the first item in this series.]

Revised   A Central Processing Unit (CPU) has a fixed repertoire of instructions for carrying out tests involving data manipulation, logical decision making, and control of the computer.

4   Eliminate commas that split paired sentence elements.

Confusing   The police assisted**,** the emergency crew.
Revised   The police assisted the emergency crew.

A comma is not placed between a subject and verb—even if the subject is lengthy.

Faulty   What has sometimes been dramatically termed "the clash of civilizations**,**" is merely different societies' interpretations of the same acts. [The noun clause subject should not be split from its verb *is*.]

Revised   What has sometimes been dramatically termed "the clash of civilizations" is merely different societies' interpretations of the same acts.

A comma is not placed between a verb and its object or complement, nor between a preposition and its object.

Faulty   One culture may organize**,** its social relations around rites of initiation. [The comma should not come between the verb and its object.]

Revised   One culture may organize its social relations around rites of initiation.

Faulty   The principle of mutual respect among**,** neighboring peoples requires flexibility and tolerance. [The comma should not come between the preposition and its object.]

Revised   The principle of mutual respect among neighboring peoples requires flexibility and tolerance.

5   Eliminate misuse of commas with quotations.

Confusing   "Is anyone home**?,**" he asked.
Revised   "Is anyone home**?**" he asked.

A comma is not used after a quotation that ends with a question mark or an exclamation point.

Faulty   "Get out!," cried the shopkeeper.

Revised   "Get out!" cried the shopkeeper.

Faulty   "Is this the way home?," asked Arthur.

Revised   "Is this the way home?" asked Arthur.

A comma is not used to set apart words quoted (or italicized) for emphasis.

Faulty   The Governor's list of, "exemplary," citizens includes a
              convicted felon.

Revised   The Governor's list of "exemplary" citizens includes a
              convicted felon.

EXERCISE 6

Supply the commas for this dialogue between a young child and her nurse, adapted from Amy Tan's *The Joy Luck Club*.

> I tugged Amah's sleeve and asked "Who is the Moon Lady?"
> "Chang-o" replied Amah "who lives on the moon and today is the only day you can see her and have a secret wish fulfilled."
> "What is a secret wish?" I asked her.
> "It is what you want but cannot ask" said Amah.
> "Then how will the Moon Lady know my wish?" I wanted to know.
> "Because she is not an ordinary person" Amah explained.

EXERCISE 7

Correct the misuse of commas in the sentences that follow (from a parody of an anthropological study). Place a check before the sentences in which commas are used correctly.

> *Example:*   The daily body ritual, performed by the Nacirema people
>   includes a mouth-rite.
>
>   The daily body ritual performed by the Nacirema people
>   includes a mouth-rite.

1. Despite the fact that these people are so punctilious about the care of the mouth, this rite involves, a practice which strikes the uninitiated stranger as revolting.

2. It was reported to me that the ritual consists of inserting a small bundle of hog hairs into the mouth, along with certain magical powders, and then moving the bundle in a highly formalized series of gestures.

3. In addition to! the private mouth-rite, the people seek out a holy-mouth-man once, or twice a year.

4. These practitioners have an impressive set of paraphernalia, consisting of a variety of, augers, awls, probes, and prods.

5. The use of these objects in the exorcism of the evils of the mouth involves, almost unbelievable ritual torture of the client.

6. The holy-mouth-man opens the client's mouth and using the above-mentioned tools enlarges any holes which decay may have created in the teeth.

7. Magical materials are put into, these holes.

8. If there are no naturally occurring holes in the teeth, large sections of one or more teeth are gouged out so that the supernatural substance, can be applied.

9. In the client's view, the purpose of these ministrations is to arrest decay, and to draw friends.

10. The extremely sacred and traditional character of the rite is evident in the fact that the natives return to the holy-mouth-men year after year, despite the fact that their teeth continue to decay.

EXERCISE 8

25.3

Correct the misuse of commas in the following paragraph. In making your corrections, you may need to add or delete words. You should feel free to combine sentences.

Example: The humidity level which was extremely high made the air feel as if it were 117 degrees.

The humidity level, which was extremely high, made the air feel as if it were 117 degrees.

It's no illusion that the earth has been getting hotter lately. For example the 1980s witnessed the hottest years since meteorological records began to be kept in the nineteenth century, in fact, the 1990s which so far have been a continuation of the same trend promise to remain just as warm and maybe even warmer. As one scientific observer put it "Planet Earth is running a fever." The killer heat wave, that claimed 566 lives in Chicago in July 1995, could have been a freak event but climatologists don't think so. They fear that the big heat wave of 1995 is actually a harbinger of more serious weather disturbances to come.

CHAPTER

26

Semicolons

Weblink
http://webster.commnet.edu/
grammar/marks/semicolon.htm
The semicolon: Its proper care and feeding.

emicolons are used to separate independent sentence elements. They represent a middle choice between commas and periods because they create a partial break while maintaining a relationship between the elements.

26a | **Use a semicolon, not a comma, to join independent clauses that are intended to be closely related.**

Secretariat won the race; Lucky Stars finished second.

Joining independent clauses with a semicolon is one of four basic ways to establish a relationship between clauses. (See the Critical Decisions box on page 455.) Never use a comma to join independent clauses. (See Chapter 13 on comma splices.)

Faulty In 1852 Mt. Everest was identified as the world's highest mountain, shortly thereafter it was named in honor of Sir George Everest.

Revised In 1852 Mt. Everest was identified as the world's highest mountain; shortly thereafter it was named in honor of Sir George Everest.

Use semicolons to join closely related independent clauses, not to string unconnected statements together.

Semicolons can be overused. By themselves, they are not enough to make close connections among a series of statements that are simply added together.

Overused In 1852 Mt. Everest was identified as the world's highest mountain; at the time it was believed to be 29,002 feet; its actual altitude is 29,028 feet.

Revised Mt. Everest, identified in 1852 as the world's highest mountain, was believed at the time to be 29,002 feet; its actual altitude is 29,028 feet.

CRITICAL DECISIONS

Using a Period to Separate Sentences Versus a Semicolon or Comma (with a Conjunction) to Link Sentences

26.1

As a writer, you can use punctuation to communicate degrees of linkage between sentences. In making decisions, pose these questions.

■ **Why separate sentences with a period?**

Use a period to show a full separation between sentences.

> Dante Alighieri was banished from Florence in 1302. He wrote the *Divine Comedy* in exile.

■ **Why link sentences with a semicolon?**

Use a semicolon, alone, to join sentences balanced in content and structure. Also use a semicolon to suggest that the second sentence completes the content of the first. The semicolon suggests a link but leaves it to the reader to infer how sentences are related.

| **Balanced sentence** | Agriculture is one part of the biological revolution**;** the domestication of animals is the other. |
| **Suggested link** | Five major books and many articles have been written on the Bayeux tapestry**;** each shows just how much the trained observer can draw from pictorial evidence. |

■ **Why link sentences with a conjunctive adverb and a semicolon or period?**

Use a semicolon with a conjunctive adverb (*however, therefore*, etc.) to emphasize one of the following relationships: addition, consequence, contrast, cause and effect, time, emphasis, or condition. With the semicolon and conjunctive adverb, linkage between sentences is closer than with a semicolon alone. The relationship between sentences is made clear by the conjunctive adverb.

> Patients in need of organs have begun advertising for them**; however,** the American Medical Association discourages the practice.

Use a period between sentences to force a pause and then to stress the conjunctive adverb.

> Patients in need of organs have begun advertising for them. **However,** the American Medical Association discourages the practice.

■ **Why link sentences with a comma and a coordinating conjunction?**

Use a comma and a coordinating conjunction to join sentences in a co-ordinate relationship that shows addition, choice, consequence, contrast, or cause (see 19a). Since two sentences are fully merged into one following this strategy, linkage is complete.

> Robotics has increased efficiency in the automobile industry, **but** it has put thousands of assembly-line employees out of work.

Use a semicolon, not a comma, to join two independent clauses that are closely linked by a conjunctive adverb.

I had planned to call London; however, the circuits were busy.

Eric arrived late the first day; thereafter, he was on time.

A conjunctive adverb is often used to establish a close connection between independent clauses. (See 19a and the Critical Decisions box on page 455.) With conjunctive adverbs, use a semicolon (or a period) between the clauses, never a comma. (Refer to Chapter 13.)

Faulty   Historians cannot control the events they research, indeed, they often cannot find enough documentation to learn all the facts. [The comma after *research* makes a comma splice.]

Revised   Historians cannot control the events they research; indeed, they often cannot find enough documentation to learn all the facts.

Note: When independent clauses are closely connected with a conjunctive adverb, the semicolon always falls between the clauses, no matter where the conjunctive adverb is located.

Option   Chlorophyll extracted from plant cells and exposed to light momentarily absorbs light energy; *however*, this energy is almost immediately reradiated as light.

Option   Chlorophyll extracted from plant cells and exposed to light momentarily absorbs light energy; this energy is almost immediately reradiated as light, *however*. [The semicolon falls between the independent clauses, even if the adverb is moved to the end of the sentence.]

Note: The use of a conjunctive adverb does not necessarily mean that there must be a semicolon between clauses. You can always make a full break between clauses with a period.

Option   Chlorophyll extracted from plant cells and exposed to light momentarily absorbs light energy. This energy, however, is almost immediately reradiated as light.

26c **Join independent clauses with a semicolon before a coordinating conjunction when one or both clauses contain a comma or other internal punctuation.**

After the Shuttle landed, Perkins tried calling the President; but he didn't get through.

Short or uncomplicated independent clauses joined by coordinating conjunctions do not normally use a semicolon. However, internal commas can create confusion and misreading. In such cases the clauses need stronger separation with a semicolon before the coordinating conjunction.

> Agnosognosia, a normally temporary condition that often afflicts right-hemisphere stroke victims, manifests itself as the patient's denial of the physical existence of the paralyzed limb; and it is for this reason that neuroscientists are studying agnosognosia for clues about how the brain constructs reality.

26d Use a semicolon to separate items in a series when each item is long or when one or more items contain a comma.

I sent the letters to Baltimore, Maryland; Portland, Oregon; and Dallas, Texas.

Short or uncomplicated items in a series are normally separated only by commas (see Chapter 25). However, when the units to be separated include internal punctuation or are made up of complex clauses, it is necessary to provide stronger separation with a semicolon.

> One neuroscientist interested in the functions and malfunctions of the brain has investigated the neural wiring of vision; the riddle of agnosognosia; and, through research into the "phantom limb" phenomenon experienced by amputees, the ways in which the brain reconfigures itself during learning.

26e Place semicolons *outside* of end quotation marks.

We read "Ode to the West Wind"; we then discussed the poem in detail.

A semicolon that separates independent clauses and other major elements is not part of a direct quotation.

> One neurologist remarks that "we are used to thinking of our bodies as our selves"; in other words, unlike agnosogniacs, we "own" our body parts and have no trouble with expressing that ownership.

26f Edit to avoid common errors.

> Use a comma, not a semicolon, after an introductory subordinate clause.

Use semicolons to link independent clauses. Never use them to link subordinate to independent clauses (see Chapter 19).

Edit to Avoid Common Errors 457

Faulty	When a writer begins a new project**;** the blank page can present a barrier.
Revised	When a writer begins a new project**,** the blank page can present a barrier.

2   **Use a colon, not a semicolon, to introduce a list.**

Faulty	The writing process consists of three stages**;** planning, drafting, and revision.
Revised	The writing process consists of three stages**:** planning, drafting, and revision.

EXERCISE I

Join the following pairs of sentences with a semicolon, with a semicolon and conjunctive adverb, or with a period and conjunctive adverb. Explain your decision.

> *Example:*   Politics and social realism have not been the hallmarks of the film industry in Hollywood.
>
> Yet there was a time when liberal, conservative, and radical organizations made films for a mass audience aimed at politicizing millions of viewers.
>
> Politics and social realism have not been the hallmarks of the film industry in Hollywood**;** yet there was a time when liberal, conservative, and radical organizations made films for a mass audience aimed at politicizing millions of viewers.

The sentences are closely enough related in meaning to warrant their being joined into a single, compound sentence. For this reason, the semicolon is appropriate. The conjunction *yet* is kept to establish the contrasting relationship between clauses. Without the conjunction this relationship might not be obvious to a reader.

1. During the early years of the twentieth century, leisure assumed an increasingly important role in everyday life.

   Amusement parks, professional baseball games, nickelodeons, and dance halls attracted a wide array of people anxious to spend their hard-earned cash.

2. Of all these new cultural endeavors, films were the most important.

   Even the poorest worker could afford to take his family to the local movie theater.

3. Cinemas took root in urban working-class and immigrant neighborhoods.

   They then spread to middle-class districts of cities and into small communities throughout the country.

4. As early as 1910 the appeal of movies was so great that nearly one-third of the nation flocked to the cinema each week.

   Ten years later, weekly attendance equaled fifty percent of the nation's population.

5. As is true today, early films were primarily aimed at entertaining audiences.

   But then, entertainment did not always come in the form of escapist fantasies.

6. Many of the issues that dominated Progressive-era politics were portrayed on the screen.

   While most of these films were produced by studios and independent companies, a significant number were made by what we might call today "special-interest groups."

7. The modest cost of making one- or two-reel films allowed many organizations to make movies to advance their causes.

   Moreover, exhibitors' need to fill their daily bills with new films meant these films would be seen by millions.

WWW

26.2

EXERCISE 2

In very long sentences semicolons are used in place of commas to prevent misreading. Combine, repunctuate, or otherwise revise the following sentences by using semicolons.

> *Example:* The traditional view of the diffusion of Indo-European languages over wide areas holds that as nomadic mounted warriors conquered indigenous peoples, they imposed their own proto-Indo-European language, *which*, in turn, evolved in local areas into the various languages we know today.
>
> But many scholars have become dissatisfied with this explanation.
>
> The traditional view of the diffusion of Indo-European languages over wide areas holds that as nomadic mounted warriors conquered indigenous peoples, they imposed their own proto-Indo-European language; *this language*, in turn, evolved in local areas into the various languages we know today. But many scholars have become dissatisfied with this explanation.

1. Linguists divide the languages of Europe into families: the Romance languages include French, Italian, Spanish, Portuguese, and Romanian.

   The Slavonic languages include Russian, Polish, Czech, Slovak, Serbo-Croat, and Bulgarian. The Germanic languages include German, Norwegian, Danish, and Swedish.

2. Many archaeologists accept a theory of "Kurgan invasions" as an explanation of the spread of Indo-European languages.

   But others dispute it because the archaeological evidence is not convincing, the core words, which resemble each other from place to place, may have changed meaning over time, and the hordes of mounted warriors would have had no obvious reason for moving west at the end of the Neolithic period.

3. There are four models of how language change might occur according to a process-based view: initial colonization, by which an uninhabited territory becomes populated, linguistic divergence arising from separation or isolation, which some think explains the development of the Romance languages in Europe, linguistic convergence, whereby languages initially quite different become increasingly similar to each other, and, finally, linguistic replacement, whereby indigenous languages are gradually replaced by the language of people coming from the outside.

www

26.3

EXERCISE 3

Correct the misuse of semicolons and, if necessary, the wording in the following sentences. Place a check by any sentence in which a semicolon is used correctly.

Example: Until the period of the Enlightenment, most Christians believed that an entity called the Devil existed**;** that he was not just a metaphor for evil but rather was evil incarnate.

   Until the period of the Enlightenment, most Christians believed that an entity called the Devil existed **and** that he was not just a metaphor for evil but rather was evil incarnate.

1. Some sociologists have argued that belief in a literal devil is a matter of social class; a Princeton professor explains: "If you see Cadillacs in the church parking lot, you won't hear Satan preached inside;" but "if you see a lot of pickup trucks, you will."

2. Late twentieth-century American culture; however, is by and large devoid of a sense of an actual Devil.

3. Our preference is to explain the existence of evil in scientific or pseudoscientific terms; serial murderers, terrorists, and bloodthirsty dictators are explained as psychopaths or sociopaths; evil is not perceived as punishment for our sins but rather as arbitrary and meaningless.

4. One cultural critic regards this loss of a sense of pure, radical evil as regrettable, he sees the disappearance of Satan as a "tragedy of the imagination."

Apostrophes

The **apostrophe** (') is used to show possession, mark the omission of letters or numbers, and mark plural forms. Decisions about the use of apostrophes involve questions of function and placement.

27a Using apostrophes to show possession with single nouns

1 For most nouns and for indefinite pronouns, add an apostrophe and the letter *s* to indicate possession.

Bill**'s** braces	somebody**'s** cat
history**'s** verdict	everyone**'s** business

For singular nouns ending with the letter *s*, *show possession by adding an apostrophe and s* if this new construction is not difficult to pronounce.

Ellis**'s** Diner	hostess**'s** menu	Diane Arbus**'s** work

CRITICAL DECISIONS

Using Apostrophes According to Convention

In almost every case, apostrophes are required by the conventions explained in this chapter. Their use is rarely governed by questions of style. You must, therefore, make sure that you clearly understand when apostrophes are needed (and not needed) and where they are correctly inserted. Many regard misuse of apostrophes as a mark of extreme carelessness if not downright incompetence.

Note: The possessive construction formed with *'s* may be difficult to read if the *s* at the end of the original word is sounded like *z*. If this is the case, you have the option of dropping the *s* after the apostrophe.

Acceptable   Orson Welle**s'** movie   or   Orson Welles**'s** movie

Whichever convention you adopt, be consistent.

2	**Eliminate apostrophes that are misused or confused with possessive pronouns.**

Personal pronouns have their own possessive case forms (see Chapter 8). They *never* use apostrophes to show possession.

Possession with personal pronouns

your book	The book is *yours.*
their book	The book is *theirs.*
her book	The book is *hers.*
our book	The book is *ours.*
his book	The book is *his.*
its binding	*Whose* book is this?

Distinguish personal pronouns in their possessive form from personal pronouns that are contractions.

Weblink

http://www.apostrophe.fsnet.co.uk/
Home page of the Apostrophe Protection Society, created to preserve correct usage of this "much abused punctuation mark."

For many readers, the most annoying mixup with apostrophes occurs when personal pronouns meant to show possession are confused with personal pronouns that are contractions formed with the verb *be*, as shown here. (See the guidelines for making contractions in 27c.)

Personal pronouns: Contractions formed with Be

It's [It is] doubtful he will arrive.
Who's [Who is] planning to attend?
You're [You are] mistaken.
They're [They are] home.

Edit to eliminate apostrophes from personal pronouns that are meant to show possession, not contraction.

Faulty   You're order has arrived.
Revised   Your order has arrived.

> **3**
>
> For a plural noun ending with *s*, add only an apostrophe to indicate possession. For a plural noun not ending with *s*, add an apostrophe and the letter *s*.

bricklayer**s'** union
children**'s** games

teacher**s'** strike
men**'s** locker

EXERCISE 1

Read the following sentences. As needed, use an apostrophe or an apostrophe and the letter *s* to make possessive each noun or pronoun in parentheses.

> *Example:* With Windows, even the simple task of switching your computer off is serious business—you have to follow the (System) commands for shutdown.
>
> With Windows, even the simple task of switching your computer off is serious business—you have to follow the System**'s** commands for shutdown.

1. In fact, you can't hit that off switch until Windows tells you that (its) safe to do so.
2. If you make it a habit to close each window once you've finished with it, you'll find that (you're) work space is maximized.
3. The (Welcome window) function is to provide you with a new Windows tip each time you start a new session.
4. In Windows, a (file name) length can be as long as you want to make it.
5. Older (systems) file names had to be kept to an 8-character length (with a 3-character extension).
6. That long file name option sounds like a real advantage until you realize that if the particular program you are using still follows the 8-character rule, your (files) names are not going to be any longer; Windows can't override your program.
7. On the other hand, the 8-character parameter challenges the (user) creativity—how else would you end up with a file name like "taxoops," a file that is actually a letter to the Internal Revenue Service.
8. Software developers know that Windows is not the cure-all for all computer ills and that awful things—like crashes—are still going to happen; (CyberMedia) software package, *First Aid for Windows*, promises to doctor your ailing system.
9. *(First Aid for Windows)* packaging even features the familiar Red Cross logo.

10. With PC healthcare systems readily available, the "DUMMIES" user need worry no more about a (device-driver) incompatibility.

11. The user doesn't have to wait for what seems like hours, waiting for the technical support (staff) advice.

27b Using apostrophes to show possession with multiple nouns

Multiple nouns showing possession can be tricky to punctuate, since the apostrophe and the letter *s* will indicate who—and how many people—own what, either separately or together. Punctuate so that your sentences express your exact meaning.

 To indicate possession when a cluster of words functions as a single noun, add an apostrophe and the letter *s* to the last word.

brother-in-law**'s** car   Chief Executive Officer**'s** salary

 To indicate possession of an object owned jointly, add an apostrophe and the letter *s* to the last noun (or pronoun) named.

Smith and Thompson**'s** interview notes are meticulous. [The notes belong jointly to, they were gathered jointly by, Smith and Thompson.]

 To indicate individual possession by two or more people, add an apostrophe and the letter *s* to each person named.

Judy**'s** and Rob**'s** interview notes are meticulous. [The reference is to two sets of notes, one belonging to Judy and the other to Rob.]

27c Using apostrophes in contractions to mark the omission of letters and numbers

When you join words into a contraction, you omit letters to indicate a more rapid, informal pace of pronunciation. The omission *must* be marked in writing with an apostrophe. Similarly, when you omit numbers in a date, use an apostrophe. Because many readers consider contractions an informality, you may want to avoid using them in academic writing.

CRITICAL DECISIONS

Distinguishing Between Plurals and Possessives

Apply the following tests to determine whether you should be using an apostrophe and *s* (*'s*) or the suffix *-s*, with no apostrophe.

Is the noun followed by a noun? If so, then you probably intend to show possession. Use the possessive form *'s*.

government's <u>policy</u>   family's <u>holiday</u>

Is a noun followed by a verb or a modifying phrase? If so, then you probably intend to make the noun plural. Use the suffix *-s*, with *no* apostrophe.

governments <u>in that part of the world</u>

famil*ies* <u>having two or more children</u>

But if an omitted word is involved, you may need a possessive form.

Eric's friends attend Central High. Frank's attend Northern.

[In the second sentence, the omitted noun *friends* is clearly intended as the subject of the sentence. The *'s* is needed to show whose friends—*Frank's*.]

WWW

27.1

1   Use an apostrophe to indicate the omission of letters in a contraction.

can**'t** = can not   won**'t** = will not   you**'ve** = you have

2   Use an apostrophe to indicate the omission of numbers in a date.

the **'**60s   the **'**80s   the **'**90s

3   Eliminate apostrophes from verbs in their -s form.

The *-s* ending used in regular verb formation does *not* involve the omission of any letters (see 9a). Any apostrophe that creeps into such verb endings should be eliminated.

Faulty   He walk's with a limp.   A cat eat's mice.

Revised   He wal**ks** with a limp.   A cat ea**ts** mice.

EXERCISE 2

Correct the use of apostrophes in the following sentences by adding or deleting apostrophes as needed. Place a check by the sentences in which apostrophes are used correctly.

> *Example:* Rough weather sailing can be exciting, but only if you're crew is well prepared for it.
>
> Rough weather sailing can be exciting, but only if your crew is well prepared for it.

1. Bad weather inevitably puts you're crew**'s** lives in danger.
2. Obviously their likely to be wetter and colder; foul weather gear should be available and distributed *before* the first splash lands in the cockpit.
3. Its equally important to take precautions to prevent risk of injury to limbs and body.
4. Those who normally lead a sedentary life are much more liable to injuries than those whose muscles are well exercised to withstand rubs, bumps, and twists.
5. Inadequate footwear, or none at all if you're feet are not hardened to such treatment, can lead to real pain if a toe is stubbed against a deck bolt or stanchion.
6. Make sure you have a working man-overboard pole—you're attention to safety could save someone's life.
7. Bad weather is particularly tiring and can result in seasickness; keep a watch to see whose becoming sick.
8. Seasickness and exhaustion combined can lead to a state of not caring what happens next to your boat and crew.
9. An exhausted sailor huddled in a wave- and windswept cockpit, peering into the murk, can easily come to see Poseidon, whose lashing the waves to fury out of spite.
10. Perhaps the easiest precaution to avoid problems in raw weather is to bring a crew whose not afraid of the tense environment faced while sailing in rough seas.

27d Using apostrophes to mark plural forms

If we were to follow the convention of using the letter *s* or letters *es* to show the plural of letters or symbols, we would quickly create a puzzle of pronunciation: *How many les in Lilliputian?* We avoid the confusion by using apostrophes.

Use an apostrophe and the letter *s* to indicate the plural of a letter, number, or word referred to as a word.

The letter, number, or word made plural should be underlined if typewritten or set in italics if typeset. Do *not* underline or italicize the apostrophe or the letter *s*.

```
Mind your p's and q's.    How many 5's in sixty?
The frequent in's and with's reduced the effectiveness
of his presentation.
```

Exception: When forming the plural of a proper noun (e.g., someone's name), omit the apostrophe but retain the letter *s*. Using an apostrophe in this case would mistakenly suggest possession and thus confuse a reader.

At the convention I met three *Frank***s** and two *Maude***s**.

2

Use an apostrophe and the letter *s* to indicate the plural of a symbol, an abbreviation with periods, and years expressed in decades.

Do *not* underline or italicize the symbol, the abbreviation, or the decade.

Joel is too fond of using &**'s** in his writing.

With all the M.D.**'s** at this conference, I feel safe.

Computer-assisted software engineering will be important in the 1990**'s**.

Option: Some writers omit the apostrophe before the letter *s* when forming the plural of decades, abbreviations without periods, and symbols.

1900**s**   IBM**s**   %**s**

Whichever convention you adopt, be consistent.

Eliminate any apostrophes misused to form regular plurals of nouns.

An apostrophe is never used to create a plural form of a regular noun.

Faulty plural   Cat**'s** eat meat.   Idea**'s** begin in thought.
Revised plural   Cat**s** eat.   Idea**s** begin.

EXERCISE 3

Follow the instructions in parentheses after each sentence to clarify possession.

Example: The *governor office personnel* have formed some close friendships. (Use apostrophes to indicate that the people who have become friends work in the office of the governor.)

The governor**'s** office personnel have formed some close friendships.

1. Isabelle Locke works at the State House as the *governor Press Secretary.* (Use apostrophes to indicate that the Press Secretary for the governor is Isabelle Locke.)

2. *Mrs. Locke and her husband Ted house* is replete with pictures of government officials posing with the Locke family. (Use apostrophes to indicate that Mrs. Locke and Ted own their house together.)

3. The governor lives around the corner, in the *Governor Mansion.* (Use apostrophes to indicate that the governor lives in the mansion.)

4. *Isabelle Locke and the governor homes* are decorated similarly, both in a colonial style. (Use apostrophes to indicate that two different homes are being referred to.)

5. Often they'll have dinner together, cooked by *Isabelle and the governor husbands.* (Use apostrophes to indicate that the two husbands cook together.)

EXERCISE 4

Decide whether an apostrophe is needed to form plurals for the following letters, numbers, or words.

Example: b

b̲'s (or *b*'s if typeset)

1. &
2. 42
3. 7
4. j
5. d
6. Karen

EXERCISE 5

Read the following paragraph about Donald Duck. Provide apostrophes and rewrite words as needed.

Theirs one basic product never stocked in Disneys store: parents. Disneys is a universe of uncles and grand-uncles, nephews and cousins. The male-female relationships existence is found only in eternal fiancés. Donald Duck and Daisy relationship, like

Mickey Mouse and Minnie relationship, is never consummated or even legitimized through the all-American institution of marriage. More troubling, though, is the origin of all of the nephews and uncles in the Disney Comics worlds. Huey, Dewey, and Louie Uncle Donald is never known to have a sister or sister-in-law. In fact, most of Donald relatives are unmarried and unattached males, like Scrooge McDuck. Donalds own parents are never mentioned, although Grandma Duck purports to be the widowed ancestor of the Duck family (again no husband-wife relationship). Donald and Mickey girlfriends, Daisy and Minnie, are often accompanied by nieces of their own. Since these women are not very susceptible to men or matrimonial bonds, Disneys "families" are necessarily and perpetually composed of bachelors accompanied by nephews, who come and go. A quick look at Walt Disneys own biography demonstrates a possible reason for his comics anti-love, anti-marriage sentiments: Disneys mother is rarely mentioned, and his wifes role in his life was minimal at best. As for the future of the Magic Kingdoms demographic increases, it is predictable that they will be the result of extrasexual factors.

27.2

CHAPTER **28**

Quotation Marks

Q uoting the words of others is a necessary, essential fact of academic life. For the sake of both accuracy and fairness, your quotations must be managed precisely. (See 35f on quoting sources in research.) Correctly using quotation marks involves decisions about when they are (and are not) required and where and how they are placed.

CRITICAL DECISIONS

Knowing Not to Substitute Apostrophes for Quotation Marks

Apostrophes and quotation marks do not serve the same functions. While few writers would be likely to substitute quotation marks for apostrophes in error, it is not uncommon for writers to use a single quotation mark, which has the same form as an apostrophe ('), where double quotation marks are required. American usage differs in some respects from English and other British-influenced usage. Be sure that you use quotation marks in all instances described in this chapter.

28a Quoting prose

1 Use double quotation marks (" ") to set off a short direct quotation from the rest of a sentence.

Weblink

http://owl.english.purdue.edu/
handouts/grammar/g_quote.html
A page on quotation marks, from the Purdue University Online Writing Lab.

Short quotations—those that span four or fewer lines of your manuscript—may be incorporated into your writing by running them in with your sentences as part of your normal paragraphing. When quoting a source, you reproduce exactly the wording and punctuation of the quoted material, indicating **direct discourse.**

470

| **Direct** | In a letter to his sister, Russian playwright Anton Chekov wrote, "When one is traveling, one must absolutely be alone." |
| | Eric asked, "Can I borrow the car?" |

Note: Indirect discourse occurs when you quote the words of someone inexactly. Such quotes are never set off with quotation marks:

| **Indirect** | Eric asked if he could borrow the car. |

Altering a quotation: Quotation marks denote the *exact* reproduction of words written or spoken by someone else. Changes that you make to quoted material (such as words omitted or added) must be announced as such—either with brackets or with ellipses (see 29d and e)

2 Use single quotation marks (' ') to set off quoted material or the titles of short works within a quotation enclosed by double (" ") marks.

Original passages

The "business" of school for first-grade students is to learn the distinction between intellectual play and playground play.

In preparation for class next week, read the first two chapters of our "In Flight" manual.

Quotations

As educator Monica Landau says, "The 'business' of school for first-grade students is to learn the distinction between intellectual play and playground play."

The class coordinator said that for next week we should "read the first two chapters of our 'In Flight' manual."

If you find it necessary to quote material within single quotation marks, use double marks once again.

3 Use commas to enclose explanatory remarks that lie outside the quotation.

Place a comma after an explanatory remark that introduces a quotation.

According to Bailey, "Competition was the key term in the formula—remove it and there was no rating, dating, or popularity."

When a remark interrupts a quotation, a pair of commas or a comma and a period should be used. The comma preceding the explanatory remark is placed inside the quotation. The comma or period following the remark precedes the continuing quotation. Use a comma following the remark when the remark interrupts a sentence. Use a period when the second part of the quotation begins a new sentence.

> "Rating, dating, popularity, competition," writes Bailey, "were catch-words hammered home, reinforced from all sides until they seemed a natural vocabulary."

> "You had to rate in order to date, to date in order to rate," she adds. "By successfully maintaining the cycle, you became popular."

Note: When the word *that* introduces a direct quotation, or when an introductory remark has the sense of a "that" construction but the word itself is omitted, do not use a comma to separate the introduction from the quoted material. In addition, do not capitalize the first letter of the quotation.

Faulty   Bailey discovered that, "The Massachusetts *Collegian* (the Massachusetts State College student newspaper) ran an editorial against using the library for 'datemaking.'"

Revised   Bailey discovered that "the Massachusetts *Collegian* (the Massachusetts State College student newspaper) ran an editorial against using the library for 'datemaking.'"

COMPUTER TIPS

Smart Quotes

Most word processors offer you a set of fancy typesetter's quotation marks and apostrophes. These smart quotes or curly quotes (" " and ' ') are different from the inch and foot marks (" and ') available on typewriters. For material that will ultimately be submitted in print, use the typesetter's quotes, which look more attractive on the page. However, if the material is to be e-mailed, or published on the World Wide Web, use the old-style typewriter marks, because the curly quotes use nonstandard characters that are interpreted differently by different computers. For example, if you type *a baker's dozen* in your e-mail message, it may appear on your reader's computer as *a bakerUs dozen*. Most good word-processing programs allow you to turn the curly quotes on or off, and some even allow you to convert the quotes in a piece of text from curly to typewriter style.

4 Display—that is, set off from text—lengthy quotations. Quotation marks are *not* used to enclose a displayed quotation.

Quotations of five or more lines are too long to run in with sentences in a paragraph. Instead they are displayed in a block format in a narrower indentation, without being enclosed by quotation marks.

In his remarks, Bill Bradley spoke on the impressive economic growth of East Asia:

> East Asia is quickly becoming the richest, most populous, most dynamic area on earth. Over the last quarter century, the East Asian economies grew at an average real growth rate of 6 percent annually while the economies of the United States and the countries of the European Community grew at 3 percent. East Asia's share of gross world product has more than doubled during the last twenty years, rising from 8 percent to 20 percent.

Manuscript form for displayed quotation

- Double space the displayed quotation and indent ten spaces from the left margin.
- Punctuate material as in the original text.
- Keep quotation marks inside a displayed quotation, using double (" ") marks.
- Do not indent the first word of the paragraph if one paragraph is being displayed. If multiple paragraphs are being displayed, indent the first word of each paragraph three additional spaces (that is, thirteen spaces from the left). However, if you are quoting multiple paragraphs and the first sentence quoted does not begin a paragraph in the original source, then do not indent the first paragraph in your paper.

A displayed quotation is best introduced with a full sentence, ending with a colon.

5 Place periods and commas inside the end quotation mark.

"The big question is whether this kind of growth is sustainable," says Bradley.

He adds, "Asian nations can no longer count as heavily on expanding exports to the United States to fuel their growth."

Exception: When a pair of parentheses enclosing some comment or page reference appears between the end of the quotation and the end of the sentence, use quotation marks to note the end of the quoted text, place the parentheses, and then close with a period.

He adds, "Asian nations can no longer count as heavily on expanding exports to the United States to fuel their growth" **(1).**

| | **6** | Place colons, semicolons, and footnotes outside end quotation marks. |

Colon   Bradley asserts that "the futures of Asia and the United States are inextricably intertwined": Asian countries profit by U.S. growth, and the U.S. must profit by Asian growth.

Semicolon   Bradley believes that the United States must look to the East with the intention of forming a "strong, lasting partnership"; moreover, we must do so without condescension.

Footnote   Bradley believes that the United States and the East must form a "strong, lasting partnership."[4]

| | **7** | Place question marks and exclamation points inside or outside end quotation marks, depending on meaning. |

Mark applies to quoted material only

Naturalist José Márcio Ayres began his field work with this question: "How do these primates survive almost exclusively on the pulp and seeds of fruit, when the forests in which they live are flooded much of the year?"

Mark applies both to quoted material and to sentence as whole

How can we appreciate the rigors of field research when even Ayres remarks, "Is the relative protection of the ukaris's habitat at all surprising in light of the enormous swarms of mosquitoes one encounters?"

Mark applies to sentence as a whole but not to quotation

Ayres reports that among ukaris males looking for mates fights are frequent and that "after all this trouble, copulation may last less than two minutes"!

| | **8** | Place dashes inside quotations only when they are part of the quoted material. |

Part of quoted material

Competitors such as "brocket deer, peccaries, agoutis, armadillos, and pacas—mammals common in upland habitats—" do not inhabit the ukaris's forest.

Separate from quoted material

Each afternoon the ukaris descend from the upper canopy of trees—"where the temperature is uncomfortably high"—to forage for seedlings.

EXERCISE 1

Use double quotation marks (" ") and single quotation marks (' ') to punctuate the sentences that follow. Words to be quoted are underlined.

> *Example:* According to Carla Fernandez, <u>One third of all offenders are in prison because of property offenses such as larceny, car theft, and burglary.</u>
>
> According to Carla Fernandez, "One third of all offenders are in prison because of property offenses such as larceny, car theft, and burglary."

1. Half of the prison population has been incarcerated for <u>violent crimes such as assault, homicide, and rape.</u>

2. The remaining 20 percent of offenders have been convicted of <u>offenses against public order,</u> such as drug dealing.

3. In a speech on March 2, 1992, New York corrections official Stuart Koman voiced a widely held view: <u>Overcrowded prisons not only do not rehabilitate offenders, they teach offenders to reject the law-abiding life. One individual who has spent 13 of his 25 years behind bars said to me that "I learned my techniques in jail. You know, the tools of my trade."</u>

4. As sociologist Lauren Rose concludes, <u>Efforts to reform prisons and to make them real *penitentiaries*—institutions of penitence— have failed (Jacobs 341).</u>

5. <u>One dilemma that we now face,</u> according to Rolf Hanson, <u>is to understand whether we want incarceration to correct criminal behavior or to punish it.</u>

28.1

28b Quoting poetry, dialogue, and other material

> Run-in brief quotations of poetry with your sentences.
> Indicate line breaks in the poem with a slash (/).
> Quote longer passages in displayed form.

A full quotation of or a lengthy quotation from a poem is normally made in displayed form (see 28a-4).

In "My Heart Leaps Up," William Wordsworth meditates on the importance of our enduring connection to nature:

> My heart leaps up when I behold
>   A rainbow in the sky:
> So was it when my life began;
> So is it now I am a man;
> So be it when I shall grow old,
>   Or let me die!

> The child is father of the Man;
> And I could wish my days to be
> Bound each to each by natural piety.

If you omit a line or lines, show the omission with an ellipsis: a line of spaced periods approximately the same length as other lines in the poem.

> My heart leaps up when I behold
>   A rainbow in the sky:
> So was it when my life began;
> . . . .
> The child is father of the Man;
> And I could wish my days to be
> Bound each to each by natural piety.

When quoting four lines or fewer, you can run the lines into the paragraph, using the guidelines for quoting prose (see 28a). However, line divisions are shown with a slash (/) with one space before and one space after. Note that omitted lines are indicated with an ellipsis—the same convention used when altering quoted prose. (See 29e.)

> In "My Heart Leaps Up," William Wordsworth meditates on the importance of our enduring connection to nature: "My heart leaps up when I behold / A rainbow in the sky: / So was it when my life began; / So is it now I am a man. . . ."

CRITICAL DECISIONS

Knowing When and How Much to Quote

Quote other writers when you find their discussions to be particularly lively, dramatic, or incisive or especially helpful in bolstering your credibility (see 35f). In general, quote as little as possible so that you keep readers focused on *your* discussion. The examples in this box draw on the following passage about shopping malls by the noted anthropologist Richard Stein *(The New American Bazaar)*.

> When they are successful, shopping malls in American cities fulfill the same function as *bazaars* did in the cities of antiquity. The bazaars of the ancient and medieval worlds were social organisms—if we mean by this term self-contained, self-regulating systems in which individual human lives are less important (and less interesting) than the interaction of hundreds, and sometimes thousands, of lives.

■ **Quote a word or a phrase, if this will do.**

> Anthropologist Richard Stein refers to the American shopping mall as a "social organism."

- **Quote a sentence, if needed.**

    Stein sees in shopping malls a modern spin on an ancient institution: "When they are successful, shopping malls in American cities fulfill the same function as *bazaars* did in the cities of antiquity."

- **Infrequently quote a long passage as a "block."**

    Limit your use of block quotations, which tempt writers to avoid the hard work of selecting for quotation *only* the words or sentences especially pertinent to a discussion. Always introduce a block quotation with a full sentence and a colon, such as the following introduction to the passage previously quoted.

    Various commentators have claimed that shopping malls serve a social function. Anthropologist Richard Stein compares the mall to the bazaar in cities of old:

---

2   Use quotation marks to quote or write dialogue.

28.2

When quoting or writing dialogue, change paragraphs to note each change of speaker. When using explanatory comments, place commas and periods following the conventions for quotations as outlined in 28a-1.

"Nobody sees you any more, Helen," Nat began. "Where've you disappeared to?"

"Oh, I've been around," she said, trying to hide a slight tremble in her voice. "And you?"

"Is somebody there where you're talking that you sound so restrained?"

"That's right."

—BERNARD MALAMUD, *The Assistant*

In a speech of two or more paragraphs, begin each new paragraph with opening quotation marks to signal your reader that the speech continues. Use closing quotation marks *only* at the end of the final paragraph to signal that the speech has concluded.

3   Indicate the titles of brief works with quotation marks: chapters of books, short stories, poems, songs, sections from newspapers, essays, etc.[1]

I read the "Focus Section" of the *Boston Sunday Globe* every week.

"The Dead" is, perhaps, Joyce's most famous short story.

"Coulomb's law" is the first chapter in volume two of Gartenhaus's text, *Physics: Basic Principles*.

[1]The titles of longer works—books, newspapers, magazines, long poems—are underlined in typewritten text and italicized in typeset text. (See Chapter 37.)

Manuscript form

The title of a paper you are submitting to an instructor or peers should *not* be put in quotation marks. Only use quotation marks when you are quoting a title *in* a paper or if your title itself contains a title—a reference to some other work. For example, if the title of your paper included a reference to a poem, the title would look like this:

> Loneliness in Stephen Crane's "The Black Riders"

This same title, referred to *in* a sentence:

> In his essay "Loneliness in Stephen Crane's 'The Black Riders,'" Marcus Trudeau argues that Crane's universe is unknowable and indifferent.

When a title is included in any other quoted material, change double quotation marks (" ") to single marks (' ').

4   **Use quotation marks occasionally to emphasize words or to note invented words.**

An uncommon usage of a standard term or a new term that has been invented for a special circumstance can be highlighted with quotation marks. Once you have emphasized a word with quotation marks, you need not use the marks again with that word.

> We can designate as "low interactive" any software title that does not challenge learners to think. Low-interactive titles may be gorgeous to look at, but looking—not thinking—is what they invite learners to do.

Words that will be defined in a sentence, or that are referred to as words, are usually italicized, though they may be set in quotations. Definitions are generally placed in quotation marks.

> The meaning of the Latin injunction *carpe diem* is "seize the day."

28c   Eliminating misused or overused quotation marks

1   **Eliminate phrases using quotation marks to note slang or colloquial expressions.**

If your use of slang is appropriate for your paper, then no quotation marks are needed. If, on the other hand, you are uncomfortable with slang or colloquial expressions and choose to show your discomfort by using quotation marks, then find another, more formal way to express the same thoughts.

Overused   Kate promised she would "walk that extra mile" for Mark.
Revised   Kate promised to help Mark in any way she could.

2 Eliminate phrases using quotation marks to make ironic comments.

Express your thoughts as directly as possible through word choice.

Misused   Dean Langley called to express his "appreciation" for all I had done.

Revised   Dean Langley called to complain about the accusations of bias I raised with reporters.

3 Eliminate quotation marks used to emphasize technical terms.

Assume your readers will note technical terms as such and will refer to a dictionary if needed.

Misused   "Electromagnetism" is a branch of physics.

Revised   Electromagnetism is a branch of physics.

4 Eliminate quotation marks that are overused to note commonly accepted nicknames.

Overused   "Ted" Kennedy is a powerful senator.

Revised   Ted Kennedy is a powerful senator.

Reserve your use of quotation marks for unusual nicknames, which often appear in parentheses after a first name. Once you have emphasized a name with quotation marks, you need not use the marks again with that name.

Ralph ("The Hammer") Schwartz worked forty years as a longshoreman in San Francisco.

EXERCISE 2

28.3

Correct the use of quotation marks to emphasize specific words in the following paragraph. Two of the eight expressions in quotation marks are emphasized correctly.

We can designate as "high interactive" any software that requires direct, active engagement on the part of the learner. "High-interactive" titles must not only look good, they must present learners with real "puzzles" to solve. "Real" in this sense means "thinking" problems that are not solved by mere computation (which on-screen calculators can manage) or by quick reference to a passage of text (which basic "search" engines can easily do); "real" problems are ones that invite unique, learner-specific answers to problems that at first may seem unsolvable. The computer screen will not "give away" the answers. No: for a problem to be real, the learner, not the teacher, must solve it.

Eliminating Misused or Overused Quotation Marks   **479**

EXERCISE 3

Following is a passage on Columbus by naval historian J. H. Parry. Quote from the paragraph, as instructed here.

1. Introduce a quotation with the word *that*.
2. Introduce a quotation with a phrase and a comma. End the quotation with a page reference (which you will invent), noted in parentheses.
3. Introduce a quotation with a sentence and a colon.
4. Interrupt a quotation with the phrase "Parry states."
5. Follow a quotation with an explanatory remark.

Columbus was not concerned with theory for its own sake, but with promoting a practical proposal. He did not study the available authorities in order to draw conclusions; he began with the conviction—how formed, we cannot tell—that an expedition to Asia by a westward route was practicable and that he was the man destined to lead it. He then combed the authorities known to him, and selected from them any assertion which supported his case. The practicability of the voyage—assuming that no major land mass barred the way—depended partly on the pattern of winds and currents likely to be encountered, but mainly on the distance to be covered. Columbus had to show that the westward distance from Europe to Asia was within the operating range of the available ships. We can trace, from what is known of his reading, from his own later writings, and from a biography written by his son Hernando, how he set about it.

CHAPTER 29

Other Marks

This chapter reviews the information you need to make decisions about using colons, dashes, parentheses, brackets, ellipses, and slashes.

CRITICAL DECISIONS

Choosing Colons, Dashes, or Parentheses
In some instances, you will have a choice between using a colon or a dash—for example, with an appositive or a summary at the end of a sentence. And in some instances you will have a choice between using dashes and parentheses to set off nonessential elements within a sentence. Keep in mind that the colon and parentheses are generally considered more formal punctuation marks, whereas the dash is somewhat more informal.

THE COLON

29a Using the colon

The **colon** is the mark of punctuation generally used to make an announcement. In formal writing, the colon follows only a *complete* independent clause and introduces a word, phrase, sentence, or group of sentences (as in a quotation).

Edit to eliminate colons misused
within independent clauses.

29.1

A colon must always follow a complete statement or independent clause. The mark must never be used as a break inside an independent clause.

Faulty	If one is depressed, the best two things in life are: eating and sleeping.
Revised	If one is depressed, the best two things in life are eating and sleeping.
Revised	If one is depressed, only two things in life matter: eating and sleeping.

> **2**   Use a colon to announce an important statement or question.

You create emphasis in a paragraph when you end one sentence with a colon to introduce another sentence.

How can it be that 25 years of feminist social change have made so little impression on preschool culture? Molly, now 6 and well aware that women can be doctors, has one theory: children's entertainment is made mostly by men.

—KATHA POLLITT

> **3**   Use a colon to introduce a list or a quotation.

Place a colon at the conclusion of an independent clause to introduce a list or a quotation.

A list

According to Cooley, the looking-glass self has three components: how we think our behavior appears to others, how we think others judge our behavior, and how we feel about their judgments.

A quotation

A New England soldier wrote to his wife on the eve of the First Battle of Bull Run: "I know how great a debt we owe to those who went before us through the Revolution. And I am willing, perfectly willing, to lay down all my joys in this life, to help maintain this government, and to pay that debt."

A colon can introduce material that is set off and indented, either a quotation (see 28a-4) or a list.

Chip designers use increased packing density of transistors in one of two ways:

1. They increase the complexity of the computers they can fabricate.
2. They keep the complexity of the computer at the same level and pack the whole computer into fewer chips.

4 Use a colon to set off an appositive phrase, summary, or explanation.

Appositive

In addition to bats, only a few species are known to display food sharing: wild dogs, hyenas, chimpanzees, and human beings.

Summary

Bats create a fluid social organization that is maintained for many years: vampire bats are remarkably social.

Explanation

When Calais surrendered, King Edward (of England) threatened to put the city to the sword, then offered the people a bargain: he would spare the city if six of the chief burghers would give themselves up unconditionally.

 5 Use a colon to distinguish chapter from verse in Biblical citations, hours from minutes, and titles from subtitles or subsidiary material.

Biblical citation

Fragments of Phoenician poetry have survived in the Psalms, where the mountains are described as "a fountain that makes the gardens fertile, a well of living water" (Song of Songs 4:15).

Hours from minutes

8:15 A.M.   12:01 P.M.

Titles from subtitles or subsidiary material

The New American Bazaar: Shopping Malls and the Anthropology of Urban Life

6 Use a colon after the salutation in a formal letter, and in bibliographic citations.

Dear Ms. King:

Dear Dr. Hart:

Bikai, Patricia. "The Phoenicians." *Archaeology* Mar./Apr. 1990: 30.

EXERCISE 1

Correct the use of colons in these sentences. Add or delete colons as needed.

> *Example:* Increasingly, grade-school Little League coaches of base-ball, soccer, and football are confronting an uncomfortable problem rabid parents.
>
> Increasingly, grade-school Little League coaches of base-ball, soccer, and football are confronting an uncomfortable problem: rabid parents.

1. Youth soccer games provide an illustration: teenagers serving as ref-erees: have been confronted in the most obnoxious way by parents snarling their disapproval at missed calls.

2. Adult coaches are used to parents whose egos interfere with their ability to watch a game: Young referees can be taught strategies to neutralize obnoxious parents. But no amount of preparation can avert the most serious damage caused by rabid parents the crushed ego of an 8-year-old whose father screams, "You're such a wimp!"

3. Communities around the country have begun to print pamphlets with titles like this "Helping Your Child to Enjoy Recreational Sports A Guide."

EXERCISE 2

Write brief sentences, as instructed.

1. Write a sentence with a colon that introduces a list.
2. Write a sentence with a colon that announces an emphatic statement.
3. Write a sentence with a colon that sets off an appositive phrase, summary, or explanation.

THE DASH

29b Using dashes for emphasis

On the typewritten page, the dash is written as two hyphens (--). The space between these hyphens closes when the dash is typeset (—).

| 1 | Use dashes to set off nonessential elements. |

Use dashes to set off modifiers and appositives. Dashes emphasize these nonessential elements set off in a sentence (see 14e).

Modifiers

Within the past ten years, a new generation of investigators—armed with fresh insights from sociobiology and behavioral ecology—have learned much about social organization in the birds of paradise.

Appositives

Sometimes the present can help us to clarify the past. So it is with a San-speaking people known as the !Kung—a group of what were once called African Bushmen.

Note: Use dashes to set off appositives that contain commas. In particular, when an appositive is made up of a series separated by commas, dashes prevent misreading.

Confusing   Over the years, the percentage of information workers, bankers, insurance agents, lawyers, science journalists, has gone from a trickle to a flood.

Revised   Over the years, the percentage of information workers—bankers, insurance agents, lawyers, science journalists—has gone from a trickle to a flood.

CRITICAL DECISIONS

Deciding When to Use Dashes

On seeing the dash, readers pause; then they speed up to read the words you have emphasized. Then they pause once more before returning to the main part of your sentence:

Effective   Zoologist Uwe Schmidt discovered that vampire bat pups are given regurgitated blood—in addition to milk—by their mothers.

Use the single dash to set off elements at the beginning or end of a sentence and a pair of dashes to set off elements in the middle. When elements are set off at the end of a sentence or in the middle, you have the choice of using commas or parentheses instead of dashes. Whatever punctuation you use, take care to word the element you set off so that it fits smoothly into the structure of your sentence. For instance, in the following sentence the nonessential element would be awkward.

Awkward   Vampire bat pups are given regurgitated blood—they drink milk too—by their mothers.

Better   Bat pups are given regurgitated blood—in addition to milk—by their mothers.

29b —

2 Use dashes to set off a significant repeating structure or an emphatic concluding element.

Repeating structure

To me the vitality of the bird of paradise's mating display was—and continues to be—one of nature's most thrilling sights. [The verb is repeated.]

Emphatic concluding remark

Once disposed of in the landfill, garbage is supposed to remain buried for eternity. So it was in Collier County, Florida—until we found several good reasons to dig it up again. [The dash sets off a sharply contrasting element, in this case a subordinate clause that functions as an adverb.]

Use dashes—with care. [This brief qualifying tag, a prepositional phrase, functions as an adverb.]

3 Use a dash to set off an introductory series from a summary or explanatory remark.

Pocket change, ball-point pens, campaign buttons—humanity's imprint continues to be recorded on the grassy slopes of the Boston Common. [This sentence structure, which begins with a series, is relatively rare.]

COMPUTER TIPS

Em Dash and En Dash

You probably already know that the dash is different from the hyphen. On a typewriter, to indicate a dash, you typed two hyphens with no spaces between, before, or after--like this. In addition, there are *two different* dashes that professional typesetters use, and most newer computers can generate both. One is called the "en dash," because it's the width of a capital N; the other is called the "em dash," because it's wider—roughly the width of a capital M. The en dash is used to indicate a span of some sort: 9:30–10:45. It's not a hyphen. It is customarily preceded and followed by very small spaces, but not full spaces. The em dash is used to indicate a break in thought or a parenthetical comment—like this—and it's neither preceded nor followed by spaces. Find out how to type in these special dashes on your particular computer.

Other Marks

4   Use a dash to express an interruption in dialogue.

A dash used in dialogue shows interruption—speakers interrupting themselves or being interrupted by others.

> Adam studied his brother's face until Charles looked away. "Are you mad at something?" Adam asked.
> "What should I be mad at?"
> "It just sounded— "
> "I've got nothing to be mad at. Come on, I'll get you something to eat."
>
> —JOHN STEINBECK

5   Use a dash to set off an attribution (by name) following an epigram.

> At blows that never fall you falter,
> And what you never lose, you must forever mourn.
>
> —GOETHE

Epigrams—succinct, provocative quotations—may be placed at the beginning of a paper as a vehicle for the introduction. Typically, the writer opens such a paper with a direct reference to the epigram.

EXERCISE 3

Add a dash or a pair of dashes to the following sentences.

> *Example:*   Many innovations the Chinese slipper, the Perrault godmother with her midnight injunction and her ability to change pumpkin into coach became incorporated in later versions of "Cinderella."
>
> Many innovations—the Chinese slipper, the Perrault godmother with her midnight injunction and her ability to change pumpkin into coach—became incorporated in later versions of "Cinderella."

1. The chapbooks of the eighteenth century and nineteenth century, crudely printed tiny paperbacks, were the source of most children's reading in the early days of our country. Originally, these were books imported from Europe. But slowly American publishing grew. In the latter part of the nineteenth century one firm stood out McLoughlin Brothers.

2. Golden Press's *Walt Disney's Cinderella* set the new pattern for America's Cinderella. This book's text is coy and condescending. (Sample: "And her best friends of all were guess who the mice!")

3. There is also an easy-reading version published by Random House, *Walt Disney's Cinderella*. This Cinderella commits the further heresy of cursing her luck. "How I did wish to go to the ball," she says. "But it is no use. Wishes never come true."

But in fairy tales wishes have a habit of happening *wishes accompanied by the proper action*, bad wishes as well as good.

EXERCISE 4

Write brief sentences, as instructed.

1. Write a sentence with a nonessential series placed mid-sentence, set off by a pair of dashes.
2. Write a sentence in which a nonessential element is set off at the end by a dash.
3. Write a sentence in which a dash or pair of dashes sets off a significant repeating structure or emphatic statement.

PARENTHESES

29.2

 29c **Using parentheses to set off nonessential information**

Parentheses ( ) are used to enclose and set off nonessential dates, words, phrases, or whole sentences that provide examples, comments, and other supporting information. The remark enclosed by parentheses presents the reader with an aside, an interesting but by no means crucial bit of information.

> Use parentheses to set off nonessential information: examples, comments, appositives.

Examples

The ground beetle *Pterostichus pinguedineus* survives in Alaska, in the Yukon, and in a series of isolated alpine refuges in the northern Appalachians (for example, the peak of Mt. Washington in New Hampshire).

Comments—explanatory or editorial

Beetles (especially those species that scavenge or that prey on other arthropods) are among the first organisms to invade terrain opened up by changing climates.

Appositives

The information content of a slice of pizza **(**advertising, legal expenses, and so on**)** accounts for a larger percentage of its cost than the edible content does.

2 Use parentheses to set off dates, translations of non-English words, and acronyms.

Dates

Thomas Aquinas **(**b. 1225 or 1226, d. 1274**)** is regarded as the greatest of scholastic philosophers.

Translations

The look on the faces of the Efe tribesmen made it clear that they could think of nothing worse than to have a *muzungu* **(**foreigner**)** living with them.

Acronyms

Lucy Suchman is staff anthropologist of Xerox's Palo Alto Research Center **(**better known as PARC**)**. [Typically, an acronym is placed in parentheses directly after the first mention of a term or title subsequently referred to by its acronym.]

3 Use parentheses to set off numbers or letters that mark items in a series when the series is run in with a sentence.

Interactive learning is student-centered in two ways: **(1)** students set the pace of their own learning; and **(2)** students set the depth of their own learning.

When the series appears in list form, omit the parentheses. Follow the numbers with periods instead.

4 Punctuate parentheses according to convention.

When a parenthetical remark forms a sentence, the remark should begin with an uppercase letter and end with an appropriate mark (period, question mark, or exclamation point) placed *inside* the end parenthesis.

The Bakhtiari think of themselves as a family, the descendents of a single founding-father. **(**The ancient Jews had a similar belief.**)**

In all other cases, end punctuation should be placed outside the end parenthesis.

Faulty   The Bakhtiari think of themselves as a family, the sons of a single founding-father. (as did the ancient Jews)

Revised   The Bakhtiari think of themselves as a family, the sons of a single founding-father (as did the ancient Jews).

EXERCISE 5

Add parentheses to the following sentences to enclose nonessential information.

> *Example:*   Nearly all twin-lens reflex cameras and a few single-lens reflex SLR cameras are designed to accommodate roll film somewhat wider than 35 millimeters.
>
> Nearly all twin-lens reflex cameras and a few single-lens reflex (SLR) cameras are designed to accommodate roll film somewhat wider than 35 millimeters.

1. Because of their size and the "look-down" viewing systems, twin-lens reflexes are not good for quick action candid shooting. An SLR is best in these situations.

2. The look-down viewing system is better for carefully composed photographs in a studio or home, for example when time is not of the essence.

3. For my money, the Canon AE-1 originally designed in 1971 remains one of the best and most flexible workhorse cameras that an amateur photographer could want.

4. I still cannot understand why any amateur photographer would want anything besides a good, reliable, single-lens reflex camera usually referred to as an SLR.

BRACKETS

29d   Using brackets for editorial clarification

Use **brackets** [ ] to clarify or insert comments into quoted material. Throughout this section the following passage will be altered to demonstrate the various uses of brackets. For an extended discussion of using quotations in a research paper, see 35f. Specifically, see 35f-3 for more on using brackets.

Elephant sounds include barks, snorts, trumpets, roars, growls, and rumbles. The rumbles are the key to our story, for although elephants can hear them well, human beings cannot. Many are below our range of hearing, in what is known as infrasound.

The universe is full of infrasound: It is generated by earthquakes, wind, thunder, volcanoes, and ocean storms—massive movements of earth, air, fire, and water. But very low frequency sound has not been thought to play much of a role in animals' lives. Intense infrasonic calls have been recorded from finback whales, but whether the calls are used in communication is not known.

Why would elephants use infrasound? It turns out that sound at the lowest frequency of elephant rumbles (14 to 35 hertz) has remarkable properties—it is little affected by passage through forests and grasslands. Does infrasound, then, let elephants communicate over long distances?

1   Use brackets to insert your own words into quoted material.

When you alter the wording of a quotation either by adding or deleting words, you must indicate as much with appropriate use of punctuation.

Brackets to clarify a reference

When quoting a sentence with a pronoun that refers to a word in another, nonquoted sentence, use brackets to insert a clarifying reference into the quotation. Delete the pronoun and add bracketed information; or, if wording permits (as in this example), simply add the bracketed reference.

> According to Katherine Payne, "Many [elephant rumbles] are below our range of hearing, in what is known as infrasound."

Brackets to weave quoted language into your sentences

You will sometimes need to alter a quotation if its structure, point of view, pronoun choices, or verb forms differ from those of the sentence into which you are incorporating the quotation. Show any changes to quoted text in brackets. Directly substituting one or two clarifying words (or letters) for the author's original language requires no use of ellipses to show an omission. (See 29e.)

> At frequencies of 14 to 35 hertz, elephant rumbles have "remarkable properties—[they are] little affected by passage through forests and grasslands" (Payne 67).

The bracketed verb and pronoun have been changed from their original singular form to plural in order to agree in number with the plural *elephant rumbles.*

Brackets to show your awareness of an error in the quoted passage

When you quote a sentence that contains an obvious error, you are still obliged to reproduce exactly the wording of the original source. To show your awareness of the error and to show readers that the error is the quoted author's, not yours, place the bracketed word *sic* (Latin, meaning "thus") after the error.

"Intense infrasonic calls have been recorded from finback whales, but weather [sic] the calls are used in communication is not known."

Brackets to note emphasis

You may wish to underline or italicize quoted words. To show readers that the emphasis is yours and not the quoted author's, add the bracketed expression *emphasis added, italics added,* or *italics mine.*

"The universe is *full* of infrasound: It is generated by earthquakes, wind, thunder, volcanoes, and ocean storms—massive movements of earth, air, fire, and water [italics mine]."

---

2 | **Use brackets to distinguish parentheses inserted within parentheses.**

Katherine Payne reports that "sound at the lowest frequency of elephant rumbles (14 to 35 hertz [cycles per second]) has remarkable properties—it is little affected by passage through forests and grasslands."

ELLIPSES

29e Using an ellipsis to indicate a break in continuity

Just as you will sometimes add words in order to incorporate quotations into your sentences, you will also need to omit words. The overall rule to bear in mind when you alter a quotation is to present quoted material in a way that is faithful to the meaning and sentence structure of the original. Your omission should not confuse an author's meaning or misrepresent the author's sentence structure.

To indicate such omissions, use an ellipsis—three spaced periods (. . .). The spaced periods show that you have omitted either words or entire sentences. The following passage will be altered to demonstrate several uses of ellipses.[1]

The successful capitalist was a man who could accurately estimate a firm's potential profits. The investors who survived were the ones who knew how to take "risks" in such a way that there was no actual risk at all. They profited through interest and dividends and through the in-

---

[1]Your instructor may ask for the addition of brackets [ ] around the ellipsis to indicate that the student writer, *not* the source author, has used the ellipsis. If you quote a passage in which the source author uses an ellipsis and you add a further ellipsis, then place your ellipsis in brackets.

creased value of their holdings, which multiplied as the national economy grew. Under Tom Scott's tutelage, Carnegie learned to collect interest rather than pay it, and he became a shrewd judge of the growth potential of investment opportunities.

—HAROLD C. LIVESAY, *Andrew Carnegie and the Rise of Big Business*

1   Know when *not* to use ellipses.

Do *not* use ellipses to note words omitted from the beginning of a sentence if it is obvious that you are quoting a fragment of the original.

Faulty   As Carnegie's biographer points out, Carnegie himself "... became a shrewd judge of the growth potential of investment opportunities" (Livesay 48).

Revised   As Carnegie's biographer points out, Carnegie himself "became a shrewd judge of the growth potential of investment opportunities" (Livesay 48).

Do *not* use an ellipsis if the passage you quote ends with a period and ends your sentence as well. Readers take for granted that the quoted sentence exists in a paragraph in which other sentences follow.

Faulty   Livesay writes that capitalists "who survived were the ones who knew how to take 'risks' in such a way that there was no actual risk at all...." (48)

Revised   Livesay writes that capitalists "who survived were the ones who knew how to take 'risks' in such a way that there was no actual risk at all" (48).

2   Use an ellipsis to indicate words omitted from the middle of a sentence.

According to Livesay, "The investors who survived ... knew how to take 'risks' in such a way that there was no actual risk at all" (48).

3   Use an ellipsis to indicate words omitted from the end of a sentence.

When you omit words from the end of a quoted sentence and the quotation concludes *your* sentence, follow with a sentence period and then place the ellipsis. Put no space before the initial period or after the final period.

Livesay makes the point that successful investors "profited through interest and dividends and through the increased value of their holdings...."

But note the placement of the sentence period—and the insertion of a space before the initial ellipsis period—when a parenthetical citation is present:

Livesay makes the point that successful investors "profited through interest and dividends and through the increased value of their holdings . . ." (48).

When the altered quotation appears in the middle of your sentence, skip one space after the last quoted word, follow with the ellipsis, and continue with your own sentence.

"Under Tom Scott's tutelage," Carnegie's biographer writes, "Carnegie learned to collect interest rather than pay it . . . "(Livesay 48), which is part of what accounted for his vast fortune.

4	Use an ellipsis to indicate the omission of whole sentences or parts of sentences.

When omitting an entire sentence (or sentences), place the ellipsis at the spot of the omission. Observe the placement of the sentence-ending period *before* the ellipsis:

As Carnegie's biographer points out, "The investors who survived were the ones who knew how to take 'risks' in such a way that there was no actual risk at all. . . . Under Tom Scott's tutelage, Carnegie learned to collect interest rather than pay it, and he became a shrewd judge of the growth potential of investment opportunities" (Livesay 48).

When omitting the end of one sentence through to the end of another sentence, follow the convention at 29e-3.

According to Livesay, "The investors who survived were the ones who knew how to take 'risks.' . . . Under Tom Scott's tutelage, Carnegie learned to collect interest rather than pay it, and he became a shrewd judge of the growth potential of investment opportunities" (Livesay 48).

When omitting the end of one sentence through to the middle of another sentence, place the author's punctuation mark (if any) after the last word of the initially quoted sentence, follow with an ellipsis, and continue with the remainder of the quotation.

Writing about the railway boom of the mid 1800s, Carnegie's biographer observes, "The investors who survived . . . profited through interest and dividends and through the increased value of their holdings, which multiplied as the national economy grew" (Livesay 48).

5	Use an ellipsis to show a pause or interruption.

When *you* are writing dialogue or prose—that is, when you are *not* quoting a source—you can use an ellipsis (with *no* brackets) to indicate a brief pause or delay. Within a sentence, use three spaced periods. Between sentences, end the first sentence with a period and then set the ellipsis—four spaced periods in all.

In dialogue that you write

"No," I said. I wanted to leave. "I . . . I need to get some air."

In prose that you write

When I left the seminary, I walked long and thought hard about what a former student of divinity might do. . . . My shoes wore out.

THE SLASH

> **I** Use slashes to separate the lines of poetry run in with the text of a sentence.

Retain all punctuation when quoting poetry. Leave a space before and after the slash when indicating line breaks.

> The narrator of William Blake's "The Tyger" is struck with wonder: "Tyger! Tyger! burning bright **/** In the forests of the night. **/** What immortal hand or eye, **/** Could frame thy fearful symmetry?"

> **2** Use slashes to show choice.

Use slashes, occasionally, to show alternatives, as with the expressions *and/or* and *either/or.* With this use, do not leave spaces before or after the slash.

> *Either/Or* is the title of a philosophical work by Kierkegaard.

> The Unsung Hero/Best Sport award was given to Abbey King.

If your meaning is not compromised, avoid using the slash; instead, write out alternatives in your sentence.

> Send a telegram and/or call to let us know you're well.

The sense, here, is that there are three options: send a telegram, call, *or* send a telegram *and* call. When two options are intended, rewrite the sentence.

> Send a telegram and call to let us know you're well.

> Send a telegram or call to let us know you're well.

> **3** Use a slash in writing fractions or formulas to note division.

> The February 1988 index of job opportunities (as measured by the number of help wanted advertisements) would be as follows:
> $(47,230/38,510) \times 100 = 122.6$
> $1/2$ $5/8$ $20\ 1/4$

29.3

EXERCISE 6

Construct sentences, as directed, in which you quote from the following passage by Sigmund Freud.

(1) As to the origin of the sense of guilt, the analyst has different views from other psychologists; but even he does not find it easy to give an account of it. (2) To begin with, if we ask how a person comes to have a sense of guilt, we arrive at an answer which cannot be disputed: a person feels guilty (devout people would say "sinful") when he has done something which he knows to be "bad." (3) But then we notice how little this answer tells us. (4) Perhaps, after some hesitation, we shall add that even when a person has not actually *done* the bad thing but has only recognized in himself an *intention* to do it, he may regard himself as guilty; and the question then arises of why the intention is regarded as equal to the deed. (5) Both cases, however, presuppose that one had already recognized that what is bad is reprehensible, is something that must not be carried out. (6) How is this judgement arrived at?

Example: Quote sentence 1, but delete the phrase "As to the origin of the sense of guilt."

According to Sigmund Freud, "the analyst has different views from other psychologists; but even he does not find it easy to give an account of it."

1. Quote sentence 2, beginning with "a person feels." Delete the parenthetical note.

2. Quote sentence 4 but delete the end of the sentence, beginning with "and the question."

3. Quote sentence 1 and use a bracketed reference to clarify the second use of the pronoun *it*.

4. Quote sentence 5 and show your awareness of the spelling error.

CHAPTER **30**

Capitals and Italics

Weblink
http://ccc.commnet.edu/grammar/
capitals.htm
A brief guide to capitalization.

Capitals and italics are primarily graphic devices that give readers cues on how to read: where to look for the beginning of a new thought, which words in a sentence are emphasized, which words form titles or proper names, and so on. Capitals and italics are also very useful for special designations that can only be shown in writing.

CAPITALS

Before the late nineteenth century, printers manually composed words by placing molded letters in type holders, taking letters from individual compartments, or type cases, set on a nearby wall. Letters used most often (vowels, for instance) were kept on the wall's lower cases, within easy reach. Letters used less often (capital letters, for instance) were kept in a slightly less convenient location in upper cases. In spite of innovations that have made manual typesetting obsolete, we still retain the printer's original designations, upper and lower case, when referring to the appearance of type on a page.

CRITICAL DECISIONS

Understanding Conventions for Using Capitals
Decisions about using capitalization are generally based on convention—that is, in order to use capitals appropriately, you simply have to learn and follow the rules for their use. Misuse of capitals can seriously undercut your authority as a writer.

| 30a | Capitalize the first letter of the first word in every sentence. |

The most basic use of capitals is to signal the start of sentences.

When a box of mixed-grain-and-nut cereal is shaken, large particles rise to the top—just as stones will rise to the top of a field.

1   Reproduce capitalization in a quoted passage.

Capitalize the first word of quoted material when you introduce a quotation with a brief explanatory phrase.

According to archaeologist Douglas Wilson, "Most of what archaeologists have to work with is ancient trash."

Do not capitalize the first word of a quotation run into the structure of your sentence. When you change capitalization in a quoted text, indicate the change with brackets.

Wilson says that archaeologists who dig through modern trash must come "[e]quipped with rubber gloves, masks, and booster shots."

2   Capitalize the first word in a parenthetical statement if the remark is a sentence.

Once a sleepy suburban town whose workers commuted to Chicago every morning, Naperville, Illinois, has acquired its own employment base. (It has become an "urban village," a "technoburb.")

If the parenthetical remark forms a sentence but is placed inside another sentence (this is a relatively rare occurrence), *do not* capitalize the first word after the parenthesis and *do not* use a period. However, do use a question mark or exclamation point if the parenthetical remark requires it.

Naperville has grown so robustly (who could have predicted such growth ten years ago?) that city services are strained.

3   In a series of complete statements or questions, capitalize the first word of each item.

When a series is formed by phrases or incomplete questions, capitalization of the first word is optional.

| **Capitals** | What causes air sickness? Is it inner-ear disturbance? Is it brain waves? |
| **Optional** | Air Force scientists want to know what causes motion sickness. Is it inner-ear disturbance? brain wave anomalies? disorienting visual signals? |

Optional   Air Force scientists want to know what causes motion sickness. Is it inner-ear disturbance? Brain wave anomalies? Disorienting visual signals?

In a series of phrases run in with a sentence, the phrases are *not* capitalized.

The program for sustainable agriculture has three objectives: (1) to reduce reliance on fertilizer; (2) to increase farm profits; and (3) to conserve energy.

In a displayed series, capitalization of the first word is optional.

Optional   The program for low-input sustainable agriculture that has emerged from a recent federal study has three objectives:

1. To reduce reliance on fertilizer.
2. To increase farm profits.
3. To conserve energy.

The word *to* could also be lowercase in each number of the displayed series.

30.1

ACROSS THE CURRICULUM

The Importance of Grammar, Style, and Usage in Chemistry

In its *Style Guide** for authors and editors, the American Chemical Society makes it clear that the "seemingly trivial elements" of language such as grammar, style, and usage are crucially important for writers:

Many authors ask why we have a style for seemingly trivial elements like capitalization, hyphenation, abbreviations, and so on. Why can't each author do it his or her own way? A consistent style provides unity and coherence to the journal or book and makes communication clear and unequivocal; thus it saves readers time and effort by not allowing a variety of styles for the same thing to distract them from the content. If readers must pause, even for a moment, to think about matters of style, it will take a lot longer to read the article.

*The ACS Style Guide: A Manual for Authors and Editors (Washington: ACS, 1986), 11.

---

4   Capitalizing the first word of a sentence following a colon is optional.

Optional   The program has two aims: The first is to conserve energy.
Optional   The program has two aims: the first is to conserve energy.

30b   Capitalize words of significance in a title.

Do not capitalize articles (*a, an, the*) or conjunctions and prepositions that have four or fewer letters, except at the title's beginning. *Do* capitalize the first and last words of the title (even if they are articles, conjunctions, or prepositions), along with any word following a colon or semicolon.

> *Pride and Prejudice*   *The Sound and the Fury*
> "The Phoenicians: Rich and Glorious Traders of the Levant"

Do not capitalize the word *the* unless it is part of a title or proper name.

> the Eiffel Tower   *The Economist*

The first word of a hyphenated word in a title is capitalized. The second word is also capitalized, unless it is very short.

> "The Selling of an Ex-President"   *Engine Tune-ups Made Simple*

30c   Capitalize the first word in every line of poetry.

Lines of poetry are conventionally marked by initial capitals. The interjection *O*, restricted for the most part to poetry, is always capitalized. The word *oh* is capitalized only when it begins a sentence.

> Break, break, break,
>   On thy cold gray stones, O Sea!
>
> —TENNYSON, from "Break, Break, Break"

Note: Very often in contemporary poetry the initial capital is *not* used. When quoting such poets, retain the capitalization of the original.

30d   Capitalize proper nouns—people, places, objects; proper adjectives; and ranks of distinction.

In general, capitalize any noun that refers to a *particular* person, place, object, or being that has been given an individual, or proper, name.

I   Capitalize names of people or groups of people.

Names of people are capitalized, as are titles showing family relationships *if* the title is part of the person's name.

> Tom Hanks   Martha Washington

Aunt Millie   Uncle Ralph

Names of family relations—brother, aunt, grandmother—are not capitalized if not used as part of a particular person's proper name.

He phoned his grandmother, Bess Truman.

I saw my favorite aunt, my mother's sister, on a trip to Chicago.

Names of political groups and of formal organizations are capitalized.

Democrats	the Left
Republicans	the Right
Communists	Socialists

2   **Capitalize religions, religious titles and names, and nationalities.**

Religions, their followers, and their sacred beings and sacred documents are capitalized.

Judaism	Jew	the Bible
Catholicism	Catholic	the New Testament
Islam	Muslim	the Koran
God	Allah	Buddha

Nations and nationalities are capitalized.

America	Americans	Native Americans
Liberia	Liberians	Hispanic Americans
Czech Republic	Czechs	

Note: The terms *black* and *white*, when designating race, are usually written in lowercase, though some writers prefer to capitalize them (by analogy with other formal racial designations such as Mongolian and Polynesian).

3   **Capitalize places, regions designated by points on the compass, and languages.**

Places and addresses

Cascades	Asia
Idaho	England
Joe's Diner	Philadelphia
Main Street	Lake Erie

Note: Capitalize common nouns such as *main* or *center* when they are part of an address.

Names of regions and compass points designating the names
of regions

Appalachia	the frozen Northwest
Mid-Atlantic	the Sun Belt

Note: A compass point is capitalized only when it serves as the name of
a particular area of the country. As a direction, a compass point is not
capitalized.

No capital   I'll be driving northeast for the first part of the trip. [The
word *northeast* is a modifier and indicates a direction, not a
region.]

We made a course to the northeast, but soon turned to
the north. [These are compass points, not the names of
regions.]

Capital   I'll be vacationing in the Northeast this year. [The word
Northeast is the name of an area of the country.]

Names of languages

English	Arabic	Swahili
Spanish	Greek	Italian

 4 Capitalize adjectives formed from proper nouns.
Capitalize titles of distinction that are part of proper names.

Proper adjectives formed from proper nouns

English tea	French perfume
Cartesian coordinates	Balinese dancer

Note: Both *Oriental* and *oriental* are considered correct, though the capitalized form is more common. Both *Biblical* and *biblical* are considered
correct.

Do not capitalize the name of an academic discipline or group of
disciplines unless it is derived from a proper noun:

humanities	social science
English	French

Titles of distinction

Capitalize a title of distinction when no words separate it from a
proper noun. Do not capitalize most title designations if they are followed by the preposition *of*.

Governor Ventura	Jesse Ventura, governor of Minnesota
Pastor Sue Wellman	Sue Wellman, pastor of my church

Note: When titles of the highest distinction are proper names for a specific office—President, Prime Minister—they often remain capitalized, even if followed by a preposition and even if not paired with a specific name.

Jacques Chirac, President of France

The President arrived at two o'clock.

The Prime Minister's role is to lead both party and government.

A prime minister may do as she pleases. [A specific office is not being named.]

Capitalize titles and abbreviations of titles when they follow a comma—as in an address or closing to a letter.

Martha Brand, Ph.D.   Fred Barnes, Sr.

Sally Roth, M.D.   David Burns, Executive Vice-President

---

5 Capitalize the names of days, months, holidays, and historical events or periods.

Monday   New Year's Day
December   Revolutionary War
Christmas   Middle Ages

Note: When written out, centuries and decades are not capitalized.

the nineteenth century   the fifties   the twenty-third century

Seasons are capitalized only when they are personified.

spring semester   Spring's gentle breath [The season is personified.]

---

6 Capitalize particular objects and name-brand products.

Jefferson Memorial   USS *Hornet*
Aswan Dam   Sam Rayburn Building
Bic pen   Toyota Camry
Whopper   Apple computer

---

7 Use capitals with certain abbreviations, prefixes, or compound nouns.

Capitalize abbreviations only when the words abbreviated are themselves capitalized.

Mister James Wolf	Mr. James Wolf
1234 Rockwood Avenue	1234 Rockwood Ave.

Capitalize acronyms and abbreviations of companies, agencies, and treaties.

FAA (Federal Aviation Administration)

ABM Treaty (Anti-Ballistic Missile Treaty)

DEC (Digital Equipment Corporation)

The prefixes *ex, un,* and *post* are capitalized only when they begin a sentence or are part of a proper name or title.

a post-Vietnam event	the Post-Vietnam Syndrome
an un-American attitude	the Un-American Activities Committee

30.2

Capitalize a number or the first word in a compound number that is part of a name or title.

Third Avenue

the Seventy-second Preakness

EXERCISE 1

Correct the capitalization in these sentences. As needed, change lower-case letters to uppercase and change uppercase to lowercase.

New orleans, the louisiana city associated with the pre-lenten celebration of mardi gras, has also been the site of an even more unusual quasi-Religious festival. This one takes place on november 1, which in the church's calendar is the feast of all saints, otherwise known as all saints' day. The custom of this day in new orleans is the Washing of the Tombs. Since the city was built on the Bayou, the land is quite swampy. Thus most of the City's dead have, over the years, been buried in above-ground vaults. On all saints' day these vaults are cleaned, whitewashed, and decorated with flowers and wreaths. The favored flower is the Chrysanthemum. Despite all of the work going on, the atmosphere has been described as quite festive. Vendors do quite well peddling food, balloons, and even miniature skeletons.

ITALICS

Weblink

http://www.ac.wwu.edu/
~bgoebel/mini-lessons/
underlining%20mini%20lesson.htm

A student's guide for when to use italics/un-derlining and when to use quotation marks.

A word set in italics calls attention to itself. On the typewritten (or hand-written) page, words that you would italicize are underlined. However, most word processors allow you to italicize text.

30e Underline or italicize words if they need a specific emphasis.

Words that you underline or set in italics are given particular emphasis. As a stylistic tool, italicizing will work well only if you do not overuse it.

Cultural relativity does *not* mean that a behavior appropriate in one place is appropriate everywhere.

Italicized words can be useful to create emphasis and change meaning in sentences, especially when writing attempts to duplicate the emphasis of speech.

"You're going to the movies with *him?*" [Why would you go with him?]

"You're going to the *movies* with him?" [Why aren't you going to the theater?]

CRITICAL DECISIONS

Italicizing for Emphasis

Decisions about using italics for emphasis require considerable care. Overuse lessens the impact of italics and makes your writing appear overexcited and unconvincing. The best way to create emphasis is not to simulate emotion with typeface, but to make your point with words.

Overused   The narrator of Charles Baxter's short story "Gryphon" is *overcome* with anger after a classmate reports Miss Ferenczi to the principal. He *wants* to believe the substitute teacher's stories no matter how outlandish they may be.

Reworded   The narrator of Charles Baxter's short story "Gryphon" is furious after a classmate reports Miss Ferenczi to the principal. It is crucial for him to believe the substitute teacher's stories no matter how outlandish they may be.

30f Underline or italicize words, letters, and numbers to be defined or identified.

l   Use italics for words to be defined.

Words to be defined in a sentence are usually underlined or set in italics. (Occasionally, such a word is set in quotation marks.)

The *operating system* runs a computer as a sort of master organizer that can accept commands whenever no specific program is running.

2 Use italics for expressions recognized as foreign.

Underline or italicize foreign expressions that have not yet been assimilated into English but whose meanings are generally understood.

amore [Italian]	*Doppelgänger* [German]
enfant terrible [French]	*e pluribus unum* [Latin]
goyim [Hebrew]	*hombre* [Spanish]

No underlines or italics are used with foreign expressions that have been assimilated into English. The following is a brief sampling of such words.

alter ego [Latin]	blitz [German]
fait accompli [French]	kayak [Eskimo]
kibitz [Yiddish]	maestro [Italian]

3 Use italics to designate words, numerals, or letters referred to as such.

Underline or italicize words when you are calling attention to them as words.

Many writers have trouble differentiating the uses of the words *lie* and *lay*.

Italicize letters and most numerals when they are referred to as such.

She crosses the *t* in *top*.

Shall I write a *1* or a *2?*

The combination of italics (or underlining) and an apostrophe with the letter *s* is used to make numbers and letters plural.

Cross your *t*'s and dot your *i*'s.

We saw *1*'s on the scoreboard each inning—a good sign.

 30g Use underlining or italics for titles of book-length works separately published or broadcast, as well as for individually named transport craft.

1 Use italics for books, long poems, and plays.

A Discovery of the Sea [book]	*Twelfth Night* [play]
The Rime of the Ancient Mariner [long poem]	

COMPUTER TIPS

Don't Underline; Use Italics

Like many conventions left over from the typewriter era, underlining was at one time a way around a typewriter's limitations—in this case, the inability to italicize. Writers had to underline to indicate to the typesetter which text should be italicized. But word processors can actually do the italicizing themselves, so you should use that capability whenever you type the title of a book, play, or movie, or at other times italics are called for. Simply highlight the material you want to italicize, and then click on the symbol in the menu bar for italics (an *I* in most programs). You can also use italics or boldface type for emphasis (sparingly). Use the underline function only if you are writing instructions or exercises or doing some other kind of work that requires a variety of typographical distinctions.

The titles of sacred documents (and their parts) as well as legal or public documents are frequently capitalized (see 30d) but are not set in italics.

30.3

the Bible	the New Testament
the Magna Carta	the Bill of Rights
the Koran	Book of Exodus

2   Use italics for newspapers, magazines, and periodicals.

the *Boston Globe*	Brookline *Citizen*
Time	*Journal of the American Medical Association*

With newspapers, do not capitalize, underline, or set in italics the word *the*, even if it is part of the newspaper's title. Italicize or underline the name of a city or town only if it is part of the newspaper's title. Titles of particular selections in a newspaper, magazine, or journal are set in quotation marks.

3   Use italics for works of visual art, long musical works, movies, and broadcast shows.

Rodin's *The Thinker*	*The Last Judgment*
Van Gogh's *The Starry Night*	the *Burghers of Calais*
Mozart's *The Magic Flute*	the *German Requiem*

Note: Underline or set in italics the article *the* only when it is part of a title.

Movies and television or radio shows are italicized.

Late Show with David Letterman   *All Things Considered*

Life Is Beautiful   *Star Wars: Episode 1*
                                             The Phantom Menace

> **4** Use italics for individually named transport craft:
> Ships, trains, aircraft, and spacecraft.

USS *Hornet* (a ship)   the *Montrealer* (a train)

Apollo X (a spacecraft)   *Spirit of St. Louis*
                                             (an airplane)

30.4

Do not underline or italicize USS or HMS in a ship's name.

EXERCISE 2

Correct the use of italics in these sentences. Circle words that should not be italicized. Underline words that should be italicized. Place a check beside any sentence in which italics are used correctly.

> ***Example:*** The most important tool of the navigator is an ⟨*accurate,*⟩ ⟨*current*⟩ ⟨*chart,*⟩ without which it is virtually impossible to navigate successfully.

1. Navigation is the art of staying *out* of trouble.

2. You can keep your charts as current as possible by subscribing to Local Notices to Mariners, a weekly publication of the U.S. Coast Guard.

3. The key to successful navigation is to navigate *continuously,* that is, *always* be able to determine the position of your boat on the chart.

4. *Landmarks* (smokestacks, water towers, buildings, piers, *etc.*) and *aids to navigation* (beacons, lighthouses, buoys) help relate what you see from your boat to items found on the chart.

5. Aids to navigation are installed and maintained by the Coast Guard *specifically* to help you relate your surroundings to the appropriate symbols on the chart.

6. A *beacon* will be denoted on the chart by a triangle and the letters *Bn.*

31

Abbreviations and Numbers

U se an **abbreviation**—the shortened form of a word followed (for the most part) by a period—only in restricted circumstances, as discussed below.

CRITICAL DECISIONS

Writing in Other Disciplines

Writers working in an unfamiliar discipline should consult the standard manuals of reference, style, and documentation for guidance in using abbreviations and numbers in the field. Many such reference works are listed in Chapter 37, Documenting Research, with conventions shown in Chapters 38–40 on writing in each of the major discipline areas.

ABBREVIATIONS

31a	**Abbreviating titles of rank both before and after proper names**

The following titles of address are usually abbreviated before a proper name.

Mr.   Mrs.   Dr.

31.1

Though not an abbreviation, *Ms.* is usually followed by a period. Typically, the abbreviations *Gen.*, *Lt.*, *Sen.*, *Rep.*, and *Hon.* precede a full name—first and last.

Faulty	Gen. Eisenhower	Sen. Kennedy
Revised	General Eisenhower	Senator Kennedy
Revised	Gen. Dwight D. Eisenhower	Sen. Ted Kennedy

Following the Modern Language Association's conventions, the abbreviations of academic titles appearing after a name are not followed by periods or spaces:

BA   MA   MS   PhD   EdD   MD

Follow other abbreviations with periods:

Jr.   Sr.   subj.   vol.   Amer.   min.

Place a comma after the surname, then follow with the abbreviation. If more than one abbreviation is used, place a comma between abbreviations. But check differing conventions for making abbreviations, depending on the expectations of your audience.

Lawrence Swift, Jr., MD

Abbreviations of medical, professional, or academic titles are *not* combined with the abbreviations *Mr.*, *Mrs.*, or *Ms.*

Faulty	Ms. Joan Warren, MD	Ms. Mindy Lubber, EdD
Revised	Dr. Joan Warren	Mindy Lubber, EdD
	or Joan Warren, MD	*or* Dr. Mindy Lubber

Other than for direct reference to academic titles such as *PhD* (Doctor of Philosophy), *MA* (Master of Arts), and *MS* (Master of Science), do not use freestanding abbreviated titles that have not been paired with a proper name.

Acceptable	Jane Thompson earned her PhD in biochemistry. [A degree is referred to separately.]
Faulty	Marie Lew is an MD [The degree should either be referred to separately or attached to the person's title.]
Revised	Marie Lew, MD, graduated from Harvard.

31b   Abbreviating specific dates and numbers

With certain historical or archaeological dates, abbreviations are often used to indicate whether the event occurred in the last two thousand years. Following MLA style, use no periods with the abbreviations below:

Ancient times (prior to two thousand years ago)

BC   (before the birth of Christ)

BCE   (before the common era)

Both abbreviations follow the date.

Modern times (within the last two thousand years)

CE   (of the common era)

AD   (*Anno Domini,* "in the year of the Lord," an abbreviation that precedes the date)

Augustus, the first Roman Emperor, lived from 63 BC (*or* BCE) to AD 14 (*or* CE).

When the context of a paragraph makes clear that the event occurred in the last two thousand years, it would be redundant, even insulting, to write "A.D. 1820."

Clock time uses abbreviations in capitals or in lowercase.

5:44 P.M. (or p.m.)   5:44 A.M. (or a.m.)

When numbers are referred to as specific items (such as numbers in arithmetic operations or as units of currency or measure), they are used with standard abbreviations.

No. 23 or no. 23 $2 + 3 = 5$ 54%
$23.01   99 bbl. [barrels]

Abbreviations for time, numbers, units, or money should be used only with reference to specific hours, dates, or amounts.

Faulty   The sun rises in the A.M.
Revised   The sun rises in the morning.

Faulty   This happened in the BC era.
Revised   This happened almost three thousand years ago.

Faulty   The % of dropouts has decreased this year.
Revised   The percentage of dropouts has decreased this year.

31c **Using acronyms, uppercase abbreviations, and corporate abbreviations**

An **acronym** is the uppercase, pronounceable abbreviation of a proper noun. Periods are not used with acronyms. The following are some familiar acronyms.

NATO   North Atlantic Treaty Organization
MADD   Mothers Against Drunk Driving
NASA   National Aeronautics and Space Administration
NOW   National Organization for Women

Weblink

http://acronymfinder.com/
A searchable database of thousands of acronyms and abbreviations.

Other uppercase abbreviations use the initial letters of familiar persons or groups to form well-known "call letter" designations conventionally used in writing.

Helping Readers to Understand Acronyms

Unless an acronym or uppercase abbreviation is common knowledge, courtesy obligates you to write out the full word, term, or organizational name at its first mention. Then, in a parenthetical remark, you give the abbreviation—as is illustrated in the beginning of this article from the journal *Archaeology*. (In subsequent references, use the abbreviation.)

To the end of the Early Intermediate Period (EIP), the appearance of stunning, elaborately decorated ceramics . . . suggests that tribal leaders possessed and exchanged prestige items as a way of consolidating their claims to political power.

In lengthy documents where you will be using many uppercase abbreviations and acronyms, consider creating a glossary, placed at the end of the paper as an appendix, in addition to defining abbreviations the first time you use them.

JFK	John Fitzgerald Kennedy
NAACP	National Association for the Advancement of Colored People
MVP	Most Valuable Player
VFW	Veterans of Foreign Wars

Abbreviations used by companies and organizations are a matter of preference. When referring directly to a specific organization, use its own preferred abbreviations for words such as *Incorporated (Inc.)*, *Limited (Ltd.)*, *Private Corporation (P.C.)*, and *Brothers (Bros.)*.

31d Using abbreviations for parenthetical references

Abbreviations from Latin are conventionally used in footnotes, documentation, and sometimes in parenthetical comments. All of these Latin expressions should be replaced in a main sentence by their English equivalents.

e.g. (*exempli gratia*)	for example
et al. (*et alii*)	and others
i.e. (*id est*)	that is
N.B. (*nota bene*)	note well
c. or ca. (*circa*)	about
etc. (*et cetera*)	and such things; and so on

Avoid the extremely vague abbreviation *etc.* unless a specific and obvious sequence is being indicated, as in *They proceeded by even numbers (2, 4, 6, 8, etc.).* Even here the phrase *and so on* is preferable.

Informal A growing portion of our National Income is composed of government transfer payments (e.g., welfare payments).

Formal A growing portion of our National Income is composed of government transfer payments (for example, welfare payments).

Bibliographical abbreviations are commonly used in documentation to provide short forms of reference citations, but they should not be used in sentences of a paragraph. The following are some of the most frequently used abbreviations.

p./pp.	page(s)	Jan.	January
ed./eds.	editor(s)	Feb.	February
n.d.	no date (for a publication	Mar.	March
	lacking a date)	Apr.	April
ch./chs.	chapter(s)	Aug.	August
ms./mss.	manuscript(s)	Sep./Sept.	September
col./cols.	column(s)	Oct.	October
vol./vols.	volume(s)	Nov.	November
		Dec.	December

Each discipline has specific conventions for abbreviations in documentation. For example, the months May, June, and July are not abbreviated in MLA style; other conventions are discussed in Chapter 37.

31.2

ACROSS THE CURRICULUM

Writing in the Disciplines

Conventions differ in the disciplines about when and how much writers should use abbreviations—and about which abbreviations are common knowledge and need not be defined. Across disciplines, abbreviations are avoided in titles. For specific abbreviations lying beyond common knowledge, writers follow the convention of defining the abbreviation on first use. As a demonstration, a sketch of conventions for abbreviating in some of the science disciplines is provided here. For detailed information about conventions in a specific discipline, see the style manuals recommended in 38f, 39e, and 40e, or consult your professor.

■ In scientific writing, courtesy dictates that writers define words that are later abbreviated.

Some 800 species of bats live in diverse habitats and vary greatly in behavior and physical characteristics. Their biosonar pulses also differ, even among species within the same genus. Nevertheless, these pulses can be classified into three types: constant frequency (CF), frequency modulated (FM), and combined (CF-FM). *(continued)*

Writing in the Disciplines *(continued)*

- Units of measure are generally abbreviated when they are paired with specific numbers. When not thus paired, the units are written out.

  In the next stage, 14 g were added. Several grams of the material were sent away for testing.
- Abbreviations of measurements in scientific writing need not be defined on first use.
- Symbol abbreviations are standardized, and you will find lists of accepted abbreviations in the *CBE Style Manual* published by the Council of Biology Editors (now known as CSE, or Council of Science Editors). Generally, the use of abbreviations in titles is not accepted in science writing. Limited abbreviations—without definition—are accepted in tables.

3Ie | **Revise to eliminate all but conventional abbreviations from sentences.**

In sentences, no abbreviations are used for the names of days or months, units of measure, courses of instruction, geographical names, and page/chapter/volume references. These abbreviations are reserved for specific uses in charts and data presentations that require abbreviated treatment in each discipline.

Faulty   Come see me on the first Mon. in Aug.

Revised   Come see me on the first Monday in August.

Faulty   He weighed 25 lbs.

Revised   He weighed 25 pounds.

Exception: Abbreviations of standard, lengthy phrases denoting measurement are common in formal writing: miles per hour (mph or m.p.h.) and revolutions per minute (rpm or r.p.m.).

Faulty   We enrolled in bio. and soc. next semester.

Revised   We enrolled in biology and sociology next semester.

Faulty   NYC is a haven for writers.

Revised   New York City is a haven for writers.

Faulty   The reference can be found in Vol. 6, sec. 5, p. 1. [These abbreviations are used in bibliographies and documentation only.]

Revised   The reference can be found in Volume 6, section 5, page 1.

EXERCISE I

Correct the use of abbreviations in these sentences. When appropriate, write out abbreviations.

Example: You can create your own home pg. on the World Wide Web—just consult the appropriate chap. in a self-help manual.

You can create your own home page on the World Wide Web—just consult the appropriate chapter in a self-help manual.

1. The World Wide Web was developed mostly at the European Laboratory for Particle Physics, near Geneva, Switz.
2. The Web project was really a spin-off of Apple Comp. Corp.'s HyperCard program.
3. Netscape, which some users claim is the most popular Web browser, has versions for both Windows and Mac. users.
4. Even if you don't have access to a Web browser, you can type in an e-mail address that will do the job; for example, you can tap into the system at Univ. of Kansas.
5. Best of all, you don't have to be a pHd. To figure out how to do some exciting Web browsing.

NUMBERS

The use of numbers as part of written work follows patterns and conventions that may vary in different disciplines. Here are the standard usages that apply in the humanities.

CRITICAL DECISIONS

Citing Numbers Accurately

Using numbers in writing—statistics, dates, measurements, monetary amounts—requires precision on the writer's part. Whenever you cite numbers in your work, make sure to check your source, or your own count, for accuracy.

31f Write out numbers that begin sentences and numbers that can be expressed in one or two words.

Weblink
http://ccc.commnet.edu/grammar/numbers.htm
Using numbers and writing lists.

One to ninety-nine

nineteen   seventy-six

Fractions

five-eighths   two and three-quarters

Large round numbers

twenty-one thousand   fifteen hundred

Decades and centuries

the sixties   or   the '60s
the twenty-first century or   the 21st century

Numbers that begin sentences should be written out.

Faulty	57 percent of those attending the meeting fell asleep.
Revised	Fifty-seven percent of those attending the meeting fell asleep.

When it is awkward to begin a sentence by writing out a long number, rearrange the sentence.

Awkward	Forty-two thousand eight hundred forty-seven was the paid attendance at last night's game.
Revised	The paid attendance at last night's game was 42,847.

31g   Use figures in sentences according to convention.

Numbers longer than two words

1,345   2,455,421

Units of measure

Rates of speed	**Temperature**	**Length**	**Weight**
60 mph	32° F	24¼ in.	21 pounds

Money

$.02   2¢ $20.00 $1,500,000 $1.5 million

Amounts of money that can be written in two or three words can be spelled out.

two cents

twenty dollars

Scores, statistics, ratios

The game ended with the score 2–1.

The odds against winning the weekly lottery are worse than 1,000,000 to 1.

Addresses

Apartment 6   2nd Avenue
231 Park Avenue   East 53rd Street
New York, New York 10021

Telephone numbers

301-555-1212

Volume, page, and line references

Volume 6   act 1 scene 4 line 16
pages 73–99   99–115   100–03

Military units

the 41st Tactical Squadron   the 6th Fleet

Dates

481–470 B.C.   (Full dates before A.D. 1.)   A.D. 70
from 1991 to 1992   1991–92
1998–2003   2003–04

Time

Write out numbers when using the expression *o'clock*.

10:00 a.m.   but   ten o'clock in the morning
10:02 p.m.   but   two minutes past ten in the evening

31h | **Edit to eliminate numbers and figures mixed together in one sentence unless these have different references.**

Faulty A spacecraft orbiting Earth travels at seventeen thousand miles per hour, but the images seen through its window appear to be moving not much faster than images seen from a car traveling 60 mph.

Revised A spacecraft orbiting Earth travels at 17,000 mph, but the images seen through its window appear to be moving not much faster than images seen from a car traveling 60 mph.

EXERCISE 2

Correct the use of numbers in these sentences. Write out numbers in some cases; use figures in others.

> *Example:* On August thirty-first, 1995, Bass PLC sold its distribution network to Tradeteam.
>
> On August 31, 1995, Bass PLC sold its distribution network to Tradeteam.

1. An enterprising British brewery has decided to try out home delivery on its customers with the claim that at least 24 cans of beer will be on the customer's doorstep within forty-eight hours once the order has been placed.

2. 3 cities have been targeted for the service so far—London, Nottingham, and Birmingham.

3. Customers must order a minimum of one crate (24 cans), and they can expect to pay 17.99 pounds with a delivery charge of 1.99£ added on.

4. The service will be tested for 3 months and then evaluated for profitability and consumer satisfaction.

5. Nottingham and Birmingham beer drinkers don't have much of a choice of brands—only one is available—but Londoners can choose from among 8 premium beers.

CHAPTER

32

Hyphens

A small but important mark, the **hyphen** (-) has two uses: to join compound words and to divide words at the end of lines.

32a Using hyphens to make compound words

Compound words are created when two or more words are
brought together to create a distinctive meaning and to function grammatically as a single word. Many compounds occur together so often
that they have become one word, formed without a hyphen, and many
words appearing in pairs remain separate.

sandbox	outline	casework	aircraft
sand toys	out loud	case study	air conditioning

Use a hyphen to link words when a compound expression would
otherwise confuse a reader, even if only momentarily.

Confusing	Helen's razor sharp wit rarely failed her. [Helen's *razor* is not the subject; Helen's *wit* is.]
Clear	Helen's razor-sharp wit rarely failed her.

> **1** Form compound adjectives with a hyphen to prevent misreading when they precede the noun being modified.

The following hyphenations make compound or multiple-word modifiers out of words that might otherwise be misread.

low-interest loan   state-of-the-art technology   hoped-for success

Note that when a **compound adjective** is positioned *after* the noun it modifies, it does not need hyphenation.

Helen's wit was razor sharp.

A compound modifier is not hyphenated when its first word ends with the distinctive suffix of a modifier.

Helen's impressively sharp wit rarely failed her.

Because of its ending, the first word in this compound modifier is not misread. In this case, the *-ly* suffix marks *impressive* as an adverb, and the reader knows that *impressively* will not function as the subject. Because there is no possibility of misreading, no hyphen is used. The same analysis holds when the first word of the compound is a comparative or superlative modifier (see 11e).

Weblink

http://www.superconnect.com/
wordsmit/hyphens.htm

A lighthearted page on "hyphenphobia," false notions about the use of the hyphen.

The least expensive item in that store cost more than I could afford.

The sweetest sounding voice in the choir belonged to a child of ten. [*By contrast:* The sweet-sounding voice belonged to a child of ten.]

> **2** Form compound nouns and verbs with a hyphen to prevent misreading.

Use a hyphen with **compound nouns** and **compound verbs** when the first word of the compound might be read as a separate noun or verb. Hyphenated nouns and verbs are marked as such in a dictionary.

cross-reference (n)   cross-examine (v)   runner-up (n)   shrink-wrap (v)

> **3** Use hanging hyphens in a series of compound adjectives.

Hang—that is, suspend—hyphens after the first word of compound adjectives placed in a parallel series.

The eighth-, ninth-, and tenth-grade classes went on the trip.

4 Follow conventions in hyphenating numbers, letters, and units.

Hyphenate fractions and the numbers twenty-one through ninety-nine.

> one-fourth   seven-thousandths   forty-six

Hyphenate figures and letters joined with words to form nouns or modifiers.

> 4-minute mile   B-rated   U-turn

Hyphenate units of measure.

> light-year   kilowatt-hour

5 Hyphenate compounds formed by prefixes or suffixes according to convention.

Use a hyphen with the prefixes *ex*, *quasi*, and *self*, with the suffix *elect*, and with most uses of *vice*. (Consult a dictionary for specifics.)

> ex-President   quasi-serious   self-doubt

Use a hyphen with the prefixes *pro*, *anti*, and *pre* only when they are joined with proper nouns.

No hyphen	**Hyphen with proper noun**
prochoice	pro-Democracy
antimagnetic	anti-Maoist

But use a hyphen with a prefix or suffix that doubles a vowel or that triples a consonant.

No hyphen	**Hyphen with doubled or tripled letters**
antiseptic	anti-intellectual
childlike	bell-like

32.1

6 Hyphenate to avoid misreading.

> re-form (to form an object—such as a clay figure—again)
> reform (to overhaul and update a system)

32b Using hyphens to divide a word at the end of a line

To the extent possible, avoid dividing words at the end of a line. When you must divide words, do so only at syllable breaks (as indicated in a dictionary). Even when given suggestions for hyphenation by word-processing software, you often face a choice concerning hyphenation that could make a difference in clarity. The following conventions improve comprehension.

- Divide compound words at the hyphen marking the compound.
- Divide words at a prefix or suffix.
- Eliminate hyphenations that hang a single letter at the beginning or end of a line.
- Avoid hyphenating a word the first syllable(s) of which forms another word (man-age, for-tune) and could confuse readers.
- Never hyphenate single-syllable words.
- Do not hyphenate abbreviations, contractions, or multiple-digit numbers.

32.2

EXERCISE I

Use hyphens in the sentences that follow to form compound adjectives; to mark prefixes or suffixes; to note fractions, numbers less than one hundred, or words formed with figures; and to prevent misreading. Place a check beside any sentence in which hyphens are used correctly.

> *Example:* Following WWII, Pepsi Cola Company succeeded in recruiting Alfred N. Steele, a tough talking, two fisted, pin-striped warrior with a unique grasp of the mood of the fifties.
>
> Following WWII, Pepsi-Cola Company succeeded in recruiting Alfred N. Steele, a tough-talking, two-fisted, pin-striped warrior with a unique grasp of the mood of the fifties.

1. Steele was uniquely qualified to lead the Pepsi Cola Company when it began to falter because of its outdated marketing campaign; he had been educated at the world's greatest soft drink institution—the Coca-Cola Company.

2. Beginning his career running a circus, he moved into advertising and then jumped to a vice presidency at Coca Cola.

3. Subsequently, Steele accepted the more lucrative offer from Pepsi-Cola, though in his first quarter at the company it lost $100,000 as Coca-Cola pulverized the entire industry with a 67% stranglehold on the soft drink market.

4. Coca Cola was the darling of the ever expanding middle class, while Pepsi was a favorite of the downtrodden who couldn't afford to sacrifice Pepsi's extra ounces for Coke's prestige.

5. Thus, Steele set his sights on getting Pepsi into America's living rooms, and to that end redesigned Pepsi's standard 12 ounce bottle.

CHAPTER

33

Understanding the Research Process

R esearch begins with a question, with a need to *know*. You will enjoy your work as a researcher more if you can manage to take an assignment from your teacher and make it your own by formulating a question that you, personally, want to answer. Then, you will spend your time locating and examining sources because you are truly interested in your topic, not simply because you are fulfilling an assignment.

This is the first of five chapters devoted to research. This chapter provides the basic strategies for posing the questions that launch research and for seeking information, both inside and outside the library, that will help you to answer your questions in the form of a research paper. Chapter 34 gives you the necessary background for conducting electronic searches. Chapter 35 discusses the ways you will actually *use* the source materials you find: by taking notes, summarizing, paraphrasing, and quoting. Chapter 36 provides guidance on arranging materials and writing your paper. And Chapter 37 acquaints you with the process of documenting sources—acknowledging in your papers that you have drawn on the work of others.

Weblink

http://www.researchpaper.com/

One of the best Internet resources for help with research papers. Check out the Idea Directory and Discussion Area for help getting started.

33a Making your research worthwhile

1 Personal interest justifies effort.

The process of conducting research takes time. For a research project to be worthwhile, you're going to have to justify it as a reasonable investment. What will make the investment worthwhile? In a word, *interest*. Any efforts you make at the beginning and through the early stages of the research process to become interested in your work will pay handsome dividends.

CRITICAL DECISIONS

Adopting Strategies to Motivate Yourself as a Researcher

The best research is conducted by those who are fully interested in their topic. Interest will motivate you to look for sources, find connections among them, and evaluate them in ways that will eventually lead to your research question. Interest and motivation are clearly functions of critical thinking, as discussed in Chapter 1:

- Read actively: Be alert to similarities and differences. See 1a.
- Challenge yourself and your sources. See 1b.
- Place particular events or ideas in a broader context. See 1c.
- Evaluate what you read. See 1g.

Motivation is easy to talk about in theory. In practice, generating personal interest in a research topic may be more difficult. Let's assume that you have been given an assignment on the social relationships made possible on the Internet, the topic of the student research paper you'll see developed throughout this section of the book. You've surfed the Net. You've corresponded by e-mail. What's to know? Why write about *this* topic?

Such a response is legitimate; but given that a teacher expects you to write a research paper, you will have work to do, and you may as well enjoy it by finding something interesting about which to write. To generate interest where none (or little) exists, try the strategies in the next box.

2 Personal interest improves writing.

Your effectiveness as a writer is directly related to your motivation:

- Motivated writers work hard with their sources, staying with each one long enough to form a definite, critical response.
- Motivated writers return to a library or make an additional call to locate promising sources.
- Motivated writers are willing to tinker with the various ways in which sources might be related. These relationships can provide original insights for the final paper.

The investment of personal interest pays two types of dividends: you enjoy and actively learn from the process of research, and you produce higher quality work.

3 Using essay writing as a foundation for research writing

The process of writing a research paper is similar to that of writing an essay. Both require that you think critically, not only about the

Generating Personal Interest in a Topic

With a bit of effort, you can discover enthusiasm for many topics, even those that you do not choose yourself.

- **If you find the topic interesting:** If you are drawn to the topic, so much the better. Divide it into several well-defined parts. Ask: Which part do I want to learn more about? Use your answer to locate general sources. Then read.
- **If you are repelled by an assigned topic:** Try to understand your negative response. Negative reactions, as well as positive ones, can lead to an effective paper. Again, divide the topic into well-defined parts. Ask: What information could help me to understand my reaction? Use your answer to locate general sources. Then read.
- **If the topic leaves you feeling neutral:** At the beginning stages, you may not know enough about a topic to be interested. When you learn even a little about the topic, you may discover possibilities. So go to a general source—an encyclopedia or an introductory book—or try a general index (for example, the *Readers' Guide to Periodical Literature*) to locate two or three promising articles to read.

  1. Based on your reading, identify as many angles of approach to the topic as you can. Discovering an approach you never considered may spark your interest.
  2. Generate as many questions as you can, based on what you read. Perhaps one will become your research focus.
  3. Read in "hyper-alert" mode. Actively respond to multiple points in the article. Perhaps one response will become your research focus.

sources you read but also about the positions you take as you develop your ideas.

In Chapter 3, you will find a diagram that models the writing process (see 3a-1). This illustration shows writing and thinking as circular, recursive activities. *Recursive* means looping back on itself. That is, while the writing process has identifiable stages, you will *not* work through these stages in a straight-line fashion. You will devote time to each of the following stages, but not necessarily in this order and not necessarily one stage at a time. You will

- define your purpose and audience;
- generate ideas and organize information;
- write a draft; and
- revise the draft.

A personal commitment to your topic will motivate you not only to challenge your sources but also to challenge yourself. Student researcher Logan Kole initially asked, *Is there anything unique about electronic communication?* His initial answer was *no*, aside from the fact that e-mail communication takes place over the phone wires. But as Logan learned through his research, and as you will see demonstrated through his paper, computer-based communication is both similar to and different from face-to-face communications in ways that have commentators both excited and deeply concerned. Given his initial research, Logan came to a new, revised question: *What are the ways in which the Internet is changing how people interact and form relationships?* In response to this revised question, Logan completed his research and wrote a successful paper.

Your original ideas are essential.

Writing a research paper involves a process of drafting and revision, in much the same way that writing an essay does—but with a difference: in research writing, you not only have the process itself to help clarify your thinking, but also you have source materials, which will help you test the soundness of your ideas as they evolve. Writing a research paper is *not* a process of locating a certain number of sources and then stitching them together mechanically. The process requires original, active thinking. The successful paper must be based on an original idea: *your* idea.

For more information on the process of writing, see Chapter 3. For an in-depth look at revising and rethinking, see Chapter 4.

EXERCISE 1

Interview two of your instructors. Ask what kinds of research they do and why their research interests them personally. Ask what, if any, "burning questions" have directed their research. Why do these questions burn for them? Take notes during the interviews. Then review these notes and write three paragraphs: two paragraphs devoted to summarizing the interviews; and one paragraph in which you make observations about the research your instructors do and their personal relationships to that research.

33b | **Determining the scope of your paper and identifying a research question**

1 | Determining the scope of your paper

Try to avoid two frustrating experiences: squeezing a great deal of research into a paper, only to feel that you've treated the material superficially, and, conversely, trying to pump extra material into a paper for which the topic seems too slight. To avoid these problems, you will need to understand several factors that affect the scope of your work: assignment, audience, topic, and intended level of detail.

■ Your *assignment* helps to set the scope of your project: specific tasks, length, and number and variety of sources expected. In 44b, you will find a list of key verbs associated with essay questions. These same verbs—such as *compare*, *discuss*, and *justify*—will be found in typical research assignments, so you should be aware of them and their definitions.

■ Your *audience* will determine key elements of your paper, ranging from tone, to vocabulary, to structure. Who is your audience? Will you be writing for specialists or nonspecialists? For college students or readers of the OP-ED page? Are your readers likely to agree with you or not? See 3a-3 for specific questions to help you analyze your audience and its needs and to make subsequent decisions in your paper.

■ Your *topic*, and the ways in which you can divide it into subtopics, will also help to define the scope of your paper. Almost immediately on beginning your research, you will learn enough about your topic to define several component parts. In your research paper, you will need to decide how many parts to work with. Your decisions will affect the scope of your paper.

■ Your *intended level of detail* for the paper will also affect the scope of your work and your selection of topics (or subtopics). A single topic can be discussed in minute detail at great length, or briefly in a quick overview. Be clear about the level of detail you will be bringing to your paper, or to specific sections of the paper.

2	Identifying your key research question

As you continue to read about your topic, you will sift through your questions and eventually arrive at one that interests you most—the question that you will answer by conducting still more research. The advantage of working with a question, as opposed to a thesis, at this point, is that you are acknowledging that you still have to discover the answer(s), rather than just find evidence to support a prematurely established conclusion. How can you tell if your research question is a good one? Consider the advice in the following box:

Weblink

http://courses.ncsu.edu/classes/
hi482001/step2.htm

Hypertext guide to Forming a Research Question, specifically for History courses, but applicable to any field.

CRITICAL DECISIONS

Do You Have a Good Research Question?

Devise a question that you, personally, **need** to answer to ensure that your research project will be interesting to you. As you reflect on what you think will be your main research question, consider the following:

1. Have any of your sources answered the question completely and, in your view, comprehensively?
   - If *no*, then your question is a good one—your research efforts will provide an answer that does not yet exist.
   - If your sources *have* completely and comprehensively answered your research question, try to find some aspect of the question that is *not* yet answered, to ensure that your efforts are original.

2. Does your question linger with you? Do you find yourself thinking about this question at odd times—on the way to the mailbox or the cafeteria?
   - If *yes*, then stay with your question: it has engaged you. Frequently, it is in these "off" hours, when you are not formally working, that important insights occur.
   - If *no*, then reexamine your question. Make sure it fascinates you sufficiently to continue letting it guide your research.

3. Does investigating your question give you opportunities to make connections from one source to another—connections that the sources themselves don't seem to be making?
   - If *yes*, then stay with your question: it is prompting efforts of *synthesis*—you are piecing elements of a puzzle together, which is what researchers do.
   - If *no*, then reexamine your question. Make sure the question encourages you to forge connections.

---

3 Understanding strategies for writing arguments in different disciplines

Writing a research paper in one discipline or another involves arguing and using evidence in ways that are appropriate to that discipline. Are you asking questions and providing evidence like a sociologist or a biologist? like an engineer? Conventions for constructing arguments change from one discipline to the next, and you should be aware of these conventions while writing your research papers. Discussions in this book will help: see Chapters 38, 39, and 40 for details on writing arguments in the humanities, the social sciences, and the sciences. Look for these key distinctions across disciplines:

Social sciences: Writers in business and in the social sciences (as described in 39a), often try to present significant social or economic patterns and to make arguments as to why those patterns are significant.

Humanities: As you will see in 38a, writers in the humanities make statements of interpretation about texts in all their variety, including stories, dramas, movies, sacred literature, correspondence, personal or government records, and the work of others (in the humanities). Textual materials become evidence in interpretive arguments. The goal is to persuade others that interpretations are valid.

Science: As you will see in 40a-2, writers in the sciences often make arguments that involve two claims. The first: *X is a problem,* or *X is puzzling.* The second claim takes this form: *X can be explained as follows.*

Writers and researchers in each of these broad discipline areas pose distinctive types of questions. Familiarize yourself with these questions and use them in your research.

EXERCISE 2

Working with roommates, classmates, or friends, generate a collection of assignments from different disciplines that call for writing. Examine the wording of these assignments with care, and answer these questions: What are the key verbs in each assignment? How do these verbs set an action plan for the writer? Does the role of the writer as originator of ideas change from one assignment to the next? What is discipline-specific about the assignment: its topic? method of analysis? presentation of findings?

33c Generating ideas for the paper

Perhaps you have selected a broad subject, which you may have already begun to restrict and focus. Or you may have started with a question and have begun to follow it up with additional questions. Here, we consider ways of further focusing your work and of searching for information sources about your topic (see 3a-1). Specifically, we will consider (1) how to keep an ongoing research log of your ideas; (2) how to develop a search strategy for preliminary reading; and (3) how to develop a search strategy for more focused reading, leading toward the development of your working thesis.

1 Keep a research log.

Many students find it valuable to keep track of their ideas in a research log. They write down their initial questions in this log and update it as often as possible. The log becomes a running record of all their inspirations, false starts, dead ends, second thoughts, breakthroughs, self-criticisms, and plans.

One technique that is particularly useful at the outset of a project is called *nonstop writing*. Nonstop writing (sometimes called *brainstorming* or *freewriting*) requires you to put pen to paper, consider your topic, and write down anything that occurs to you. Generate as many ideas as you possibly can within ten or fifteen minutes. At the end of the session, you may have some useful ideas to pursue. Here, for example, are some initial ideas generated by brief brainstorming sessions about computer-based communication.

> computer-based communication—may be more honest than face-to-face because you can't rely on appearance. Less edited than letters written by hand. Could it help people stay in touch? What about the coldness of it? Could it ever take the place of face-to-face contact?

Even though these ideas are in crude form, you can see a paper beginning to take shape here. As you proceed with your research, keep your log updated. You will want to do this not just to preserve a record of your research (often valuable in itself), but also to allow you to return to initially discarded ideas, which, at a later stage in the paper, may assume new relevance or importance.

Researchers use a log for other purposes, as well.

1. To jot down *sources* and possible sources—not only library sources, but also names and phone numbers of people to interview.
2. To freewrite their *reactions* to the material they are reading and to the people they are interviewing; these reactions may later find their way into the finished paper.
3. To jot down *questions* that occur to them in the process of research, which they intend to pursue later. (For example, how many people communicate by e-mail? Are there any first-person accounts of relationships started online?)
4. To try out and revise ideas for *theses* as their research progresses.

Avoid using your log for actually taking notes on your sources. It is best to do this on notecards or on your computer, so that you can freely rearrange notes as you prepare to write your first draft.

2	Talk with your instructor or with other authorities.

Before starting your research, do not neglect another important resource: your instructor. Schedule a conference or visit your instructor during office hours. Your conference may turn into a kind of verbal freewriting session, with several unresolved questions remaining at the end of the session—one of which may become the focus of your paper.

Generating Ideas for Your Paper

The following are three additional strategies for generating ideas. Each will help you consider ways in which to divide a broad topic into smaller, more manageable parts. You will probably be more specific and imaginative in thinking about *parts* of a topic than you will be in thinking about the topic as a whole.

- **Reading:** Read general works that survey your topic. The survey will suggest subdivisions.
- **Web browsing:** Browsing the Web can be an excellent springboard to ideas. You might check, first, with one of the general subject directories, such as Yahoo! <http://www.yahoo.com> to see how the editors create categories and subcategories of information, in the process providing an overview of an entire subject area. You will be linked to Web documents, which can also spark ideas.
- **Brainstorming:** Place your topic at the top of a page and, working for five or ten minutes continuously, list any related phrases or words that come to mind. After generating your list, group related items. Groups with the greatest number of items indicate areas that should prove fertile in developing your paper.
- **Listing attributes:** In a numbered list, jot down all of the attributes, or features, that a broad topic possesses. Then ask of every item on your list: What are its uses? What are its consequences?

You have now focused on one or more research questions. You have done some preliminary reading and perhaps have talked to one or two authorities on the subject. You have begun generating some written ideas. At this point, you have followed the basic writing process by focusing on a topic (3a-1) and have given some thought to your purpose and audience (3a-2, 3).

Remember that having selected a research question, you are under no obligation to zealously guard it against all changes. Quite possibly, you will need to adjust your focus—and therefore your key question—as your research and your thinking on a subject develop.

EXERCISE 3

Choose a subject and develop some ideas about it, using one or more of the strategies discussed in this section. Read at least two relevant sources, and then develop a research question for a paper on the subject.

33d Developing a strategy for preliminary research

I Beginning systematic research

Effective search strategies often begin with the most general reference sources: encyclopedias, bibliographic listings, biographical works, and dictionaries. These general sources are designed for people who want to familiarize themselves relatively quickly with the basic information about a particular subject. Authors of general sources assume that their readers have little or no prior knowledge of the subjects covered and of the specialized terminology used in the field. By design, they review a subject in less depth than do specialized sources. So you'll want to read the more general sources relatively early in your search.

Weblink

http://encyclopedia.com/

A free searchable site with more than 17,000 articles from the Columbia Concise Electronic Encyclopedia.

Consult librarians as a resource.

Librarians have made it their career to know how to find information quickly and efficiently. This does not mean that they will do your research for you. It means they will be happy to direct you to the tools with which to do your own research. Frequently, the key to getting the information you need is simply knowing where to look. The next sections will provide some assistance in this area. Your reference librarian will be able not only to supplement our list of sources (see 33-f), but also to tell you which ones are best for your purposes.

Weblink

http://www.s9.com/biography/

This searchable free online biographical dictionary includes more than 28,000 biographies.

2 Refining your thinking with systematic research

Systematic reading can help you to refine your thinking about a topic. New sources can lead you to a revised research question. Again, Logan Kole's experience provides a good illustration.

A bit too early in the process, Logan settled on a research question that significantly restricted his information gathering: *What are the ways in which people use the Internet to deceive others?* As it happened, the majority of Logan's sources discussed both the advantages and the disadvantages of communicating online. His initial focus on Internet deception might have worked to guide the writing of a paper. But the more Logan read, the more convinced he became that deception and ill-intent describe only part of a story that many people find promising and exciting. In fact, to dwell exclusively on the negatives would have misrepresented, in Logan's view, the source materials he had gathered.

Understanding the Research Process

His initial research therefore led him to a newly revised question that, in turn, organized the remainder of his research and the writing of his paper: *What are the ways in which the Internet is changing how people interact and form relationships?*

3   Bringing your research to an end

You should recognize that any diagram of the search strategy or of the focusing procedure makes these processes look neater than they generally are. In practice, they are often considerably less systematic, because writing is such a recursive process—as shown in 3a-1 and 3d-3.

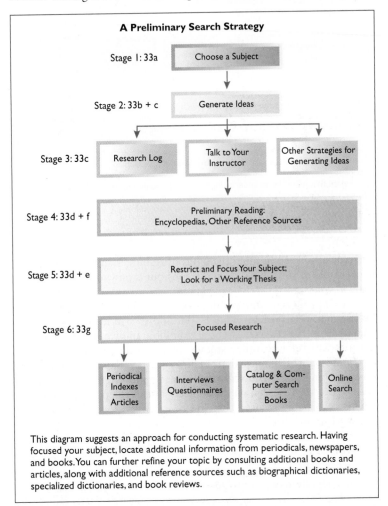

A Preliminary Search Strategy

Stage 1: 33a — Choose a Subject

Stage 2: 33b + c — Generate Ideas

Stage 3: 33c — Research Log | Talk to Your Instructor | Other Strategies for Generating Ideas

Stage 4: 33d + f — Preliminary Reading: Encyclopedias, Other Reference Sources

Stage 5: 33d + e — Restrict and Focus Your Subject; Look for a Working Thesis

Stage 6: 33g — Focused Research

Periodical Indexes / Articles | Interviews Questionnaires | Catalog & Computer Search / Books | Online Search

This diagram suggests an approach for conducting systematic research. Having focused your subject, locate additional information from periodicals, newspapers, and books. You can further refine your topic by consulting additional books and articles, along with additional reference sources such as biographical dictionaries, specialized dictionaries, and book reviews.

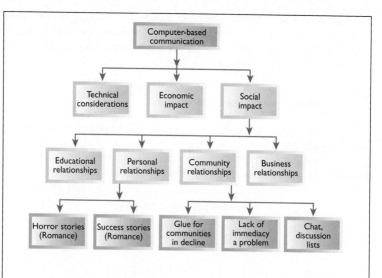

This diagram illustrates the focusing and selection process of student researcher Logan Kole. Selection and focusing brings Logan to his initial topic of computer-based communication. He quickly sees from his initial reading on the topic that he can take his research in three very different areas and therefore needs to restrict the topic still more. Guided by additional reading, he identifies four areas of interest: educational, personal, community, and business relationships. Any of these areas would provide an appropriate scope for his paper.

Aware that he might be undertaking too broad a topic, Logan nonetheless decides to focus on the boundary between two areas—community relationships and personal relationships. He reasons that groups are comprised of individuals and that a discussion of one will aid his discussion of the other.

It is crucial to keep in mind the kinds of resources and procedures that are available to you, and—given the constraints on your time—to use as many as you can.

As you proceed, you will discover that research is to some extent a self-generating process. That is, one source will lead you—through references in the text, citations, and bibliographic entries—to others. Authors will refer to other studies on the subject. Frequently, they will indicate which ones they believe are the most important, and why. At some point you will realize that you have already looked at most of the key research on the subject. This is the point at which you can be reasonably assured that the research stage of your project is nearing its end.

EXERCISE 4

Working with your topic, begin preliminary research. Start keeping a research log. Read one or two general reference sources; from these, try restricting the focus of your topic. As you do so, identify several sources that more specifically address your research needs. Having read one or more of these sources, can you refine your research question? Check on your success in focusing your topic by creating a diagram similar to the one above.

Devising a working thesis

1 Answering your research question

During your preliminary reading you began to focus on a *research question*. Recall Logan Kole's question: *What are the ways in which the Internet is changing how people interact and form relationships?* As you continue to read about your subject, you should begin to develop your own ideas about it. Answer your research question, at least provisionally, and you will have a *working thesis* (see 3d): the clearest, most succinct statement thus far of your paper's main idea.

This thesis is *provisional:* it is subject to change as you come across new material and as your thinking about the subject develops. For now, however, this working thesis is the main idea that shapes your thinking. The working thesis will also influence the focused reading of your subsequent research. By defining relevant areas and eliminating irrelevant ones, it narrows the scope of your search for supporting evidence.

For the sake of convenience, let's examine four working theses. Here are four discipline areas, and four narrowed topics:

For a paper in the *humanities,* the topic is nineteenth-century literature about the potential excesses of science, for example, in *Frankenstein* and *Dr. Jekyll and Mr. Hyde.*

For a paper in *business,* the issue is who owns the information contained in genetic algorithms.

For a paper in the *social sciences,* the topic is social and ethical issues in technological intervention in human reproduction.

For a paper in *science,* the topic is whether genetically altered food products are safe.

2 Taking a stand: The working thesis as a statement to be proven

Weblink
http://www.indiana.edu/~wts/wts/thesis.html
An extended look at the process of composing and revising a thesis statement.

So far, these are only *topics*—not theses. To develop a working thesis from each of these topics, you will need to make a *statement* about the topic (after surveying a good deal of source material). Here are four statements that can be used as working theses:

Humanities: Frankenstein was perhaps the first in a long line of books to exploit people's nervousness about scientific progress.

Business: Companies employing genetic engineers try to be diligent about patenting their discoveries.

Social Sciences: Safeguards need to be strengthened to protect infertile couples being promised "miracle cures" from the latest expensive medical procedure.

Science: Biotechnology promises to improve the *quantity* of food, but quantity will mean little unless we can guarantee the safety of genetically altered foods.

Note that while each thesis requires that the writer support his or her opinion, the first two theses tend to be *informative*, whereas the second two tend to be *argumentative*. That is, in each of the first two cases, the thesis itself is not a particularly controversial one. It is not a proposition that normally generates strong emotions. In the latter two cases, however, the writer will argue one side of a fairly controversial issue. These are issues on which it is sometimes difficult to get people to change their minds, even after considering the evidence, because they have strong underlying feelings about them. As you write the thesis, understand whether you are writing an informative or argumentative research paper. If you are writing an argument, consult Chapter 6 for guidance.

EXERCISE 5

Based on your preliminary reading in general sources (Exercise 4), develop two working thesis statements about your topic: an *informative thesis* and an *argumentative thesis*. Make sure that each thesis takes the form of a *statement* about the topic.

33f Doing preliminary research and reading

If you follow the strategy for preliminary research presented earlier, you will begin your research efforts with a systematic review of general sources. In this section, we will review some of the most useful general sources. Note: While all of the sources mentioned here have a print format, many (such as the major encyclopedias) are migrating to the World Wide Web. Check with your librarian to see if your school has access to these Web-based resources.

Encyclopedias, bibliographies, dictionaries

Encyclopedias

A general encyclopedia is a comprehensive, often multivolume work that covers events, subjects, people, and places across the spectrum of human knowledge. The articles, usually written by specialists, offer a broad overview of the subjects covered. From an encyclopedia you may discover a particular aspect of the subject that interests you and see how that aspect relates to the subject in general. Encyclopedia entries on major subjects frequently include bibliographies.

Keep in mind that encyclopedias—particularly general encyclopedias—are frequently not considered legitimate sources of information for college-level papers. Thus, while you may want to use an encyclopedia article to familiarize yourself with the subject matter of the field and to locate specific topics within that field, you probably should not use it as a major source, or indeed, for anything other than background information.

One disadvantage of encyclopedias is that since new editions are published only once every several years, they frequently do not include the most up-to-date information on a subject. Naturally, this is of more concern in some areas than others: if you are writing on the American Revolution, you are on safer ground consulting an encyclopedia than if you are writing on whether doctors consider alcoholism a disease. Still, the nature of scholarship is that *any* subject—including the American Revolution—is open to reinterpretation and the discovery of new knowledge, so use encyclopedias with due caution. Following are some of the most frequently used general encyclopedias:

Academic American Encyclopedia

Collier's Encyclopedia

Columbia Encyclopedia

Encyclopedia Americana

Encyclopædia Britannica

COMPUTER TIPS

The Library Without Books

More and more, libraries are beginning to resemble computer labs rather than book repositories. Many of the indexes you may be used to consulting, such as the *Readers' Guide to Periodical Literature* and many others, are now available electronically through your library's online subscription, the Internet, or CD-ROM. Often these electronic resources do more than find titles and brief descriptions of articles and other sources of information; they also allow you to retrieve the full text of the article. Ask your reference librarian for a listing of these electronic resources, and for instructions on how to access them and print out articles.

Biographical sources

Frequently, you have to look up information on particular people. Note that some biographical sources are classified according to whether the person is living or dead. The following are some of the most common biographical sources:

For persons still living

American Men and Women of Science

Contemporary Authors: A Biographical Guide to Current Authors and Their Works

Current Biography

Directory of American Scholars

International Who's Who

For persons living or dead

American Novelists Since World War II

American Poets Since World War II

Biography Almanac

Contemporary American Composers: A Biographical Dictionary

McGraw-Hill Encyclopedia of World Biography

National Academy of Sciences, Biographical Memoirs

Webster's Biographical Dictionary

Dictionaries

Dictionaries enable you to look up the meaning of particular terms. As with encyclopedias, dictionaries may be either general or specialized in scope. Some of the more common dictionaries are listed in 22b-1.

2 Other print sources of information

In addition to encyclopedias, biographical sources, and dictionaries, you may find the following sources useful.

Guides to the literature enable you to locate and use reference sources within particular disciplines. Here are five examples:

Business Information Sources

Guide to Historical Literature

How and Where to Look It Up: A Guide to Standard Sources of Information

Reference Books: A Brief Guide

Sources of Information in the Social Sciences

Handbooks provide facts and lists of data for particular disciplines. Here are several examples:

The Allyn & Bacon Handbook (covers grammar and style)

Gallup Poll: Public Opinion

Handbook of Basic Economic Statistics

Handbook of Chemistry and Physics

Statistical Abstract of the United States

Almanacs also provide facts and lists of data, but are generally issued annually:

Almanac of American Politics

Congressional Quarterly Almanac

Dow Jones Irwin Business Almanac

Information Please Almanac (general)

The World Almanac (general)

Yearbooks, issued annually, update data already published in encyclopedias and other reference sources:

Americana Annual

Britannica Book of the Year

Statesman's Yearbook

Atlases and gazetteers provide maps and other geographical data:

National Atlas of the United States of America

Times Atlas of the World

Citation indexes indicate when and where a given work has been cited *after* its initial publication; these are useful for tracing the influence of a particular work:

Humanities Citation Index

Science Citation Index

Social Science Citation Index

Book review indexes provide access to book reviews. These are useful for evaluating the scope, quality, and reliability of a particular source:

Book Review Digest (includes excerpts from reviews)

Book Review Index

Government publications are numerous and frequently offer recent and authoritative information in a particular field:

American Statistics Index

Congressional Information Service

The Congressional Record

Government Manual

Guide to U.S. Government Publications

Information U.S.A.

Monthly Catalogue of U.S. Government Publications

Consult your librarian for information on guides to the literature, almanacs, and other reference guides relevant to your subject.

Library of Congress Subject Headings

If you are making a systematic search to refine your subject, you should probably check the *Library of Congress Subject Headings.* This set of volumes indicates how the subjects listed according to the Library of Congress System are broken down. For example, drug abuse is broken down into such subtopics as "religious aspects," "social aspects," and "treatment." You can use the *Library of Congress Subject Headings* as you would use encyclopedia entries or the *Bibliographic Index* below. First, you can survey the main aspects of that subject. Second, you can select a particular aspect that interests you. Third, you can focus your subject search (in both the book and periodical indexes) on the particular aspect or subtopic that interests you, since these subtopics indicate the headings to look under in these indexes.

Weblink

http://www.access.gpo.gov/
su_docs/locators/cgp/index.html

The Catalog of U.S. Government Publications: A search and retrieval service that provides bibliographic records of U.S. Government information resources.

Bibliographic Index

Although we will cover periodical indexes later (see 33g-2), it is appropriate to mention here the *Bibliographic Index* is an excellent research tool both for browsing through some of the subtopics of a subject and for directing you to additional sources. The *Bibliographic Index* is an annual bibliography of bibliographies (that is, a bibliography that lists other bibliographies), arranged by subject. Shown on page 541, for example, is the listing under "Computer-mediated communication" in the 2001 *Bibliographic Index.*

Each of these listings represents a bibliography that appears in another source—a book, a pamphlet, or an article. In most cases, the bibliography appears as a source of additional readings at the conclusion of the book, the chapter, or the article. In some cases, however, the bibliography stands by itself as an independent publication. If you browse through a few successive years of listings on a subject, you will probably discover some topics that interest you, as well as a source of readings on that topic.

Main heading
(redirects user
to another
main heading)

Computer-mediated communication *See* Telematics

Telematics

Main heading

> George, G. and Sleeth, R. G. Leadership in
> computer-mediated communication: implica-
> tions and research directions. *J Bus Psychol*
> v15 no2 p305-10 Wint 2000

Title of periodical

Volume, number,
page number(s)

Author

> Joinson, A. N. Self-disclosure in computer-
> mediated communication: the role of self-
> awareness and visual anonymity. *Eur J Soc
> Psychol* v31 no2 p191-2 Mr/Ap 2001

Date of periodical

> Jordan, T. Language and libertarianism: the poli-
> tics of cyberculture and the culture of cyber-
> politics. *Sociol Rev* v49 no1 p15-17 F 2001

---

3 **General electronic sources**

There are two types of electronic database resources: CD-ROM
disks and online material. Most periodical indexes that are available in
print (such as *Readers' Guide* and *Humanities Index*) are also available on
CD-ROM. Since a CD can store several years' worth of indexes, a CD
search takes less time and effort than a search through several bound
volumes. Many general reference print materials, such as *The Oxford
English Dictionary* and various encyclopedias, are currently available on

33.1

COMPUTER TIPS

Bookmarks

One of the most convenient time savers for using the
Internet is the "bookmark," a record of a URL that
you'd like to remember. URLs are often complex and
unwieldy, so to copy them down and later type them in again by hand
invites mistakes. Instead, let your Web browser keep a list of them for
you. In the course of your research, when you access a Web page from
which you use information or one that you think you may need to access again, add a bookmark to your list. Then, when you need to return
to the page, all you have to do is click on that bookmark. Most browsers
let you examine your bookmarks, so your list can function as a readily
accessible record of the URLs you'll need for your bibliography.

Using General Sources

- Use *encyclopedias* to get a broad overview of a particular subject.
- Use *biographical sources* to look up information about persons living or dead.
- Use *general dictionaries* to look up the meaning of particular terms.
- Use *guides to the literature* to locate reference sources in particular disciplines.
- Use *handbooks* to look up facts and lists of data for particular disciplines.
- Use *almanacs* to look up annually updated facts and lists of data.
- Use *yearbooks* to find updates of data already published in encyclopedias and other reference sources.
- Use *atlases* and *gazetteers* to find maps and other geographical data.
- Use *citation indexes* to trace references to a given work after its initial publication.
- Use *book review indexes* to look up book reviews.
- Use *government publications* to look up recent and authoritative information in a given field.
- Use *bibliographic sources* to locate books and articles on a particular subject.
- Use *electronic sources* to locate large databases and current information.

CD-ROM—a format that allows users to make rapid cross-references and searches.

One important index is InfoTrac (originally on CD but migrating to the Web), which provides access to articles in over 1,000 business, technological, and general-interest periodicals, as well as the *New York Times* and the *Wall Street Journal*. Some specialized reference works on CD-ROM can be particularly interesting and rich in resources, depending on your research topic; a renowned example is the *Perseus* CD-ROM program from Harvard University Press, a large compendium of material on the classical world, including social, archaeological, literary, and linguistic material from classics scholarship.

Consult your librarian, who will have a listing of CD-ROMs and Internet resources that you can use in your research. See Chapter 34 for a detailed discussion on searching electronic sources.

EXERCISE 6

Use your working thesis to guide your access to one or more of the reference materials listed in this section. Keep a record of the sources used (keep full bibliographic information, including electronic access information if you browse the Internet or use an online service). Take notes on each source.

Focused research: Print sources and interviews

Once you have looked through a number of general sources and developed a working thesis, you have some basic knowledge about your subject and some tentative ideas about it. But there are limits to your knowledge—which correspond to the limits of the kinds of sources you have relied on so far. You need more specific information to pursue your thesis.

1 **Looking for specific sources**

General sources are not intended to provide in-depth knowledge, nor can they explore more than a few of the often numerous aspects of a subject. Refer back to the diagram on page 534. If you were researching the subject of the social impact of computer-based communication, your general sources might be sufficient to get you to the third level of the diagram, but the sources' inherent limitations would prevent them from taking you any further. For information about the kind of topics on the fourth level—details on the particular successes and failures of online communication—you would need to do more focused reading. You need a strategy for locating information in articles and books, either online or in the library, or via interviews.

2 **Finding print materials in libraries**

The following overview of available sources will help you focus on the ones that best address your working thesis. Periodical indexes are often preferable to the main library catalog as a first step in conducting focused research. Note that the search process for most print sources involves searching by author, title, and subject. For good *subject* topics, refer back to the *Library of Congress Subject Headings*, described in 33f-2.

General periodical indexes: Magazines

Periodicals are magazines and newspapers published at regular intervals—quarterly, monthly, daily. Periodical articles often contain information available from no other source and are generally more up-to-date than books published during the same period. You are probably familiar with the *Readers' Guide to Periodical Literature* as a means of locating magazine articles, but there are numerous other periodical reference guides.

For example, consider *Ulrich's International Periodicals Directory*. This is not a periodical index, but rather a subject guide to periodicals;

that is, it directs you to periodicals on a given subject. To find out more about the nature or scope of a particular magazine, check *Katz's Magazines for Libraries*. This reference tool lists the most commonly used magazines and offers basic descriptive and evaluative information about each.

Like encyclopedias, periodical indexes are of two types: *general* and *specialized*. The most commonly used general periodical index is, of course, the *Readers' Guide to Periodical Literature*, which indexes magazines of general interest such as *Time, Newsweek, U.S. News and World Report, The New Republic, Sports Illustrated, Commonweal*. Here, for example, is a *Readers' Guide* entry for "Internet—social use." The first entry is from the print volume; the one that follows, from the *Readers' Guide* online database, provides details on one particular reading selection.

INTERNET—*cont.* ——————————————————————— Main heading

Subheading ———————————————— **Social use**

            See also

Related main ——— Foreign Affair (Web site)
headings   Online dating

      E-mail and mom. Touré. por *Essence* v29 no11 p66 Mr 1999

      Geeks [J. Dailey and E. Twilegar] J. Katz. il pors *Rolling Stone*   no 811 p 48-50+ Ap 29 1999   — Includes picture

Title of   Home sweet virtual home. N. Gross. il *Business Week* no3649
periodical —   p 200+ O 4 1999

      Logging on. il *Fortune* special issue p29-30 Wint 2000

      The Net is a family affair. D. Brady. il map *Business Week*   no3659 p EB80-EB82+ D 13 1999

      Turkish delight [M. Cagri] il por *People Weekly* v52 no21 p84 —— Volume, pages,   N 29 1999   date of issue

ONLINE DATING

      For a good man, click here [dating] S. Schlosberg. il *Health*   (*San Francisco, Calif.: 1992*) v13 no7 p78+ S 1999

      They've got love [online dating leads to marriage] il *People*   *Weekly* v51 no6 p46-51 F 15 1999   Subject of

      Valley of the doll-less [Internet dating thrives in Silicon Valley]   article, if not
Author ——— B. Stone. il *Newsweek* v134 no7 p59 Ag 16 1999   clear from title

      What do guys think about meeting girls over the Internet? il   '*Teen* v43 no2 p36 F 1999

If you had located the second-to-last entry on an electronic search, the screen or printout would look like this:

TITLE
    Valley of the doll-less
OTHER TITLES
    Augmented title: Internet dating thrives in Silicon Valley
PERSONAL AUTHOR
    Stone, Brad
JOURNAL NAME
    Newsweek
SOURCE
    Newsweek v 134 no7 Aug 16 1999. p. 59.
PUBLICATION YEAR
    1999
PHYSICAL DESCRIPTION
    il
ISSN
    0028-9604
LANGUAGE OF ARTICLE
    English
ABSTRACT
    California's Silicon Valley has the highest percentage of unmarried men in the United States, with the result that Internet dating services are booming. For a nominal monthly fee, clients gain access to such sites as <http://www.match.com> and <http://www.matchmaker.com>, which allow users to post their profile and picture on the Web and sort through thousands of other user profiles. Male clients claim to get three to four emails a week, whereas women say they receive several every day. The disadvantages of using Internet dating agencies are discussed.

DESCRIPTORS
    Online dating; Silicon Valley Calif
DOCUMENT TYPE
    Feature-Article

Another useful general periodical index is the *Essay and General Literature Index*, which indexes (by subject, author, and sometimes by title) articles and essays that have been collected into books. The index is especially useful in that it gives you access to material that might not otherwise have surfaced in your search. These articles and essays generally would be classified under the humanities, but some deal with social science issues as well.

General periodical indexes: Newspapers

Most libraries have back issues of important newspapers on microfilm. The *New York Times Index* may be used to retrieve articles in the *Times* as far back as 1913. There are also indexes for the *San Francisco*

Chronicle, the *Los Angeles Times*, and the *Wall Street Journal* (an important source of business news). The *Newspaper Index* lists articles from the *Chicago Tribune*, the *New Orleans Times-Picayune*, the *Los Angeles Times*, and the *Washington Post*. You can print out "hard copies" (from microfilm) of articles you need. If you're looking for articles in newspapers other than these, check dates of stories in the *New York Times Index*, or see whether the newspaper has a search service.

Following is a sample entry on "Computers and the Internet" from the *New York Times Index*. The entry cross-refers readers to more than fifty related topics, one of which is "Marriages."

COMPUTERS AND THE INTERNET. See also
Abortion, S 30
Acquired Immune Deficiency Syndrome, J1 19
Advertising, J1 19,21,28, Ag 9,16,21
Afternic.com, S 16
Aged, Ag 3
Airlines and Airplanes, J1 6,19, Ag 1,2,10,23, S 6,9,22,24,25
Alcoholic Beverages, J1 9, Ag 16
Allergies, S 21
Animals, J1 6
Apparel, J1 12,13, Ag 29, S 18,21,25,28
Architecture, J1 23, Ag 10,17

. . .

Lizards, J1 27
Lotteries, J1 18
Love (Emotion), J1 23
Magazines, J1 20, Ag 28,29
Magic and Magicians, J1 6
Marbles, J1 20
Marriages, Ag 17

Listed under "Marriages" is the entry noted above for August 17, 2000:

Description of story —

Many Indian- and Pakistani-Americans are eliminating their parents as marriage brokers by turning to Internet Websites like Internet Matrimonials, A1 Matrimonials, IndianMarriages and Suitable Match; find the impersonal, direct communication through such sites to be more efficient and more in keeping with contemporary attitudes; most still judge potential mates by the criteria their parents would apply: religion, caste, subcaste and graduate degrees; photo; drawing (M), Ag 17,G,1:2

Date of story section no., page no., column no.

The library catalog

Almost certainly, your library's catalog has been converted to electronic form, allowing you to search for items far more quickly than you could when they were filed on cards. You can search the catalog by *author*, by *title*, or by *subject*. Many library catalog terminals also allow access to magazine and newspaper databases such as MAGS and

NEWS. In some cases, you can view (or print out) abstracts or even complete texts of particular items that you locate in such indexes. Electronic catalogs are more current than print indexes, since they are updated far more frequently. In addition, electronic magazine and newspaper catalogs generally allow you to search more publications at once than their print counterparts, and they almost always cover a greater period of time—usually several years. The disadvantage is that electronic databases generally don't include information more than ten years old. Thus you would still have to rely largely on print indexes for information about—for example—the Watergate scandal of the 1970s.

Weblink

http://www.ipl.org/

The Internet Public Library is the first public library of the Internet.

Browsing through some of the subject entries is a good way of locating books on your topic. But before you do this, you should have at least begun to narrow your subject. Otherwise, you could be overwhelmed with the sheer number of books available. (There may be several hundred books on various aspects of Internet communication.)

The convenience of electronic catalog searching should not blind you to the old-fashioned advantages and pleasures of going into the stacks and browsing among the shelves in your area of interest. Browsing is not an efficient or comprehensive substitute for methodical catalog searching. Some important books may be checked out or shelved in another area. But opening promising titles and examining the contents may reveal valuable sources that you might otherwise have overlooked. Here is a computer-display entry for a book that Logan Kole used in researching and writing his paper.

Computer display

Title:	Life on the screen: identity in the age of the Internet / Sherry Turkle.
Author:	Turkle, Sherry
Published:	New York: Simon & Schuster, 1997, c 1995.
Description:	347 p.; 25 cm.
Edition:	First Touchstone Edition, 1997.
Notes:	"A Touchstone Book"
	Includes bibliographical references (p. [271]-320) and index.
Subject:	Computers and civilization.
	Computer networks–Psychological aspects.
ISBN:	0684833484
DBCN:	AGR-4402

LOCATION	CALL NO.	STATUS
South Florida	QA76.9.C66 T87 1997	Available
CC/MAIN/CIR	(book) c.1	

The computer display reproduces the information on a card in the card catalog. The display will (often) list the status of the source: checked in, checked out, or on reserve. Accurately note the call number (on this display QA79.9.C66 T87 1997) and consult a library map before going to retrieve the source.

Book Review Digest

An invaluable source for determining the quality of books is the *Book Review Digest*. This publication, collected into annual volumes, indexes many of the most important books published during a given year by author, title, and subject. More important, it provides lists of reviews of those books, as well as brief excerpts from some of the reviews. Thus, you can use the *Book Review Digest* to quickly determine not only the scope of a given book (each entry leads off with an objective summary) but also how well that book has been received by reviewers. If the reviews are almost uniformly good, that book will be a good source of information. If they are almost uniformly bad, stay away. If the reviews are mixed, proceed with caution.

Trade bibliographies and bibliographies of books

For books too recent to have been acquired by your library or that the library does not have, you may wish to consult *Books in Print* and *Paperbound Books in Print*. These volumes, organized by author, title, and subject, are available in some libraries and in most bookstores. For books that your library does not have, but that may be in other libraries, consult the *Cumulative Book Index* and the *National Union Catalog*.

EXERCISE 7

Researching either the topic you have been working on or some other topic, locate at least five books and ten articles on the subject. Provide complete bibliographic information for these sources (see 35b). Locate several reviews of at least one of the books, and summarize the main responses in a paragraph.

3 Finding material through interviews and surveys

Although you will probably conduct most of your research in the college library, remember that professional researchers do most of their work *outside* the library—in the field, in labs, in courthouses, and in government and private archives. Consider the possibilities of conducting original research for your own paper, by interviewing knowledgeable people and devising and sending out questionnaires. (Many subjects have been extensively discussed by experts on television news programs, talk shows, and documentaries. It may be possible to borrow videocassettes or to obtain printed transcripts of such programs.)

Focused Reading for Print Material

- To locate articles in general-interest magazines, use the *Readers' Guide to Periodical Literature*, the *Readers' Guide CD-ROM Index*, *InfoTrac*, or another database index.
- To locate articles in newspapers, use the *New York Times Index* or other indexes for particular newspapers.
- To identify periodicals specializing in a given subject, use *Ulrich's International Periodicals Directory*.
- To determine the scope of a particular magazine, use *Katz's Magazines for Libraries*.
- To locate books and government publications, use the *library catalog*.
- To determine how a given subject is subclassified in the library catalog, use the *Library of Congress Subject Headings Index*.
- To locate reviews of books, see the *Book Review Digest*.

Interviews

Interviews allow you to conduct primary research and to acquire valuable information unavailable in print sources. By recounting the experiences, ideas, and quotations of people who have direct knowledge of a particular subject, you add considerable authority and immediacy to your paper. You can conduct three types of interviews: (1) by phone, (2) by e-mail, or (3) in person.

Those you select to interview may include businesspeople, government officials, doctors, professors, community activists, or your own grandparents. If you would like to talk to a business executive or a government official but do not have a particular individual in mind, call the public relations office (in a business) or the public information office (in a government agency) and ask for the names of possible interviewees. Then, call the individual and try to schedule an appointment. Even busy people can usually find some time to give an interview. Many will be glad to talk to someone about their experiences. But if you are turned down, as sometimes happens, try someone else.

It is important to prepare adequately for your interview. Devise most of your questions in advance. You can improvise with other questions during the interview, according to the turns it takes. Avoid *leading* questions that presume certain conclusions or answers:

> Why do you think that American workers are lazier today than they were a generation ago?

> What do you think of the fact that the present administration wants to burden small businesses with added health-care costs?

Instead, ask *neutral* questions that allow the interviewee to express his or her own observations:

What changes, if any, have you noticed in the work habits of your present employees from those who worked here in the 1960s?

To what extent has government funding of genetic research changed during the present administration?

Also avoid *dead-end* questions that require yes/no answers or *forced choice* questions that impose a simplistic choice on the interviewee:

Do you think that this was an important experiment? (dead end)

What should take priority, in your view: jobs or the environment? (forced choice)

Instead, ask *open-ended* questions that allow the interviewee to develop her or his thoughts at some length:

In what way was this an important experiment for you?

How do you think it is possible to deal with the seemingly conflicting needs of jobs and the environment?

Factual questions can be useful for eliciting specific information:

When did your restaurant begin offering a salad bar?

How many parade permits has the city denied during the past year?

33.2 Ask follow-up questions when appropriate, and be prepared to lead your respondent through promising, though unplanned, lines of inquiry. Throughout the interview show your interest in what your respondent is saying. On the other hand, keep in mind that your own reactions may unintentionally create cues that affect your subject's responses. Your subject, for instance, may begin to tell you what he or she thinks you

---

Checklist for Interviews

■ Determine what kind of information you need from the person, based on the requirements of your paper and its thesis.

■ Make an appointment, telling the person what your paper is about and how long the interview will take.

■ Become knowledgeable about the subject so that you can ask informed questions. If the person has written a relevant article or book, read it.

■ Prepare most of your questions in advance.

■ Take pen, pencil, and a hardback notebook to the interview. If you take a tape recorder, ask the person's permission to record the interview. Even if you do record the conversation, take notes on especially important comments.

■ At the end of the interview, thank the person for his or her time. Promise to send a copy of the finished paper. Soon afterward, send a follow-up thank you note.

want to hear (even if it is not quite accurate), based on how you have previously reacted. For this reason, trained interviewers try not to specifically respond to the interviewee's answers.

Surveys

Surveys are useful when you want to measure behavior or attitudes of a fairly large, identifiable group of people—provided that both the group and the measurements are carefully specified. An identifiable group could be freshmen on your campus, Democrats in town, Asian Americans in a three-block area, or autoworkers in two factories. Measuring attitudes or behavior could mean obtaining records and comparing the frequency of responses made to specific and carefully worded questions. On the basis of measured comparisons among the responses to questions, a researcher might venture some broad claims about patterns of response as indicators of attitudes or behaviors within the population measured (it is not safe to generalize beyond the group actually measured without rigorous statistical procedures). Such generalizations are usually made in quantitative terms: "Fewer than two-thirds of the respondents said they feel threatened by the possibility of contracting AIDS."

To get honest answers to your questions, it is essential to guarantee your respondents' anonymity. Most frequently, questions and answers to surveys are written, though occasionally they may be oral (as when, for example, you ask students entering the library for their attitudes on current American military activities). When you devise questions for a survey, apply some of the same considerations you do for interviews. For example, do not ask *loaded* questions that lead the respondent toward a particular answer ("Do you think that the money the university is spending to upgrade the president's residence would be better spent to reduce class size?"). For surveys, short-answer questions are better than open-ended questions, which are difficult to compare precisely or to quantify. It is relatively easy to quantify yes/no responses or responses on a five-point scale ("How concerned do you feel about the threat of AIDS? 5—extremely concerned; 4—very concerned; 3—moderately concerned; 2—somewhat concerned; 1—unconcerned").

CHAPTER

Using Electronic Resources

A s you are probably well aware, the Internet holds a universe of searchable information that can enrich your research papers. On the Internet you can—

- Find up-to-the-minute information on your topic.
- Locate pertinent charts, tables, graphs, and pictures for your papers.
- Participate in discussion groups in which experts exchange information.
- Identify and contact experts and conduct virtual interviews.
- Post questions on bulletin boards and in discussion groups with a reasonable expectation that experts will respond.

CRITICAL DECISIONS

Using Internet Sources
While you can find a wealth of information online, Internet-based research is a *supplement* to, and does not replace, print-based research. Only a fraction of the world's printed resources—books, newspapers, and periodicals— are available electronically. Unlike print libraries, the Internet is a decentralized, often chaotic environment in which to work. The search strategies that you use in libraries to locate sources must be adapted when you begin searching online. Finally, unlike the books and journal articles you find in your college library, resources on the Internet are not necessarily edited for fairness or accuracy—and you must take special care before using online sources in your papers. Good researchers develop the habit of evaluating the legitimacy of *all* sources. This obligation is especially important when working with online sources.

Online research differs from print-based research, requiring that you adjust both your research technique and your perspective on what you will find. As you will see, the strategies discussed in this chapter for launching your Internet searches build on techniques discussed in Chapter 33. The following general process of finding online resources will be familiar to you if you have searched for information in print-based libraries:

1. Begin by investigating broad topics.
2. Scan numerous sites, some of which will strike you as immediately promising.
3. Browse these sites and pursue links to other, related sites.
4. Narrow your search and locate Web pages on your specific topic.
5. Along the way, collect pertinent material—in this case not by photocopying articles or checking books out from the library, but by downloading computer files or taking notes electronically. (Some online material is archived onto CD-ROMs and is often conveniently available in CD form in libraries.)

Commercial and Professional Information Services Beyond the Internet

Libraries often subscribe to professional and commercial information services that archive in searchable form vast numbers of magazine and newspaper articles, journal articles, abstracts, monographs, and books or sections of books. These commercial services charge a fee for accessing their archives, but as a member of a college community you can (usually) gain access for free. Check in your school library's periodical room to determine which subscription databases are available. Here are a few of the more heavily used, commercial databases:

- Lexis–Nexis: locates news or government publications.
- InfoTrac: locates full-text newspaper and journal articles.
- DIALOG: provides access to more than 300 million items in over 400 separate databases in the humanities, the social sciences, the natural sciences, and business.
- PsychINFO: references items in journals of psychology.
- ERIC: references items in educational journals and reports.
- Arts and Humanities Search: references items in arts and humanities journals.
- WILSONLINE: provides electronic access to the printed indexes published by H. W. Wilson Co., including *Readers' Guide to Periodical Literature*, *Education Index*, and *Social Science Index*.

34a Finding the right online resources

In this section you will find definitions and tips on accessing the basic online resources: e-mail, Usenet discussion groups (or "newsgroups"), discussion lists (or "listservs"), synchronous communication (MOOs), anonymous ftp, and the World Wide Web. As with any information you locate in a search, you will need to assess the reliability of materials found online.

I E-mail

Definition. If you've used the Internet at all, it has probably been with e-mail—sending and receiving messages to and from friends and family. But e-mail can benefit you as a researcher as well. More and more authorities (university and private researchers, journalists, government officials) have and regularly use e-mail. Many (not all, of course) would welcome an inquiry from a student and would respond with an informed and authoritative reply. Don't overlook the research potential of e-mail. Through e-mail you can do the following:

- Conduct interviews.
- Exchange computer files that are not available to the general Internet user (text, graphics, charts, statistics, and so forth) with people who have such information to share.
- Read the current draft of a new project or an old unpublished conference paper that the scholar would be willing to share with you.

Reliability. Judge the reliability of an e-mail source as you would that of any person you've interviewed. When referring to this source in your paper, provide some background context. Who is this person? What is his or her area of expertise? Why is he or she qualified to speak on your topic? If possible, use an attributive phrase to establish the credibility of your source *in* the paper.

Access. How do you find e-mail addresses of people with whom you would like to correspond?

- Simply ask them. Note that some universities and businesses maintain e-mail phone books.
- The e-mail addresses of people who contribute to newsgroups and discussion lists are included in the headers of the messages they send. Save one or two messages and you will have their addresses.
- Use an Internet e-mail directory such as Bigfoot <http://www.bigfoot.com> or WhoWhere <http://www.whowhere.com>.

2 Usenet discussion groups or "newsgroups"

Definition. The easiest way to visualize a newsgroup is to think of a standard cork bulletin board hanging on a wall. Anyone can walk by and tack up a message, and anyone else can come by and read the message, respond to it, or put up a new message. Newsgroups on the Internet are electronic versions of that cork bulletin board. Anyone with an Internet account can use a newsreader to follow a continuing discussion, read the current messages, and post a reply or a new message. Newsgroups can provide an excellent forum for trying out your ideas on others before you commit to these ideas in your paper.

Reliability. Because they are a radically democratic forum in which everyone—the unknowing and the expert—can offer an opinion, newsgroups vary in reliability. Use material gathered from this resource with caution. If you want to refer to a newsgroup posting in a paper, first try to confirm from other sources the reliability of that information. You may also want to interview the person who posted the message by e-mail.

Access. If your school subscribes to a newsfeed, a central computer where all the messages are stored and fed to other providers, you will have access to a newsreader of some kind and you will be able to choose which newsgroups to follow (remember, there are well over 10,000). Newsgroup addresses read hierarchically, much like domain names, in a series of units separated by dots (see the box on page 566). For example, the newsgroup address "rec.music.bluenote.blues" is read as follows:

Its type is "recreation."

Its subtype is "music."

Its particular category is "bluenote."

Its topic is "blues."

That is, "rec.music.bluenote.blues" is a discussion group about blues music. When you join in on the conversation of a newsgroup, you will be able to read and reply to messages, just as you can with e-mail. Remember that in newsgroup posts, what you write is public.

3 Discussion lists or "listservs"

Definition. Academic discussion lists are similar to newsgroups, with one significant difference: you must actively subscribe to the list, and then you receive the messages directly as individual e-mail messages. The mailing of the discussions is essentially managed by automated computer programs that receive all incoming messages and immediately forward them to everyone who subscribes to the list; one of the most common of these automated programs is called "Listserv."

Reliability. Lists usually stick to their stated topics; although theoretically anyone can subscribe to any discussion list, usually contributors are serious about their commitment to the topic. They tend to be knowledgeable—though, as with any source, you will want to verify information before citing it as credible. The mere appearance of information on a discussion list does not ensure its reliability.

Access. To find a listing of currently active academic listservs, use your WWW browser to access the URL http://www.liszt.com (see 34a-5 for accessing WWW sites). If you find a list to which you would like to subscribe, address an e-mail message *to the listserv* (the machine that manages the list), not to the list itself. The machine will ignore the "subject" line of the e-mail box and read only the message, which must contain the following information:

- Type the word "subscribe". Don't use the quotation marks. Simply type the word as the first word in an e-mail message.
- Next, type the name of the list to which you want to subscribe.
- Finally, type your first name, followed by your last name.

The message must contain absolutely nothing else. (Added words can confuse the machine.) For example, if your name were Mary Rose, you would send the basic message "subscribe deos-l Mary Rose" (again, no quotation marks) to the listserv's address to subscribe to the Distance Education list. After you have subscribed, you will receive further instructions about using the list and posting to it. Note that some newsgroup or listserv discussions are password protected and are not open to the general public.

Communicating away from "real time"

Weblink

http://tile.net/listserv/

To find listservs on your chosen topics, check out this searchable listing of e-mail discussion groups.

A listserv is an *asynchronous* means of communication. That is, the discussion that occurs in this environment does not occur in real time—as spoken conversations do in person or by phone. On a newsgroup or listserv, one participant may post a comment on Monday; a second participant may post a response on Wednesday; and other responses may follow. All responses following the initial posting are called a "thread," and on a given listserv several threaded discussions may occur simultaneously. Asynchronous communication lacks the immediacy of face-to-face conversation, of course, but it also fosters an extended exchange of ideas in which points, counterpoints, and counter-counterpoints blossom over time. Moreover, asynchronous communication fosters this exchange of ideas among participants who live in different time zones and who maintain different schedules.

Definition. On the computer, you can enjoy real-time, synchronous communications with others in several ways: by participating in a chat room via an online service such as America Online; through software programs such as Microsoft's NetMeeting; or by connecting to a server (a host computer somewhere on the Internet) and entering a text-based virtual world called a MOO.

34.1

MOO is an abbreviation for **M**ultiuser dimension, **O**bject **O**riented—a more accessible version of an earlier shared virtual space called a MUD, which stands for **M**ultiuser **D**imension. These virtual spaces permit those who have logged on to them to have text-based conversations in real time. Unlike chat rooms in which virtual participants converse (via the keyboard) in a single location, MOO environments offer multiple "rooms" in the environment that participants can enter.

Educators have been quick to realize the potential of real-time, multiuser, virtual environments. Conducting classes virtually makes a great deal of sense when, for reasons of geography or economics, it is impossible for people to meet face-to-face. Increasingly, MOOs are used as meeting places for virtual conferences in which participants enter into different discussions in different rooms. In a MOO space, classes comprising students from around town or around the world can meet in real time and discuss the day's lessons. You may take a composition course in a MOO:

- Meet as a class to critique a paper.
- Meet group mates virtually in a MOO (or private chat room), instead of meeting face-to-face in the library.
- Arrange to conduct a real-time interview by inviting an expert to log on to a MOO environment.
- Log on to a MOO-based writing lab in Pittsburgh, Pennsylvania, to get some real-time help on a paper you are working on in Madison, Wisconsin.

A particular advantage of the MOO is its written record. Because all exchange is typed, you can record whatever people have communicated that is of interest. This capability is especially helpful when conducting interviews or peer critiques.

Reliability. MOOs can be more or less academic in the discussions you find taking place in them. The reliability of MOO-based information as source material for a paper will therefore vary considerably. Let common sense be your guide. If you use a MOO space to conduct a synchronous interview with an expert source, then you will regard the resulting information with the same authority as you would had it been recorded in a face-to-face interview. Bring the same standards to bear on sources located in MOOs that you would to information found in class discussions, interviews, and so on. In all cases, you will want to verify that sources have the background needed to speak with authority.

Access. You can connect to MOOs in either of two ways. First, using software available at your school, you can link to the server (or host

Weblink

http://www.du.org/dumoo/
moohelps.htm

An introduction to MOO use.

computer) on which the MOO exists. In this type of connection, exchanges will be entirely text-based. Very likely, your school's computer help desk will have a document that can get you started with a hookup for MOOs.

A more recent development is the presence of MOOs on the World Wide Web, an environment that gives MOOs the capability to relay real-time sound and graphics. To gain access to a Web-based MOO, you need a browser. Then, you can get onto any of several general search engines, type MOO as the query, and receive an ample listing of possibilities. For starters, you might try these sites, which provide links to numerous MOOs:

Educational MOOs and MUDs	http://www.daedalus.com/net/moolist.html
The Lost Library of MOO	http://lucien.berkeley.edu/moo.html
A Nice Big List of MOOs	http://members.tripod.com/adm/popup/roadmap.shtml
Rachel's Super MOO list	http://cinemaspace.berkeley.edu/~rachel/moolist/edu.html

A note on MOO etiquette: When you log on to a MOO, be aware that it is a social world whose participants see what you have typed as you type it. Therefore, you should bring the same sense of respect and decency to MOOs that you do to face-to-face gatherings.

---

5   World Wide Web

Definition. Currently the most popular way of browsing and searching the Internet is via the World Wide Web. Its popularity derives both from its hypertext interface (clicking on the screen brings you to a new page of information) and its ability to display color and graphics. In addition, the Web has subsumed all previous Internet modes. Here are some key terms worth knowing:

- *Webservers:* specially configured computers, worldwide, on which information for the WWW is stored.
- *Web page or home page* (or simply *page*): individual documents on the WWW.
- *Web site or site:* a collection of pages.
- *URL:* the acronym (for Uniform Resource Locator) that designates particular characters used to locate a Web site. The URL is a Web site's "http://" address.

■ *Hypertext:* links from information on one Web page to related information on another Web page—perhaps located on another Web server in a different school, country, or continent. Hypertext links are often underlined in blue. Icons and photographs can also serve as links. If you see something on a Web page that you'd like to explore further and it's underlined in blue or looks like a link, click your mouse on it and you're there.

■ *Browsing:* linking from one Web document to another, following your interests. Software such as Netscape or Microsoft Explorer are used as browsing tools, or "browsers."

■ *Downloading:* Some links on a Web page may not be hypertext links but, rather, links that prompt you to download a file—that is, to transfer a file from the Web server (the machine on which the Web page resides) to your computer. Click on the link and the browser will display a message box asking if you would like to save the file.

■ *Search engines:* The Web has many different search engines, but all work on the keyword principle. You type a word or phrase into the search engine's subject box and the engine scans the Internet for Web pages. Different engines specialize in finding particular types of information. So it is best to conduct several searches using different engines. The next section, 34b, offers extensive guidance on using Internet search engines to find what you want online.

34.2

Reliability. The quality and reliability of information you find on the Web will vary considerably. Individuals, commercial operations, and organizations create their own Web sites. So, while you may find research reports and government documents and online medical journals, you may also find unsubstantiated opinion, self-serving advertisements, and propaganda. Judge your materials carefully—and see section 34c for extensive guidance on evaluating Web-based sources.

Access. Most likely, you will gain access to the Web through a browser such as Netscape Navigator or Microsoft Internet Explorer. You will move from document to document on the Web by following hypertext links. If the trail you follow begins to seem fruitless, you can back out of it by clicking the mouse on the "back" key (the left-pointing arrow near the top of the screen) in your browser. With enough backward steps like this, eventually you'll return to where you began, for a fresh start. (You can also click on "home" or "search" to start your search over.)

6 Anonymous FTP

Definition. "FTP" stands for "File Transfer Protocol." It's the standard method for transferring files (text documents, graphics, computer software) over the Internet. Normally, if you find a file you want to transfer to your own computer for viewing, you need to be able to access the computer where the information resides, in which case you would theoretically need an account on that computer and a password. However, many computer systems worldwide have been made partially accessible on the Web to "anonymous" users, people who don't have accounts. Hence, anonymous FTP provides a means for you to retrieve files from computers to which you normally would not have access. Knowing how to use FTP enables you to exchange or distribute lengthy documents for collaborative projects. It also permits you to store Internet files on your own computer so that you can access them more easily as you write.

Reliability. Information gathered through anonymous FTP is usually as reliable as print information in a library. Often it will consist of government documents, research reports, statistical tabulations of data, and so on. You may actually access visual and graphical information: pictures from the Hubble Space Telescope are available from NASA by anonymous FTP, for example.

Access. There are several ways of transferring files, but the easiest is to use your Web browser. Both Netscape and Microsoft Internet Explorer use FTP by downloading a file when you click a link on a Web page. Links can be set up not only to take you from one page to another, but also to start a file transfer.

EXERCISE 1

Working with the topic you have been researching in Chapter 33, use two of the following Internet resources to locate online materials that might prove useful in writing your research paper: e-mail, Usenet discussion groups or newsgroups, discussion lists or listservs, synchronous communication, or anonymous FTP.

EXERCISE 2

Use both of the online directory assistance programs mentioned in 34a-1 ("Bigfoot" and "WhoWhere") to locate your name and e-mail address and that of a friend who is attending another school. How useful do you find these services? Next, identify *one* expert on the topic of your research whom you would consider interviewing, if you had his or her e-mail address. (Select your candidate from one of the articles or books you identified in Chapter 33.) Find the expert's contact information. Compose a *brief* e-mail note, introducing yourself and your project. Send the note to the expert and ask for an interview—either by phone or e-mail. If the interview is granted, consult the advice at 33g-3.

There is no electronic card catalog for the Web, no Dewey Decimal or Library of Congress system by which each document added to the Web is assigned to its appropriate subcategory of knowledge and given a distinct retrieval code. The most frustrating aspect of the Internet for those seeking information is the difficulty of locating the information they're looking for. Typically, people will type in a query to one of the search services and then find themselves deluged with possible sites.

For example, a search for "black holes" on AltaVista, one of the most popular search engines, yielded 2,621,748 "hits." A search on HotBot yielded a more manageable, but still impractical 78,484 sites. In fact, the first of these 78,484 sites was for "The Capitalist Pig," a company that designs Web pages for businesses, and which has nothing to do with black holes, but whose opening paragraph is addressed to potential clients trying to navigate their Web browsers around "black holes of pages that just won't load." Why was such a useless response returned for this query? The search engine was looking only for the text string "black holes." It found such a string at the beginning of the document and, having no judgment of its own, had no way of knowing that the site in which it appeared had nothing to do with astronomy or astrophysics.

As an online researcher, *you* must provide the judgment that search engines lack. The way you express this judgment is to construct a precise query—the single most important key to a successful search. Good queries yield good results; poor queries yield poor results. This section will help you to devise good, focused search queries.

	Determine the type of information you need; choose appropriate search tools.

When conducting online searches, approach your task not as a single search but as a *series of related* searches—each focusing on *different* sources of information. The type of information you need in any particular search will determine the type of tools you use. For instance, if you

---

[1] Section 34b is based on our adaptations of two excellent sources on conducting Internet searches. The first is Keith Gresham's "Surfing with a Purpose" from the September/October 1998 issue of *Educom Review*, which provides our overall strategy for conducting Internet research. Gresham is an instruction librarian at the University of Colorado at Boulder. The second source for this section is "Guide to Effective Searching of the Internet," a tutorial on keyword searching prepared in 1998 by Michael Bergman of The Web Tools Company. Suggestions for Web links were provided by Prentiss Riddle, Web Master for Rice University. Visit and launch searches from the Rice University Internet Page at <www.rice.edu/Internet> to get updated advice on the best Internet search tools as they become available.

A Process for Conducting Research on the Internet

We recommend the search process devised by instruction librarian Keith Gresham (University of Colorado at Boulder). The section that follows this summary box is organized around Gresham's four-step process:

1. **Determine the type of information you need; choose appropriate search tools.** Do you need news? Government reports? Industry statistics? Journal articles? Magazines? Choose carefully among general search engines, specialty search engines, and subject directories.
2. **Create a list of search terms.** Search terms are those specific words or phrases that best describe the major concepts of your topic.
3. **Construct a search statement and conduct your search.** Depending on the search tool you are using, search by individual key words, by exact phrases, or by Boolean search expressions.
4. **Evaluate search results and revise the query (if needed).** Even carefully constructed searches retrieve irrelevant results or result lists with thousands of hits. If you don't locate useful information within the first fifteen retrieved sites, revise the query. Construct new search statements using different combinations of search words or phrases.

are looking for a very current topic in the news, you would choose to work with search engines such as NewsBot or TotalNews that search news sites on the Web. Using a general search engine such as AltaVista, which searches the entire Web (non-news sites included), would not be productive. You should realize that the information you need may not be freely available on the Web. Assuming your school has access, you might want to check your library's reference room for Internet-based subscription services such as Lexis–Nexis. However, if you are turning to the Web as a resource, be aware that Web search tools are classified into two types: subject directories and search engines.

Subject directories

Directories classify Web pages into types, according to a subject breakdown. For example, *Yahoo*, the most well-known directory, classifies Web sites into categories such as Arts and Humanities, Business and Economy, Education, Government, Health, News and Media, Reference, and Science. Each category is divided into subcategories: for example, Science includes sites on Astronomy, Biology, and Oceanography. Oceanography is further subdivided into sites such as Coral Reefs, Marine

Biology, and Meteorology. The subdividing continues (for example, "sea-grasses" is a subdivision of Marine Biology) until there are no more sub-classifications, at which point Yahoo provides hyperlinks to one or more relevant sites. Here are the URLs for several popular directories:

Argus Clearinghouse	http://www.clearinghouse.net
Internet Public Library	http://ipl.sils.org
LookSmart	http://looksmart.com
About.com	http://www.about.com
WWW Virtual Library	http://vlib.org
Yahoo	http://www.yahoo.com

COMPUTER TIPS

Carriage Returns, Linefeeds, and Formatting Problems

Each major type of computer system used in schools, businesses, and on the Internet—Unix, MS-DOS and Windows, and Macintosh—has a different method for breaking lines on the screen and for printing. As a result, what looks like perfectly formed text on one machine may wind up looking like a series of short, choppy little lines or perhaps like a long line trailing off the screen. When you retrieve text from the Internet, be prepared for such short or long lines, added spaces, and other strange formatting problems which will persist as you cut and paste text into your paper. Take time to reformat as you work, using your delete function and format menu. If necessary, delete multiple spaces with your word processor's search-and-replace function.

Search engines

Search engines index words and terms in Web pages and feature "spiders" or "robots" to retrieve documents containing these terms. The number of keywords queried by search engines is virtually unlimited, as opposed to the finite number of classifications used by directories (Yahoo has about 1,400). If a Web page's topic doesn't easily fall into one of the pre-established classifications, it may not be accessible through the directory. But the relatively smaller number of sites located through a directory may be an advantage in researching topics that are easily classifiable by the directory. The search for "black holes" in Yahoo, for example, yielded a very manageable 65 sites—in contrast to the thousands, or even millions of sites returned by the search engines.

Many search services are hybrids: Yahoo allows users to search by keywords, and Excite has some features associated with directories. Here are URLs for some of the most highly used general search engines.

General search engines

AltaVista	http://www.altavista.digital.com
Excite	http://www.excite.com
Google	http://www.google.com
Hotbot	http://www.hotbot.com
Infoseek	http://www.infoseek.com
Lycos	http://www.lycos.com
WebCrawler	http://Webcrawler.com

As a rule of thumb, remember: use *several* search services—a variety of search engines and subject directories—in any given search to assure that you don't miss important sites and sources of information.

Depending on your need for specific types of information, you may want to use more specialized search engines, as follows.

Searching to access multiple WWW indexes

Dogpile	http://www.dogpile.com
MetaCrawler	http://www.metacrawler.com

Searching for news

Weblink

http://www.askjeeves.com/

This unique meta-search engine allows you to enter your query in plain English in the form of a question.

When you are searching a topic of current interest in the news (as opposed to more static topics such as the Great Depression), consider using search engines that query news sources exclusively. The following tools will help you to search a variety of news sources.

CNN	http://www.cnn.com
NewsDirectory.com	http://www.newsdirectory.com
Google News	http://www.google.com/news
NewsIndex	http://www.newsindex.com
TotalNews	http://totalnews.com

And you may want to register at the *New York Times* site <http://www.nytimes.com/> for free access to the last year's *Times* online.

Searching mailing lists and Usenet news groups

Google Groups	http://groups.google.com
Liszt Directory of E-Mail Discussion Groups	http://www.liszt.com
WWW forums	http://www.forumone.com

Searching for people

Anywho Reverse Telephone Search	http://www.anywho.com/rl.html
Bigfoot	http://www.bigfoot.com
Finger (by Internet Site)	http://www.cs.indiana.edu/finger/gateway
Personal Web Pages	http://www.utexas.edu/world/personal
Switchboard	http://www.switchboard.com/bin/cgiqa.dll
WhoWhere?	http://www.whowhere.lycos.com
Yahoo! People Search	http://people.yahoo.com

Plan for multiple Internet searches.

Given the Internet's vast, unwieldy structure, it is certain that no single search tool will locate all the materials available. If you get into the habit of conducting *multiple* searches whenever you set out to find information, you increase the likelihood of locating useful materials.[2]

Use general search engines.

Google	http://google.com
AltaVista	http://www.altavista.com
HotBot	http://www.hotbot.com

General search engines cast the largest possible net over the Internet, searching through the largest databases available of Web sites. The retrieval lists for the general search engines tend to be large—unless you can limit the search by date or topic.

Use general search engines to find specialized sites.

Use the same general search engines, as above, but use the advanced search features to limit the retrieval list by specifying narrower searches. As part of the advanced search features of various engines, you can specify the domain (for instance, ".gov" or ".mil") that you wish to search, the dates, and types of publications. For more on domain names, see the box on page 566.

Use specialized news search engines.

NewsBot	http://www.newsbot.com
NewsIndex	http://www.newsindex.com
TotalNews	http://www.totalnews.com

---

[2]This discussion is based on the work of Keith Gresham, Instruction Librarian at University of Colorado at Boulder. Material is adapted from his article, "Surfing with a Purpose," in *Educom Review* 33.5 (Sept/Oct 1998): 22–29.

A specialized set of search engines will exclusively search news outlets for matches with your topic. These engines are particularly useful when you are searching topics of a rapidly changeable nature.

Use subject directories.

Yahoo!	http://www.yahoo.com
LookSmart	http://www.looksmart.com

The largest subject directories index tens of thousands of Web sites. If you can find your topic in the directory structure, you will likely discover useful information that you may not have found using any of the standard search engines.

Use engines that search discussion lists.

Google Groups	http://groups.google.com
ForumOne	http://www.forumone.com

The Internet Domain Name System

Accuracy in typing an Internet address is essential: a missed period or transposed letters will frustrate your efforts. To appreciate *why* this is so, read about the Domain Name System.

The naming system

The Domain Name System allows for each computer on the Internet to have its own address, much like the post office's system of states, cities, streets, and house numbers allows each building to have its own unique address. Internet addresses are composed of units separated by the symbol "." (pronounced "dot"). The Internet address "www.gsfc.nasa.gov" is read as follows:

- The abbreviation "gov" means this Internet site is located at a government agency;
- The particular agency is "nasa";
- The particular computer where the Internet service resides is named "gsfc"; and
- The service provided is particular to the World Wide Web ("www").

The major domain names are as follows:

com—companies and commercial sites

edu—educational institutions

gov—government organizations

mil—military organizations

net—Internet service providers and users

org—nonprofit institutions

If you are searching a topic that is likely to generate an ongoing Internet discussion, use one of these search engines to locate the discussion. You can join the discussion list and monitor the conversation about this topic (if the discussion is current), or you can access an archived discussion of your topic. Either way, the text of the discussion is available for you to copy and paste it into a word processor.

EXERCISE 3

Determine the type of online information you need to complement the print-based research that you began in Chapter 33. Using the information in this section, choose appropriate research tools—general search engines, specialized search engines, or subject directories. Plan (but do not yet begin) to conduct multiple Internet searches. Identify the tools you will be using.

2 Create a list of search terms.

The key to getting good results from Web searches and not wasting effort sifting through irrelevant sources is to formulate precise queries. Even the most accurate queries are unlikely to yield a significant number of usable documents, and poorly conceived ones are going to yield considerably worse results. Queries are poorly conceived when they are overly vague or when they employ an insufficient number of keywords. Most users submit an average of 1.5 keywords in their queries—not enough to produce fruitful results. This section will help you to select keywords, which you can then combine in various ways into a search statement (step 3, below).

Weblink

http://www.monash.com/
spidap.html

Detailed explanations of how search engines work and how to get the most out of them.

An Index to Keywords

To select keywords

1. Ask the five Ws and generate a list.
2. Strip out prepositions, articles, etc.
3. Classify the words remaining: nouns, actions, modifiers.
4. Focus on a noun: a person, place, or thing.
5. Narrow the search with a modifier to create a phrase.
6. Find synonyms.
7. Find the right level of generality.

We'll dramatize the process of formulating queries by presenting a scenario. One spring day, Jan, an office worker in downtown Minneapolis, notices that the fingers of her right hand feel strained when she bends them, and that her wrist is stiff. Later that day, at home, she applies ice but finds that her wrist and fingers still hurt. She decides to do some investigating on the Web.

Ask the five Ws.

A good way to begin formulating an accurate query is to jot down the *who, what, where, when, how,* and *why*. Considering her mystery ailment, Jan jots down the following:

- Who/What?—sore fingers, stiff wrist, injury, an accident
- Where?—at workplace, on-the-job pain
- When?—during typing
- How?—when I bend, painful fingers and wrist
- Why?—related to work at a keyboard? typing? safety?

Strip out prepositions, articles, and so on.

The next step is to break down the query by identifying key words. Note that common words such as *and, about, the, of, an, in, as, if, not, is, it* are ignored by search engines since they appear so frequently in connection with any subject. Eliminating such words leaves

sore	job	keyboard	injury
fingers	office	workplace	safety
stiff	typing	bend	accident
wrist	painful	pain	

Classify words.

Now let's further classify these terms by arranging them into three categories: *nouns (persons/places/things), actions,* and *modifiers.*

Person/Place/Thing		Actions	Modifiers
fingers	office	typing	stiff
wrist	job	bend	sore
workplace	pain		painful
injuries	keyboard		
accident	safety		

Focus on a noun—a person, place, or thing.

The most important terms in your query should be *objects*—that is, tangible "things." The thing (or person or place) you want to learn more about becomes the center of your search: your subject. Recall that much of the Internet is searched and classified by comprehensive subject directories such as Yahoo! and the Mining Company. As they scan the Web, the editors of those directories look for subjects that can be classified in categories and subcategories. Search engines will search the entire Web for documents, document summaries, or document titles. Every search will be based on a subject—a person, place, or thing—against which the engine will be computing matches. By narrowing in on a subject yourself and focusing on a noun (a person, place, or thing), you will align your search needs with the logic of the search tools on the Web.

In the example search, there are ten potentially useful keywords:

fingers, office, wrist, job, workplace,
pain, injuries, keyboard, accident, safety

But selecting a single keyword will not (in most cases) be sufficient for getting the results you want. Very often such one-word searches yield an unmanageably large return list. To conduct a successful search, you need to qualify your search term with a modifier.

Narrow the search with a modifier to create a phrase.

When you begin to qualify and make more precise your search terms by combining them in meaningful ways, Internet searches become more useful. For instance, narrowing "injuries" by including the modifier "workplace" yields the new search term "workplace injuries." Narrowing the keyword "wrist" by converting it to a modifier that qualifies the noun "pain" yields the new search term "wrist pain." Focusing the keywords in these ways had impressive results:

AltaVista search on "injuries": 849,750 hits

AltaVista search on "workplace injuries": 2,704 hits

HotBot search on "wrist": 27,680

HotBot search on "wrist pain": 9,834

Narrowing a search by using a modifier can help in two ways:

1. The narrowed search may directly yield the information you want.
2. The narrowed search may yield information that enables you to focus the search still further, bringing you that much closer to the information you want.

To illustrate: the first returned hit on the HotBot search of "wrist pain" listed a Web site for a product that relieved wrist pain—particularly "carpal tunnel syndrome" and "repetitive stress injuries." As it turned out for Jan, who was doing research on her wrist ailment, she suffered from what she suspected was carpal tunnel syndrome. A search on that term brought her to a wealth of pertinent information.

Using quotation marks: You may want to make sure that a search engine regards the words you have entered as an exact phrase or text string, rather than as individual words. For example, assume that Jan wanted a search engine to search for all occurrences of the word "workplace" when it appeared directly before the word "safety." She did *not* want the search to return all documents with only one of these words or even both of them—if they did not occur together in the desired sequence. You can instruct a search engine to treat words as an exact phrase by enclosing the words within quotation marks. Thus, you would type **"workplace injuries"** into the query box and click "Go" or "Submit." (Note that not all search engines recognize quotation marks as a means of defining phrases.)

Use the results of the five W exercise (see p. 568) to generate two- or three-word phrases that can function as the starting point for your Internet searches. Typically, one of these words will be a noun—a person, place, or thing; and one of these words will be a modifier that limits, or focuses, the noun. Working from her list of individual words, Jan generated several useful search phrases:

workplace injuries	workplace accidents
job safety	typing injuries
work-related pain	

Find synonyms.

Spend a few moments thinking of synonyms for your keywords. If you're having trouble thinking of synonyms, use a thesaurus (available on most Word processors—check under "tools," where you'll also find Spell checkers). Synonyms allow a search engine a greater chance to identify sources related to your query. In constructing a search relating to her stiff fingers and wrist, Jan settled on the synonym "occupation" and "occupational" for "job" and "work." She settled on the synonym "accident" for "injury"—not an exact synonym but an approximation she thought might yield more results.

Find the right level of generality.

One key to effective searching on the Internet is to search at the level of generality that will yield useful results. Recall our earlier discussion of directories, when we saw how Yahoo subdivides one of the disciplinary areas of **science** as follows:

Science

>**oceanography**

>>**marine biology**

>>>**seagrasses**

Clearly, keywords at too high a level—the level of *science*—will yield too many documents in an Internet search. Conversely, keywords at too low a level of generality—*seagrasses*—may yield too few documents, should your topic include other aspects of marine biology.

If you are using a keyword or phrase and the search returns too many or too few documents, shift your level of generality up or down, accordingly. When you are overwhelmed with hits in the tens of thousands, shift the level of generality *down* by experimenting with different modifiers that will limit the keyword. When you have the opposite problem—*no* hits—broaden the search term. For help in developing a sense of generality and specificity of search terms, go to Yahoo! or another subject directory (see the recommended lists earlier in this chapter) and work yourself up and down the directory structures.

EXERCISE 4

Use the suggestions in this section to create a list of search terms for your topic. Ask the five Ws and generate a list; strip out prepositions; classify the words as nouns, actions, or modifiers; focus on nouns; narrow the focus with a modifier to create a phrase; find synonyms and the right level of generality. At the completion of this exercise, you should have generated a list of search terms.

---

3   Construct the search statement and conduct your search.

You have devoted effort to identifying keywords or key phrases for your search. Now, depending on the search engine you use, you can refine these words and phrases further in an effort to improve your search results. The search engines themselves are increasingly providing a "refine" function—sometimes called "advanced" search tools or "power" searches. The refine function allows you to narrow searches by date, type of publication, and type of Web site—for instance, you might instruct the engine to search only organizations, government, or military sites. Refining your searches is easy: locate the advanced feature set and fill in (or, in some cases, click to check) a box. At the Excite search engine, once you type in a keyword and launch a search, the engine will prompt you to refine the search by offering additional terms that you can check off to include in your search.

Beyond using these "refine" functions that are built into the various search engines, you can refine your queries in two additional ways: use "wildcards" on word stems and use Boolean connectors between keyword terms.

Use "wildcards" on word stems.

You want to be able to select relevant documents containing *work*, but you also want to select documents containing *workplace*. To avoid having to use two similar keywords for the same concept (since it's best to limit the number of keyword terms to about three), you can "truncate" (cut off) the keyword to its stem—in this case *work*. Adding an asterisk to the stem produces *work**. Your search engine can now look for documents containing variants of the keyword—including variant spellings. For instance, some sources spell "carpal" (in carpal tunnel syndrome) as "carpel." Instructing the engine to search for *carp** would locate Web pages with variant spellings of the keyword. But note that the wildcard strategy, if not used carefully, will sometimes yield unintended and unwanted results: for example, a search on *carp** will retrieve documents about fish. Using *cit** in a query to search for documents containing *city* and *cities* will also select documents containing *citadel, citation, cite, citizen, citizenship, citric,* and *citronella.*

Use Boolean connectors between keyword terms.

One of the most effective ways to narrow your search is to use Boolean connectors between keywords. (The name comes from George

Weblink

http://www.ithaca.edu/library/
course/expert.html

A basic introduction to Boolean logic with Venn diagrams.

Boole, a nineteenth-century mathematician and logician, who developed Boolean algebra.) Such terms are called *operators* and the way they are used to connect keywords is called *syntax.* Note that the "refine" or "advanced" features of several search engines seamlessly incorporate Boolean logic into the search query, eliminating the need to master Boolean terminology. Still, Boolean logic underlies most search functions, so it's a good idea to be familiar with the terms. Note also that not all search engines support the full range of Boolean operators, though almost all recognize **AND, OR,** and **AND NOT** in queries. The main Boolean operators are listed in the box on page 573.

Constructing *multiple* Internet searches

Remember this important tip for effective Internet searching: Once you have settled on a topic, search the Internet *multiple* times, using different search tools. Here are two Web sites on carpal tunnel syndrome, found in different searches using different search tools:

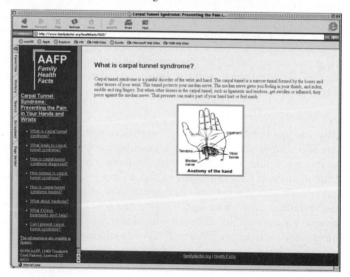

A second search found the Carpal Tunnel Syndrome home page, a vast resource of Web links on defining, preventing, discussing, and treating the disorder.

Using Boolean Logic

- **AND** Terms on both sides of this operator must be present somewhere in the document to be scored as a result. **AND** may be used more than once in a query to narrow a search: thus, using **London AND "Big Ben" AND "Buckingham Palace" AND Trafalgar** would yield only documents containing all four terms.
- **OR** Terms on EITHER side of this operator are sufficient to be scored as a result. **OR** means that the document may contain either term, but not necessarily both. In most cases, then, **OR** will yield too many results. It is mainly useful at the introductory stages of a search.
- **AND NOT** Documents containing the term that occurs AFTER this operator are rejected from the results set. (For instance, you might search on "Queen Elizabeth AND NOT ship.") **AND NOT** is a means of weeding out irrelevant documents. *Note:* Only one instance of an unwanted term is sufficient to eliminate a document from consideration.
- **NEAR** Similar to AND, only both terms have to occur within a specified word distance from one another to be scored as a result. You might search on "Diana NEAR Wales" or "Diana NEAR Charles."

(continued)

Using Boolean Logic *(continued)*

- **BEFORE** Similar to NEAR, only the first (left-hand) term before this operator has to occur within a specified word distance *before* the term on the right side of this operator in order for the source document to be scored as a result.
- **AFTER** Similar to NEAR, only the first (left-hand) term before this operator has to occur within a specified word distance *after* the term on the right side of this operator in order for the source document to be scored as a result.

See 34b-2 on using quotation marks with a search string to search for an exact sequence of words.

EXERCISE 5

Using the Internet tools that you identified in Exercise 3, conduct *multiple* searches on your topic. If your search tools allow, consider refining the search by date, Boolean operators (see the box in this section), or domain name. (For example, you might limit certain searches to URLs that end with "edu" or "gov".) Experiment with search terms, using different phrases to generalize or limit the search. Revise your search query if you do not locate useful information in the first fifteen retrieved sites. Switch to a different search tool if, after five revisions, you do not locate useful information.

4 **Evaluate search results and revise the query if needed.**

Even carefully constructed searches retrieve irrelevant results or results lists with thousands of hits. *If you don't locate useful information within the first fifteen retrieved sites,* revise the query. Construct new search statements using different combinations of search words or phrases that move up and down the level of generality that you would expect to find, for instance, in a subject directory. An example: if you are overwhelmed with the retrieval list of a keyword search on "computers," refine the keyword with a modifier and try "laptop computers." If that search is similarly overwhelming, add the word "reviews" to the keyword and search on "laptop computer reviews." Soon enough, you will reduce the list of retrieved Web sites to a manageable number. Each new combination of keywords will retrieve different results. *If after five revisions of your keyword you still aren't finding useful information, consider switching to a different search tool.* Then begin the search process again.

To illustrate this process of revision, consider the following example: Using the Alta Vista search engine, you could search on "repetitive stress injury" and have 6,813 documents retrieved—far too many "hits" to sort through in any meaningful, systematic way. Alta Vista offers an "Advanced

Search" feature that allows the researcher to limit the query. By directing the search engine to look for matches between specific dates (3/20/97–6/20/02), and specifying that the engine search only government documents (with a URL ending in ".gov"), you could narrow the retrieval list to 486 items.

One item in the retrieval list in the Alta Vista search was a site from the federal government's Occupational Safety and Health Administration (OSHA). This Web site is published by a credible source (an agency of the federal government) and opens with a definition of ergonomics that would prove very useful in a paper on repetitive stress disorders. Here is that Web page:

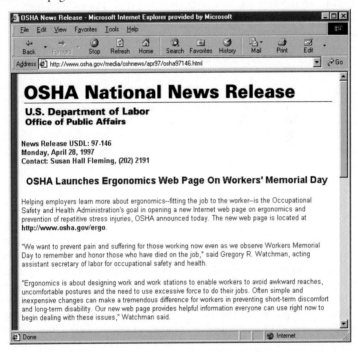

As this example illustrates, you should expect to revise your Internet searches. Very likely, useful information on your topic resides somewhere on the Internet, waiting for you to discover it. But the process of discovery typically takes several attempts with any given tool, such as Alta Vista or Excite. Recall from 34b-1 that you do well to launch *multiple* searches on your topic, using different tools. With each tool, expect to be somewhat overwhelmed with the initial retrieval list. Use the tool's "refine" or "advanced search" feature to fine-tune the search. More reliably, you can fine-tune a search using the techniques discussed in 34b-2 and 34b-3.

How do you assess the accuracy, reliability, and overall quality of information you find on the Web? In general, the same criteria that apply to print information (see 1g-1–2) also apply to Web-based information. Most major print journals, magazines, and newspapers have Web sites that post current and archived articles, and evaluating articles on these sites presents the same challenges as evaluating a printed article. However, a good deal of information on the Internet presents an additional set of challenges for evaluation primarily because anyone can "publish" on the Web: anyone with an ax to grind, anyone who imagines his or her words are worth broadcasting to the world, can do so with relatively little effort and expense, and with no outside review.

Moreover, self-published Internet authors may post their sites anonymously. Academic research is premised on the reader's ability to check facts and verify methods. Thus, when you encounter anonymously published Web sites, you face the task not only of determining the accuracy and fairness of the material, but also of inferring clues about the author's credibility. Students who refer to such sites in their research run the risk of using sources that are not valid. You should, therefore, avoid quoting from anonymously published sites unless you are instructed to view them as part of your coursework.

1   Evaluating Web pages

You will find a great deal of value on the Web. But as a researcher you should approach Web-based sources with caution—both for the above-mentioned reasons and because of the distinctive nature of electronic information on the Internet: Web search engines frequently retrieve irrelevant or questionable pages. Subsidiary pages may also be retrieved out of context, that is, apart from their "home" pages. Web pages that appear to be informational may actually be "infomercials" for products or services. Web pages may not be regularly updated, and may become outdated. Page hyperlinks may be outdated or inactive. Hyperlinks in otherwise reliable Web pages may lead to pages of doubtful reliability or accuracy at other sites. Web pages are inherently unstable; they can change or even disappear without warning. And outdated browser software, or software without necessary "add-ons" or "plug-ins," may not allow you to view certain Web pages accurately.

Weblink

http://www.netskills.ac.uk/
TonicNG/cgi/sesame?detective

Internet Detective—an extended look at the skills needed to evaluate Internet information critically.

A highly useful approach to evaluating information on the Web has been provided by Jan Alexander and Marsha Tate, reference librarians at the Wolfgram Memorial Library at Widener University. Alexander and Tate categorize Web pages into five major types. Following their explanation of these types, you will find questions to pose of each.

■ **Advocacy Web Page:** "one sponsored by an organization attempting to influence public opinion (that is, one trying to sell ideas). The URL address of the page frequently ends in .org (organization)."[3] *Examples:* National Abortion and Reproductive Rights Action League <www.naral.org>, The National Right to Life Committee <www.nrlc.org>, the Democratic Party <www.democrats.org>, the Republican Party <www.rnc.org>.

—What is the site advocating? Is the advocacy reasonable in tone?

—What does the organization have to gain through its advocacy?

—How does the organization characterize its opponents?

■ **Business/Marketing Web Page:** "one sponsored by a commercial enterprise (usually it is a page trying to promote or sell products). The URL address of the page frequently ends in .com (commercial)." *Examples:* Adobe Systems, Inc. <www.adobe.com>, Coca Cola Co. <www.cocacola.com>, Oxyfresh <www.oxyfresh.com>.

—Is advertising clearly differentiated from content?

—How does the commercial sponsor profit from the content on the site?

—Is the validity of the information compromised by commerce?

■ **News Web Page:** "one whose primary purpose is to provide extremely current information. The URL address of the page usually ends in .com (commercial)." *Examples:* USA Today <www.usatoday.com>, *Washington Post* <www.washingtonpost.com>, CNN <www.cnn.com>.

—Could you verify the news on the site from a print source?

—Are sources of information clearly listed so that you can verify them?

—How current is the page? When was it last revised?

—Are editorial opinions clearly distinguished from news items?

■ **Informational Web Page:** "one whose purpose is to provide factual information. The URL address frequently ends in .edu or .gov, as many of these pages are sponsored by educational institutions or

---

[3]This section is taken in large part from the Web site "Evaluating Web Resources," (http://muse.widener.edu/Wolfgram-Memorial-Library/webevaluation/webeval.htm, copyright 1996–1999, revised 25 July 2001) which complements the book *Web Wisdom: How to Evaluate and Create Information Quality on the Web* (1999) by Janet Alexander and Marsha Ann Tate.

government agencies." *Examples:* U.S. Census Bureau <www.census.gov/>, dictionaries <www.webster.com>, Health and Human Services (HHS) <www.cdc.gov/tobacco/sgr/sgr_forwomen/factsheet_outcomes.htm>, Buddhist Studies <www.ciolek.com/WWWVL-Buddhism.html>.

—How current is the information? When was it last revised?

—Can you verify the information?

—How reputable are the sources of information?

■ **Personal Web Page:** "one published by an individual who may or may not be affiliated with a larger institution. Although the URL address of the page may have a variety of endings (e.g., .com, .edu, etc.) a tilde (~) is frequently embedded somewhere in the URL."

—Does the individual have any obvious biases?

—Is the site free of obvious errors in grammar, punctuation, and usage?

—On the basis of what experience does the individual publish on the Web?

The first step in evaluating a Web site is to understand its type, and to then pose appropriate questions—some of which have been suggested above. You will find a more complete set of questions in Chapter 1, which is devoted to critical thinking.

2 Evaluating Usenet postings

Usenet postings present the greatest challenge to your critical evaluation skills because of the amount of "noise" you have to filter through to get information. Usually, Usenet posters are just average people expressing their opinions—informed, misinformed; rational, biased; thoughtful, off-the-cuff. Occasionally there will be a posting by experts in a particular field who have substantial information to offer, but this is not common. Ultimately, recognizing misleading, inaccurate, or useless postings is a matter of skill, experience, and taste (different people will place more or less trust in the posting of an enthusiastic Rush Limbaugh supporter, for example), but here are some guidelines that may help as you gain experience in the Usenet world:

1. Consider your first impulse if the posting you're reading appears to contradict what you believe, what you've seen and heard firsthand, or what most other posters in the group are saying. Start with your gut feeling.
2. What are the motivations, biases, and outright prejudices of the poster?
3. This is the hardest part: if you agree with the poster, or most other authorities you've read appear to agree, put yourself in the position

of someone who disagrees with you. How would that person react to this particular posting?

4. Try to verify with a second source any information you get from Usenet. How much of what a poster writes is verifiable fact, how much is well-considered opinion, and how much is just mindless ranting and raving?

5. Does the poster use inflammatory or blatantly prejudiced language?

6. Who is the poster? What do you know about him or her? A poster who signs herself as an employee of the Environmental Protection Agency has at least a head start on authority and believability compared with one who signs himself as a member of "Free Americans to Eliminate Government."

EXERCISE 6

Working with the criteria set out in this section, evaluate the usefulness of any three of the Web sites (or other online destinations) you found in Exercises 3 through 5. Be sure to classify each Web page as an Advocacy page, a Business/Marketing page, a News page, or an Information page. Distinguish Web pages from Usenet postings. Pose questions for evaluation appropriate to the types of materials you have gathered.

EXERCISE 7

Evaluate one or more of the following sites.[4] Apply the criteria of *authority*, *accuracy*, *objectivity*, *currency*, and *coverage* to this site. Note: to fully evaluate a site, once you have arrived at a home page, you will need to follow some of the links to other pages.

The "Alternative" White House	http://www.whitehouse.net
The Official White House	http://www.whitehouse.gov
Chips Ahoy	http://www.chipsahoy.com
Joe Boxer	http://www.joeboxer.com
The Minuteman Press Online	http://www.afn.org/~mpress/
ITI Information Center	http://www.itimiami.com
HHS News	http://www.cdc.gov/tobacco/ sgr/sgr_forwomen/factsheet_ outcomes.htm
Philadelphia Online	http://www.phillynews.com
Timothy Burke's Home Page	http://www.swarthmore.edu/ SocSci/tburke1

---

[4]These sites are taken from a list compiled by Janet Alexander and Marsha Ann Tate (http://www2.widener.edu/Wolfgram-Memorial-Library/examples.htm, copyright 1996–1999).

34d URLs for researchers

Below is a list of URLs for a handful of extremely useful sites that you will want to check while conducting research online. Because of the certainty that sites will change URLs or vanish altogether, the more extensive—and continually updated—list of URLs for researchers is posted on this *Handbook*'s companion Web site.

1 General research sites

NewsDirectory.com	http://www.newsdirectory.com
WWWVirtual Library	http://www.virtuallibrary.com

2 Desktop references

CIA World Factbook	http://www.cia.gov/cia/publications/factbook/index.html
Hypertext Webster Interface	http://www.webster.com
Refdesk.com	http://www.refdesk.com

www

34.4

3 Writing help

Allyn & Bacon's Compsite	http://abacon.com/compsite
Online Writing Lab Links	http://www.witc.tec.wi.us/write/owl.htm

35

Using Sources

This chapter will offer you strategies for using sources with care. To keep matters in perspective, realize that you will present sources in a paper for one reason only: to support and advance your original thinking. Without your guiding, independent purpose, a research paper has no reason for existing. Clearly, a paper that stitches together the words and ideas of others, but that is guided by no original effort, cannot be called research.

35a	Finding sources for authoritative opinions, facts, and examples

1 Authoritative opinions

When linking the words of experts to your own words, you shift the basis on which you ask readers to accept key statements. Without authoritative support, you ask readers to take you at your word—which some may be willing to do. But skeptical readers will want proof. By offering authoritative opinions, you ask readers to accept your view because experts also believe it to be true. Writer Jennifer Wolcott illustrates this strategy in the example passage in the box on page 582.

2 Facts

Certain statements about the world exist in the category of things that are demonstrably true or false. Either the aurora borealis is caused by sunspots or it is not; either London is a more northerly city than New York or it is not. When you make statements such as these, readers want assurance that the statements are accurate. You can provide this assurance by turning to sources for factual support.

3 Examples

Turn to sources for examples that clarify and support your points. Indeed, it is often *through* a well-chosen example, which your source materials can provide, that readers remember your point. Consider this

CRITICAL DECISIONS

Citing Authoritative Sources

When should you refer to authorities in your writing?
Consider the following statement.

Online chat can sprout real-life romances that begin
with surprisingly honest communication.

The writer asks us to accept a statement as true. Should we believe it? If we know relatively little or nothing about a topic, how are
we to judge the accuracy of statements made about it? Read the following expanded version of the example sentence.

> Online chat can sprout real-life romances that begin with surprisingly honest communication and realistic expectations, traits that
> many traditional relationships lack at first, according to an Ohio
> University sociologist who is studying relationships that begin in
> cyberspace. "I really feel the basis of these relationships is better and
> deeper than many real-life meetings because the couples are honest
> with each other in their writings," says Andrea Baker, assistant professor of sociology at Ohio University's Lancaster campus. . . .
> Baker's study suggests the written word tends to promote frank conversation in cyberspace, especially between couples who eventually
> want to meet face-to-face. Study participants said this immediate
> sincerity when meeting online was a pleasant switch from the typical
> blind date scenario. "Couples say this kind of honesty is absolutely
> necessary to forming a good relationship," Baker says. "In most
> cases, they are extremely honest and really cover the downsides as
> well as the upsides so there won't be any surprises when they
> meet."*

With a source added for support, the statement is more convincing than the original, sourceless version. Carefully used sources can
provide authoritative opinions, facts, and examples that will advance
the ideas of your research papers.

*Jennifer Wolcott, "Click Here for Romance," *The Christian Science Monitor* 13 Jan. 1999,
23 Feb. 2000 <http://www.csmonitor.com/durable/1991/01/13/fp11s1-csm.shtml>.

paragraph from a discussion of nervousness during college interviews.
The writer, Anthony Capraro, III, directs a college counseling service:

> **Nervousness** . . . is absolutely and entirely normal. The best way
> to handle it is to admit it, out loud, to the interviewer. Miles Uhrig,
> director of admission at Tufts University, sometimes relates this true
> story to his apprehensive applicants: One extremely agitated young
> applicant sat opposite him for her interview with her legs crossed,
> wearing loafers on her feet. She swung her top leg back and forth to
> some inaudible rhythm. The loafer on her top foot flew off her foot,
> hit him in the head, ricocheted to the desk lamp and broke it. She
> looked at him in terror, but when their glances met, they both dissolved in laughter. The moral of the story—the person on the other

Using Sources

side of the desk is also a human being and wants to put you at ease. So admit to your anxiety and don't swing your foot if you're wearing loafers! (By the way, she was admitted.)[1]

A well-chosen example can etch the point you want to make in your reader's mind.

Classifying sources: Primary and secondary

When attempting to determine the value and quality of a source, keep in mind the distinction between *primary* and *secondary* sources. Primary sources are written by people who have *direct* knowledge of the events or issues under discussion: they were participants in or observers of those events. Examples of primary sources are letters, diaries, autobiographies, oral histories, historical records or documents, and works of literature. Here is a primary source—an announcement for a Fourth of July celebration in 1871 on the Kansas frontier:

> A great 4th of July at Douglas, 1871, everybody is invited to come and bring filled baskets and buckets. There will be a prominent speaker present, who will tell of the big future in store for southern Kansas. Grand fire works at night! Eighteen dollars worth of sky rockets and other brilliant blazes will illuminate the night! There will also be a bunch of Osage Indians and cowboys to help make the program interesting. After the fire works there will be a big platform dance, with music by the Hatfield Brothers.
>
> —qtd. in JOANNA L. STRATTON, *Pioneer Women: Voices from the Kansas Frontier* (New York: Touchstone, 1981) 135

Authors of secondary sources have *indirect* knowledge, only. They rely on primary or other secondary sources for their information. Examples of secondary sources include biographies, textbooks, historical surveys, and literary criticism. A historian studying nineteenth century Wild West shows in America and Europe might use the Independence Day announcement as a source. Working with the question "How would 'a bunch of Osage Indians and cowboys . . . help make the program interesting'?" the historian might investigate what attitudes are revealed about Native Americans in this and similar announcements from the era. If you were writing a research paper on Wild West shows of the nineteenth century, your reference to the historical study would be to a secondary source. The original announcement would remain a primary source.

Can a source be both primary and secondary?

A source can be considered both primary and secondary, depending on how it is used. Consider the historical study of Wild West shows—for

---

[1]Anthony F. Capraro, III, "The Interview." *Barron's Profiles of American Colleges*, 19th ed. (Hauppauge, New York: Barron's Educational Series, 1992) 12.

your purposes a secondary source, assuming you were writing a paper on this topic. Now imagine a second writer (Writer B) who has begun a research project on the ways in which historians gather evidence. The same historical study of Wild West shows would become for Writer B a *primary* source. Writer B's interest would not concern the shows themselves but rather the ways in which evidence was used and a story was told. Presumably, in Writer B's project, other historical accounts would be treated as primary sources. In certain contexts, then, a secondary source can be approached as a primary source. How that source is used determines the classification.

Advantages and disadvantages of primary and secondary sources

Primary sources are not necessarily superior (or inferior) to secondary sources, but it is good to recognize the strengths and limitations of each.

Primary sources

- provide facts and viewpoints that are not generally available from other sources;
- often have immediacy and drama; but
- may be colored by the bias of the authors, who want to inflate their own importance or to justify questionable decisions.

Secondary sources

- may offer a broader perspective, with their distance from original events;
- tend to be less affected by intense passions of the moment than those who participated in those events; but
- may write with a strong, interpretive bias that you will need to evaluate carefully.

Source by source, you will need to make your decisions on reliability, determining whether you consider the material to be primary or secondary.

35c Reading sources critically

Your ability to write a research paper depends on your being able to use sources with care. And your ability to use sources, the subject of this chapter, depends *entirely* on your being able to read well. Because effective reading is a foundational skill on which the success of all research rests, you should turn to Chapter 1 if you are not fully comfortable with the prospect of reading to understand, respond, and forge relationships. Careful, strategic reading is a skill you can teach yourself; once learned, it will serve you well.

Consider how the strategies for critical reading described in Chapter 1 might help as you work with source materials for your research papers.

| 1 | **Reading to understand and respond** |

Your main goal during this stage is to familiarize yourself with your sources and to determine their *relevance* for your research project.

■ *Understand.* Preview the source by skimming its contents. Read the table of contents, the introduction or preface, the conclusion, headings, and selected topics.

■ *Respond.* Read your source carefully enough to *react* and to *ask questions.* Check the credentials of the author and the critical reception of his or her work. Does the author's background or professional affiliation suggest to you the point of view he or she will take? Identify the author's stance on the subject: Is she or he pro, con, or neutral? relatively detached or passionately involved (or something in-between)? Is the tone angry, cynical, witty, solemn, or earnest? Does the author have a personal stake in the issue under discussion? If so, how might this affect your acceptance of her or his arguments?

Highlight important questions, particularly those most relevant to your research question, and make notes in the margins. Take notes, looking for important quotations that you might be able to use in the paper. Identify arguments and the positions of people involved. Finally, be alert to *differences* and *similarities* among sources. After critical reading and additional research, you will probably want to discuss such differences.

| 2 | **Reading to evaluate and synthesize** |

Your goal during this stage of critical reading is to clearly assess each source and to consider your sources together, so that you can begin to find patterns of meaning that emerge. As you continue to read with your research question in mind, you will begin to develop a thesis for your paper.

■ *Evaluate.* Determine the *reliability* of your sources. This involves attempting to separate fact from opinion in the source; identifying and assessing the author's assumptions; and evaluating both the evidence offered by the author in support of his or her argument and the logic by which the conclusions are reached (see 6h).

Consider the source. Reading to evaluate also involves considering the source of publication for an article or book. Was the article published in a popular magazine (intended for a general audience) or an academic or professional journal (intended for a specialized audience)? Articles in journals will probably be more difficult to read, but will tend to carry more authority and credibility. Is the book or pamphlet published by a commercial or academic publisher, or by a publisher with a special interest (a chemical company, for example, or a nonprofit agency such as the pro-environmental Earth First! or the American

Civil Liberties Union)? Special-interest publications should not necessarily be discounted, but you should consider the source and be aware of potential biases. For more specific advice, see the box in 6d-2, "Using Authoritative Sources."

■ *Synthesize.* Determine how the evidence from one source is related to evidence from other sources. You must compare what you find in your sources, evaluate the information and assumptions in each, and form your own ideas about the most important relationships among them. The skills for doing this are demonstrated in detail in Chapters 1 and 2 (see 1h and 2d). Your discussion will require cross-references among sources, noting where one author refers to ideas discussed by any others. When possible, establish a relationship among them through comparing, contrasting, defining concepts or examples, or making connections by process or cause and effect. In this way you *synthesize* the sources to let them support your answers to the research question and your argument for the paper's provisional thesis.

3 Evaluating electronic sources

In 34b–c, you will find an extensive discussion on locating, accessing, and evaluating the reliability of electronic sources. When you draw on these sources, be very careful to assess their validity and credibility, keeping the following considerations in mind:

■ Reliability of evidence varies considerably across electronic sources, so judge each source on its merits—as you would any source.
■ Sources gained through anonymous FTP tend to have the same status as print information in the library.
■ Information gained from newsgroups and Web pages can be helpful but also unreliable. Any person or organization can create and post documents on the Internet. The material you find may have been produced for an expressly commercial, political, racial, or religious motive. Carefully consider each source.

35d Creating a working bibliography

Your **working bibliography** is a list of all of the sources you locate in preparing your paper. This includes books, articles, entries from biographical sources, handbooks, almanacs, electronic sources, and the various other kinds of sources cited in Chapter 34. The bibliography should also include sources you locate in indexes that you intend to check later. Your working bibliography differs from your **final bibliography** in that it is more comprehensive. The final bibliography consists only of those sources that you actually use in writing the paper.

It is absolutely essential that you prepare your working bibliography *at the same time* that you are compiling and consulting your sources. That way you can be sure to have accurate and complete information when the time comes to return to your sources to obtain more information or to double-check information, and to compile your final bibliography. It is enormously frustrating to be typing your list of references (quite possibly, the night before your paper is due!) and to suddenly realize that your notes do not contain all the information you need.

Making bibliographic notes

We recommend that you compile a working bibliography on 3" × 5" index cards or by computer record. What you take notes on is less important than your ability to quickly and effortlessly alphabetize entries or to arrange them in any other order (such as by topic and subtopic order, or by sources you have already examined and ones you have not) that is most useful to you during the research and writing process. As you consult each new source, carefully record key information:

1. full name of author (last name first)
2. title (and subtitle)
3. publication information:
   a. place of publication
   b. name of publisher
   c. date of publication
4. inclusive page numbers

In case you have to relocate the source later, indicate the library call number (in the upper right-hand corner) and the name and date of the index where you located the source (at the bottom). It is also a good idea to include a brief annotation (either below the publication information or on the back of the card), in which you describe the contents of that source or the author's main idea, and indicate your reaction to the source and how you might use it in your paper. By surveying your annotations as you proceed with your research, you will quickly be able to see how much you have already found on your subject and what else you still need to look up. Your annotations may also prevent you from wasting time looking up the same sources twice. Finally, you should assign a code number to each bibliographic entry. Then, when you are taking notes on the source, you can simply put that code number in the upper right-hand corner of the note, rather than recopying the complete bibliographic information.

Using your records to create a final bibliography

When the time comes to prepare your final bibliography, you can simply arrange the cards for the sources you used in alphabetical order and type up the pertinent information as a list. If your records are on a computer, you may use "sort" (for database) or "Find" and "cut and paste" functions to alphabetize the entries. Here's a sample bibliography record for a book:

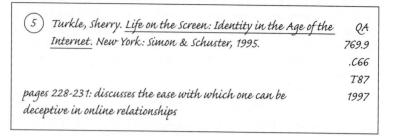

⑤ Turkle, Sherry. *Life on the Screen: Identity in the Age of the Internet.* New York: Simon & Schuster, 1995.

QA
769.9
.C66
T87
1997

pages 228-231: discusses the ease with which one can be deceptive in online relationships

Here is a sample bibliography record for an article:

⑧ Branscum, Deborah. "Life at High-Tech U." *Newsweek* 27 Oct. 1997: 78-80.

makes point that a study of first-year college students found that ordinarily reserved students were more comfortable joining into classroom debates online

Creating an annotated bibliography

Some instructors may ask for an **annotated bibliography** as an intermediate step between your working bibliography notes and the final bibliography. In effect, an annotated bibliography is a fully annotated working bibliography in manuscript form; it records the same information demonstrated above in card form, presenting it in alphabetical sequence on manuscript sheets for your review and for suggestions from collaborators, peers, or your instructor.

A note on photocopying: Most periodicals and reference books can't be checked out of the library. Therefore, you may find yourself photocopying articles or book chapters. Remember to photocopy or record all pertinent bibliographic data. You will find it handy to photocopy the title page of a book or a periodical's contents page (or whichever page has dates, volume numbers, and other publication information). Two additional reminders may save you hours of retracing your steps late in the writing process:

- Check to see that you've photocopied *all* relevant words on each page. (You'll save yourself the frustration of discovering at a later time that the machine has missed the first five letters of each line.)
- For books that have endnotes, photocopy the corresponding notes at the end of the chapter or end of the book. This way, you won't have to find the source again if you have to track down a reference.

EXERCISE I

Compile a working bibliography—both books and articles—of twenty to twenty-five items for one of the subjects you have been researching for Chapter 33. Or if you prefer, research a new subject. Record key information (as indicated above) on 3" × 5" cards or in your electronic database (if the latter, you will need a printout). Include content annotations for at least five items.

35e Taking notes: Summarizing and paraphrasing

Use your computer's notetaking software or 4" × 6" cards for taking notes. Again, any system will work as long as you are able to (1) clearly identify the source from which the note is taken and (2) sort through and rearrange notes with ease.

Researchers use various formats for recording their notes, but the following elements are most important:

1. a *code number* corresponding to the code number on your bibliography record *or* the bibliographic reference itself;
2. a *topic* or *subtopic* label (these enable you to easily arrange and rearrange your records in topical order);
3. the *note* itself; and
4. a *page reference*.

Do not attempt to include too much information in a single note record. For example, do not summarize an entire article or chapter in one record, particularly if you are likely to use information from a single record in several places throughout your paper. By limiting each note to a single point or illustration, you make it easier to arrange the records according to your outline, and to rearrange them later if your outline changes. Here is a sample note for *Life on the Screen*, by Sherry Turkle. The code number in the upper-right corner of the note corresponds with the bibliography record for the book from which the note is taken. See page 588 for the bibliography record.

Deception in online relationships   ⑤

Relationships online allow people an opportunity to pretend to be someone very different from who they really are. While some may regard this as deception, others believe that creating a separate online identity is all part of the fun, that there are no rules requiring one to be honest. So if someone gets hurt when the deception is found out, opinion differs as to who is responsible. (228)

There are three methods of notetaking: *summarizing, paraphrasing,* and *quoting.* These methods can be used either individually or in combination with one another.

1 Summarizing sources

A *summary* is a relatively brief, objective account, in your own words, of the main idea in a source passage. You summarize a passage when you want to extract the main ideas and use them as background material in your own paper. For details on the process of writing summaries, see 2a. Here is a section of an article by Ron Kling, which Logan Kole refers to in his research paper on computer-mediated communication:

> In the United States, communities seem to be deteriorating from a complex combination of causes. In the inner cities of big urban centers, many people fear street crime and stay off the streets at night. In the larger suburban and post-suburban areas, many people hardly know their neighbors and "latch key" children often have little adult contact after school. An African proverb which says that "it takes a whole village to raise a child" refers to a rich community life with a sense of mutual responsibility that is difficult to find in many new neighborhoods. Some advocates believe that computer technology in concert with other efforts could play a role in rebuilding community life by improving communication, economic opportunity, civic participation, and education.
>
> —RON KLING, "Social Relationships in Electronic Forums: Hangouts, Salons, Workplaces, and Communities." *CMC Magazine,* July 22, 1996.

Here is a summary of this source:

> CMC is potentially so powerful a medium of exchange that some believe it can promote dialogue within communities that are declining. A community, after all, is built on people acting in the interests of their neighbors for the common good. Via e-mail, online newsgroups, and e-forums, neighbors will have new ways of looking out for one another.

2 Paraphrasing sources

A paraphrase is a restatement, in your own words, of a passage of text. Paraphrases are sometimes the same length as the source passage, sometimes shorter. In certain cases, particularly if the source passage is written in densely constructed or jargon-laden prose—the paraphrase may even be longer than the original.

You paraphrase a passage when you want to preserve all (or virtually all) the points of the original, major and minor, and when—perhaps for the sake of clarity—you want to communicate the ideas in your own words. Keep in mind that only an *occasional* word (but not whole phrases) from the original source appears in the paraphrase, and that the paraphrase's sentence structure does not reflect that of the source.

Original passage

Parents need to be able to talk to their children about where they are going and what they are doing. This same commonsense rule applies to their children's lives on the screen. Parents don't have to become technical experts, but they do need to learn enough about computer networks to discuss with their children what and who is out there and lay down some basic safety rules.

—SHERRY TURKLE, *Life on the Screen: Identity in the Age of the Internet*, page 227.

Paraphrase

Just as parents should make sure they know their children's whereabouts and activities in real life, so should they monitor their children's online activities. Without having to master the complexities of these new technologies, they can still become familiar enough with online systems to talk with their children about their online activities. In doing so, they should also establish guidelines for their children to follow. (227)

This paraphrase is as long as Turkle's original passage, with roughly the same level of detail.

EXERCISE 2

Write a 250- to 400-word summary of one of the sources you have located for your working bibliography (Exercise 1). Then write a paraphrase of several sentences from a section of text in the same source.

35f Quoting sources

You may decide to quote from a passage when the author's language is particularly well chosen, lively, dramatic, or incisive, and when you think you could not possibly express the same idea so effectively. Or you may decide to quote when you want to bolster the credibility of your argument with the reputation of your source. By the same token, you may occasionally decide to discredit an opposing argument by quoting a discredited or notorious source.

I Avoiding overquoting

Knowing how much to quote is an art in itself. If you underquote, your paper may come across as dry. If you overquote, your paper may come across as an anthology of other people's statements ("a cut-and-paste job"), rather than an original work. Some instructors have developed rules of thumb on quoting. One such rule is that for a ten-page paper, there should be no more than two extended quotations (i.e., indented quotations of more than 100 words); and each page should contain no more than two short quotations. If this rule of thumb makes sense to you (or to your instructor), adopt it. Otherwise, modify it to whatever extent you think reasonable.

CRITICAL DECISIONS

 Deciding When to Summarize, Paraphrase, or Quote a Source

Summarize

■ to present the main points from a relatively long passage
■ to condense information essential to your discussion

Paraphrase

■ to clarify complex ideas in a short passage
■ to clarify difficult language in a short passage

Quote

■ when the language of the source is particularly important or effective
■ when you want to enhance your credibility by drawing on the words of an authority on the subject

---

2 Deciding how to quote

www

35.1

When you quote a source, you need to record the author's wording *exactly;* the conventions for altering quotations with ellipses and with bracketed words (that you provide) are discussed below and in 29e. Here is a passage from Brittney Chenault, "Developing Personal and Emotional Relationships Via Computer-Mediated Communication" (*CMC Magazine*, May 1998):

> People meet via CMC every day, exchange information, debate, argue, woo, commiserate, and support. They may meet via a mailing list or newsgroup, and continue the interaction via e-mail. Their relationships can range from the cold, professional encounter to the hot, intimate rendezvous.

What you consider to be quotable depends on the purpose of your research. Logan Kole read this section of Chenault's article to investigate the ways computer-mediated communication will affect the way we communicate and the quality of our relationships. For Logan, the following quotation was most useful:

Kinds of online relationships

> "People meet via CMC every day, exchange infor-
> mation, debate, argue, woo, commiserate, and
> support. . . . Their relationships can range
> from the cold, professional encounter to the
> hot, intimate rendezvous."

Note that this writer has used an ellipsis in the place of a deleted sentence. Ellipses are discussed in the next section.

Sometimes you may wish to quote a passage that has itself been quoted by the source author. Generally, you should try to locate the original author when you want to quote. However, this won't always be practical: the original source may not be available at your library or may not be available at all (if the original source was quoted from an unpublished interview or from a lecture). The following passage appears in a *New York Times on the Web* article by Bonnie Rothman Morris: "You've Got Romance! Seeking Love Online: Net-Based Services Change the Landscape, If Not the Odds, of Finding the Perfect Mate," 26 Aug. 1999, 23 Feb. 2000 <http://www.nytimes.com/library/tech/yr/mo/circuits/index.html>.

> Tom Buckley didn't have much use for a dating service, or so he thought. "I didn't need to pay a company to help set me up to get a date, a girlfriend, a fiancée, a wife," said Buckley, 30, a steel broker in Portland, Ore., who plays rugby in his spare time. But after a lonely Thanksgiving dinner where he was the only single adult at the family dinner table, Buckley signed up for a free week on Match.com. What ensued on the matchmaking service was an e-mail romance with Terri Muir, a schoolteacher on Vancouver Island in British Columbia. "Anybody who knew us would never have thought we would have gone down that road," Buckley said in a telephone interview. Reflecting on the couple's instant attraction, he said, "e-mail made it easier to communicate because neither one of us was the type to walk up to someone in the gym or a bar and say, 'You're the fuel to my fire.'"

If you decided not to use any of the commentary by Bonnie Morris but, rather, only the quotation by Tom Buckley that Morris quoted, your note would appear as follows. The single quotation marks *within* double quotation marks shows a quotation within a quotation. (Further quotations within single quotation marks—a relatively rare event that happens to be illustrated in the current example—are noted with double quotation marks.)

Online dating club as an alternative way to meet

Note #12

> Successfully cyber-matched man, Tom Buckley of Port-
> land, Oregon, relates the usefulness of an Internet
> dating service (Match.com) and e-mail as a way to
> meet his (future) wife:

```
" 'Anybody who knew us would never have thought we
would have gone down that road,' Buckley said in a
telephone interview. Reflecting on the couple's in-
stant attraction, he said, 'e-mail made it easier to
communicate because neither one of us was the type
to walk up to someone in the gym or a bar and say,
"You're the fuel to my fire."'" (qtd. in Morris)
```

These are the *exact* words from the original. The student has added nothing, omitted nothing, and changed nothing. Here's how Logan Kole put the quoted passage from Morris to use in his paper:

```
Tom Buckley of Portland, Oregon, met his wife after signing
up with Match.com. Buckley noted that the Internet helped
him to meet his wife because "neither one of us was the type
to walk up to someone in the gym or a bar and say, 'You're
the fuel to my fire'" (qtd. in Morris).
```

3   Using brackets and ellipses in quotations

Sometimes for the sake of clarity, conciseness, or smoothness of sentence structure, you will need to make additions, omissions, or changes to quotations. For example, suppose you wanted to quote a passage beginning with the following sentence: "In 1979, one week after receiving a 13.3% pay raise, she received a call from the company president." To clarify the pronoun *she*, you would need to replace it with the name of the person in question enclosed in a pair of brackets: "In 1979, one week after receiving a 13.3% pay raise, [Virginia Rulon-Miller] received a call from the company president." (See 29d.)

Note that when using brackets, you do not need to use the ellipsis to indicate that the pronoun (*she*) has been omitted. Brackets surrounding proper nouns imply that one word (or set of words) has replaced another. For more on altering quotations with ellipses and brackets, see Chapters 28 and 29, especially 29d–e.

Sometimes you need to change a capital letter to a lowercase one in order to smoothly integrate the quotation into your own sentence. For example, suppose you want to quote the following sentence: "Privacy today matters to employees at all levels, from shop-floor workers to presidents." You could smoothly integrate this quotation into your own sentence by altering the capitalization, as follows.

The new reality, as John Hoerr points out, is that "[p]rivacy today matters to employees at all levels, from shop-floor workers to presidents."

4 Smoothly integrating quotations into your sentences

Using attributive phrases to introduce quotations

Whether or not you alter quotations by means of ellipses or brackets, you should strive to integrate them smoothly into your own sentences. Use attributive phrases (phrases that attribute, or point to the origin of, the quoted source). Here is a quotation from Adam Gopnik, writing on the topic of e-mail for "Talk of the Town" in *The New Yorker* (12 Dec. 1999):

> E-mail has succeeded brilliantly for the same reason that the videophone failed miserably: what we actually want from our exchanges is the minimum human contact commensurate with the need to connect with other people.

The quotation can be integrated into the text of a paper in any of several ways:

1. According to one commentator, "E-mail has succeeded brilliantly for the same reason that the videophone failed miserably: what we actually want from our exchanges is the minimum human contact commensurate with the need to connect with other people" (Gopnik 17).

2. "E-mail has succeeded brilliantly for the same reason that the videophone failed miserably," according to Adam Gopnik (17).

3. "[W]hat we actually want from our exchanges," says Adam Gopnik, "is the minimum human contact commensurate with the need to connect with other people" (17).

4. Writing an ironic and well-researched commentary in *The New Yorker*, Adam Gopnik suggests that we generally don't desire human connection as much as we've been led to believe: "what we actually want from our exchanges is the minimum human contact commensurate with the need to connect with other people" (17).

5. "E-mail has succeeded brilliantly for the same reason that the videophone failed miserably," writes Adam Gopnik. "[W]hat we actually want from our exchanges is the minimum human contact commensurate with the need to connect with other people" (17).

6. Adam Gopnik argues that people want the "minimum human contact commensurate with the need to connect with other people" (17).

An attributive remark ("According to___") can be shifted around in a sentence from beginning to end. Place a comma after the remark when it introduces a sentence; place a comma before the remark when it ends a sentence; place a *pair* of commas around the remark when it interrupts the quoted sentence. In the fourth example, a sentence (not a phrase) introduces the quotation, so a colon is the appropriate punctuation (to avoid a comma splice or a run-on).

Using statements with present-tense verbs to introduce quotations

Notice that in example 4 above, the quotation is introduced by a sentence. In examples 3 and 5, the quotation is woven into the structure of a sentence. In these cases, the convention is to use a main sentence verb in the *present* tense (see 9e-1). Even though your source has already been written (and so technically, the author has already declar*ed* or stat*ed* or conclud*ed*), when quoting sources you should use the present tense (declares, states, concludes). This convention applies even if you are discussing a literary work; thus you would say that Hamlet ponder*s:* "To be or not to be." The only exception to the use of the present tense would be if you were reporting the historical progress of some development or debate and you wished to emphasize that certain things were said at a particular point in time. ("The Senator assert*ed:* 'I do not intend to dignify these scurrilous charges by responding to them.'")

5 Using block quotations

You should integrate most quotations into your own text, using quotation marks. If a quotation runs longer than four lines, however, you should set it apart from the text by indenting it ten spaces from the left margin. Quotation marks are not required around block quotations. Block quotations should be double spaced, like the rest of the text (see 28a).

Verbs That Help You Attribute Quotations

Attributive phrases use verbs in the present tense. To vary attributive phrases, you might consider verbs such as these:

adds	defends	points out
agrees	denies	rejects
argues	derides	relates
asks	disagrees	reports
asserts	disputes	responds
believes	emphasizes	reveals
claims	explains	says
comments	finds	sees
compares	holds	shows
concedes	illustrates	speculates
concludes	implies	states
condemns	insists	suggests
considers	maintains	thinks
contends	notes	warns
declares	observes	writes

35g Weaving summaries, paraphrases, and quotations into your paragraphs

To complete the integration of source materials into your paper, devote your attention to the paragraph level, where ideas are developed *across* sentences. The following approach can help you to integrate summaries, paraphrases, and quotations into the overall scheme of your paper. You will want to vary the approach, but here are the basics:

Sources and Cycles of Development

■ Introduce your idea into a paragraph before you introduce a source. Working with your paragraph's idea, create a context into which you can fit the source.

■ Having created the context, steer the reader directly to your source using an attributive phrase or a sentence with a present-tense verb.

■ Quote, summarize, or paraphrase the source.

■ *Use* the source by commenting on it, responding to it, or explaining its significance.

When you apply these principles to individual paragraphs, you create what can be called a "cycle of development" for using source materials. A full cycle will ensure that your reader is properly prepared for the source and that the source will advance your paragraph's idea, which originates with you, without overwhelming that idea. The important concept is that your idea comes first; then you follow with, and integrate, your sources. These principles are illustrated below, using a paragraph from Logan Kole's research paper.

Cycle of development

Proponents of CMC confidently point to examples in which the new technologies of communication bring people together in meaningful, healthy ways. In a study of first-year college students, researcher Richard Holeton of Stanford University found that students who were ordinarily reserved were able to come out of their shells and participate in Internet debates (Branscum 79). Similarly, the Internet can serve as a way for people who are having trouble dating to find partners. For instance, Tom Buckley of Portland, Oregon, met his wife after signing up with Match.com. Buckley noted that the Internet helped him to meet his wife because "neither one of us was the type to walk up to someone in the gym or a bar

The writer introduces an idea and sets a context.

The writer steers the reader to a summary that supports and develops the idea.

The writer steers the reader to a second summary and to a quotation that supports and develops the paragraph's main idea.

and say, 'You're the fuel to my fire'" (qtd. in Morris).
Holeton's research and Buckley's experience suggest
that the Internet may provide a way for otherwise
timid individuals to express themselves.

— Comment.

This paragraph illustrates a cycle of development with two summaries and a quotation. Paragraphs will vary in their cycles: some will be built on a summary only, or on a quotation or a paraphrase. But all will set a context, steer a reader to a source, *use* that source to support the paragraph's main idea, and make a comment.

EXERCISE 3

The following passage appears in the book *Taking Laughter Seriously* by John Morreall. Read the paragraph and then follow the directions below, which ask you to work with the text in various ways. For activities 3–5, create a context in which quoting from Morreall's paragraph makes sense. Pretend you are writing a paper on laughter and that your quotations would fit into that paper.

(1) When the person with a sense of humor laughs in the face of his own failure, he is showing that his perspective transcends the particular situation he's in, and that he does not have an egocentric, overly precious view of his own endeavors. (2) This is not to say that he lacks self-esteem—quite the contrary. (3) It is because he feels good about himself at a fundamental level that this or that setback is not threatening to him. (4) The person without real self-esteem, on the other hand, who is unsure of his own worth, tends to invest his whole sense of himself in each of his projects. (5) Whether he fails or succeeds, he is not likely to see things in an objective way; because his ego rides on each of the goals he sets for himself, any failure will constitute personal defeat and any success personal triumph. (6) He simply cannot afford to laugh at himself, whatever happens. (7) So having a sense of humor about oneself is psychologically healthy. (8) As A. Penjon so nicely said, it "frees us from vanity, on the one hand, and from pessimism on the other by keeping us larger than what we do, and greater than what can happen to us."

Assume for your answers to the following activities that a "Works Cited" list exists that includes a full entry for Morreall's book. When you quote from Morreall, you should provide a parenthetical citation, the format of which you will find explained in 37a-1. (The above paragraph appears on page 106 of *Taking Laughter Seriously*.)

Morreall, John. *Taking Laughter Seriously*. Albany: State University of New York, 1983.

1. Write a summary of this passage: limit, 50 words.
2. Write a paraphrase of this passage: limit, 140 words.

3. Write a sentence in which you quote any phrase from Morreall's paragraph.

4. Write a sentence in which you quote from the beginning of one of Morreall's sentences and from the end of the same sentence—omitting the middle. Remember to communicate to readers that you've altered Morreall's original language.

5. Quote A. Penjon. Note that the sentence you are quoting appears in a book by Morreall. (See 37a on in-text citations for "Material quoted in your source.")

Plagiarism is an unpleasant subject, but one that must be confronted in any discussion of research papers. In its most blatant form, **plagiarism** is an act of conscious deception: an attempt to pass off the ideas or the words of another as your own. To take an extreme example, a student who buys a research paper from a commercial "paper mill" or borrows a paper written by someone else and turns it in for academic credit is guilty of the worst kind of plagiarism. Only slightly less guilty is the student who copies into his paper passages of text from his sources without giving credit or using quotation marks.

35.2

The penalties for plagiarism can be severe—including a failing grade in the course or even a suspension from school. Graduate students guilty of plagiarism have been dropped from advanced degree programs. Even professionals no longer in school can see their reputations damaged or destroyed by charges of plagiarism. During the 1988 presidential campaign, a Democratic candidate was forced to drop out of the race when it was revealed that some of the material in his campaign speeches was copied from a speech by a prominent British politician.

Much plagiarism is unintentional. But unintentional or not, the effect of plagiarizing is the same, so you'll want to avoid the problem. Here are two general rules to help you avoid unintentional plagiarism:

1. Whenever you *quote* the exact words of others, place these words within quotation marks and properly cite the source.

2. Whenever you *paraphrase* or *summarize* the ideas of others, do not use whole phrases, or many of the same words, or sentence structures similar to the original. You must identify the source of the paraphrased or summarized material. You are obligated to credit your source even if you change the wording of the original statement or alter the sentence structure.

1   Determining what is common knowledge

The only exception to the second rule stated above is if the information summarized or paraphrased is considered common knowledge. For example, you need not cite the source of the information that General Lee commanded the Confederate forces during the Civil War, or the fact that Mars is the fourth planet from the sun, or the fact that Ernest Hemingway wrote *The Sun Also Rises*. If, on the other hand, you are summarizing one particular theory of why Lee's forces faced almost certain defeat, or the geological composition of the Martian surface, or how the critical assessment of Hemingway's *The Sun Also Rises* has shifted over the years, then you are obliged to cite the sources of your information or ideas, whether or not you quote them directly.

The key issue underlying the question of common knowledge is the likelihood of readers mistakenly thinking that a certain idea or item of information originated with you when, in fact, it did not. If there is *any* chance of such a mistake occurring, you should cite the source.

Your decision regarding what to consider common knowledge depends, partly, on audience. Suppose you are writing on a technical subject, computer software, for an audience of engineers. There's a great deal of technical information you might find in your sources, perhaps about computer languages, that you might reasonably decide would be common knowledge for readers who are specialists. They would clearly know that the information in question did *not* originate with you. Writing on the same topic for nonspecialists, however, you would want to cite the source of that same information, given the likelihood that your technically less sophisticated readers could reasonably mistake the information as yours.

The obligation is yours, then, *with every new research project,* to anticipate what your audience knows and what assumptions they will make about your knowledge. Let a spirit of honesty and fairness guide you, and you will make the right decisions.

2   Identifying blatant plagiarism of a source

We will use the sample passage below to illustrate what can happen when source ideas undergo several possible levels of intentional or unintentional plagiarism in the student examples that follow. The passage is from Steven F. Bloom's "Empty Bottles, Empty Dreams: O'Neill's Use of Drinking and Alcoholism in *Long Day's Journey into Night*," which appears in *Critical Essays on Eugene O'Neill*, edited by James J. Martine (Boston: G. K. Hall, 1984).

> In *Long Day's Journey into Night*, O'Neill captures his vision of the human condition in the figure of the alcoholic who is constantly and repeatedly faced with the disappointment of his hopes to escape or

transcend present reality. As the effects of heavy drinking and alcoholism increase, the alcoholic, in his attempt to attain euphoric forgetfulness, is repeatedly confronted with the painful realities of dissipation, despondency, self-destruction, and ultimately, death. This is the life of an alcoholic, and for O'Neill, this is the life of modern man.

Here is a plagiarized student version of this passage. Plagiarized phrases are underlined:

> *Long Day's Journey into Night* shows O'Neill's <u>vision of the human condition</u> in the figure of the alcoholic who is <u>constantly faced with the</u> disappointment of his hopes to escape. <u>As the effects of heavy drinking and alcoholism increase, the alcoholic, in his attempt to attain forgetfulness, is repeatedly confronted with the painful realities of dissipation</u>, semidestruction, and, <u>ultimately, death. This is the life of an alcoholic, and for O'Neill, this is the life of modern man.</u>

This is the most blatant form that plagiarism can take. The student has copied the passage almost word for word and has made no attempt to identify the source of either the words or the ideas. Even if the author *were* credited, the student's failure to use quotation marks around quoted material would render this version unacceptable.

---

3 Avoiding unintentional plagiarism of a source

At times, the well-intentioned writer may attempt to put the ideas of others into his or her own words but may produce an effort that still too closely resembles the original and would constitute plagiarism. Remember, for the material to be your own, you must follow basic procedures:

- The language should be your own—with rare exceptions for a quoted word or a brief, exactly quoted phrase.
- The sentence structures should be your own. Do not reproduce the author's sentences, substituting words for the author's original wording.
- The sequence of ideas that you present (with attribution) from the original source should be your own.

The following paragraph illustrates a failed attempt to make legitimate use of the source on Eugene O'Neill. Plagiarized phrases are underlined.

> The figure of the disappointed alcoholic who <u>hopes to escape reality</u> represents <u>the human condition</u> in *Long Day's Journey into Night.* Trying to forget his problems, the alcoholic, while drinking more and more, is <u>confronted with the realities</u> of his <u>self-destructive</u> condition, <u>and, ultimately, with death. For Eugene O'Neill,</u> the life of the alcoholic represents <u>the life of modern man.</u>

In this version, the writer's attempt to put the ideas of Steven Bloom into his own words still too closely resembles the original in sentence structure, the sequence of ideas, and the use of key phrases. For example, Bloom's "confronted with the painful realities of dissipation" becomes "confronted with the realities of his self-destructive condition." The writer's very slight reworking of Bloom's original would still count as plagiarism even if Bloom were given proper credit in a parenthetical citation—that is, even had the first sentence begun "According to Steven F. Bloom." The student may not have intended to plagiarize—he may, in fact, believe this to be an acceptable rendition—but it would still be considered plagiarism.

4   Making legitimate use of a source

The following use of the source passage is entirely acceptable:

According to Steven F. Bloom, alcoholism in *Long Day's Journey into Night* is a metaphor for the human condition. The alcoholic drinks to forget his disappointments and to escape reality, but the more he drinks, the more he is faced with his own mortality. "This is the life of an alcoholic," asserts Bloom, "and for O'Neill, this is the life of modern man" (177).

The student has carefully attributed both the paraphrased idea (in the first part of the passage) and the quotation (in the second part) to the source author, Steven Bloom. The student has also taken special care to phrase the idea in her own language.

Of course, you cannot avoid keeping *some* key terms. Obviously, if you are going to paraphrase the ideas in this passage, you will need to use words and phrases such as "alcoholic," "heavy drinking," "the human condition," and so on. However, what you say *about* these terms should be said in your own words.

It is crucial that you give your readers no cause to believe that you are guilty either of intentional or unintentional plagiarism. When you are summarizing or paraphrasing a particular passage, you must do more than change a few words. You must fully and accurately cite your source, by means of parenthetical citations or by means of attributive phrases, such as "According to Bloom, ..."

5   Quoting accurately

When you do quote material directly, be certain that you quote it accurately. For example, consider a student quotation of the preceding passage (which follows the student's introduction).

Long Day's Journey into Night is O'Neill's "vision of the human condition," according to Steven F. Bloom:

> As the effects of his heavy drinking and alcoholism increase, the alcoholic, attempting to achieve forgetfulness, is repeatedly

confronted with all the painful realities of dissipation, self-destruction, and death. This is the life of an alcoholic for O'Neill and it is also the life of modern man.

At first glance, this quotation may seem to be accurate. But it is not. The student has *omitted* some words that were in the source passage (in the first sentence, "euphoric" and "despondency"; in the second sentence, "and"); has *changed* other words (in the first sentence, "attempting to achieve," instead of "in his attempt to attain"; in the second, "it," instead of "this"); has *added* some words that were not in the original (in the first sentence, "all"; in the second sentence, "also"); and has also omitted punctuation (in the second sentence, the comma after "O'Neill").

These changes may seem trivial and may not seem to essentially change the meaning of the passage, but once you place a passage within quotation marks (or indent it if it is a block quotation), you are obligated to copy it *exactly*. Deleted material should be indicated by an ellipsis . . . (see 29e); your own insertions should be indicated by brackets [ ] (see 29d). Otherwise, the material within your quotation marks must be word for word, punctuation mark for punctuation mark, *identical* to the original.

Copyright Matters

Even when you diligently attribute your use of a source, take care not to violate copyright law. It is illegal to reproduce all, or most, of a copyrighted work whether it appears in print or on the Web.

With a spirit of honesty and careful attention to accuracy, you will avoid problems with unintentional plagiarism. Develop the habit of proofreading your papers when they are all but final. Compare your typed copy of all quotations, paraphrases, and summaries with your original notes and with photocopies of sources (if you have these). Then enjoy the accomplishment of having used your sources well to advance the ideas of your paper.

EXERCISE 4

Paraphrase a short passage from one of the sources you have located during your research. Then write a short paragraph explaining what you have done to eliminate all possibility of inadvertent plagiarism in your paraphrase.

CHAPTER **36**

Writing the Research Paper

The material in this chapter parallels that in Chapters 3 and 4 on planning, writing, and revising the essay. Because the *process* of writing a research paper is in many (but not all) respects similar to that of writing an essay, the discussion of process here will be brief and cross-referenced with earlier sections of the book.

CRITICAL DECISIONS

Preparing to Write a Research Paper

As you complete your research and prepare to write a paper, you probably have more information than you can possibly absorb. How will you get from the many notes you've taken—on notecards or on computer—to a finished paper? Here is where you must do your work as a critical thinker, synthesizing your sources in ways that advance the single idea at the heart of your paper. At this point in the process, you should be working with a question that interests you, one that motivates you to sift through all your notes in search of a satisfying answer. If you care about your work, the writing and the research will come more easily. With your question in mind, you will work with source materials until you formulate a satisfying answer—a thesis, which will be the core idea of your paper.

36a   Refining the thesis

In 33e you saw the usefulness of devising a working thesis. *Working,* here, means preliminary. A working thesis offers a provisional idea with which to begin sifting through your notes; with this idea, you can begin to look at new materials in a more focused way. The discussion here will follow the progress of student writer Logan Kole as he works through the process of writing a research paper on the ways in which the Internet has affected interpersonal relationships. After looking through his materials, Logan came up with the following:

36.1

Initial working thesis

     The Internet is changing the ways people interact and
form relationships.

Read sources and rework your thesis.

In 3d, and again in 33e, you saw that the job of the thesis is to
communicate both to you and to readers the ideas you are developing
in a paper. While you cannot definitively know, before the act of writing, what the final thesis will be (a thesis is often discovered in the very
act of writing a first draft), it is also true that the clearer you can be
with your ideas for an initial working thesis, the more surefooted
you'll be when beginning your draft.

    Logan's initial working thesis is far too broad and too obvious.
Unless he suggests *how* the Internet will change the ways in which
people will interact, he gives himself too little direction for starting
to write. The way for Logan—and you—to become more definite
about a working thesis is to read more about the topic at hand.
Here is what Logan Kole wrote about the process of refining his
working thesis. Note especially how his review of source materials
helped him:

I looked over each of my initial reading selections and
located the main points of each. Then I reviewed all of
these points and observed that they addressed several
different kinds of relationships the authors believe are
affected by Computer-Mediated Communication (CMC): communal relationships, relationships between long-distance
friends, those between students and instructors, and love
relationships. Some authors discuss positive experiences,
some negative. I wanted to reflect this variety in my
working thesis. I had to be more definite about the ways
in which the Internet is changing interpersonal relations.

Reading over his sources, therefore, gave Logan the knowledge he
needed to refine his working thesis:

Refined working thesis

With so many computer users forming a variety of online
relationships, no one can deny that this new technology is
affecting our modes of communication. However, reactions to
these changes range widely from excitement over abilities
to forge global connections, to fear that such connections
will prove much less satisfying than old-fashioned human
interactions.

A refined working thesis, reflecting as it does your response to at least several of the sources you've collected, is more sophisticated than an initial working thesis. A refined working thesis moves you closer to developing a plan for your paper and writing a first draft. Logan's reworking is long—and it will be revised again before he is through—but it is detailed enough to give him a direction as he begins to write.

Characteristics of a Working Thesis

- The subject of the thesis is *narrow* enough in scope that you can write a detailed paper without being constrained by the page limits of the assignment (3d-1).
- The predicate of the working thesis communicates a relationship you want to clarify about your subject, based on your understanding of the information you have generated (3d-2).
- The main statement of your thesis may involve one or more (but not many more) of the following relationships: sequential order, definition, classification, comparison, contrast, generalization, or causation.
- The thesis clearly suggests the patterns of development you will be pursuing in your paper. (The types of paragraphs you write in your paper will be directly tied to the relationships you develop in your thesis; see 3d-2, 3.)
- The thesis will clearly communicate your intellectual ambitions for the paper (3d-3).

36b   Developing a plan

Keeping your refined working thesis in mind, once again review all the notes you have taken, this time consolidating them into categories that will help you create a plan for your first draft.

Organize your notes into groups.

If you have been supplying headings for your notecards or computerized records, your task will be considerably easier. Stack the cards, or electronically move your records, into clusters. Logan Kole devised two main categories: pros and cons of online communities and pros and cons of online personal relationships.

If you have not already written headings on your notecards or computer records, write them as you review your notes with your refined working thesis in mind. There are at least two ways to do this. You can write headings on your notecards, group notes according to headings, and then use these groupings to construct an outline for your first draft.

Or you can sketch a first draft by converting sections of the outline as your headings, and then turning to your notes to organize them in a way that fits your outline. Either way (or if you devise some other way), your goal by this point is to have a refined working thesis, a sketch of your first draft, and notes to draw on as you write each section of this draft.

Outlines

Outlines and sketches for a paper come in all shapes and sizes (see 3d-4). A sketch may be a logically arranged map of key topics and their relationships. If your instructor asks for an *informal outline*, it will generally have only two levels: topics and subtopics. For example:

Online communities
    —pros/advantages
    —cons/disadvantages

Formal outlines have several levels (3d-4). The most common type employs a combination of Roman and Arabic numerals and letters.

I. Major topic
  A. Subtopic
    1. Minor subtopic
      a. sub-subtopic (or illustration)
        (1) illustration, example, explanation
        (2) illustration, example, explanation
    2. Minor subtopic
  B. Subtopic
II. Major topic

For more information on how to write outlines, see 3d-4 and 18e; for a discussion on how to work from outlines as you write a first draft, see 3e-2.

Make room for changes.

No matter how much care you take in assembling an outline or map of the paper *before* you write, it will inevitably change, to a greater or lesser extent, as you write the draft. Don't be discouraged by these changes. They are part of the writing process. With each successive draft beyond the first, your changes will tend to point you in a single direction: to a final thesis and a completed paper.

36c   Drawing on your sources to support *your* idea

Sources in a research paper exist to help you to advance a thesis that *you* have defined. One purpose of research is for you to make connections across sources where few or no clear connections currently exist.

These connections, and what you have to say about them, are what will make your paper original. No matter how many sources you use, focus on the ways that *you* synthesize them. Focus on the points *you* want to make.

Three ways of treating sources

As discussed in Chapter 35, there are three ways of dealing with source materials: summary, paraphrase, and quotation. Avoid writing a paper that stitches these methods together and leaves no room for you. You can do this by continually asking yourself: What is my overall point? How does this particular source serve the purpose of my paper by advancing that point? If you can keep the focus on your ideas and your connections across sources, then you will avoid letting your sources overwhelm you.

Filling in gaps

After you have developed your outline and arranged notecards to correspond to the outline, you will probably discover that in some areas you have more information than you need, while in other areas you do not have enough. In the latter case, go back to the library to fill in the gaps or take another look at material you have already gathered. In the former case (too much information), you will have to make some hard decisions. After accumulating so much material, you may be tempted to use it *all*. Resist that temptation.

If you provide *too* much information, you risk inundating your reader and drowning out your unique point of view in the paper. Both problems can defeat communication. Your job is to sift through source materials, select from among them those elements that will advance your idea, and incorporate them into your paper. Balance is the key: you want to establish key relationships but not overwhelm your reader.

36d   Determining your voice

How do you want to come across to your readers? As a student investigating a topic that *fascinates* you? As an authority speaking to specialists? As an authority speaking to nonspecialists? As a critic writing for a magazine? The option you select determines the *voice, tone,* and *register* of your writing. (See 3a-4 and 21e.)

Deciding on tone: Formal vs. informal

Consider, for example, the voice of a passage written by Sonia Maasik and Jack Solomon, which Logan Kole decided to quote in his paper (see 36h, "Works Cited"):

The unreal world of virtual culture . . . is being substituted for a social reality made up of real human beings. And such a world, based entirely on the transmission of electronic signals, is potentially a world in which human beings will be unable to conceive of others as human beings. When all interaction is electronic, [the critics] ask, where is the ground for true human empathy and relatedness?

The voice of this passage is serious, academic, and authoritative. The authors make little attempt to entertain their readers. But entertainment is not their purpose. Though the material is dry and the vocabulary somewhat elevated, the passage is clear and precise. Kole uses it in his paper to make an important point about the skeptics' view of computer-mediated communication.

Now consider an informal tone from a feature newspaper story entitled "Click Here for Romance" by Jennifer Wolcott (see 36h, "Works Cited"):

Honesty is what most appealed to California resident John Dwyer about the online approach. Disillusioned with the bar scene, he decided to give it a whirl. He posted a personal ad and photograph, got hundreds of responses, and eventually connected with Debbie.

Becoming sensitive to differences in tone

The difference in voice between these passages is pronounced. Wolcott's voice is casual, with conversational phrasings like "bar scene" and "give it a whirl." Wolcott is writing a story for a major newspaper *(The Christian Science Monitor)*, and has a story to tell. She must do so clearly, but she uses a nonacademic tone for her (presumably) nonacademic audience. By contrast, Maasik and Solomon write for an academic audience. Each author's voice is appropriate for the intended purpose and audience.

When writing your paper, choose a tone that is appropriate both for your attitudes toward your paper and for *your* audience (see 3a-4). Think of your readers as intelligent people who are interested in the issue on which you are writing, but who still expect to be engaged, as well as informed. A good academic paper should be like one side of an intelligent conversation—a conversation in which both participants take pleasure. (See 3a-4 for more on determining your own voice.)

36e Writing a draft

Sections 3b–e and 5a provide detailed discussions of strategies that will help you to write a first draft. You will need a method for working (or not working) from your outline, for writing a group of related paragraphs at a single sitting, and for recognizing and responding to obstacles as they arise.

COMPUTER TIPS

 Cut, Don't Delete

In freewriting, in early exploratory drafts, and in other initial stages of writing, you may find it useful not to delete information at first. If you've typed a paragraph that you decide you probably don't need, don't be hasty—you *may* need it later. Instead, use your word processor's *cut* function to remove the text. Unlike deleted text, cut text remains in your computer's memory in case you want it back. A word of caution: in nearly all word processors, only one chunk of cut text at a time can stay in memory. Cutting a second chunk of text automatically deletes the first chunk from memory forever. So before you cut a second chunk of text, use your computer's *paste* function to place the first one in some permanent location—perhaps at the very end of your paper or in another "notepad" file. Once your revisions are nearly finished and you're sure of the information you need, then you can delete material you haven't used.

You are finally ready to write:

- You have conducted systematic research on a subject in which you are interested;
- You have accumulated a stack of notes, in which you have summarized, paraphrased, and quoted relevant material;
- You have developed and revised a thesis; and
- You have prepared a careful sketch or an outline, on the basis of which you have organized your notes.

In short, you have become something of an expert on the subject. There is no reason to be anxious at this point. You are not writing the final draft. You are simply preparing a rough draft that will be seen by no one but yourself (and possibly some friends whose advice you trust). You will have plenty of opportunity to revise the rough draft.

Writing a skeleton draft and incorporating sources

To avoid overreliance on sources, as well as to clarify the main lines of a paper's argument, some researchers write their first drafts referring only to their outlines—and not to their source notes. As they write, they mark the places where source material (in summarized, paraphrased, or quoted form) will later be inserted. Drafts written in such a manner are simply skeletons or scaffolds. But by examining the skeleton, you can see whether the logic of your paper is sound. Does the argument make sense to you? Does one part logically follow from another? It should, even without the material from your notes. Remember your purpose and your audience: tell readers, as if you were having a conversation, what they should know about your subject and why you believe as you do.

At some point you will turn to your notes and consider how sources can help advance your ideas. Here are some considerations:

- Try arranging source notes in the order in which you intend to use them, but avoid simply transcribing your notes onto your rough draft.
- If you think you have made your point, move on, and skip any additional, unused notes on the topic or subtopic.
- Once you have completed a draft, you can revisit your notes and decide to substitute particularly effective unused notes for less effective ones used in the draft.

To avoid having to transcribe lengthy quotations or notes onto your draft, consider taping or stapling these notes (or photocopies of the quotations) directly onto the appropriate spots on the draft. When you do incorporate sources, remember to transfer bibliographic codes and page numbers, so that later you can enter the correct citations.

Starting in the middle

Many writers skip the introduction on the rough draft and get right into the body of the paper, believing that they are in a better position to draft the introduction later—when they know exactly what they are introducing. If you believe that you must begin at the beginning and work systematically all the way through, then do that. Whichever approach you take (and neither one is inherently preferable), remember that this is only a *rough* draft. Nothing at this stage is final.

36f Revising and editing

In 4a–d, you will find a discussion on revising and editing. Keep in mind that revision literally means "re-seeing." You should not consider revision simply a matter of fixing punctuation and spelling errors and improving a word or phrase here and there. Revision is, rather, a matter of looking at the whole paper from top to bottom and trying to determine whether you have presented material effectively.

Weblink

http://www.bc.edu/bc_org/avp/ulib/ ref/Research_Guide/Ch7-Web. html#REVISING%20YOUR%20PAPER

Covers the priorities in revising: Begin with the higher order concerns, the aspects of writing most responsible for the quality of the paper.

Some writers think of revision as a twofold process: *Macro revision* concerns the essay as a whole (its purpose, its voice, its structure), including its larger component units—the section and the paragraph. *Micro revision* concerns sentence structure, grammar, punctuation, and mechanics.

Others consider revision to be a four-stage process, in which writers revise (1) the essay as a whole; (2) individual paragraphs; (3) individual sentences; and (4) individual words.

These strategies are means to the same goal: ensuring that you consider *every* component of your essay, from largest to smallest, as you work to improve it.

Arriving at a final thesis

Before writing a draft, you start with a rough working thesis, which provides enough focus to help you sift through the materials you've gathered. More thinking about your sources may require you to refine your thesis. The act of writing a draft will help you to refine and focus still more. Ask yourself these questions as you reread your work:

- What is the main question of this research project?
- Is the question suitably complex for the subject I've defined?
- Is my answer to this question—my thesis—clear?
- Have I stated my thesis clearly in the draft?

Responding to these questions, and making corresponding adjustments in your paper, will help to guide your revision. These questions helped Logan Kole devise a final thesis concerning computer-mediated communication (CMC):

Final thesis

While many praise CMC's potential to bridge barriers and promote meaningful dialogue, others caution that CMC is fraught with dangers.

In the course of writing his first draft, Logan realized that his refined thesis (see p. 605), enabling him though it did to begin a draft, was not wholly accurate. First, none of his source materials actually discussed the "global" dimension to the interpersonal connections forged on the Internet. Second, his statement that some "fear such connections" did not adequately relate the negative views he encountered regarding CMC. As well, his working thesis was too long. Taking all of these matters into consideration, he decided to be less specific with his final thesis.

The process of writing worked well for Logan Kole. He formulated an initial thesis, refined it sufficiently so that he could write a first draft, and then—in preparation for a final draft—fashioned a tight fit between the information his sources gave him and a new, final thesis.

Working with feedback from readers and peer editors

When revising your paper, get as much feedback as possible from others. It is difficult even for professional writers to get perspective on what they have written immediately after they have written it. You are likely to

Writing the Research Paper

be too close to the subject, too committed to your outline or to particular words to be very objective at this point. Show your draft to a friend or classmate whose judgment you trust and to your instructor. Obtain reactions on everything from the essay as a whole to the details of word choice.

36g Understanding the elements of documentation

Writers can use several systems of documentation to credit their sources (see Chapter 37). The system used depends on the discipline in which they are writing—social sciences, humanities, science and technology, or business—or on the preferences of the audience.

Documenting sources is a two-part process:

1. Cite the source *in your paper* to identify it and give credit immediately after its use. This is called an *in-text* citation.
2. Cite the source *at the end of your paper*, in the form of a list of references that readers can pursue in more detail.

For three of the four documentation systems reviewed in Chapter 37—MLA, APA, and CSE—in-text citations are usually placed within parentheses. For the CMS—footnote and endnote—system, you make in-text citations with a small superscript numeral, and references are listed in notes.

Use Documentation to Give Fair Credit and to Assist Your Reader

Why go to the trouble of documenting your sources?

- *To give credit where it is due.* Ethics demands that the originators of ideas and information be credited.
- *To allow readers to gauge the accuracy and reliability of your work.* Any research paper will stand or fall according to how well (how perceptively, accurately, or selectively) you use sources.
- *To avoid charges of plagiarism.* You certainly do not want to give your readers the impression that you are claiming credit for ideas or words that are not yours.
- *To allow interested readers to follow up on a point.* Readers will sometimes want to pursue a point you have raised by going to your sources. Therefore, give readers the clearest possible directions for where to look.

All information and ideas should be documented—not just the sources that you quote directly. Summaries or paraphrases also require acknowledgment. The only exception to this rule is that *common knowledge*—as determined in part by the nature of your audience's level of expertise—need not be documented. (See 35h-1 for a discussion of what counts as common knowledge; and see paragraphs B and C in the sample paper.) For detailed information on documentation styles, see Chapter 37.

A sample research paper: "Computer-Mediated Communication: How Will It Affect Interpersonal Relationships?"

36h

The following research paper (pages 615–626) demonstrates the process of research and writing discussed in these chapters. The student writer, Logan Kole, chose to direct his efforts toward answering a key research question: How will the Internet affect interpersonal relationships? This key research question (see 33b-2) led to a working thesis (see 33e-1) and then to a refined thesis (see 36a); but, throughout, Logan retained the question as the focal point for his paper. He describes his motivation for this project as follows:

www

36.2

A few months ago, I checked out a dating service online. I had been so swamped with school work that any thought of a social life seemed impossible. But I had this need to connect and wondered, since I was logged on, if I couldn't meet this need online. Was this a moment of weakness for me, I wondered later, or was online chatting a legitimate way to meet people? The question fascinated me.

Kole's paper conforms to Modern Language Association (MLA) documentation style.

Cover-page format

Computer-Mediated Communication: How Will
It Affect Interpersonal Relationships?

1/3 down from
top of page.

by
Logan Kole

Center each line
of information.

Professor Kelley
English 160, Section 8
3 September 2002

1/3 up from
bottom of page.

First-page format for a paper with *no* cover page

Kole 1

Logan Kole
Professor Morrison
English 160, Section 8
3 September 2002

Note: no comma
or abbreviation
for "page."

Computer-Mediated Communication: How Will It
Affect Interpersonal Relationships?

Double-space all
information.

From the home, to the workplace, to the
classroom, the Internet has clicked its way into
our everyday lives. Today's students can e-mail
as file attachments their end-of-term papers to
their professors and can then turn around and
use e-mail to gather a group of friends for a
party or to celebrate the term's completion. These

Kole i

Outline

<u>Thesis statement:</u> While many praise CMC's potential to bridge barriers and promote meaningful dialogue, others caution that CMC is fraught with dangers.

Introduction: Increasingly, Americans are getting online to check their e-mail. This new medium has begun to take the place of face-to-face communications, a development that excites some people and concerns others.

I. Pros and cons of online communities
   A. Pros
      1. Advocates argue that CMC makes old methods of communication more efficient and gives rise to new methods (chat rooms and discussion lists).
      2. Communities in decline can benefit from online discussion.
   B. Cons
      1. Skeptics don't believe CMC can provide the basis of lasting relationships.
      2. Relationships may need physical immediacy to succeed.

II. Pros and cons of online relationships
   A. Pros
      1. Shy people can overcome their shyness online and find their voice.
      2. The Internet may promote honest communication.

Note the lower-case Roman numeral

Begin the outline with the thesis.

Place the outline immediately after the cover page.

Papers with no cover page do not have an outline.

Major sections: I, II, III

Subsections: A, B, C

Outline highlights unity and coherence.

Kole ii

B. Cons

    1. Online, people can easily deceive others about their identity and intentions--creating dangers for the unsuspecting.

    2. Online "love" is for some a fantasy preferable to the difficulties of real-life relationships.

Conclusion: Both online and offline, relationships succeed and fail; experts do not yet know whether CMC aids or hinders relationships--or both. Until the experts are more sure, people should exercise caution when meeting others online.

Supporting points: 1, 2, 3

Papers that do not outline easily may have logic problems.

Outline uses parallel elements: all phrases or all sentences.

Kole 1

Computer-Mediated Communication:
How Will It Affect
Interpersonal Relationships?

From the home, to the workplace, to the classroom, the Internet has clicked its way into our everyday lives. Today's students can e-mail as file attachments their end-of-term papers to their professors and can then turn around and use e-mail to gather a group of friends for a party or to celebrate the term's completion. These online exchanges, called CMC (or computer-mediated communication), sound fairly commonplace at the turn of the millennium. But what we have yet to discover is how CMC might change both the ways we communicate and the quality of our relationships. While many praise CMC's potential to bridge barriers and promote meaningful dialogue, others caution that CMC is fraught with dangers.

Very soon, half of America will communicate via e-mail, according to analysts (Singh 283). We can only assume that figure will grow--rapidly--as children who have matured in the Internet era move to college and into careers. With e-mail becoming an increasingly common form of communication, people are discovering and conversing with one another in a variety of ways that bring a new twist to old, familiar patterns. Using e-mail, people meet "to exchange pleasantries and argue, engage in intellectual discourse, conduct commerce, exchange knowledge, share emotional support, make plans, brainstorm, gossip, feud, [and] fall in love" (Chenault). That is, through

Thesis

A

Paragraph A (Reference to a single source, no quotation): You must cite all source material, even when you are not quoting it. In this case, the writer notes the source of his statistic about the growing use of e-mail. Notice Logan Kole's placement of the source information—author and page number (no comma between them)—at the end of the sentence, before the period.

Paragraph A (Citing an unpaginated source): The writer quotes an Internet source. Since the source (Chenault) provides no page numbers, Logan Kole provides no page numbers in his citation. Readers can locate the full reference to this source in the "Works Cited" list at the end of the paper. If you cite an alphabetized source (an encyclopedia article, for instance) or a one-page source, there is no need to provide page numbers in an in-text citation.

Paragraph A (Citing common knowledge): When you find the same information presented in several sources without debate, you can assume that information is "common knowledge"—that is, publicly available and not the intellectual property of any one person. You are free to use this information without attributing it to a source. In Paragraph A, Logan Kole found many expressions of excitement and concern about e-mail communication in his sources, and he therefore correctly decided not to provide any in-text citation.

e-mail people do what they have always done: communicate. But the medium of that communication has changed, which excites some people and concerns others.

A

Common knowledge: no citation needed

Advocates argue that the Internet has not only made existing types of communication faster, more convenient, more efficient, and less expensive; it has also made possible "new forms of community life," such as chat rooms and discussion lists, in which people from all over the country, and world, gather to share information and exchange points of view (Kling). CMC is potentially so powerful a medium of exchange that some believe it can promote dialogue within communities that are declining. A community, after all, is built on people acting in the interests of their neighbors for the common good. Via e-mail, online newsgroups, and e-forums, neighbors will have new ways of looking out for one another (Kling).

Section 1: Pros and cons on online communities

B

Still, skeptics aren't convinced that electronic communication can provide the basis of lasting personal relationships, primarily because relationships initiated on a cathode ray tube lack immediacy and physical presence. What may be missing in the electronic village say the critics is "an essential core of humanity" (Maasik and Solomon 701):

C

> The unreal world of virtual culture . . . is being substituted for a social reality made up of real human beings. And such a world, based entirely on the transmission of electronic signals, is potentially a world in which human beings will be unable to

Paragraph B (Summary): In an earlier draft, Logan Kole quoted a long passage from Ron Kling, a specialist in information systems and information science. As Logan continued working with his notes, he identified another source (Maasik and Solomon—see paragraph C) that he felt was even more compelling. He did not want to include two lengthy block quotations in his paper, so he chose to summarize the passage by Kling. Here is Kling's original:

> In the United States, communities seem to be deteriorating from a complex combination of causes. In the inner cities of big urban centers, many people fear street crime and stay off the streets at night. In the larger suburban and post-suburban areas, many people hardly know their neighbors and "latch key" children often have little adult contact after school. An African proverb which says that "it takes a whole village to raise a child" refers to a rich community life with a sense of mutual responsibility that is difficult to find in many new neighborhoods. Some advocates believe that computer technology in concert with other efforts could play a role in rebuilding community life by improving communication, economic opportunity, civic participation, and education.
>
> —R<small>ON</small> K<small>LING</small>, "Social Relationships in Electronic Forums: Hangouts, Salons, Workplaces, and Communities." CMC Magazine, July 22, 1996.

Logan Kole's summary begins with "CMC is potentially so powerful" and runs to the end of the paragraph.

Paragraph C (Block quotation with ellipsis): Quotations of five or more lines should be displayed in a block. Note that you do not use quotation marks for a block quotation, and you set the parenthetical citation *outside* of the final mark of punctuation.

In this block quotation, Logan decided to delete part of the original source. The original quotation read as follows, with the material to be deleted underlined.

> The unreal world of virtual culture, <u>they believe, the world in which you can pretend to be just about anything,</u> is being substituted for a social reality made up of real human beings.

Logan noted his alteration to the quoted passage with a bracketed ellipsis. See 29e for detailed advice on using the ellipsis.

Paragraph C (Bracketed clarifying remark in a quoted passage): In the block quotation, Logan Kole clarified what for his readers would have been an ambiguous pronoun. Here is the sentence from the original:

> When all interaction is electronic, they ask, where is the ground for true human empathy and relatedness?

Logan understood that his readers would wonder who "they" were. He therefore altered the quotation with a clarifying remark set in brackets. The brackets alert readers that the change in language was Logan's, not the source author's.

A Sample Research Paper

Kole 3

conceive of others as human beings.
When all interaction is electronic,
[the critics] ask, where is the ground
for true human empathy and relatedness? (Maasik and Solomon 701)

Reference set outside end punctuation in block quotation

The fact that people communicate--via e-mail,
snail (written) mail, or in person--does not
guarantee that their exchanges lead to community. Members of a community trust and care for
one another; they extend themselves and offer
help (Kling). Critics of CMC argue that the
supporters gloss over this important distinction
when they assume that electronic forums are
"building new forms of community life" (Kling).
Talking, electronically or otherwise, marks only
the beginning of a process. Community building
is hard work and takes time.

Notwithstanding these concerns, proponents of CMC confidently point to examples in
which the new technologies of communication
bring people together in meaningful, healthy
ways. In a study of first-year college students, researcher Richard Holeton of Stanford
University found that students who were ordinarily reserved were able to come out of their
shells and participate in Internet debates
(Branscum 79). Similarly, the Internet can
serve as a way for people who are having trouble dating to find partners. For instance, Tom
Buckley of Portland, Oregon, met his wife after signing up with Match.com. Buckley noted
that the Internet helped him to meet his wife
because "neither one of us was the type to
walk up to someone in the gym or a bar and
say, 'You're the fuel

Section 2: pros and cons of online relationships

to my fire'" (qtd. in Morris). Holeton's research and Buckley's experience suggest that
the Internet may provide a way for otherwise
timid individuals to express themselves.

Summary of
two sources

Beyond simply providing a safe and lower-
stress place to meet, the Internet may actually
promote honest communication. An Ohio State
sociologist, Andrea Baker, concluded from her
research that individuals who begin their romance online can be at an advantage: writing
via e-mail can promote a "better and deeper"
relationship than one begun in person because
writing itself promotes a frank, honest exchange (qtd. in Wolcott). Certainly this was
the experience of John Dwyer, a Californian
who tired of meeting women in bars and decided
instead to post an advertisement online. He
eventually met the woman who would become his
wife, Debbie, who said: "If you are honest
when talking online, you can strip away all
the superficial stuff and really get to know
someone" (qtd. in Wolcott). When it works,
CMC can promote a sincere exchange among
those looking for lasting relationships.

Shows that Wolcott
is the source of the
Dwyer quotation

Yet, as MIT professor Sherry Turkle notes,
online relationships allow people an opportunity
to pretend to be someone very different from who
they really are; in fact, some see creating a
separate online identity as all part of the fun
(228). Obviously, such deception can lead to
emotional or financial betrayal. Take, for
instance, the experience of Robert Spradling.
He met and formed a romantic attachment to a
Ukrainian woman online. She encouraged the
romance via e-mail and eventually asked for

Source author's
name is in
the sentence,
so citation
omits name.

money to set up a business. He sent $8,000 and
later, again online, asked her to marry him.
She agreed, they met in Kiev, and after
Spradling returned home she disappeared--his
money gone and his heart broken (Morris). Perhaps Spradling was one of the Internet roman-
tics for whom it is wiser to avoid face-to-face
meetings. That way, he could have enjoyed the
interactive fantasy of a "cyber-lover" without
ever having to ruin the fun with the uncomfortable truths of real life (Suler).

> Summary of the Spradling example; paraphrase would be too long

It is far from certain, then, that all or
even most relationships begun online develop
positively. Closer to the truth is that both online and offline, some relationships begin--and
end--in deceit while others blossom. Experts do
not yet know whether computer-mediated communication, because of its electronic format, alters
relationships as they are forming or, rather, is
simply a new territory in which to find others.
Time will tell. In the meantime, the advice that
loved ones give us when we set off to find new
friends--Be careful!--makes sense whether we are
looking in the virtual world or down the street.

> Conclusion

Kole 6

Works Cited

Branscum, Deborah. "Life at High-Tech U."
    Newsweek 27 Oct. 1997: 78-80.

Chenault, Brittney G. "Developing Personal
    and Emotional Relationships Via Computer-
    Mediated Communication." _CMC Magazine_
    May 1998. 8 Aug. 2002 <http://
    www.december.com/cmc/mag/1998/may/
    chenault.html>.

Kling, Rob. "Social Relationships in Electronic
    Forums: Hangouts, Salons, Workplaces and
    Communities." _CMC Magazine_ July 1996.
    12 Sept. 2002 <http://www.december.com/cmc/
    mag/1996/jul/kling.html>.

Maasik, Sonia, and Jack Solomon, eds. _Signs of
    Life in the USA_. Boston: Bedford Books,
    1997.

Morris, Bonnie R. "You've Got Romance! Seeking
    Love Online: Net-Based Services Change the
    Landscape, If Not the Odds, of Finding the
    Perfect Mate." _New York Times Online_ 26
    Aug. 1996. 8 Aug. 2002 <http://
    oak.cats.ohiou.ed/~bakera/ArticleE.htm>.

Singh, Sanjiv N. "Cyberspace: A New Frontier
    for Fighting Words." _Rutgers Computer and
    Technology Law Journal_ 25.2 (1999): 283.

Suler, John. "Cyberspace Romances: Interview
    with Jean-Francois Perreault of Branchez-
    vous." _The Psychology of Cyberspace_
    Dec. 1996. 14 Aug. 2002 <http://
    www.rider.edu/users/suler/psycyber/
    psycyber.html>.

References list.
See Chapter 7
for details.
Magazine entry

Electronic
publication

Journal

Internet
Web site

Turkle, Sherry. Life on the Screen: Identity
    in the Age of the Internet. New York:
    Simon, 1995.

Wolcott, Jennifer. "Click Here for Romance."
    Christian Science Monitor 13 Jan. 1999. 23
    Sept. 2002 <http://www.csmonitor.com/
    archive/archives.html>.

Book entry

Writing the Research Paper

CHAPTER 37

Documenting Research

Any time you use material derived from specific sources, whether quoted passages or summaries or paraphrases of fact, opinion, explanation, or idea, you are ethically obligated to let your reader know who deserves the credit. Further, you must tell your readers precisely where the material came from so that they can locate it for themselves. Often readers will want to trace the facts on which a conclusion is based, or to verify that a passage was quoted or paraphrased accurately. Sometimes readers will simply want to follow up and learn more about your subject.

There are basically two ways for a writer to show a "paper trail" to sources. The most widely used format today is the parenthetical reference, also called an *in-text citation*. This is a telegraphic, short-hand approach to identifying the source of a statement or quotation. It assumes that a complete list of references appears at the end of the paper. Each entry in the list of references includes three essential elements: authorship, full title of the work, and publication information. In the references, entries are arranged, punctuated, and typed to conform to the bibliographic style requirements of the particular discipline or of the instructor. With this list in place, the writer is able to supply the briefest of references—a page number or an author's name—in parentheses right in the text, knowing that the reader will be able to locate the rest of the reference information easily in the list of references. The second method for showing a paper trail is the footnote style—which is less often used today than the parenthetical system.

WWW

37.1

For more detailed information on the conventions of style in the humanities, social sciences, business disciplines, and sciences, refer to these style manuals:

- Gibaldi, Joseph. *MLA Style Manual and Guide to Scholarly Publishing.* 2nd ed. New York: MLA, 1998 and Gibaldi, Joseph. *MLA Handbook for Writers of Research Papers.* 6th ed. New York: MLA, 2003.
- *Publication Manual* (of the American Psychological Association). 5th ed. Washington, DC: APA, 2001.
- *Chicago Manual of Style.* 14th ed. Chicago: University of Chicago Press, 1993.
- *Scientific Style and Format: The CBE Manual for Authors, Editors, and Publishers.* 6th ed. New York: Cambridge University Press, 1994.
- Walker, Janice, and Todd W. Taylor. *The Columbia Guide to Online Style.* New York: Columbia University Press, 1998.

An Overview of the Four Documentation Systems Presented in This Chapter

37a Using the MLA system of documentation (see detailed index on 629–31)

1. Making in-text citations in the MLA format   631
2. Preparing a list of references in the MLA format   637
   Listing books in the MLA "Works Cited" format   638
   Listing periodicals in the MLA "Works Cited" format   641
   Listing other sources in the MLA "Works Cited" format   644
3. Listing electronic sources in the MLA "Works Cited" format   646
   Online sources   646
   CD-ROMs and diskettes   651

37b Using the APA system of documentation (see detailed index on 652–53)

1. Making in-text citations in the APA format   653
2. Preparing a list of references in the APA format   655
   Listing books in the APA format   656
   Listing periodicals in the APA format   657
   Listing other sources in the APA format   659
3. Listing electronic sources in the APA format   660

37c Using the CMS style of documentation (see detailed index on 663)

1. Making the first and subsequent references in CMS notes   663
2. Following the CMS note style   664
   Citing books in the CMS note style   664
   Citing periodicals and other sources in the CMS note style   665

37d Using the CSE systems of documentation (see detailed index on 667)

1. Making in-text citations in the CSE formats   667
   The name-year system   667
   The citation-sequence system   668
2. Preparing a list of references using CSE systems   669
   Listing books in the CSE format   669
   Listing periodicals in the CSE format   671
   Listing electronic sources in the CSE format   673

628   Documenting Research

The Modern Language Association (MLA) publishes a style guide that is widely used for citations and references in the humanities. This section gives detailed examples of how the MLA system of parenthetical references provides in-text citation. In addition, a later section (37c) will show how to use the Chicago Manual of Style (CMS) system of documentation (formerly used in MLA publications), where complete information on each source is given every time a source is cited.

In a research paper, either of these systems of source citation is followed at the end by a list of references. In the MLA system, the list of references is called "Works Cited." Keep in mind that the complete information provided in the list of references will be the basis of your in-text citations. The parenthetical form provides minimal information and sends the reader to the list of references to find the rest. By contrast, the footnote or endnote system virtually duplicates the information in the list of references but uses a slightly different arrangement of the elements in the entry. Following is an index to this section on the MLA system of documentation.

| **1** | **Making in-text citations in the MLA format** |

When you make a parenthetical in-text citation, you assume that your reader will look to the list of "Works Cited" for complete references. The list of references at the end of your paper will provide three essential pieces of information for each of your sources: author, title, and facts of publication. Within your paper, a parenthetical citation may point to a source considered as a whole or to a specific page location in a source. Here is an example of an MLA in-text citation referring to a story as a whole.

```
In "Escapes," the title story of one contemporary author's
book of short stories, the narrator's alcoholic mother makes
a public spectacle of herself (Williams).
```

The next example refers to a specific page in the story. In the MLA system, no punctuation is placed between a writer's last name and a page reference.

```
In "Escapes," a story about an alcoholic household, a key
moment occurs when the child sees her mother suddenly appear
on stage at the magic show (Williams 11).
```

Here is how the references to the Williams story would appear as described in the list of references or "Works Cited."

```
Williams, Joy. "Escapes." Escapes: Stories. New York:
    Vintage, 1990. 1-14.
```

Deciding when to insert a source citation and what information to include is often a judgment call rather than the execution of a mechanical system. Use common sense. Where feasible, incorporate citations smoothly into the text. Introduce the parenthetical reference at a pause in your sentence, at the end if possible. Place it as close to the documented point as possible, making sure that the reader can tell exactly which point is being documented. When the in-text reference is incorporated into a sentence of your own, always place the parenthetical reference *before* any enclosing or end punctuation.

```
In Central Africa in the 1930s, a young girl who comes to
town drinks beer with her date because that's what everyone
does (Lessing 105).
```

In a realistic portrayal of Central African city life in the
1930s (Lessing), young people gather daily to drink.

When a quotation from a work is incorporated into a sentence of
your own, the parenthetical reference *follows* the quotation marks, yet
precedes the enclosing or end punctuation.

At the popular Sports Club, Lessing's heroine finds the
"ubiquitous glass mugs of golden beer" (135).

Exception: When your quotation ends with a question mark or exclamation point, keep these punctuation marks inside the end quotation
marks, then give the parenthetical reference, and end with a period.

Martha's new attempts at sophistication in town prompted
her to retort, "Children are a nuisance, aren't they?"
(Lessing 115).

COMPUTER TIPS

Citation Format Software

Software programs such as Daedalus, Inc.'s *BiblioCite*
and others now on the market allow you to plug in
standard bibliographic information (author's name, title, and so on) to generate a perfectly formatted "Works Cited" or
"References" page. If you have access to such software, use it. Following the conventions of standard bibliographic formats is the kind of
tedious organizational task at which computers excel. Be sure to
check, however, to be sure that your program is set up to comply with
the latest formats for Internet sources. If not, then be prepared to do
some manual editing to update your citations.

Naming an author in the text

When you want to emphasize the author of a source you are citing,
incorporate that author's name into your sentence. Unless you are referring to a particular place in that source, no parenthetical reference is
necessary in the text.

Biographer Paul Mariani understands Berryman's alcoholism as
one form of his drive toward self-destruction.

Naming an author in the parenthetical reference

When you want to emphasize information in a source but not especially the author, omit the author's name in the sentence and place it in
the parenthetical reference.

Biographers have documented alcohol-related upheavals in John Berryman's life. Aware, for example, that Dylan Thomas was in an alcohol-induced coma, dying, Berryman himself drank to escape his pain (Mariani 273).

When you are referring to a particular place in your source and have already incorporated the author's name into your sentence, place only the page number in parentheses.

Biographer Paul Mariani describes how Berryman, knowing that his friend Dylan Thomas was dying in an alcohol-induced coma, himself began drinking to escape his pain (273).

Documenting a block quotation

For block quotations, set the parenthetical reference—with or without an author's name—*outside* of the end punctuation mark.

The story graphically portrays the behavior of Central African young people gathering daily to drink:

> Perry sat stiffly in a shallow chair which looked as if it would splay out under the weight of his big body . . . while from time to time--at those moments when laughter was jerked out of him by Stella--he threw back his head with a sudden dismayed movement, and flung half a glass of liquor down his throat. (Lessing 163)

A work by two or three authors

If your source has two or three authors, name them all, either in your text or in a parenthetical reference. Use last names, in the order they are given in the source, connected by *and*.

Critics have addressed the question of whether literary artists discover new truths (Wellek and Warren 33-36).

One theory claims that the alcoholic wants to "drink his environment in" (Perls, Hefferline, and Goodman 193-94).

A work by four or more authors

For a work with four or more authors, name all the authors, or use the following abbreviated format with *et al.* to signify "and others."

Some researchers trace the causes of alcohol dependence to "flawed family structures" (Stein, Lubber, Koman, and Kelly 318).

Some researchers trace the causes of alcohol dependence to "flawed family structures" (Stein et al. 318).

Stein and his coeditors trace the causes of alcohol dependence to "flawed family structures" (318).

Reference to two or more sources with the same authorship

When you are referring to two or more sources written by the same author, include a shortened form of each title so that references to each text will be clear. The following example discusses how author Joy Williams portrays the drinking scene in her fiction. Note that a comma appears between the author's name and the shortened title.

She shows drinking at parties as a way of life in such stories as "Escapes" and "White Like Midnight." Thus it is a matter of course that Joan pours herself a drink while people talk about whether or not they want to survive nuclear war (Williams, "White" 129).

Distinguishing two authors with the same last name

Use one or more initials to supplement references to authors with the same last name.

It is no coincidence that a new translation of Euripides' The Bacchae should appear in the United States (C. K. Williams) at a time when fiction writers portray the use of alcohol as a means of escape from mundane existence (J. Williams).

Two or more sources in a single reference

Particularly in an introductory summary, you may want to group together a number of works that cover one or more aspects of your research topic. Separate one source from another by a semicolon.

Studies that confront the alcoholism of literary figures directly are on the increase (Mariani; Dardis; Gilmore).

A corporate author

A work may be issued by an organization or government agency with no author named. Cite the work as if the name given is the author's. Since the name of a corporate author is often long, try incorporating it into your text rather than using a parenthetical note. In this example the corporate author of the book is Alcoholics Anonymous. The book will be listed alphabetically under "Alcoholics" in "Works Cited."

Among publications that discuss how to help young people cope with family problems, Al-Anon Faces Alcoholism, put out by Alcoholics Anonymous, has been reissued frequently since 1974 (117-24).

A multivolume work

When citing a page reference to a multivolume work, specify the volume by an Arabic numeral followed by a colon, a space, and the page number. The Trevelyan history is in four volumes.

Drunkenness was such a problem in the first decades of the eighteenth century that it was termed "the acknowledged national vice of Englishmen of all classes" (Trevelyan 3: 46).

A literary work

Well-known literary works, particularly older ones now in the public domain, may appear in numerous editions. When referring to such a work or a part of one, give information for the work itself rather than for the particular edition you are using, unless you are highlighting a special feature or contribution of the edition.

For a play, supply act, scene, and line number in Arabic numerals, unless your instructor specifies using Roman numerals for act and scene (II. iv. 118–19). Below, the first numeral in the title refers to the first of two plays that Shakespeare wrote about Henry IV, known as parts 1 and 2.

Shakespeare's Falstaff bellows, "Give me a cup of sack, rogue. Is there no virtue extant?" (1 Henry IV 2.4.118-19).

To cite a modern editor's contribution to the publication of a literary work, adjust the emphasis of your reference. The abbreviation *n* stands for *note*.

Without the editor's footnote in the Riverside Shakespeare explaining that lime was sometimes used as an additive to make wine sparkle, modern readers would be unlikely to understand Falstaff's ranting: "[Y]et a coward is worse than a cup of sack with lime in it. A villainous coward!" (1 Henry IV 2.4.125-26n).

Material quoted in your source

Often you will want to quote and cite material that you are reading at second hand—in a work by an intermediate author. Quote the original material and refer to the place where you found it.

Psychoanalyst Otto Fenichel included alcoholics within a general grouping of addictive personalities, all of whom use addictive substances "to satisfy the archaic oral longing, a need for security, and a need for the maintenance of self-esteem simultaneously" (qtd. in Roebuck and Kessler 86).

An anonymous work

A work with no acknowledged author will be alphabetized in a list of references by the first word of its title. Therefore cite the anonymous work in the same way in your parenthetical reference. The title in this example is *The Hidden Alcoholic in Your Midst.*

```
People who do not suffer from addiction often can be
thoughtless and insensitive to the problems of those around
them. That is the message of an emotional and thought-
provoking pamphlet (Hidden), whose author writes anonymously
about the pain of keeping his alcoholism secret.
```

Page locations for electronic sources

You will find that some electronic sources and documents from the Internet have page numbers; others have paragraph numbers; many have neither. Since you need to provide specific information to show readers where to locate and examine sources, you can follow these general guidelines—an extension of those developed by the Modern Language Association for print sources. Examples are hypothetical.

- Begin the parenthetical citation by referring to the author or title of the source, as you would with any other in-text citation (provided these are not previously mentioned in your sentence).
- Refer to a page number in the electronic source, if provided.

```
Leading scientists have called for a moratorium on the
release of genetically engineered organisms into the en-
vironment (Weiss 12).
```

- If the electronic source has no page numbers, refer to paragraph numbers (if provided). If your citation begins with the author's name or a title, place a comma and follow with the abbreviation *par.* or *pars.*, and indicate the paragraph(s) used.

```
Hardy reports that many geneticists object to the idea
of a moratorium and have formed their own lobbying
groups to fight such moves (par. 14).
```

- If no pagination or paragraph numbering is provided, you can use abbreviations like those used for classic literary works to refer to a structural division within the source: "pt." for part; "sec." for section; "ch." for chapter; "vol." for volume.

```
In the absence of agreement within the scientific commu-
nity, Norman Stein, director of Genetics Watch, has
called for a "sensible government policy" (qtd. in Lub-
ber sec. 5).
```

- If the electronic source provides no pagination, no paragraph numbering, and no internal structural divisions, cite the source by name only. At the "Works Cited" page, readers will see that the electronic source was not paginated.

```
Scientists prefer to govern themselves; historically, the
threat of government intervention has prompted voluntary
restraints from scientific organizations (Wesley).
```

- Finally, when you are citing a one-page electronic source or an electronic source in which entries are arranged alphabetically (such as a CD-based or online encyclopedia), no in-text reference to a page or paragraph is needed. The following reference is to a "Works Cited" list that names an anonymously written article in an online encyclopedia.

```
For centuries, farmers have manipulated "genetic materi-
als to achieve desired changes in plants and animals"
("Genetic Engineering").
```

Following MLA parenthetical style, these in-text citations of electronic sources refer readers to detailed entries in the "Works Cited" list. See 37a-3 for guidelines on creating these detailed entries.

| 2 | Preparing a list of references in the MLA format |

In research papers following MLA format, the list of references is called "Works Cited" when it includes those sources you have referred to in your paper. Be aware that some instructors request a more comprehensive list of references—one that includes every source you consulted in preparing the paper. That list would be titled "Bibliography."

The examples in this section show how entries in the "Works Cited" list consist of three elements essential for a list of references: authorship, full title of the work, and publication information. In addition, if the work is taken from an electronic (online) source, consult 37a-3. The basic format for each entry requires the first line to start at the left margin, with each subsequent line to be indented five typed spaces from the left margin.

Not every possible variation is represented here. In formatting a complicated entry for your own list, you may need to combine features from two or more of the examples.

The "Works Cited" list begins on a new page, after the last page of your paper, and continues the pagination of your paper. Entries in the list are alphabetized by the author's last name. An anonymous work is alphabetized by the first word in its title (but disregard *A*, *An*, and *The*). Center "Works Cited" on the page and double space entries.

Listing books in the MLA "Works Cited" format

The MLA "Works Cited" list presents book references in the following order:

1. *Author's name:* Put the last name first, followed by a comma and the first name (and middle name or initial) and a period. Omit the author's titles and degrees, whether one that precedes a name (Dr.) or one that follows (PhD).

2. *Title of the book:* Underline the complete title. If there is a subtitle, separate it from the main title by a colon and one typed space. Capitalize all important words, including the first word of any subtitle. The complete title is followed by a period.

3. *Publication information:* Name the city of publication, followed by a colon and one typed space; the name of the publisher followed by a comma; the date of publication followed by a period. This information appears on the title page of the book and the copyright page, on the reverse side of the title page.

If the city of publication is not well known, add the name of the state, abbreviated as in the zip code system. Shorten the name of the publisher in a way that is recognizable. "G. P. Putnam's Sons" is shortened to "Putnam's." For university presses use "UP" as in the example "U of Georgia P." Many large publishing companies issue books under imprints that represent particular groups of books. Give the imprint name first, followed by a hyphen and the name of the publisher: Bullseye-Knopf.

Any additional information about the book goes between author and title or between title and publication data. Observe details of how to organize, abbreviate, and punctuate this information in the examples below.

A book with one author

The basic format for a single-author book is as follows:

Mariani, Paul. <u>Dream Song: The Life of John Berryman</u>. New York: Morrow, 1990.

A book with two or three authors

For a book with two or three authors, follow the order of the names on the title page. Notice that first and last name are reversed only for the lead author. Notice also the use of a comma after the first author.

Roebuck, Julian B., and Raymond G. Kessler. <u>The Etiology of Alcoholism: Constitutional, Psychological and Sociological Approaches</u>. Springfield: Thomas, 1972.

A book with four or more authors

As in the example under in-text citations (see 37a-1), you may choose to name all the authors or to use the abbreviated format with *et al.*

```
Stein, Norman, Mindy Lubber, Stuart L. Koman, and Kathy Kelly.
     Family Therapy: A Systems Approach. Boston: Allyn, 1990.
Stein, Norman, et al. Family Therapy: A Systems Approach.
     Boston: Allyn, 1990.
```

A book that has been reprinted or reissued

In the following entry, the date 1951 is the original publication date of the book, which was reprinted in 1965.

```
Perls, Frederick, Ralph F. Hefferline, and Paul Goodman.
     Gestalt Therapy: Excitement and Growth in the Human
     Personality. 1951. New York: Delta-Dell, 1965.
```

A dictionary or encyclopedia

If an article in a reference work is signed (usually by initials), include the name of the author, which is spelled out elsewhere in the reference work (usually at the beginning). The first example is unsigned. The second article is signed (F.G.H.T.).

```
"Alcoholics Anonymous." Encyclopaedia Britannica: Micropae-
     dia. 1991 ed.
Tate, Francis G. H. "Rum." Encyclopaedia Britannica.
     1950 ed.
```

A selection from an edited book or anthology

For a selection from an edited work, name the author of the selection and enclose the selection title in quotation marks. Underline the title of the book containing the selection, and name its editor(s). Give the page numbers for the selection at the end of your entry.

```
Davies, Phil. "Does Treatment Work? A Sociological Perspec-
     tive." The Misuse of Alcohol. Ed. Nick Heather et al.
     New York: New York UP, 1985. 158-77.
```

When a selection has been reprinted from another source, include that information too, as in the following example. State the facts of original publication first, then describe the book in which it has been reprinted.

```
Bendiner, Emil. "The Bowery Man on the Couch." The Bowery
     Man. New York: Nelson, 1961. Rpt. in Man Alone: Alien-
     ation in Modern Society. Ed. Eric Josephson and Mary
     Josephson. New York: Dell, 1962. 401-10.
```

Two or more works by the same author(s)

When you cite two or more works by the same author(s), you should write the author's full name only once, at first mention, in the reference list. In subsequent entries immediately following, substitute three hyphens and a period in place of the author's name.

Heilbroner, Robert L. The Future as History. New York:
    Harper Torchbooks-Harper, 1960.

---. An Inquiry into the Human Prospect. New York: Norton,
    1974.

A translation

When a work has been translated, acknowledge the translator's name after giving the title.

Kufner, Heinrich, and Wilhelm Feuerlein. In-Patient Treat-
    ment for Alcoholism: A Multi-Centre Evaluation Study.
    Trans. F. K. H. Wagstaff. Berlin: Springer, 1989.

A corporate author

If authorship is not individual but corporate, treat the name of the organization as you would the author. This listing would be alphabetized under "National Center."

National Center for Alcohol Education. The Community Health
    Nurse and Alcohol-Related Problems: Instructor's
    Curriculum Planning Guide. Rockville: National
    Institute on Alcohol Abuse and Alcoholism, 1978.

Signaling publication information that is unknown

If a document fails to state place or date of publication or the name of the publisher, indicate this lack of information in your entry by using the appropriate abbreviation.

Missing, Andrew. Things I Forgot or Never Knew. N.p.:
    n.p., n.d.

In the above example, the first *n.p.* stands for "no place of publication." The second *n.p.* means "no publisher given," and *n.d.* stands for "no date."

An edition subsequent to the first

Books of continuing importance may be revised substantially before reissue. Cite the edition you have consulted just after giving the title.

Scrignar, C. B. Post-Traumatic Stress Disorder: Diagnosis,
    Treatment, and Legal Issues. 2nd ed. New Orleans:
    Bruno, 1988.

A book in a series

If the book you are citing is one in a series, include the series name (no quotation marks or underline) followed by the series number and a period before the publication information. You need not give the name of the series editor.

```
Schuckit, Marc A., ed. Alcohol Patterns and Problems. Series
    in Psychological Epidemiology 5. New Brunswick: Rutgers
    UP, 1985.
```

An introduction, preface, foreword, or afterword

When citing an introductory or concluding essay by a "guest author" or commentator, begin with the name of that author. Give the type of piece—Introduction, Preface—without quotation marks or underline. Name the author of the book after giving the book title. At the end of the listing, give the page numbers for the essay you are citing. If the author of the separate essay is also the author of the complete work, repeat that author's last name, preceded by *By*, after the book title.

```
Fromm, Erich. Foreword. Summerhill: A Radical Approach to
    Child Rearing. By A. S. Neill. New York: Hart, 1960.
    ix-xiv.
```

In the following book, the editors also wrote the introduction to their anthology.

```
Josephson, Eric, and Mary Josephson. Introduction. Man
    Alone: Alienation in Modern Society. Ed. Josephson and
    Josephson. New York: Dell, 1962. 9-53.
```

An unpublished dissertation or essay

An unpublished dissertation, even of book length, has its title in quotation marks. Label it as a dissertation in your entry. Naming the university and year will provide the necessary publication facts.

```
Reiskin, Helen R. "Patterns of Alcohol Usage in a Help-
    Seeking University Population." Diss. Boston U, 1980.
```

Listing periodicals in the MLA "Works Cited" format

A *periodical* is any publication that appears regularly over time. A periodical can be a daily or weekly newspaper, a magazine, or a scholarly or professional journal. As with listings for books, a bibliographical listing for a periodical article includes information about authorship, title, and facts of publication. Authorship is treated just as for books, with the author's first and last names reversed. Citation of a title differs in that the title of an article is always enclosed in quotation marks rather than underlined; the title of the periodical in which it appears is always underlined. Notice that the articles *a, an,* and *the*, which often begin the name of a periodical, are omitted from the bibliographical listing.

The facts of publication are the trickiest of the three elements because of the wide variation in how periodicals are dated, paginated, and published. For journals, for example, the publication information generally consists of journal title, the volume number, the year of publication, and the page numbering for the article cited. For newspapers, the listing includes name of the newspaper, full date of publication, and full page numbering by both section and page number(s) if necessary. The following examples show details of how to list different types of periodicals. With the exception of May, June, and July, you should abbreviate the names of months in each "Works Cited" entry (see 31d).

A journal with continuous pagination through the annual volume

A continuously paginated journal is one that numbers pages consecutively throughout all the issues in a volume instead of beginning with page 1 in each issue. After the author's name (reversed and followed by a period), give the name of the article in quotation marks. Give the title of the journal, underlined and followed by a typed space. Give the volume number, in arabic numerals. After a typed space, give the year, in parentheses, followed by a colon. After one more space, give the page number(s) for the article, including the first and last pages on which it appears.

```
Kling, William. "Measurement of Ethanol Consumed in Dis-
     tilled Spirits." Journal of Studies on Alcohol 50
     (1989): 456-60.
```

In a continuously paginated journal, the issue number within the volume and the month of publication are not included in the bibliographical listing.

A journal paginated by issue

```
Latessa, Edward J., and Susan Goodman. "Alcoholic Offenders:
     Intensive Probation Program Shows Promise." Corrections
     Today 51.3 (1989): 38-39+.
```

This journal numbers the pages in each issue separately, so it is important to identify which issue in volume 51 has this article beginning on page 38. The plus sign following a page number indicates that the article continues beyond the last-named page, but after intervening pages.

A monthly magazine

This kind of periodical is identified by month and year of issue. Even if the magazine indicates a volume number, omit it from your listing.

```
Waggoner, Glen. "Gin as Tonic." Esquire Feb. 1990: 30.
```

Some magazines vary in their publication schedule. *Restaurant Business* publishes once a month or bimonthly. Include the full date of publication in your listing. Give the day first, followed by an abbreviation for the month.

```
Whelan, Elizabeth M. "Alcohol and Health." Restaurant Busi-
     ness 20 Mar. 1989: 66+.
```

A daily newspaper

In the following examples, you see that the name of the newspaper is underlined. Any introductory article (*a*, *an*, and *the*) is omitted. The complete date of publication is given—day, month (abbreviated), year. Specify the edition if one appears on the masthead, since even in one day an article may be located differently in different editions. Precede the page number(s) by a colon and one typed space. If the paper has sections designated by letter (A, B, C), include the section before the page number.

If the article is unsigned, begin your entry with the title, as in the second example ("Alcohol Can Worsen Ills of Aging").

Welch, Patrick. "Kids and Booze: It's 10 O'Clock--Do You
        Know How Drunk Your Kids Are?" Washington Post 31 Dec.
        1989: C1.

The following entry illustrates the importance of including the particular edition of a newspaper.

"Alcohol Can Worsen Ills of Aging, Study Says." New York
        Times 13 June 1989, natl. ed.: 89.
"Alcohol Can Worsen Ills of Aging, Study Says." New York
        Times 13 June 1989, late ed.: C5.

A weekly magazine or newspaper

An unsigned article listing would include title, name of the publication, complete date, and page number(s). Even if you know a volume or issue number, omit it.

"A Direct Approach to Alcoholism." Science News 9 Jan.
        1988: 25.

A signed editorial, letter to the editor, review

For these entries, first give the name of the author. If the piece has a title, put it within quotation marks. Then name the category of the piece—Letter, Rev. of (for Review), Editorial—without quotation marks or underline. If the reference is to a review, give the name of the work being reviewed with underline or quotation marks as appropriate.

Fraser, Kennedy. Rev. of Stones of His House: A Biography of
        Paul Scott, by Hilary Spurling. New Yorker 13 May 1991:
        103-10.
James, Albert. Letter. Boston Globe 14 Jan. 1992: 61.
Stein, Norman. "Traveling for Work." Editorial. Baltimore
        Sun 12 Dec. 1991: 82.

An abstract of an article

Libraries contain many volumes of abstracts of recent articles in many disciplines. If you are referring to an abstract you have read rather than to the complete article, list it as follows.

```
Corcoran, K. J., and M. D. Carney. "Alcohol Consumption and
    Looking for Alternatives to Drinking in College Stu-
    dents." Journal of Cognitive Psychotherapy 3 (1989):
    69-78. Abstract. Excerpta Medica 60 (1989): item 4136.
```

A government publication

Often, a government publication will have group authorship. Be sure to name the agency or committee responsible for writing a document.

```
United States. Cong. Senate. Subcommittee to Investigate Ju-
    venile Delinquency of the Committee on the Judiciary.
    Juvenile Alcohol Abuse: Hearing. 95th Cong., 2nd sess.
    Washington: GPO, 1978.
```

An unpublished interview

A listing for an unpublished interview begins with the name of the person interviewed. If the interview is untitled, label it as such, without quotation marks or underlining. Name the person doing the interviewing only if that information is relevant. An interview by telephone or e-mail can be noted as part of the interview citation.

```
Bishop, Robert R. Personal interview. 5 Nov. 1987.
Bly, Robert. E-mail interview. 10 Dec. 1993.
```

An unpublished letter

Treat an unpublished letter much as you would an unpublished interview. Designate the recipient of the letter. If you as the writer of the paper were the recipient, refer to yourself as "the author."

```
Bishop, Robert R. Letter to the author. 8 June 1964.
```

If a letter is housed in a library collection or archive, provide full archival information.

```
Bishop, Robert R. Letter to Jonathan Morton. 8 June 1964.
    Carol K. Morton papers. Smith College, Northampton.
```

A film or videotape

Underline the title, and then name the medium, the distributor, and the year. Supply any information that you think is useful about the performers, director, producer, or physical characteristics of the film or tape.

Alcoholism: The Pit of Despair. Videocassette. Perf. Gordon
    Jump. AIMS Media, 1983. VHS. 20 min.

A television or radio program

If the program you are citing is a single episode with its own title, supply the title in quotation marks. State the name and role of the foremost participant(s). Underline the title of the program, identify the producer and list the station on which it first appeared, the city, and the date.

"Voices of Memory." Li-Young Lee, Gerald Stern, and Bill
    Moyers. The Power of the Word with Bill Moyers. Exec.
    prod. Judith Davidson Moyers and Bill Moyers. Public
    Affairs TV. WNET, New York. 13 June 1989.

An interview that is broadcast, taped, or published

Treat a published interview as you would any print source. A broadcast or taped interview can be treated as a broadcast program.

"The Broken Cord." Interview with Louise Erdrich and Michael
    Dorris. Dir. and prod. Catherine Tatge. A World of
    Ideas with Bill Moyers. Exec. prod. Judith Davidson
    Moyers and Bill Moyers. Public Affairs TV. WNET, New
    York. 27 May 1990.

A live performance

Identify the "who, what, and where" of a live performance. If the "what" is more important than the "who," as in a performance of an opera, give the name of the work before the name of the performers or director. In the following example, the name of the speaker, a cofounder of AA, comes first.

Golda's Balcony. By William Gibson. Dir. Scott Schwartz.
    Perf. Tova Feldshuh. Manhattan Ensemble Theatre, New
    York. 12 May 2003.

A work of art

Underline the title of a work of art referred to, and tell the location of the work. The name of the museum or collection is separated from the name of the city by a comma.

Manet, Edouard. The Absinthe Drinker. Ny Carlsberg Glyptotek,
    Copenhagen.

Computer software

Like a printed book, computer software has authorship, a title, and a publication history. Include this in any bibliographical listing, along with relevant information for your reader about the software and any hardware it requires. Underline the title of the program. Identify the title as computer software. In the example, the name of the author and the location of the company would be added if they were known.

<u>TrueSync Information Manager</u>. Computer software. Starfish
    Software, 1997.

A separately issued map, chart, or graph

Even a freestanding map or poster generally tells something about who published it, where, and when. Give the title, underlined, and any identifying information available. Use the abbreviation *n.d.* any time a date is lacking in publication information.

<u>Roads in France</u>. Map. Paris: National Tourist Information
    Agency, n.d.

3   **Listing electronic sources in the MLA "Works Cited" format**

The Modern Language Association (MLA) style for documenting electronic sources varies slightly, depending on whether you access sources via the Internet or a CD-ROM (or diskette). The guidelines here are based on the 2003 *MLA Handbook for Writers of Research Papers*, 6th edition.

Weblink

http://www.mla.org

Although the complete MLA Style Manual is not online, the guidelines for documenting electronic sources are online.

Online sources

The MLA offers a standard citation form for a source taken from an Internet site. Supply as much information as is available and pertinent.

Last name, First name. "Title of Work." Specifics on print in-
    formation history if any. Specifics on electronic informa-
    tion history, including underlined title of the site and
    date of creation or last update. Date of access <URL>. <u>Key</u>-
    <u>word</u> or <u>Path</u>: with path markers separated by a semicolon.
"Academic Advising." <u>Disability Resource Center</u>. 2001.
    California Polytechnic State U, San Luis Obispo. 10
    Apr. 2003 <http://sas.calpoly.edu/drc/>. Path: Support
    Services; Academic Advising.
<u>Ellis Island On-Line</u>. 2000. The Statue of Liberty-Ellis Island
    Foundation. 12 May 2003 <http://www.ellisisland.org/>.

Because the information available to you online will vary from site to site, be flexible in your approach to creating citations. If, for instance, you wished to reference an entire Web site (as in the Ellis Island entry), you might have no author information. If you did not follow links or search on keywords to locate a source, you would omit the "Path" or "Keyword" information. If your Internet document listed no author, you would begin with the title of the work, set in quotation marks. If the work appeared (or appears concurrently) in print, you would provide that information, following guidelines in 37a-2. Be as thorough as you can be with the information at hand. Some specifics to bear in mind:

■ **Publication dates:** The content of Web-based sources may change from one user's access to another's. Thus, provide *two* dates in each citation, if possible: the date the document was last updated (sometimes unavailable) and the date of your access. Note: If you provide print information as well, your entry may have *three* dates.

■ **Uniform Resource Locators:** If a long URL invites errors when a reader copies it to a browser, provide the URL of the search page from which you found the source. Readers will launch their own search. If you searched from a database service such as InfoTrac and no URL exists for your source *or* if the URL contains the name of the institution you searched from, making the URL useless to your readers, then provide the URL of the home page of the search service. If you can't determine the home page, end with the access date. To prevent introducing errors into a citation's URL, break a URL only at a forward slash mark (/). Do not add dots (.) or hyphens (-). Remember to enclose the URL in angle brackets < >.

■ **Other information:** Because information on the Internet is changeable, sites you visit today may be altered or gone tomorrow. Therefore, to ensure later access, print out Web-based sources that you intend to use. In your citation provide the following information, when available, as an aid to readers: (1) Title of the site, underlined—for instance, a scholarly project or online journal. For sites without a title, be descriptive: write "Home page," for instance. (2) Name of a sponsoring institution—such as a university or a research center. (3) Name of an editor or translator—using the abbreviation *ed.* or *trans.* (4) The pertinent paragraph, page, or section number. (5) Version or volume numbers. (6) Name of the subscription service used—for instance, *EBSCO*.

A scholarly project

Underlined Title of Project. Database editor. Specifics on
      electronic publication, including date of creation or
      revision, versions, organizations. Date of access <URL>.
The Life and Works of Herman Melville. Ed. J. Madden. 10
      Apr. 1997. Multiverse. 3 June 1998 <http://
      www.melville.org/melville.htm>.

A short work within a scholarly project

Last name, First name. "Title of Short Work." Specifics on
      print information if any. Underlined Title of Project.
      Database editor. Specifics on electronic publication,

including date of creation or revision, versions, organizations. Date of access <URL>.

O'Brien, Fitz-James. "Our Young Authors--Melville." <u>Putnum's
Monthly Magazine</u> Feb. 1853. <u>The Life and Works of Herman Melville</u>. Ed. J. Madden. 10 Apr. 1997. Multiverse.
3 June 1998 <http://www.melville.org/obrien.htm>.

An online book published independently

Last name, First name. <u>Title of Work</u>. Editor or translator if
any. Specifics on print information if any. Specifics on
electronic publication, including date of creation or
revision, versions, organizations. Date of access <URL>.

Twain, Mark. <u>The Adventures of Tom Sawyer</u>. Ed. Internet
Wiretap. 1993. 15 Jan. 1998 <http://www.cs.cmu.edu/
People/rgs/sawyr-table.html>.

Home pages: Academic department, Course, Personal

English. Dept. home page. New York U. 15 Jan. 2003. 12 June
2003<http://www.nyu.edu/gsas/dept/english/>.

McIntyre, Ronald. Existentialism. Course home page. Spring
2000. Dept. of Philosophy, California State U, North-
ridge. 15 May 2003 <http://www.csun.edu/~vcoao087/
index.htm>.

Tamaj, Sara. Home page. 12 Feb. 2002. 21 Mar. 2003
<http://www.edam.upenn.edu/2149~student_account.html>.

An article in a scholarly journal

Last name, First name. "Title of Work." <u>Name of Periodical</u>
Print information such as volume and issue number (Year
of publication): Number of paragraphs or pages if
given. Date of access <URL>.[1]

Badt, Karin Luisa. "The Roots of the Body in Toni Morrison:
A Matter of 'Ancient Properties.'" <u>African American
Review</u> 29.4 (1995): 11 pp. 5 Mar. 1998 <http://
thunder.northernlight.com/cgi-bin/
pdserv?cbrecid=LW19970923040189466&cb=0>.

An article in a magazine

Connolly, Brian. "Puzzling Pastimes." <u>IntellectualCapital.com</u>
28 May 1998. 2 Aug. 1998 <http://
www.intellectualcapital.com/issues/98/0528/iccyberrep.asp>.

---

[1]Use the abbreviation "pp." for pages and "pars." for paragraphs. If no paragraph or
page numbers are given for the article, use a period instead of a colon after the year
of publication and follow with the date of access.

Gray, Paul. "Paradise Found." Time 19 Jan. 1998. 5 Feb. 1998
     <http://www.pathfinder.com/time/magazine/1998/dom/
     980119/cover1.html>.

An article in a newspaper

Meyers, Laura. "Britain Backs U.S. on Iraq." Los Angeles
     Times 3 June 1998. 17 June 1998 <http://
     www.latimes.com/HOME/NEWS/AUTOAP/tCB00V0294.1.html>.

An unsigned editorial

"Flirting with Disaster." Editorial. New York Times on the
     Web 3 June 1998. 18 July 1998 <http://
     www.nytimes.com/yr/mo/day/editorial/03wed3.html>.

A signed editorial

Klayman, Larry. "No Special Treatment." Editorial. USA Today
     3 June 1998. 3 June 1998 <http://www.usatoday.com/news/
     comment/ncoppf.htm>.

A letter to the editor

Fletcher, Anthony Q. Letter. New York Times on the Web 3 June
     1998. 3 June 1998 <http://www.nytimes.com/yr/mo/day/
     letters/1fletc.html>.

A review

Lipschutz, Neal. "Buchanan's Anti-Trade Tirade." Rev. of The
     Great Betrayal, by Patrick Buchanan. IntellectualCapital.
     com 3.21 (1998): 2 pp. 28 Aug. 1998 <http://
     www.intellectualcapital.com/bibliotech/rev-052898.asp>.

Electronic mail

Chadima, Steve. "Re: Business as Poker." E-mail to Leonard
     J. Rosen. 14 Aug. 1998.

Online postings

You may want to cite a contribution to an e-mail discussion list or
a posting to an online news group or listserv. Generally, follow this
format:

Last name, First name. "Title of Posting from Subject Line."
     Online posting. Date of electronic posting. Name of on-
     line group. Date of access <URL or, if none, e-mail ad-
     dress of group's moderator>.

Nostroni, Eric. "Collaborative Learning in a Networked
    Environment." Online posting. 8 Sept. 1997. Electronic
    Forum. 9 Nov. 1997 <eforum@cgu.edu>.

Rand, Marc. "Watching the Humans Watching Whales." Online
    posting. 26 May 1998. AnimalRights News. 29 May 1998
    <news:rec.animals>.

Tuttle, AnneMarie. "Waltzing toward the Millennium." Online
    posting. 14 Sept. 1998. The Millennium Project Conference.
    4 Oct. 1998 <http://www.ryu.org/mem~tuttle/ waltz.html>.

Synchronous communications: MOOs, MUDs, IRC

Richardson, Lea. Online debate. "The Politics of Recycling."
    16 Aug. 1997. EnviroMOO. 16 Aug. 1997 <telnet://
    enviro.moo.greenearth.org:42557>.

Computer software

Q-Notes for Windows 95. Vers. 1.0.1A. 15 Nov. 1997. Brook-
    line: Q-Corp, Inc. 1997.

Online service

You may locate and use source materials from an online service,
such as America Online (AOL), EBSCO, or Lexis-Nexis. If you do so,
and the service provides a URL for the source, follow the format above
for citing online sources. When you access a source through a keyword
or a path and no URL is provided, use the following format—recording
as much information as is provided:

Author's Last name, First name. "Name of article" Underlined
    title of source in which the article appears. Version or
    date of creation including page numbers. Name of Online
    Service. Date of access. Keyword or Path (no italics, fol-
    lowed by a colon): Write the keyword, followed by a pe-
    riod, or the pathway (separating items with a semicolon).

Fenwick, Ben. "Oklahoma Twister Survivors Face Long Recov-
    ery." Reuters. 9 May 1999. America Online. 10 May 1999.
    Path: News; U.S. and World.

Hunter, James. "Odysseus." Encyclopedia Mythica. 1999. Amer-
    ica Online. 10 May 1999. Keyword: Mythica.

If you are citing material found on a premium search service such
as UMI's ProQuest Direct or Lexis-Nexis, present as much of the
following information as is available: begin with information from

the print edition—author, title, publication date and page(s). Follow with the name of the database, underlined; the name of the search service; the abbreviated name of the library and its location (with state, if needed for clarification); date of access; and URL of the service.

Targett, Simon. "Oxford to Offer Degree Courses over Inter-
    net." Financial Times 20 July 1998: 1. Proquest Direct.
    Bentley Coll. Lib., Waltham, MA. 20 May 1999
    <http://proquest.umi.com/pqdweb>.

CD-ROMs and diskettes

CD-ROMs and diskettes issued as a single publication (analogous to the publication of a book)

As when citing an online source, cite as much of the recommended information as is pertinent and available. Follow this general format:

Last name, First name. "Title of Article." Title of Specific
    Collection. Editor of collection if given. Publication
    information for printed text if given. Title of CD-ROM
    or Diskette. Publication medium--i.e., CD-ROM or
    Diskette. Edition or version number if given. Place of
    publication: Name of publisher, year of publication.

Chin, Jeffrey. "The Role of Impermanence in American Dating
    Ritual." Sociological Review of Dating and Marriage:
    1990-1998. Ed. Ellen Markham. Dating and Marriage: A
    Cross-Disciplinary Approach. CD-ROM. Rel. 1.2. Newton,
    MA: Westhill Wired, 1999.

"Industrial Revolution." Concise Columbia Encyclopedia.
    CD-ROM. Redmond: Microsoft, 1994.

Miller, Arthur. The Crucible. CD-ROM. New York: Penguin, 1994.

Pirsig, Robert M. Zen and the Art of Motorcycle Maintenance
    and Lila: An Inquiry into Morals. Diskette. New York:
    Voyager, 1992.

CD-ROMs and diskettes updated periodically (analogous to the publication of a magazine or journal)

Last name, First name. "Title of Article." Publication in-
    formation for printed text if given. Title of CD-ROM or
    Diskette. Publication medium--i.e., CD-ROM or Diskette.
    Name of publisher. Month and year of electronic
    publication.

Bureau of the Census. "Exports to Germany, East: Merchandise
  Trade-Exports by Country." National Trade Statistics
  (1995): 85-96. National Trade Databank. CD-ROM. U.S.
  Bur. of Census. Aug. 1995.

Gillette. "Gillette Co.: Balance Sheet, 12/31/93-9/30/95."
  Compact Disclosure. CD-ROM. Digital Library Systems,
  Inc. Oct. 1995.

37b Using the APA system of documentation

The American Psychological Association's *Publication Manual* has
set documentation style for psychologists. Writers in other fields, especially those in which researchers report their work fairly frequently in
periodicals and edited collections of essays, also use the APA system of
documentation. Whichever style of documentation you use in a given
research paper, use only one. Do not mix features of APA and MLA (or
any other format) in a single paper.

APA documentation is similar to the MLA system in coupling a
brief in-text citation, given in parentheses, with a complete listing of information about the source at the end of the paper. In the APA system
this list of references is called "References." In the in-text citation itself,
APA style differs by including the date of the work cited. The publication date is often important for a reader to have immediately at hand in
psychology and related fields, where researchers may publish frequently,
often modifying conclusions reached in prior publications. Date of publication also serves to distinguish readily among publications for authors
who have written numerous titles. Following is an index to this section
on the APA system of documentation.

Making in-text citations in the APA format

For every fact, opinion, or idea from another source that you quote, summarize, or otherwise use, you must give credit. You must also give just enough information so that your reader can locate the source. Whether in the text itself or in a parenthetical note, APA documentation calls for you to name the author and give the date of publication for every work you refer to. When you have quoted from a work, you must also give the page or page numbers (preceded by *p.* or *pp.*, in APA format). Supply the page number(s) immediately following a quotation, even if the sentence is not at a pause point.

In the sample paragraphs that follow, you will find variations on using APA in-text citation. Notice that, wherever possible, reference information is incorporated directly into the text and parentheses are used as a supplement to information in the text. Supply the parenthetical date of publication immediately after an author's name in the text. If you refer to a source a second time within a paragraph, you need not repeat the information if the reference is clear. If there is any confusion about which work is being cited, however, supply the clarifying information. The full reference should be provided the next time the source is cited in a new paragraph.

Dardis's study (1989) examines four twentieth-century American writers--three of them Nobel Prize winners--who were alcoholics. Dardis acknowledged (p. 3) that American painters too include a high percentage of addicted drinkers. Among poets, he concludes (p. 5) that the percentage is not so high as among prose writers.

However, even a casual reading of a recent biography of poet John Berryman (Mariani, 1990) reveals a creative and personal life dominated by alcohol. Indeed, "so regular had [Berryman's] hospital stays [for alcoholism] become . . . that no one came to visit him anymore" (Mariani, p. 413). Berryman himself had no illusions about the destructive power of alcohol. About his friend Dylan Thomas he could write, "Dylan murdered himself w. liquor, tho it took years" (qtd. in Mariani, p. 274). Robert Lowell and Edna St. Vincent Millay were also prominent American poets who had problems with alcohol (Dardis, 1989, p. 3).

A work by two authors

To join the names of two authors of a work, use *and* in text but use the ampersand (&) in a parenthetical reference. Notice how the parenthetical information immediately follows the point to which it applies.

Roebuck and Kessler (1972) summarized the earlier research (pp. 21-41).

A summary of prior research on the genetic basis of alcoholism (Roebuck & Kessler, 1972, pp. 21-41) is our starting point.

Two or more works by the same author

If the work of the same author has appeared in different years, distinguish references to each separate work by year of publication. If, however, you refer to two or more works published by the same author(s) within a single year, you must list the works in alphabetical order by title in the list of references, and assign each one an order by lowercase letter. Thus,

(Holden, 1989a)

could represent Caroline Holden's article "Alcohol and Creativity," while

(Holden, 1989b)

would refer to the same author's "Creativity and Craving," published in the same year.

A work by three to five authors

Use names of all authors in the first reference, but subsequently give only the first of the names followed by *et al.* Use the *et al.* format for six or more authors.

Perls, Hefferline, and Goodman (1965) did not focus on the addictive personality. Like other approaches to the study of the mind in the '50s and '60s, Gestalt psychology (Perls et al.) spoke of addiction only in passing.

A work by a corporate author

Give a corporate author's whole name in a parenthetical reference. If the name can be readily abbreviated, supply the abbreviation in brackets in the first reference. Subsequently, use the abbreviation alone.

Al-Anon Faces Alcoholism (Alcoholics Anonymous [AA], 1974) has been reissued many times since its initial publication.

One of the books most widely read by American teenagers (AA, 1974) deals with alcoholism in the family.

Distinguishing two authors with the same last name

Distinguish authors with the same last name by including first and middle initials in each citation.

(J. Williams, 1990)

(C. K. Williams, 1991)

Two or more sources in a single reference

Separate multiple sources in one citation by a semicolon. List authors alphabetically within the parentheses.

We need to view the alcoholic in twentieth-century America from many perspectives (Bendiner, 1962; Dardis, 1989; Waggoner, 1990) in order to understand how people with ordinary lives as well as people with vast creative talent can appear to behave identically.

2   Preparing a list of references in the APA format

In research papers following the APA system, the list of references (which is alphabetized) is called "References." Within an entry, the date is separated from the other facts of publication. The APA list of references includes only those works referred to in your paper.

Listing books in the **APA format**

Leave two typed spaces to separate items in an entry. Double-space the list throughout. Start each entry at the left margin; if the entry runs beyond one line, indent subsequent lines five spaces—that is, create a "hanging indent." The following order of presentation is used:

1. Author's name(s): Put the last name first, followed by a comma. Use first—and middle—initial instead of spelling out a first or middle name.
2. Date: Give the year of publication in parentheses followed by a period. If your list includes more than one title by an author in any one year, distinguish those titles by adding a lowercase letter (a, b, etc.) to the year of publication (as in 1989a and 1989b).
3. Title of the book: Italicize the complete book title, if possible; otherwise underline. Capitalize only the first word in a title or subtitle (which typically follows a colon), in addition to proper names.
4. Publication information: Name the city of publication, followed by a colon. Give the full name of the publisher, but without the "Co." or other business designation.

```
Dardis, T. (1989). The thirsty muse: Alcohol and the Ameri-
     can writer. New York: Ticknor & Fields.
```

A book with two authors

Invert both names; separate them by a comma. Use the ampersand (&).

```
Roebuck, J. B., & Kessler, R. G. (1972). The etiology of al-
     coholism: Constitutional, psychological and sociologi-
     cal approaches. Springfield, IL: Charles C. Thomas.
```

A book with three to six authors

List *all* authors, treating each author's name as in the case of two authors. Use the ampersand before naming the last. (This book was first published in 1951, then reissued without change.)

```
Perls, R., Hefferline, R. F., & Goodman, P. (1951/1965).
     Gestalt psychology: Excitement and growth in the human
     personality. New York: Delta-Dell.
```

If there are seven or more authors, list only the first six, followed by a comma and et al.

A selection from an edited book or anthology

Italicize the title of the book. The selection title is not underlined or enclosed in quotation marks. (In APA style, spell out the name of a university press.)

```
Davies, P. (1985). Does treatment work? A sociological per-
    spective. In N. Heather (Ed.), The misuse of alcohol
    (pp. 158-177). New York: New York University Press.
```

A corporate author

Alphabetize the entry in the references list by the first significant word in the name, which is given in normal order.

```
National Center for Alcohol Education. (1978). The community
    health nurse and alcohol-related problems: Instructor's
    curriculum planning guide. Rockville, MD: National In-
    stitute on Alcohol Abuse and Alcoholism.
```

An edition subsequent to the first

Indicate the edition in parentheses, following the book title.

```
Scrignar, C. B. (1988). Post-traumatic stress disorder:
    Diagnosis, treatment, and legal issues (2nd ed.).
    New Orleans: Bruno.
```

A dissertation

In contrast with MLA style, the title of an unpublished dissertation or thesis is italicized.

```
Reiskin, H. R. (1980). Patterns of alcohol usage in a help-
    seeking university population. Unpublished doctoral
    dissertation, Boston University.
```

If you are referring to the abstract of the dissertation, the style of the entry differs because the abstract itself appears in a volume (volume number italicized).

```
Reiskin, H. R. (1980). Patterns of alcohol usage in a help-
    seeking university population. Dissertation Abstracts
    International, 40, 6447A.
```

Listing periodicals in the APA format

A journal with continuous pagination through the annual volume

The entry for a journal begins with the author's last name and initial(s), inverted, followed by the year of publication in parentheses. The title of the article has neither quotation marks nor underline. Only the first word of the title and subtitle are capitalized, along with proper nouns. The volume number, which follows the italicized title of the journal, is also italicized. Use the abbreviation *p.* or *pp.* when referring to page numbers in a newspaper. Use no abbreviations when referring to the page numbers of a magazine or journal.

```
Kling, W. (1989). Measurement of ethanol consumed in dis-
     tilled spirits. Journal of Studies on Alcohol, 50,
     456-460.
```

A journal paginated by issue

In this example, the issue number within volume 51 is given in parentheses. Give all page numbers when the article is not printed continuously.

```
Latessa, E. J., & Goodman, S. (1989). Alcoholic offenders:
     Intensive probation program shows promise. Corrections
     Today, 51(3), 38-39, 45.
```

A monthly magazine

Invert the year and month of a monthly magazine. Write the name of the month in full. (For newspapers use the abbreviations *p.* and *pp.*)

```
Waggoner, G. (1990, February). Gin as tonic. Esquire, 30.
```

A weekly magazine

If the article is signed, begin with the author's name. Otherwise, begin with the article's title. (You would alphabetize the following entry under *d*.)

```
A direct approach to alcoholism. (1988, January 9). Science
     News, 25.
```

A daily newspaper

```
Welch, P. (1989, December 31). Kids and booze: It's 10
     o'clock--Do you know how drunk your kids are? The
     Washington Post, p. C1.
```

A review or letter to the editor

Treat the title of the review or letter as the title of an article, without quotation. Use brackets to show that the article is a review or letter. If the review is untitled, place the bracketed information immediately after the date.

```
Fraser, K. (1991, May 13). The bottle and inspiration [Re-
     view of the book Stones of his house: A biography of
     Paul Scott]. The New Yorker, 103-110.
```

Two or more works by the same author in the same year

If you refer to two or more works published by the same author(s) within a single year, list the works in alphabetical order by title in the list of references, and assign each one an order by lowercase letter.

Chen, J. S., & Amsel, A. (1980a). Learned persistence at 11-12 days but not at 10-11 days in infant rats. *Developmental Psychobiology, 13*, 481-492.

Chen, J. S., & Amsel, A. (1980b). Retention under changed-reward conditions of persistence learned by infant rats. *Developmental Psychobiology, 13*, 469-480.

Listing other sources in the APA format

An abstract of an article

Show where the abstract may be found, at the end of the entry.

Corcoran, K. J., & Carney, M. D. (1989). Alcohol consumption and looking for alternatives to drinking in college students. *Journal of Cognitive Psychotherapy, 3*, 69-78. Abstract obtained from *Excerpta Medica*, 1989, *60*, Abstract No. 1322.

A government publication

U.S. Senate Judiciary Subcommittee. (Hearing, 95th Congress, 2nd sess.). (1978). *Juvenile Alcohol Abuse*. Washington, DC: U.S. Government Printing Office.

A film or videotape

For nonprint media, identify the medium in brackets just after the title.

Brackett, C. (Producer), & Wilder, B. (Director). (1945). *The lost weekend* [Motion picture]. United States: Paramount Pictures.

A television or radio program

Moyers, B. (Producer). (1990, May 27). The broken cord [Interview with Louise Erdrich & Michael Dorris]. *A world of ideas with Bill Moyers* [Television series]. New York: Public Affairs TV, WNET.

An information service

Weaver, D. (1988). *Software for substance abuse education: A critical review of products* (Report No. NREL-RR-88-6). Portland, OR: Northwest Regional Educational Lab. (ERIC Document Reproduction Service No. ED 303 702)

Computer software

Begin your reference to a computer program with the name of the author or other primary contributor, if known.

```
Cohen, L. S. (1989). Alcohol testing: Self-help [Computer
     software]. Baltimore, MD: Boxford Enterprises.
```

3 Listing electronic sources in the APA format

Weblink

http://www.apastyle.org/elecref.html

Current APA guidelines on how to cite documents retrieved from the World Wide Web.

APA guidelines require that a reference to an Internet source include, at least, the document's title or a description; a date—either the date the document was published or updated or the date it was retrieved (or both); and its universal resource locator, or URL. When identified, authors' names should be included as well.

Information should be presented in the following order: author name, if given; date of publication or posting; article title; title of source, in italics; edition, volume number, version, and so forth, if relevant; and date of retrieval, followed by the URL.

Internet article based on a print source

Because many journal articles accessed online are exact copies of their print versions, APA style allows writers to reference such sources just as they would the original print source, with the bracketed information "Electronic version."

```
Tent, J. (1995, February 3). Citing e-texts summary [Elec-
     tronic version]. Linguist List, 6, 210.
```

If, however, the article may have been modified in any way for its online posting, include the date of retrieval and the URL. Note that the citation does not end with a period because the URL does not end with a period.

```
Tent, J. (1995, February 3). Citing e-texts summary.
     Linguist List, 6, 210. Retrieved July 15, 2002, from
     http://www.lam.man.deakin.edu.au/citation.txt
```

Article in an Internet-only journal

```
Mitra, A., & Schwartz, R. L. (2001). From cyber space to
     cybernetic space: Rethinking the relationship between
     real and virtual spaces. Journal of Computer-Mediated
     Communication, 7(1). Retrieved March 10, 2002, from
     http://www.ascusc.org/jcmc/vol7/issue1/mitra.html
```

Web site

Dice, R. (1998, June 15). *Web Database Crash course--Lesson 1*. Retrieved May 3, 2002, from http://www.hotwired.com/webmonkey/98/24/index0a.html?tw=frontdoor

Li, X., & Crane, N. (1996a, May 20). *Bibliographic formats for citing electronic information*. Retrieved July 2, 2002, from http://www.uvm.edu/~ncrane/estyles

Online newspaper

McDowell, R. (1999, April 21). Colorado students struggle to understand rampage. *The Boston Globe*. Retrieved April 25, 2002, from http://www.globe.com/news/daily/21/school.htm

Online magazine article

Dubow, C. (1999, April 21). Turning acorns into trees. *Forbes*. Retrieved January 12, 2002, from http://www.forbes.com/tool/html/99/apr/0421/feat.htm

Abstract of an online article

Jacobs, D. R., Hisashi, A., Mulder, I., Kromhout, D., Menotti, A., Nissinen, A., & Blackburn, H. (12 April 1999). Cigarette smoking and mortality risk: Twenty-five-year follow-up of the seven countries study. *Archives of Internal Medicine, 159*, 733-740. Abstract retrieved July 1, 2002, from http://www.medstudents.com.br/jornal/index.htm

E-mail or online posting

E-mail messages and other nonarchived online communication should be identified in your text as personal communications but not included in your reference list. The parenthetical citation would read, for example, (personal communication, May 1, 2002). For communications that your readers could retrieve, use the following formats.

Message from an electronic mailing list

Kosten, A. (1998, April 7). Major update of the WWWVL migration and ethnic relations. Message posted to ERCOMER News, archived at http://www.ercomer.org/archive/ercomernews/00002.htm

Message from an online forum or discussion group

Hamman, R. (2001, August 2). Poll results for cybersociology
     [Msg 516]. Message posted to http://groups.yahoo.com/
     group/cybersociology/message/516

37c Using the CMS style of documentation

The parenthetical reference mode of in-text citation is neat and easy to use. The physical and biological sciences, as well as many social sciences, have used it for decades. However, in many of the humanities (including history, philosophy, and art history), in some social sciences (including economics, communication, and political science), as well as in most business-related disciplines, many writers have long preferred the system of endnotes or footnotes developed in *The Chicago Manual of Style*, fourteenth edition, and the closely related system that is offered as an alternate system in the *MLA Handbook for Writers*, fifth edition. (The MLA footnote/endnote system differs from CMS in some details of punctuation and spacing as noted below.)

To use footnotes or endnotes, signal a citation in the text by a raised numeral (superscript) at the appropriate point, preferably after a comma or period. The citation information signaled with this numeral is placed in a separate note numbered to match the one in the text. Both CMS and MLA systems prefer citation information to be collected as *endnotes* at the end of your paper, though some publications continue to use *footnotes* placed at the bottoms of pages where in-text citations are signaled.

Place endnotes in double-spaced form at the end of your paper on a separate page, with the heading "Notes" appearing before any listed Bibliography. Indent the start of each note five spaces, and continue the note on subsequent lines with a return to the left margin. The number preceding each endnote should be the same size and alignment as its text (not a superscript), followed by a period and a space. Here is an endnote or footnote in the recommended CMS format (the MLA format omits the comma before page numbers):

     3. Paul Mariani, Dream Song: The Life of John Berryman
(New York: Morrow, 1990), 45-49.

If footnotes are used, they are placed at the bottom of a page, four line spaces below the text, in single-space format, with a double space to separate footnotes on the same page. While CMS recommends numbering footnotes in the same manner as endnotes, the old MLA style and other traditional formats specify that they be numbered with superscript numerals like those in the text. Many word processing programs are able to handle these formatting conventions automatically, along with the placement of footnotes at the bottoms of pages. A citation note in the CMS style contains essentially the same information—author, title, publication facts—as an entry in a list of references in the MLA "Works Cited" format. There are differences in order and punctuation, and the note, unlike an entry in "Works Cited," concludes with a page reference. A note need not tell the span of pages of a source article when that information appears in a bibliography included at the end of the paper.

The Chicago Manual of Style advises the use of italics for the titles of books and journals. In this discussion, you will find books and journals underlined. If you are working with a computer and can show italics, you may choose to do so.

Here is an index to this section on CMS style:

I	**Making the first and subsequent references in CMS notes**

The first time you cite a source in a CMS paper, you will give complete information about it. If you refer to that source again, you need give only the briefest identification. Usually, this is the author's name and a page reference.

In the following sample paragraph, the first CMS note refers to an entire book. The second note cites a particular passage in a review, and refers to that page only. The third note refers to a work already cited in note 2.

Alcohol has played a destructive, painful role in the lives of numerous twentieth-century writers. Among poets, Dylan Thomas is often the first who comes to mind as a victim of alcoholism. John Berryman, too, suffered from this affliction.[1] Among novelists who battled alcohol was the great British writer Paul Scott, author of the masterpiece The Raj Quartet. A reviewer of a new biography of Scott faults the biographer for not understanding fully the effect of alcoholism on Scott and his wife and daughters.[2] Scott's own mother, out of a kind of bravado, encouraged Paul to drink gin at the age of six.[3]

1. Paul Mariani, Dream Song: The Life of John Berryman (New York: Morrow, 1990).

2. Kennedy Fraser, review of Stones of His House: A Life of Paul Scott, by Hilary Spurling, New Yorker, 13 May 1991, 110.

3. Fraser, 108.

Compare the format of these CMS footnotes with their corresponding entries in the MLA "Works Cited" list.

Fraser, Kennedy. Rev. of Stones of His House: A Biography of Paul Scott, by Hilary Spurling. New Yorker 13 May 1991: 103-10.

Mariani, Paul. Dream Song: The Life of John Berryman. New York: Morrow, 1990.

2 Following the CMS note style

Citing books in the CMS note style

A book with two or three authors

1. Julian B. Roebuck and Raymond G. Kessler, The Etiology of Alcoholism: Constitutional, Psychological and Sociological Approaches (Springfield, IL: Thomas, 1972), 72.

A book with four or more authors

Name each author, or use the *et al.* format.

2. Norman Stein et al., Family Therapy: A Systems Approach (Boston: Allyn, 1990), 312.

A corporate author

3. National Center for Alcohol Education, <u>The Community Health Nurse and Alcohol-Related Problems: Instructor's Curriculum Planning Guide</u> (Rockville: National Institute on Alcohol Abuse and Alcoholism, 1978), 45–49.

A multivolume work

4. G. M. Trevelyan, <u>Illustrated English Social History</u> (Harmondsworth: Pelican-Penguin, 1964), 3:46.

Two sources cited in one note

5. Joy Williams, <u>Escapes</u> (New York: Vintage, 1990), 57–62; C. K. Williams, <u>The Bacchae of Euripides: A New Version</u> (New York: Farrar, 1990), 15.

An edition subsequent to the first

6. C. B. Scrignar, <u>Post-Traumatic Stress Disorder: Diagnosis, Treatment, and Legal Issues</u>, 2nd ed. (New Orleans: Bruno, 1988), 23–28.

A selection in an edited book or anthology

7. Emil Bendiner, "The Bowery Man on the Couch," in <u>Man Alone: Alienation in Modern Society</u>, ed. Eric Josephson and Mary Josephson (New York: Dell, 1962), 408.

An introduction, preface, foreword, or afterword

8. Erich Fromm, foreword to <u>Summerhill: A Radical Approach to Child Rearing</u>, by A. S. Neill (New York: Hart, 1960), xii.

Citing periodicals and other sources in the CMS note style
A journal with continuous pagination through the annual volume

9. William Kling, "Measurement of Ethanol Consumed in Distilled Spirits," <u>Journal of Studies on Alcohol</u> 50 (1989): 456.

A monthly magazine

10. Glen Waggoner, "Gin as Tonic," <u>Esquire</u>, February 1990, 30.

A weekly magazine

11. "A Direct Approach to Alcoholism," <u>Science News</u>, 9 January 1988, 25.

A daily newspaper

12. "Alcohol Can Worsen Ills of Aging, Study Says," New York Times, 13 June 1989, late edition, p. C5.

A dissertation abstract

13. Helen R. Reiskin, "Pattern of Alcohol Usage in a Help-Seeking University Population" (Ph.D. diss., Boston University, 1980), abstract in Dissertation Abstracts International 41 (1983): 6447A.

Computer software

14. Alcohol and Pregnancy: Protecting the Unborn Child Ver. 2.1, Student Awareness Software, Cambridge, MA.

A government document

15. United States Senate Judiciary Subcommittee, Juvenile Alcohol Abuse: Hearing, 95th Cong., 2nd sess. (Washington, DC: GPO, 1978), 3.

Internet sources

16. Laura Meyers, "Britain Backs U.S. on Iraq," Los Angeles Times, <http://www.latimes.com/HOME/NEWS/AUTOAP/tCB00V0294.1.html>, 17 June 1998.

Weblink

http://www.msoe.edu/gen_st/style/

Since The Chicago Manual of Style has not been revised since 1993, citation of electronic sources is inadequate. This guide is based on The Chicago Manual of Style with extensions to cover electronic sources.

For further guidance on citing Internet sources in CMS format, consult "A Brief Citation Guide for Internet Sources in History and the Humanities," which you can find at <http://www.h-net.msu.edu/~africa/citation.html>. The site is maintained by Melvin Page (Professor of History at East Tennessee State University) and has been endorsed by H-Net (Humanities and Social Sciences Online).

37d Using the CSE systems of documentation

The Council of Science Editors (CSE)[3] systems of documentation are standard for the biological sciences and, with minor or minimal adaptations, are also used in many of the other sciences. See *Scientific Style and Format: The CBE Manual for Authors, Editors, and Publishers*, 6th

[3]The CSE was formerly known as the Council of Biology Editors (CBE).

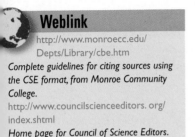

ed., 1994. You will find many similarities between the CSE styles of documentation and the APA style, which was derived from the conventions used in scientific writing. As in APA and MLA styles, any in-text references to a source are provided in shortened form in parentheses. For complete bibliographic information, readers expect to consult the list of references at the end of the document. Following is an index to this section on the CSE systems for documentation.

1   Making in-text citations in the CSE formats[4]

The *CBE Manual for Authors, Editors, and Publishers* presents three formats for citing a source in the text of an article. Your choice of format will depend on the discipline in which you are writing. Whatever format you choose, remain consistent within any one document.

The name-year system

The CSE convention that most closely resembles the APA conventions is the name-year system. In this system a writer provides in parentheses the name of an author and the year in which that author's work was published. Note that, in contrast to the APA system, no comma appears between the author's name and the year of publication.

[4]Note: When this book was going to press, CSE announced its intention (on the CSE Web site) to update *Scientific Style and Format*, particularly with respect to citing electronic sources. Periodically consult the CSE Web site (www.councilscienceeditors.org/index.shtml) for guidance on the latest formats.

```
Slicing and aeration of quiescent storage tissues induces a
rapid metabolic activation and a development of the membrane
systems in the wounded tissue (Kahl 1974).
```

If an author's name is mentioned in a sentence, then only the year of publication is set in parentheses.

```
Jacobsen et al. found that a marked transition in respira-
tory substrate occurs in sliced potato tissue that exhibits
the phenomenon of wound respiration (1974).
```

If your paper cites two or more works published by the same author in the same year, assign a letter designation (a, b, etc.) to inform the reader of precisely which piece you have cited. This form of citation applies both to journal articles and to books.

```
Chen and Amsel (1980a) obtained intermittent reinforcement
effects in rats as young as eleven days of age. Under the
same conditions, they observed that the effects of intermit-
tent reinforcement on perseverance are long lived (Chen and
Amsel 1980b).
```

When citing a work by an organization or government agency with no author named, use the corporate or organizational name in place of a reference to an individual author. Provide the year of publication following the name as indicated previously.

```
Style guides in the sciences caution that the "use of nouns
formed from verbs and ending in -tion produces unnecessarily
long sentences and dull prose" (CBE Style Manual Committee
1983).
```

The citation-sequence system

The briefest form of parenthetical citation is the citation-sequence system, a convention in which only an Arabic numeral appears in parentheses to identify a source of information. There are two variations on the citation-sequence system. With references *in order of first mention*, you assign a reference number to a source in the order of its appearance in your paper. With references *in alphabetized order*, you assign each source a reference number that identifies it in the alphabetized list of references at the end of the paper.

If possible, use superscripts—a raised number slightly smaller than the regular text—to make your number citation. The second of the following examples shows the citation-sequence system with superscripts. If your word processor or typewriter does not permit the use of superscripts, set each citation number in parentheses. Place the parenthetical number immediately following the word, phrase, or sentence to which it refers, as in this first example:

Citation for a reference list in order of first mention

According to Kahl et al., slicing and aeration of quiescent
storage tissues induces a rapid metabolic activation and a
development of the membrane systems in the wounded tissue
(1). Jacobson et al. found that a marked transition in respiratory substrate occurs in sliced potato tissue that exhibits the phenomenon of wound respiration (2).

Citation for a reference list in alphabetized order

According to Kahl et al., slicing and aeration of quiescent
storage tissues induces a rapid metabolic activation and a
development of the membrane systems in the wounded tissue.[2]
Jacobson et al. found that a marked transition in respiratory substrate occurs in sliced potato tissue that exhibits
the phenomenon of wound respiration.[1]

2 Preparing a list of references using CSE systems

In the sciences the list of references appearing at the end of the paper is often called "Cited References." If you adopt the name-year system for in-text citation (see 37d-1), the entries in your list of references
are alphabetized, much as with the APA system, rather than numbered.

If you adopt one of the citation-sequence systems for in-text citation (see 37d-1), you will either number entries alphabetically or in order of appearance in the paper. A numbered entry, beginning with the
numeral, starts at the left margin. Place a period after the number, skip
two spaces, and list the author's last name followed by the rest of the entry. For the spacing of the second or subsequent lines of a numbered entry, align the second line directly beneath the first letter of the author's
last name. For style guides in the specific sciences, see 40e. The following are some of the basic formats for listing sources in the CSE systems.

Listing books in the CSE format

In preparing a list of references in the CSE format, leave two typed
spaces between each item in an entry. Sequence the items in an entry as
follows:

- *Number:* If you are using the citation-sequence system, assign a
  number to the entry.
- *Author's name:* Put the last name first, followed by a space and the
  initials of the first and middle names. Leave no space between initials. After the initial(s), place a period. For a book with two or
  more authors, place a comma after the initial(s) of each co-author.
  Do *not* use an ampersand (&) or the word *and* between authors.

■ *Title of book:* Do not use underlining or italics. Capitalize the first letter of the first word only. End the title with a period. If the work is a revised edition, abbreviate the edition: 2nd ed., 3rd ed., 4th ed., and so on.

■ *Publication information:* Name the city of publication (and state, if needed to clarify). Place a colon and give the abbreviated name of the publisher. Place a semicolon, and give the year of publication followed by a period. Provide number of pages in the book, followed by the letter *p* and a period.

If you refer to more than one work published by the same author(s) in the same year, list the works in order of earliest to latest. Assign the lower-case letter *a* to the earliest work, *b* to the next earliest work, and so on. If you refer to more than one work published by the same author in different years, list the earliest work first.

In CSE, the format of entries for books in "Cited References" changes slightly depending on whether you are using the citation-sequence system or the name-date system.

A book by an individual author or multiple authors

Citation-sequence system

Entries are listed in the order of their citation in the paper.

1. Goodwin TW, Mercer EI. Introduction to plant biochemistry. Elmsford, NY: Pergamon; 1972. 643 p.

2. Beevers H. Respiratory metabolism in plants. Evanston, IL: Row, Peterson; 1961. 935 p.

Name-year system

Notice that these *un*numbered entries are alphabetized and the date follows the author's name.

Beevers H. 1961. Respiratory metabolism in plants. Evanston, IL: Row, Peterson. 935 p.

Goodwin TW, Mercer EI. 1972. Introduction to plant biochemistry. Elmsford, NY: Pergamon. 643 p.

A book by corporate authors

Citation-sequence system

3. CBE Style Manual Committee. Scientific style and format: the CBE manual for authors, editors, and publishers. 6th ed. New York: Cambridge Univ Pr; 1994. 825 p.

Name-year system

CBE Style Manual Committee. 1994. Scientific style and format: the CBE manual for authors, editors, and publishers. 6th ed. New York: Cambridge Univ Pr. 825 p.

A book by compilers or editors

Citation-sequence system

4. Smith KC, editor. Light and plant development. New York: Plenum; 1977. 726 p.

Name-year system

Smith KC, editor. 1977. Light and plant development. New York: Plenum. 726 p.

A dissertation or thesis

Citation-sequence system

5. Reiskin HR. Patterns of alcohol usage in a help-seeking university population [dissertation]. Boston: Boston University; 1980. 216 p. Available from: Boston: Boston Univ Pr.

Name-year system

Reiskin HR. 1980. Patterns of alcohol usage in a help-seeking university population [dissertation]. Boston: Boston University. 216 p. Available from: Boston: Boston Univ Pr.

Option: The five numbered entries in the "Cited References" page are formatted for a paper following the citation-sequence system, with entries listed in the order in which they are first cited in the text of the paper. A variation on the citation-sequence system: number citations in a paper can refer to alphabetized entries in the "Cited References" page, in which case these five references would be numbered—but alphabetized.

Listing periodicals in the CSE format

Leave two typed spaces between each item in an entry. Sequence the items as follows:

- *Number:* Assign a number to the entry if you are using a citation-sequence system.
- *Author's name:* Put the last name first, followed by a space and the initials of the first and middle names. Leave no space between initials. After the initial(s), place a period. For an article with two or more authors, place a comma after the initials of each co-author. Do *not* use an ampersand (&) or the word *and* between authors.
- *Title of the article:* Do not use underlining or quotation marks. Capitalize the first letter of the first word only.

■ *Journal name:* Abbreviate the name, unless it is a single-word name (such as *Nature*); do not underline. *The Journal of Molecular Evolution* would be abbreviated as J. Mol. Evol.

■ *Publication information:* Format depends on whether you are using the citation-sequence system or the name-year system.

Journals

Citation-sequence system

Follow this format, observing spacing conventions.

```
Author(s). Article title. Journal title year;volume num-
ber:inclusive pages.
```

6. Coleman RA, Pratt LH. Phytochrome: immunological assay of
   synthesis and destruction in plants. Planta 1974;
   119:221-231.

Name-year system

Follow this format, observing spacing conventions. Notice the placement of the year.

```
Author(s). Year. Article title. Journal title volume:in-
clusive pages.
```

```
Coleman RA, Pratt LH. 1974. Phytochrome: immunological
assay of synthesis and destruction in plants. Planta
119:221-231.
```

Newspaper and magazine articles

Citation-sequence system

Follow this model (as quoted from *Scientific Style and Format*, 658). Observe spacing conventions.

```
Author(s). Article title. Newspaper title and date of pub-
lication;section designator:page number(column number).
```

7. Welch P. Kids and booze: it's 10 o'clock--do you know how
   drunk your kids are? Washington Post 1989 Dec 21;Sect
   C:1(col 3).

```
Author(s). Article title. Magazine title and date of
publication:page numbers.
```

8. Waggoner G. Gin as tonic. Esquire 1990 Feb:30.

Name-year system

Follow this model (as quoted from *Scientific Style and Format*, 658). Observe spacing conventions.

```
Author(s). Date of publication. Article title. Newspaper
title;section designator:page number(column number).
```

```
Welch P. 1989 Dec 21. Kids and booze: it's 10 o'clock--
do you know how drunk your kids are? Washington
Post;Sect C:1(col 3).
```

```
Author(s). Date of publication. Article title. Magazine
title:page numbers.
```

```
Waggoner G. 1990 Feb. Gin as tonic. Esquire:30.
```

Listing electronic sources in the CSE format

When citing sources from the Internet or other electronic media, the CSE recommends listing access location (URLs) and date accessed. Follow the formats above for books, journals, and newspapers. After the journal, magazine, newspaper, or book title, place brackets and list the type of electronic medium—for instance, *serial online*. Then conclude the entry with the following information.

Write *Available from* (no italics, followed by a colon). Provide the electronic citation (or URL).

Write *Accessed* (no italics, not followed by a colon). Provide year abbreviated month day, followed by a period.

Citation-sequence system

```
9. McDowell R. Colorado students struggle to understand ram-
   page. Boston Globe [newspaper online]. 1999 Apr 21.
   Available from: http://www.globe.com/news/daily/21/
   school.htm Accessed 1999 Apr 23.
```

Name-year system

```
McDowell R. 1999 Apr 21. Colorado students struggle to
understand rampage. Boston Globe [newspaper online].
Available from: http://www.globe.com/news/daily/21/
school.htm Accessed 1999 Apr 23.
```

37.2

CHAPTER **38**

Writing and Reading
in the Humanities

THE HUMANITIES

The humanities are characterized by some of the following features:

Overall Object of Study
- The world of human creations

Disciplines
- Literature, history, philosophy, fine arts, art history, music, classics, languages, film, American studies

Types of Questions
- Who are we?
- What are our responsibilities to ourselves? To others?
- What is a good life?
- How do we know what we know?
- How do works of art communicate truth? Beauty?

Assumptions
- Analyzing texts/creations produced by humans helps provide answers to the "large questions."
- Though we may not agree on answers to these "large questions," the processes involved in asking and seeking answers are inherently worthwhile.

- Patterns and similarities can be found in texts—and the values and ideas they express—across cultures and time.

Methods of Study
- Observation and analysis— "close reading"

Specific Objects of Study
- Literary works such as poems, plays, novels, short stories
- Historical documents such as letters, journals, treaties, transcripts of proceedings
- Philosophical treatises and theories
- Musical compositions and recordings
- Paintings and sculptures

Examples of Recent Research
- Sacvan Bercovitch, *Reconstructing American Literary History*
- Robert S. MacElvaine, *Eve's Seed: Biology, the Sexes, and the Course of History*
- Martha Nussbaum, *Upheavals of Thought: The Intelligence of Emotions*

The humanities address many puzzles of life and human nature, frequently by posing "large," difficult questions to which there are seldom definite answers. Difficult questions lend themselves to difficult and varied answers, and answers in the humanities change from one culture to the next and from one generation to the next. Even within generations and cultures, answers vary.

Ask two philosophers *how do we know what we know?* and you will likely get different responses. The same would hold if you approached two historians about the causes of the Civil War or two critics about the literary merit of Kate Chopin's novel *The Awakening*. Indeed, historians, philosophers, and literary critics may fiercely debate among themselves exactly which "large" questions should be asked and how one should go about investigating them. Still, whatever their specific character, the large questions remain.

The importance of texts

In this formulation, history is the discipline in which readers question texts to learn what is revealed about a past event and what about that event might be pertinent to the present. Philosophy is the discipline in which readers study the articles and books (the *texts*) of those who, with rigorous and careful reasoning, have reflected on ideas important to understanding human nature. Literature is the discipline in which readers study a work of drama, poetry, or fiction to gain entry into an imaginative world and to learn how this text and its world is constructed, how it might reflect circumstances of the author's experience, and how it might comment on and force questions about the *reader's* experience. For the historian, philosopher, and student of literature, texts are the point of entry into the three-way relationship of text, creator/author, and audience. For a student in the humanities there is always the relationship; there is always the implicit understanding that texts are important and that as we read, view, listen to, and write about them, we create meaning ourselves. In the humanities, we *create* new texts as we study older ones. We carry on a tradition of raising and investigating difficult questions and, through our efforts, seek to grow more aware of who we are and what we have done (Frankel 8–9).[1]

38a   Writing in the humanities

1   Expressing and informing in the humanities

Writing to express

Students in the humanities write for many purposes, two of which are to express and to inform. Expressive writing, often beginning as a personal response to an individual text, discusses questions such as these:

---

[1]In-text citations in Chapters 38–40 refer to the list of References and Works Cited found in this book's Web site.

- What do I feel when reading this material?
- Why do I feel the way I do?
- How am I changed in response to this text?
- How can I account for differences I have observed between this text and others, or between this text and my own experience?

Readers may find themselves so involved with a text that they want to respond in writing. You might consider keeping a reading journal in which you record responses to texts and, based on your entries, develop ideas for papers. Much of what is best about writing in the humanities begins as a personal response.

Writing to inform

All writing in literature, history, and philosophy courses is, at least in part, informative. Working as a historian, you may need to sift through documents in order to establish a sequence of events on which to base a narrative—perhaps the story of how your grandparents came to this country. As a student of literature, you may *compare* and *contrast* works of the same author, responding to assignments such as this: *Choose two of Hawthorne's short stories and discuss his treatment of the origins and consequences of sin.* In a philosophy course, you might be asked to *classify* discussions on a topic, such as education, according to the types of arguments authors are making. In informing readers, you will often *define* and illustrate a term by referring to specific passages in a text.

2   Making arguments

Frequently in the humanities, you will use informative writing to make arguments. The purpose of making arguments in literature, history, and philosophy is to *interpret* texts and to *defend* interpretations as reasonable.[2] No one will expect your arguments to end all discussion of a question, but as in any discipline, your arguments should be compelling and well supported. The purpose of reading stories, of retelling the past, or of puzzling through large questions is not to arrive at agreement (as in the sciences) but to deepen individual perception and to see the ways in which we fit into the larger human community. The goal of an argument in the humanities is reached

---

[2]This discussion is based directly on the work of Stephen Toulmin, Richard Rieke, and Allan Janik in *Introduction to Reasoning* (Upper Saddle River, N.J.: Prentice Hall, 1997). See Chapter 12, their "Introduction" to fields of argument; and Chapter 15, "Arguing about the Arts." For a related discussion, see Richard D. Rieke and Malcolm O. Sillars, *Argumentation and Critical Decision Making*, 5th ed. (New York: Longman, 2001).

when readers can acknowledge that they understand the point of view expressed and find it reasonable. You should therefore not expect to read—or write—a single, correct interpretation of a play. History professors will urge you to reject single, apparently definitive versions of the past. Philosophy professors will urge you to reject the notion that any one answer to the question *What is a good life?* could satisfy all people.

Consensus is not the goal of arguments in the humanities. But this is not to say that all arguments are equally valid. Arguments must be supported and well reasoned. They can be plainly wrong and they can be irresponsible, as when someone insists: "Since discussions in this course are based on personal opinions, my opinion is as good as anyone else's." Not true. One interpretation, argued well, can be clearly superior to and more compelling than another. In each of the humanities this is so, notwithstanding the fact that students of literature, history, and philosophy pose different questions and examine texts using different methods. As a student of literature, you might investigate living conditions during the Great Depression by reading novels such as *The Grapes of Wrath*. In a history class, you might work with oral accounts such as the one compiled by Studs Terkel in *Hard Times: An Oral History of the Great Depression*. In a philosophy course, you might read and debate discussions of a society's obligations to its poor. You would in every case be arguing for an interpretation, and in every case your argument would be more or less convincing, in light of the conventions for arguing in that discipline.

Critical thinking and arguments

You can help yourself focus on the purpose of argumentation in your humanities classes by posing these questions:

- What sorts of questions will I investigate in this course?
- How do the texts I study help to focus my attention on these questions?
- How do students in this discipline make claims about a text?
- What kinds of sources (books, films, letters, interviews, works of art, or pieces of music) are used to support those claims?

Claims and evidence

In making a *claim* in the humanities, a writer usually interprets a text. That is, the writer attempts to explain how the text is meaningful—how, for instance, a poem's images direct the reader's attention to certain themes, how an essay confirms or contradicts our understanding of some historical event. One much-relied-on process for making and supporting claims in the humanities goes something like this:

Discovering and supporting claims

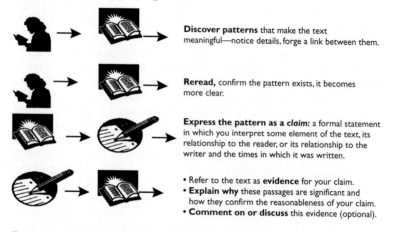

Discover patterns that make the text meaningful—notice details, forge a link between them.

Reread, confirm the pattern exists, it becomes more clear.

Express the pattern as a _claim:_ a formal statement in which you interpret some element of the text, its relationship to the reader, or its relationship to the writer and the times in which it was written.

- Refer to the text as **evidence** for your claim.
- **Explain why** these passages are significant and how they confirm the reasonableness of your claim.
- **Comment on or discuss** this evidence (optional).

Examples of claims and evidence in the humanities

Consider the following examples of how claims are made and supported in major areas of the humanities.

A literary study

In a paragraph from her book _Redefining the American Dream: The Novels of Willa Cather_, literary scholar Sally Peltier Harvey claims that Cather's _My Ántonia_ endorses an alternative to the traditional American Dream. Instead of locating success in the realm of property and social prestige, _My Ántonia_ proposes an American Dream wherein success and happiness are to be found in a simple life of family and communal connection. As you read, notice Harvey's pattern of claim and support: she offers her interpretation—her claim—and follows that with supporting evidence from the novel:

See 38d for hints on detecting patterns in literary works.

See the discussion of thesis at 3d and "argumentative thesis" at 6d.

Throughout _My Ántonia_, Cather sets up contrasts between those characters who achieve the American Dream of material success, and those such as Ántonia and her husband, whose sense of fulfillment relies neither on fame, fortune, nor even on the competitive drive that pushed Thea Kronborg. The characters in _My Ántonia_ who have the strongest sense of self and find the deepest satisfaction are, not surprisingly, the ones whose material success seems only modest. Cather most fully explores this idea in the contrast between Ántonia and Jim Burden. In the introduction, we meet Jim Burden, a successful lawyer who lives in New York and has married well by society's standards. The narrator, who "grew up" with Jim in Black Hawk, notes that Jim's wife "is handsome, energetic, executive," a patron of the arts, a woman with "her own fortune." But Jim Burden's apparent success has left him empty, as Cather suggests by juxtaposing the description of Jim's wife in this statement: "As for Jim, disappointments have not changed him." Thus, before *My Ántonia* even begins, we see Jim Burden [. . .] as a success in the world's eyes, but as an unhappy vagabond of the soul, who has found no fulfillment in either his career or his personal life. Jim comes home to himself only when he experiences with Ántonia [Cuzak] and her family a sense of belonging that success has not brought: "My mind was full of pleasant things: trips I meant to take with the Cuzak boys. . . . There were enough Cuzaks to play with for a long while yet" (370–71).[3]

—SALLY P. HARVEY, *Redefining the American Dream*

Notice that Harvey makes a broad claim—that Cather contrasts characters who have achieved "material success," but are personally unfulfilled, with characters like Ántonia and her husband, whose success is based on a "sense of belonging" rather than material prosperity. Here, Harvey focuses on supporting one element of the broad claim with which she opens the paragraph: Jim's outward success but inward sense of "disappointment." Subsequent paragraphs further flesh out the claim by citing contrasting examples of Ántonia's strong sense of self and inner fulfillment.

Be assured that Harvey's awareness of this aspect of Cather's novel did not always exist. There must have been some point before which Harvey—like any reader—simply did not think about the contrasts between Jim Burden and Ántonia. We can assume that Harvey has read the novel many times; we can imagine that during one rereading she began to see a pattern emerging in various passages. We can further imagine that on noticing this pattern, Harvey was able to confirm and refine it by rereading various passages. At this point, she was prepared to write: to convert the patterns she had detected (then confirmed) into a claim, which she then used as the basis for an argument.

In one paragraph, Sally Harvey demonstrates the cycle of claim, reference, and comment that is basic to writing about literature.

> To make a claim about literature, first find a pattern of meaning in a text. Confirm and refine that pattern and then make a claim. To support this claim, return to the text and discuss specific passages. An analysis of a literary text is built by linking many such cycles according to an overall plan or thesis. (See 38d for more on writing about literature.)

[3]While Harvey's use of ellipsis does not conform to current MLA style (see 29e) in that she does not mark her omission of quoted text with a bracket around the ellipsis, her use does conform with conventions for altering quotations at the time this passage was written. The page numbers in parentheses at the end of this passage refer to Willa Cather's *My Ántonia* (Boston: Houghton Mifflin, 1941).

A historical study

The historian Joanna Stratton supports a claim in the following passage by referring to a source (information from a letter or journal) but does not comment on the source in the same way Harvey does for a literary text. In her book on pioneer women of the American Frontier, Stratton worked with interviews, letters, and journals that her great-grandmother had collected in the 1920s.

> For the most part, the cavelike dugout provided cramped and primitive quarters for the pioneering family. Damp and dark year round, it was practically impossible to keep clean, for dirt from the roof and the walls sifted onto everything. Although its thick earthen walls did afford warm insulation from the cold and strong protection from the wind, in rain the dugout became practically uninhabitable.
>
> "Father made a dugout and covered it with willows and grass," wrote one settler, "and when it rained, the water came through the roof and ran in the door. After the storms, we carried the water out with buckets, then waded around in the mud until it dried up. Then to keep us nerved up, sometimes the bull snakes would get in the roof and now and then one would lose his hold and fall down on the bed, then off on the floor. Mother would grab the hoe and there was something doing and after the fight was over Mr. Bull Snake was dragged outside. Of course there had to be something to keep us from getting discouraged."
>
> —JOANNA L. STRATTON, *Pioneer Women*

Often in a historical account the writer wants to maintain focus on the narrative or story, and so withholds immediate comment on a source quotation except in footnotes or in specialized analysis. *To make a claim in history, writers make interpretations of available records from the past and try to reconstruct them into a meaningful pattern.*

Sometimes the presentation of a claim in historical writing may seem not to be an interpretation at all:

> [I]n the rain the dugout became practically uninhabitable.

This claim reads as a fact, but actually it is a generalization Stratton has reached based on available evidence, one example of which she provides with a supporting quotation. Other historians examining the same or different evidence might reach a different conclusion. The importance of a historian's interpretations becomes obvious when you read the conflicting accounts of the events immediately before and after Lincoln's assassination. While historians agree on the facts—Lincoln *was* shot at Ford's Theatre on April 14, 1865—the precise circumstances of and reason for the shooting are subject to historical debate—or interpretation.

A philosophical study

The philosopher Richard Rorty makes a claim in the following passage without reference to any written text, but rather to the meaning that is attached to words ("morality," "obligation," "natural feelings") and to the patterns of human thought and activity that can be observed in connection with those words. In the process, Rorty himself created a philosophical text, one that later became a subject of interpretation and claim by other philosophers. In this passage, Rorty examines the different ways in which we define our feelings and behavior toward members of our families and toward those outside our families. He does so in the larger context of discussing questions of morality and moral obligation.

> Do I have a moral obligation to my mother? My wife? My children? "Morality" and "obligation" here seem inapposite. For doing what one is obliged to do contrasts with doing what comes naturally, and for most people responding to the needs of family members is the most natural thing in the world. Such responses come naturally because most of us define ourselves, at least in part, by our relations to members of our family. Our needs and theirs largely overlap; we are not happy if they are not. We would not wish to be well fed while our children go hungry; that would be unnatural. . . .
>
> By contrast, I may feel a specifically *moral* obligation to deprive both my children and myself of a portion of the available food because there are starving people outside the door. The word "moral" is appropriate here because the demand is less natural than the demand to feed my children. It is less closely connected with my sense of who I am. But the desire to feed the hungry stranger may of course *become* as tightly woven into my self-conception as the desire to feed my family. Moral development in the individual, and moral progress in the human species as a whole, is a matter of re-marking human selves so as to enlarge the variety of the relationships which constitute those selves. . . .
>
> Should this progress ever be completed, the term "morality" would drop out of the language. For there would no longer be any way, nor any need, to contrast doing what comes naturally with doing what is moral. . . . The term "moral obligation" becomes increasingly less appropriate to the degree to which we identify with those whom we help: the degree to which we mention them when telling ourselves stories about who we are, the degree to which their story is also our story.
>
> —RICHARD RORTY, "Ethics Without Principles"

As Rorty discusses the differences between "natural feelings" toward our family members and "moral obligation" to help those outside of our families, he builds on his claim (one that he goes on to elaborate upon in subsequent paragraphs not included here): that the more we "identify with" others, the more natural it will be to extend help to them. If we felt connected to others as we feel to our own children, if we "re-mark[ed] human selves so as to enlarge the variety of the relationships which constitute those selves," we would cease to have a use for the term "morality." This claim has all kinds of larger implications for humanity and for the practice of philosophy itself.

Using claims and evidence

As a student of philosophy, you will sometimes generate your own evidence for arguments; but more often, you will refer to and build on the work of the philosophers you are studying. Learning to make claims in philosophy can be especially demanding for those with little experience in the discipline. In literature and history, sources and what one writes about them are connected in concrete ways to a story, imagined or actually lived. Philosophy has no elements of story as such. To support a claim in philosophy, you will focus on ideas and their relation to other ideas. Arguments, consequently, can become quite abstract. For instance, Rorty contrasts "natural feelings" toward one's children with "moral obligation" toward others' children. Also, in portions of his argument not reproduced here, he refers to claims made by other philosophers—both ancient and contemporary.

The three examples of claims made by Harvey, Stratton, and Rorty do not begin to represent the variety of claims you will encounter in your study of literature, history, and philosophy. These examples are meant to suggest that variety; they suggest, as well, a common concern in the humanities: interpretation. As you read and study in your courses, try to identify the specific types of claims that are made and the methods of evidence used to support them. To aid this process, pose these questions:

- What sorts of claims (interpretations) do people make in this subject?
- In what ways do writers use sources (books, films, historical documents, works of art, or pieces of music) to support their claims?

38b Reading in the humanities

Primary and secondary sources

When you read a poem, a story, a letter, or an autobiography, you are working with a primary source. Of the preceding examples, only the one by Rorty is a **primary source**. The writings of Harvey and Stratton are examples of **secondary sources**, the work of scholars who themselves have interpreted primary sources such as particular poems, novels, stories, or letters. If you were writing a paper on *My Ántonia*, you might refer to Harvey's interpretations. In doing so, you would need to read with care in order to understand and evaluate her ideas and to distinguish them from your own. In deciding whether to cite Harvey in your paper, you might ask:

- What point is she making?
- How well does she make it?
- Are her observations well grounded in the text that she quotes?
- On what basis do I agree or disagree with her?

Reading from a disciplinary perspective

A given source or text in the humanities can be studied from several perspectives within a discipline or across disciplines. For example, consider how differently Benjamin Franklin's *Autobiography* is studied in the following examples: as political philosophy or as a historical event.

Philosophy

Philosopher Ralph Ketchem approaches the *Autobiography* as an expression of the author's philosophy on the power of individual initiative in politics:

> As a public philosopher, Franklin assumed that the traditional personal values have political relevance. He shared the Aristotelian belief that government exists for the sake of the good life and that its powers can be used to that end. A good citizen, guided by the virtues Franklin encouraged in *Poor Richard's Almanack* and in his *Autobiography*, would undertake civic improvement and participate disinterestedly in government. In an expanding country filled with opportunity, Franklin saw individual initiative as the essential engine of progress, but he did not hesitate to seek whatever seemed required for the public good through government. His confidence in the virtue of the citizens of the United States caused him to favor government by consent, but he was not a simple democrat who believed majority will should be omnipotent. He accepted democracy because he thought it would yield good government; if it did not, he readily rejected it.

Ketchem shows how the *Autobiography* was part of Franklin's overall ambition to promote the role of the individual and of personal values as a force in political life. He supports his claims by focusing on Franklin's ideas about individual values in relation to other ideas about the role of government.

History

Another viewpoint, from social historian and English professor John G. Cawelti, looks at the origins of the title of Franklin's work in the essay "Who Named Franklin's *Autobiography*?"

> One of the minor literary mysteries of the nineteenth century is the question of who named that major American classic, Benjamin Franklin's *Autobiography*. Though Franklin referred to the work as his "Memoirs" and other early editions call it the "Life," it has been most widely known since the later nineteenth century as *The Autobiography of Benjamin Franklin*. In fact, under this title the work inspired a number of other "autobiographies," such as that of Andrew Carnegie, which not only call themselves autobiographies, but follow the Franklinian pattern of an account of how an individual created himself.
>
> It is a moot point whether Franklin would have chosen the title of *Autobiography*, since he almost certainly did not know the word. Franklin died in 1790; the first recorded use of "autobiography" is from 1797 in a context that clearly indicates that it is considered a

rather bizarre neologism. Other uses of the word suggest that it did not become widely current until the 1830s when Carlyle, for example, noted the phenomenon by referring to "these Autobiographical times of ours" (1831). Yet, the vision of himself that Franklin so brilliantly narrated in his account of his own life is exactly what "autobiography" has come to mean: a self-generated account of how an individual created him/herself.

Cawelti's essay goes on to present evidence about who may have named the *Autobiography*, supporting his claims by citing historical evidence about the publishing history of the work.

Two claims about Franklin's Autobiography

Ketchem and Cawelti interpret a single text differently, according to their separate disciplinary perspectives. Each makes a claim—a statement that expresses the pattern of meaning each author found in the work he was examining.

Ketchem   As a public philosopher, Franklin assumed that the traditional personal values have political relevance.

Cawelti   [T]he vision of himself that Franklin so brilliantly narrated in his account of his own life is exactly what "autobiography" has come to mean: a self-generated account of how an individual created him/herself.

38c   Types of writing assignments in the humanities

I   The analysis

An **analysis** is an investigation that you conduct by applying a principle or definition to an activity or to an object in order to see how that activity or object works, what it might mean, or why it might be significant. As a writer, your job is to identify and discuss particular parts, or features, of the text that you feel are especially meaningful.

> The writing assignments you will most often encounter in humanities courses have in a general way been addressed in Chapter 2, "Critical Thinking and Writing." The discussion here will introduce the special requirements of these assignments in the humanities and will refer you to pertinent sections of Chapter 2.

As a student of literature, philosophy, and history, you will use features specific to these disciplines in conducting your analyses. The more you study in a discipline, the more you will learn which features of a text are important to that discipline and, hence, which are worth analyzing.

The following general pattern serves as a model for writing an analysis, regardless of discipline. Placement of one or more of these elements in a paper may vary according to discipline; but when writing an analysis you can expect to touch on the following:

- Introduce the work being analyzed and the interpretation you will make (your claim).
- Introduce the features you will use to analyze the text. Your choice of features will depend on the discipline in which you are writing.
- Conduct your analysis by discussing one feature of a text (or idea) at a time. For literary texts, quote specific passages and *comment* on the ways the passage supports your interpretation (see 38a-2).
- Conclude by summing up the evidence for your interpretation. Show how the features you have discussed separately reinforce one another in creating the effect or quality you have argued for.

Applying principles or theories in analysis

Section 2c discussed analysis as an investigation conducted by systematically applying a set of *principles*. In introductory courses to literature, this set of principles will be general if you are interpreting a poem or story according to standard features such as theme. (Other standard features are suggested in 38d-4.) In advanced literature courses, and also in philosophy and history courses, you may be asked to analyze a text or some situation by applying a much-discussed theory. In a philosophy course, for example, you might be asked to apply Richard Rorty's notion of moral obligation to some situation other than the ones he describes. In this instance, your professor would be asking that you analyze a situation, based on principles laid out in a specific source.

www

38.2

2 The book review

You may be asked to read and review a book for your courses, both inside and outside of the humanities. The purpose of a review is to make a judgment about the worth of a text and to communicate and justify that judgment—or *evaluation*—to a reader. Before writing to evaluate you should *read* to evaluate. That is, you should understand what an author has written so that you can summarize main points; you should distinguish an author's facts from opinions; and you should distinguish your assumptions from those of the author. Your overall assessment of a book will rest largely on the extent to which you and the author share assumptions about the subject being discussed.

See 2b for an extended discussion on preparing and writing a review (which in 2b is called an *evaluation*).

A research paper calls on you to investigate some topic, using both primary and secondary sources. Often, a research paper in the humanities is an analysis (see 38c-1) that you set in a broader context. In writing an analysis, you typically read and interpret a single text—in the paper that follows, it is a short story ("A Shameful Affair") by Kate Chopin. Broadening your effort into a research paper, you would analyze the story and also draw on available scholarship as an aid to your analysis. Research will also help provide a context for your thesis. By reviewing the literature on your topic, you tap into the conversation that has taken place concerning it. Aware of what others have written, you can add your voice (through your paper) and contribute to the conversation.

For her paper on "A Shameful Affair," Brandy Brooks turned to the work of two Chopin scholars, Joyce Dyer and Martin Simpson. In a research paper, you remain responsible for developing and supporting an interpretation. You draw on sources, as needed, to help make your points.

What You Need to Know to Write Research Papers

- Gather sources on a topic and use them judiciously, according to a plan—see 2d for a discussion of writing a synthesis based on multiple sources.
- Read multiple sources on a topic, understand the main points of each, and then link these points to one another and to your own guiding interpretation, or thesis—see Chapter 1, "Critical Thinking and Reading."
- See also Chapters 33, 34, and 35 on the research process.
- Chapter 37 contains a discussion on how to cite sources when writing a paper. In the humanities, you will generally follow the MLA form for documenting sources.

38d Writing about literature[4]

To write knowledgeably about a literary work—about a poem, a play, a short story, or a novel—you need to understand, generally, how arguments are made in the humanities. In 38a-2 you saw that arguments

---

[4]In this discussion, the term *literature* refers to works of art *in writing*: poems, plays, and fiction. The expression "review of the literature," common in the humanities, social sciences, and sciences, refers to a writer's presentation of prior research on a topic. Such a presentation is usually meant to set a broader context for a paper and to demonstrate the need for additional research.

Weblink

http://www.uky.edu/ArtsSciences/
Classics/Harris/rhetform.html

A searchable and browsable site offering definitions of literary and rhetorical terms.

in the humanities depend on a cycle of claim, reference to a text, and comment. In that same discussion and in 38b you found examples of such arguments about literary texts (about *My Ántonia* and Franklin's *Autobiography*). The cases illustrated a cycle of claim, reference, and comment. If you have not already done so, read these sections of the chapter. The discussion here assumes your familiarity with the terms *claim, text, refer/ reference,* and *comment*.

	First reading: Respond

> On a *first* reading, respond to the text.

Personal response is fundamental to the critical reading of any text. Pose these questions to a text:

- What can I learn from this selection?
- What is my background on the subject of this selection?
- What is the origin of my views on the topics of this text?
- What new interest, or what new question or observation, does this text spark in me?

Developing a personal response requires that you read a text closely, in such a way that you are alert to details that make the text meaningful. At the risk of stating the obvious, you should prepare for a close reading by finding a block of uninterrupted time when you are feeling alert and able to concentrate on what you read. Realize that close reading involves *multiple* readings. Expect that you will read a full text twice and selected parts of the text three or more times. On your first reading, disregard for the moment the paper you intend to write and read to be engaged, even moved. If you have not thought about what you have read, if you have not responded to it personally, you can hardly expect to write about it with conviction.

See Chapter 1 for a discussion of critical reading generally, and of the importance of responding.

Questions to prompt a personal response on a first reading

- What do I feel when reading this material? Why do I feel this way?
- Does this text make me *want* to read? Why or why not?
- What about this text is worth reading a second time?
- How am I challenged by or changed in response to this text?
- With what questions does this text leave me?
- What differences do I see between the author's observations of the world and my own? How can I explain these differences?

Personal responses based on these and related questions can make you want to know more about what you have read. For instance, if on completing a story, drama, or poem you find yourself *moved, offended, challenged, saddened, confused, needled,* or *intrigued,* you will have an immediate and even pressing reason to return for a second reading. And it is the second reading in which you will discover the patterns that will enable you to write a worthwhile paper. Sometimes, you may need to brainstorm after a first reading in order to understand your particular response to a text. What follows is Kate Chopin's short story "A Shameful Affair." Brandy Brooks, whose paper you will read in 38e, demonstrates the kinds of responses generated to the story on a first reading. Read Chopin's story, along with Brooks's marginal notes from her first reading:

See 3b-2 on
brainstorming.

A Shameful Affair
Kate Chopin

Kate Chopin (1851–1904) is a much-admired nineteenth-century American writer known widely for her novel *The Awakening* (1899) and for two collections of short stories, *Bayou Folk* (1894) and *A Night in Arcadie* (1897). Chopin began her career as a published writer when she was thirty-eight years old, after her husband died and she was left to care for six children.

Mildred Orme, seated in the snuggest corner of the big front porch of the Kraummer farmhouse, was as content as a girl need hope to be.

1

This was no such farm as one reads about in humorous fiction. Here were swelling acres where the undulating wheat gleamed in the sun like a golden sea. For silver there was the Meramec—or, better, it was pure crystal, for here and there one might look clean through it down to where the pebbles lay like green and yellow gems. Along the river's edge trees were growing to the very water, and in it, sweeping it when they were willows.

2

Beautiful, I can see the river.

The house itself was big and broad, as country houses should be. The master was big and broad, too. The mistress was small and thin, and it was always she who went out at noon to pull the great clanging bell that called the farmhands in to dinner.

3

From her agreeable corner where she lounged with her Browning or her Ibsen, Mildred watched the woman do this every day. Yet when the clumsy farmhands all came tramping up the steps and crossed the porch in going to their meal that was served within, she never looked at them. Why should she? Farmhands are not so very nice to look at, and she was nothing of an anthropologist. But once when the half dozen men came along, a paper which she had laid carelessly upon the railing was blown across their path. One of them picked it up, and when he had mounted the steps restored it to her. He was young, and brown, of course, as the sun had made

4

him. He had nice blue eyes. His fair hair was dishevelled. His shoulders were broad and square and his limbs strong and clean. A not unpicturesque figure in the rough attire that bared his throat to view and gave perfect freedom to his every motion.

Mildred did not make these several observations in the half second that she looked at him in courteous acknowledgment. It took her as many days to note them all. For she singled him out each time that he passed her, meaning to give him a condescending little smile, as she knew how. But he never looked at her. To be sure, clever young women of twenty, who are handsome, besides, who have refused their half dozen offers and are settling down to the conviction that life is a tedious affair, are not going to care a straw whether farmhands look at them or not. And Mildred did not care, and the thing would not have occupied her a moment if Satan had not intervened, in offering the employment which natural conditions had failed to supply. It was summer time; she was idle; she was piqued, and that was the beginning of the shameful affair.

5

"Who are these men, Mrs. Kraummer, that work for you? Where do you pick them up?"

6

"Oh, ve picks 'em up everywhere. Some is neighbors, some is tramps, and so."

7

"And that broad-shouldered young fellow—is he a neighbor? The one who handed me my paper the other day—you remember?"

8

"Gott, no! you might yust as vell say he was a tramp. Abet he vorks like a steam ingine."

9

"Well, he's an extremely disagreeable-looking man. I should think you'd be afraid to have him about, not knowing him."

10

"Vat you vant to be 'fraid for?" laughed the little woman. "He don't talk no more un ven he vas deef und dumb. I didn't t'ought you vas sooch a baby."

11

"But, Mrs. Kraummer, I don't want you to think I'm a baby, as you say, a coward, as you mean. Ask the man if he will drive me to church tomorrow. You see, I'm not so very much afraid of him," she added with a smile.

12

The answer which this unmannerly farmhand returned to Mildred's request was simply a refusal. He could not drive her to church because he was going fishing.

13

"Aber," offered good Mrs. Kraummer, "Hans Platzfeldt vill drive you to church, oder verever you vants. He vas a goot boy vat you can trust, dat Hans."

14

"Oh, thank him very much. But I find I have so many letters to write tomorrow, and it promises to be hot, too. I shan't care to go to church after all."

15

She could have cried for vexation. Snubbed by a farmhand! a tramp, perhaps. She, Mildred Orme, who ought really to

16

have been with the rest of the family at Narragansett—who had come to seek in this retired spot the repose that would enable her to follow exalted lines of thought. She marveled at the problematic nature of farmhands.

After sending her the uncivil message already recorded, and as he passed beneath the porch where she sat, he did look at her finally, in a way to make her positively gasp at the sudden effrontery of the man. **17**

But the inexplicable look stayed with her. She could not banish it. **18**

II

It was not so very hot after all, the next day, when Mildred walked down the long narrow footpath that led through the bending wheat to the river. High above her waist reached the yellow grain. Mildred's brown eyes filled with a reflected golden light as they caught the glint of it, as she heard the trill that it answered to the gentle breeze. Anyone who has walked through the wheat in midsummer-time knows that sound. **19**

Again, I can see this. M. into the wheat.

In the woods it was sweet and solemn and cool. And there beside the river was the wretch who had annoyed her, first, with his indifference, then with the sudden boldness of his glance. **20**

"Are you fishing?" she asked politely and with kindly dignity, which she supposed would define her position toward him. The inquiry lacked not pertinence, seeing that he sat motionless, with a pole in his hand and his eyes fixed on a cork that bobbed aimlessly on the water. **21**

"Yes, madam," was his brief reply. **22**

"It won't disturb you if I stand here a moment, to see what success you will have?" **23**

"No, madam." **24**

She stood very still, holding tight to the book she had brought with her. Her straw hat had slipped disreputably to one side, over the wavy bronze-brown bang that half covered her forehead. Her cheeks were ripe with color that the sun had coaxed there; so were her lips. **25**

All the other farmhands had gone forth in Sunday attire. Perhaps this one had none better than these working clothes that he wore. A feminine commiseration swept her at the thought. He spoke never a word. She wondered how many hours he could sit there, so patiently waiting for fish to come to his hook. For her part, the situation began to pall, and she wanted to change it at last. **26**

"Let me try a moment, please? I have an idea." **27**

"Yes, madam." **28**

"The man is surely an idiot, with his monosyllables," she commented inwardly. But she remembered that monosyllables belong to a boor's equipment. **29**

She laid her book carefully down and took the pole gingerly that he came to place in her hands. Then it was his turn to **30** stand back and look respectfully and silently on at the absorbing performance.

"Oh!" cried the girl, suddenly, seized with excitement upon seeing the line dragged deep in the water.   **31**

"Wait, wait! Not yet."   **32**

He sprang to her side. With his eyes eagerly fastened on the tense line, he grasped the pole to prevent her drawing it, as her intention seemed to be. That is, he meant to grasp the pole, but instead, his brown hand came down upon Mildred's white one.   **33**

He started violently at finding himself so close to a bronze-brown tangle that almost swept his chin—to a hot cheek only a few inches away from his shoulder, to a pair of young, dark eyes that gleamed for an instant unconscious things into his own.   **34**

Then, why ever it happened, or how ever it happened, his arms were holding Mildred and he kissed her lips. She did not know if it was ten times or only once.   **35** The moment! Kiss

She looked around—her face milk white—to see him disappear with rapid strides through the path that had brought her there. Then she was alone.   **36**

Only the birds had seen, and she could count on their discretion. She was not wildly indignant, as many would have been. Shame stunned her. But through it she gropingly wondered if she should tell the Kraummers that her chaste lips had been rifled of their innocence. Publish her own confusion? No! Once in her room she would give calm thought to the situation, and determine then how to act. The secret must remain her own: a hateful burden to bear alone until she could forget it.   **37**

III

And because she feared not to forget it, Mildred wept that night. All day long a hideous truth had been thrusting itself upon her that made her ask herself if she could be mad. She feared it. Else why was that kiss the most delicious thing she had known in her twenty years of life? The sting of it had never left her lips since it was pressed into them. The sweet trouble of it banished sleep from her pillow.   **38**

But Mildred would not bend the outward conditions of her life to serve any shameful whim that chanced to visit her soul, like an ugly dream. She would avoid nothing. She would go and come as always.   **39**

In the morning she found in her chair upon the porch the book she had left by the river. A fresh indignity! But she came and went as she intended to, and sat as usual upon the porch amid her familiar surroundings. When the Offender passed her by she knew it, though her eyes were never lifted. Are there only sight and sound to tell such things? She discerned it by a wave that swept her with confusion and she knew not what besides.   **40**

She watched him furtively, one day, when he talked with Farmer Kraummer out in the open. When he walked away   **41** she remained like one who has drunk much wine. Then un-hesitatingly she turned and began her preparations to leave the Kraummer farmhouse.

When the afternoon was far spent they brought letters to her. One of them read like this: **42**

"My Mildred, deary! I am only now at Narragansett, **43** and so broke up not to find you. So you are down at that Kraummer farm, on the Iron Mountain. Well! What do you think of that delicious crank, Fred Evelyn? For a man must be a crank who does such things. Only fancy! Last year he chose to drive an engine back and forth across the plains. This year he tills the soil with laborers. Next year it will be something else as insane—because he likes to live more lives than one kind, and other Quixotic reasons. We are great chums. He writes me he's grown as strong as an ox. But he hasn't men-tioned that you are there. I know you don't get on with him, for he isn't a bit intellectual—detests Ibsen and abuses Tolstoi. He doesn't read 'in books'—says they are spectacles for the short-sighted to look at life through. Don't snub him, dear, or be too hard on him; he has a heart of gold, if he is the first crank in America."

Mildred tried to think—to feel that the intelligence which this **44** letter brought to her would take somewhat of the sting from the shame that tortured her. But it did not. She knew that it could not.

In the gathering twilight she walked again through the wheat **45** that was heavy and fragrant with dew. The path was very long and very narrow. When she was midway she saw the Offender coming toward her. What could she do? Turn and run, as a little child might? Spring into the wheat, as some frightened four-footed creature would? There was nothing but to pass him with the dignity which the occasion clearly demanded.

But he did not let her pass. He stood squarely in the path-way before her, hat in hand, a perturbed look upon his face. **46**

"Miss Orme," he said, "I have wanted to say to you, every **47** hour of the past week, that I am the most consummate hound (He's no that walks the earth." farmhand.)

She made no protest. Her whole bearing seemed to indicate **48** that her opinion coincided with his own.

"If you have a father, or brother, or any one, in short, to **49** whom you may say such things—"

"I think you aggravate the offense, sir, by speaking of it. I **50** shall ask you never to mention it again. I want to forget that it ever happened. Will you kindly let me by."

"Oh," he ventured eagerly, "you want to forget it! Then, **51** maybe, since you are willing to forget, you will be generous enough to forgive the offender some day?"

"Some day," she repeated, almost inaudibly, looking seem- **52** ingly through him, but not at him—"some day—perhaps; when I shall have forgiven myself."

He stood motionless, watching her slim, straight figure lessening by degrees as she walked slowly away from him. He was wondering what she meant. Then a sudden, quick wave came beating into his brown throat and staining it crimson, when he guessed what it might be.

Why crimson?

> **2** Second reading: Analyze the text—find patterns of meaning in it based on your response.

> Ask *why* and *how* of your personal response, and you will have a specific, guiding question to lead you through a second reading. Your goal with this question is to understand your response by finding a pattern that makes the text meaningful.

Thoughtful writing about literature is based on your reading of the literary work. Response is the first component of this reading; analysis, based on that response, is the second.

See Chapter 2 for an extended discussion of the ways in which thoughtful writing is based on a close, critical reading of a text.

You can approach a second reading of a text by working with the response that most interested you in your first reading. Convert that response into a pointed question by asking *Why? How? What are some examples?* Guided by this question, return to the text and analyze it (see 2c-2). If your analysis succeeds, it will yield insights into how the text works, how you think it achieves its meaning in one particular way (with respect to your question). As you read a second time, make notes in the margin wherever you feel the text provides details that can help you answer your guiding question. These notes, considered in light of your question, can suggest a pattern that makes the text meaningful. You can write a successful paper by presenting this same pattern to your reader.

See 2c for a general discussion on writing analyses.

During her first reading of "A Shameful Affair," Brandy Brooks was most struck by the vivid use of color in the story, and she noticed that color seemed associated with drama and emotion in the characters. Based on what she believed might be a pattern, she formulated a question to guide her second reading: *How does Chopin use colors in this story to communicate Mildred's emotions and her growing awareness?* With this question in mind, Brooks reread the story, finding more examples of colors and the ways in which Chopin uses them.

Writing about Poetry

Approach poems as literary texts—apply the principles and guidelines discussed in this chapter to analysis of poems.

■ Read the poem several times and respond.
■ Continue to read the poem, looking for a pattern of meaning.
■ Express the pattern as a claim; cite lines of the poem to support your claim.

---

3   Construct a pattern of meaning:
     Making claims and providing evidence

> Refine the pattern you have found and make a claim. Locate passages in the text that support this claim.

Based on your first and second readings of a text, you are ready to make a claim: to state for your readers the pattern you have found and your reasons for believing this pattern is worth your time pursuing and your reader's time considering. With her first and second readings of Chopin's "A Shameful Affair," in mind, Brandy Brooks developed this claim:

In "A Shameful Affair," Kate Chopin communicates Mildred
Orme's sexual awakening through descriptions of a farm and,
particularly, through the colors one finds there.

Brooks has found a pattern that helps make Chopin's story meaningful to her, and she formally expresses this pattern as a claim. That Brooks found this pattern and not another should not suggest that other patterns do not exist. Many do. "A Shameful Affair" is a story rich with meaning and, like any literary work, lends itself to numerous interpretations. The point to remember is that whatever pattern a student of literature finds in a text, she or he is obliged to show readers why, given all the patterns that *could* be found, this one is reasonable and worth the reader's consideration. A writer demonstrates the worthiness of a pattern, or claim, by repeatedly referring the reader to the text—a primary source—and when pertinent, to secondary sources. (See 38a and b.) Again, you have seen in examples in this chapter (38a-2) how claims in the humanities in general, and claims about literary texts in particular, are supported. Often, before planning an argument in support of a claim, the writer will prepare a sketch. Here's how Brooks planned to support the claim above, based on both her reading of the text and her reading of two secondary sources.

```
Intro
    Chopin: sexual awakening, symbolism, importance
      of location
    Claim
Plot summary
1st demonstration of color being important—farm setting
      Reference to Joyce Dyer--symbolism of farm, nature
2nd demo of color--intro of Fred Evelyn
3rd demo of color--Mildred into the wheat, to see Fred
4th demo of color--but color not used (after kiss)
5th demo of color--reintroduced at key point, the end
Conclusion
      Reference to Martin Simpson
```

When you read the paper in 38e, you will see that Brooks used this sketch as a guide to selecting passages in "A Shameful Affair" and in secondary sources that helped her to support her claim about Chopin's use of color.

CRITICAL DECISIONS

Writing and Incorporating Plot Summaries

A common feature in papers written about literature, a plot summary is a brief description of characters and events that provides readers, some of whom may be unfamiliar with the story, context enough to follow a discussion.

Plot summaries are written in the historical present tense. Consider this sentence from Brooks's paper (present-tense verbs are underlined):

Mildred sees the farmhands every day as she sits reading on the Kraummer's porch.

At times you may need to vary from the present tense to clarify sequences of events; but plot summaries are written predominantly in the present tense because the events of a text are always present to a reader—the same actions occur in the same order in the text no matter how many times that text is read. Remember that the purpose of the plot summary is to allow the writer to refer to a text and in this way support a claim. Typically, the writer's observation about the text immediately follows the plot summary, sometimes in the same sentence:

(continued)

As of yet, Mildred's chosen farmhand is without a name;
but like the retouched color rose in a black-and-white
photograph, this young man stands apart from the
farmhands that cross Mildred's path, none of whom have
been described in terms of color.

The clause beginning "but like the retouched color rose" is not part of Brooks's summary but is one of her observations about the story that supports her claim and follows from her guiding question (*How does Chopin use colors in this story to communicate Mildred's emotions and her growing awareness?*).

---

4 Literary criticism: More formal readings of texts

How do you find a pattern?

What counts as a detail worth noting in a poem, story, or play? What counts as a pattern of details worth discovering? Answers depend on the questions a reader poses. You will see (in 38d-5) that Brandy Brooks observed details of "A Shameful Affair" and fit them together in a pattern based on a question built from her *personal response* to the story. Other, more formal questions that can be put to a literary text are based on the philosophies of various "schools" of literary criticism, each of which regards texts differently and, based on its approach, poses distinctive questions.

If you major in literature, and especially if you go on to graduate school, you will learn about schools of literary criticism. For the moment, even without the benefit of a literary critic's carefully prepared questions (some of which will be presented below), you can gain lasting insights into a poem, play, or work of fiction by finding in it a pattern based on your own personal responses.

Posing more formal questions for a second reading

You may find yourself writing papers for literature courses in which you approach the study of literature according to the viewpoints of various schools of literary criticism. Without naming those schools here and introducing you to complicated terminologies and methods, following are some additional questions you might pose to a text.

- What circumstances of the author's life does the text reflect?
- In what ways does the text exist in a relationship with other texts by the same author and with other texts from the same time period?
- How might the text shift its meaning from one reader to the next? From one audience to the next over time?

- What is the reader's role in making this text meaningful?
- How does the text reflect certain cultural assumptions (about gender or culture, for instance) in the author's and the readers' times?
- What psychological motives underlie the characters' actions?
- What are the economic or power relationships among the characters?

When you want to maintain your focus on a poem, play, or work of fiction itself, then you can pose the following questions, arranged by category. These questions are often appropriate for introductory survey courses in literature.

- *Theme* What large issues does this text raise? Through which characters, events, or specific lines are the questions raised? To what extent does the text answer these questions?

- *Characterization* Who are the main characters? What are their qualities? Is each character equally important? Equally well developed?

- *Plot* How does the writer sequence events so as to maintain the reader's attention? Which actions are central? How are other, subsidiary actions linked to the central ones? What patterning to the plot do you see? In what ways are the plot's structure and theme related?

- *Language* What devices, such as rhyme (identical sounds), meter (carefully controlled rhythms), and pauses, does the author use to create special emphasis? How does the author use metaphors and choose words to create visual images? In what ways are these images tied to the meaning of the text?

- *Narrator, Point of View* Who is speaking? What is the narrator's personality and how does this affect the telling? Is the narrator omniscient in the sense that he or she can read into the thoughts of every character? If not, how is the narrator's vision limited?

- *Structure* In what ways can you (or does the author) divide the whole poem or story into component parts—according to theme? plot? setting? stanza? How are these parts related?

- *Symbolism* Are any symbols operating, any objects that (like a flag) create for readers emotional, political, religious, or other associations? If so, how do these symbols function in the poem, story, or play?

---

5   Write the paper: Synthesize the details you have assembled.

> Demonstrate the reasonableness of your claim by making observations about the text; if appropriate, refer to secondary sources and the observations of others. Synthesize these observations into a coherent argument.

See 2d for a discussion on writing syntheses. The principles reviewed there apply here.

The goal of a paper in a literature course is to show that your interpretation—the pattern of meaning you have found—is reasonable and can help others understand the text. Your observations about the text and, if you use them, the observations of others, are the details that you will *synthesize* into a coherent argument.

38e Sample student paper: "The Role of Color in Kate Chopin's 'A Shameful Affair'"

In the paper starting on page 699, Brandy Brooks examines the ways in which Kate Chopin uses colors and descriptions of nature to suggest the sexual awakening of the character Mildred Orme. Throughout the paper, you will find Brooks following the pattern of claim and support common in literary criticism: Brooks makes a claim, refers to a passage, and then comments on the passage in order to cement its relationship to the claim. She carefully develops an interpretation of the story and, when she finds the need, draws on secondary sources. (Page references are to "A Shameful Affair" as printed in this *Handbook*, on pages 688–693.)

1"

Brandy H. M. Brooks

Dr. Glenn Adelson

English 16

25 October 1998 — Double space   Title centered

The Role of Color in Kate Chopin's

"A Shameful Affair"

Indent 5 spaces

Kate Chopin is a writer of self-discoveries--
of characters who awaken to desires buried deep
within and only dimly understood (if understood at
all). In leading the reader through a character's
discovery, Chopin often prefers powerful descriptive images to explicit speeches or action. The
setting in which a character finds herself, for
instance, can reflect or influence her development
of self-awareness. In "A Shameful Affair," Chopin
communicates Mildred Orme's sexual awakening
through descriptions of a farm and, particularly,   The thesis
through the colors one finds there.

    Mildred Orme is a twenty-year-old sophisti-   Plot Summary
cated beauty who seeks simple country life for a   (present tense)
summer of quiet reading and reflection. With the
rest of her family vacationing at Narragansett
Bay, Mildred arrives at the Kraummers' farm as a
mature young woman who is temporarily free of her
parents' restrictions and fully aware that she's
placed herself in the company of strong, young
men. Mildred sees the farmhands every day as she
sits reading on the Kraummers' porch. While at
first "she never look[s] at them" (688), one day
one of the men returns a slip of paper blown from
her side by a gust of wind. She notices him. And
"that," writes Chopin, is "the beginning of the
shameful affair" (689).

    At the farm, Mildred finds herself immersed
in a rich, fertile natural world that distracts

1"

her from the "exalted lines of thought" (690)
she had intended to pursue during her visit. The
pull of nature is strong and sensual:

> Here were swelling acres where the undu-
> lating wheat gleamed in the sun like a
> golden sea. For silver there was the
> Meramec--or, better, it was pure crys-
> tal, for here and there one might look
> clean through it down to where the peb-
> bles lay like green and yellow gems.
> Along the river's edge trees were grow-
> ing to the very water, and in it, sweep-
> ing it when they were willows. (688)

These colors are bright and gleaming. There is a
"golden sea," a river described as "silver" or
"pure crystal," and pebbles that sparkle like
gemstones. With her use of color, Chopin draws
our attention to the farm and its natural setting, to its physical beauty as a place into which
Mildred, ready for sexual awakening, has stepped.
According to critic Joyce Dyer, the farm is a
symbol "of natural growth and fertility . . . that
will help us understand the force that
drives Mildred toward Fred Evelyn" (448).

Chopin continues to control the use of
color when introducing Mildred's young man. We
learn that Fred "was young, and brown"; "[h]e
had nice blue eyes. His fair hair was dishevelled" (689). As of yet, Mildred's chosen farmhand is without a name; but like the retouched
color rose in a black-and-white photograph, this
young man stands apart from the farmhands that
cross Mildred's path, none of whom have been described in terms of color. Chopin gives to Fred
the "brown" of the earth and the "blue" of

Margin annotations:

1" · Indent 1" · 1" · 1/2" · 1"

1st demonstration of color in the story

Reference to a secondary source in support of the thesis

2nd demonstration of color in the story

the sky, making him as much a part of the
natural ripeness of the Kraummer farm as the
"swelling acres" of wheat (688).

Indirectly, through Mrs. Kraummer, Mildred asks Fred to drive her to church the next
day--Sunday. Fred won't because he has plans
to go fishing. The refusal stings Mildred. On
Sunday she abandons her plans for church and
decides, instead, on a walk. And where should
she go but to the river? For reasons Mildred
does not yet understand but that nonetheless
compel her, she must be near Fred Evelyn. The
scene into which she plunges is rich with the
colors of ripe, fertile nature:

> High above her waist reached the
> yellow grain. Mildred's brown eyes
> filled with a reflected golden light
> as they caught the glint of it, as
> she heard the trill that it answered
> to the gentle breeze. (690)

And Mildred herself takes on color as she works
her way toward the river, drawing closer to the
man she unconsciously desires. Chopin describes
how as her hat "slipped disreputably to one
side," her "wavy bronze-brown bang . . . half
covered her forehead." Her "cheeks were ripe
with color that the sun had coaxed there," and
her "brown eyes" reflect "golden light" (690).
Mildred, the wheat fields, the stream, and Fred
Evelyn are all <u>alive</u> with natural energy, as
communicated by Chopin through the use of
color. Without ever stating explicitly that
Mildred is on the threshold of discovering her
sexuality, Chopin prepares us for the moment.

At the river, Fred Evelyn is fishing.
Mildred asks if she can try--and promptly

*Sentences of
plot summary
(present tense)*

*3rd
demonstration
of color in the
story*

*Sentence of
plot summary
(present tense)*

catches a fish. In the excitement that follows, Fred's "brown hand [comes] down upon Mildred's white one" (691). The contrast of colors increases our tension: after the long build-up, two people (two colors), touch. What will happen? Fred cannot restrain himself, so close is he "to a bronze-brown tangle that almost swept his chin . . . to a pair of young, dark eyes that gleamed for an instant unconscious things into his own" (691). Without thinking, he reaches for Mildred and kisses her lips.

Just as Chopin uses color in this story to prepare us for her character's fulfillment of sexual desire, she uses the <u>absence</u> of color to suggest the dampening effect of society on that desire. Immediately after the kiss, color drains from Mildred's once-ripe cheeks. She turns, "her face milk white" (691), to watch Fred run back to the farm. Confusion sweeps over her: she stares blankly, with shock and shame. She cries that night, wanting to forget the kiss but unable to--and is frightened that it was "the most delicious thing she had known in her twenty years of life" (691).

4th demonstration of color; this time, color *not* used

During and following this emotional ordeal, Chopin stops using color in the story. All the luscious ripeness of nature is gone while Mildred struggles with the social consequences of her act. Color returns when she meets Fred a final time in the wheat field. Before this meeting, we gain a crucial piece of information: in a letter from her family, Mildred learns that Fred belongs to her same social class. He has come to do farm work in an effort "to live more lives than one kind" (692). Suddenly, he is no longer a rough farmhand to whom she was drawn physically, but an adventurer and a potential partner--someone who might gain the approval of her parents. Her next meeting with him, the last of the story, promises a final drama: not only might they discuss their kiss, they might discuss their future.

But the young woman and man awkwardly stammer their words. Fred apologizes (in language very unlike that of a farmhand): "I have wanted to say . . . that I am the most consummate hound that walks the earth" (636). Responding to a request that she forgive him, Mildred says: "[S]ome day--perhaps; when I shall have forgiven myself" (692). Fred ponders her meaning. "Then a sudden, quick wave came beating into his brown throat and staining it crimson, when he guessed what it might be" (693).

Color--the blood-red color of animal life-- returns at precisely the moment a physical, natural connection between the young woman and man once again becomes possible. Through her use of color in the final moment of the story, Chopin pulls us away from social worries about kissing and thrusts us back into nature, into the world of "undulating wheat." Mildred's "some day" suggests that she may not simply wish to forget Fred. The moment he understands this, color floods him. Where color is present in this story, sexual fulfillment is possible.

Biographer Joseph Rosenblum has written that Chopin explores "the mental landscapes of her heroines and . . . the power of sexual passion at a time when even male American authors generally shunned this subject" (2). These explorations, which he calls "revolutionary" for late-nine-teenth-century America, are clearly at work in "A Shameful Affair," in which Chopin uses vivid

Final demonstration of color in the story

Conclusion

Brooks 6

description to trace the path of Mildred Orme's
sexual awakening. In a few brief pages, we watch
her "drawn out of the world of sheltered social
convention and into a natural world that is rich
with sensuous physical surroundings" (Simpson
59). Chopin carefully, and subtly, uses color
to heighten the drama of each moment in which
Mildred grows in sexual awareness.

Reference to a secondary source in support of the thesis

Brooks 7

Works Cited

Chopin, Kate. "A Shameful Affair." The Awakening
and Other Stories. Ed. Lewis Leary. New
York: Holt, 1970. 31-37.

Dyer, Joyce. "Symbolic Setting in Kate Chopin's
'A Shameful Affair.'" Southern Studies: An
Interdisciplinary Journal of the South 20
(1981): 447-52.

Rosenblum, Joseph. "Kate Chopin." Cyclopedia of
World Authors. Pasadena: Salem, 1 Jan.
1989. Northern Light. 21 Oct. 1998
<http://secure.northernlight.com/search>.

Simpson, Martin. "Chopin's 'A Shameful Affair.'"
The Explicator 45.1 (1986): 59-60.

38f   Reference materials in the humanities

Style guides

The following sources offer discipline-specific guidance for writing
in the humanities.

Barnet, Sylvan. *A Short Guide to Writing About Literature.*
8th ed. Glenview: Scott, 1999.
Blanshard, Brand. *On Philosophical Style.* South Bend, IN:
St. Augustine's, 2000.
Daniels, Robert V. *Studying History: How and Why.* 3rd ed.
Englewood Cliffs, NJ: Prentice, 1981.

Specialized references

The following specialized references will help you to assemble information in a particular discipline or field within a discipline.

Encyclopedias provide general information useful when beginning a search.

WWW

38.3

Cassell's Encyclopedia of World Literature rev. ed.

Encyclopedia of American History

Encyclopedia of Art

Encyclopedia of Bioethics

Encyclopedia of Dance and Ballet

Encyclopedia of Philosophy

Encyclopedia of Religion and Ethics

Encyclopedia of World Art

An Encyclopedia of World History: Ancient, Medieval, and Modern

International Encyclopedia of Film

International Standard Bible Encyclopedia

The New College Encyclopedia of Music

Oxford Companion to Art

Oxford Companion to Film

Oxford Companion to Canadian Literature (there are also *Oxford Companion* volumes for Classical, English, French, German, and Spanish Literature)

Oxford Companion to Music

Penguin Companion to American Literature (there are also *Penguin Companion* volumes for English, European, Classical, Oriental, and African Literature)

Princeton Encyclopedia of Poetry and Poetics

Dictionaries provide definitions for technical terms.

A Handbook to Literature

Concise Oxford Dictionary of Ballet

Dictionary of American History

Dictionary of Films

Dictionary of Philosophy

Harvard Dictionary of Music

Interpreter's Dictionary of the Bible

McGraw-Hill Dictionary of Art

New Grove Dictionary of Music and Musicians

Periodical indexes list articles published in a particular discipline over a particular period. *Abstracts,* which summarize the sources listed and involve a considerable amount of work to compile, tend to be more selective than indexes.

Abstracts of English Studies

America: History and Life

Art Index

Arts and Humanities Citation Index

British Humanities Index

Cambridge Bibliography of English Literature and New Cambridge Bibliography of English Literature

Essay and General Literature Index

Film Literature Index

Historical Abstracts

Humanities Index

Index to Book Reviews in the Humanities

International Index of Film Periodicals

MLA International Bibliography of Books and Articles on Modern Languages and Literatures

Music Index

New York Times Film Reviews

Philosopher's Index One: Periodicals

Religion Index

Year's Work in English Studies

Humanities resources on the World Wide Web

The following URLs provide a useful, Web-based starting point for researchers in the humanities. For a complete and continuously updated URL list, see the Handbook's companion Web site.

Academic Research Engine (developed by Student Advantage) (http://navisite.collegeclub.com/channels/academics/)

H-Net: Humanities and Social Sciences Online (University of Michigan) (http://www2.h-net.msu.edu/)

Horus's Web Links to History Resources (University of California, Riverside) (http://horus.ucr.edu/horuslinks.html)

The Internet Encyclopedia of Philosophy (http://www.utm.edu/research/iep/)

Literary Resources on the Internet (http://www.andromeda.rutgers.edu/~jlynch/Lit/)

Voice of the Shuttle (access to humanities Web links) (http://vos.ucsb.edu)

World Religion Gateway (http://www.academicinfo.net/religindex.html)

CHAPTER 39

Writing and Reading
in the Social Sciences

THE SOCIAL SCIENCES

The social sciences are characterized by some of the following features:

Overall Object of Study
- The human social world

Disciplines
- Psychology, sociology, political science, economics, anthropology, communications

Types of Questions
What patterns underlie human behavior?
Why do we behave the way we do—individually and in groups?

Assumptions
- Human behavior is patterned, rule-governed behavior that can be explained.
- Individuals exist in a complex array of social systems—large and small.
- Individuals within systems interact; systems themselves interact and are evolving, dynamic entities.
- Individuals and social systems evolve—they change over time. Present behavior can be traced to prior causes.

Methods of Study
- Observation and experimentation

- Quantitative and qualitative analysis

Specific Objects of Study
- *Sociology:* The ways in which groups interact and influence each other
- *Psychology:* Individual development, behavior, emotional and mental processes
- *Political Science:* Types and functioning of governmental systems
- *Anthropology:* The physical and cultural features of humans and human civilizations

Examples of Recent Research
- Dylan Evans, *Emotions: The Science of Sentiment*
- Ella Edmondson Bell & Stella Nkomo, *Our Separate Ways: Black and White Women and the Struggle for Professional Identity*
- Stuart Henry & Roger Eaton, *Degrees of Deviance: Student Accounts of Their Deviant Behavior*

ocial scientists attempt to discover patterns in human behavior that illuminate the ways we behave as members of groups: as members of family or community groups; as members of racial, ethnic, or religious groups; and as members of political or economic groups. The belief that behavior is patterned suggests that a person's actions in his or her social setting are not random but rather are purposeful—whether or not the actor explicitly understands this. Social scientists do not claim that human behavior can be known absolutely—that, for instance, given enough information we can plot a person's future. They speak, rather, in terms of how and why a person or group is likely to behave in one set of circumstances or another. Social science is not mathematically precise in the manner of the natural sciences, and yet it is similar to those disciplines in the way that claims are based on what can be observed.

At any given moment, each of us exists within a broad constellation of systems: economic, political, cultural, psychological, and familial. The fabric of our lives is so complex that, in order to speak meaningfully and in detail about how we interact, social scientists carve up the social world according to the separate systems that constitute it. But no one of the social sciences is dominant: each contributes a partial understanding to what we know of human society.[1]

39a   Writing in the social sciences

I   Writing to inform

Before we can find significance in social behavior, we must accurately describe behavior and, when appropriate, objectively measure it. A great deal of what social scientists do when they write is to *inform* readers with precise descriptions. Consider, for instance, an ethnographer's account of cowboys' work with cattle on Nevada ranches:

> Other important tasks are performed at the same time as branding: castration, ear marking, wattling, dehorning, and the administration of vaccinations, medicine, or vitamin serums with modern injection guns. All six pieces of work can be done in quick succession by several men working as a team. One person ropes and throws the cow and holds the rope taut. A second person lops a piece of ear off with a pocket knife while holding the cow's head down with one knee. That "knife man" (man or woman) can then move around to accomplish castration (if necessary) and also cut the wattle mark. In ear marking, a crop, slit, split, or bob of the cow's ear is made with the penknife blade, and portions of the ear are

[1]To the extent that historical inquiry is based on an interpretation of texts, history is regarded as one of the humanities. Many historians, though, consider themselves to be social scientists in that they use procedures such as statistical analysis to find meaningful patterns in the past. In this book, history is discussed as one of the humanities. See Chapter 38.

removed or cut according to the established precedent in the brand book. The wattle is a special knife cut on the fatty portion of the cow's neck, jaw, or brisket area; the cut hide heals and hangs down in a certain position. Like the iron itself, ear mark styles and wattles are considered a rancher's property and can be used by other ranchers only if purchased and duly recorded with the state brand inspector's office. Ear marks and wattles are efficient identification methods in foul weather, under dusty conditions, or when cows are bunched up together.

—HOWARD W. MARSHALL, *Buckaroos in Paradise*

As in other disciplines, informative writing in the social sciences is built on recognizable patterns. One such pattern is the *process* by which some activity takes place. Howard W. Marshall's account of the process by which cattle are marked and medicated is precise and authoritative—in a word, informative. Similarly, informative accounts can be found in any of the disciplines in the social sciences. A psychologist, for instance, might *compare* and *contrast* the different motivations people have for joining groups. In the course of this discussion, the psychologist might *classify* types of people according to their need for group identity. Such a discussion might begin or end with an attempt to *define* the term *group*. All of the techniques discussed in Chapter 3 for informing writers are put to use in social science writing.

2 Making arguments

When social scientists report their findings in journals, they make arguments. Achieving general agreement about the causes of human behavior may be a distant goal of researchers, but achieving this goal is unlikely, inasmuch as the subjects that social scientists study—humans—are willful beings whose behavior is determined by numerous, overlapping causes. Researchers acknowledge the complexity of human behavior by avoiding cause-and-effect explanations. They prefer, instead, to express findings in terms of their probability of being correct—in terms of the "significance level."

Some key terms in social science research

Significance level	Expresses the statistical probability that findings are correct. A level of .05, for instance, signifies that there is a less than 5 out of 100 possibility that the researcher's findings occurred by chance.
Correlation	A statistical measure of the degree of association between two phenomena. Correlations are expressed numerically, ranging between 1.00 and –1.00. Positive correlations between two things, for instance, study time and grade point average, mean that an increase in study time is *associated* with an increase in GPA. A negative correlation signifies that an increase in study time is associated with a decrease in GPA. Correlation does not show whether one thing *causes* another, however.

Variable	The thing being measured in an experiment or study.
Experiment	A method of study in which the researcher controls the variables in order to ascertain the cause-and-effect relationship (causation) between variables.
Dependent variable	The variable being measured in an experiment. In an experiment measuring the effect of study time on GPA, GPA would be the dependent variable—the response or effect that is caused by the variable acting upon it (the independent variable).
Independent variable	The variable that acts upon the dependent variable. In an experiment, the researcher manipulates the independent variable in order to measure its effect upon the dependent variable. In our example, the independent variable study time could be varied in order to assess how it affects the dependent variable, GPA.
Extraneous variable	"A factor that may influence the dependent variable, though it has nothing to do with the independent variable." In order for an experimenter to be able to assert a causal relationship between dependent and independent variables, he or she must "eliminate or control any extraneous variables that could affect the results" (Worchel, Cooper, and Goethals 19). In our study time/ GPA example, extraneous variables that would have to be controlled for might be class attendance, student IQ, students' extracurricular activities, and so on.

Arguments are the means by which knowledge is built in the social sciences. Various subdisciplines within each discipline carry on these arguments, and each one frames questions differently, uses distinctive methods, and subscribes to different theories.

For instance, the discipline of anthropology is broadly understood as the study of humankind in its physical and cultural setting. The diagram indicates the two main divisions in anthropology:

Anthropology

—*the study of humankind in its physical and cultural setting*
—*includes ethnographers, ethnologists, geographers, linguists, archaeologists, and others*

Two main branches

Physical Anthropology
—*the study of humans as a biological species that evolved from earlier forms (such as* Australopithecus*) to its present form* (Homo sapiens).

Cultural Anthropology
—*the study of artifacts of civilization in order to understand how various peoples have organized their lives socially, economically, technologically, or linguistically.*

Both specialists can be termed anthropologists in that they share basic assumptions—for instance, about the value of studying the physical and/or cultural development of humankind. Nonetheless, both within and between subfields of anthropology, researchers will disagree on how to study human culture or biology. As a student in one of the social sciences, you will learn to read, think, and write in the context of arguments made in a particular field. The more courses you take in a discipline, the more you will learn how to produce arguments and to think like researchers in that discipline.

Claims and evidence

See the general discussion of claims and evidence in 3d and 6d-1.

A *claim* is an arguable statement that a writer is obliged to support with evidence. *Claims in the social sciences will often commit you to observing the actions of individuals or groups and to stating how these actions are significant, both for certain individuals and for the people responding to them* (Braybrooke 11). The variety of human behavior is, of course, vast, and researchers have developed methods for gathering data both in controlled laboratory settings and in field settings. The interview and the survey are two widely used techniques that allow researchers to observe aspects of behavior that remain largely invisible such as attitudes, beliefs, and desires. Researchers carefully develop questionnaires, trying not to skew responses by the way questions are framed. If successfully developed and administered, questionnaires yield information about behavior that can be quantified and grouped into categories. These categories, in turn, can be analyzed statistically so that logical and reliable comparisons or contrasts can be drawn. Statistics can then be used as *evidence* in social science arguments to show whether a proposed connection between behaviors is significant.

Qualitative and quantitative research

The logic by which social scientists argue and connect evidence to claims will also depend on the method of investigation. In the next section of this chapter (39b), you will read a summary of two social scientific arguments—one quantitative (a researcher's number-based analysis of experiments in a laboratory or natural setting), and the other qualitative (a researcher's perceptions of life lived in its natural social setting). You will see in each the interplay between method of observation, type of evidence, and logic that connects evidence to a claim.

Examine the definitions of quantitative and qualitative research:

	Quantitative research	**Qualitative research**
Definition	A research technique that produces numerical data	A research technique that produces "data that must be described by their qualities or distinguishing characteristics" (Hansen 45).
Typical methods	Experiments and surveys	Observations (including field studies and case studies) and in-depth interviews
Typical setting	Controlled laboratory setting	Natural social setting—out in "the field."
Sample size	Large sample size	Small sample size—very time intensive, generates large amounts of data.
Generaliz-ability	Large amounts of data can be generalized to large population.	Small amounts of data have limited generalizability.
Depth of data	Does not produce in-depth data. Good at showing *that* things occur, but not *why*.	Produces in-depth data that can be used to understand *why* things occur.
Research question examples	"What is the impact of AIDS on the U.S. economy?" This question lends itself to a quantitative approach since the economy is measured with numbers (Patten 21).	"What is the emotional impact of AIDS on at-risk health care workers?" This question lends itself to a qualitative approach since it focuses on emotions— something difficult to measure numerically (Patten 21).

Critical thinking and arguments

Social scientists have developed numerous methods for investigating human behavior, and, accordingly, many types of evidence are used in a variety of arguments. You can help orient yourself to your courses in the social sciences by understanding the special characteristics of arguments.

Questions to pose in your social science classes

- Does this class focus on a subdiscipline within a larger social science discipline (e.g., social psychology in sociology; clinical psychology in psychology)?
- What questions about human behavior are studied in this discipline?
- What methods of investigation do researchers in this discipline use to study these questions?

- How are researchers' claims related to methods of investigation?
- In this discipline, what types of information count as evidence in support of a claim?

Expect a variety of answers to these questions, even when you ask them of a single discipline. Given the many subspecialties in the social sciences, you are likely to find researchers using several methods to investigate a particular question.

CRITICAL DECISIONS

Taking Different Sociological Approaches to an Issue
Social science researchers may take differing approaches to an issue.

Issue: Sociologists examining the relationship between violence on television and the activities of children.

Sociologist 1: sets up a lab experiment in which a group of children, closely monitored for their reactions, watches violent and nonviolent programs.

Sociologist 2: goes with a team of researchers into the field to videotape children watching television programs at home.

Sociologist 3: collects, analyzes, and draws conclusions about the state of published research on television violence and behavior of children (Rieke and Sillars 245-6).

Each of these studies would properly be described as "sociological," but each would have its own distinct method and would, accordingly, lead to different claims and different sorts of evidence offered in support of these claims.

39b Reading in the social sciences

The sources you read in the social sciences will represent the variety of investigations carried out by researchers. Aside from textbooks and other general surveys of the disciplines, you will read reports of carefully controlled laboratory experiments as well as field and case studies. These two broad categories of source types parallel the two major strategies for generating information in the social sciences: quantitative and qualitative research (see page 712).

When social scientists study human behavior by conducting controlled experiments in a laboratory, they seek evidence for their claims by making careful observations and measurements in a lab. Based on statistical evidence (often questionnaire responses represented numerically), researchers are able to argue that the relationships they claim exist among various behaviors in fact *do* exist and are very likely not due to chance. Equally important can be the finding that no relationship exists between variables. Quantitative studies can also be conducted in a natural setting. For instance, when survey questionnaires ask people "closed-ended" questions, that is, questions for which there are a limited choice of responses ("yes/no," "strongly agree" to "strongly disagree"), researchers generate quantitative data that are analyzed using statistical formulas.

In the following summary of an experimental report, you will see how a group of researchers began their study with a specific question about human behavior. They wondered if people would be more likely to meet their goals for increased physical exercise if they wrote out their intentions, examined their perceived barriers to meeting these goals, and planned specific ways to meet the barriers. The researchers devised a quantitative experimental study to answer this question. As you read, notice the authors' claims—the answers to their research question—and the evidence they use to support those claims. Also notice the structure of the report: It follows the typical scientific report format of *Introduction*, *Methods*, *Results*, and *Discussion*.

Experimental report

Title

"Facilitating Changes in Exercise Behavior: Effect of Structured Statement of Intent on Perceived Barriers to Action." This title, typical of those used in experimental reports, is long and highly descriptive of what a reader can expect from this paper.

Authors

D. Craig Huddy, Jaimie L. Hebert, Gerald C. Hyner, Robert L. Johnson. In the social sciences and the sciences, teams of researchers often work together to conduct and then write the report for a study.

Abstract

The authors provide a one-paragraph summary of their study's goals, methods, and findings. Abstracts help other researchers sort through the mass of published studies, providing a quick guide so that they can decide whether to read further. Here is the authors' abstract:

Two groups of worksite employees (58 in a control, 53 in an experimental group) underwent three 90-min. educational sessions designed to increase participation in exercise. At the end of the third session, experimental subjects were asked to complete a structured statement of exercise intention which addressed the major barrier to exercise. Two weeks following the program, chi-square analysis [2] showed that the two groups were proportionately different in changes in frequency and intensity of exercise such that the experimental group in both cases showed greater changes than the control. Experimental subjects showed a twofold increase in frequency and intensity of exercise over the control group. Pearson r [3] indicated a statistically significant association between the completeness of structured statements of intention and an increase in frequency of exercise. We conclude that structured statements of intention are useful for distinguishing between contrived barriers to exercise (excuses) and actual barriers that require practical solutions.

Introduction

The first section of the report sets up the importance of the issue under examination, reviews relevant past research, discusses theories employed by the researchers, and states the research question(s) and hypotheses. Huddy et al. start their introduction by stating that finding effective ways of helping people modify unhealthy behaviors is one of the key challenges facing health practitioners. Such unhealthy behaviors include cigarette smoking, lack of exercise, and high-fat diets. The researchers go on to discuss the theoretical perspectives they used to inform their study's methodology:

> Studies employing the Health Belief Model have indicated that perceptions of barriers to action is the single best predictor of preventive health behavior (Janz & Becker, 1984). Presumably, the fewer the barriers or the less threatening the barriers, the more likely a person is to undertake a recommended health behavior. For [health care] practitioners, the implication is that clients require assistance to find ways of circumventing identified barriers. Part of this process involves the realization that many identified barriers may be imagined or contrived, i.e., rationalizations or excuses, and others real, i.e., actual impediments to a healthy lifestyle requiring well-conceived strategies for management.
>
> The theory of reasoned action stipulates that a person's stated intention corresponds well with probability of behavior when certain criteria are satisfied. The more complete the intention, i.e., the more fulfilled the criteria, the more likely is a corresponding behavior (Fishbein, 1980). When the criteria are vague or incomplete, the likelihood of the behavior diminishes. The utility of these intentional criteria for practitioners is that clients may be helped to clarify their thinking and move away from vague commitments toward stronger, less ambiguous intentions.

[2]Chi-square is a statistical method for testing differences between sets of data, often by comparing a theoretical distribution with the observed data from a sample population.

[3]Pearson *r* is a type of correlation coefficient—a number between −1 and 1 that measures the degree to which two variables are linearly related. In this study, Pearson *r* was used to measure the association between scores on intent to exercise and actual frequency, duration, and intensity of exercise.

The authors go on to describe how they put these theories into practice by using a behavior modification technique, the contract, to help the study participants clearly articulate their specific goals for exercise.

Huddy et al. end their introduction by stating two hypotheses:

> The first hypothesis was that the employees who completed a statement of exercise intention (experimental group) would show proportionately more changes in exercise behaviors than those employees who did not complete such a statement (control group). The second hypothesis was that there would be proportionately more changes in exercise behavior within the experimental group for those employees who had the most complete statements of intention.

Method

This section of the report is broken into several subsections including "Subjects," "Research Design and Protocol," "Follow-up," and "Analysis." The authors describe the details of their study method so that readers can assess the validity of their claims, and so other researchers might test those claims by replicating their experiment.

The researchers recruited 58 volunteers from one company and assigned them to a control group; 53 volunteers from another company were assigned to an experimental group. Both groups participated in three 90-minute sessions designed to educate them about health and exercise. Data were gathered on the participants' current health and exercise behaviors. At the last session, titled "Barrier Identification,"

> participants completed a measure of barriers to exercise and were encouraged to share their feelings about their personally identified barriers to regular exercise. Strategies for circumventing identified barriers were discussed extensively and practical suggestions for implementing these strategies emphasized. Participants in the experimental group were then asked to complete a structured statement of intention to exercise.

Two weeks later, the researchers assessed participants' changes in exercise behavior, and used sophisticated statistical techniques to compare the experimental group's behavior to the level of detail and specificity in participants' structured statements of intention to exercise.

Results and discussion

In this section, the authors report the results of their statistical analyses, noting that both of their hypotheses were supported. They include tables listing and comparing the self-reported changes in frequency and intensity of exercise. Summing up the support for hypothesis 1, the authors write:

> Twenty-five percent of both groups combined showed an increase in frequency of exercise, but the experimental group had a 34% increase in frequency while the control had only a 17% increase.

After reporting the results, the authors discuss the implications of their findings:

This study was successful in showing the utility of structured statements of intention to exercise in a worksite health-promotion program designed to assist employees in the identification and management of barriers to exercise. Participants who were more specific (less vague) in their intentions were more likely to increase their frequency of exercise. . . .

The real utility of the process of identification of barriers and the subsequent application of structured statements of intention to exercise lies in the recognition of contrived barriers (excuses) and the discovery of actual barriers that require solutions. The implication is that practitioners need to engage clients in identification of barriers (resulting in the establishment of priorities) before stated intentions to act become bona fide intentions.

References

This section lists all the sources cited within the study, following standard APA guidelines for documenting sources. Here are two examples:

Fishbein, M. (1980). Factors influencing health behaviors: A theory of reasoned action. In M. Fishbein (Ed.), *Understanding attitudes and predicting social behavior* (pp. 223–260). Englewood Cliffs, NJ: Prentice-Hall.

Janz, N., & Becker, M. (1984). The health belief model: A decade later. *Health Education Quarterly, 11,* 1–47.

Huddy et al. began their study with a specific question about human behavior: Are people more likely to achieve their exercise goals when they specify their intentions for increased exercise, and when they examine—and plan ways to meet—the barriers they perceive to fulfilling their intentions? Their report represents a particular instance of social scientists observing the actions of individuals and stating how these actions are significant.

2 Field (qualitative) studies

Quite different from experimental research, which takes place under controlled conditions and generates quantifiable data, field studies situate researchers among people in a community or group setting in order to observe life as it is lived in its natural social context. The result is a *qualitative* study built on an observer's descriptions and interpretations of behavior. Based on observations and/or in-depth interviews, the field researcher writes reports and discusses the possible general significance of the behavior he or she has seen, offering what in many cases is a fascinating glimpse into unfamiliar cultures, or new perspectives on familiar ones.

Read the following summary of a qualitative report, and examine the author's claims and the evidence he provides in support of those claims. Notice that, like the quantitative study in the last section, this report also follows the scientific report format of *Introduction, Methods, Results,* and *Discussion.* Be aware, however, that not all qualitative studies are formatted in this fashion.

Field study

Title

"Role Transitions, Objects, and Identity"

Author

Ira Silver

Abstract

In this one-paragraph summary, Silver notes his study's goals, methods, and findings. Abstracts help other researchers sort through the mass of published studies, providing a quick guide so that they can decide whether to read further.

ABSTRACT: *Most research on role transitions, following a tradition pioneered by van Gennep, regards these major turning points in the life course primarily as times when people move between different sets of social networks. While these studies acknowledge that rites of passage occur within particular physical spaces in which material objects are present, the importance of such objects has received little attention. I explore one particular role transition— moving away to college—and illustrate that objects play a central role in how students construct their identities. Students at "Midwestern" University make strategic choices about which objects to leave home as anchors of prior identities and which ones to bring to school as markers of new identities. Moreover, I suggest that the meanings of these two categories of objects differ by gender. I argue that this case opens up the possibility that objects play a much more central part in role transitions than social scientists have acknowledged. This study also challenges existing assumptions about different processes of identity formation. Therefore, it engenders the need for additional research about how people reinterpret objects during role transitions, and about the different meanings that objects may have for the constructions of masculinity and femininity.*

Introduction

Silver's study looks at the experience of going to college as a particular instance of "role transition." He opens his study in the following manner:

In his classic anthropological study, Arnold van Gennep (1960 [1909]) demonstrated that the various stages of the life course are distinguished by a series of role transitions. During such transitions, he argued, individuals engage in particular acts and ceremonies that initially separate them from their former roles, and subsequently reintegrate them into new statuses. He described, for example, male puberty rites among natives of the African Congo:

He is taken into the forest, where he is subjected to seclusion, lustration, flagellation, and intoxication with palm wine, resulting in anesthesia. Then come the transition rites, including bodily mutilations and painting of the body. The trial period is followed by rites of reintegration into the previous environment. . . . The initiates pretend not to know how to walk or eat and, in general, act as if they were newly born and must relearn all gestures of ordinary life. Before they enter the relearning process, which takes several months, the initiates bathe in a stream, and the sacred hut is burned. (van Gennep 1960 [1909], p. 81)

These "rites of passage," as van Gennep termed them, are characterized by a number of symbols: the palm wine, the painting of the body, the stream, and the sacred hut. Moreover, these rites occur in a particular physical space: the forest. Yet, although van Gennep descriptively attended to the environments where these rites occur, this symbolic landscape is ignored theoretically in his analysis.

Silver goes on to claim that objects and physical spaces facilitate role transitions, and should be studied by sociologists and anthropologists:

In this paper, I present data concerning a particular role transition—going to college—to illustrate that objects and the processes individuals use to reinterpret them are more central to successful integration into new social roles than existing research on role transitions acknowledges. I show that because objects are tangible evidence testifying to the salient characteristics of personal identity—places, events, and social relationships—the college students I studied incorporated objects into their new social roles. In so doing, these students used objects to construct their identities as coherent and continuous, even though their roles were profoundly changing. I argue that these data engender a need for researchers to pay greater attention to the importance of objects during role transitions.

In the remaining portion of the introduction, Silver discusses at length some theories about identity and role transitions.

Data and method

In this section, Silver describes his study procedure. He explains that he conducted focused interviews with 22 students at a Midwestern university. Most of the students were white and affluent. He makes the following observation:

This sample is, of course, neither socioeconomically nor racially representative of all college students. Yet, it is not intended to serve as conclusive evidence of how college students, or any group for that matter, accomplish role transitions. Rather, I use it to illustrate a theoretical argument about the need for researchers to give greater attention to the important process by which people invest meanings in objects during role transitions.

Silver continues to discuss his interview procedure, describing why focused interviews were the best method for obtaining the type of data he needed, and how he went about conducting these interviews.

Results and discussion

Overall, Silver found that objects were seen by students as "crucial constituents of their identities." Students left certain "anchors" at home in order to keep a connection to their prior identities and also to avoid being stigmatized as immature at college. Such objects included doll collections and stuffed animals (women), and football trophies, comic books, and baseball card collections (men).

While making the transition to their new college identities, Silver reports that students carefully considered what types of objects to bring with them and display in their dorm rooms. The most commonly found "markers" students chose were photographs and music, including photo albums, specially prepared photo collages, framed photos, CD and tape collections, and posters depicting musicians.

In the last subsection of his results, "Fusing Physical and Social Space," Silver comments on what he observed and quotes from some of the interviews:

> My room says a lot about who I am. Honestly, it's as much for me as for others. I was going to get the James Dean poster, but everyone else has it. So, I simply couldn't bring myself to getting it. This room does not completely reflect who I am, but it's the only extension I have of myself. . . .

Although these students strived to express their uniqueness to others, they still used conventional genres—posters and music—to do so. Students sought to manage the impressions they made in the eyes of their peers by bringing to school certain genres of objects that fit within their perceptions of what was appropriate for a college room.

Conclusions

Silver ends his study with a section summing up the overall findings of his interviews with college students, and discusses the implications of these findings for theories of identity formation and role transition. He reiterates his claim that researchers need to take the functions served by objects into account when they study the processes of role transition.

References

This section lists all the sources cited within the study, following standard APA guidelines for documenting sources. Here are two sample entries:

Katriel, T., & Farrell, T. (1991). Scrapbooks as cultural texts: An American art of memory. *Text and Performance Quarterly 11*, 1–17.

van Gennep, A. (1960). *The rites of passage* (M. B. Vizedom & G. L. Caffee, Trans.). Chicago: University of Chicago Press. (Original work published 1909)

Silver began his study with an idea: that previous researchers had neglected to examine the functions performed by objects and physical space in role transitions. He suspected such objects were an important element in such transitions, and his interviews with college students suggested he is right. Notice the word "suggested" here: he hasn't *proven* anything, but he has found enough evidence to warrant further study into the role that objects and physical space play when people make transitions to new social identities.

39c Types of writing assignments in the social sciences

The assignments you will most often be given in your social sciences courses have in a general way been addressed in Chapter 2, "Critical Thinking and Writing," as well as in other chapters. The discussion here will introduce the special requirements of assignments in the social sciences and will provide references to other sections of the book.

1 The experimental report (quantitative research)

Experimental researchers in the social sciences have patterned their writing of lab reports on those done in the sciences. Section 40c-1 discusses the general requirements of each section of the standard lab report: *Introduction, Methods, Results,* and *Discussion*. In the social sciences, you will encounter more variability than in the sciences in titling the various sections of an experimental report. See 39b-1 for an example experimental report in the social sciences—and a discussion of the logic underlying each section of the report.

www

39.2

2 The field report and case study (qualitative research)

The field report

Many inquiries in the social sciences do not lend themselves to statistical analysis but rather to observations of social interactions in the

Manuscript Form for Research Reports in the Social Sciences

These are guidelines established in the *Publication Manual of the American Psychological Association*, 2001. Individual instructors or departments might have slightly different preferred formats.

Title page: Center your title one-third of the way down the page. On subsequent centered lines enter (a) your first name, middle initial, and last name; (b) the name of the department in which you are taking the course; (c) the name of your college or university; (d) the date. Each of these lines should be double-spaced. Some instructors may prefer that you substitute the course title and the instructor's name for b. and c.

Page numbering: Place numbers in the upper right-hand corner of each page, starting with the title page. Use your word processor's "header" function to format page numbering and add a running head preceding the page number. This head should consist of a shortened version of your paper's title. For example, the study by Huddy et al. (see 39b-1) might have a running head reading Changes in Exercise Behavior.

Abstract: Place the abstract on a separate page following the title page. Center the word Abstract, double-space, and begin, writing the abstract as a single paragraph.

Headings and subheadings: Each heading, such as Methods, or Results, is centered and given its own line. Each subheading, such as Participants, Procedures, or Analysis, is given its own line, is underlined or italicized, and is placed flush to the left margin.

Tables and figures: Each table or figure should be numbered, titled, and placed on its own page at the end of the report, after the References list. (In a published report, tables and figures appear in the body of the report.) When referring in your report to a particular table or figure, capitalize the T and F.

communities where they occur. See 39b-2 for an example field study report—and a discussion of the logic underlying its sections.

One outcome of field research is the field report, which provides a rich and detailed description of the behaviors observed as well as an analysis that discusses the possible significance of those behaviors.

The Case Study

A set of field observations may be put to other uses. When they concern a "relatively short, self-contained episode or segment of a person's life," field notes may be used in a *case study*, a focused narrative ac-

Weblink

http://www.nova.edu/ssss/QR/
QR2-3/presenting.html

An introduction to presenting the results of qualitative research.

count that becomes the occasion for an analysis (Bromley 1). The case may provide the basis for making a recommendation: for example, concerning the placement of a drunk driver in a rehabilitation program (as opposed to jail) or concerning the placement of a child in an appropriate class. You will find case studies used as the basis of recommendations in most disciplines, but especially in the social sciences and the business and medical professions.

You may also be given cases to analyze. In this instance, your professor will present a snapshot narrative of some behavior in its social context: perhaps observations of a child in a daycare setting or observations about employee morale at a business. Your job will be to sort through the information presented just as if you had made and recorded the observations yourself. Then you select the most important information to include in your case analysis, based on a theoretical approach recently read or reviewed in class.

39.3

---

3   The library research paper

See 33a-1 and, generally, Chapter 33, "Understanding the Research Process."

Just as in other disciplines, your library research paper in the social sciences should be guided by a central "burning" question. You will base your library research on secondary sources of the sort you found illustrated in 39b.

Depending on your topic, you will read journal articles and books that are both qualitative and quantitative in their method. You will generally be expected to use sources to support a thesis, or claim, of your own design. You will read sources and relate them to each other and to your thesis. As you synthesize material, try to arrange your discussion by *topic* or *idea*, not by source (see 2d). For suggestions of discipline-specific sources, see 39e.

For help in conducting library research, consult Chapters 33, 34, and 35. For the conventions of documenting sources in the social sciences, see 37b.

39d   Sample student paper: "A History of Child Labor on the Farm"

The following library research paper, written by a student for her sociology class, investigates the social history of child labor in agricultural settings. Tara Burgess read several books to support her thesis that "[f]arm work has, for a very long time, exploited its workers in general and children in particular." Notice that Burgess organizes her paper by *idea*, not by source—one clear indication of which is her use of headings in the paper. Each heading develops one part of her thesis. Notice as well her use of the American Psychological Association's (APA's) format for documenting sources.

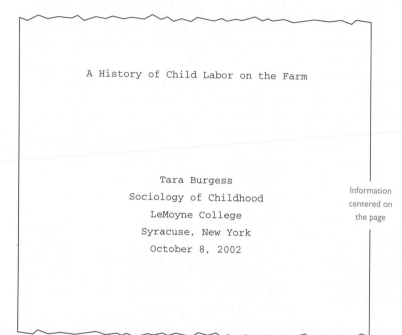

A History of Child Labor on the Farm

Tara Burgess
Sociology of Childhood
LeMoyne College
Syracuse, New York
October 8, 2002

Information centered on the page

Writing and Reading in the Social Sciences

Burgess 1

The Social-Historical Perspective

Traditionally, historians have primarily concerned themselves with the lives of prominent figures and the course of important events (Gordon,
1978, p. 1). This limited historical view, which
has dominated the way in which people think about
social life past and present, has been highly
criticized by many social scientists. As one
sociologist, Alan Johnson, wrote:

> Probably the most important basis for socio-
> logical practice is to realize that the in-
> dividual perspective . . . doesn't work. . . .
> An individualistic model is misleading
> because it encourages us to explain human
> behavior and experience from a perspective
> that's so narrow it misses most of what's
> going on. (1997, pp. 21-22)

Therefore, sociologists approach childhood as
a subcategory of society, like social class or age
group. Although individual children experience
childhood for a limited time, childhood as an institution is a permanent element of society despite the fact that its members are ever changing
(Corsaro, 1997, p. 4). Today, much social history,
especially that of childhood and the family, is
the product of collaboration among sociologists
and historians. One fruitful area of research has
been child labor--and, particularly, child labor
on the farm.

Child Labor on the Farm

The role of the child has always been important in agrarian societies. As sociologist Viviana
Zelizer stated, "The birth of a child . . . was

Annotations in right margin:

Introduction sets up the sociological perspective that guides this research.

Extended block quotation

Transition to the paper topic

welcomed as the arrival of a future laborer and as
security for parents in later life" (1985, p. 5).
Beyond economic considerations, farming has taken
on mythical associations, especially in America.
Children on the farm are thought to enjoy the advantages of working hard, working alongside family, and working outdoors. But these romanticized
views are flawed. <u>Farm work has, for a very long
time, exploited its workers in general and
children in particular.</u>

APA format for documenting sources

Thesis

The Nineteenth Century

In the nineteenth century, as industry in Europe and North America expanded at a fast pace,
agriculture similarly experienced rapid growth.
Great Britain led both the Industrial Revolution
and advancement in agriculture. For much of its
history, agriculture had been the greatest single
occupation in the United Kingdom. In the early
1800s, it employed nearly half of the British labor force (Hopkins, 1994, p. 11). Similarly, between 1870 and 1900, farmers across the United
States added "more than 430 million acres of . . .
farmland," which was "more than had been settled
during the previous 263 years" (West, 1996, p.
33). This vast expansion created much new work.

Claims supported by references to social sciences literature

Children played a vital role in the success
of these new farms. Boys who were physically
strong enough, often as young as 10 years old,
contributed to the building of houses and barns,
the tilling of fields, and the harvesting of bulky
crops. Girls not only engaged in working the
fields and caring for animals but also had innu-
merable domestic responsibilities from churning
butter to sewing clothes to canning and pickling
food for winter eating. Youngsters began to do

Focus on a sociological group, not on individuals

such "chores" as early as four or five years of
age (West, 1996, p. 34).

By the middle of the century, owing to the
work of Charles Dickens among others, child labor
had become a major concern in the United Kingdom.
In response to the rising alarm, the British
government commissioned several investigations
of work environments, including one on the employment of women and children in agriculture in
1843 (Hopkins, 1994, p. 13). Examiners reported
that, although workdays were long (12 hours or
more during much of the year), the limited hours
of daylight in the winter countered this problem.
Overall, the inquiry downplayed the risks of farm
work to children. Still, concerns did not disappear.

Chronological development within the section

By the late nineteenth century, industrialization had found its way into farming, creating a
highly commercialized "new agriculture." Rapid
changes in the technology of farming posed a new
threat to the stability of the family farm and to
all people who worked in the trade. Traditional
horse- and oxen-drawn farm equipment was gradually
replaced by dangerous motorized machinery. Trac-
tors and other equipment were widely used by the
early twentieth century.

The Twentieth Century

Section head communicates chronological arrangement.

The census of 1900 revealed that 60 percent
of all "gainfully employed" children between the
ages of 10 and 15 were agricultural workers
(Zelizer, 1985, p. 77). By the 1920 census, the
number of working children had dropped significantly. But these figures were probably
underestimated, because they fail to take into
account children under 10, part-time laborers,

and seasonal differences (West, 1996, p. 31). To
be sure, fewer workers (and farms) were needed to
produce the same, if not a larger, amount of
goods as new devices became more widely used on
farmlands (West, 1996, p. 209). Many small farms
and/or poor families could not afford to keep up
with all of the technological advancements. Consequently, thousands left their farms every year,
resulting in fewer children performing agricultural work. For those children who remained on
the farm, many of the tasks stayed much the same
as in the past (West, 1996, p. 208)--but, now,
with new dangers posed by mechanization and
chemical fertilizers and pesticides.

The traditional view of farm work began to
change as investigations uncovered some of the
dangers of child farm workers. In 1918, the United
States Children's Bureau examined rural children
in several North Carolina counties. From sunrise
to sundown, families worked with only an hour break
for dinner. Excessive children's farm work was
feared to put undue strain on a child's strength,
interrupt schooling, and potentially affect health
(Zelizer, 1985, p. 79). Many doctors did not know
how to detect injuries, illnesses, or even deaths
that resulted from contact with or inhalation of
chemicals. Yet it was much more difficult for the
gruesome details of farm accidents caused by
machinery to go unnoticed.

Despite continuing tragedies on the farm,
legislation concerning children in agriculture
remained unchanged and the dangers of such jobs
were generally ignored (Taylor, 1973, pp. 7-8;
West, 1996, p. 302). By 1930, compulsory public
schooling had removed many children from the

workforce, putting a majority of children under age 14 in school. In addition, the Fair Labor Standards Act (FLSA) of 1938 made it illegal to employ children under age 16 while school was in session, and it prohibited children from working in the most "hazardous jobs" (Taylor, 1973, p. 7; West, 1996, p. 299). However, agricultural labor lagged behind the general population, due in part to legislative exceptions, which made allowances for child farm workers.

In Maine, for instance, schools took a "cropping vacation" so children can harvest potatoes. In Texas, where school starts two months before migrant families return, special migrant schools that begin in November operate 8 a.m. to 5 p.m. to squeeze a full year of schooling into migrant children before they must leave for the spring planting. The rationale behind these accommodations was that youngsters who are "an economic asset to their parents" would otherwise simply work and not attend school at all (Taylor, pp. 9-10).

Specific examples offered

Legislators quick to compromise the schooling of child farm laborers also suffered under the romanticized view that farm labor was "good work," a view maintained even by members of Congress (including some who opposed child labor in factories) and many child labor reformers. This romanticized view "was carefully preserved by the powerful farming interests, yet it was also the result of an equally influential cultural consensus" (Zelizer, 1985, p. 77). Into the twentieth century, then, child labor on the farm remained an important economic asset. In fact, "a family without child workers was in serious trouble" (West, 1996, p. 213).

Burgess 6

It was not until the 1960s that widespread concern was renewed about the safety of children in American agriculture. Efforts to tighten the FLSA brought angry protest from rural America. These people implied that child farm work was primarily being done by children of farmers and by urban/suburban youth in search of pocket money. While it is true that some of the farm labor included such children, the great majority of children working on farms did (and do) so not for pocket change but for family survival (Taylor, 1973, pp. 5-6).

Conclusion

Today, government regulations about child farm labor remain weak. The main federal child labor legislation only restricted farm labor by boys and girls under 16 during school hours. This has meant that they can be hired to work "at any age and under any conditions" throughout the summer and after school. The law does not apply to children who work for their families, and there are no federal restrictions on "piece" work or the number of hours children can work (West, 1996, p. 301). While some states have stricter limitations on children employed on farms, most exempt agriculture from child labor legislation (Taylor, 1973, p. 8). As West noted, "Even those lenient laws, however, have been widely violated" (1996, p. 301).

Paper has brought the reader through to the current day.

Agriculture continues to employ the largest number of children in the West and throughout the world. Though much has changed over the centuries to make farming more productive, child labor remains a serious problem. Until legislators summon the courage to resist economic pressures and the wisdom to reject romanticized views, children who work on farms will continue to suffer educationally and physically.

A solution is urged.

References

Corsaro, W. A. (1997). *The sociology of childhood.*
    Thousand Oaks, CA: Pine Forge Press.
Gordon, M. (Ed.). (1978). *The American family in
    social-historical perspective* (2nd ed.). New
    York: St. Martin's Press.
Hopkins, E. (1994). *Childhood transformed:
    Working-class children in nineteenth-
    century England.* Manchester and New York:
    Manchester University Press.
Johnson, A. G. (1997). *The forest and the trees:
    Sociology as life, practice, promise.*
    Philadelphia: Temple University Press.
Taylor, R. B. (1973). *Sweatshops in the sun: Child
    labor on the farm.* Boston: Beacon Press.
West, E. (1996). *Growing up in twentieth-century
    America: A history and reference guide.* West-
    port, CT: Greenwood Press.
Zelizer, V. A. (1985). *Pricing the priceless
    child: The changing social value of children.*
    New York: Basic Books.

APA format

39e Reference materials in the social sciences

Style guides

The following sources offer general or discipline-specific guidance
for writing in the social sciences.

Bart, Pauline, and Linda Frankel. *The Student Sociologist's Handbook.*
    4th ed. NY: Random, 1986.

Becker, Howard S., with a chapter written by Pamela Richards.
    *Writing for Social Scientists: How to Start and Finish Your
    Thesis, Book, or Article.* Chicago: U of Chicago P, 1986.

Cuba, Lee J. *A Short Guide to Writing About Social Science.* 4th ed. NY: Longman, 2001.

Jolley, Janina M., Peter A. Keller, and J. Dennis Murray. *How to Write Psychology Papers: A Student's Survival Guide for Psychology and Related Fields.* Sarasota: Professional Resource Exchange, 1993.

McCloskey, Donald. *The Writing of Economics.* NY: Macmillan, 1987.

Publication Manual of the American Psychological Association. 5th ed. Washington: American Psychological Association, 2001.

Richlin-Klonsky, Judith, and Ellen Strenski, coordinators and eds. *A Guide to Writing Sociology Papers.* NY: Worth, 2001.

Specialized references

The following specialized references will help you to assemble information in a particular discipline or field within a discipline.

Encyclopedias provide general information useful when beginning a search.

Editorial Research Reports (current events)

Encyclopedia of Crime and Justice

Encyclopedia of Education

Encyclopedia of Human Behavior

Encyclopedia of Psychology

Encyclopedia of Social Work

Encyclopedia of Sociology

Guide to American Law

International Encyclopedia of Higher Education

International Encyclopedia of Psychiatry, Psychology, Psychoanalysis, and Neurology

International Encyclopedia of Social Sciences

Dictionaries provide definitions of technical terms.

Black's Law Dictionary

Dictionary of the Social Sciences

McGraw-Hill Dictionary of Modern Economics: A Handbook of Terms and Organizations

The Encyclopedic Dictionary of Psychology

The Prentice-Hall Dictionary of Business, Finance and Law

Writing and Reading in the Social Sciences

Periodical indexes and abstracts list articles published in a particular discipline over a particular period. *Abstracts*, which summarize the sources listed and involve a considerable amount of work to compile, tend to be more selective than indexes.

Abstracts in Anthropology

Current Index to Journals in Education (CIJE)

Education Index

Key to Economic Science

Psychological Abstracts

Public Affairs Information Service (PAIS)

Social Science Citation Index

Social Science Index

Social Work Research and Abstracts

Sociological Abstracts

Women's Studies Abstracts

Social science resources on the World Wide Web

The following URLs provide a useful, Web-based starting point for researchers in the Social Sciences. For a complete and continuously updated URL list, see the Handbook's companion Web site.

Academic Research Engine (developed by Student Advantage)
(http://navisite.collegeclub.com/channels/academics/)

Anthropology Web Sites
(http://www.anth.ucsb.edu/links/pages/)

Economics Virtual Library
(http://www.helsinki.fi/WebEc/)

Political Science Information Resources
(http://www.lib.sfu.ca/kiosk/corse/poli.htm)

Psychology Web Resources
(http://www.skidmore.edu/~hfoley/resources.htm)

Social Sciences Virtual Library
(http://www.clas.ufl.edu/users/gthursby/socsci/)

Yahoo! Sociology
(http://dir.yahoo.com/social_science/sociology/)

40

Writing and Reading in the Sciences

THE SCIENCES

The sciences are characterized by some of the following features:

Overall Object of Study

- The world of nature

Disciplines

- Biology, chemistry, physics, earth science, astronomy, medicine, geology, mathematics

Types of Questions

- What kinds of things exist in the world of nature?
- What are these things composed of, and how does their makeup affect their behavior or operation?
- How did these things come to be structured as they are?
- What are characteristic functions of each natural thing and/or its parts? (Toulmin, Rieke and Janik 231).

Assumptions

- "Things and events in the universe occur in consistent patterns that are comprehensible through careful, systematic study;
- Knowledge gained from studying one part of the universe is

applicable to other parts" (American Association 25).

Methods of Study

- Empirical observation and experimentation
- Quantitative analysis

Specific Objects of Study

- *Microbiology:* the study of microorganisms and their effect on other organisms
- *Physics:* the study of matter and energy and the interactions between them
- *Chemistry:* the study of the structure, properties, and reactions of matter
- *Astronomy:* the study of matter in outer space

Examples of Recent Research

- Mark Ridley, *The Cooperative Gene: How Mendel's Demon Explains the Evolution of Complex Beings*
- Franklin M. Harold, *The Way of the Cell: Molecules, Organisms, and the Order of Life*
- Vera C. Rubin, *Bright Galaxies, Dark Matters*

cientists work systematically to investigate the world of nature—at scales so small that they are invisible to the naked eye and at scales so vast that they are equally invisible. A scientist's investigations are always built on observable, verifiable information, known as *empirical evidence*. Scientists devise experiments in order to gather information through observation and measurement, and, on the basis of carefully stated predictions, or **hypotheses,** they conduct analyses and offer explanations, or claims. Scientists make claims (usually) of fact or definition, about *whether* a thing or a phenomenon exists and, if it does, *what* it is or *why* it occurs. Questions that cannot be answered by an appeal to observable, quantifiable fact may be important and necessary to ask (for example, "What makes *Moby Dick* a great novel?" or "What are a society's responsibilities to its poor?"), but these are not matters for scientific investigation.

40a Writing in the sciences

I Writing to inform

A major function of scientific writing is to *inform*. Scientists try to be precise in their descriptions of the world, writing, when possible, with *mathematical* or *quantifiable* precision. A researcher would report the temperature of water as 4° C, not as "near freezing"—an inexact expression, the meaning of which would change depending on the observer. Precise measurements taken from a thermometer or some other standard laboratory instrument help readers of scientific literature to know exactly what has been observed or what procedures have been followed so that, if necessary, experiments can be repeated.

www
40.1

Patterns scientists use to inform

As in other disciplines, informative writing in science is built on recognizable patterns.

- One of the ways in which a scientist may inform is by writing a precise *description*—for example, of experimental methods and materials or of observations made in the lab or field.
- A description may involve presenting a *sequence* of events—perhaps the sequence by which volcanic islands are born.
- Presenting information can also take the form of a *comparison and contrast*—for example, between the organization of the human brain and that of a computer.
- Scientists also *classify* the objects they study. When entomologists report on newly discovered insects, they identify each discovery with respect to a known species of insect.
- If no closely related species exists, researchers may attempt to *define* a new one.

A scientist's efforts to inform readers are very often part of a larger attempt to persuade. In every discipline arguments are built on claims, evidence, and the logical relationships that connect them. But the characteristics of these elements change from one discipline to the next and also within disciplines as theoretical perspectives change.[1] Geneticists working on techniques of tissue analysis argue differently from astronomers. Each discipline uses different methods and different tools of investigation. Each asks different questions and finds meaning in different sorts of information. Within any one discipline you will find that multiple perspectives give rise to competing communities or schools of thought. Within any one scientific community the purpose of argument will be to achieve agreement about the way in which some part of the universe works.

The process of scientific inquiry

The process of scientific inquiry generally goes like this: once investigators make their observations in a laboratory or in a natural setting, they report their findings to colleagues in articles written for scientific and technical journals. In these articles, scientists argue for the validity of their particular *claim*. The scientific community will not accept these reports as dependable until independent researchers can recreate experiments and observe similar findings. As scientists around the world try to replicate the experiments and confirm results, a conversation—an argument—develops in which researchers might publish a challenge or addition to the original findings. In this way, a body of literature—of writing on a particular topic—grows.

The process of building knowledge in the sciences

| Natural phenomenon... | Observed in a natural setting or a laboratory by investigators who then... | Report their findings in academic journal articles. | Independent researchers repeat experiments and test claims. If claims are supported in repeated testing... | Claims are accepted by larger scientific community. |

[1]This discussion is based directly on the work of Stephen Toulmin, Richard Rieke, and Allan Janik in *Introduction to Reasoning* (Upper Saddle River, NJ: Prentice, 1997). See Chapter 12, their "Introduction" to fields of argument, and Chapter 14, "Argumentation in Science." For a related discussion, see Richard D. Rieke and Malcolm O. Sillars, *Argumentation and Critical Decision Making*, 5th ed. (NY: Longman, 2001).

As an undergraduate student in the sciences, you will be introduced to scientific thinking and to the ways in which scientists argue. In each of your science classes, try to identify the purposes of argumentation.

Pose these questions in your science classes:

■ In this area of science, what are the particular issues on which researchers seek to gain agreement?

■ What questions do researchers pose and why are these questions useful?

Claims

Scientific arguments often involve two sorts of claims. The first takes the form *X is a problem* or *X is somehow puzzling*. This claim establishes some issue as worthy of investigation, and it is on the basis of this claim (which must be supported) that experiments are designed.

40.2

Recognizing a difference or anomaly often begins the process of scientific investigation. The process continues when you make a second claim that attempts to explain the anomaly. Such a claim takes this form: *X can be explained as follows.*

Scientific investigation

Generally, when you are reading or writing in the sciences, these questions will help you to clarify how arguments are made:

■ What is the question being investigated? What problem or anomaly is said to exist?

■ What explanation is offered in response to this problem or anomaly?

Logic and evidence

As in any discipline, writers in science use various principles of logic to examine raw data and to select *particular* information as significant. The variety of logical principles that scientists have available to them in trying to make sense of their research is vast and complex, and if you major in a science it will be the purpose of your entire undergraduate career to train you to understand which principles of logic are appropriately applied in which circumstances. For purposes of demonstration, observe the application of one common logical principle—concerning *types*. Watch how certain kinds of evidence are assembled on the basis of this logic.

Investigations begin with a puzzle or anomaly.

All the flowers and vegetables in my garden—except for mums and turnips—have wilted after the first hard frost. Why weren't the mums and turnips harmed?

A variety of information is available.

My garden is above-ground, 3 feet deep, 5 feet wide, and 10 feet long. The garden gets full morning sun but is largely shaded each afternoon. I grow tomatoes, beans, peas, cucumbers, turnips, table flowers, geraniums, mums, and morning glories. The soil tests slightly acidic, and it is well fertilized. Turnips are my sweetest crop, high in sugar. All the plants except the turnips grow above ground. The mums differ from the other above-ground plants in that their crown is located below ground. I water the garden twice daily, morning and evening.

The investigator applies a logical principle as an aid to sifting through the available information.

A frost-resistant plant is a type of plant that exhibits two or three of these features: (1) The plant is high in sugar content; solutions high in sugar resist freezing. (2) The cell walls of the leaves are thick and fibrous and are not easily punctured by ice crystals. (3) The crown—the portion of the plant from which the above-ground plant grows—is located below ground and is not harmed until the temperature drops to 25° F.

The investigator uses the principle to distinguish meaningful information—potential evidence—from meaningless information.

Based on the principle above, I see that mums exhibit features 2 and 3, while turnips exhibit features 1 and 3.

Working with an inference and carefully selected evidence, a writer can support a claim (or conclusion).

Of all the *types* of plants in my garden, only mums and turnips can be classified as frost resistant in that only they exhibit two of the three features characteristic of frost-resistant plants.

Each different logical pattern an investigator might use prompts him or her to look for a certain patterning among available information. You can better understand the workings of a science by identifying the varieties of logical principles researchers use in making arguments. As a student reading or writing in a scientific discipline, pose these questions:

■ What logical principles are used in this discipline to make meaningful, supportable connections between observed facts and claims?

■ What observable, measurable evidence can help to support a scientific claim?

40b Reading in the sciences

Scientists work with written sources all the time. Accurate written records of experiments are essential in the process of reaching consensus about questions of scientific interest. As a student of science, you will read journal articles and textbooks, and you will do well to establish a strategy for reading both. First of all, adopt the general strategies suggested in Chapter 1 of this book, especially in 1e, "Reading to understand."

Textbooks

In introductory courses your reading will be primarily in textbooks, where the writing is directed to students and should, therefore, be more accessible than the writing in journal articles. In the sciences, textbooks play a special role in synthesizing available knowledge in an area and presenting it, with explanations, to students. The material in texts will grow increasingly technical as you move from introductory to specialized courses. Read your texts in science courses closely (see 1e), monitoring your progress frequently to ensure that you understand the material. Highlight any concepts or terms that confuse you, and seek clarification from classmates or a professor.

Journal articles

Journal articles are written by researchers for colleagues, not for students, and you can expect the language, concepts, and methodologies in journals to be challenging. The use of equations and sophisticated statistical techniques in a study's Results section may leave you baffled. But you can still develop a general, useful understanding of an article (if not a critical response to the author's research methodology) by reading as follows:

Read the article's Abstract, the Introduction, and the Discussion—in this order. If these sections prove interesting, then read the middle sections (the Materials and Methods, and the Results), which will probably contain the article's most technical elements. As you read, pose these questions:

- What is the purpose of this study?
- What is the researcher's perspective—for instance, biologist, chemist, or electrical engineer—and how does this perspective influence the study?
- What is the researcher's claim or conclusion?
- What seems significant about the research?

The following section summarizes a scientific report. The authors present the purpose, methods, and results of an experiment on the use of oral nicotine inhalers for reducing smoking. The format in which they present their study is typical of scientific reports.

Title

"Smoking Reduction with Oral Nicotine Inhalers: Double Blind, Randomised Clinical Trial of Efficacy and Safety." This title, typical of those used in experimental reports, is long and highly descriptive of what a reader can expect from this paper.

CRITICAL DECISIONS

Verb Tense in Scientific Writing

The special conventions regarding verb tenses in scientific writing can be very sticky. It is important because proper usage derives from scientific ethics.

Use of present tense

When a scientific paper has been validly published in a respected journal, it thereby becomes knowledge. Therefore, whenever you quote previously published work, ethics require you to treat that work with respect. You do this by using the present tense. It is correct to say "Streptomycin inhibits the growth of *M. tuberculosis* (13)."

Use of past tense

Your own present work must be referred to in the past tense. Your work is not presumed to be established knowledge until *after* it has been published. If you determined that the optimal growth temperature for *Streptomyces everycolor* was 37° C, you should say, "*S. everycolor* grew best at 37° C." If you are citing previous work, possibly your own, it is then correct to say "*S. everycolor* grows best at 37° C."

Mixture of tenses

In the typical paper, you will normally go back and forth between the past and present tenses. Most of the Abstract should be in the past tense, because you are referring to your own present results. Likewise, the Materials and Methods and the Results sections should be in the past tense, as you describe what you *did* and what you *found*. On the other hand, most of the Introduction and much of Discussion should be in the present tense, because these sections usually emphasize previously established knowledge.

Source: Robert Day, *How to Write and Publish a Scientific Paper*, 5th ed. (Phoenix: Oryx Press, 1998).

Authors

Chris T. Bolliger, Xandra van Biljon, Andre P. Perruchoud, Jean-Pierre Zellweger, Annik Robidou, Tobias Danielsson, Ake Westin, and Urbain Sawe. In the sciences and the social sciences, teams of researchers often work together to conduct and then write the report for a study.

Abstract

The authors provide a one-paragraph summary of their study's objectives, methods, results, and conclusions. Abstracts help other researchers sort through the mass of published studies, providing a quick guide so that they can decide whether to read further.

ABSTRACT: *Objectives: To determine whether use of an oral nicotine inhaler can result in long-term reduction in smoking and whether concomitant use of nicotine replacement and smoking is safe. Design: Double blind, randomised, placebo controlled trial. Four-month trial with a two year follow up. Setting: Two university hospital pulmonary clinics in Switzerland. Participants: 400 healthy volunteers, recruited through newspaper advertisements, willing to reduce their smoking but unable or unwilling to stop smoking immediately. Intervention: Active or placebo inhaler as needed for up to 18 months, with participants encouraged to limit their smoking as much as possible. Main outcome measures: Number of cigarettes smoked per day from week six to end point. Decrease verified by a measurement of exhaled carbon monoxide at each time point compared with measurement at baseline. Results: At four months sustained reduction of smoking was achieved in 52 (26%) participants in the active group and 18 (9%) in the placebo group (P<0.001; Fisher's test). Corresponding figures after two years were 19 (9.5%) and 6 (3.0%) (P=0.012). Conclusion: Nicotine inhalers effectively and safely achieved sustained reduction in smoking over 24 months. Reduction with or without nicotine substitution may be a feasible first step towards smoking cessation in people not able or not willing to stop abruptly.*

Introduction

Bolliger et al. open their report by noting that because of their dependence on nicotine—a highly addictive drug—many cigarette smokers find it impossible to quit smoking. In such cases, reduction of tobacco consumption is a useful strategy for reducing health risks and possibly moving smokers closer to quitting. They end their introduction with the following statements:

The oral nicotine inhaler, which is one of the newer nicotine replacement products, has been shown to be an effective aid for smoking cessation. [12] [13][2] Use of a nicotine inhaler by smokers unwilling or unable to stop smoking completely might be a good approach to reducing cigarette consumption as the inhaler imitates some aspects of cigarette smoking and contains nicotine. We tested the efficacy and safety of the nicotine inhaler in achieving sustained smoking reduction.

Methods

This section is broken into subsections. First the authors describe their "study design" as a "two center, double blind, placebo controlled, randomised clinical trial." They solicited participants through newspaper advertisements asking for smokers who were "unwilling or unable to quit but were interested in reducing their smoking."

---

[2]These bracketed numbers refer readers to sources numbered and listed on the report's References page. The authors use the CBE (Council of Biology Editors) "citation-sequence" system for in-text citations (see 37d-1).

In the remaining five subsections, titled "Participants," "Treatment," "Assessment," "Measures of Outcome," and "Statistical Analysis," the authors describe various elements of their study methods. Out of a total of 400 participants who fit established criteria, half were given active (nicotine-containing) inhalers, and half were given placebo (non-nicotine-containing) inhalers. Members of each group were not informed whether their inhalers were active or placebo. At one, two, three, and six weeks, and four, six, 12, 18, and 24 months the participants' smoking levels were assessed and compared to a baseline level established for each participant at the start of the study. The researchers measured success as

> self reported reduction of daily cigarette smoking by at least 50% compared with baseline from week six to month four, the duration for which the study was powered. This reduction was verified by decreased carbon monoxide concentrations at week six and months three and four.

Results

The authors provide a number of charts and tables to help with the presentation of their results. They also describe these results in subsections including "Baseline characteristics and rate of follow-up," "Treatment compliance," and "Efficacy." The most significant findings were that participants in the active treatment group showed more significant reduction of cigarette use than those in the placebo group from week two onward. However, researchers found the following:

> [S]ustained rates of complete abstinence were low in both groups, with no significant differences between groups. [. . .] With regard to changes in participants' interest to quit smoking, no difference could be detected between reducers or non-reducers or active and placebo treatment.

Discussion

Here the researchers discuss the significance, or meaning of their results. They write,

> This trial confirmed that it is possible to achieve a sustained reduction in cigarette smoking in people unable or not willing to quit. Although the overall success rates were relatively small, active treatment with the nicotine inhaler was more effective in obtaining this reduction than placebo over the entire period of two years.

The authors also note that since 38 (10%) of the participants in their study who were unwilling or unable to stop smoking at the start of the study were abstinent from nicotine two years later, there is support "to the idea that smoking reduction can be a step towards abstinence."

References

This section lists all the sources cited within the study, following standard CSE guidelines for documenting sources. Here are two examples, corresponding to bracketed numbers in the Introduction:

12. Tonnesen P, Nørregaard J, Mikkelsen K, Jorgensen S, Nilsson F. A double-blind trial of a nicotine inhaler for smoking cessation. JAMA 1993; 269: 1268-1271.

13. Hjalmarson A, Nilsson F, Sjostrom L, Wiklund O. The nicotine inhaler in smoking cessation. Arch Intern Med 1997; 157: 1721-1728.

40c Types of writing assignments in the sciences

As an undergraduate, you will most often be assigned two kinds of writing: a report of a laboratory experiment and a literature review. The purpose of writing in both cases will be to introduce you to methods of scientific thinking and the ways that scientists argue.

I The lab report

A laboratory experiment represents a distinct (empirical) strategy for learning about the world. Experimental researchers agree on this basic premise: that research must be *replicable*—that is, repeatable. Knowledge gained through experiment is based on what can be *observed*; and what is observed, if it is going to be accepted universally as a fact, must be observed by others: hence the need for *reporting on* and *writing* original research. Reports of experimental research usually consist of four parts: *Introduction*, *Methods*, *Results*, and *Discussion*. Even when scientific papers do not follow this structure, they will mirror its problem-solution approach. Robert A. Day, author of a highly readable and authoritative guide to writing scientific papers, characterizes the logic of the four-part form this way:

> What question (problem) was studied? The answer is the Introduction. How was the problem studied? The answer is the Methods. What were the findings? The answer is the Results. What do these findings mean? The answer is the Discussion. (7)

Introduction

- The Introduction of a scientific paper should clearly define the problem(s) and/or state the hypothesis you are investigating, as well as the point of view from which you will be investigating it. Establishing your point of view will help readers to anticipate the type of experiment you will be reporting on, as well as your conclusions.
- Your Introduction should also state clearly your reasons for investigating a particular subject. This is common practice in journal

> See 37d for the conventions on citing and documenting sources in the sciences.

articles, where researchers will cite pertinent literature in order to set their current project in a context.

■ In references to prior work in which the same or similar problems or processes have been reported, you will cite sources. These references will help you to establish a context as well as a need for the present experiment.

Materials and Methods

The Methods section of the lab report is given slightly different names in different discipline areas: Experimental Details, Experimental Methods, Experimental Section, or Materials and Methods (American Chemical Society [ACS] 6); and Methods and Materials (CBE 590).

■ Whatever heading your instructor prefers, it is in the Materials and Methods section that you provide readers with the basis on which to reproduce your experimental study. Unless you have some reason for not doing so, describe your experimental methods chronologically.

■ When reporting on the Materials and Methods of *field studies* (investigations carried out beyond the strictly controlled environment of the lab), describe precisely *where* you conducted your study, *what* you chose to study, the *instruments* you used to conduct the study, and the *methods of analysis* you employed.

■ As you set up and conduct your experiment, keep detailed records that will allow you to report precisely on your work when the time comes for writing. Both student and professional experimenters keep a *lab notebook* for this purpose. Even though you may be tempted to make quick, shorthand entries, write in precise and complete sentences that will allow you to retrace your steps. The notebook should be complete, containing the information necessary to write your lab report.

Results

■ The Results section of your paper should precisely set out the data you have accumulated in your research. The statements you make in this section will provide the basis on which you state conclusions in the Discussion section to follow. Your presentation of results, therefore, must be both clear and logically ordered. (Instructors will usually review in class what constitutes clear and logical ordering of results in their disciplines.)

■ As in the Materials and Methods section, when your discussion of results is lengthy, use subheadings to organize the presentation.

Discussion

The purpose of the Discussion section in your report is to interpret experimental findings and to discuss their implications. In the

Discussion, your main task is to address the *So what?* question. Readers should know, clearly, what you have accomplished (or failed to accomplish) and why this is significant.

■ If you believe your research findings are significant, say so and give your reasons. If appropriate, suggest directions for future study.

■ As in the Introduction, set your experimental findings in a context by relating them to the findings of other experiments.

■ When your results differ from those you expected or from results reported by others, explain the difference.

The Abstract

The Abstract is the *briefest possible* summary of an article (see 2a). Typically, it includes the following:

■ The subject of the paper, its purpose and objectives

■ The experimenter's materials and methods, including the names of specific organisms, drugs, and compounds

■ Experimental results and their significance

Most often, the Abstract excludes the following:

■ References to literature cited in the paper

■ References to equations, figures, or tables (AIP 5; CBE 20)

Weblink

http://utoronto.ca/hswriting/
abstract.htm

Hypertext guide to writing an abstract from the University of Toronto.

When writing the Abstract of your lab report, consider devoting one sentence of summary to each of the major headings (Introduction, Materials and Methods, Results, and Discussion). If necessary, end your four-sentence Abstract with a concluding sentence.

---

2 The Literature Review

For general advice on the skills necessary or conducting a Literature Review, see "Reading to evaluate" (1g), "Reading to synthesize" (1h), and "Writing a synthesis" (2d). These same principles also apply to writing Literature Reviews in the social sciences and humanities.

The Literature Review, a prominent and important form of writing in science, synthesizes current knowledge on a topic. Unlike a term paper, which draws on a limited number of sources in order to support a thesis, a Literature Review covers and brings coherence to the range of studies on a topic. A review may also evaluate articles, advising readers pressed for time about which articles merit attention. While every experimental report begins with a review of pertinent literature, only the Literature Review makes this discussion its main business.

Instructors assigning review papers will not ask that you conduct an exhaustive search of literature on a topic. Your search should be limited

Manuscript Form for Lab Reports in the Sciences

Check with your instructor about the specific form your lab report should take. Here are some general guidelines:

Title page: Center your title one-third of the way down the page. On subsequent centered, double-spaced lines enter your name, the title of the course, and the date. Use a descriptive and precise title for your report.

Page numbering: Place numbers in the upper right-hand corner of each page, starting with the title page. Use your word processor's "header" function to format page numbering and add a running head preceding the page number. Some instructors will want you to use a shortened version of your paper's title as your running head; other instructors may prefer you place your last name next to the page number.

Margins and spacing: Use one-inch margins all around, and double-space your entire report—including your abstract, footnotes, and references list.

Abstract: Place the abstract on a separate page following the title page. Center the word Abstract, double-space, and begin, writing the abstract as a single paragraph.

Headings and subheadings: Each heading, such as "Materials" and "Methods," or "Results," is centered and given its own line. Some instructors will want to see each major section begin on a new page. Subheadings should be placed on the left margin, and given their own line.

Tables and figures: Each table or figure should be numbered, titled, and placed either in the body of the report, or on its own page at the end of the report, after the references list.

in such a way that it will both introduce you to a topic and acquaint you with scientific ways of thinking. Your topic should not be so broad that you overwhelm yourself with vast amounts of reading material.

Writing the paper

Writing a Literature Review in the sciences involves several steps. Once you have a topic in mind, you will need to read widely to be able to ask a fruitful research question and begin to conduct more focused research. Reading scholarly review articles is an excellent place to begin, since by definition they survey a great many potential sources for you and, better still, point out themes and raise questions that you can take up in your own review. Review articles are published for most of the sciences. Locate them by searching for the word review in the various publications that abstract and index journal articles, such as *Microbiological Abstracts*, *Chemical Abstracts*, *Engineering Index Annual*, *Physics Abstracts*, and *Science Abstracts*.

If you are unfamiliar with the process of conducting research, then before attempting a Literature Review, skim Chapter 33 for general strategies on writing a research paper. A Literature Review, like any good synthesis or research paper, is usually organized by *ideas*, not by sources. In Literature Reviews, you will not find a simple listing of summaries: these are the substance of annotated bibliographies, which are themselves useful tools to researchers. The review should represent your best effort at inferring themes, problems, trends, and so on. When referring to sources, use the citation form appropriate to your discipline. See 37d for information on citing and documenting sources in the sciences.

40d Sample student paper: "Black Hole Flares"

Following is a report on a summer research project on the black holes, undertaken by physics student Ryan Hernandez. Often, undergraduate experiments in the sciences do not create new knowledge but, rather, the opportunity to learn how scientists approach problems: how to pose questions, set up experiments, make observations, and draw conclusions. Later, students who master basic techniques may, in fact, go on to make original contributions. In the present example, Ryan Hernandez sets out to create new knowledge—to photographically record a "flare event" at the center of galaxies in order to demonstrate the existence of black holes. Note that he is not reporting on an experiment already concluded but, rather, on his intentions for an experiment about to begin.

Here are several features you might look for when reading Ryan Hernandez's paper. Though he is reporting on a project in physics, he follows a classic approach adapted by investigators across many scientific disciplines:

- Hernandez grounds his intended work in the work of others. See Sections 1 and 2 and the citation.
- Observe how a problem—a question—lies at the heart of this project. Hernandez states the problem guiding his research at the end of the first paragraph in his "Background" section.
- Hernandez proposes a solution to the problem guiding his research (see "Background," paragraph 2) and then defines a procedure to test that solution.

- Note the intention to use a discipline-appropriate tool—a powerful Remote Optical Telescope—to collect data. Students of other disciplines will use other discipline-appropriate tools in their research.
- Hernandez has in place a plan, guided by an equation, to analyze the data he collects. See his Section 4: "Reduction and Analysis of Images." Notice his use of a computer programming language to help in his analysis.
- Hernandez incorporates graphics into his report. Generally, scientists use graphs, tables, and photographs to communicate results.

Black Hole Flares

Ryan O. Hernandez

Summer ARC Project
Department of Physics
University of California, Santa Barbara
8 October 2002

Hernandez 2

Abstract

This project is a search for black holes at the center of prospective galaxies. First, we will automate the process of photographing and analyzing galaxies. Then, we will research which galaxies are good candidates for harboring a black hole. Once chosen, these candidates will be monitored for what amounts to a "flare" at the center of the galaxy. The flare is believed to occur when a star from the galaxy surrounding the black hole is torn apart and consumed by the black hole. Although it is believed that there is a black hole at the center of most galaxies, catching the flare event requires repeated observations of over 10,000 galaxies. We will monitor these galaxies over the next few years in our search of a black hole flare.

Writing and Reading in the Sciences

1 Introduction

Scientists believe that at the center of some galaxies there might be a "dead quasar." "Dead quasars are massive black holes now starved of fuel, and therefore quiescent" (Rees 817). Although these dead quasars are quiescent, it is possible to see them under special circumstances. We will discuss those special circumstances and the relationship between a quasar, a black hole, and a galaxy.

To find a dead quasar we will be examining approximately 10,000 galaxies. The problem with viewing so many galaxies is that one would have to stay up all night, every night just to photograph them. We don't have the people or the resources to hire someone to do this. Also, once we do have the images we want, we will need to find a way of checking each individual image to see if a flare event has occurred. These processes are pretty time consuming even for one image. Since we will be analyzing over a hundred images each night, we must find a process that will cut the time immensely.

2 Background

Since quasars were first discovered, people have been questioning the mechanism that powers them. "The best explanation to date is that quasars are powered by super-massive black holes that accelerate matter to relativistic velocities giving off powerful jets of luminous material" (Rees 817) (Figure 1). This would explain how such luminosity could be created in such a compact space. Observations suggest that most galaxies have a super-massive black hole at their centers. The problem with this explanation comes when we examine the distances at which quasars are found. Quasars are

found to be at a high red shift, which corresponds
to being in the distant past. If this is so, why
are these galaxies not also luminous like quasars?

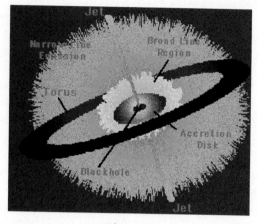

Figure 1

The resolution to this problem is an easy
one: quasars may just be a part of the evolution
of a galaxy. During the early part of the galaxy's
lifetime, there is a lot of matter near the center
of the galaxy, near the black hole. This matter is
drawn into the black hole and forms an accretion
disk and the luminous jets that are characteristic
of a quasar. Once all the matter near the black
hole has been consumed, the galaxy quiets down and
appears as the galaxies we observe today. If this
hypothesis is true, we might expect that, every
now and then, an unlucky star wanders too close
to the center of a galaxy and gets "eaten" by the
black hole. This would cause a flare in the black
hole, a "mini-quasar." Calculations estimate that
in a typical galaxy this type of event should occur every 10,000 years. Since it would be impractical to observe a single galaxy for 10,000 years,

we will monitor thousands of galaxies over a few
years and expect to see one of these galaxies un-
dergoing a period of activity.

3 Remote Optical Telescope

The Remote Optical Telescope (ROT) is based
on the top of Broida Hall at the University of
California, Santa Barbara. ROT is controlled in
the Remote Access Astronomy Project trailer by
computer. The main telescope is a Celestron with a
14-in lens. It has a Schmidt-Cassegrain Reflecting
design and dark sky sensitivity from 18th to 20th
magnitude. ROT also has a main camera used for
guiding and photographing.

On computer all the parameters including
coordinates, filters, and exposure times for photographing one's image are inputted. There is an
effort underway by another group member to automate
this procedure. To do so, the telescope will have
to account for what time of night and year it is.
Once the telescope is automated to do this, we hope
that the galaxy will be centered in the image. This
will make the analysis of the images easier to do.

4 Reduction and Analysis of Images

Once the telescope has photographed the
galaxies, the images are saved on computer. The
next task at hand is to reduce the images. This is
a process that rids the images of defects caused
by dust, electronics, and pixel-to-pixel variations. The equation below shows the derivation of
a reduced image.

$$\text{Reduced Image} = (\text{Raw Image} - \text{Dark Raw Image}) / (\text{Flat Image} - \text{Dark Flat})$$

After the image is reduced, it is analyzed to
see if it contains a black hole flare. This is

Hernandez 6

done by subtracting the new reduced image from a previously photographed control image. But, before the two photographs can be subtracted, they must be aligned exactly. The whole process of reduction and analysis of images is not too difficult; however, it is time consuming, considering 10,000 galaxies will be photographed.

To save a lot of time the process will be automated using the programming language, Interactive Data Language (IDL). A program will be written using this language that will

(1) Load the image and name it;

(2) Reduce the image;

(3) Align the reduced image with the control image;

(4) Subtract the reduced image from the control image;

(5) Designate whether or not a flare occurred.

To see what a flare might look like we simulated an image of the dwarf elliptical galaxy,

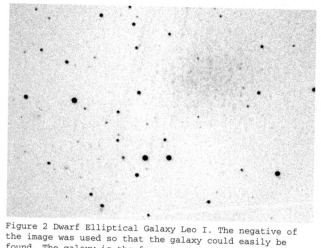

Figure 2 Dwarf Elliptical Galaxy Leo I. The negative of the image was used so that the galaxy could easily be found. The galaxy is the fuzzy part on the top right.

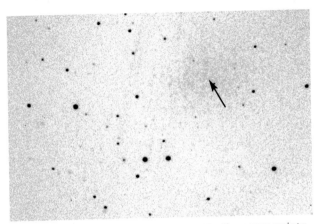

Figure 3 Dwarf Elliptical Galaxy Leo I. The arrow points to where the artificial flare was added.

Leo I (Figure 2). Using IDL, one of the stars surrounding Leo I (the fuzzy part on the top right of the image) was cut and added to the center of the galaxy to create an artificial flare (Figure 3). Before we begin photographing galaxies, we hope to determine what minimum brightness a star can have so that it will be detected. We will incorporate this information into our program so that we may be able to utilize the telescope to its full potential.

5 Future Work

We are slowly building the foundation for this research project. We still have a lot of work to continue just so that we may begin photographing galaxies. Once we are able to begin, we will have to decide what galaxies are good candidates. And remember, we want to investigate 10,000!

If we fail to discover a flare after observing many types of galaxies, we'll most likely move onto other astronomical objects like globular

```
                                    Hernandez 8
clusters. Globular clusters are systems of between
100,000 and 1,000,000 gravitationally bound stars.
Since black holes are known to be collapsed stars,
we are confident that globular clusters are a wise
choice for our next candidate.

                      Reference
Rees, Martin J. "'Dead Quasars' in Nearby
      Galaxies?" Science 247 (Feb. 1990):
      817-823.
```

40e Reference materials in the sciences

Style guides

A source of excellent general advice for writing papers in the sciences is Robert Day's *How to Write and Publish a Scientific Paper*, 5th ed. (Phoenix: Oryx Press, 1998). For discipline-specific advice on writing, consult the following works:

> *AIP [American Institute of Physics] Style Manual.* 4th ed. NY: AIP, 1990.
>
> *Scientific Style and Format: The CBE Manual for Authors, Editors, and Publishers.* 6th ed. Cambridge, UK: Cambridge UP, 1994.
>
> Dodd, Janet S., et al. *The ACS [American Chemical Society] Style Guide: A Manual for Authors and Editors.* 2nd ed. Washington: ACS, 1998.
>
> Michaelson, Herbert B. *How to Write and Publish Engineering Papers and Reports.* 3rd ed. Philadelphia: ISI Press, 1990.

Specialized references

The following specialized references will help you to assemble information in a particular discipline or field within a discipline.

Encyclopedias provide general information useful when beginning a search.

> *Cambridge Encyclopedia of Astronomy*
> *Encyclopedia of Biological Sciences*
> *Encyclopedia of Chemistry*
> *Encyclopedia of Computer Science and Engineering*
> *Encyclopedia of Computer Science and Technology*

Encyclopedia of Earth Sciences
Encyclopedia of Physics
Grzimek's Animal Life Encyclopedia
Grzimek's Encyclopedia of Ecology
Harper's Encyclopedia of Science
Larousse Encyclopedia of Astronomy
McGraw-Hill Encyclopedia of Environmental Science
McGraw-Hill Yearbook of Science and Technology
Stein and Day International Medical Encyclopedia
Universal Encyclopedia of Mathematics
Van Nostrand's Scientific Encyclopedia

Dictionaries provide definitions of technical terms.

Computer Dictionary and Handbook
Condensed Chemical Dictionary
Dictionary of Biology
Dorland's Medical Dictionary
Illustrated Stedman's Medical Dictionary
McGraw-Hill Dictionary of Scientific and Technical Terms

Periodical indexes and abstracts list articles published in a particular discipline over a particular period. *Abstracts*, which summarize the sources listed and involve a considerable amount of work to compile, tend to be more selective than indexes.

Applied Science and Technology Index
Biological Abstracts
Biological and Agricultural Index
Cumulative Index to Nursing and Allied Health Literature
Current Abstracts of Chemistry and Index Chemicus
Engineering Index
General Science Index
Index Medicus
Index to Scientific and Technical Proceedings
Science Citation Index

Computerized periodical indexes are available for many specialized areas and may be faster than leafing through years of bound periodicals. Access to these databases may be expensive.

Science and Technology Databases

Agricola (agriculture)
Biosis Previews (biology, botany)

CA Search (chemistry)

Compendix (engineering)

NTIS (National Technical Information Search)

ORBIT (science and technology)

SciSearch

SPIN (physics)

Science Resources on the World Wide Web

The following URLs provide a useful, Web-based starting point for researchers in the sciences. For a complete and continuously updated URL list, see this book's companion Web site.

Academic Research Engine (developed by Student Advantage) (http://navisite.collegeclub.com/channels/academics/)

AstroWeb
(http://www.cv.nrao.edu/fits/www/astronomy.html)

Information Resources for Biology
(http://www.library.ucsb.edu/subj/bio1.html)

Information Resources for the Sciences
(http://www.library.ucsb.edu/subj/sciences.html)

Physics Encyclopedia
(http://members.tripod.com/~IgorIvanov/physics/)

Yahoo! Chemistry
(http://dir.yahoo.com/Science/chemistry/)

CHAPTER 41

Writing for the Web

T he World Wide Web is a radically democratic publishing forum. Anyone can create and post Web sites, spreading information both across campus and continent. This chapter will introduce you to the basic elements of Web publishing so that you can take the first steps necessary to post your work.

CRITICAL DECISIONS

Planning Your Web Document

Web documents differ fundamentally from printed texts. Although it may seem obvious, the fact that they are presented on a computer screen is tremendously important. Internet audiences have new choices about how to read documents; these should be considered carefully as you plan to post work on the Web. Here are some suggestions that will help you to prepare your document for the Web:

1. *Anticipate multiple audiences.* Although your document may be intended for classmates or a professor, other people may stumble upon it via a search engine or a link from another page. Therefore, it's a good idea to provide a context for your work—provide your name and the title of the document on each page, and consider adding links to the home page for your course or university.
2. *Use brief units of thought.* The unit of thought in an essay is, at its briefest, a paragraph. In print documents, paragraphs are frequently strung together in lengthy sections. Since Web readers can quickly scroll through a document or jump around using links, you can make your text easier to read by keeping your "thought units" brief, and by indexing them with hyperlinks.
3. *Anticipate a nonlinear development of ideas.* Readers *will* jump through your text and, if you provide links, to other Web sites. Providing a clear outline and section titles within your text can ease confusion for this sort of reader. *(continued)*

Planning Your Web Document *(continued)*

4. *Make navigation easy.* People may skim through your Web essay searching for specific facts or simply to gain a quick overview of your ideas. Consider providing a site map, or simply a hyperlinked outline, that will facilitate navigation to various parts of your document.

5. *Be conscious of design.* You can optimize your document for legibility on various computers and Web browsers by following basic onscreen design principles. Additionally, provide a version of your work for users who may want to print it out and read it the old-fashioned way.

EXERCISE 1

Take an essay that you have written and break it into "thought units"— that is, groupings of related paragraphs. Working with index cards, give each section of the paper a title and place these titles on separate cards. Place the thesis of the paper on its own card. Finally, arrange the cards in the order in which the paper is presented. (In Exercise 3, you will compare the organization of your print-based essay to an essay that you will restructure for the Web.)

41a Plan the content.

41.1

As the author of an essay, you have done all of the required research and writing—therefore, you are a content expert. You can work with a Web designer (or take on that role yourself) to identify items that will serve as links to other Web pages. You will probably develop a new organizational plan for your essay, breaking with the structure that you used for print and the expectation that your document will be read linearly. Anticipating multiple navigation paths through your site, you can create brief, interconnected but independent "thought units" of text and images.

You can use your knowledge of the essay's subject matter to enhance the text content, making it a uniquely Internet-based document. Anecdotes, related article references, and other materials that you didn't have room to accommodate in your print essay can all be included here alongside the main text, or as links to separate Web pages.

■ **Identify links:** Your text probably contains references that could be linked to other places on the Internet. You can link citations in a text to their online sources, not only in the formal bibliography, but also within the text itself. Mark these links: you will enhance them with special HTML tags later.

- **Consider visual aids:** When you post a document on the Internet, you can give it extra meaning through the incorporation of charts, graphs, illustrations, and photographs. Whether you create this artwork yourself, get permission from another source to use it, or link to it elsewhere on the Internet, now is the time to identify it.
- **Provide a feedback mechanism:** Let your users talk back to you. They'll let you know if a feature isn't working or if your site is somehow unclear. You might provide your e-mail address at the bottom of each page, or create a feedback form in HTML.

41b Create the Web site's structure.

It's a good idea to map out your Web site on paper before you actually commit to anything in a digital format. Professional Web designers always lay everything out this way because experimentation with pencil and paper always saves them time. Collect all of your information and other materials and then begin to plan the site's structure.

1 Make a site map.

A Web site consists of many, sometimes thousands of, individual Web pages. A site map is a logistical illustration of all of the pages in a site and how they are linked to each other. On page 760, you'll find a site map created by student Marie Hobahn as she prepared to make a Web-based version of her essay, "Women and Computing: Beyond the Glass Ceiling," which you will find in Chapter 6. (See page 770 for the first page of her Web-based version of the essay.)

This site map restructures Marie's original essay that she wrote for a composition class. Although she hopes that readers will begin from her home page, which includes her introduction, thesis, and links to the other major "thought units," she understands that on the Internet, readers might be entering her argument from several points. Therefore, Marie links each thought unit to the others, so that readers may navigate to different areas as they please.

Site maps are as useful as you allow them to be. Some are pencil scrawls on a single sheet of paper, while others are the size of conference room tables and contain color-coded areas, elaborate illustrations, and hundreds of link arrows marching back and forth. Regardless of how complex or simple the site map looks, it is the most important step in building a Web site.

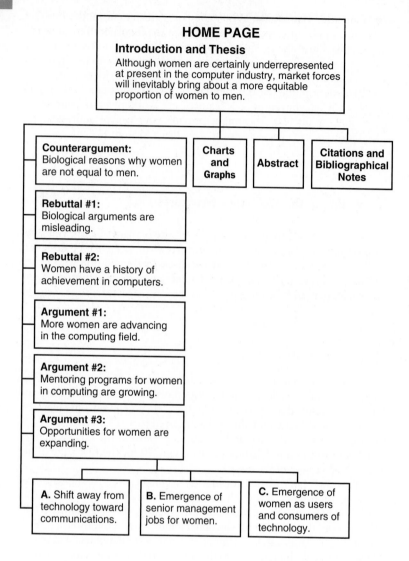

HOME PAGE

Introduction and Thesis

Although women are certainly underrepresented at present in the computer industry, market forces will inevitably bring about a more equitable proportion of women to men.

Counterargument: Biological reasons why women are not equal to men.

Charts and Graphs

Abstract

Citations and Bibliographical Notes

Rebuttal #1: Biological arguments are misleading.

Rebuttal #2: Women have a history of achievement in computers.

Argument #1: More women are advancing in the computing field.

Argument #2: Mentoring programs for women in computing are growing.

Argument #3: Opportunities for women are expanding.

A. Shift away from technology toward communications.

B. Emergence of senior management jobs for women.

C. Emergence of women as users and consumers of technology.

EXERCISE 2

Compare Marie Hobahn's site map for her Web-based essay with her print-based essay, which you will find at the beginning of Chapter 6. Observe closely how she dissects the print essay into briefer thought units, which then become separate Web pages in the site she is planning.

The (Messy) Process of Web Page Design and Production

Every page of a well-designed Web site is built on sketches, maps, and megabytes of digital revisions. Much as the essay-writing process benefits from thoughtful outlining of ideas and multiple rewrites, the Web design and construction process involves a great deal of planning and a commitment to iterative design.

Iterative design is an approach to creation that occurs in cycles:

1. Create a rough estimate of what the page ought to look like and contain.
2. Present this work to others for critique.
3. Revise your plans based on the feedback.
4. Re-present your ideas.
5. Continue revising again and again until, finally, a polished product is created.

Like the iterative process of writing an essay, designing a Web site is a messy process: typically sites are built up and then partially torn down, only to be redesigned, rebuilt, and torn down again. Constant refinement improves the end product.

EXERCISE 3

Working with the sections of your print-based essay, which you defined in Exercise 1, take two sections of the essay and create briefer thought units, each a paragraph or two in length. Give each paragraph a title, and place these titles on separate index cards. Again, place the thesis on its own card. Using Marie Hobahn's site map as a guide, try drawing links (you might use lengths of string) between the thesis and paragraphs, and between paragraphs themselves. How many ways, other than start-to-finish, can you think of for a reader to navigate through these parts of your essay?

---

2   Create blueprints for your site.

It isn't unusual to walk into an Internet development office and find dozens of sketches of page elements taped onto the wall. Sometimes, designers sketch directly onto yellow sticky notes, since these are easier to rearrange. Moveable paper sketches give developers the opportunity to experiment with the placement of elements, changing their locations from here to there until the whole vision of the Web site makes sense.

Once developers are sure what goes where, they will create page blueprints. These are detailed sketches indicating, for each page, the following information:

- What artwork will be used, and how large it is;
- Where the links to other pages will be located;
- How much text needs to fit on the page.

Drawing blueprints does not require art talent! These are simply schematics that help you anticipate the amount of content on each page.

Here's a blueprint of the first page of Marie Hobahn's Web-based essay, which incorporates many of the elements described so far, including a feedback mechanism, a title, links, and a navigational system.

41c Design the pages.

One of the exciting aspects about Web publishing is how easy it is to create a unique look for your document by making simple decisions about colors, fonts, and artwork. You don't have to be an artist to make your Web pages look good. Careful design decisions can make the difference between an inviting page that is easy to read and a Web page that readers leave immediately.

| **Collect and prepare artwork.**

An all-text Web page will probably look dull to readers. When it's possible, try including relevant images, like charts, photographs, or illustrations, alongside your text content.

41.2

Images are of course widely available all over the Internet and are easily found using search engines. (Make sure you see the note on citing sources, at the end of this section.) To save an image from a Web page, right click on the image (or, if you're using a Macintosh, click and hold your mouse over the image). Select the Save Image menu item, give it a name, and save it in a place on your computer where you will keep all of your HTML files.

Most computer stores sell CD-ROM collections of clip art that you can use without paying royalties. Many Web sites specialize in this sort of stock photography and clip art. Here are a few examples:

- http://www.picturerequest.com
- http://www.photostogo.com
- http://www.digitalartshop.com

Once you are at a Web site that specializes in images, you can usually perform keyword searches (for instance, "Eiffel Tower") and find dozens of potential photographs or illustrations. In general, these sites allow you to download a small version of the artwork (called a "comp") for free. If you choose to download a larger, high-resolution version, you will have to pay a royalty fee.

You can also scan photographs and illustrations into your computer, or create new art in such programs as Photoshop or Illustrator.

Once you select an appropriate image, you may need to alter it to fit into your Web page. Use a program like Photoshop to resize the image as desired, or crop out the unimportant parts. It's also a good idea to limit the file size of your images by keeping them as small as possible, and by saving them with compression. The larger and more complex your art is, the more your Web pages will "weigh," forcing your users to wait a long time to download them. You can check an image's file size by right-clicking its name to view its Properties on a PC, or by highlighting it and selecting the Get Info command on a Macintosh.

Finally, you will need to save the image into a Web-ready format. All artwork should be either a GIF (pronounced "giff" or "jiff") or a JPEG (pronounced "jay-peg"). In general, when you're preparing images, you should save photographs as JPEGs, and cartoonish artwork or simple charts as GIFs. These formats were created with these purposes in mind.

Since Web pages are stored on computers that don't understand the difference between image files and other kinds of files, you have to give your images names like "paris.gif" or "eiffeltower.jpg." The three-letter extension at the end of the name tells the computer that it is handling a piece of art.

Remember to cite sources: An image on the Web is likely to be the unique creation of the person who made the page. Unless that image is clearly labeled as available for public use, you may need to secure written permission from the copyright holder to reproduce it on your Web site. Regardless of circumstances, you should always credit your source.

---

2   **Make graphic design and typography decisions.**

Online, no two people will see your page in exactly the same way. In designing pages for the Web, you should be aware of general design principles (see Chapter 42) and the unique constraints that technology adds to your project. Here are some to consider:

- Not everyone with an Internet connection views the Web through the same size screen that you do. Some people have large screens capable of displaying large amounts of information at once, while other people work on laptops and must scroll repeatedly to view your entire Web page.
- Not everyone has a fast Internet connection. People reading Web pages from their offices or computer labs may download fancy animations in a snap, while others dial up from home on 28.8 modems and become frustrated at pages that "weigh" too much.
- Eyesight varies from person to person, especially in an onscreen environment.

There are a few basic design principles that you can adopt to create the most accessible Web pages possible:

Color and contrast are key.

- Use high contrast between your type and your background colors. People can read best when type is in a dark color set against a light background. Books have been printed with black ink on white pages for hundreds of years for a good reason!
- Keep your content on a solid-colored background. It is difficult to read text when there are images in the background competing for attention.

■ Pick a link color that is sufficiently different from your normal text color so that readers can easily see the hyperlinks in your text.

All things in moderation (especially artwork)

■ Don't use too many images on one Web page. They can take a long time to download. If you absolutely need to include a large number of graphics on one page, consider using thumbnail versions that link to the full-sized files in another window.

■ Use animation judiciously—to explain a concept or just to make your user smile. More than one or two animations on a page can be overwhelming. Free GIF animation software is easily found online and is easy to use. Two good programs are GifBuilder for Macintosh and Animagic GIF for the PC. You'll find these programs at shareware sites like www.download.com.

■ Too many links make navigation confusing. Try to consolidate possibilities into five to seven choices per page. Also, consider using linked images rather than words or phrases. For instance, if your document is about a Caribbean cruise, why not use a clickable map of the route as a way to navigate through the content?

Viewing environments are diverse.

■ Make sure that you preview your Web pages on both a Macintosh and a PC computer, and in different popular Web browsers. Oftentimes, pages look much different in these environments.

■ Imitate your users and test out your page on a slow Internet connection as well as a fast one.

41d Build the site.

Once you know what is going to be contained on each of your Web pages, you're ready to move ahead with creating HTML pages, and posting them to a Web server. There are entire books available about this process, but the basics can be learned in just a few hours with a little practice.

www

41.3

1 Create the HTML pages.

HTML is short for **H**yper**T**ext **M**arkup **L**anguage. The word "language" may sound formidable, but HTML is not a true programming language and it doesn't take a computer science major to understand it. In fact, complete beginners can usually make their first Web page in a matter of twenty minutes.

HTML is a *markup* language. Creating a Web page involves taking your content and marking it up with special "tags." These tags are instructions to a Web browser that explain how to display your text. For an example of how this works, take a look at this very simple Web page:

Here is the HTML that makes this page viewable as a Web document. Note that the HTML tags are enclosed in angle brackets:

```
<HTML>
<HEAD>
<TITLE>hello, world</TITLE>
</HEAD>
<BODY>
Hello, world.
</BODY>
</HTML>
```

HTML code instructs browsers on how to interpret and display information. Content without proper tagging will not be displayed when a browser attempts to open it. Let's examine each HTML tag involved in this example page:

- **<HTML>** This tag announces to the browser that the content that follows is formatted in HTML.
- **<HEAD>** This tag announces that key information about the Web page will follow. For example, you might include the document's title, its author, subject matter, and date of publication.
- **<TITLE>** All text between the opening tag <TITLE> and the closing tag </TITLE> will appear at the top of the browser window when the page loads. The forward slash character (/) marks the ending for all tagged elements that occur in pairs, such as </HEAD> and </TITLE>.
- **<BODY>** This tag opens the body of the document. All text and graphics following this tag will appear in the Web page. After you have entered all of the text and art that should be contained in the body of the page, you must close this portion of the document with the tag </BODY>. Finally, you can complete the entire page with the tag </HTML>.

2 Add your text.

Adding the text of your essay to your Web page is as easy as cutting and pasting it in between the BODY tags of your HTML document. Once you've done that, you can start adding links and formatting tags that will make your work a real hypertext document.

First, create the hyperlinks that you planned for your document. Links are added through special HTML tags, as shown in this example:

Here is a sample sentence on a Web page. When users click <A HREF="page2.html">here</A>, they will go to another Web page.

Here is how this tagged example text will look on an actual Web page:

Here is a sample sentence on a Web page. When users click here, they will go to another Web page.

The underlined here is now a hyperlink. In HTML, the tag <A HREF="page2.html"> tells the browser that all text until the closing tag </A> should be linked to the page in quotation marks. The A stands for *anchor*, because the tagged text is anchored to another HTML page. HREF means *hypertext reference*.

To make the link in this example work, you'll need to create two HTML pages: "page1.html" is the page that will contain this sentence, and "page2.html" is the page to which the link will take the user.

As a writer, you may often want a link that simply allows a reader to jump down a page. This is a good strategy for dealing with footnotes. These links are called jump links, and are created in HTML like this:

Jump down the page to my footnote by clicking <A HREF="#footnote1">here</A>.

<A NAME="footnote1">Here</A> is the footnote.

One last kind of link that you may want to use is the "mailto" link. This is how you can include your e-mail address on a Web page.

<A HREF="mailto:marie.hobahn@nyu.edu">e-mail me!</A>

When clicked, the words "e-mail me!" (contained between the two HTML tags) will initiate an e-mail message to the address in the quotation marks.

There are dozens of formatting HTML tags that you can use to make your text look good. Some that you might find useful include:

- <B> and </B> Everything between these tags will appear as bold type.
- <I> and </I> Everything between these tags will appear as italicized type.
- <U> and </U> Everything between these tags will appear as underlined type.
- <P> and </P> Use these tags to surround a new paragraph.
- <FONT SIZE="+1"> and </FONT> All type between these tags will appear one size larger than other type.
- <FONT SIZE="−1"> and </FONT> All type between these tags will appear one size smaller than other type.
- <FONT COLOR="red"> and </FONT> Experiment with different colors in this tag to create colorful text.

EXERCISE 4

Take one paragraph, or thought unit, from the print essay with which you have been working in Exercises 1 and 3, and develop HTML code for it as if you were going to post it to the Internet. Use as many HTML tags reviewed in this section as you can, and create at least one hyperlink.

3 Add your images.

It's easy to add images to your HTML document. Simply find the area in the text where you'd like to include the image, and use a tag like this one:

<IMG SRC="myimage.gif">

IMG is short for image, and SRC is short for source. Add the name of your image between the quotation marks, and you're all set.

If you'd like to be more precise about positioning your image, you can add detail to the IMG SRC tag. For instance, to place your image in a Web-based résumé like the one found on page 792, you would code the image as follows:

<IMG SRC="myimage.gif" HEIGHT="200" WIDTH="150" BORDER="0" ALIGN="LEFT">

Add the dimensions of your image to help the browser leave the right amount of space. To change the size of your image, you can experiment with inputting different dimensions that will shrink or stretch the artwork.

Include a border if you like. By changing the contents of the BORDER="" part of this tag, you can create a thick black border around your artwork. Experiment and see how you prefer to display your images.

If you want to position your image to the right or the left, include the information ALIGN="LEFT" or "RIGHT" or "CENTER."

Source Code for One Page from Marie Hobahn's Web-based Essay (on page 770)

```
<HTML>
<HEAD>
<TITLE>Women and Computing: Beyond the Glass Ceiling</ TITLE>
</HEAD>
<BODY BGCOLOR="#FFFFFF">

<center><b>Women and Computing: Beyond the Glass Ceiling</b>
<br>By Marie Hobahn (<a
href="mailto:marie.hobahn@nyu.edu">marie.hobahn@nyu.edu</a>)
</center>

<p><b>Argument #3: Opportunities for Women Are Expanding</b>
<p>Opportunities are expanding for women, and gains are being made.
In the next few years these gains will broaden as three important
changes sweep through the computer industry.
<p>A. <a href="3a.html">Shift away from technology towards com-
munications</a>
<br>B. <a href="3b.html">Emergence of senior management jobs for
women</a>
<br>C. <a href="3c.html">Emergence of women as users and con-
sumers of technology</a>
<br><a href="3c.html"></a>
<p><IMG  SRC="navigation-map.gif"  BORDER=0  height=224
width=192>

</BODY>
</HTML>
```

A page from Marie Hobahn's Web-based essay

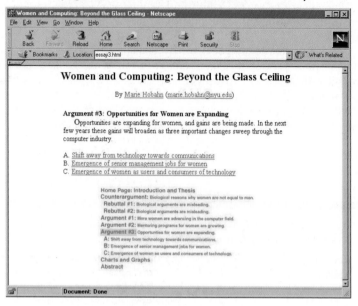

Creating Web Pages Automatically

If you don't want to learn HTML, you can still create Web pages using one of several commercially available programs.

1. Word processors. Some word-processing applications like Microsoft Word allow writers to automatically save their documents in HTML format.
2. WYSIWYG (What You See Is What You Get) programs. These programs were designed for easy Web site creation through ready-to-use drag and drop page elements. You might try Macromedia's Dreamweaver and Adobe's GoLive.

Why bother learning HTML when there are programs like this available? Familiarity with the tags will empower you to make more creative decisions than these programs allow. Also, you'll be able to make changes from any computer, rather than relying on your own computer that has this software installed.

If you've tried out your Web pages in a browser, and they look good to you, it's time to upload them to a Web server. Web servers are computers configured to hold the thousands of HTML files, images, and other materials that make up Web sites. These computers are permanently connected to the Internet, so that PCs in homes and libraries can access them and request pages.

Many universities maintain Web servers where students can post their Web sites. When preparing a site for a course, make sure to ask your instructor if the department has server space allocated for your use. If not, you can rent space from an Internet Service Provider (ISP). There are thousands of these firms, and you can search for one that suits your budget on the Web.

As an alternative, you might consider posting your pages on a free Web site hosting service. These services give you space to house your materials free of charge, but they will insert advertising into your pages. Some examples are:

■ http://www.freeservers.com
■ http://geocities.yahoo.com
■ http://www.tripod.lycos.com

Not all servers can support the same Web site features. If your pages contain elements like java applets, animations, video, or sound, make sure to ask a technical support professional if the Web server is appropriate for you.

When you're ready to make your HTML available on the Web, you'll need to transfer the files from your own computer to the server of your choice. You'll do this using File Transfer Protocol, or FTP. Your instructor, or a technical support person at your ISP, can show you how to use an FTP program to move files from one computer to another and where to put them. The process is usually very straightforward, even when the Web server that will receive your files is located halfway across the world!

4 l e   A note for advanced Web developers

The information in this chapter offers a general overview of Web publishing. For a more complete introduction, and tips on creating Web pages with advanced features, consult the following books and Web sites:

Books

HTML 4 for the World Wide Web: Visual QuickStart Guide (2000). This guide by Elizabeth Castro is a wonderful HTML self-help book with easy-to-follow lessons and good illustrations.

Designing Web Graphics.3 (1999). This book by Lynda Weinman is a good resource for Web graphic design and production. It contains many illuminating examples and useful, everyday techniques for creating graphics.

Learning Perl, 3rd edition, by Randal L. Schwartz and Tom Phoenix (2001) is the definitive book for starting to program in CGI with Perl. The book is practical, easy to read, and often very funny.

Web sites

Webmonkey (http://hotwired.lycos.com/webmonkey/) offers tips on Web design and construction with a fun attitude and great examples.

Project Cool (http://www.devx.com/projectcool/developer) is a friendly reference and tutorial site with tips and examples for many new technologies. The site also covers multimedia production issues.

World Wide Web Consortium (http://w3c.org) is a "command center" for the Web, where you will find the official specifications for HTML and related technologies. It is very technically oriented.

42

The Visual Design
of Documents

Your goal in writing is to communicate a particular content. If your content is clear, readers will understand—and your efforts will have succeeded. Everything you have read in this book encourages you to communicate clearly, through words. Here we consider how document design—the use of art, graphics, typeface, and format—can make your content more accessible to readers.

CRITICAL DECISIONS

Designing Documents to Support Content

The design of any document should, above all else, support the content the writer is presenting. Without content, you have no reason for writing, and no amount of flashy design will conceal a lack of content. Therefore, understand your content first. Articulate it as clearly as you can, with words. Then, look to the ways effective design can help you to deliver that content. Remember: *Every design element in a document should help readers to understand the content.*

42a Design elements and the audiences for your documents

When you write papers for your college courses look for design conventions in Appendix A, "Manuscript Form and Preparation," and also in the example student papers for the humanities, social sciences, and sciences in Chapters 38, 39, and 40. There you will find discussions and illustrations of basic visual elements of academic writing:

- Titles—to focus attention on your topic and argument
- Headings—to provide summary organizers for sections of a paper

- Displayed (or "block") quotations—to emphasize key words of others
- Graphs, charts—to synthesize often complex data into visual form

Design elements for nonacademic audiences

42.1

When you address readers in the world of business, government, or technical fields beyond academic settings, it is especially important to make the unity and coherence of your writing accessible, and a well-planned design can help. The following types of documents will benefit from carefully designed visual elements:

- Presentation pieces intending to educate, technically train, or persuade business or government audiences
- Special reports, especially proposals in the science and business worlds
- Promotional, public relations, and marketing pieces
- Newsletters and public information bulletins in print and on electronic media

Readers of these types of documents have many demands on their time. They will first skim articles and reports to determine if there is anything of use to them. Only then will they read sections (if not an entire piece) slowly and carefully. You must therefore try to focus the attention of these readers, capturing their interest so that they will give your document consideration. You can focus attention by using titles, headings, block quotations, and graphs and charts. You can also focus attention in more visually exciting ways.

- Emphatic type—to highlight key words and phrases
- Art and photos—to express information, mood, and ideas
- Layout and use of white space—to ensure a balanced, open look

This chapter can help you look for basic ways to ensure that visual interest and clarity are part of your writing. You also can consult a number of books for detailed help on document design for business and technical communication: K. W. Houp et al., *Reporting Technical Information*, 9th edition, 1998; M. J. Killingsworth, *Information in Action: A Guide to Technical Communication*, 2nd edition, 1999; or P. W. Agnew et al., *Multimedia in the Classroom*, 1996 (all Boston: Allyn & Bacon).

42b   Effective headings and typography emphasize content.

Clearly worded, brief headings will communicate the logic of your document's organization. The combination of clear typeface and carefully worded headings will bring a visual coherence to your work that suggests coherent ideas.

Typeface

A type "face" is the name given to the distinctive design and shape of a family of lettering used for text. A face or design usually includes several "fonts," or lettering of different sizes and styles, including italics or boldface. As a general principle, the fewer the typefaces in one document, the better.

Assigning different typefaces to specific functions

Sometimes, when you need to distinguish one kind of text function from another, a distinctive typeface can be assigned for each function, adding coherence as well as visual interest to a document. As a second principle, when you introduce a different typeface, assign each face a single function.

42.2

The typography of this textbook illustrates the point. Notice that the book has only three typefaces or designs (though it uses different fonts and type sizes). Each clearly signals that a different category of information is being presented.

- You are now reading the regular typeface used for the text.
- When you read the color-printed headings, you see a slightly different, thicker font used only for these emphatic headlines.
- When student writing is shown, as in the papers for Chapters 38 to 40, you see the student text in a very different face (called Courier, seen in typewriters or in e-mail) to show a distinctive kind of writing.

Type size

Your word processor will be able to vary emphasis and readability by expanding or contracting type sizes. These sizes are commonly designated with numbers from as low as 6 or 8 "points" (a typesetter's unit of measure) to 10, 11, or 12, commonly seen for basic text in books or magazines, up to point sizes as large as the 30-, 40-, or even 50-point headings seen in advertising.

If you vary type size in your document, again bear in mind the principle of orderliness. Assign specific type sizes to specific functions. Relative to the size of the standard type size you are using in your document, you may want to assign section headings a larger size and chapter titles an even larger size, while footnotes and index entries might receive a smaller size. You can see several varieties of type sizes in this book, each for a distinct purpose.

Highlighting with boldface, italics, and boxes

Again, the principle of restraint holds: less is usually more. If you want boldfaced, italicized, or boxed words and phrases to receive special emphasis, then use these tools sparingly. Maintain a "base" of plain text that contrasts clearly with any emphatic type, and try to establish a convention for its use. For instance, you could reserve boldfaced words for headings; you could reserve italics for words that are being defined; you could draw a box around material that you consider crucially important. Overuse of these tools will quickly diminish their effectiveness and disorient your readers with a cluttered document.

In this text, italicized words are used only to emphasize important terms, to identify key words in examples, and for conventional usage in titles. Boldface type is restricted to terms that are included in the glossary. Boxed information appears with the stepwise procedures in 38d and the one key principle in this chapter:

> Every design element in a document should help readers to understand the content.

Overall format and heading structure

A coherent overall plan

Plan an overall structure for your document in such a way that its internal logic, and its key points, are quickly communicated to anyone who takes a few minutes to scan the pages. To communicate structure and idea, divide your content into well-connected chunks of varying sizes: major units, sections, subsections, paragraphs. Communicate these chunks of material with format elements such as these:

- Table of contents—For longer, formal presentations, a listing of titles or topics can provide a map and overview of your document's plan. Schematic overviews or charts can also be used—as on the endpapers of this book.
- Unit or chapter titles—Units that begin on new pages will focus attention on the main elements of your presentation.
- Unit or chapter openings—Brief overviewing paragraphs can set out the unit's plan—as typified by the opening of Chapter 29 in this book.
- Section titles—Headings at different levels of emphasis can focus the reader's attention on broad ideas and specifics. (See the next section.)
- Unit summaries—When clearly marked and located at the end of a unit, or possibly at the opening of a chapter and called an "abstract" (see 39b or 40b, c), summary restatements can distill key points.

When you choose format elements for your document, be consistent in structure, heading scheme, and typeface. Readers will understand these visual elements and will come to depend on them as cues to your content.

Headings

Headings—words or brief phrases or sentences—announce the content of your presentation. The wording of headings should forecast the main issues or thesis ideas to come in each section. Here is a check-list of questions to help you to plan a heading scheme:

- How many levels of heads will you use? Consult your outline and try to reduce the number of hierarchical levels to a simple scheme.
- Will you number the heads? Avoid numbering except in complex reference or technical works.
- What typographical emphasis will you give the hierarchy of headings? For each level, make a consistent scheme for distinctive treatment of size, typeface, boldface, italics, or color, with all headings made distinct from your text.
- In addition to heads, will you use software to make "headers" or "footers"—brief identifying phrases that appear at the top or bottom of pages, usually on the line with page numbers?

A warning: When your final document is laid out in pages, survey it to make sure that headings at the bottom of a page are not left alone ("widowed"), but have at least two or three lines of text following. If need be, break pages to run a short page and push the lone heading to the top of a new page.

Itemized lists

Lists, outlines, and bullet points are effective visual tools for concentrating the reader's attention on the content you deem important. For lists and bullet points, bear these considerations in mind:

- List items that you can express in a sentence or two.
- Use a bullet (•), a dash (—), or an asterisk (*) for briefer material that you can express in one or two indented lines.
- Keep listed and bulleted items grammatically parallel. The rules of parallelism for outlining apply especially to lists, and often to a series of headings as well. (See 18e-1, 2.)
- Indent the listed numbers or bullet points to set them off from your text.
- Use bullet points if the order of items is unimportant; otherwise, use numbers.
- For the left margins of lists, either use the list format on your word processor, or else the "hanging indent" form, with second and subsequent lines indented back from the initial word, number, or bullet, and aligned as in this example.

If your list or your bullet points run longer than seven or eight items, consider regrouping material and presenting two lists or sets of bullet points, each with its own heading. As with other formatting elements, it is important to make a consistent plan for functional use of itemized or bulleted lists, avoiding visual confusion from inconsistency or overuse.

Using white space

Too much text on a page tires readers' eyes as they scan the page looking for important information. Some experts on page design (especially for documents intended for nonacademic audiences) suggest that writers devote no more than 60 percent of a page to text. The remainder of the page should consist of graphical elements and white space.

42c Graphic material in reports, presentations, or proposals

Quite aside from the visual variety graphics contribute to a document, flowcharts, tables, charts, graphs, photographs, and art can actually be the clearest and most compact way of delivering information. As with your use of headings and typography to focus a reader's attention, strive in your use of graphics for a simple, consistent, and clean design framed by plenty of white space.

Graphic elements and their functions

Ideally, your use of graphics will complement—but not repeat—the material you've already written. To achieve an effective visual balance in your documents, plan the document's layout in advance. Understand in broad terms the balance you want to achieve between text and graphics. When you do incorporate graphical elements, refer in your text to these elements at the earliest opportunity. Try to not wait until your reader has completed reading your text to present related graphics. Consider using these graphical forms for the following specific purposes:

TO review, preview, emphasize, or prioritize	USE a flowchart, table list, outline list
TO orient readers in terms of space or sequences	USE a chart, diagram, map, photo views
TO show flow of functions or actions	USE a flowchart, diagram, photo
TO add emphasis to key relationships	USE a bar graph, pie chart, simple table
TO analyze or summarize key data	USE a complex graph, table, diagram
TO illustrate original data and sources	USE a facsimile recreating your source
TO help motivate	USE a photo, image, drawing, cartoon

For a detailed look at how to organize and present the types of graphical materials just mentioned, see the following texts: K. W. Houp et al., *Reporting Technical Information*, 9th edition, 1998, Chapter 10, "Graphical Elements," and M. J. Killingsworth, *Information in Action: A Guide to*

Technical Communication, 2nd edition, 1999, Chapter 6, "Developing Purposeful Graphics" (both Boston: Allyn & Bacon).

Tables, charts, graphs

Tables present data that usually show a relationship between at least two sets of varying quantities, listed in columns. To show a table's relationships clearly, each set of quantities in each column or section of data is labeled. The often dense, complex data in tables need simple, direct labels. Any qualifying or complex elements should be explained in footnotes.

Tables are the best vehicle for displaying large blocks of dense quantitative data. When you need a vivid display of critical changes or patterns of relationships in the table, a graph is the next option. Using software packages, you can convert tabular data into line, bar, or circle graphs.

Consider the following examples showing similar material displayed in a line graph, a bar graph, and a circle graph. All three graphs compress a great deal of numerical information into a readily understood visual format. While the graphs show similar material relating to Medicare/Medicaid finances, each type offers a different emphasis and different options for the presentation best suited to your data and the points you wish to emphasize.

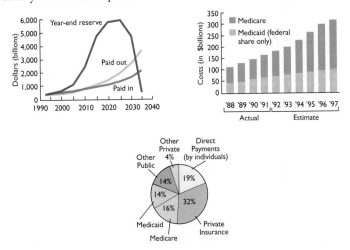

Note that in all three presentations there is a brief label, similar to those for tables, that identifies the significance of the quantities in each dimension of the graph. In constructing line or bar graphs, it is very important to plan the proportions you attach to the vertical and horizontal scale of quantities being displayed. If either dimension appears too short or too long, readers are likely to challenge the relationship you are showing between the graphed quantities, especially if the graph looks steeper or flatter than seems warranted by the data.

Graphic Material in Reports, Presentations, or Proposals   779

A line graph can show complex relationships, trends, and changes over space or time—in this case money paid into and out from federal Medicaid/Medicare funds, with surpluses and projected deficits shown. The scales on both axes of the graph are proportionally chosen to represent the abruptness of change.

When your message consists of simpler, less dense information, consider converting line graphs to bar graphs or pie charts. A bar graph emphasizes simple contrastive relationships among distinct units being compared, rather than the continuous trend relationships of line graphs. A pie chart is good for showing proportional parts of a whole entity—especially percentages.

Diagrams and images

Use diagrams, photographs, and images to help readers focus on your content and to amplify its meaning. For example, this book's "Thinking and Writing Wheel" graphic in Chapter 3 (see particularly 3a and 3b) is a schematic diagram that complements the text in those sections, giving readers a conceptual "map" and overview of a complex process. Use graphical elements with care, positioning them where you think they will best enhance the reader's understanding of your content.

42d Designing newsletters

www
42.3

You may find yourself working in organizations that produce pamphlets, brochures, newsletters, or their electronic cousin—Web pages. For all of these formats, the basic principles from preceding sections for typography, headings, organizing schemes, and graphic elements are even more important than for reports and technical documents. If your job description calls for you to produce these types of documents, the success of which depends heavily on good visual design, then you should consult a specialized book such as J. J. Yopp and K. C. McAdams, *Reaching Audiences: A Guide to Media Writing* (Boston: Allyn & Bacon, 1999).

Newsletters

Organizations of all sorts use newsletters to disseminate information both internally, to employees, and externally, to the public. The newsletter is often presented in an 8½ × 11 inch format that takes advantage of the various design tools discussed in this chapter. One distinctive feature is the newsletter's newspaper-like column width for text, which you see in the example on the next page from the New England office of the Environmental Protection Agency. Notice the use of type style and size, headers, a box, white space, ruled lines of varying thickness, and images to achieve unity, balance, and proportion. Attractively designed, this first page of the newsletter invites readers to continue reading inside.

Fact Sheet/March 2000

Connecticut River

Photo: Steve Delany, CS EPA

www.epa.gov/OWOW/
heritage/rivers.html

The American Heritage Rivers Initiative program was announced by the White House in 1998 as a new program to help communities restore and revitalize waters and waterfronts. Americans will look more in the future to our rivers as a source for improving community life. This initiative will integrate the economic, environmental and historic preservation programs and services of federal agencies to benefit communities in efforts to protect their rivers.

▶ **Connecticut River Navigator Contact**
Dan Burke
(413) 548-9420 ext. 34
burke.dan@epa.gov

▶ **Connecticut River Watershed Council, Inc. Contact**
Whitty Sanford
(413) 529-9500
CRWC@croker.com

⊕EPA
New England Office

Customer Call Center
888-372-7341
www.epa.gov/region1

What Makes the Connecticut River Watershed Special?

▶Watershed encompasses roughly two-thirds of New England. The river is 410 miles long and is the source of 70% of Long Island Sound's fresh water.

▶Land uses: commerce, agriculture and industry, with 80% of the watershed being forested and 11% of the watershed in agricultural use.

▶Ninety-nine cities and towns border the Connecticut River, including Springfield, MA and Hartford, CT.

▶Watershed contains one of the least disturbed tidal marsh systems in the nation and is a key habitat for a wide variety of birds and wildlife.

Why Was The CT River Selected for the American Heritage River Initiative (AHRI)?

▶Nominating communities demonstrated an existing framework to adopt the goals of AHRI. The nomination also received enormous support from over 250 communities and institutions as well as strong state support.

▶One of 124 nominations nationally solicited and one of the 14 rivers ultimately selected by President Clinton.

What is the Long Term Goal?

▶To support community-based efforts to restore and protect the environmental, economic, cultural and historic values of the Connecticut River.

Progress/Goals for the Future

What Partnership Progress Has Been Made?

▶EPA hired the full-time "Navigator" position, Dan Burke. Navigator's role is to help communities identify federal programs and resources to help carry out action plans for the river.

▶In July 1999, an agreement was signed establishing a framework for and demonstrating the commitment of federal, state and local partners.

▶EPA funded a watershed outreach and education project, CT water quality monitoring, restoration of fish passage in CT, nonpoint source/stormwater mangement projects in Hartford, CT area and in 1999 funded $50,000 for sustainable riverbanks and $31,000 for livable communities and smart growth.

What EPA Actions are Planned for 2000?

▶**CSO's:** Work with Interstate CT River Coalition to develop a pilot program for CSO control using watershed-based source reduction controls for stormwater.

▶**Sustainable Riverbanks:** Inventory erosion sites, restore worst sites and establish conservation easements on riverfront properties.

▶**Energy and Recreation:** Participate in relicensing efforts by 2001 of hydroelectric dams on the river.

▶**Hartford Urban Riverfront Revitalization:** Assist in streamlining the permitting process where possible.

▶**Communications:** Contribute to creation of a CT River website.

▶**Issue Report Card:** Provide assistance for an annual CT River report card.

43

Writing in a Business Environment

I n a business environment, much is accomplished based on writing alone. When you enter this environment by writing a letter or memo, you must understand that businesspeople have many demands placed on them simultaneously. When reading, they must know a writer's purpose and they must be given a motivation for continuing to read. Lacking either of these qualities, a document will not represent itself as *important* enough to merit attention, and the reader will simply turn to more pressing concerns.

CRITICAL DECISIONS

Writing Letters and Memos That Succeed

In writing for busy people in the professional world, make sure that your work is direct, concise, and clearly organized. A *direct* letter or memo will state in its opening sentence your purpose for writing. A *concise* letter or memo will state your exact needs in as few words as possible. A *well-organized* letter or memo will present only the information that is pertinent to your main point, in a sequence that is readily understood. Keep this in mind as you plan, draft, and revise.

The writing process in a business environment

Direct, concise, and clearly organized writing takes time, of course, and is seldom the effort of a single draft. Writing a document in a business setting involves a process, just as your writing a research paper in an academic setting involves a process. It may seem counterintuitive, but you will spend less time writing a letter twice (producing both rough and revised drafts) than you will trying to do a creditable job in a single draft. Generally, you will do well to follow the advice in Chapters 3 and

4 on planning, developing, drafting, and revising a paper. For every document that you write, aside from the simplest two- or three-line notes, you should prepare to write, write a draft, and then revise.

43a Standard formats, spacing, and information in a business letter

Standard formats

Use unlined, white bond paper ($8\frac{1}{2} \times 11$ inches) or letterhead stationery for your business correspondence. Prepare your letter on a typewriter or word processor, and print on one side of the page only. Format your letter according to one of three conventions: full block, block, and semi-block—terms describing the ways in which you indent information. The six basic elements of a letter—return address, inside address and date, salutation, body, closing, and abbreviated matter—begin at the left margin in the *full block* format. Displayed information such as lists begins five spaces from the left margin. In the *block* format, the return address and the closing are aligned just beyond the middle of the page, while the inside address, salutation, new paragraphs, and abbreviated matter each begin at the left margin. (See the "Letter of Inquiry" on page 787 for an example of block format.) The *semi-block* format is similar to the block format except that each new paragraph is indented five spaces from the left margin and any displayed information is indented ten spaces. (See the "Letter of Application" on page 789 for an example of a semi-block format.)

43.1

Standard spacing

Maintain a one-inch margin at the top, bottom, and sides of the page. Single-space the document for all but very brief letters (two to five lines), the body of which you should double-space. Skip one or two lines between the return address and the inside address; one line between the inside address and the salutation (which is followed by a colon); one line between the salutation and opening paragraph; one line between paragraphs; one line between your final paragraph and your complimentary closing (which is followed by a comma); four lines between your closing and typewritten name; and one line between your typewritten name and any abbreviated matter.

Standard information

Return address and date

Unless you are writing on letterhead stationery (on which your return address is preprinted), type as a block of information your return address—street address on one line; city, state, and zip code on the next; the date on a third line. If you are writing on letterhead, type the date only, centered one or two lines below the letterhead's final line.

Inside address

Provide as a block of information the full name and address of the person to whom you are writing. Be sure to spell all names—personal, company, and address—correctly. Use abbreviations only if the company abbreviates words in its own name or address.

Salutation

Begin your letter with a formal greeting, traditionally *Dear _____:* Unless another title applies, such as *Dr.* or *Senator,* address a man as *Mr.* and a woman as *Miss* or *Mrs.*—or as *Ms.* if you or the person addressed prefer this. When in doubt about a woman's marital status or preferences in a salutation, use *Ms.* If you are not writing to a specific person, avoid the gender-specific and potentially insulting *Dear Sirs.* Many readers find the generic *Dear Sir or Madam* and *To whom it may concern* to be equivocal, and you may want to open instead with the company name, *Dear Acme Printing,* or with a specific department name or position title: *Dear Personnel Department* or *Dear Personnel Manager.* See the discussion at 31a for the conventions on abbreviating titles in a salutation or an address.

Body of the letter

Develop your letter in paragraph form. State your purpose clearly in the opening paragraph. Avoid giving your letter a visually dense impression. When your content lends itself to displayed treatment (if, for instance, you are presenting a list), indent the information. You may want to use bullets, numbers, or hyphens. (See, for example, the "Letter of Inquiry" on page 787.)

Closing

Close with some complimentary expression such as *Yours truly,* *Sincerely,* or *Sincerely yours.* Capitalize the first word only of this closing remark and follow the remark with a comma. Allow four blank lines for your signature, then type your name and, below that, any title that applies.

Abbreviated matter

Several abbreviations may follow at the left-hand margin, one line below your closing. If someone else has prepared your letter, indicate this as follows: the preparer should capitalize your initials, place a slash, then place his or her initials in lowercase—*LR/bb.* If you are enclosing any material with your letter, type *Enclosure* or *Enc.* If you care to itemize this information, place a colon and align items as in the example letter on page 789. If you are sending copies of the letter to other readers (known as a *secondary audience*), write *cc:* (for *carbon copy*) and list the names of the recipients of the copies, as in the example letter on page 796.

The second page

Begin your letter's second page with identifying information so that if the first and second pages are separated the reader will easily be able to match them again. The blocked information should consist of your name, the date, and the page number presented in a block at the upper left-hand corner of the page.

```
Jon Lipman
February 8, 2002
Page 2

and in the event of your coming to Worcester,
I would be happy to set up an interview with you
here. Perhaps the week of May 17 would be conve-
nient, since I will be traveling to eastern
Massachusetts.
```

Envelope

Single-space all information. If you are not using an envelope with a preprinted return address, type your return address at the upper left-hand corner. Center between the right- and left-hand sides the name and address of the person to whom you are writing. Vertically, type the address just below center.

```
Jon Lipman
231 Gray Street
Worcester, Massachusetts 01610

              Ms. Hannah Marks
              Equipment Design, Inc.
              1254 Glenn Avenue
              Arlington, Massachusetts 02174
```

43b Letters of inquiry

A letter of inquiry (see page 787) is based on a question you want answered. Presumably, you have done enough research to have identified a person knowledgeable in the area concerning you. Do not ask for too much information or for very general information that you could readily find in a library. If you are inquiring about price or product information, simply ask for a brochure.

- Begin the letter with a sentence that identifies your need. State who you are, what your general project is (if the information is pertinent), and the reason for your writing.
- Follow with a sentence devoted to how you have learned of the reader or the reader's company and how this person or company could be of help.
- Pose a few *specific* questions. Frame these questions in such a way that you demonstrate you have done background research.
- State any time constraints you may have. Do not expect your reader to respond any sooner than two or three weeks.
- Close with a brief statement of appreciation. If you feel it would expedite matters, you might include a self-addressed, stamped envelope.

43c Letters of complaint

When you have a problem that you want remedied, write a letter of complaint. No matter how irate you may be, keep a civil but firm tone and do not threaten. If the time comes to take follow-up action, write a second letter in which you repeat your complaint and state your intentions. Your letter of complaint should be clear on the following points:

- Present the problem.
- State when and where you bought the product in question (if this is a consumer complaint). Provide an exact model number. If this is a complaint about poor service or ill treatment, state when and where you encountered the unacceptable behavior.
- Describe precisely the product failure or the way in which a behavior was unsatisfactory.
- Summarize the expectations you had when you bought the product or when you engaged someone's services. State succinctly how your expectations were violated and how you were inconvenienced (or worse).
- State exactly how you want the problem resolved.

Block format: Letter of inquiry

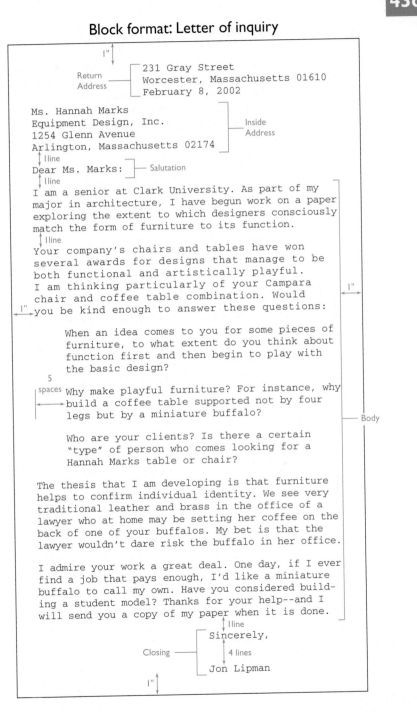

1"

Return Address — 231 Gray Street
Worcester, Massachusetts 01610
February 8, 2002

Ms. Hannah Marks
Equipment Design, Inc. — Inside Address
1254 Glenn Avenue
Arlington, Massachusetts 02174

1 line

Dear Ms. Marks: — Salutation

1 line

I am a senior at Clark University. As part of my major in architecture, I have begun work on a paper exploring the extent to which designers consciously match the form of furniture to its function.

1 line

Your company's chairs and tables have won several awards for designs that manage to be both functional and artistically playful. I am thinking particularly of your Campara chair and coffee table combination. Would you be kind enough to answer these questions: 1"

1"

When an idea comes to you for some pieces of furniture, to what extent do you think about function first and then begin to play with the basic design?

5 spaces

Why make playful furniture? For instance, why build a coffee table supported not by four legs but by a miniature buffalo?   — Body

Who are your clients? Is there a certain "type" of person who comes looking for a Hannah Marks table or chair?

The thesis that I am developing is that furniture helps to confirm individual identity. We see very traditional leather and brass in the office of a lawyer who at home may be setting her coffee on the back of one of your buffalos. My bet is that the lawyer wouldn't dare risk the buffalo in her office.

I admire your work a great deal. One day, if I ever find a job that pays enough, I'd like a miniature buffalo to call my own. Have you considered building a student model? Thanks for your help--and I will send you a copy of my paper when it is done.

1 line

Sincerely,

Closing — 4 lines

Jon Lipman

1"

43d   Letters of application

When seeking employment, whether for summertime work or for a full-time job after graduation, your first move may well be to write a letter of application in which you ask for an interview. A successful letter of application will pique a prospective employer's interest by achieving a delicate balance. On the one hand you will present yourself as a bright, dependable, and resourceful person while on the other you will avoid sounding like an unabashed self-promoter.

As you gather thoughts for writing, think of the employer as someone in need of a person who can be counted on for dependable and steady work, for creative thinking, and for an ability to function as a member of a team. Avoid presenting yourself merely as someone who has a particular set of skills. You are more than this. Skills grow dated as new technologies become available. You want to suggest that your ability to learn and to adapt will never grow dated.

- Keep your letter of application to one typewritten page.
- Open by stating which job you are applying for and where you learned of the job.
- Review your specific skills and work experience that make you well suited for the job.
- Review your more general qualities (in relation to work experience, if appropriate) that make you well suited for the job.
- Express your desire for an interview and note any constraints on your time: exams, jobs, and other commitments. Avoid statements like "you can contact me at_____." You will provide your address and phone number on your résumé.
- Close with a word of appreciation.

When you have written a second draft of your letter, seek out editorial advice from those who have had experience applying for jobs and particularly from those who have been in a position of reading letters of application and setting up interviews. Here are a few questions you can put to your readers: What sort of person does this letter describe? Am I emphasizing my skills and abilities in the right way? How do you feel about the tone of this letter? Am I direct and confident without being pushy? Based on editorial feedback, revise. Proofread two or three times so that your final document is direct, concise, well organized, and letter-perfect with respect to grammar, usage, and punctuation.

Write your letter in a block or semi-block format (see pages 787 and 789) on bond paper. Use paper with at least a twenty-five percent cotton fiber content, which you will find at any stationery store. Use an envelope of matching bond paper.

Semi-block format: Letter of application

231 Gray Street
Worcester, Massachusetts 01610
February 8, 2002

Ms. Hannah Marks
Equipment Design, Inc.
1254 Glenn Avenue
Arlington, Massachusetts 02174

Dear Ms. Marks:

5 spaces ⟶ I would like to apply for the marketing position you advertised in Architectural Digest. As you know from our previous correspondence, I am an architecture major with an interest in furniture design. As part of my course work I took a minor in marketing, with the hope of finding a job similar to the one you have listed.

For the past two summers I have apprenticed myself to a cabinet maker in Berkshire County, Massachusetts. Mr. Hiram Stains is 70 years old and a master at working with cherry and walnut. While I love working in a shop, and have built most of the furniture in my own apartment (see the photographic enclosures), I realize that a craftsman's life is a bit too solitary for me. Ideally, I would like to combine in one job my woodworking skills, my degree in architecture, and my desire to interact with people.

Your job offers precisely this opportunity. I respect your work immensely and am sure I could represent Equipment Design with enthusiasm. Over time, if my suggestions were welcomed, I might also be able to contribute in terms of design ideas.

I would very much like to arrange an interview. Final exams are scheduled for the last week of April. I'll be preparing the week before that, so I'm available for an interview anytime aside from that two-week block. Thank you for your interest, and I hope to hear from you soon.

Sincerely,

Jon Lipman

Jon Lipman

enc.: photographs
writing sample

⎤ Align
⎟ itemized
⎦ enclosures

Weblink

http://leo.stcloudstate.edu/
resumes/index.html

*Hypertext guide to writing a résumé, from
the Write Place at St. Cloud State U.*

A résumé (see page 791) highlights information that you think employers will find useful in considering you for a job. Typically, résumés are written in a clipped form. Although word groups are punctuated as sentences, they are, strictly speaking, fragments. For instance, instead of writing "I supervised fund-raising activities" you would write "Supervised fund-raising activities." Keep these fragments parallel. Keep all verbs in either the present or the past tense; begin all fragments with either verbs or nouns.

Not parallel	Supervised fund-raising activities. Speaker at three area meetings on the "Entrepreneurial Side of the Art World." [The first fragment begins with a verb; the second begins with a noun.]
Parallel	Supervised fund-raising activities. Spoke at three area meetings on the "Entrepreneurial Side of the Art World." [Both fragments begin with a verb in the past tense.]

43.2

A résumé works in tandem with your job application. The letter of application establishes a direct communication between you and your prospective employer. Written in your voice, the letter will suggest intangible elements such as your habits of mind and traits of character that make you an attractive candidate. The résumé, by contrast, works as a summary sheet or catalog of your educational and work experience. The tone of the résumé is neutral and fact oriented. The basic components are these:

- Your name, address, and telephone number—each centered on a separate line at the top of the page.

Provide headings, as follows:

- *Position Desired* or *Objective*. State the specific job you want.
- *Education.* Provide your pertinent college (and graduate school) experience. List degrees earned (or to be earned); major; classes taken, if pertinent; and your grade point average, if you are comfortable sharing this information.
- *Work Experience.* List your jobs, including titles, chronologically, beginning with your most recent job.
- *Related Activities.* List any clubs, volunteer positions, or activities that you feel are indicative of your general interests and character.
- *References.* Provide names and addresses if you expect the employer to contact references directly. If you are keeping references on file at a campus office, state that your references are available upon request.

```
                    Jon Lipman
                  231 Gray Street
          Worcester, Massachusetts 01610
                  508-555-8212


Objective:    Marketing position in an arts-
              related company

Education:    Clark University, Worcester,
              Massachusetts
              Bachelor of Arts in Architecture,
              May 2002
              Minor in Marketing, May 2002
              Grade point average (to date) 3.3/4.0

Work          September 2001-present: Directed
Experience:   marketing campaign for campus-based
              artists' collective and supervised
              fund raising. Spoke at three area
              meetings on the "Entrepreneurial
              Side of the Art World."

              May 2001-August 2001: Studied cabi-
              net making with Hiram Stains, mas-
              ter cabinet-maker in Berkshire
              County, Massachusetts. Applied de-
              sign principles learned in school
              to cabinet construction.

              September 2000-April 2001: Organized
              artists' collective on campus and
              developed marketing plan.

              May 2000-August 2000: Studied cabi-
              net making with Hiram Stains.
              Learned tool use and maintenance.

Related       Supervised set design for theater pro-
Activities:   ductions on campus. Donated services
              as carpenter to local shelter.

References:   Mr. Hiram Stains
              Route 16
              Richmond, Massachusetts 01201

              Ms. Amanda Lopez
              Center Street Shelter
              Worcester, Massachusetts 01610

              Dr. Edward Bing
              Department of Architecture
              Clark University
              Worcester, Massachusetts 01610
```

Principles for Writing an Online Résumé

Increasingly, job applicants are creating résumés for view on the World Wide Web, where the résumé is one hyperlink on the applicant's home page. While the goal of any résumé is to introduce the applicant in a favorable light, Web-based résumés differ from traditional paper résumés in important ways. Most of these differences, you'll find, will work to your advantage. Some tips:

43.3

1. Adhere to basic strategies and design principles for creating Web sites. See Chapter 41 for advice.

2. Include links to your work. Whether you have posted writing samples or other efforts online, here is a superb opportunity to showcase your work. Add hyperlinks within the body of your résumé, or create a special links area.

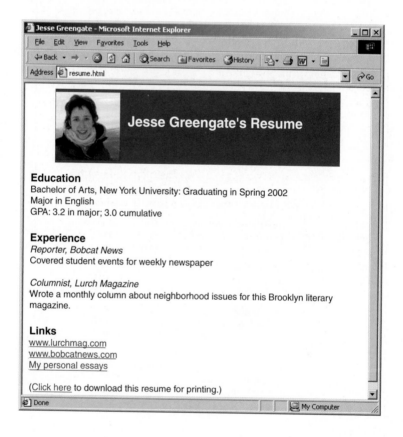

3. Because readers may not have the patience to click through multiple pages on the Web, try to keep your key information—contact information, education, and work experience—well organized and on one page.

4. Place the most important items of your résumé in the topmost 300 pixels of the screen—the area that every Web user should be able to read without scrolling down the page. It is the area of highest impact.

5. Include an e-mail link on the page (if you are comfortable doing so). A reason not to do so: anyone who finds your page, including advertisers, can use your e-mail address.

6. Incorporate relevant graphics into your résumé: showcase projects (such as artwork) with scanned photographs or images from a digital camera.

7. Give your page an informative title, such as "Marie Hobahn's Résumé," so that users who bookmark it will recognize that this is your résumé.

8. Include the date that you have most recently updated the page. Users will want to know that your résumé is current.

9. **The Scannable Résumé:** Provide a non-Web version of your résumé in downloadable form for readers who want to print the résumé or scan it into a résumé database. (You might, at an employer's request, attach a scannable résumé to an e-mail message.) Prepare a résumé for scanning as follows:

   ■ Eliminate design elements: avoid boldface and italics; remove photos and hyperlinks; remove boxes, underlining, and tab spaces; run text flush to the left margin.

   ■ Use a standard typeface (such as Times Roman), with a 12-point font.

   ■ Use standard résumé headings, including Education, Work Experience, References.

   ■ Separate categories of information with one line of white space.

   ■ Add a "keywords" section (after your contact information) with nouns that represent your achievements: for example, biology major, student representative, field hockey player, hospice volunteer, dean's list member. Make sure to use the individual keywords throughout the résumé, so that database search engines will produce your name when a prospective employer searches on a particular keyword.

   ■ See the example scannable résumé on page 794.

Scannable résumé

Jon Lipman
231 Gray Street
Worcester, Massachusetts 01610
Phone: (508) 555-8212
E-mail: jonl@clark.edu

Keywords: architecture, marketing, fund raising,
wood working, speaker, project organizer, leader,
set design

Objective
Marketing position in an arts-related company

Education
Clark University, Worcester, Massachusetts
B.A. in Architecture, May 2002
Minor in Marketing, May 2002
Grade point average: 3.3/4.0

Work Experience
September 2001-present: Directed marketing campaign
for campus-based artists' collective and supervised
fund raising. Spoke at three area meetings on the
"Entrepreneurial Side of the Art World." Generated
community interest in the work of campus artists by
organizing a fair and a direct mail campaign.

43f Memoranda

Memoranda, or memos, are internal documents written from one employee to another in the same company to announce or summarize a meeting, set a schedule, request information, define and resolve a problem, argue for funding, build consensus, and so on. Because they are written "in-house," memos tend to be less formal in tone than business letters. Still, they must be every bit as direct, concise, and well organized, or readers will ignore them. When writing a memo longer than a few lines, follow the process discussed earlier of preparing to write, writing, and revising. A memo will differ from a business letter in the following ways:

- The memo has no return address, no inside address, and no salutation. Instead, the memo begins with this information:

    (Date)
    To:
    From:
    Subject:

- The memo follows a full block format, with all information placed flush to the left margin.
- The memo is often divided into headings that separate the document into readily distinguished parts.
- Portions of the memo are often displayed—that is, set off and indented when there are lists or other information lending itself to such treatment.
- Some companies highlight the information about distribution of memo copies to others, either placing the *cc:* line under the *To:* line or adding a subsection titled *Distribution:* with the opening section.

If your memo is three-quarters of a page or longer, consider highlighting its organization with headings, as in the example memo on page 796. Headings work in tandem with the memo's subject line and first sentence to give readers the ability to scan the memo and quickly—within thirty seconds—understand your message. Once again, realize that your readers are busy. They will appreciate any attempt to make their job of reading easier.

February 14, 2002

TO: Linda Cohen

FROM: Matthew Franks

SUBJECT: Brochure production schedule

Thanks for helping to resolve the production schedule for our new brochure. Please review the following production and distribution dates. By return memo, confirm that you will commit your department to meeting this schedule.

Production dates

Feb. 19	2002	First draft of brochure copy
March 1	2002	First draft of design plans
March 8	2002	Second draft of brochure copy and design
March 15	2002	Review of final draft and design
March 17	2002	Brochure to printer

Distribution dates

April 4	2002	First printing of 10,000 in our warehouse
April 11	2002	Mailing to Zone 1
April 14	2002	Mailing to Zone 2
April 17	2002	Mailing to Zones 3 and 4

Please let me hear from you by this Friday. If I haven't, I'll assume your agreement and commitment. It looks as though we'll have a good brochure this year. Thanks for all your help.

cc: Amy Hanson

CHAPTER 44

Writing Essay Exams

Increasingly, professors across the curriculum are using essay exams to test student mastery of important concepts and relationships. A carefully conceived exam will challenge you not only to recall and organize what you know of a subject but also to extend and apply your knowledge.

CRITICAL DECISIONS

Selecting What to Include in Essay Exams

Essay exams will require of you numerous responses. But the one response to *avoid* is the so-called information dump in which at first glimpse of a topic you begin pouring onto the page *everything* you have ever read or heard about it. A good answer to an essay exam question requires that you be selective in choosing the information you discuss. What you say about that information and what relationships you make with it are critical. As is often the case with good writing, less tends to be more—provided that you adopt and follow a strategy.

44a A strategy for taking essay exams

Prepare

Ideally, you will have read your textbooks and assigned articles with care *as* they were assigned during the period prior to the exam. If you

Weblink

http://owl.english.purdue.edu/
handouts/general/gl_essay.html

Overview, with discussion and examples, of techniques for writing an essay exam, from the Purdue Online Writing Lab.

have read closely, or "critically" (see 1e–h), your preparation for an exam will amount to a *review* of material you have already thought carefully about. Skim assigned materials and pay close attention to notes you have made in the margins or have recorded in a reading log. Take new notes based on your original notes: highlight important concepts from each assignment. Then reorganize your notes according to key ideas that you think serve as themes or focus points for your course.

List each idea separately, and beneath each, list any reading that comments on or provides information about that idea. In an American literature course this idea might be "innocence lost." In a sociology course the idea might be "social constructions of identity."

Turn next to your class notes (you may want to do this *before* reviewing your reading assignments), and add information and comments to your lists of key ideas. Study these lists. Develop statements about each idea that you could, if asked, support with references to specific information. Try to anticipate your instructor's questions.

Read the entire exam before beginning to write.

44.1 Allot yourself a certain number of minutes to answer each essay question, allowing extra time for the more complex questions. As you write, monitor your use of time.

Adopt a discipline-appropriate perspective.

Essay exams are designed in part to see how well you understand particular ways of thinking in a discipline. If you are writing a mid-term exam in chemistry, for instance, appreciate that your professor will expect you to discuss material from a chemist's perspective. That is, you will need to demonstrate not only that you know your information but also that you can *do* things with it: namely, think and reach conclusions in discipline-appropriate ways.

Adapt the writing process according to the time allotted for a question.

Assuming that you have thirty minutes to answer an essay question, spend at least five minutes of this allotted time in plotting an answer.

- Locate the assignment's key verb and identify your specific tasks in writing. (See the box on pages 799–800.)
- Given these tasks, list information you can draw on in developing your answer.
- Examine the information you have listed and develop a thesis (see 3d), a statement that directly answers the question and that demonstrates your understanding and application of some key concept associated with the essay topic.
- Sketch an outline of your answer listing the major points you will develop in support of your thesis and in what order.

Spend twenty minutes of your allotted time on writing your answer. When you begin writing, be conscious of making clear, logical connections between sentences and paragraphs. Well-chosen transitions (see

5d-3) not only will help your instructor follow your discussion but also will help you to project your ideas forward and to continue writing. As you do in formal papers, develop your essay in sections, with each section organized by a section thesis (see 5a). Develop each section of your essay by discussing *specific* information.

Save five minutes to reread your work and ensure that its logic is clear and that you address the exam question from a discipline-appropriate point of view. Given the time constraints of the essay exam format, instructors understand that you will not submit a polished draft. Nevertheless, they will expect writing that faces the question and that is coherent, unified, and grammatical.

44b The importance of verbs in an essay question

In reading an essay assignment, you can often identify exactly what an instructor expects by locating a key verb in the assignment such as *illustrate, discuss,* or *compare.* Following is a guide to students on "Important Word Meanings" in assignments. Developed by the History Department at UCLA, this guide was intended to help students develop effective responses to essay questions.

Important Word Meanings in Essay Assignments

Good answers to essay questions depend in part upon a clear understanding of the meanings of the important directive words. These are the words such as *explain, compare, contrast,* and *justify,* which indicate the way in which the material is to be presented. Background knowledge of the subject matter is essential. But mere evidence of this knowledge is not enough. If you are asked to *compare* the British and American secondary school systems, you will get little or no credit if you merely *describe* them. If you are asked to *criticize* the present electoral system, you are not answering the question if you merely *explain* how it operates. A paper is satisfactory only if it answers directly the question that was asked.

The words that follow are frequently used in essay examinations:

summarize	sum up; give the main points briefly. *Summarize the ways in which humans preserve food.*
evaluate	give the good points and the bad ones; appraise; give an opinion regarding the value of; talk over the advantages and limitations. *Evaluate the contributions of teaching machines.*

(continued)

Important Word Meanings in Essay Assignments (continued)

contrast | bring out the points of difference. *Contrast the novels of Jane Austen and William Makepeace Thackeray.*

explain | make clear; interpret; make plain; tell "how" to do; tell the meaning of. *Explain how humans can, at times, trigger a full-scale rainstorm.*

describe | give an account of; tell about; give a word picture of. *Describe the Pyramids of Giza.*

define | give the meaning of a word or concept; place it in the class to which it belongs and set it off from other items in the same class. *Define the term "archetype."*

compare | bring out points of similarity and points of difference. *Compare the legislative branches of the state government and the national government.*

discuss | talk over; consider from various points of view; present the different sides of. *Discuss the use of pesticides in controlling mosquitoes.*

criticize | state your opinion of the correctness or merits of an item or issue; criticism may approve or disapprove. *Criticize the increasing use of alcohol.*

justify | show good reasons for; give your evidence; present facts to support your position. *Justify the American entry into World War II.*

trace | follow the course of; follow the trail of; give a description of progress. *Trace the development of television in school instruction.*

interpret | make plain; give the meaning of; give your thinking about; translate. *Interpret the poetic line, "The sound of a cobweb snapping is the noise of my life."*

prove | establish the truth of something by giving factual evidence or logical reasons. *Prove that in a full-employment economy, a society can get more of one product only by giving up another product.*

illustrate | use a word picture, a diagram, a chart, or a concrete example to clarify a point. *Illustrate the use of catapults in the amphibious warfare of Alexander.*

Source: Andrew Moss and Carol Holder, *Improving Student Writing: A Guide for Faculty in All Disciplines* (Dubuque, IA: Kendall/Hunt, 1988) 17–18.

CHAPTER 45

Making
Oral Presentations

In the classroom and in other settings, you have probably already had the experience of listening to speakers who give effective oral presentations as well as to those who do not. Effective oral presentations are clearly organized, easy to follow in terms of transitions and verbal cues, and delivered articulately and dynamically. They include helpful visuals, if necessary, to emphasize or explain key points. Both in your college courses and later, as a working professional, you will likely be called upon to make effective oral presentations. This chapter provides advice for doing so.

CRITICAL DECISIONS

Considering Audience and Purpose

Thinking about your audience and your purpose is a key component in preparing and delivering oral presentations. Solid preparation will help you connect with your audience and achieve your purpose. Pose these questions to help define your audience and anticipate their needs:

■ How can you introduce your topic so as to spark your audience's immediate interest?

■ What verbal cues will help your audience follow the thread of your ideas?

■ What can you use to focus your audience's attention and enhance their understanding?

■ How can you conclude so that your audience comes away satisfied?

■ If your purpose is to persuade, what style should you adopt—in both your text and your delivery—to best achieve this goal?

45a Planning oral presentations

1 Drafting

Some experienced public speakers can effectively make an oral presentation based only on an outline and some notes. For most speakers, however, an oral presentation should be drafted and revised in detail just as an essay is (see Chapters 3 and 4). You'll need to—

- determine or focus your topic;
- brainstorm or use other techniques to generate ideas;
- do research, if required;
- develop a thesis and, perhaps, a tentative outline;
- compose a draft to use as a starting point.

Understand the needs of listeners (vs. readers).

As you are drafting, keep in mind that listeners, unlike readers, cannot go back to review what you said if they become confused. For this reason, even more so than in writing, you should begin each section of your presentation clearly. Introductory remarks such as "The first point I'd like to make . . ." or "Let me move on to my second point . . ." are generally unnecessary, even awkward, in written work, as can be introductory questions such as "Why is this important?" In oral presentations, however, such verbal cues marking the development of your talk can help enhance your listeners' understanding. Of course, you need not rely exclusively on such formulaic expressions, but you do need to make sure that each section begins in a way that listeners won't miss the transition.

The same is true of section conclusions, which should clearly summarize the points made in that section. One age-old bit of advice for public speakers is "Tell the audience what you're going to say, say it, and then tell them what you've said." Again, while this advice may be overly formulaic, it does suggest the essential need for public speakers to adapt to the special needs of listeners.

Carefully organize the presentation.

Oral presentations also need a very clear organizational structure—from least important point to most important, chronological order, problem-solution order, and so forth. In addition, oral presentations benefit from balanced sentence constructions that listeners find easy to follow (see Chapter 18).

2 Revising

Your first step in revising a draft of an oral presentation should be to read it out loud as though you were delivering it for an audience. Watch for problems of delivery:

- If you have to pause within a sentence to catch your breath, then that sentence is likely too long for readers to follow. Revise to shorten, or express the idea in more than one sentence.
- If you verbally stumble while reading your presentation, your sentence structure may be too complex or your word choice too elevated to seem natural as speech. Again, revise to simplify and shorten.

The goal in oral presentations is to express your ideas so that listeners can follow and understand every word. Stylistic complexity that may be appropriate for a reading audience can cause a listening audience to miss crucial points.

In terms of content, however, revising a draft of an oral presentation is much the same as revising a draft of an essay to be read. See Chapter 4 and in particular the box "Strategies for Early Revision" on page 98.

| 3 | Refining your introduction and conclusion |

Introduction: Capture your audience's imagination.

Unlike a reading audience, a listening audience is often captive, so **45.1** you want to assure them right away that what you will be speaking about is going to interest them—or at least that your presentation will make them interested in the topic. You can immediately involve your audience in a variety of ways:

- Offer a fact that your audience will find surprising.
- Present an intriguing question.
- Persuade or amuse the audience with an appropriate anecdote.
- Refer to the audience's own self-interest.

Then you should go on to clearly establish the main point you plan to make and briefly note how you are going to develop that point. Such forecasting helps listeners better follow your organization. In general, keep your introduction relatively brief—no more than three minutes for a fifteen-minute presentation.

Conclusion: Make it memorable.

When working on your conclusion, think carefully about what you want your audience to take away from your presentation:

- Reiterate key points, but in a way that brings them to life and makes them concrete and meaningful.
- Conclude in a way that will strengthen your case, not simply restate it.
- Consider referring back to an important point made in your introduction.
- Signal that you are about to conclude.

Most public speaking experts advise against leading off with the phrase "In conclusion" because audience members tend to stop listening once they hear it. But a question like "What does all this suggest?" or a cue such as "What all this shows is that . . ." can effectively serve to indicate you are leading up to your conclusion.

4 Preparing graphics and visual aids

Use visual aids to support the text of your presentation, not to substitute for it or overwhelm it. Remember that using visual aids requires careful preparation and extra rehearsal time. Consider a range of aids:

- Prepare handouts for your audience.
- In advance of your talk, make notes on a chalkboard.
- Create posters or flip-chart pages containing visual information (but be sure to have an easel or a place to tape the pages).
- Transfer visual material onto transparencies for use with an overhead projector.
- Use slides (prepared yourself or obtained from a library or commercial service).
- Use software programs, such as PowerPoint, to manipulate images and text that you can then project.

Whatever aids you choose, make sure that they are large enough for everyone to see. There is no better way to frustrate audience members than to make references to images they don't have access to.

Academic versus business presentations

Business presentations often incorporate visual aids that repeat words from the text of the speech in order to reinforce key points or to motivate the audience. In academic settings, visuals made up only of words from your text are not generally as useful, unless you are actually teaching a class. Unless you have good reasons to do otherwise, in academic settings limit your use of visual aids to tables, graphs, pictures, and so forth that make verbal information easier to understand in visual form. For example, a presentation on the distribution of your school's tuition receipts would be enhanced by pie charts and other such graphics. A presentation on the work of a particular artist or on the phases of the moon would clearly benefit from representative visual images.

Don't feel that you must include visual aids unless your topic truly calls for them (or unless they are required by your instructor). Well used, visual aids are an invaluable tool for aiding an audience's understanding. Poorly designed or used, they can undermine a presentation.

See 42c for advice on creating visual aids.

Present from full text.

You may choose to rehearse—and to deliver your final presentation—from a complete copy of your text that you have highlighted to prompt you on which words to emphasize and where to pause. Rehearse sufficiently to become familiar with your material so that you do not simply read it. To keep yourself on track throughout the presentation, look down at your text only occasionally.

Present from notes.

You might also summarize or outline the text of your presentation on notecards and rehearse and deliver your presentation without worrying about sticking to the exact wording of the full written text. As you rehearse, though, do not punctuate your presentation with filler words such as "you know" and "like" and with verbal pauses ("uuh"), which can annoy listeners.

Monitor your pitch, tone, and gestures.

Think carefully about varying the pitch and tone of your voice. Avoid delivering your presentation in an unvarying monotone. Also think about gestures, and try to integrate these naturally into your verbal presentation.

Get feedback.

If possible, ask a friend to listen to your presentation and make comments. You might also consider taping or videotaping yourself delivering the presentation. (Even though many people cringe at hearing their own voice on tape, disregard those feelings. Concentrate on your effectiveness in delivering your presentation.)

Finally, be sure to practice with all your visual aids. Monitor the length of your presentation to make sure it is within any assigned time limits.

45b   Delivering oral presentations

1   Preparing

- Briefly check your script or notes in advance, making sure that your pages or cards are in the correct order.
- Also check that any posters or slides are right side up and in the proper order. If you are using any electronic equipment, be sure that it is in working order and that you can easily plug it into a wall outlet.

2   Dealing with nervousness

- Be prepared, but realize that even the best-prepared speakers may feel some nervousness.
- Relax and breathe deeply. Stretch your neck and shoulders. Shake out your hands. If possible, take a short walk to relieve nervous energy.
- Think positively. In most situations, you will be facing a supportive or, at least, neutral audience, not a hostile one.
- Be confident, knowing you have something interesting to say to your audience.

45.2

3   Making the presentation

- Set up any visual aids, if you have not been able to do so in advance. Distribute any handouts, giving audience members a moment to look at them so they won't miss the beginning of your presentation.
- Get in place, and take a moment to gather your thoughts.
- Make eye contact at a point near the back of the audience, and open your presentation in a clear, firm voice loud enough to reach the entire audience. When gesturing toward visual aids, be sure not to turn your back on the audience.
- At your conclusion, survey the audience briefly. Say "Thank you." But do *not* say, "That's it." Carefully retrieve any visual aids, and exit the speaking area at a relaxed pace.

CHAPTER

46

Using English Nouns, Pronouns, and Articles

The next three chapters are designed to supplement the rest of the *Handbook*. They provide basic information on structural and idiomatic features of the English language that students from an English as a Second Language (ESL) background may need for reference.

These chapters assume that ESL students are now working in a basic English composition course alongside native speakers, and that they have already completed a college-level course of instruction (or its equivalent) in using English as a Second Language. The role of this material is not to provide primary ESL instruction but to give students help in three ways: (1) to identify key topics and problems that persistently cause difficulties for ESL students from many different backgrounds; (2) to propose standard usage guidelines and remedies for such problems (with the assistance of exercises); and (3) to refer ESL students to sections of Chapters 1–45 that will give particular help with difficult language and usage issues in English. Students should also notice that Chapters 7–33 have been furnished with topical "ESL Note" references, which briefly describe key issues and refer readers to pertinent sections of these supplementary chapters.

The following chapters cover topics in the three functional areas of English language usage: Chapter 46—nouns and noun-related structures (including articles and determiners); Chapter 47—verbs, verbals, and related structures (including particles with phrasal verbs); and Chapter 48—usage for modifiers and modifying structures. Prepositions—perhaps the most troublesome feature of English—are treated in connection with the structures that determine them in each chapter of this part. (Prepositions determined by nouns are discussed in 46c; those determined by phrasal verbs are discussed in 47f; and those governed by adjectives are discussed in 48b.)

Using the different classes of English nouns

English nouns name things, abstractions, or people that are considered either countable or not countable in English. English also distinguishes whether a noun names a person or thing that is specific, or something that is generic.

I   Identifying and using count nouns

In English, **count nouns** name things or people that are considered countable. They identify one of many possible individuals or things in the category named. Count nouns have three important characteristics.

- Singular count nouns can be preceded by *one,* or by *a/an*—the indefinite articles that convey the meaning "one (of many)."

  one car   a rowboat   a truck   an ambulance

  Singular count nouns can also be preceded by demonstrative pronouns *(this, that),* by possessive pronouns *(my, your, their),* and often by the definite article *(the).*

- Plural count nouns can be preceded by expressions of quantity *(two, three, some, many, a few)* and can use a plural form.

  two cars   some rowboats   many trucks   a few ambulances

- A count noun used as a singular or plural subject must agree with a singular or plural verb form.

  This *car stops* quickly. [A singular subject and verb agree.]

  Other *cars stop* slowly. [A plural subject and verb agree.]

  (See 10a for guidelines on subject–verb agreement.)

2   Forming plurals with count nouns

Plural count nouns are either regular or irregular. Regular nouns form the plural with *-s* or *-es.* Irregular plural forms—such as *man/men, tooth/teeth, wolf/wolves, medium/media*—follow the models shown in 23e. (See rules for plural forms in 10a and in the spelling sections in 23e-1, 3, and 5.)

3   Identifying and using noncount (mass) nouns

In English, **noncount (mass) nouns** name things that are being considered as a whole, undivided group of items not being counted. Noncount (mass) nouns name various kinds of individuals or things that are considered as group categories in English, such as these:

    Using English Nouns, Pronouns, and Articles

abstractions: courage, grammar
fields of activity: chemistry, tennis
natural phenomena: weather, dew, rain
whole groups of objects: rice, sand, oxygen, wood, oil

Objects that are considered too numerous or shapeless to count are often treated as noncount nouns, as with the word *rock* in this sentence.

We mined dense rock in this mountain.

As such objects become individually identifiable, the same word may be used as a count noun.

Four *rocks* fell across the road.

Some nouns name things that can be considered either countable or noncountable in English, depending on whether they name something specific or something generic.

Countable (and specific)	A *chicken* or two ran off.
	A *straw* or two flew up.
Noncountable (and generic)	*Chicken* should be cooked well.
	Straw can be very dry.

Nouns that name generalized or generic things often occur in noncountable form, but may also occur in singular form in scientific usage (see 46a-5).

Three characteristics distinguish noncount (mass) nouns:

■ Noncount nouns never use the indefinite article *a/an* (or *one*). (Articles are discussed in detail in 46b.)
■ Noncount nouns are never used in a plural form.
■ Noncount nouns always take singular verbs. (See 10a for guidelines on subject–verb agreement.)

46.1

4	Using expressions of quantity with count and noncount nouns

Expressions of quantity—such as *many, few, much, little, some,* and *plenty*—are typically used to modify nouns. Some expressions are used to quantify count nouns; some are used with noncount nouns; and others are used with both kinds of nouns.

Count nouns	Noncount nouns	Both count and noncount nouns
many potatoes	*much* rice	*lots of* potatoes and rice
few potatoes	*little* rice	*plenty of* potatoes and rice
		some, any potatoes and rice

When the context is very clear, these expressions can also be used alone as pronouns.

Do you have *any* potatoes or rice?

I have *plenty* if you need *some.*

<h2>5   Using nouns in specific and generic senses</h2>

English nouns show differences in usage between nouns that name specific things or people and nouns that name generalized or generic things.

A definite noun	The whale migrated thousands of miles.
	The whales migrated thousands of miles. [When a noun names something very specific, either singular or plural, it is preceded by the **definite article** (or by demonstrative pronouns *this/that*).]
An indefinite noun	A whale surfaced nearby; then several whales surfaced. [When a noun names something indefinite but countable, the **indefinite article** is used.]
Generic usage	Whales are migratory animals.
	A whale is a migratory animal. [When the reference is to a general group, nouns often use either the **plural with no article** or the **singular with an indefinite article.**]
Scientific usage	The whale is a migratory animal.
	Whales are migratory animals. [A generic noun may also be singular or plural with a definite article (see 46b-2).]

<h2>6   Distinguishing pronouns in specific and indefinite or generic uses</h2>

Most pronouns, including personal pronouns, rename and refer to a noun located elsewhere that names a specific individual or thing. However, indefinite pronouns, such as *some, any, one, someone,* or *anyone,* may refer to a noun in an indefinite or generic sense.

Personal pronoun	Where are my pencils? I need *them.* [Meaning: I need specific pencils that are mine.]
Indefinite pronoun	Where are my pencils? I need *some.* [Meaning: I need generic, indefinable pencils; I will use any I can find.]

(The list in 7a-7 gives terms that describe various classes of pronouns.)

46b   Using articles with nouns

Articles are the most important class of words used in English to show whether nouns are being used as count or noncount nouns, or as specific or generic nouns. There are three articles in English: *a*, *an*, and *the*. *Some*, the indefinite pronoun, is occasionally used as if it were an indefinite article.

I   Nouns sometimes take the indefinite articles *a* and *an*.

Weblink

http://leo.stcloudstate.edu/
grammar/useartic.html

The Use and Nonuse of Articles, from LEO: Literacy Education Online.

The indefinite articles *a* and *an* are grammatically the same. They are singular indefinite articles that mean "one (of many)," and they are used only with singular count nouns. Pronunciation determines which to use. *A* precedes a noun beginning with a consonant or a consonant sound (a bottle, a hotel, a youth, a user, a xylophone). *An* precedes a noun beginning with a vowel or vowel sound (an egg, an hour, an undertaker).

A is sometimes used with the quantifiers *little* and *few*. Note the differences in the following examples.

Example	Meaning
a little, a few	a small amount of something
a few onions	
a little oil	
little, few	a less-than-expected amount of something
few onions	
little oil	

A and *an* are rarely used with proper nouns, which usually identify a unique individual rather than one of many. The indefinite article occasionally appears with a proper noun in a hypothetical statement about one of many possible persons or things in the category named, as in this sentence.

> Dr. King dreamed of *an America* where children of all colors would grow up in harmony. [We may dream of more than one possible "America."]

---

2   Nouns sometimes take the definite article *the*.

Use *the* with specific singular and plural count nouns and with noncount nouns.

Specific nouns

I need *the tool* and *the rivets*. [one singular and one plural noun]

I need *the equipment*. [a noncount noun]

I need *the tool* on *the top shelf*.
I need *the tools* that are painted orange.
I need *the smallest tool* on *that shelf*.

[Note the modifiers, clauses, and phrases that make the nouns specific.]

Generic nouns

I need tools for that work. [In this case, no article is used.]

(For varieties of usage with generic nouns, see 46a-5.)

Use *the* in a context where a noun has previously been mentioned, or where the writer and the reader both know the particular thing or person being referred to.

I saw a giraffe at the zoo. *The giraffe* was eating leaves from a tree.

I stopped at an intersection. When *the light* turned green, I started to leave. [The sentence assumes the existence of a particular traffic light at the intersection.]

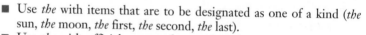

Other uses of the definite article

46.2

- Use *the* with items that are to be designated as one of a kind (*the* sun, *the* moon, *the* first, *the* second, *the* last).
- Use *the* with official names of countries when it is needed to give specific meaning to nouns such as *union, kingdom, state(s), republic, duchy,* and so on (*the* United States, *the* Republic of Cyprus, *the* Hashemite Kingdom of Jordan). No article is needed with certain other countries (Cyprus, Jordan, Japan, El Salvador).
- Use *the* when a noun identifies institutions or generic activities *other than sports*, and in certain usages for generic groups (see 46a-5).

  We called *the* newspapers, *the* radio, and *the* news services.

  Sergei plays *the* piano, *the* flute, and *the* guitar.

  The whales are migratory animals.   *The* birds have feathers.

  Without an article   Nadia plays basketball, hockey, and volleyball.

- Use *the* with names of oceans, seas, rivers, and deserts.

  the Pacific   *the* Amazon   *the* Himalayas   *the* Sahara

  Without an article   Lake Michigan   Mt. Fuji

- Use *the* to give specific meaning to expressions using the noun *language*, but not for the proper name of a language by itself.

  He studied the Sanskrit language, not the Urdu language.

  Without an article   He studied Sanskrit, not Urdu.

■ Use *the* with names of colleges and universities containing *of.*

He studied at *the* University *of* Michigan.

Without an article (typically) He studied at Michigan State University.

3	Nouns sometimes take no article.

Typically no article is needed with names of unique individuals, because they do not need to be made specific and they are not usually counted as one among many. In addition, nouns naming generalized persons or things in a generic usage commonly use no article:

Managers often work long hours.

Whales are migratory animals.

(See 46a-5.)

Some situations in which no article is used are shown in 46b-2. Here are some others.

■ Use no article with proper names of continents, states, cities, and streets, and with religious place names.

Europe   Alaska   New York   Main Street   heaven   hell

■ Use no article with titles of officials when accompanied by personal names; the title effectively becomes part of the proper noun.

President Truman   King Juan Carlos   Emperor Napoleon

■ Use no article with fields of study.

Ali studied literature.   Juan studied engineering.

■ Use no article with names of diseases.

He has cancer.   AIDS is a very serious disease.

■ Use no article with names of magazines and periodicals, unless the article is part of the formal title.

Life   *Popular Science*   *Sports Illustrated*

BUT: *The New Yorker* [The article is part of the proper name.]

46c	Using nouns with prepositions

Some of the complex forms of prepositions in English are determined by their use with nouns. Nouns that follow prepositions are called **objects of prepositions** (see 7a-8 and 8b-1); this grouping forms a modifying **prepositional phrase** (7d-1). The distinctive function of such modifying phrases often determines which preposition to choose in an English sentence.

1 Using the preposition *of* to show possession

The preposition *of* is often widely used to show possession as an alternative to the possessive case form (*I hear a man's voice. I hear the voice of a man*). It is also widely used to show possession for many nouns that do not usually take a possessive form. For example, many inanimate nouns, as well as some nouns naming a large group of people (*crowd, mob, company*) or a location (*place, center*), are not typically used with a possessive case form, and are likely to show possession with the preposition *of.*

Faulty   I washed the *car's hood.*
Correct   I washed the *hood of her car.*

Faulty   *The Information Center's* location is unknown.
Correct   The location *of the Information Center* is unknown.

The preposition *of* is not used with proper nouns.

Faulty   I washed the *car of Luisa.*
Correct   I washed *Luisa's car.*

2 Using prepositions in phrases with nouns or pronouns

The distinctive function of a modifying prepositional phrase often determines which preposition to choose in an English sentence. Here are a few typical functions for prepositional phrases, with distinctive prepositions in use.

Function	Preposition	Example/Explanation
Passive voice (9g)	*by* the cook	He was insulted *by* the cook.
	with a snowball	I was hit *with* a snowball.
Time expressions	*on* January 1	use for specific dates
	on Sundays	use for specific days
	in January	use for months
	in 1984	use for years
	in spring	use for seasons
	at noon, *at* 5 P.M.	use for specific times
	by noon, *by* 5 P.M.	use to indicate *before* a specific hour
	by April 15	use to indicate *before* a specific date
Locations	*at* 301 South Street	use for an address
	in the house	
	on the floor	

Directions *onto* the floor
           beside the library
           through the window
           into the air

For information on verbs with prepositions, see 47f; for information on adjectives with prepositions, see 48b.

EXERCISE 1

Complete the following sentences with *a, an, the,* or *some,* or write *X* for no article.

www

46.3

1. Please pass me _____ butter. I usually eat _____ bread with lunch.
2. Today we watched _____ police officer arguing with _____ driver. _____ driver didn't understand _____ English.
3. You need _____ furniture. You should buy _____ chair and borrow _____ round green table in my house.

Choose the correct form.

1. He admired (Sam's motorcycle/the motorcycle of Sam), which stood in the (driveway's center/center of the driveway).
2. Meet me (on/in/at) March 15 (on/at) the theater (on/in/at) six o'clock.

CHAPTER 47

Using English Verbs

47a Distinguishing different types of verbs and verb constructions

Weblink

http://vwebl.hiway.co.uk/ei/
intro.html

The English Institute's Preliminary Grammar Book *has an extensive discussion with examples of English verbs, aimed at second-language speakers.*

A verb, the main word in the predicate of an English sentence, asserts the action undertaken by the subject or else the condition in which the subject exists. The four types of verbs include transitive verbs (which take direct objects), intransitive verbs (which do not take direct objects), linking verbs, and helping or auxiliary verbs (which show tense or mood). Although only transitive verbs can show passive voice, most verbs can show various tenses and mood. (See Chapter 9 for a discussion of verb usage.)

I Transitive and intransitive verbs work differently.

A **transitive verb** can take an object. Examples of transitive verbs include *throw* and *take*.

| subject | verb | object | subject | verb | object |
| He | throws | a pass. | They | took | the ball. |

Because transitive verbs can take an object, most of them can operate in both the active and passive voices.[1] The active and the passive forms of the verb may be similar in meaning, but the emphasis changes with the rearrangement of the subject and object, as well as with changes in the verb form (to the past participle with *be*).

subject	verb	object	subject	verb	modifiers
Workers in Ohio make Hondas.			Hondas are made (by workers) in Ohio.		
active voice			passive voice		

[1]**Exceptions:** Transitive verbs *have, get, want, like,* and *hate* are seldom used in passive voice.

Notice how the active-voice object *Hondas* in the first sentence becomes the passive-voice subject in the second. In a passive-voice sentence the original performer of the action (*workers* in the example) is not emphasized and may even be omitted. (See 9g on the uses of passive constructions.)

By contrast, an **intransitive verb** never takes an object and can never be used in the passive voice. Examples of intransitive verbs include *smile* and *go*.

subject   verb   subject verb

The politician smiled.   He went into the crowd.

47.1

2	Linking verbs are used in distinctive patterns.

Linking verbs, the most common example of which is *be*, serve in sentences as "equals signs" to link a subject with an equivalent noun or adjective. Some other linking verbs are *appear, become,* and *seem*. (See 11d for a full list and description of linking verbs; see also 7b, Pattern 5.)

Things *seem* unsettled.

Shall I *become* a doctor?

Expletives

Linking verbs also serve in a distinctive English construction that uses changed word order with an **expletive** word, *there* or *it*. Expletives are used only with linking verbs, as in these sentences.

It *is* important to leave now.   It *appears* unnecessary to do that.

There *seems* to be a problem.   It *seems* important.

There and *it* form "dummy subjects" or filler words that occupy the position of the subject in a normal sentence; the true subject is elsewhere in the sentence, and the verb agrees with the true subject (see 10a-8).

Expletive in subject position	**True subject**
There is a cat in that tree.	*A cat* is in that tree.
There are some cats in the tree.	*Some cats* are in the tree.
It is convenient to use the train.	*To use the train* is convenient.

The expletive *it* also has a unique role in expressing length of time with *take* followed by an infinitive.

It takes an hour to get home by car.   *It took* us forever.

Expletive constructions are important in and useful for several other expressions, including time, distance, or weather.

It is three o'clock and it's raining.   It's a long way home from here.

Expletives are often used to form subject complements, sometimes with an infinitive, as well as to make short or emphatic statements.

It is fun to ride a sleigh. It is a tale of great sorrow. There were no survivors.

However, in complex and formal English sentences, the "dummy subject" expletive becomes an unnecessary word obscuring the true subject. The expletive also encourages using linking verbs instead of more direct, active verbs—transitive or intransitive verbs. To eliminate wordiness and promote the clear, direct style that is preferred in English academic prose, try to avoid expletives; revise sentences to restore normal word order (see 17a-3).

3 Verbs in the active versus the passive voice

Verbs using the **active voice** emphasize the actor of a sentence as the subject. (See section 9g.)

Brenda *scores* the winning goal. Tom *plays* the violin.

When a transitive verb occurs in the **passive voice,** the sentence reverses its order: the verb converts to a past participle with an auxiliary, the original subject may be expressed in a phrase with *by,* and the original object of the sentence is moved to the front of the new sentence and is emphasized (see 9g):

The winning goal *is scored* by Brenda. The violin *is played* by Tom.

In a further transformation of the active-voice sentence, the original actor/subject can be made to disappear entirely by omitting the prepositional phrase.

The winning goal *is scored.* The violin *is played.*

The many uses and disadvantages of the passive voice are shown in detail in sections 9g-1 and 9g-2, as well as 16b-3 and 17b-1.

47b Changing verb forms

Verb forms express *tense,* an indication of when an action or state of being occurs. The three basic tenses in English are the past, the present, and the future. (See 9a and 9b for a discussion of the forms of English verbs, and 9e-1, 2 for a basic discussion of tenses.) Section 9e presents a useful "time line" chart of English verb tenses and verb forms that express time relationships.

1 Not all verbs use progressive tense forms.

Each of the three basic tenses has a progressive form, made up of *be* and the present participle (the *-ing* form of the verb). The progressive tense emphasizes the *process* of doing whatever action the verb asserts. The tense is indicated by a form of *be*: present progressive (I *am going*), past progressive (I *was going*), past perfect progressive (I *had been going*), future progressive (I *will be going*). For examples, see 9e and 9f.

Certain verbs are generally *not* used in the progressive form; others have a progressive use only for process-oriented or ongoing meanings of the verb.

Words that are rarely seen in a progressive form

- **Think** (in the sense of "believe"): "I think not."

    Exception: The progressive form can be used for a process of considering something.

    Faulty   I *am thinking* it is wrong.

    Correct   I *am thinking* about changing jobs. [considering]

- **Believe, understand, recognize, realize, remember:** "You believe it."

    Exception: The last four can sometimes use the progressive form if a process of recognition or recollection is meant: "He is slowly realizing the truth." "He is gradually remembering what happened."

- **Belong, possess, own, want, need:** "We want some." "We once owned it."

- **Have:** "You have what you need."

    Exception: The progressive form can be used in the sense of "experiencing."

    Faulty   Maria *is having* a car.

    Correct   Mary *is having* a baby. [experiencing childbirth]
    Maria *is having* success in her project.

- **Be, exist, seem:** "This seems acceptable."

    Exception: The progressive form is used only with an abstract emphasis on a process of "being" or "seeming": "He was just existing from day to day."

- **Smell, sound,** and **taste** as intransitive verbs, as in "It smells good"; "It sounds funny"; "It tastes bad."

- **Appear** in the sense of "seem": "It appeared to be the right time."

    Exception: Sometimes the progressive form is used in the sense of presenting itself/oneself over a time period. "She's appearing nightly as the star actress."

- **See:** "I can never see why you do it."

    Exception: The progressive form is used in the sense of interviewing someone or witnessing or experiencing something.

Changing Verb Forms   **819**

Faulty	I *am seeing* an airplane now.
Revised	I *am seeing* a new patient. [interviewing]

■ **Surprise, hate, love, like:** "It surprises me"; "I hate lima beans."

<table>
<tr><td>2</td><td>Using the perfect forms</td></tr>
</table>

The perfect tense is made up of *have* and the past participle (the *-ed* form of the verb). The form of *have* indicates the tense: present perfect (*has* worked), past perfect (*had* worked), and future perfect (*will have* worked). (See 9e and 9f; also 9b, irregular past participles.)

Sometimes students confuse the use of the simple past with the use of the present perfect. The present perfect is used when an action or state of being that began in the past continues to the present; it is also used to express an action or state of being that happened at an indefinite time in the past.

Present perfect Linda has worked in Mexico since 1987.

Present perfect Ann has worked in Mexico. [The time is unspecified.]

By contrast, the simple past is used when an action or state of being began *and ended* in the past.

Simple past Linda worked in Mexico last year. [She no longer works there.]

Since or *for* with perfect tenses in prepositional phrases of time

A phrase with *since* requires using the present perfect (*has worked*) or past perfect tenses (*had worked*); it indicates action beginning at *a single point in time* and still continuing at the time shown by the verb tense.

She [has/had worked]   *since* noon
  since July
  since 1991
  since the end of the school year
  since the last storm
  since the baby was born

A time phrase with *since* cannot have a noun object that shows plural time; *since* phrases must indicate a single point in time.

Faulty	He lived here since three months.
	I am here since May.
Revised	He has lived here *for* three months.
	I have been here since May.

Also, a time phrase with *since* cannot modify a simple past tense or any present tense.

Faulty   He worked here since six months.

Revised   He *had worked* here since February.

The perfect tenses can have a time modifier with a prepositional phrase formed either with *since* or *for*.

> He has worked since noon.

> He had worked for a month.

A modifying phrase with *for* indicates action *through a duration of time*.

> He [has/had worked]   *for* three hours
> *for* a month and a half
> *for* two years
> *for* a few weeks

When a phrase uses a plural noun, thus showing duration of time, the plural signals that the preposition in the modifier must be *for*, not *since*.

Faulty   I had worked on it since many years.

Revised   I had worked on it for many years.

---

3   Using the varied forms of English future tenses

The following list shows different ways of expressing the future.

Verb form	*Explanation*
She *will call* us soon. She *is going to* call us soon.	These examples have the same meaning.
The movie *arrives* in town tomorrow. The next bus *leaves* in five minutes. The bus *is leaving* very soon.	The simple present and the present progressive are used to express definite future plans, as from a schedule.
Your flight *is taking off* at 6:55. The doctor *is operating* at once. I *am calling* them right now.	The present progressive is sometimes used to make strong statements about the future.
Hurry! The movie *is about to* begin. Finish up! The bell *is about to* ring.	The "near" future is expressed by some form of *be* plus *about to* and a verb.
It's cold. *I'm going to* get a sweater. It's cold. *I'll lend* you a sweater.	"Going to" suggests a plan. "Will" suggests a willingness.

In choosing forms of future tenses, be alert to time expressions such as "soon," "five minutes," or "tomorrow" as context clues to events that will require use of future forms. Verbs expressing thoughts about future actions, such as *intend* and *hope*, are not used in any future tense, and the verb *plan* uses a future tense only in the idiomatic *plan on* (to make or follow a plan).

Faulty   I will intend to meet my friends tomorrow.

Revised   I intend to meet my friends tomorrow.
I plan to attend college.

See 47b-5 for guidelines on expressing future time in conditional sentences.

Using verb tenses in sentences with a sequence of actions

In complex sentences that have more than one verb, it is important to adjust the sequence of verb tenses to avoid confusion. See the discussion on verb tense combinations in 9f.

Verb tenses with reported speech

Reported speech, or indirect discourse, is very different from directly quoted speech, which gives the exact verb tense of the original.

Direct speech   Ellie said, "He is taking a picture of my boat."

Indirectly quoted speech may occasionally be reported immediately.

Reported speech   Ellie just said [that] he is taking a picture of her boat.

Some kinds of reported speech can be summarized with verbs such as *tell, ask, remind,* and *urge,* followed by an infinitive:

Reported speech   Ellie asked him to take a picture of her boat.

Most often, however, reported speech has occurred sometime before the time of the main verb reporting it. In English, the indirect quotation then requires changes in verb tense and pronouns.

Reported speech   She said [that] he had taken a picture of her boat.

In this situation, the reported speech itself takes the form of a *that* noun clause (although the word *that* is often omitted); its verb tense shifts to past tense, following the guidelines shown in 9f-1 for tense sequences. See also the Critical Decisions box at 16d for a chart of verb forms needed to express direct speech versus reported speech. Punctuation for quotations is discussed at 28a-1.

Using verb tenses in conditional and subjunctive sentences

Conditional sentences talk about situations that are either possible in the future or else unreal (contrary to fact) in the present or past. Conditional sentences typically contain the conjunction *if* or a related conditional term (*unless, provided that, only if, (only) after, (only) when,* etc.). The following are guidelines for using verb forms in conditional sentences.

Possible or real statements about the future

Use the present tense to express the condition in possible statements about the future; in the same sentence, use the future to express the result of that condition.

	conditional + present future	*(will + base form)*
Real statement	*If I have* enough money,	*I will go* next week.
	When I get enough money,	*I will go.*
	[Meaning: The speaker may have enough money.]	

Unreal conditional statements about the future

Use the past subjunctive form (which looks like a past tense) with sentences that make "unreal" conditional statements about the future; in the same sentence, use the past form of a modal auxiliary (usually *would*, *could*, or *might*) to express an unreal result of that stated condition.

	If + past	*past form of modal (would)*
Unreal statement	*If you found* the money,	*you would go* next week.
	[Meaning: The speaker now is fairly sure you will not have the money.]	

Unreal conditional statements about the past

Use the subjunctive with appropriate perfect tense verb forms with sentences that make unreal conditional statements about the past. Use the past perfect tense for the unreal statement about the past. In the same sentence, use the past form of the modal auxiliary plus the present perfect to express the unreal result.

	If + past perfect	*past modal +*	*present perfect*
	(had made)	*(would)*	*(have gone)*
Unreal statement	*If I had made* money,	*I would have gone* last week.	
	[Meaning: At that time the speaker did not have the money.]		

For more on the subjunctive, see 9h-1; for more on modal auxiliaries, see 47d.

6	**Expressing a wish or suggestion for a hypothetical event**

In stating a wish in the present that might hypothetically occur, use the *past subjunctive* (which looks like the past tense) in the clause expressing the wish. (The object of the wish takes the form of a *that* clause, although the word *that* is often omitted.)

present	[that]	*past subjunctive (like past tense)*
He *wishes*	[that]	she *had* a holiday.
I *wish*	[that]	I *were* on vacation.

Changing Verb Forms   823

The auxiliaries *would* and *could* (which have the same form in the present and past tenses) are often used to express the object of a wish.

present	[that]	*would/could* + base form
I *wish*	[that]	she *would stay*.
We *wish*	[that]	we *could take* a vacation day.

In stating a wish made in the past or present for something that hypothetically might have occurred in the past, use the past perfect in the *that* clause. (The verb *wish* may be expressed either in the past or in the present tense.)

present OR past	[that]	past perfect *(had worked)*
I wished	[that]	I *had* not *worked* yesterday.
I wish	[that]	it *had been* a holiday.

See 9h-4 for guidelines on using the subjunctive mood with *that* clauses.

Expressing a recommendation, suggestion, or urgent request

In stating a recommendation, suggestion, or urgent request, use the *present subjunctive*—the base form of the verb *(be, do)*—in the *that* clause (see 9h).

present	[that]	present subjunctive = base form
We *suggest*	[that]	he *find* the money.
We *advise*	[that]	you *be* there on time.

(See 9h-4 for comments on the subjunctive in this form.)

EXERCISE I

Circle the appropriate verb form.

1. Sam insisted that she (wants/wanted) something to drink.
2. For some reason it (smelled/was smelling) very strange.
3. Many years ago I (heard/have heard) an unusual story.
4. Perhaps if you (had wanted/would have wanted) the job, you (would have gotten/had gotten) to the interview on time.
5. She wishes that she (could do/can do) a good job.

47c **Changing word order with verbs**

> **I** Invert the subject and all or part of the verb to form questions.

The subject and verb are inverted from normal order to form questions. The following patterns are used with the verb *be*, with modal auxiliaries, with progressive forms, and with perfect forms.

	Normal Statement Form	Question Form
Be	He *is* sick today.	*Is he* sick today?
Modals	She *can* help us.	*Can she* help us?
Progressive	They *are* studying here.	*Are they* studying here?
Perfect	It *has* made this sound before.	*Has it* made this sound before?

Questions (and negatives) with the auxiliary *do/does*

Verbs other than those shown above use the auxiliary verbs *do/does* to form questions, and also to form negatives with *not*. In this form, when the auxiliary verb *do/does* is added, the verb changes to the base form (the dictionary form). Use this pattern for the simple present and simple past:

Question form/negative form: *do* + base form

Statement	He *gets on* this bus.
Question	*Does* he *get on* this bus?
Negative	He *does not get on* this bus.
Avoid	Does he *gets on* this bus? [Needs a base form.]

Statement	She *finishes* at noon.
Question	*Does* she *finish* at noon?
Negative	She *does not finish*.
Avoid	Does she *finishes* at noon? [Needs a base form.]

Statement	It *ran* better yesterday.
Question	*Did* it *run* better yesterday?
Negative	It *did not run* better.
Avoid	Did it *ran* better yesterday? [Needs a base form.]

Statement	They *arrived* at noon.
Question	When *did* they *arrive?*
Negative	They *did not arrive*.
Avoid	When do they *arrived?* [Needs a base form.]

For more on auxiliary verbs, see the listings in 9c and in 47d.

---

2   **Invert the subject and verb in some emphatic statements.**

The question form is also used with auxiliaries or expletives in some emphatic statements that begin with adverbs such as *never, rarely,* and *hardly,* producing a negative meaning.

Normal	Emphatic
There is never an easy answer.	Never *is there* an easy answer.
They have rarely come to check.	Rarely *have they* come to check.

Using the helping verbs: Auxiliaries and modal auxiliaries

1 **Auxiliary verbs, or helping verbs, are part of basic grammar.**

The basic auxiliary verbs *(be, will, have, do)* are used to show tense, to form questions, to show emphasis, and to show negation.

To show tense, or aspect *(be, will, have)*: He is driving. She has driven.

To form questions *(do/does)*: Do they drive? Why do you drive?

To show emphasis *(do/does)*: She does drive sometimes.

To show negation *(do + not)*: I do not drive.

2 **Use modal auxiliaries for a wide range of meanings.**

Modal auxiliaries include *can, could, may, might, should, would,* and *must*, as well as the four modals that always appear with the particle *to: ought to, have to, able to,* and *have got to*. The base form of the verb (the dictionary form) is always used with a modal auxiliary, whether the time reference is to the future, present, or past. For a past time reference, use the modal plus the past perfect *(have* + the past participle).

Some idiomatic expressions with modals

Some other idiomatic expressions with modals are expressed in the following list.

Example	Meaning
I *would rather* drive than fly.	I prefer driving to flying.
We *would talk* for hours.	We always talked for hours then.
She has car keys, so she *must* drive.	[must = probably does]
Shall we dance again?	I'm inviting you to dance again.
Would you mind turning the heat up?	[would you mind = would you object to]
Do you mind turning it off?	Please turn it off.

Meaning Expressed	Present Time or Past Time	Modal + Past Perfect
ability and permission	She can drive. She could drive.	She could have driven.
possibility	She may drive. She might drive.	She might have driven.
advisability	She should drive. She ought to drive. She had better drive.	She should have driven. She ought to have driven.
necessity	She must drive. She has to drive.	She had to drive.
negative necessity versus prohibition*	She does not have to drive. [she need not] She must not drive. [she is not allowed]	

*Note that the two negatives above have very different meanings.

47e Choosing gerunds and infinitives with verbs

There are three types of verbals: infinitives, gerunds, and participles (see 7a-4).

1 Using infinitives and gerunds as nouns

Use an infinitive or a gerund to function either as a subject or as an object.

As subjects   *To be one of the leaders here* is not really what I want.
His being one of the leaders here is unacceptable.

As objects   I don't really want *to be one of the leaders here*.
I don't accept *his being one of the leaders here*.

Note: The possessive case is used with gerunds; see 8c-2. (See 7a-4 and 7d-2, 3 for basic definitions and examples of verbals. See 48a-1 for participles that function as modifiers, and 47b-1 for participles in the progressive form of English verbs.)

2 Learning idiomatic uses of verb/verbal sequences

Sometimes it is difficult to determine which verbs are followed by a gerund, which are followed by an infinitive, and which can be followed by either verbal. This usage is idiomatic and must be memorized; there are no rules to govern these forms. Note in the following examples that verb tense does not affect a verbal.

Verb + Gerund	Verb + Infinitive	Verb + Either Verbal
enjoy	**want**	**begin**
I enjoy swimming.	I want to swim now.	Today I begin swimming. Today I begin to swim.
go	**agree**	**continue**
I went swimming.	I agreed to swim.	I continued swimming. I continued to swim.
enjoy + gerund	want + infinitive	begin + either verbal
go + gerund	agree + infinitive	continue + either verbal
finish + gerund	decide + infinitive	like + either verbal
recommend + gerund	need + infinitive	prefer + either verbal
risk + gerund	plan + infinitive	start + either verbal
suggest + gerund	seem + infinitive	love + either verbal
consider + gerund	expect + infinitive	hate + either verbal
postpone + gerund	fail + infinitive	can't bear + either verbal
practice + gerund	pretend + infinitive	can't stand + either verbal

Note: There is no difference in meaning between *I begin to swim* and *I begin swimming*. However, sentences with other verbs differ in meaning depending on whether a gerund or an infinitive follows the verb. This difference in meaning is a function of certain verbs. See the following examples.

Example	Meaning
I always remember *to lock* the car.	I always remember to do this.
I remember *locking* the car.	I remember that I did this.
They stop *to drink* some water.	They stopped in order to drink.
They stopped *drinking* water.	They didn't drink anymore.

Information on idiomatic usage is provided in ESL dictionaries such as the *Longman Dictionary of American English: Your Complete Guide to American English*, 1997.

EXERCISE 2

Circle the appropriate verb form.

1. I am certain that you (have to/might) walk to town.
2. They all need (doing/to do) some daily exercise.
3. You might consider (walking/to walk) to town.
4. Doesn't she (get/gets) angry sometimes?
5. We can postpone (doing/to do) the hard work till later.

www

47.2

47f Using two- and three-word verbs, or phrasal verbs, with particles

Phrasal verbs consist of a verb and a *particle*. Note that a particle can be one or more prepositions (off, up, with) or an adverb (away, back). English has many phrasal verbs, often built on verbs that have one basic meaning in their simple one-word form, but different meanings when particles are added.

The coach *called off* the game because of the storm.

He *left out* some important details.

The meaning of a phrasal verb is idiomatic; that is, the words as a group have a different meaning from each of the words separately. Most of these varied meanings are found in a standard English dictionary. Here are some examples of sentences with two-word and three-word verbs.

I *got ready* for work.

She didn't go to the party because she didn't *feel up to* it.

The doctor told him to *cut down on* red meat.

They *did without* a television for a few years.

---

1 Some phrasal verbs are separable.

With separable phrasal verbs, a noun object either can separate a verb and particle or follow the particle.

noun object	noun object

Correct I *made out* a check to the IRS. I *made* a check *out* to the IRS.

However, a pronoun object always separates the verb and the particle. A pronoun never follows the particle.

  pronoun object

Faulty I *made out* it to the IRS.

Revised I *made* it *out* to the IRS.

Other separable phrasal verbs include the following:

call off	hand out	prevent from
check out	leave in, out	set up
divide up	look up [research]	sign on, up
find out	pick up	start over, up
fill in	put over	take on
fit in	[present	throw out
give back, up	deceptively]	turn on, off,
hang out, up	put up to [promote]	up, down
[suspend:	put back	wake up
trans.]	put off	write down

2   **Some phrasal verbs are nonseparable.**

With nonseparable phrasal verbs, a noun or pronoun object always follows the particle. For these verbs it is not possible to separate the verb and its particle with a noun or pronoun object.

	noun object		pronoun object
Faulty	I ran Mary into.	**Faulty**	I ran her into.
Revised	I ran into Mary.	**Revised**	I ran into her.

Other nonseparable phrasal verbs include the following:

bump into	call on	do without
get into	get over	get through
keep on	keep up with	hang out [= stay]
refer to	see about	

Several verbs in their basic form are intransitive, but can become transitive phrasal verbs when a nonseparable prepositional particle is added to them.

Intransitive   The politician *smiled* sheepishly, then quickly *apologized*.

Transitive   He *smiled at* me sheepishly, then *apologized* quickly *for* being late.

Other examples of this kind of verb include the following:

complain about	laugh at	participate in
feel up to	look at, into	run into
insist on	object to	walk around, down, up, into, etc.

Note: An adverb, but not a noun or pronoun, may separate the verb from its particle.

He *apologized* quickly *for* being late.

The following are nonseparable two-word verbs that are intransitive, but that can be made transitive if still another particle is added to them:

run around with   *get ready* for   *get by* with
get away with   *drop out* of   *look out* for
read up on

---

3   **Some phrasal verbs can be either separable or nonseparable.**

Some phrasal verbs can be either separable or nonseparable. The meaning of a phrasal verb will change, depending on whether or not the phrase is separated by an object. Note the difference in meaning that appears with the placement of the object in the similar verbs below.

Examples	*Meaning*
I *saw through* it. [nonsep.]	I found it transparent.
I *saw* it *through.* [sep.]	I persisted.
She *looked over* the wall. [nonsep.]	She looked over the top of it.
She *looked* the wall *over.* [sep.]	She examined or studied it.
I *turned on* him. [nonsep.]	I turned to attack him.
I *turned* it *on.* [sep.]	I flipped a switch.
I *turned* him *on.* [sep.]	I aroused his passion.
They *talked to* us. [nonsep.]	They spoke to us.
They *talked* us *into* staying. [sep.]	They convinced us to stay.

Note: Standard dictionaries usually list verbs with the meanings of most particles (indicating whether or not they are transitive), but they usually do not indicate whether a phrasal verb is separable or nonseparable. However, this information is provided in ESL dictionaries such as the *Longman Dictionary of American English: Your Complete Guide to American English*, 1997.

EXERCISE 3

Circle the appropriate verb form.

1. Can you (fit in it/fit it in) to your busy schedule?
2. If you (call on her/call her on), she may not be home.
3. We may want to (wake up her/wake her up) early today.
4. I forgot to tell you something; I (left out it/left it out) of my note yesterday.
5. Will you (set up him/set him up) to do the job?

CHAPTER

Using Modifiers
and Connectors
in English Sentences

odifiers expand sentences in a variety of ways. The two types of
modifiers are adjectives and adverbs, as well as phrases and clauses
that function as adjectives or adverbs. There are two types of adverbs, descriptive and conjunctive. For basic discussions of the types of
modifiers, how they function, and how they are placed or located in
sentences, see 7a-5 and 6, and 7c. (For more on adjectives, see 11a-1
and 11e. For more on descriptive adverbs, see 11e and f. For more on
conjunctive adverbs, see 19a-3.)

48a   **Using single-word adjectives and nouns as modifiers of nouns**

A modifier of a noun must be placed as close to the noun modified
as possible (11a-1; 15a). Single-word adjectives are normally placed before a noun or after a linking verb.

Before a noun   The *bored student* slept through the *boring lecture.*
After a linking verb   Jack *is bored.* The lecture he heard *was boring.*

1   **Using the present and past participle forms of verbs as adjectives**

The present participle and the past participle forms of verbs are often used as single-word adjectives. The choice of form has an important
impact on meaning. In the following examples, notice that these forms
can be very different—almost opposite—in meaning.

Past participle	Meaning
a tired student	The student is tired.
damaged buildings	The buildings are damaged.
a frightened passenger	The passenger is frightened.
excited tourists	The tourists are excited.
an accredited school	The school is accredited.

Present participle	Meaning
a tiring lecture	The lecture causes a feeling of being tired.
a damaging explosion	The explosion caused the damage.
a frightening storm	The storm causes the fright.
an exciting tour	The tour caused excitement.
an accrediting board	This group gives accrediting status.

---

2 **Using nouns as modifiers**

When two nouns are combined in sequence, the last is considered **48.1**
to be the noun modified; the first is the modifier. (This follows the pattern for single-word adjectives mentioned earlier.) The importance of sequence is evident in the following examples, where the same nouns are combined in different order to produce different meanings.

Modifier	+ Noun modified	Meaning
a car	company	a company whose business involves cars
a company	car	a car provided to someone by the business
a light	truck	a small truck
a truck	light	a light attached to a truck
a game	parlor	a place where indoor games are played
a parlor	game	a type of game, such as chess, played indoors

When more than two nouns are combined in sequence, it is increasingly difficult to determine which noun is modified and which is a modifier; see 48f-2. For this reason, it is best to avoid overusing nouns as modifiers (see 11g).

48b **Using adjectival modifiers with linking verbs and prepositions**

Adjectives and past-participle adjectives in sentences with linking verbs are often followed by a modifying prepositional phrase.

We are *ready*. We are *ready for* the next phase of training.

Jenny seems an *involved* person. She is *involved with* a boyfriend.

The preposition to be used in such phrases is determined by the adjective or participle adjective. With each such adjective, the choice of preposition is idiomatic, not logical; therefore, adjective/preposition combinations must be memorized. Sometimes the same adjective will change its meaning with different prepositions, as in this example.

Jenny was *involved in* planning from the start. Meanwhile, she was *involved with* a new boyfriend.

Past-participle adjective examples include the following:

excited about	acquainted with	divorced from
composed of	opposed to	scared of/by
involved in	interested in	cautioned to/against
exhausted from	done with	angry at/with

Single-word adjective examples include the following:

absent from	afraid of	mad at
bad for	clear to	sure of
crazy about	familiar with	cruel to
excited about	capable of	accustomed to
guilty of	responsible for	

Note: Standard dictionaries may not indicate which preposition is typically used with a given adjective. However, this information is provided in ESL dictionaries such as the *Longman Dictionary of American English: Your Complete Guide to American English*, 1997.

48c Positioning adverbial modifiers

I Observe typical locations for adverbs in English sentences.

Adverbs have typical or standard locations in English sentences, although these patterns can be varied for special emphasis. Adverbs are typically located immediately before a verb.

Faulty She finishes cheerfully her homework.

Revised She cheerfully finishes her homework.

Emphatic She finishes her homework—cheerfully.

Common adverbs expressing frequency or probability typically come after the verb *be* and helping verbs. In questions, such adverbs can come after the subject.

He was frequently at the gym on Fridays.

She may often discuss politics.

Does she often come here?

However, when sentences are inverted for negatives, these adverbs are usually placed before the helping verb.

Faulty   They don't frequently talk. It doesn't sometimes matter.

Revised   They frequently don't talk. It sometimes doesn't matter.

---

2   **Limiting modifiers cannot move without changing meaning.**

Although many adverbs can be located at a number of different places in a sentence without changing the meaning, positioning is quite critical with certain **limiting modifiers** such as *only, almost, just, nearly, even, simply* (see 15b).

No change in meaning	**Significant change in meaning**
Generally it rains a lot in April.	*Only* Leonid sings those songs.
It *generally* rains a lot in April.	Leonid *only* sings those songs.
It rains a lot in April, *generally*.	Leonid sings *only* those songs.
	[OR sings those songs *only*.]

See 15a–g for more on positioning modifiers. See also 47c-2 for inverted word order with adverbs—such as *rarely, never, seldom*—located at the beginning of a sentence.

48d   **Using phrases and clauses to modify nouns and pronouns**

See the guidelines for modifier placement in 15a–h.

---

1   Positioning adjective phrases and clauses

Unlike single-word adjective modifiers (which are placed before a noun and after a linking verb; 48a), clauses and most phrases functioning as adjectives must immediately *follow* the noun or pronoun they modify in order to avoid confusion with adverbial modifiers in the sentence.

Faulty   I brought the tire to the garage *with the puncture*.

            I brought the tire to the garage *that had a puncture*.

            [The modifier next to *garage* is very confusing.]

Revised   I brought the tire *with the puncture* to the garage.

            I brought the tire *that had a puncture* to the garage.

If two or more adjective phrases or clauses modify the same noun, typical patterns of sequence operate, as shown in 48f-1. (See 25d-1–3 for rules on punctuating adjective clauses.)

> **2** Avoid adding unnecessary pronouns after adjective clauses.

The subject in an English sentence can be stated only once; pronouns in the sentence refer to the subject (or to other nouns) but they do not repeat it. When a lengthy adjective clause follows the subject as a modifier, it is important not to repeat the subject with an unnecessary pronoun before the verb.

Faulty   The *person* who works in office #382 *she* decides. [The subject is repeated with an unnecessary pronoun.]

Revised   The person who works in office #382 decides.

This error is likely to occur because of a failure to observe the steps in forming a dependent clause. Here is the process for forming an adjective clause, using *who, which,* or *that* to replace the noun or pronoun of the dependent clause:

Two sentences   The person decides. *She* works in office #382.

Transform to a clause   *[she = who] who* works in office #382

Place the clause   The person *who works in office #382* decides.

The correct form for the relative pronouns *who* or *whom* in a dependent clause is discussed in 8f-2.

>   Use the relative pronoun *whose* for a clause showing possession.

An adjective clause is often constructed using the relative pronoun *whose* to show possession by the person or animate thing modified. (See 46c-1 on possession.) Students sometimes omit a step in transforming a separate possessive statement into an adjective clause with *whose.*

Faulty   The person whom her office was locked called security.

Revised   The person whose office was locked called security.

Here is the pattern for transforming a sentence showing possession to a relative clause showing possession, using *whose* to replace the possessive noun or pronoun.

Two sentences   The person called security. *Her* office was locked.

Replace possessive subject with *whose*   *whose office was locked [her = whose]*

Place the clause   The person *whose* <u>office was locked</u> called security.

The same process is used for a clause showing possession of a thing.

Two sentences	The government made a protest. *Its* ambassador was insulted.
Transform: Replace with *whose*	*[its = whose]* ambassador was insulted
Place the clause	The government *whose* <u>ambassador was insulted</u> made a protest.

48e Combining phrases and clauses with connecting words

As writers combine phrases and clauses, they choose between two basic relationships: a coordinate or a subordinate connection. Elements that have a *coordinate* connection emphasize a balance or equality between elements. (See 19a for a discussion of coordinate relationships.) Elements can also have a subordinate or dependent connection that emphasizes that the elements are unequal, with one having a dependent link to another. (See 7e and 19b for a discussion of subordinate relationships.)

Phrases and clauses are often logically linked with connecting words, **conjunctions** and **conjunctive adverbs,** that require careful consideration of the kind of connection students wish to establish.

I Choose the right connecting word for coordinate structures.

Connecting words for a coordinate, or balanced, relationship include **coordinating conjunctions** (*and, but, or, nor, so, for, yet*), **correlative conjunctions** (*either/or, neither/nor, both/and, not only/but, whether/or, not only/but also*), and many **conjunctive adverbs** (*however, nevertheless, accordingly, also, besides, afterward, then, indeed, otherwise*). These words show relationships of contrast, consequence, sequence, and emphasis; they are discussed in 19a-1–3.

After deciding on the desired relationship among sentence parts, select a *single set of connecting words*. Avoid a mixture of words that may cancel out the meaning.

Mixed	They were *both* competitive, *but however* they were well matched. [The mixed connecting words show similarity and contrast at the same time.]
Balanced	They were *both* competitive, *and* they were well matched. They were competitive; *however,* they were well matched.

See 25a-1 and 25f-1 for appropriate rules on punctuation.

Choose the subordinating conjunction that establishes the desired dependent relationship.

Subordinating conjunctions establish different relationships, including conditional relationships and relationships of contrast, cause and effect, time and place, purpose, and outcome (see Chapter 19). In your writing, choose a single subordinating conjunction, and avoid combinations that are contradictory or confusing.

Mixed   *Because* she was sick, *so* she went to the clinic. [A relation of cause and effect is confusingly combined with one of purpose or outcome.]

Clear   *Because* she was sick, she went to the clinic. [cause/effect]
She was sick, *so* she went to the clinic. [outcome]

See 19b for a full discussion on establishing clear subordinate relationships among sentence parts. See 25a-1 and 25f-1 for rules on punctuation.

48f   Arranging cumulative modifiers

I   Observing typical order of cumulative adjectives

Single-word adjective modifiers are placed close to a noun, immediately before a noun, or after a linking verb (48a).

Cumulative adjectives are groups of adjectives that modify the same noun. There is a typical order of modifiers and cumulative adjectives in an English sentence. A major disruption of typical order can be confusing.

Faulty   a beach French gorgeous tent   red light my small bulb
Revised   a gorgeous French beach tent   my small red light bulb

Although some stylistic variations from typical order in the location of cumulative adjectives are possible for emphasis, typical locations in an English sentence provide a very strong normal pattern. Here are some guidelines.

Possessives precede numbers. Ordinal numbers follow cardinal numbers.

Jill's first car   my first nine drafts

The typical order of descriptive adjectives is shown on page 839.

(1) Opinion	(2) Size	(3) Shape	(4) Condition	(5) Age	(6) Color	(7) Origin	(8) Noun
ugly		round			green		fenders
	huge		muddy				spots
lovely				old	red	Turkish	slippers
comfortable			sunny				room

Arranging cumulative phrases, clauses, or noun modifiers[1]

A single phrase or clause functioning as an adjective immediately follows the noun or pronoun it modifies to avoid confusion with any adverbial phrases in the same sentence (48b).

When accumulated adjective phrases or clauses modify the same noun, their flexible emphasis creates an extremely varied sequence, especially for issues of opinion. In a neutral context some of the same typical sequences may be observed as for single-word adjectives (above), except that the modifying phrases follow the noun.

I found *spots* that are *huge* and that are also very *muddy*.

We saw that the *rooms* were very *narrow* and yet they seemed *bright*.

When two adverbial phrases or clauses are accumulated, place phrases typically precede time phrases.

Not typical   They lived in the 1970s in Japan.

Typical   They lived in Japan in the 1970s.

Two-word modifiers of nouns

Three nouns are often combined, with the first two forming a two-word modifier for the last noun. When this happens, nouns fall into a typical arrangement somewhat comparable with that of adjectives.

Not typical   a file steel cabinet

Typical   a steel file cabinet

The sequence of two nouns to modify a third noun may be classified and arranged in this sequence.

Material, number, or location	Origin, purpose, or type	Noun modified
chapter	review	questions
two-word	noun	modifier
slate	roofing	tile
steel	file	cabinet

[1]We owe this discussion on order of modifiers to Jean Praninskas, *Rapid Review of English Grammar* (Englewood Cliffs, NJ: Prentice-Hall, 1975).

However, the categories of meaning for nouns are less clear than for adjectives and the opportunity for confusion is much greater. Students are therefore advised to avoid accumulating noun modifiers beyond this limit, and to rewrite combinations as phrases and clauses (see 11g).

EXERCISE I

Circle the correct form.

1. The girls thought the ride was (excited/exciting) and they were (interested/ interesting) in the things they saw.
2. These gang members seemed capable (of/in) any kind of violence and were cruel (at/to) their enemies.
3. Luisa (walks usually/usually walks) to her studio (even when/when even) she feels tired.
4. The famous preacher (he spoke/who spoke) at our meeting was inspiring.
5. I have lost my (yellow beautiful/beautiful yellow) umbrella with the (large Japanese/Japanese large) designs.

A

Manuscript Form and Preparation

Before readers register a word of your writing, they form an impression based on your paper's appearance. If you are committed enough to a paper to have revised it several times, surely you will want to give it a crisp appearance. A clean, well-prepared, typed manuscript is a sign of an attentive attitude taken toward all the stages of writing. Careful manuscript preparation implicitly shows respect for your readers, who will certainly appreciate any efforts to make their work easier.

Style guides in the disciplines recommend slightly different conventions for preparing manuscripts, and you should consult the specialized guides listed in 38f, 39e, and 40e when writing in the humanities, social sciences, and sciences. Consult your professor as well. The recommendations here follow the guide commonly used in the humanities, the *MLA [Modern Language Association] Handbook for Writers of Research Papers*, 5th ed.

A1   Paper and binding

Prepare your work on plain white, twenty-pound paper that measures 8-1/2 × 11 inches. For economy's sake, you might consider buying a ream (500 sheets) if you are typing the manuscript or are preparing it on a laser printer. If you are working with a dot matrix printer, buy a box of 500 or 1,000 sheets of fanfold paper. Unless your instructor advises otherwise, avoid onion skin or erasable paper, both of which will easily smudge. (For ease of preparation, though, you might type your work on erasable paper and submit a photocopy, which will not smudge.) Make a copy of your final paper to keep for your files, and submit the original to your instructor. In binding pages, affix a single paper clip to the upper left-hand corner. To ease your reader's handling of your paper, do *not* place multiple staples along the left margin, and avoid plastic folders unless otherwise directed.

A2   Page layout

Whether you adopt conventions for page layout suggested by the *MLA Handbook* or by other style guides, maintain consistent margins and spacing. Your paper's first page, subsequent pages, and reference list page(s) should be designed according to standard practice in a discipline.

Margins and line spacing

Type on one side of a page, double-spacing all text (including footnotes and endnotes). Maintain double-spacing between paragraphs and between lines of text and any displayed quotations. Leave a one-inch margin on the top and bottom of a page and a one-inch margin on both sides of a page. If you are working on a computer, set the margins as well as the running head (your last name and a page number) automatically. With each new paragraph, indent five spaces (on a computer, press the Tab key). For displayed quotations (see 28a-4), indent ten spaces and maintain that indentation for the length of the quotation.

Design of first page

Following the MLA format, you do not need to prepare a separate title page for your research papers. (This convention differs in the sciences and social sciences. See the box on page 722 as well as the example research paper beginning on page 748.) Observe the spacing of headings and title in the following example.

1"

1" ↑

1/2" ↓
Brooks 1 ← 1" →

1" →Brandy H. M. Brooks ⎤ Double space
Dr. Glenn Adelson ⎦

English 16 ⎤ Double space
25 October 1998 ⎦

Center title

The Role of Color in Kate Chopin's ⎤ Double space
"A Shameful Affair" ⎦

Indent 5 spaces
→Kate Chopin is a writer of self-discoveries-- ⎤ Double space
of characters who awaken to desires buried deep ⎦ space
within and only dimly understood (if understood at
all). In leading the reader through a character's
discovery, Chopin often prefers powerful descriptive images to explicit speeches or action. The
setting in which a character finds herself, for
instance, can reflect or influence her development
of self-awareness. In "A Shameful Affair," Chopin
communicates Mildred Orme's sexual awakening
through descriptions of a farm and, particularly,
through the colors one finds there.

Design of subsequent pages

Observe the position of the running head and the first line of text on a paper's second or subsequent page.

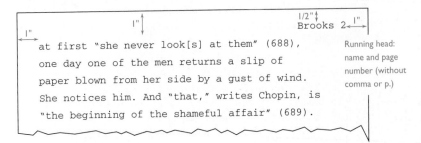

1"

1/2" ↕
Brooks 2 ←1"→

1"

at first "she never look[s] at them" (688),
one day one of the men returns a slip of
paper blown from her side by a gust of wind.
She notices him. And "that," writes Chopin, is
"the beginning of the shameful affair" (689).

Running head:
name and page
number (without
comma or p.)

Design of "Works Cited" page

Observe the position of the running head, the title "Works Cited," and the indentation of the reference entry's second line.

1"

1/2" ↕
Brooks 8 ←1"→

Works Cited — Double space

1"→ Chopin, Kate. "A Shameful Affair." "The Awakening"

5 spaces ← → and Other Stories. Ed. Lewis Leary. New York:

Holt, 1970. 31-37.

Dyer, Joyce. "Symbolic Setting in Kate Chopin's

'A Shameful Affair.'" Southern Studies: An

Interdisciplinary Journal of the South 20

(1981): 447-52.

Simpson, Martin. "Chopin's 'A Shameful Affair.'"

The Explicator 45.1 (1986): 59-60.

A3   Text preparation

Printing a manuscript on a word processor

Use Times New Roman (or another easily readable typeface) and a 12-point type size. Print on one side of the page and, if possible, use a laser printer. If none is available, use a dot matrix printer with a fresh ribbon. Keep the right-hand edge of your text ragged, or *un*justified. If your dot matrix machine is printing a light page, try photocopying the page with the photocopier adjusted to a darker than normal setting. Keep a copy of your work on disk.

COMPUTER TIPS

Widows and Orphans

When your word processor paginates a final draft for you, a page or paragraph may break in an awkward spot, leaving either a *widow*—one word alone on a line at the end of a paragraph—or an *orphan*—one short line alone at the top of a page or column. For aesthetic reasons, you should avoid these awkward breaks. Many word processors have an option that will automatically eliminate widows and orphans. If your program does not have this option, then you may have to rewrite a sentence or paragraph to eliminate them yourself.

Printing a manuscript on a typewriter

Type on one side of a page with standard typewriter fonts. Avoid typefaces giving the appearance of script, since these are difficult to read. Use a fresh ribbon with black ink.

Handwriting a manuscript

Very few instructors accept handwritten papers. If yours does, use lined, white 8½ × 11 inch paper. Do not use spiral-bound notebook paper with its ragged edges. Write neatly and legibly in pen, on one side of the page, using dark blue or black ink. Consult your instructor, who may ask you to skip every other line to allow room for editorial comments.

A4   Alterations

In a final review of your paper, when you are working away from your typewriter or word processor, you may find it necessary to make minor changes to your text—perhaps to correct a typographical error or to improve your wording. Make corrections *neatly*. When striking out a word, do so with a single line. Use a caret (^) to mark an insertion in the text, and write your correction or addition above the line you are altering. If time permits and you have worked on a word processor, enter the changes into your file and reprint the affected pages. Retype or reprint a page when you make three or more handwritten corrections on it. If your typewriter or computer keyboard lacks a particular symbol or mark that you need, handwrite that symbol on the page.

nonetheless

```
For reasons Mildred does not yet understand but that
compel her, she must be near Fred Evelyn.              ^
```

Observe the following standard conventions for spacing before and after marks of punctuation.

One space before

    beginning parenthesis or bracket

    beginning quotation mark

    period in a series denoting an omission—see ellipses, 29e

No space before (except as noted)

comma	question mark	semicolon
period[1]	apostrophe	end quotation mark
exclamation point	colon	hyphen or dash

No space after (except as noted)

    hyphen[2] or dash

    beginning parenthesis or bracket

    apostrophe[3]

One space after (except as noted)

    comma, semicolon, or colon[4]

    apostrophe denoting the possessive form of a plural

    end parenthesis or bracket that does not end a sentence

    end quotation within a sentence

    period in a series denoting an omission—see ellipses, 29e

    period marking an abbreviated name or an initial

Place one space after the following end-of-sentence punctuation marks, unless you prefer or your instructor asks you to follow these marks with two spaces—the convention used for example student papers in this text. Choose *your* convention—one or two spaces—and be consistent throughout your papers.

    final sentence period

    question mark, exclamation point

    closing quotation, end parenthesis or bracket

Exceptions (as noted above)

    [1]Unless the period occurs in a series denoting omission—see 29e.

    [2]Unless the hyphen denotes one in a pair or series of delayed adjectives, as in *a first-, second-, or third-place finish.*

    [3]Unless the apostrophe denotes the possessive form of a plural, as in *boys',* in which case skip one space.

    [4]Unless the colon denotes a ratio, as in *3:2.*

Glossary of Usage

This glossary is intended to provide definitions and descriptions of selected word usages current in formal academic writing. In consulting this kind of glossary, writers should be prepared to make informed decisions about the meaning and the level of diction that is most appropriate to their writing project.

Many entries in this glossary consist of commonly confused homonyms—words that are pronounced almost alike but have different meanings and spellings. A comprehensive listing of often-confused homonyms appears in 23a-1 in the spelling chapter.

a, an Use *a* when the article precedes a noun beginning with a consonant. For example, *At last we found a hotel.* Use *an* when the article precedes a word beginning with a vowel or an unpronounced *h*. *It was an honor to receive an invitation.* (See 7a.)

accept, except Use *accept* when your meaning is "to receive." Use *except* when you mean an exception, as in *He invited everyone except Thuan.* You can also use *except* as a verb that means "to leave out," as in *The report excepted the two episodes of misconduct.*

adverse, averse Use *averse* when you mean a person's feelings of opposition. Use *adverse* when you refer to a thing that stands in opposition or is opposed to someone or something, as in *I was not averse to taking the roofing job, but the adverse circumstances of a tight deadline and bad weather almost kept me from it.*

advice, advise Use *advice* as a noun meaning "a recommendation," as in *Longfellow gave excellent military advice.* Use *advise* as a verb meaning "to recommend," as in *Many counselors advise students to declare a double major.*

affect, effect If your sentence requires a verb meaning "to have an influence on," use *affect*. If your sentence requires a noun meaning "result," use *effect*. *Effect* can also be a verb, however. Use *effect* as a verb when you mean "to make happen," as in *He was able to effect a change in how the city council viewed the benefits of recycling.*

aggravate, irritate In formal writing, use *aggravate* when you mean "to make worse," as in *The smoke aggravated his cough.* Use *irritate* when you mean "to bother," as in *He became irritated when the drunken driver said the accident was not her fault.*

ain't Do not use *ain't* in formal writing. Use *is not, are not,* or *am not* instead.

all ready, already Use *all ready* when you mean "prepared" as in *He was all ready for an expedition to Antarctica.* Use *already* when you mean "by this time," as in *The ushers at Symphony Hall will not seat you if the concert has already started.*

all right Do not use *alright.* It is simply a misspelling.

all together, altogether Use *all together* when you mean "as a group" or "in unison," as in *Once we got the family all together, we could discuss the estate.* Use *altogether* when you mean "entirely," as in *Some of the stories about Poe's addictions and personal habits are not altogether correct.* (See 23a.)

allude, elude Use *allude* when you mean "to refer indirectly to." Use *elude* when you mean "to avoid or escape."

allusion, illusion Use *allusion* when you mean "an indirect reference," as in *The children did not understand the allusion to Roman mythology.* Use *illusion* when you mean "false or misleading belief or appearance," as in *Smith labored under the illusion that he was a great artist.*

a lot Do not use *a lot* in formal writing. Use a more specific modifier instead. When you use *a lot* in other contexts, remember that it is always two words.

among, between Use *between* when you are expressing a relationship involving two people or things, as in *There was general agreement between Robb and Jackson on that issue.* Use *among* when you are expressing a relationship involving three or more separable people or things, as in *He failed to detect a link among the blood cholesterol levels, the red blood cell counts, and the T-cell production rates.*

amongst Do not use *amongst* in formal writing. Instead, use *among.*

amount, number Use *amount* when you refer to a quantity of something that cannot be counted, as in *The amount of effort put into finding the cure for AIDS is beyond calculation.* Use *number* when you refer to something that can be counted, as in *The number of people who want to run the Boston Marathon increases yearly.*

an, and Use *an* when the article precedes a noun beginning with a vowel or an unpronounced *h.* Use *and* when your sentence requires a conjunction that means "in addition to."

and etc. Avoid using *etc.* in formal writing. When you must use *etc.* in nonformal writing, do not use *and. Et cetera* means "and so forth"; therefore, *and etc.* is redundant.

and/or Use *and* or *or,* or explain your ideas by writing them out fully. But avoid *and/or,* which is usually too ambiguous to meet the demands of formal writing.

anxious, eager   Use *anxious* when you mean "worried" or "nervous." Use *eager* when you mean "excited or enthusiastic about the possibility of doing something."

anybody, any body; anyone, any one   Use *anybody* and *anyone* when the sense of your sentence requires an indefinite pronoun. Use *any body* and *any one* when the words *body* and *one* are modified by *any*, as in *The teacher was careful not to favor any one student* and *Any body of knowledge is subject to change.*

any more, anymore   Use *any more* to mean "no more," as in *I don't want any more of those plums.* Use *anymore* as an adverb meaning "now," as in *He doesn't work here anymore.*

anyplace   Do not use *anyplace* in formal writing. Use *anywhere* instead.

anyways, anywheres   Do not use *anyways* and *anywheres* in formal writing; use *anyway* and *anywhere* instead.

apt, likely, liable   Use *apt* when you mean "having a tendency to," as in *Khrushchev was apt to lose his temper in public.* Use *likely* when you mean "probably going to," as in *We will likely hear from the Senator by Friday.* Use *liable* when you mean "in danger of," as in *People who jog long distances over concrete surfaces are liable to sustain knee injuries.* Also use *liable* when you are referring to legal responsibility, as in *The driver who was at fault was liable for the damages.*

as, like   Use *as* either as a preposition or as a conjunction, but use *like* as a preposition only. If your sentence requires a preposition, use *as* when you are making an exact equivalence, as in *Edison was known as the wizard of Menlo Park.* Use *like* when you are referring to likeness, resemblance, or similarity, as in *Like Roosevelt, Reagan was able to make his constituency feel optimism.*

as, than   When you are making a comparison, you can follow both *as* and *than* with a subjective- or objective-case pronoun, depending on meaning. For example, *We trusted O'Keeffe more than him [we trusted Smith]* and *We trusted O'Keeffe more than he [Jones trusted O'Keeffe]. O'Keeffe was as talented as he [was talented]* and *We found O'Keeffe as trustworthy as [we found] him.* (See 8g.)

as to   Do not use *as to* in formal writing. Rewrite a sentence such as *The president was questioned as to his recent decisions in the Middle East* to read *The president was questioned about his recent decisions in the Middle East.*

assure, ensure, insure   Use *assure* when you mean "to promise" as in *He assured his mother that he would return early.* Use *ensure* when you mean "to make certain," as in *Taking a prep course does not ensure success in the SATs.* Use *insure* when you mean "to make certain" in a legal or financial sense, as in *He insured his boat against theft and vandalism.*

at   Do not use *at* in a question formed with *where*. For example, rewrite a sentence such as *Where is the class at?* to read *Where is the class?*

a while, awhile   Use *awhile* when your sentence requires an adverb, as in *He swam awhile*. If you are not modifying a verb, but rather want a noun with an article, use *a while*, as in *I have not seen you in a while*.

bad, badly   Use *bad* as an adjective, as in *Bad pitching changed the complexion of the game*. Use *badly* as an adverb, as in *The refugees badly needed food and shelter*. Use *bad* to follow linking verbs that involve appearance or feeling, as in *She felt bad about missing the party*. (See 11d.)

being as, being that   Do not use either *being as* or *being that* to mean "because" in formal writing. Use *because* instead.

beside, besides   Use *beside* as a preposition meaning "next to." Use *besides* as an adverb meaning "also" or "in addition to" as in *Besides, I needed to lose the weight*. Use *besides* as an adjective meaning "except" or "in addition to," as in *Rosa Parks seemed to have nothing besides courage to support her*.

better, had better; best, had best   Do not use *better, had better, best,* and *had best* for *should* in formal writing. Use *ought* or *should* instead.

between, among   See *among, between*.

breath, breathe   Use *breath* as a noun; use *breathe* as a verb.

bring, take   Use *bring* when you are referring to movement from a farther place to a nearer one, as in *The astronauts were asked to bring back rock samples*. Use *take* for all other types of movement.

broke   Use *broke* only as the past tense, as in *He broke the Ming vase*. Do not use *broke* as the past participle; for example, instead of writing *The priceless vase was broke as a result of careless handling*, write *The priceless vase was broken as a result of careless handling*.

bunch   Use *bunch* to refer to "a group or cluster of things growing together." Do not use *bunch* to refer to people or a group of items in formal writing.

burst, bust   Use *burst* when you mean "to fly apart suddenly," as in *The pomegranate burst open*. (Notice that the example sentence doesn't say *bursted*; there is no such form of the verb.) (See 9b.)

but however, but yet   When you use *however* and *yet*, do not precede them with *but* in formal writing. The *but* is redundant.

but that, but what   When you use *that* and *what*, do not precede them with *but* in formal writing. The *but* is unnecessary.

calculate, figure, reckon   If your sentence requires a word that means "imagine," use *imagine*. Do not use *calculate, figure,* or *reckon,* which are colloquial substitutes for "imagine."

can, may   Use *can* when you are writing about the ability to do something, as in *He can jump six feet*. Use *may* when you are referring to permission, as in *He may rejoin the team when the period of probation is over*.

can't, couldn't Do not use these contractions in formal writing. Use *cannot* and *could not* instead.

can't hardly, can't scarcely See *not but, not hardly, not scarcely.*

can't help but Use *can't help* by itself; the *but* is redundant.

censor, censure Use *censor* when you mean editing or removing from the public eye on the basis of morality. Use *censure* when you mean "to give a formal or official scolding or verbal punishment."

center around Do not use *center around* in formal writing. Instead, use *center on.*

chose, choose Use the verb *choose* in the present tense for the first and second person and for the future tense, as in *They choose [or will choose] their teams carefully.* Use *chose* for the past tense, as in *The presidential candidate chose a distinguished running mate.*

compare to, compare with Use *compare to* to note similarities between things, as in *He compared the Chinese wine vessel to the Etruscan wine cup.* Use *compare with* to note similarities and contrasts, as in *When comparing market-driven economies with socialist economies, social scientists find a wide range of difference in the standard of living of individuals.*

complement, compliment Use *complement* when you mean "something that completes," as in *The wine was the perfect complement for the elegant meal.* Use *compliment* when you mean "praise," as in *The administrator savored the compliment on her organizational skills.*

conscience, conscious Use *conscience* when your sentence requires a noun meaning "a sense of right or wrong." Use *conscious* as an adjective to mean "aware of" or "awake."

consensus of opinion Do not use *consensus of opinion* in formal writing. Use *consensus* instead to avoid redundancy.

continual, continuous Use *continual* when you mean "constantly recurring," as in *Continual thunderstorms ruined their vacation days at the beach.* Use *continuous* when you mean "unceasing," as in *The continuous sound of a heartbeat, unceasing and increasing in volume, haunted the narrator.*

could of, would of, should of, might of, may of, must of In formal writing, avoid combining modal auxiliaries (*could, would, should, might, may,* and *must*) with *of.* Instead, write *could have, would have, should have, might have, may have,* and *must have.*

couple, couple of Do not use *couple* or *couple of* to mean "a few" in formal writing. Instead, write *a few.*

criteria Use *criteria* when you want a plural word referring to more than one standard of judgment. Use *criterion* when you are referring to only one standard of judgment.

data Use *data* when you are referring to more than one fact, statistic, or other means of support for a conclusion. When you are referring to a single fact, use the word *datum* in formal writing, or use *fact*, *figure*, or another term that is specific to the single means of support.

different from, different than Use *different from* when an object or phrase follows, as in *Braque's style is different from Picasso's.* Use *different than* when a clause follows, as in *Smith's position on the deficit was different when he was seeking the presidency than it was when he was president.*

differ from, differ with Use *differ from* when you are referring to unlike things, as in *Subsequent results of experiments in cold fusion differed radically from results first obtained in Utah.* Use *differ with* to mean "disagree," as in *One expert might differ with another on a point of usage.*

discreet, discrete Use *discreet* to mean "respectfully reserved," as in *He was always discreet when he entered the synagogue.* Use *discrete* to mean "separate" or "distinct," as in *The essay was a discrete part of the examination and could be answered as a take-home assignment.*

disinterested, uninterested Use *disinterested* to mean "impartial," as in *An umpire should always be disinterested in which team wins.* Use *uninterested* to mean "bored" or "not interested."

doesn't, don't Do not use *doesn't* and *don't* in formal writing; instead, use *does not* and *do not*. In other contexts, use *don't* with the first and second person singular, as in *I don't smoke*, and with the third person plural, as in *They don't smoke.* Use *doesn't* with the third person singular, as in *He doesn't ride the subway.*

done Use *done* when your sentence requires the past participle; do not use done as the simple past. For example, rewrite a sentence such as *Van Gogh done the painting at Arles* to read *Van Gogh did the painting at Arles.*

due to, due to the fact that Use *due to* to mean "because" only when it follows a form of the verb *be*, as in *The sensation of a leg falling asleep is due to pooling of the blood in the veins.* Do not use *due to* as a preposition, however. Also, do not use *due to the fact that* in formal writing because it is wordy. (See 17a.)

eager, anxious See *anxious, eager.*

effect, affect See *affect, effect.*

elicit, illicit Use *elicit* to mean "to draw out," as in *The social worker finally elicited a response from the child.* Use *illicit* to mean "illegal," as in *Illicit transactions on the black market fuel an underground Soviet economy.* (See 23a.)

emigrate, immigrate, migrate Use *emigrate* to mean "to move away from one's country." Use *immigrate* to mean "to move to another country." Use *migrate* to mean "to move to another place on a temporary basis."

ensure, assure, insure See *assure, ensure, insure.*

enthused, enthusiastic Use *enthusiastic* when you mean "excited about" or "showing enthusiasm." Do not use *enthused* in formal writing.

especially, specially Use *especially* when you mean "particularly," as in *Maria Mitchell was especially talented as a mathematician.* Use *specially* when you mean "for a specific reason," as in *The drug was intended specially for the treatment of rheumatism.*

et al., etc. Do not use *et al.* and *etc.* interchangeably. *Et al.* is generally used in references and bibliographies and is Latin for "and others." *Et cetera* is Latin for "and so forth." Like all abbreviations, *et al.* and *etc.* are generally not used in formal writing, except that *et al.* is acceptable in the context of a citation to a source.

etc. Do not use *etc.* in formal writing. Use *and so forth* instead. Or, preferably, be as specific as necessary to eliminate the phrase.

everybody, every body Use *everybody* when you mean "everyone." Use *every body* when you are using *body* as a distinct word modified by *every,* as in *Is every body of water in Canada contaminated by acid rain?*

every day, everyday Use *everyday* when your sentence requires an adjective meaning "common" or "daily," as in *Availability of water was an everyday problem in ancient Egypt.* Use *every day* when you are using the word *day* and modifying it with the adjective *every,* as in *Enrico went to the art gallery every day.*

everywheres Do not use *everywheres* in formal writing. Use *everywhere* instead.

except, accept See *accept, except.*

except for the fact that In formal writing prefer the less wordy *except that.*

explicit, implicit Use *explicit* when you mean "stated outright," as in *The Supreme Court rules on issues that are not explicit in the Constitution.* Use *implicit* when you mean "implied," as in *Her respect for the constitution was implicit in her remarks.*

farther, further Use *farther* when you are referring to distance, as in *He was able to run farther after eating carbohydrates.* Use *further* when you are referring to something that cannot be measured, such as *Further negotiations are needed between the central government and the people of Azerbaijan.*

fewer, less Use *fewer* when you are referring to items that can be counted, as in *There are fewer savings accounts at the branch office this year.* Use *less* when you are referring to things that cannot be counted, as in *I have less confidence in the administration today than I did a year ago.* (See 11e.)

figure See *calculate, figure, reckon.*

fixing to Do not use *fixing to* in formal writing. Use *intend to* instead.

former, latter Use *former* and *latter* only when you are referring to two things. In that case, the former is the first thing, and the latter is the second. If you are referring to more than two things, use *first* for the first and *last* for the last.

get   Do not overuse *get* in formal writing. Prefer more precise words. For example, instead of *get better*, write *improve*; instead of *get*, write *receive*, *catch*, or *become*; instead of *get done*, write *finish* or *end.*

gone, went   Use *gone* when your sentence requires the past participle of *to go*, as in *They had gone there several times.* Use *went* when your sentence requires the past tense of *to go*, as in *They went to the theater Friday.*

good, well   Use *good* as an adjective, as in *Astaire gave a good performance, but not one of his best.* Use *well* as an adverb, as in *He danced well.* You can also use *well* as an adjective when you refer to good health, as in *She felt well* or *She is well today.* (See 11d.)

good and   Do not use *good and* in formal writing. Use *very* or, preferably, a more precise modifier instead.

got, have; has/have got to   Do not use *got* in place of *have* in formal writing. For example, rewrite a sentence such as *I got to lose weight* to read *I have to [or I must] lose weight.*

had better, better; had best, best   See *better, had better.*

had ought   Do not use *had ought* in formal writing. Use *ought* by itself instead.

half   When you refer to half of something in formal writing, use *a half* or *one-half*, but do not use *a half a*. For example, rewrite a sentence such as *He had a half a sandwich for dinner* to read *He had a half sandwich for dinner.*

hanged, hung   Use *hanged* for the action of hanging a person, as in *The innocent man was hanged by an angry mob.* Use *hung* for all other meanings, such as *The clothes were hung on the line* and *The chandelier hung from a golden rope.* (See 9b.)

he, she; he/she; his, her; his/her; him, her; him/her   When you are using a pronoun to refer back to a noun that could be either masculine or feminine, you might use *he or she* in order to avoid language that is now considered sexist. For example, instead of writing *A doctor must be constantly alert; he cannot make a single mistake* to refer generally to doctors, you could write *A doctor must be constantly alert; he or she cannot make a single mistake.* Or you could recast the sentence in the plural to avoid this problem: *Doctors must be constantly alert; they cannot make a single mistake.* (See 10c and 21g for specific strategies on avoiding gender-offensive pronoun references.)

herself, himself, myself, yourself   Use pronouns ending in *-self* when the pronouns refer to a noun that they intensify, as in *The teacher himself could not pass the test.* Do not use pronouns ending in *-self* to take the place of subjective- or objective-case pronouns. Instead of writing, for example, *Joan and myself are good friends*, write *Joan and I are good friends.* (See 7a.)

himself   See *herself, himself, myself, yourself.*

his/her   See *he, she.*

hisself   Do not use *hisself* in formal writing. In a context such as *He hisself organized the picnic,* recast the sentence to read *He himself organized the picnic.*

hopefully   Use *hopefully* when you mean "with hope," as in *Relatives watched hopefully as the first miners emerged after the fire.* Avoid using *hopefully* as a modifier for an entire clause or to convey any other meaning. For example, avoid *Hopefully, a cure for leukemia is not far away.*

hung, hanged   See *hanged, hung.*

if, whether   Use *if* to begin a subordinate clause when a stated or implied result follows, as in *If the court rules against the cigarette manufacturers, [then] thousands of lawsuits could follow.* Use *whether* when you are expressing an alternative, as in *Economists do not know whether the dollar will rebound or fall against the strength of the yen.*

illicit, elicit   See *elicit, illicit.*

illusion, allusion   See *allusion, illusion.*

immigrate   See *emigrate, immigrate, migrate.*

impact   Use *impact* when you are referring to a forceful collision, as in *The impact of the cars was so great that one was flattened.* Do not use *impact* as a verb meaning "to have an effect on." Instead of writing *Each of us can positively impact waste reduction efforts,* write *Each of us can reduce waste.*

implicit, explicit   See *explicit, implicit.*

imply, infer   Use *imply* when you mean "to suggest without directly stating," as in *The doctor implied that being overweight was the main cause of my problem.* Use *infer* when you mean "to find the meaning of something," as in *I inferred from her lecture that drinking more than two cups of coffee a day was a health risk.*

in, into   Use *in* when you are referring to location or condition. Use *into* to refer to a change in location, such as *The famous portrait shows a man going into a palace.* In formal writing, do not use *into* for "interested in." For example, avoid a statement such as *I am into repairing engines.*

incredible, incredulous   Use *incredible* to mean "unbelievable," as in *Some of Houdini's exploits seem incredible to those who did not witness them.* Use *incredulous* to mean "unbelieving," as in *Many inlanders were incredulous when they heard tales of white people capturing men, women, and children who lived on the coast.*

individual, person, party   Use *individual* when you are referring to a single person and when your purpose is to stress that the person is unique, as in *Curie was a tireless and brilliant individual.* Use *party* when you mean a group, as in *The party of eight at the next table disturbed our conversation and* *ruined our evening.* The word *party* is also correctly used in legal documents referring to a single person. Use *person* for other meanings.

infer, imply   See *imply, infer.*

in regards to   Do not use *in regards to* in formal writing. Generally, you can substitute *about* for *in regards to.*

inside of, outside of   Use *inside* and *outside,* without *of,* when you are referring to location, as in *The roller blades were stored inside the garage.* In formal writing, do not use *inside of* to replace *within* in an expression of time. For example, avoid a sentence such as *I'll have that report inside of an hour.*

insure, assure, ensure   See *assure, ensure, insure.*

irregardless, regardless   Do not use *irregardless.* Use *regardless* instead.

is when, is where   Do not use *is when* and *is where* when you are defining something. Instead of writing *Dinner time is when my family relaxes,* write *At dinner time, my family relaxes.*

its, it's   Use *its* when your sentence requires a possessive pronoun, as in *Its leaves are actually long, slender blades.* (See 8c-1 and 27a-2.) Use *it's* only when you mean "it is." (See 23a.)

-ize   Do not use the suffix *-ize* to turn a noun into a verb in formal writing. For example, instead of writing *He is finalizing his draft,* write *He is finishing his draft* or *He is working on his final draft.*

kind, sort, type   Do not precede the singular words *kind, sort,* and *type* with the plural word *these.* Use *this* instead. Also, prefer more specific words than *kind, sort,* and *type.* (See 17a.)

kind of, sort of   Do not use these phrases as adjectives in formal writing. Instead, use *rather* or *somewhat.*

later, latter   Use *later* when you refer to time, as in *I will go to the concert later.* Use *latter* when you refer to the second of two things, as in *The latter of the two dates is better for my schedule.* (See also *former, latter.*)

latter, former   See *former, latter.*

lay, lie   Use *lay* when you mean "to put" or "to place," as in *She lays the present on the table.* Use *lie* when you mean "recline," as in *She lies awake at night,* or when you mean "is situated," as in *The city lies between a desert and a mountain range.* Also, remember that *lay* is a transitive verb that takes a direct object. (See 9d.)

learn, teach   Do not use *learn* to mean "teach." For example, rewrite a sentence such as *Ms. Chin learned us Algebra* to read *Ms. Chin taught us Algebra.*

leave, let   Use *leave* to mean "depart." Use *let* to mean "allow." You can use either *leave* or *let* when the word is followed by *alone,* as in *Leave her alone* or *Let him alone.*

less, fewer   See *fewer, less.*

liable   See *apt, likely, liable.*

lie, lay   See *lay, lie.*

like, as   See *as, like.*

like, such as   Use *like* to make a comparison, as in *Verbena is like ageratum in size and color.* Use *such as* when you are giving examples, as in *Many small flowers, such as verbena, ageratum, and alyssum, can be combined to create decorative borders and edgings.*

likely   See *apt, likely, liable.*

lose, loose   Use *lose* as a verb meaning "to misplace" or "to fail to win." Use *loose* as an adjective meaning "not tight" or "unfastened." You can also use *loose* as a verb meaning "to let loose," as in *They loosed the enraged bull when the matador entered the ring.* (See 23a.)

lots, lots of   Do not use *lots* or *lots of* in formal writing. Use *many, very many, much,* or choose a more precise word instead.

man, mankind   Do not use *man* and *mankind* to refer to all people in general. Instead, consider using *people, men and women, humans,* or *humankind.* (See 21g.)

may, can   See *can, may.*

may be, maybe   Use *maybe* to mean "perhaps." Use *may be* as a verb (or auxiliary verb), as in *William may be visiting tomorrow.* (See 23a.)**may of**   See *could of, would of, should of, might of, may of, must of.*

media   Use a plural verb with *media,* as in *The media are often credited with helping the consumer win cases against large companies. Medium* is the singular form.

might of   See *could of, would of, should of, might of, may of, must of.*

migrate   See *emigrate, immigrate, migrate.*

moral, morale   Use *moral* when you mean "an object lesson" or "knowing right from wrong." *What is the moral to the story?* Use *morale* when you mean "outlook" or "attitude." *The team's morale was high.* (See 23a.)

Ms.   Use *Ms.* to refer to a woman when a title is required and when you either know that she prefers this title or you do not know her marital status. An invented title, *Ms.* was intended to address the issue of discrimination or judgment based on marital status. In research writing, use last names alone, without any title, as in *Jenkins recommends.* In this case, do not use a title for either a man or a woman.

must of   See *could of, would of, should of, might of, may of, must of.*

myself   See *herself, himself, myself, yourself.*

nor, or   Use *nor* and *or* to suggest a choice. Use *nor* when the choice is negative; use *or* when the choice is positive. (See 7f.)

not but, not hardly, not scarcely   Do not use *not* to precede *hardly*, *scarcely*, and *but* in formal writing. Because *but*, *hardly*, and *scarcely* already carry the meaning of a negative, it is not necessary or correct to add another negative.

nothing like, nowhere near   Do not use *nothing like* and *nowhere near* in formal writing. Instead, use *not nearly*.

nowheres   Do not use *nowheres* in formal writing. Use *nowhere* instead.

number, amount   See *amount, number*.

off of   Do not use *off of* in formal writing. Use *off* or *from* alone instead, as in *She jumped off the bridge* or *He leaped from the rooftop*.

Ok, okay, O.K.   Do not use *Ok*, *okay*, or *O.K.* in formal writing as a substitute for *acceptable*.

on, upon   Use *on* instead of *upon* in formal writing.

on account of   Do not use this as a substitute for *because*. Use *because* instead.

or, nor   See *nor, or*.

outside of, inside of   See *inside of, outside of*.

party, individual, person   See *individual, person, party*.

people, persons   Use *people* to refer to a general group, as in *The people will make their voices heard*. Use *persons* to refer to a (usually small) collection of individuals, as in *The persons we interviewed were nearly unanimous in their opinion*.

per   Do not use *per* in formal writing. For example, instead of writing *The package was sent per your instructions*, it is better to write *The package was sent according to your instructions*. *Per* is acceptable in technical writing or when used with data and prices, as in *Charging $75 per hour, the consultant earned a handsome salary*.

percent (per cent), percentage   Use *percent* (or *per cent*) with a specific number. Use *percentage* with specific descriptive words and phrases, such as *A small percentage of the group did not eat meat*. Do not use *percentage* as a substitute for *part*; for example, rewrite a sentence such as *A percentage of my diet consists of complex carbohydrates* to read *Part of my diet consists of complex carbohydrates*.

person, party, individual   See *individual, person, party*.

plenty   Do not use *plenty* as a substitute for *quite* or *very*. For example, instead of writing *The Confederate troops were plenty hungry during the winter of 1864*, write *The Confederate troops were hungry [or starving] during the winter of 1864*.

plus   Avoid using *plus* as a conjunction joining independent clauses or as a conjunctive adverb. For example, rewrite *Picasso used color in a new way plus he experimented with shape; plus, he brought new meaning to ideas* *about abstract painting* to read *Picasso used color in a new way and he experimented with shape; moreover, he brought new meaning to ideas about abstract painting.* It is acceptable to use *plus* when you need an expression meaning "in addition to," as in *The costs of day care, plus the costs of feeding and clothing the child, weighed heavily on the single parent's budget.*

practicable, practical   Use *practicable* when you mean "capable of putting into practice," as in *Although it seemed logical, the plan for saving the zoo was very expensive and turned out not to be practicable.* Use *practical* when you mean "sensible," as in *Lincoln was a practical young man who studied hard, paid his debts, and dealt with people honestly.*

precede, proceed   Use *precede* when you mean "come before," as in *The opening remarks precede the speech.* Use *proceed* when you mean "go forward," as in *The motorists proceeded with caution.*

pretty   Do not use *pretty*, as in *pretty close*, to mean "somewhat" or "quite" in formal writing. Use *somewhat, rather,* or *quite* instead.

previous to, prior to   Avoid these wordy expressions. Use *before* instead.

principal, principle   Use *principal* when you refer to a school administrator or an amount of money. Use *principle* when you are referring to a law, conviction, or fundamental truth. You can also use *principal* as an adjective meaning "major" or "most important," as in *The principal players in the decision were Sue Marks and Tom Cohen.*

quotation, quote   Use *quotation* when your sentence requires a noun, as in *The quotation from Nobel laureate Joseph Goldstein was used to lend credence to the theory.* Use *quote* when your sentence requires a verb, as in *She asked Goldstein whether she could quote him.*

raise, rise   Use *raise* when you mean "to lift." Use *rise* when you mean "to get up." To help you understand the difference, remember that *raise* is transitive and takes a direct object; *rise* is intransitive. (See 9d.)

rarely ever   Do not use *rarely ever* in formal writing. Use *rarely* or *hardly ever* instead.

real, really   Use *real* as an adjective and use *really* as an adverb.

reason is because   Do not use *reason is because* in formal writing. Rewrite your sentence to say, for example, *The real reason that the bomb was dropped was to end the war quickly* or *The bomb was dropped because Truman wanted to prevent Soviet influence in the Far Eastern settlement.*

reckon   See *calculate, figure, reckon.*

regarding, in regard to, with regard to   In formal writing that is not legal in nature, use *about* or *concerning* instead of these terms.

regardless, irregardless   See *irregardless, regardless.*

respectfully, respectively   Use *respectfully* when you mean "with respect," as in *He respectfully submitted his grievances.* Use *respectively* when you mean "in the given order," as in *The chief of police, the director of the department of public works, and the director of parks and recreation, respectively, submitted their ideas for budget cuts.*

right Do not use *right* as an intensifier in formal writing. For example, instead of writing *The farmer was right tired after milking the cows,* write *The farmer was tired [or exhausted] after milking the cows.*

rise, raise See *raise, rise.*

seen Do not use *seen* without an auxiliary such as *have, has,* or *had.* For example, rewrite a sentence such as *I seen the film* to read *I have seen the film.*

set, sit Use *set* when you mean "to place." *Set* is a transitive verb that requires an object, as in *I set the book on the table.* Do not use *set* to mean "to sit" in formal writing. (See 9d.)

shall, will Use *shall* instead of *will* for questions that contain the first person in extremely formal writing, as in *Shall we attend the meeting?* In all other cases, use *will.*

should of See *could of, would of, should of, might of, may of, must of.*

should, would Use *should* when you are referring to an obligation or a condition, as in *The governor's mansion should be restored.* Use *would* when you are referring to a wish, as in *I would like to see it repainted in its original colors.*

sit, set See *set, sit.*

so Do not use *so* in formal writing to mean "very" or "extremely," as in *He is so entertaining.* Use *very, extremely,* or, preferably, a more specific intensifier instead. Or follow *so* with an explanation preceded by *that,* as in *The reaction to the Freedom Riders was so violent that Robert F. Kennedy ordered a military escort.*

some Do not use *some* to mean either "remarkable" or "somewhat" in formal writing. For example, rewrite a sentence such as *Babe Ruth was some hitter* to read *Babe Ruth was a remarkable hitter,* or use another more precise adjective to modify *hitter.* Also, rewrite a sentence such as *Wright's mother worried some about the kinds of building blocks her young child used* to read *Wright's mother worried a bit [or was somewhat worried about] the kinds of building blocks her young child used.*

somebody, some body; someone, some one Use the indefinite pronouns *somebody* and *someone* when referring to a person, such as *There is someone I admire.* Use *some body* and *some one* when the adjective *some* modifies the noun *body* or *one,* as in *We will find the answer in some body of information.*

sometime, sometimes, some time Use *sometime* when you mean "an indefinite, later time." Use *sometimes* when you mean "occasionally" or "from time to time." Use *some time* when *some* functions as an adjective modifying *time,* as in *His eyes required some time to adjust to the darkened room.*

sort   See *kind, sort, type.*

specially, especially   See *especially, specially.*

stationary, stationery   Use *stationary* to mean "standing still." Use *stationery* to mean "writing paper."

such   Do not use *such* to mean "very" or "extremely" unless *such* is followed by *that.* For example, rewrite a sentence such as *It had such boring lyrics* to read *It had extremely boring lyrics* or *It had* <u>such</u> *boring lyrics* that *I almost fell asleep half way through the song.*

such as, like   See *like, such as.*

supposed to, used to   Do not use *suppose to* or *use to* in formal writing. Use *supposed to* or *used to* instead.

sure, surely   Use *surely* instead of *sure* when your sentence requires an adverb. For example, rewrite a sentence such as *Robert Fulton was sure a genius* to read *Robert Fulton was surely [or certainly] a genius.*

sure and, sure to; try and, try to   Do not use *sure and* and *try and* in formal writing. Instead, use *sure to* and *try to.* For example, rewrite the sentence *Be sure and bring your computer* to read *Be sure to bring your computer.*

take, bring   See *bring, take.*

than, as   See *as, than.*

than, then   Use *than* when you mean "as compared with," as in *The violin is smaller than the cello.* Use *then* when you are stating a sequence of events, as in *First, he learned how to play the violin. Then he learned to play the cello.* Also use *then* when you mean "at that time" or "therefore." (See 23a.)

that there   See *this here, these here, that there, them there.*

that, which   Use *that* or *which* in an essential (or restrictive) clause, or a clause that is necessary to the meaning of the sentence, as in *This is the book that explains Locke's philosophy.* Use *which* in a nonessential (nonrestrictive) clause, or one that is not necessary to the meaning of the sentence, as in *My library just acquired Smith's book on Locke, which is not always easy to find.* (See 14e.)

their, there, they're   Use *their* as a possessive pronoun, as in *Their father prevented William and Henry James from being under the control of any one teacher for more than a year.* (See 8c-1.) Use *there* to refer to a place, as the opposite of *here.* Use *they're* to mean "they are." (See 27a-2.)

theirselves   Do not use *theirselves* in formal writing. Rewrite a sentence such as *They treated theirselves to ice cream* to read *They treated themselves to ice cream.*

them there   See *this here, these here, that there, them there.*

then, than   See *than, then.*

these here   See *this here, these here, that there, them there.*

these kind   See *kind, sort, type.*

this here, these here, that there, them there   Do not use *this here,* *these here, that there,* and *them there* in formal writing. Use *this, that, these,* and *those* instead.

thru   Do not use *thru* in formal writing. Use *through* instead.

thusly   Do not use *thusly* in formal writing. Use *thus* instead. (*Thus,* which is already an adverb, does not need an *-ly* ending.)

till, until, 'til   Do not use *'til* or *till* in formal writing. Prefer *until.*

to, too, two   Use *to* as a preposition meaning "toward"; use *too* to mean "also" or "excessively"; and use *two* as a number. (See 23a.)

toward, towards   Use *toward* instead of *towards* in formal writing. *Towards* is the British form.

try and, try to   See *sure and, sure to; try and, try to.*

type of   Do not use *type* in formal writing when you mean "type of." For example, rewrite a sentence such as *He is an anxious type person* to read *He is an anxious type of person.* (See also *kind, sort, type.*)

uninterested, disinterested   See *disinterested, uninterested.*

unique   Do not modify *unique* in formal writing. Because *unique* is an absolute, you should not write, for example, *most unique* or *very unique.*

until   See *till, until, 'til; until* is the preferred form in formal writing.

use, utilize   When you need a word that means "use," prefer *use.* *Utilize* is a less direct choice with the same meaning. (See 17a.)

used to   See *supposed to, used to.*

very   Avoid using *very* as an intensifier. Sometimes you will want to replace more than one word in order to eliminate *very.* For example, in the sentence *It was a very nice painting,* you could substitute more precise language, such as *It was a colorful [or provocative or highly abstract] painting.* (See 17a.)

wait for, wait on   Unless you are referring to waiting on tables, use *wait for* instead of *wait on* in formal writing. For example, rewrite *We grew tired as we waited on Sarah* to read *We grew tired as we waited for Sarah.*

ways   Do not use *ways* in formal writing to mean "way." Use *way* instead.

well, good   See *good, well.*

where at   See *at.*

whether, if   See *if, whether.*

which, that   See *that, which.*

which, who   Use *which* when you are referring to things. Use *who* when you are referring to people.

who, whom   Use *who* when a sentence requires a subject pronoun, as in *Who can answer this question?* Use *whom* when a sentence requires an object pronoun, as in *Whom did you invite?* (See 8f.)

who's, whose   Do not use *who's* in formal writing. Use *who is* instead. (See 27a-2.) Use *whose* to show possession, as in *Whose computer did you use?* (See 8f.)

will, shall   See *shall, will.*

-wise   Do not attach the suffix *-wise* to nouns or adjectives to turn them into adverbs in formal writing. For example, instead of writing *I am not doing well grade-wise*, you could recast the sentence to read *My grades are falling* or *My grades are low.*

would of   See *could of, would of, should of, might of, may of, must of.*

would, should   See *should, would.*

your, you're   Do not use *you're* in formal writing. Use *you are* instead. (See 27a-2.) Use *your* to show possession, as in *Your CD player is broken.* (See 8f.)

yourself   See *herself, himself, myself, yourself.*

Glossary of Terms:
Grammar and Composition

abbreviation　The shortened form of a word, usually followed by a period.

absolute phrase – See *phrase*.

abstract expression　An expression that refers to broad categories or ideas *(evil, friendship, love)*.

abstract noun　See *noun*.

acronym　The uppercase, pronounceable abbreviation of a proper noun—a person, organization, government agency, or country. Periods are not used with acronyms *(ARCO, WAVES)*. (See 31c.)

active voice　See *voice*.

adjective　A word that modifies or describes a noun, pronoun, or group of words functioning as a noun. Adjectives answer the questions: which, what kind, and how many. A single-word adjective is usually placed before the word it modifies. Pure adjectives are not derived from other words. (See 7a-5; Chapter 11.)

adjective clause　See *clause*.

adjective forms　Adjectives change form to express comparative relationships. The **positive form** of an adjective is its base form. The **comparative form** is used to express a relationship between two elements. The **superlative form** is used to express a relationship among three or more elements. Most single-syllable adjectives and many two-syllable adjectives show comparisons with the suffix *-er* (tall*er*) and superlatives with the suffix *-est* (tall*est*). Adjectives of three or more syllables change to the comparative and superlative forms with the words *more* and *most*, respectively *(more beautiful, most beautiful)*. Negative comparisons are formed by placing the words *less* and *least* before the positive form *(less interesting, least interesting)*. (See 11e.)

adverb　A word that modifies a verb, an adjective, another adverb, or an entire sentence. Adverbs describe, define, or otherwise limit the words they modify, answering the questions when, how, where, how often, to what extent, and to what degree. Adverbs (as words, phrases, or clauses) can appear in different places in a sentence, depending on the rhythm the writer wants to achieve. Most adverbs are formed by adding the suffix *-ly* to an adjective. (See 7a-6; Chapter 11.)

adverb clause   See *clause*.

adverb forms   The change of form that adverbs undergo to express comparative relationships. The **positive form** of an adverb is its base form. The **comparative form** is used to express a relationship between two elements. The **superlative form** is used to express a relationship among three or more elements. Most single-syllable adverbs show comparisons with the suffix *-er (nearer)* and superlatives with the suffix *-est (nearest)*. Adverbs of two or more syllables change to comparative and superlative forms with *more* and *most*, respectively *(more beautifully, most beautifully)*. Negative comparisons are formed by placing the words *less* and *least* before the positive form *(less strangely, least strangely)*. (See 11e.)

adverbial conjunction   See *conjunctive adverb*.

agreement   The grammatical relationship between a subject and a verb, and a pronoun and its antecedent. If one element in these pairs is changed, the other must also be changed. Subjects and verbs must agree in number and person; pronouns and antecedents must agree in number, person, and gender. (See Chapter 10.)

analogy   A figure of speech that makes a comparison between two apparently unrelated people, objects, conditions, or events in order to clarify a process or a difficult concept. The unknown entity is explained in terms of the more familiar entity. (See 5e-7; 6d-1; 21f-1.)

analysis   A close, careful reading of a text in which parts are studied to determine how the text as a whole functions. In a written analysis, in most instances, the author is obliged to support his or her interpretation with direct evidence from a text. (See 38c-1.)

antecedent   A noun (or occasionally a pronoun) that a pronoun refers to and renames. A pronoun and its antecedent must agree in number, person, and gender. (See 10b; Chapter 14.)

antonym   A word whose denotation (dictionary meaning) is opposite that of another word.

apostrophe   A punctuation mark used to show possession, mark the omission of letters or numbers, and mark plural forms. (See Chapter 27.)

appositive   A word or phrase that describes, identifies, or renames a noun in a sentence. (See 8e-2.)

appositive phrase   See *phrase*.

article   The words *a, an,* or *the*. The **indefinite article,** *a* or *an,* introduces a generalized noun. *A* appears before nouns beginning with a consonant; *an* is placed before nouns beginning with a vowel or an unpronounced *h*. The **definite article,** *the*, denotes a specific noun. Also called *determiners*.

assumption   A core belief, often unstated, that shapes the way people perceive the world. (See 1g.)

audience   The person or people who will be reading a piece of writing. Writing that takes a particular audience's needs and experience into consideration is most effective.

auxiliary verb   The verbs *be, will, can, have, do, shall*, and *may*, combined with the base form of another verb, or its present or past participle. Such auxiliary verbs are used to establish tense, mood, and voice in a sentence. Also called *helping verbs*. (See 7a-3; 9c.)

base form   The infinitive form of a verb *(to be, to go)* from which all changes are made. Also called the *dictionary form*.

bibliography   The list of sources used in writing a paper. An **annotated bibliography** is a fully annotated working bibliography in manuscript form. A **working bibliography** includes all of the sources located in researching a paper. A **final bibliography** consists of only those sources used in the actual writing of a paper. In Modern Language Association (MLA) format, the bibliography is titled *Works Cited;* in American Psychological Association (APA) format, it is called *References;* and in Council of Science Editors (CSE) format, it is called *Cited References.* (See 35d; Chapter 37.)

brackets   Punctuation marks used to clarify or insert remarks into quoted material. (See 29d.)

brainstorming   A technique of idea generation in which the writer quickly jots down words or phrases related to a broad subject. When the time limit (five or ten minutes) is reached, related items are grouped; groupings with the greatest number of items indicate potential topics for composition. (See 3b-2.)

buzzwords   Vague, often abstract expressions that sound as if they have meaning, but do not contribute anything of substance to a sentence. (See 17a-4.)

case   The change in form of a noun or pronoun, depending on its function in a sentence. The three cases are the subjective, objective, and possessive forms. Nouns and indefinite pronouns take all three cases, but change form only when they show possession (with the addition of an apostrophe and *s*). Pronouns change form in all three cases. The subjective case is used when a pronoun functions as a subject, subject complement, or as an appositive that renames a subject. The **objective case** is used when a pronoun functions as the object of a preposition, as the object or indirect object of a verb, as the object of a verbal, or as the subject of an infinitive. The **possessive case** of a noun or pronoun indicates possession or ownership. (See Chapter 8.)

chronological arrangement   A method of organizing a paper in which the writing begins at one point in time and proceeds in sequence, forward or backward, to some other point. (See 5d-1.)

clause   A grouping of words that has a subject and a predicate. An **independent clause** (or *main clause*) is a core statement that can stand alone as a sentence. A **dependent clause** (or *subordinate clause*) cannot stand alone as a sentence; it is joined to an independent clause by either a subordinating conjunction or a relative pronoun. There are four types of dependent clauses. **Adverb clauses** begin with subordinating conjunctions *(when, because, although)* and modify verbs, adjectives, and other adverbs. **Adjective clauses** begin with relative pronouns *(which, that, who, whom, whose)* and modify nouns or pronouns. **Noun clauses** are introduced by pronouns *(which, whichever, who, whoever, whom, whomever, whose)* and the words *how, when, why, where, whether,* and *whatever* and function as subjects, objects, complements, or appositives. **Elliptical clauses** have an omitted word or words (often relative pronouns or the logically parallel second parts of comparisons), but the sense of the sentence remains clear. (See 7e; 16e.)

cliché   A trite expression that has lost its impact. (See 21f-3.)

coherence   The clarity of the relationship between one unit of meaning and another. (See 4b-2.)

collective noun   See *noun*.

colloquial   Informal, conversational language. (See 21e-3.)

colon   A punctuation mark (:) generally used to make an announcement. In formal writing, the colon follows only a complete independent clause and introduces a word, phrase, sentence, or group of sentences. (See 29a.)

comma   A punctuation mark (,) used to signal that some element, some word or cluster of related words, is being set off from a main clause for a reason. (See Chapter 25.)

comma splice   The incorrect use of a comma to mark the boundary between two independent clauses. (See Chapter 13; 25f-1.)

common noun   See *noun*.

comparative form   See *adjective forms, adverb forms*.

complement   A word or group of words that completes the meaning of a subject or direct object by renaming it or describing it. A **subject complement** follows a linking verb and can be a noun, pronoun, adjective, or group of words substituting for an adjective or noun. An **object complement** typically follows verbs such as *appoint, call, choose, make,* and *show* and can be a noun, adjective, or group of words substituting for a noun or adjective.

complete predicate   See *predicate*.

complete subject   See *subject*.

complex sentence   See *sentence.*

compound adjective   Two or more words that are combined to modify a given noun. Often, when a compound adjective precedes a noun it is hyphenated to prevent misreading; when it follows the noun it modifies, it does not need hyphenation. (See 32a-1; 32a-3.)

compound-complex sentence   See *sentence.*

compound noun   Two or more words that are combined to function as a single noun. Hyphens are used when the first word of the compound could be read alone as a noun *(cross-reference)*. (See 32a-2.)

compound predicate   Two or more verbs and their objects and modifiers that are joined with a coordinating conjunction to form a single predicate.

compound sentence   See *sentence.*

compound subject   Two or more nouns or pronouns and their modifiers that function as a single subject.

compound verb   Two or more verbs that are combined to function as a single verb. Hyphens are used when the first word of the compound could be read alone as a verb *(shrink-wrap)*. (See 32a-2.)

compound words   Nouns, adjectives, or prepositions created when two or more words are brought together to form a distinctive meaning and to function grammatically as a single word. (See 32a.)

concrete expression   A vivid, detailed expression *(a throbbing headache).*

concrete noun   See *noun.*

conjunction   A word that joins sentence elements or entire sentences by establishing a coordinate or equal relationship among combined parts, or by establishing a subordinate or unequal relationship. **Coordinating conjunctions** *(and, but, or, nor, for, so, yet)* join complete sentences or parallel elements from two or more sentences into a single sentence and express specific logical relationships between these elements. **Correlative conjunctions** *(both/and, neither/nor, either/or, not only/ but also)* are pairs of coordinating conjunctions that place extra emphasis on the relationship between the parts of the coordinated construction. The parts of the sentence joined by correlative conjunctions must be grammatically parallel. **Subordinating conjunctions** *(when, while, although, because, if, since, whereas)* connect dependent clauses to independent clauses. (See 7a-9; 18b; 19a-1, 2.)

conjunctive adverb   An adverb (such as *however, therefore, consequently, otherwise,* or *indeed*) used to create a compound sentence in which the independent clauses that are joined share a logically balanced emphasis. Also called *adverbial conjunction.* (See 7a-9; 19a-3; 26b.)

connotation   The implications, associations, and nuances of a word's meaning. (See 21a.)

coordinate adjectives Two or more adjectives in a series, whose order can be reversed without affecting the meaning of the noun being modified. Coordinate adjectives are linked by a comma or by a coordinating conjunction *(an intelligent, engaging speaker).* (See 25c-2.)

coordinating conjunction See *conjunction.*

coordination The combining of sentence elements by the use of coordinating and correlative conjunctions and conjunctive adverbs. Elements in a coordinate relationship share equal grammatical status and equal emphasis. (See 19a; 20b-1.)

correlative conjunction See *conjunction.*

count noun See *noun.*

cues Words and phrases that remind readers as they move from sentence to sentence (1) that they continue to read about the same topic and (2) that ideas are unfolding logically. Four types of cues are pronouns, repetition, parallel structures, and transitions. (See 5d-2.)

cut To delete sentences because they are off the point or because they give too much attention to a subordinate point. (See 4b-3.)

dangling modifier A word, phrase, or clause whose referent in a sentence is not clearly apparent. (See 15h.)

dash A punctuation mark (—) used to set off and give emphasis to brief or lengthy modifiers, appositives, repeating structures, and interruptions in dialogue. (See 29b.)

dead metaphor A metaphor that has been used so much it has become an ordinary word.

declarative sentence See *sentence.*

demonstrative pronoun See *pronoun.*

denotation The dictionary meaning of a word. (See 21a.)

dependent clause See *clause.* Also called *subordinate clause.*

descriptive adverb An adverb used to describe individual words within a sentence. (Poverty *almost* always can be eliminated at a higher cost to the rich.)

determiner See *article.*

dialect Expressions specific to certain social or ethnic groups as well as regional groups within a country. (See 21e-2.)

diction A writer's choice of words. (See Chapter 21.)

dictionary form See *base form.*

direct discourse The exact re-creation, using quotation marks, of words spoken or written by a person. Also called *direct quotation.* (See 28a-1.)

direct object See *object.*

direct quotation See *direct discourse.*

documentation   The credit given to sources used in a paper, including the author, title of the work, city, name of publisher, and date of publication. There are different systems of documentation for various disciplines; three frequently used systems include the Modern Language Association (MLA), American Psychological Association (APA), and the Council of Science Editors (CSE) systems of documentation. (See Chapter 37.)

double comparative   An incorrect method of showing the comparative form of an adverb or adjective by adding both the suffix *-er* to the word and placing the word *more* before the adverb or adjective. Only one form should be used. (See 11f.)

double negative   An incorrect method of negation in which two negative modifiers are used in the same sentence. Only one negative should be used. (See 11f.)

double superlative   An incorrect method of showing the superlative form of an adverb or adjective by adding both the suffix *-est* to the word and placing the word *most* before the adverb or adjective. Only one form should be used. (See 11f.)

drafting   The stage in the composition process in which the writer generates the first form of a paper from a working thesis or outline. (See 3e; 36e.)

editing   The stage in the composition process in which the writer examines and, if necessary, alters the work's style, grammar, punctuation, and word choice. (See 4c-1; 36f.)

ellipses   Punctuation marks (. . .) consisting of three spaced periods that indicate the writer has deleted either words or entire sentences from a passage being quoted. (See 29e.)

elliptical clause   See *clause.*

elliptical construction   A shortened sentence in which certain words have been omitted deliberately in order to streamline communication. (See 16g.)

essential modifier   A word, phrase, or clause that provides information crucial for identifying a noun; this type of modifier appears in its sentence without commas. The relative pronoun *that* is used only in essential clauses (*who* or *which* may also be used). Also called a *restrictive modifier.* (See 14e-2; 25d-1.)

etymology   The study of the history of words. (See 22d.)

euphemism   A polite rewording of a term that the writer feels will offend readers.

euphony   The pleasing sound produced by certain word combinations.

evaluation   A judgment of the effectiveness and reliability of a text in which the writer discusses the extent of his or her disagreement with an author.

exclamation point   A punctuation mark (!) used to indicate an emphatic statement or command. (See 24c.)

exclamatory sentence   See *sentence.*

expletive   A word that fills the space left in a sentence that has been rearranged. The words *it* and *there* are expletives (filler words without meaning of their own) when used with the verb *be* in sentences with a delayed subject.

fact   Any statement that can be verified.

faulty parallelism   An error in a sentence where elements that should be grammatically equivalent are not. Faulty parallelism is indicated in a sentence when the use of a coordinating conjunction makes part of the sentence sound out of place or illogical. (See 18a.)

faulty predication   An error in a sentence indicated when the predicate part of a sentence does not logically complete its subject. Faulty predication often involves a form of the linking verb *be.*

figure of speech   A carefully controlled comparison that intensifies meaning. See *simile, analogy,* and *metaphor.*

final thesis   See *thesis.*

first person   See *person.*

formal English   The acknowledged standard of correct English. (See 21e.)

formal register   The writing of professional and academic worlds. Formal writing is precise and concise, avoids colloquial expressions, is thorough in content, and is highly structured. (See 3a-4.)

freewriting   A technique of idea generation in which the writer chooses a broad area of interest and writes for a predetermined amount of time or in a prescribed number of pages, without pausing to organize or analyze thoughts. In *focused freewriting,* the same process is followed, but a specific topic is prescribed. (See 3b-3.)

fused sentence   The joining of two independent clauses without a coordinate conjunction or proper punctuation. Also called a *run-on sentence.* (See Chapter 13.)

gender   The labeling of nouns or pronouns as masculine, feminine, or neuter.

gerund   The *-ing* form of a verb without its helping verbs; gerunds function as nouns.

gerund phrase   See *phrase.*

historical present tense   The present tense form used when referring to actions in an already existing work (a book, a movie). (See 9e-1.)

homonyms   Words that sound alike or are pronounced alike but that have different spellings and meanings. (See 23a-1.)

hyphen A punctuation mark (-) used to join compound words and to divide words at the end of lines.

hypothesis A carefully stated prediction.

idiom A grouping of words, one of which is usually a preposition, whose meaning may or may not be apparent based solely on simple dictionary definitions. The grammar of idioms is often a matter of customary usage and is often difficult to explain. (See 21b-2.)

imperative mood See *mood.*

imperative sentence See *sentence.*

incomplete sentence A sentence that lacks certain important elements—a word, subject, or predicate.

indefinite pronoun See *pronoun.*

independent clause See *clause.*

indicative mood See *mood.*

indirect discourse The inexact quotation of the spoken or written words of a person. Indirect discourse inserts the writer's voice into the quotation. Also called *indirect quotation.* (See 28a-1.)

indirect object See *object.*

indirect question A restatement of a question asked by someone else. An indirect question uses a period as punctuation, not a question mark.

indirect quotation See *indirect discourse.*

infinitive The base form of a verb, which is often preceded by the word *to.* Also called the *dictionary form.*

infinitive phrase See *phrase.*

informal register The more colloquial, casual writing of personal correspondence and journals. (See 3a-4.)

intensive pronoun See *pronoun.*

interjection An emphatic word or phrase. When it stands alone, an interjection is frequently followed by an exclamation point. As part of a sentence, an interjection is usually set off by commas. (See 7a-10.)

interrogative pronoun See *pronoun.*

interrogative sentence See *sentence.*

intransitive verb See *verb.*

irregular verb A verb that changes its root spelling to show the past tense and form the past participle, as opposed to adding *-d* or *-ed.*

jargon The in-group language of professionals, who may use acronyms and other linguistic devices to take short-cuts when speaking with colleagues. (See 21e-4.)

limiting modifier   A word that restricts the meaning of another word placed directly after it (*only, almost, just, nearly, even, simply*).

linking verb   See *verb*.

list   A displayed series of items that are logically similar or comparable and are expressed in grammatically parallel form.

logical arrangement   A method of organizing a paper in which the topic is divided into its constituent parts, and the parts are discussed one at a time in an order that will make sense to readers. (See 5d-1.)

main clause   See *clause*.

mapping   A visual method of idea generation. The topic (word or phrase) is circled and from the circle are drawn spokes labeled with the "journalist's questions" (*who, what, where, when, how, why*). The answer to each question is then queried with the journalist's questions again. This method groups and subordinates ideas, thus assisting in generating main ideas and supporting information. (See 3b-7.)

mass noun   See *noun*.

metaphor   A figure of speech that illustrates or intensifies something relatively unknown by comparing it with something familiar. (See 21f-1.)

misplaced modifier   A word, phrase, or clause whose position confuses the meaning of a sentence. A misplaced modifier is not placed next to the word(s) it is meant to modify. (See 15a.)

mixed construction   A confused sentence structure that begins with a certain grammatical pattern and then abruptly changes direction with another grammatical pattern.

mixed metaphor   An illogical comparison of two elements. (See 21f-2.)

modal auxiliary   A verb that is paired with the base form of a verb to express urgency, obligation, likelihood, or possibility (*can, could, may, might, must, ought to, should, would*). (See 9c-1.)

modifier   An adjective or adverb, in the form of a single word, phrase, or clause, that adds descriptive information to a noun or verb. A single-word adjective is often positioned directly before the noun it modifies. Adverbs can be shifted to any part of a sentence. Depending on its location, an adverb will change the meaning or rhythm of a sentence, so care must be taken to ensure that an adverb modifies the word intended. (See 7c.)

mood   The form of a verb that indicates the writer's attitude about an action. The indicative mood expresses facts, opinions, or questions. The **imperative mood** expresses commands. The **subjunctive mood** expresses a recommendation, a wish, a requirement, or a statement contrary to fact. (See 9h.)

nonessential modifier   A word, phrase, or clause that provides information that is not essential for defining a word. Commas are used to set the clause apart from the sentence in which it appears. The relative pronouns *who* and *which* may be used in nonessential clauses. Also called *nonrestrictive modifier.* (See 14e-2; 25d-2.)

nonrestrictive modifier See *nonessential modifier.*

noun A noun names a person, place, thing, or idea. Nouns change their form to show number; the plural is usually formed by adding -*s* or -*es.* Possession is indicated with the addition of an apostrophe and usually an *s.* **Proper nouns,** which are capitalized, name particular persons, places, or things. **Common nouns** refer to general persons, places, or things. **Mass nouns** denote items that cannot be counted. **Count nouns** denote items that can be counted. **Concrete nouns** name tangible objects. **Abstract nouns** name intangible ideas, emotions, or qualities. **Animate** versus **inanimate nouns** differ according to whether they name something alive. **Collective nouns** are singular in form and have either a singular or plural sense, depending on the meaning of the sentence. (See 7a-2; 10a-5.)

noun clause See *clause.*

noun phrase See *phrase.*

number A change in the form of a noun, pronoun, or verb that indicates whether it is singular or plural. (See 16a.)

object A noun, pronoun, or group of words substituting for a noun that receives the action of a transitive verb (**direct object**); is indirectly affected by the action of a transitive verb (**indirect object**); or follows a preposition (**object of a preposition**). (See 7b.)

object complement See *complement.*

objective case See *case.*

object of a preposition See *object.*

opinion A statement of interpretation and judgment.

outline A logically parallel list with further subdivision and subsections under individual items in the list. (See 18e-2.)

paragraph A group of related sentences organized by a single, controlling idea. (See Chapter 5.)

parallel case An argument that develops a relationship between directly related people, objects, events, or conditions.

parallelism The use of grammatically equivalent words, phrases, and sentences to achieve coherence and balance in writing. (See 5d-2; Chapter 18.)

paraphrase A restatement of a passage of text. The structure of a paraphrase reflects the structure of the source passage. (See 35f-2.)

parentheses Punctuation marks used to enclose and set off nonessential dates, words, phrases, or whole sentences that provide examples, comments, and other supporting information. (See 29c.)

participial phrase   See *phrase.*

participle   A verb form. The **present participle** (the *-ing* form) functions as a main verb of a sentence and shows continuing action when paired with *be;* functions as an adjective when paired with a noun or pronoun *(the loving parent);* and functions as a noun when used as a gerund *(studying takes time).* (See *gerund.*) The **past participle** (the past tense *-d, -ed, -n,* or *-en* forms) functions as the main verb of a sentence when paired with *have (I have studied for days);* forms a passive construction when paired with *be (The rock was thrown);* and functions as an adjective when paired with a noun or pronoun *(the contented cow).*

parts of speech   The categories into which words are grouped according to their grammatical function in a sentence: nouns, verbs, verbals, adjectives, adverbs, pronouns, prepositions, conjunctions, interjections, and expletives. (See glossary entries for each category and 7a-2–11.)

passive voice   See *voice.*

past participle   See *participle.*

past tense   See *tense.*

period   A punctuation mark (.) that denotes a complete stop—the end of a sentence. (See 24a.)

person   The form of a pronoun or a noun that identifies whether the subject of a sentence is the person speaking (the **first person**); the person spoken to (the **second person**); or the person spoken about (the **third person**). (See 16a.)

personal pronoun   See *pronoun.*

phrase   A grouping of words that lacks a subject and predicate and cannot stand alone as a sentence. **Verbal phrases** consist of infinitive phrases, gerund phrases, and participial phrases—all of which are built on verb forms not functioning as verbs in a sentence, along with associated words (objects and modifiers). **Infinitive phrases** consist of the infinitive form, often preceded by *to;* they function as adjectives, adverbs, or nouns. **Gerund phrases** consist of the *-ing* form of a verb and function as nouns—as subjects, objects, or complements. **Participial phrases** consist of the present or past participle of a verb and function as adjectives. **Verb phrases** consist of the combination of an auxiliary and the base form, or present or past participle, of a verb. **Noun phrases** consist of a noun accompanied by all of its modifying words. A noun phrase may be quite lengthy, but it always functions as a single noun—as a subject, object, or complement. **Absolute phrases** consist of a subject and an incomplete predicate; they modify entire sentences, not individual words. **Appositive phrases** rename or further identify nouns and are placed directly beside the nouns they refer to. (See 7d; 12c; 29a-4; 29b-1.) **Prepositional phrases** consist of a preposition combined with a noun (called an *object*), which functions in a sentence as a modifier, such as an adjective or adverb.

plagiarism   A conscious attempt to pass off the ideas or the words of another as one's own. (See 35h.)

plot summary   A brief description of characters and events that provides readers context enough to follow a discussion. Plot summaries are written in the historical present tense.

popular register   The writing typical of most general-interest magazines. The language is more conversational than formal writing, but all conventions of grammar, usage, spelling, and punctuation are adhered to. (See 3a-4.)

positive form   See *adjective forms, adverb forms.*

possession   Nouns and pronouns indicate ownership, possession, or attachment with a change in case form. Nouns indicate possession with the addition of an apostrophe and usually an *s.* (See 7a-2.)

possessive case   See *case.*

predicate   A verb and other words associated with it that state the action undertaken by a subject or the condition in which the subject exists. A **simple predicate** consists of the verb and its auxiliaries. A **complete predicate** consists of the simple predicate and its modifiers and objects. A **compound predicate** consists of two verbs and their associated words which are joined with a coordinating conjunction and share the same subject. (See 7a-1.)

prefix   A group of letters joined to the beginning of a root word to form a new, derived word. Prefixes indicate number, size, status or condition, negation, and relations in time and space. (See 22d-2; 23c.)

preposition   A word (*in, at, of, for, on, by, above, under*) that links a noun, pronoun, or word group substituting for a noun to other words in a sentence—to nouns, pronouns, verbs, or adjectives. (See 7a-8.)

prepositional phrase   See *phrase.*

present participle   See *participle.*

primary source   An original document or artifact that may be referred to in a paper, such as a story, letter, or autobiography.

principal parts   The forms of a verb built from the infinitive, from which the tenses are formed: past tense, present participle, and past participle.

pronoun   A word that takes on the meaning of and substitutes for a noun (referred to as the pronoun's *antecedent*). Pronouns show number (singular or plural) and change case depending on their function in a sentence. **Personal pronouns** (*I, me, you, us, his, hers*) refer to people or things. **Relative pronouns** (*who, which, that*) introduce dependent clauses that usually function as adjectives. The pronouns *who, which,* and *that* rename and refer to the nouns they follow. **Demonstrative pronouns** (*this, that, these, those*) point to the nouns they replace. **Interrogative pronouns** *(who, which, what, whose)* form questions. **Intensive pronouns** *(herself, themselves)* are formed with the suffix *-self* or *-selves* to repeat and emphasize a noun or pronoun. **Reflexive pronouns** *(herself, ourselves)* are formed with the suffix *-self* or *-selves* and rename or reflect back to a preceding noun or pronoun. **Indefinite pronouns** *(one, anybody)* refer to general or nonspecific persons or things. **Reciprocal pronouns** *(one another, each other)* refer to the separate parts of a plural noun. (See 7a-7; Chapter 8; Chapter 14.)

proofreading   The final stage in the composition process in which the writer rereads the final paper to identify and correct misspelled words; words (often prepositions) omitted from sentences; words that have been doubled; punctuation that may have been forgotten; and homonyms. (See 4c-2.)

proper noun   See *noun.*

quotation   See *direct discourse.*

quotation marks   These marks (" ") denote the exact reproduction of words written or spoken by someone else.

reciprocal pronoun   See *pronoun.*

redundant phrase   An expression that repeats a message unnecessarily.

reflexive pronoun   See *pronoun.*

regionalism   An expression whose meaning is specific to certain areas of the country. Use of such expressions is inappropriate in formal writing. (See 21e-2.)

register   The level of language or tone used in a paper. (See *formal register, informal register, popular register.*)

regular verbs   Verbs that change form in predictable ways, taking the suffix *-ed* to show the past tense and the past participle.

relative pronoun   See *pronoun.*

restrictive modifier   See *essential modifier.*

revision   A stage in the composition process in which the writer examines the first draft to clarify the purpose or thesis; rewrites to achieve unity and coherence; and adjusts to achieve balance by expanding, condensing, or cutting material. (See Chapter 4; 36f.)

root word   The base form of a word that contains its core meaning. Suffixes and prefixes are added to a root word to form additional words.

run-on sentence   See *fused sentence.*

-s form   The form of a verb that occurs with third-person, singular subjects when an action is in the present. This form (created by adding *-s* or *-es* to a verb) is used with the personal pronoun *he, she,* or *it;* with any noun that can be replaced by these pronouns; and with a number of indefinite pronouns (e.g., *something* or *no one*), which are often considered singular.

second person   See *person*.

secondary source   The work of scholars who have interpreted the writings of others.

section   A grouping of paragraphs that constitutes part of the larger document. (See 5a-1.)

section thesis   See *thesis*.

semicolon   A punctuation mark (;) used to denote a partial separation between independent elements. (See Chapter 26.)

sentence   A fully expressed thought consisting of a complete subject and a complete predicate. A sentence begins with a capital letter and ends with a period, question mark, or exclamation point. The four functional types of sentences include declarative, interrogative, exclamatory, and imperative sentences. A **declarative sentence** makes a statement or assertion about a subject. An **interrogative sentence** poses a question and is formed either by inverting a sentence's usual word order or by preceding the sentence with a word such as *who, which, when, where,* or *how*. An **exclamatory sentence** is used as a direct expression of a speaker's or writer's strong emotion. An **imperative sentence** expresses a command. The four structural types of sentences are simple, compound, complex, and compound-complex sentences. A **simple sentence** has a single subject and a single predicate. A **compound sentence** has two subjects and two predicates. A **complex sentence** has an independent clause and one or more dependent clauses. A **compound-complex sentence** has at least two independent clauses and one subordinate, dependent clause.

sentence fragment   A partial sentence punctuated as if it were a complete sentence, with an uppercase letter at its beginning and a period, question mark, or exclamation point at its end. A sentence fragment lacks either a subject or a predicate, and sometimes both. It can also be a dependent clause that has not been joined to an independent clause.

sexism   In writing, the use of inappropriate gender-specific words (*a biologist in his lab*) that creates biased or inaccurate characterizations linked with a male or female reference. (See 21g.)

simile   A figure of speech in which two different things, one usually familiar, the other not, are explicitly compared. The properties of the known thing help to define the unknown thing. Similes often use the words *like* or *as* to set up the comparison. (See 21f-1.)

simple future tense   See *tense*.

simple past tense   See *tense*.

simple predicate   See *predicate*.

simple present tense   See *tense*.

simple sentence   See *sentence*.

simple subject   See *subject*.

slang   The informal language peculiar to a culture or subculture; inappropriate for formal writing.

slash   A punctuation mark (/) used to separate lines of poetry run in with the text of a sentence; to show choice, as in *either/or*; and to note division in fractions or formulas. (See 29f.)

spatial arrangement   A method of organizing a paper in which the subjects are described according to their relative positions; for example, for a photograph, the foreground, middle ground, and background might be described. (See 5d-1.)

split infinitive   The insertion of an adverbial modifier between the two parts of an infinitive—the word *to* and the base form—which can disrupt the intended meaning (*to* successfully *attempt*). (See 15f.)

squinting modifier   A word, phrase, or clause that ambiguously appears to modify two words in a sentence—both the word preceding and following it.

subject   A noun, pronoun, or group of words substituting for a noun, that engages in the main action of a sentence or is described by the sentence. A **simple subject** consists of a single noun or pronoun. A **complete subject** consists of a simple subject and its modifiers. A **compound subject** consists of a multiple subject created by using the coordinating conjunction *and*.

subject complement   See *complement*.

subjective case   See *case*.

subjunctive mood   See *mood*.

subordinate clause   See *clause, dependent clause*.

subordinating conjunction   See *conjunction*.

subordination   A method for linking words, phrases, or clauses that is used to give more emphasis to one idea than to another in a sentence. The words in a dependent (subordinate) clause cannot stand alone as a sentence. (See 19b.)

suffix   A group of letters joined to the end of a root word. Suffixes change the grammatical function of words and can be used to indicate tense.

summary   A brief, objective account of the main ideas of a source passage.

superlative form   See *adjective forms, adverb forms*.

synonym   A word that has approximately the same denotation (dictionary meaning) as another word.

synthesis   A presentation that draws together material from several sources. (See 2d.)

tag question   A brief question attached to a statement, set off by a comma. Tag questions consist of a helping verb, a pronoun, and frequently the word *not (He won the match, didn't he?)*. (See 25e-5.)

tense   The change in form of a verb that shows when an action has occurred or when a subject exists in a certain state of being. Tenses are marked by verb endings and auxiliary verbs. (See 9e, f; 16b-1.) The **simple present tense** indicates an action taking place at the writer's present time. The verb's base form is used for singular or plural first- and second-person subjects, as well as for plural third-person subjects *(I go, you go, they go)*. The verb for a third-person singular subject ends with the suffix *-s (she goes)*. The **simple past tense** indicates an action completed at a definite time in the past. Regular verbs form this tense by adding *-d* or *-ed* to the base form. The **simple future tense** indicates an action or state of being that will begin in the future. All other tenses build on these basic tenses by using auxiliaries. See Chapter 9 for more information on the present, past, and future perfect tenses; the present, past, and future progressive tenses; and the perfect progressive tenses.

thesis   A general statement about a topic that crystallizes the main purpose of a writing and suggests its main parts. A **section thesis** explicitly announces the point to be addressed in a section and either directly or indirectly suggests what will be discussed relating to this point. (See 5a-2.) A **working thesis** is a statement that should prove to be a reasonably accurate summary of what will be written. A **final thesis** is an accurate, one-sentence summary of a work that will appear in the final draft. (See 3d; 33e; 36a.)

third person   See *person.*

tone   The expression of a writer's attitude toward the subject or audience. Tone is determined by word choice and quality of description, verb selection, sentence structure, and sentence mood and voice. The tone of a piece changes depending on the audience. (See 3a-4; 16c.)

topic   The subject of a piece of writing. (See 3a.)

topical development   The expansion of statements about a topic announced in the opening sentence of a paragraph. After its opening announcement, the topic is divided into two or three parts, each of which is developed at a different location in the paragraph. (See 5e.)

topic sentence   A paragraph's central, controlling idea. (See 5c.)

transition   A word, sentence, or paragraph devoted to building a smooth, logical relationship between ideas in a sentence, between sentences, between paragraphs, or between whole sections of an essay.

(Phrases include *for example, on the other hand, in addition.*) (See 4b-2; 5d-3; 20c-1.)

transitive verb   See *verb.*

usage   The prevailing, customary conditions describing how, where, and when a word is normally used in speech and writing. Usage labels in a dictionary, such as *colloquial, slang, archaic,* and *dialect,* indicate special restrictions on the conditions for using a particular meaning or form of a word.

verb   The main word in the predicate of a sentence expressing an action or occurrence or establishing a state of being. Verbs change form to demonstrate tense, number, mood, and voice. **Transitive verbs** *(kick, buy)* transfer the action from an actor—the subject of the sentence—to a direct object—a person, place, or thing receiving that action. **Intransitive verbs** *(laugh, sing, smile)* show action that is limited to the subject; there is no direct object that is acted upon. *(The rock fell.)* The same verb can be transitive in one sentence and intransitive in another. *(She runs a good business. She runs every day.)* **Linking verbs** *(is, feel, appear, seem)* allow the word or words following the verb to complete the meaning of the subject. *(Joan is a lawyer.)* (See 7a-3; Chapter 9.)

verb phrase   See *phrase.*

verbal   A verb form that functions in a sentence as an adjective, an adverb, or a noun. Verbals include infinitives, participles, and gerunds. (See *infinitive, participle, gerund;* 7a-4; 7d-2.)

verbal phrase   See *phrase.*

voice   The form of a transitive verb in a sentence that shows whether emphasis is given to the actor or to the object acted upon. **Active-voice** sentences emphasize the doer of an action. **Passive-voice** sentences emphasize the object acted upon or deemphasize an unknown subject. In passive-voice sentences the words are rearranged so that the object occupies the first position. This construction requires the use of a form of the verb *be* and the preposition *by. (The house was designed by Frank Lloyd Wright.)*

working thesis   See *thesis.*

Credits

Chapter 33
From *Bibliographic Index*, © 2000 The H.W. Wilson Company. All rights reserved.
From *Readers Guide to Periodical Literature*, © 2000 The H.W. Wilson Company. All rights reserved.
"Valley of the Doll-less" from *Readers Guide to Periodical Literature*, © 2000 The H.W. Wilson Company. All rights reserved.
From *Index*, August 17, 2000. Copyright © 2000 New York Times Co., Inc. Used with permission.

Chapter 34
Copyright © 2001 American Academy of Family Physicians. Reproduced by permission of AFP.
This site was created by Andrea L. Yager and Excellence Web Services. Copyright © 2002 CTSplace.com. Used with permission.

Chapter 35
Rob Kling, "Social Relationships in Electronic Forums," *CMC* magazine, July 22, 1996 from his book *Computerization and Controversy*, 2nd ed. © 1996 Academic Press.
Bonnie Rothman Morris "You've Got Romance" *New York Times*, August 26, 1999. Copyright © 1999 New York Times Co., Inc. Used with permission.
"Click Here for Romance" by Jennifer Wolcott, *The Christian Science Monitor*, January 13, 1999. This article first appeared in *The Christian Science Monitor* on January 13, 1999 and is reproduced with permission. Copyright © 1999 The Christian Science Monitor (www.csmonitor.com). All rights reserved.
Taking Laughter Seriously by John Morreall, © 1983 State University of New York Press.

Chapter 36
Rob Kling, "Social Relationships in Electronic Forums," *CMC* Magazine, July 22, 1996 from his book *Computerization and Controversy*, 2nd ed. © 1996 Academic Press.

Chapter 38
© Schwadron. Reprinted by permission of H. Schwadron.
From *Redefining the American Dream* by Sally P. Harvey. © 1995 Farleigh Dickinson University Press. Reprinted by permission.
Richard Rorty, *Ethics Without Principles*, © 1999 Penguin, UK
"Who Named Franklin's Autobiography?" by John G. Cawelti and Eric Atherton, *ANQ*, 8.2, 1995, pp. 17–19. Copyright © John G. Cawelti and Eric Atherton.

Chapter 39
Reproduced with permission of authors and publisher from Huddy, D.C. et al., "Facilitating Changes in Exercise Behavior: Effect of Structured Statements of Intention on Perceived Barriers to Action." *Psychological Reports*, 76 (1995): 867–875. © Psychological Reports 1995.
Ira Silver, "Role Transitions, Objects, and Identity," *Symbolic Interaction*, 19, no. 1, (1996): 1–20. Copyright © 1996 by JAI Press. Reprinted by permission.
Excerpt from *Publication Manual of the American Psychological Association*, 5th ed. (2001). Copyright © 2001 by the American Psychological Association. Reprinted (or adapted) with permission.

Chapter 40
Chris T. Bolliger et al., "Smoking Reduction with Oral Nicotine Inhalers: Double Blind, Randomised Clinical Trial of Efficacy and Safety," *British Journal of Medicine*, 321, no. 7257 (2000): 329–334. Copyright © 2000 BMJ. Reprinted by permission of the PMJ Publishing Group.

Index

883

Index

Helping verbs, 222–225, 826, 865
  base form, 185
  modal auxiliaries, 826–827
he or she, 255
here and *there*, 249–250
herself, himself, myself, yourself, 853
he/she, 853
Highlighting emphasizing words, 368–369
him/her, 853
himself, myself, yourself, herself, 853
his/her, 853
hisself, 854
Historical events or periods, reference to 503
Historical present tense, 870
Historical study
  as claims and evidence in the humanities,
    examples of, 680
  reading from disciplinary perspective,
    683–684
Holidays, reference to 503
Home page, defined, 558
Homonyms, 415–416, 424, 870
hopefully, 854
Hosting service, Web site, 771
Hours, using colon with 483
how. See Subordinating conjunctions
however, 274. *See also* Conjunctive adverbs
HTML (HyperText Markup Language)
  pages, creating, 765–767, 771
Humanities. *See also* Critical reading; Critical
    thinking
  analysis, 47–51, 684–685, 696–697
  argument, 676–682
  assignments, types of, 684–686
  book review, 685
  claims, writing, 162, 677–678, 682
  CMS documentation style, use in 662–666
  commercial and professional information
    services, 553
  comparison and contrast, 333–334
  essay exams, 797–799
  essay writing, 524–526
  essays collected in books, finding, 545
  evaluation, 20–30, 585–586
  evidence, use in, 677–682, 694–696
  expression in, 62, 675
  historical study, 680, 683
  introduction, example of, 140
  literary criticism, 696–697
    characterization, 697
    claim in, 162
    comment in, 679
    evidence in, 694–696
    plot summaries, 695–696
    structure, 697
    theme, 697
  literary study, 678–679
  overview of, 674
  philosophical study, 680, 683
  reading in, 682–684, 696–697
  reference materials, 538, 542, 704–706
    primary and secondary sources, 682
  research paper in, 686
  response to author, 43–47
  texts
    importance of, 675

patterns in, 679, 696
writing for, 675–682
  to express, 675–676
  to inform, 676
  as literary criticism, 686–698
  sample paper, 699–704
  strategies of, 797–799
  style guides, 704. *See also* CMS, MLA
    styles
  synthesis, 697–698
hung, hanged, 853, 854
Hypertext, 559
Hyphen, 871
  compound words, 519–521
  dividing word at end of line, 521–522
  manuscript spacing, 845
Hypothesis, 735, 871

-ible, 421
Ideas
  brainstorming, 68–69
  freewriting and focused freewriting,
    70–71
  generating, 529–531
  journalist's questions, 71
  journal writing, 71–72
  "many parts" strategy, 72–73
  mapping, 73–74
  reading, 66–68
  reviewing, 74–75
Idioms, 871
  awkward diction, revising, 387, 388
  dictionaries, 405
  with modal auxiliary verbs, 827–827
  parallel constructions, 332
  verb/verbal sequences, 827–829
ie/ei spelling rules, 417–418
if. See Subordinating conjunctions
if, whether, 854
if/as if/as though, 240
if because, 330
if constructions, 239–240
illicit, elicit, 851, 854
Illogical coordination, 360–361
illusion, allusion, 847, 854
Illustrate, in essay exam question, 800
Images
  in documents, 780
  downloading from Internet, 763
  in Web design, 765, 768–769
immigrate, migrate, emigrate, 851
impact, 854
Imperative mood, 239, 323, 872
Imperative sentence, 200, 877
Implication. *See* Connotation
implicit, explicit, 852
imply, infer, 854
Importance, paragraphs arranged by,
    124
in, into, 854
in addition to, 246
Inanimate noun, 207, 873
Incomplete sentence, 331–333, 871
incredible, incredulous, 854
indeed. See Conjunctive adverbs
Indefinite antecedents, renaming, 255

REVISION SYMBOLS

The symbols below indicate a need to make revisions in the areas designated. Boldface numbers and letters refer to handbook sections.

ab	abbreviation **31a-e**	ref	unclear pronoun reference **14**
ad	form of adjective/adverb **7c, 11**	rep	unnecessary repetition **17a**
agr	agreement **10**	sp	spelling error **23**
awk	awkward diction or construction **7b, 15, 21**	shift	inconsistent, shifted construction **16**
ca	case form **8**	sub	sentence subordination **7e-f, 19b**
cap	capitalization **30a-d**	t	verb tense error **9e-f**
coh	coherence **4b, 5d**	trans	transition needed **5a, 5e, 5f**
coord	coordination **7f, 18a, 19a**	var	sentence variety needed **19, 20**
cs	comma splice **13**		
d	diction, word choice **21, 22**	vb	verb form error **9, 17b**
dm	dangling modifier **15h**	w	wordy **17a**
dev	development needed **3, 4, 18d**	ww	wrong word; word choice **10c, 21, 22**
emph	emphasis needed **19, 20**	//	faulty parallelism **18**
frag	sentence fragment **7b, 12**	. ? !	end punctuation **24**
fs	fused sentence **13**	:	colon **29a**
hyph	hyphen **32**	∨̇	apostrophe **27**
inc	incomplete construction **7b, 16g-h**	—	dash **29b**
ital	italics **30e-g**	( )	parentheses **29c**
k	awkward diction or construction **7b, 11g, 15, 21**	[ ]	brackets **29d**
		. . .	ellipsis **29e**
lc	lowercase letter **30a-d**	/	slash **29f**
log	logic **6, 38a, 39a, 40a**	;	semicolon **26**
mm	misplaced modifier **7d, 15**	" "	quotation marks **28**
ms	manuscript form **36h** **Appx. A**	⌄	comma **25**
mix	mixed construction **16e-f**	⊂	close up
no ¶	no paragraph needed **5**	∧	insert a missing element
num	number **31f-h**	ℰ	delete
¶	paragraph **5**	⌐⌐	transpose order
¶ dev	paragraph development needed **5**		

SPOTLIGHT ON COMMON ERRORS

If the examples or brief explanations in the cells lead you to suspect an error, turn to the highlighted SPOTLIGHT page indicated to find quick answers, fuller explanations, and references to detailed discussions in the handbook.

I. FORMS OF NOUNS AND PRONOUNS See the SPOTLIGHT (page 204).

Apostrophes can show contraction or possession (but not with posessive pronouns).

Faulty Forms	*Revised*
The scarf is *Chris*. It is *her's*.	The scarf is *Chris's*. It is *hers*.
Give the dog *it's* collar.	Give the dog *its* collar.
Its a difficult thing.	*It's* [it is] a difficult thing.

Choose a pronoun's form depending on its use as a subject or object.

Faulty Forms	*Revised*
This is *him*. It was *me*. Is that *her*?	This is *he*. It was *I*. Is that *she*?
The ball landed between *she* and *I*.	The ball landed between *her* and *me*.
Her and *me* practice daily.	*She* and *I* practice daily.

II. VERBS See the SPOTLIGHT (page 220).

Keep verb tenses consistent when describing two closely connected events.

Inconsistent	*Revised*
She *liked* the work. Still, she *keeps* to herself.	She *likes* the work. Still, she *keeps* to herself.

(a) Choose the right verb forms with an *if* clause.
(b) Decide on which of these verb forms to use: *sit* or *set*, *lie* or *lay*, *rise* or *raise*.

Faulty Verb Form	*Revised*
(a) If it *would be* any colder, the pipes *would* freeze.	(a) If it *were* any colder, the pipes *would* freeze.
(b) *Lie* the books here. Then *lay* down.	(b) *Lay* the books here. Then *lie* down.

III. AGREEMENT See the SPOTLIGHT (page 244).

Match subjects with verbs. Make sure both are either singular or plural.

Not in Agreement	*Revised*
The *reason* she wins *are* her friends.	The *reason* she wins *is* her friends.

(a) Words joined by *and* require a plural pronoun and verb. (b) For words joined by *or/nor*, match the pronoun and verb to the nearer word.

Not in Agreement	*Revised*
(a) My friends **and** Sue *likes her* pizza hot.	(a) My friends **and** Sue *like their* pizza hot.
(b) Neither her friends **nor** Sue *like their* pizza cold.	(b) Neither her friends **nor** Sue *likes her* pizza cold.

IV. SENTENCE STRUCTURE: FRAGMENTS See SPOTLIGHT (page 273).

Mark where sentences end, usually with a period. Avoid a FRAGMENT—a word group that lacks a full subject and predicate and cannot stand alone.

Faulty	*Revised*
If our cousins arrive today. [Fragment]	Our cousins may arrive today.
	If our cousins arrive today, we'll have a picnic.